CONTENTS

TICKET
ADMIT ADULT
47438
1
JAMAICA
NATIONAL
HERITAGE
TRUST
TICKET
ADMIT ADULT
47439
1
JAMAICA
NATIONAL
HERITAGE
TRUST

GREETINGS FROM
Jamaica
MONTEGO BAY
FALMOUTH
Discovery Bay
ST. ANN'S BAY
ORACABESSA
PORT MARIA
LUCEA
DUNCANS
OCHO RIOS
NEGRIL
Sugar Cane
Dunn's River Falls
BUFF BAY
PORT ANTONIO
SAVANNA LA-MAR
MAGGOTTY
CHRISTIANA
CASTLETON
Bamboo Avenue
MANDEVILLE
Rodney's Memorial
NEWCASTLE
MANCHIONEAL
SANTA CRUZ
BLACK RIVER
MAY PEN
SPANISH TOWN
KINGSTON
Rafting on the Rio Grande
HECTORS RIVER
TREASURE BEACH
PORT ROYAL
PORT MORANT
MORANT BAY
LIONEL TOWN
CARIBBEAN SEA

Noel Hawks

Introduction

"It's a matter of great pride among the two million members of Jamaica's population that our music, reggae, is poised to become one of the most influential forms of popular music of the Seventies."

The Roots Of Reggae

This brief introduction to the music of the island from the Jamaican High Commission in London might have seemed over ambitious in 1975 but, as they say, "time will tell" and it certainly did. By the close of the decade Sebastian Clarke was able to write:

"Jamaican music has grown to such an extent that it now provides employment for a significant number of Jamaicans, meaningfully contributing to a depressed Jamaican economy. There are four pressing plants in Jamaica which employ an average of two hundred people in various capacities: factory hands, to salesmen, accountants, engineers, drivers, secretaries etc. The record industry has, in turn, created an outlet for record shops which also provide employment." **Sebastian Clarke**

During the final quarter of the Twentieth Century, and on into the new Millennium, Jamaican music would become an indelible influence on other musical genres all around the world but a great deal of the story of how this happened still belongs to "the half that's never been told". All three volumes of Jamaican Recordings, through the medium of interviews with key players and contemporary articles and reviews, attempt to document the development of Kingston's recording studios, the infrastructure and the people that made it possible.

A disregard for the past and a failure to recognise the significance or maintain a record of pivotal cultural events are not new phenomena and the importance of recording as much as possible before "we lose the receipts" is essential to an understanding of reggae.

"We like to think we're pretty smart, with our Twenty First century hair and our trainers with lights on, but most of the stuff we know is just stuff someone else found out and told us...

The Williamson tunnels are a good example of how fragile our knowledge of the past is, of how easily stuff can be forgotten... how mysterious the world of only a few generations back can be if we lose the receipts.

Robin Halstead, Jason Hazeley, Alex Morris & Joel Morris

In the Twenty First Century an appreciation of Jamaican music and its significance is seen as the mark of a cultured person and everyone everywhere, of course, 'loves' reggae but it was not always like this.

"We're supposed to like Elbow, and the XX, and to have an obscure Sixties reggae compilation we put on when we're trying to impress someone."

Richard Osman

Yet, at the time the music was being created, "a Sixties reggae compilation" would not have impressed many people as only the 'lower classes' were listening intently and I have attempted here to track its trajectory from vilification to approbation. In the early Sixties ska had been "taken uptown" and out of the Kingston ghettos. In the UK, the music's most significant overseas market, ska, rock steady and reggae first found favour outside of its expatriate West Indian audience with white working class youth, initially the mods, and then with their younger brothers and sisters who were disparagingly referred to as skinheads. It was not to be taken seriously, unlike so-called progressive or underground music, and disapproval was serious and sustained due to a combination of what, at the time, was termed 'colour prejudice' and the ubiquitous English class system.

"British disc jockeys and pop music papers loathed reggae from the start and have steadfastly ignored it as 'unprogressive'; at the time of the skinhead craze they were throwing review copies in their waste paper baskets..."

Colin McGlashan

The late John Peel, whose Top Gear radio show on Radio One was a huge influence on underground music, did actually play Andy Capp's inventive 'Pop A Top' in 1970. John would continue to champion reggae throughout his entire radio career and this was largely due to the adverse reaction to his first playing 'Pop A Top'. Many years later he told me that "any record that provoked his audience so markedly had to be worth further investigation".

"Peel did notice something interesting about 'Pop A Top' though: any time he played it he would receive venomous letters from angry listeners."
David Cavanagh

But if you were living on a council estate in one of the UK's inner city areas or suburbs in the late Sixties and early Seventies reggae was everywhere, and I mean everywhere, apart from the music papers, the television or on the radio with a handful of notable exceptions. BBC Radio One was obliged to playlist records such as 'Liquidator' and 'Return Of Django' because they had broken into the charts. But, unlike underground music, its popularity was a truly underground phenomenon as Danny Baker, one of the co-creators, with Mark Perry, of the infamous *Sniffin' Glue* punk fanzine recalled. The households that Danny refers to were in Bermondsey, south east London by the way.

"The received wisdom now is that the cool set at the time listened to reggae, Motown and soul, but that rather overlooks the fact that everybody listened to reggae, Motown and soul back then. I can't think of a household, ours included, that didn't have one of the 'Tighten Up' albums or 'Motown Chartbusters' or the Atlantic Record samplers featuring Wilson Pickett and Aretha Franklin." **Danny Baker**

Very few cultural commentators deigned to even notice the music or take it seriously enough to consider writing about it. Consequently the documentation of Jamaican music at the time of some of its greatest creativity was largely limited to the pioneering journalism of Carl Gayle in Black Music and Chris Lane and Dave Hendley in *Blues & Soul*. Everything changed following reggae's breakthrough in the wake of Bob Marley & The Wailers astonishing overground success in the mid Seventies and its eventual acceptance as a valid musical genre.

"Meanwhile I should think Bob Marley will be spending his time putting together a scrapbook of his reviews from *The Times, New Musical Express, The Guardian, Melody Maker* etc, etc so that he'll have something to read when they all find another bandwagon to jump on and remember that 'reggae all sounds the same'." **Chris Lane**

The Jamaican music business was built on the foundation of sound system operators and producers making records and not artists making music… that would come later… and this volume details the exponential expansion of recording facilities in Kingston and the role of the much maligned record producers.

"The Jamaican musical landscape was filled with record producers during the Sixties and Seventies. All were going about their business, in terms of the artistes they wanted to record, the amount they would pay them, and the type of sound they wanted to hear. It was a tricky business because there was no guarantee that the recording would be a hit, and huge amounts of cash had to be spent, leading up to and obtaining the final product… the actual vinyl record. All the funding, which involved studio time payments, musician fees, material and pressing fees were borne by the producers." **Roy Black**

"Time a gwaan and the tape a roll. A money a run this thing, you know brother..." **'Promoters Grouse' Rupie Edwards**

"A production is actually work, creativity. It's beyond just going into the studio and tell a singer 'which song can you give me?' Many people call themselves 'producer' just turn up and record any artist, any song. For me an artist or writer have fi come and say 'we have a project'. The songs you have we listen them, tell you what we like and don't like and when everything is acceptable between both of us then we work…"
Augustus 'Gussie' Clarke

Dub, first created in Kingston's recording studios, would incalculably influence the worldwide development of recorded music. In the Sixties American blues had formed the basis for the "hard rock from which all traces of black music's influence had been removed" and, in exactly the same way, dub would prove to be the foundation of Eighties and Nineties dance music.

"We'd record the rhythm on one track and the voice on the other. We never used to tie the voice and the rhythm together as that way you could run the rhythm for whatever purpose you wanted. If you dropped the voice out then the sound system deejay could talk over the rhythm.

In the beginning Dynamics and the bigger men wouldn't do it and engineers such as Byron Smith and Karl Pitterson never used to mix the dubs. Those engineers wouldn't sit down and work the board like Tubbys. In my knowledge he was the first and that's how Tubbys got such fame. All of them dub things used to carry on at Tubbys." **Roy Cousins**

Reggae's recording innovations were appropriated, time after time after time, without being acknowledged or credited. This pivotal form, dub, radically altered our understanding of music making, simultaneously transformed the mixing desk into a musical instrument in its own right and would eventually find favour with the intelligentsia too.

"...and even the rock critics began to murmur appreciatively that here, at last, was a reggae music that wasn't like a skinhead chasing you down the street." **Ian McCann**

However, it is of paramount importance to never lose sight of the people who actually made the music and their stories are here too.

"Listen! In Christendom people who attend one church consecutively refer to it as a home church and, once you start going to this tabernacle or enclosure for a while, then of course you're going to develop a relationship with your surroundings. But it's the people who create the vibes... the studio doesn't have a life of its own. It's people who breathe life into a situation so, whilst the studio might be conducive, it's the confederation of souls that makes the vibration because the place becomes a sanctuary... so to speak. So I would leave the ambience of the studio out of it. I just want to put it into perspective.

Those guys (the musicians)... they'd go around to different studios... go to Joe Gibbs and give him his set of hits and go to so and so and give them their set of hits. They could go to any studio almost as the studio band because they had access to the studios, they could record their own things, and they could work with other people because it was a freedom time. The musicians always knew better than the people with the facilities so it wasn't difficult for the people with the facilities to leave the musicians to create. So, within that perspective, one could push the envelope and do whatever you wanted to do." **Bob Andy**

As in the first volume each chapter is a self contained history of a particular studio so that, although the chapters are intended to follow chronologically, the narrative occasionally gets ahead of the stories in the subsequent chapters. I hope that this, and some inevitable repetition where a number of key events and characters overlap add to, rather than detract from, the narrative and that these histories offer a wider perspective on how Jamaican music progressed from parochial beginnings into a worldwide phenomenon.

"Contemporary Jamaican music has had a short and vigorous history and its development in terms of scope and sophistication offers a reasonably close parallel to the development of modern Jamaican society."

The Roots Of Reggae

i
roy
version
galore

Treasure Isle
33 Bond St.
Kgn., Ja.
Tel. 25629
27594
LOCK JAW
Upsetter
Tommy McCook
and The Supersonics
RECORDED AT TREASURE ISLE RECORDING STUDIO

DUKE REID
MANUFACTURED AND DISTRIBUTED BY TROJAN RECORDS LTD
B&C Music
℗ 1970
DR-2513 A
WEAR YOU TO THE BALL
HUGH ROY AND JOHN HOLT
Produced by: Duke Reid

TREASURE ISLE LIQUOR STOR
83 Bond St. Kingston
7/6
BREAKING UP

MASTERS
TIME
Glory Records
MT.002
Island
Music
HAPPY DAY
THE JOYFUL SINGERS
LYNN TATE ON ORGAN

Duke Reid
VOCAL
LET THE GOOD TIMES ROLL
(Derrick & Patsy)
DERRICK AND PATSY
MANUFACTURED BY FEDERAL RECORD MFG. CO. LTD. JAMAICA W.I.

SOUL SHOT
Side One
D. R. ENTERPRISES
B.M.I.
33 Bond St.
Kgn., Ja.
Tel. 25629
27594
MY GIRL
THE TECHNIQUES
With Tommy McCook &
The Supersonics
RECORDED AT TREASURE ISLE RECORDING STUDIO KGN. JA. W.I.

Noel Hawks

Chapter 1

Down On Bond Street : Treasure Isle

Now clap your hands and stamp your feet. 'Cause this happens to be a Treasure Isle treat..."
'Treasure Isle Time' U Roy

"Treasure Isle Recording Studio. The high quality of reproduction heard on all Treasure Isle discs emanates from this up to date control booth, with skilled technician in attendance. He calculates just the right measure of sound, with the proper addition of jump-up enthusiasm, a dash of spontaneity and a judicious sprinkle of technical inventiveness, to present you with the perfect tropical cocktail..."
'Independence Jump Up Calypso'

"Treasure Isle Recording Studios who recorded, edited and mastered this record is equipped with the most modern and up to date recording instruments."
'Come Rock With Me In Jamaica Land Of The Sea And Sun'

It is no exaggeration to state that the radical musical innovations that originated down on Bond Street altered the entire notion and understanding of the popular music making process in the closing quarter of the Twentieth Century and on into the new Millennium. The influence of the understated elegance of Duke Reid's rock steady rhythms would prove to be profound; they were the perfect starting point for the musical experiments of both deejays and dub remixing engineers. The professional, polished perfection emanating from the Treasure Isle Recording Studio provided the platform that launched a completely new style of music that not only broke the sound barriers but also overthrew countless cultural and artistic preconceptions.

In 1961 Lindon O Pottinger, a chartered accountant and entrepreneur, built a small recording studio using "a Magnetophon tape recorder" at the rear of the Pottinger family home on Sundown Crescent off Molynes Road, Kingston which would become the foundation for Duke Reid's Treasure Isle Recording Studio. Magnetophon was the brand, or model name, of the pioneering reel to reel tape recorder originally developed by the German electronics company AEG in the Thirties based on the magnetic tape invention of Fritz Pfleumer.

"Mr Pottinger was a very influential man in the business...he was very much in the business and he owned a whole heap of juke boxes and things like that in Jamaica. Yeah, man. So people must remember Mr Pottinger."

Bunny 'Striker' Lee

Sadly few do remember Mr Pottinger, "the first black man to have a studio in Jamaica", and he is usually remembered today only because his equipment was purchased by Duke Reid to set up the Treasure Isle Recording Studio which he situated on top of his liquor store at 33 Bond Street in the autumn of 1965. However, Lindon's wife, Mrs Sonia Pottinger, would go on to play a major role in the Treasure Isle story in the Seventies.

Arthur Stanley 'Duke' Reid was born 21st July 1915 in Priestman's River in the parish of Portland on Jamaica's north east coast and, at the age of seventeen, left the countryside for Kingston where he joined the Jamaica Constabulary Force. He served as a policeman for ten years and became a championship marksman but, after giving "the force ten years of sterling service", he decided "to move into other areas of interest" and resigned his post. He joined his wife Lucille, who was known, naturally enough, as the Duchess at her thriving grocery shop, Pink's Grocery, at 81 Beeston Street on the corner of Pink Lane in downtown Kingston which would later be renamed the Treasure Isle Liquor Store. "From 1953 onwards" the

'Greatest Jamaican Beat'

Duke Reid at the control during a 1958 sesison
when he again won the top award for sound systems

'Greatest Jamaican Beat'

Reid's Sound System

'Laurence Cane-Honeysett'

'Greatest Jamaican Beat'

Duke Reid is crowned King of Sounds and Blues at an explosive session featuring the top sound systems in the island at Jamaica Success Club in 1956

'Greatest Jamaican Beat'

This was 1957 when Duke Reid took the King of Sounds and Blues award at Forresters Hall, North Street

Duke played American rhythm & blues and 'local' mento music on his sponsored 'Treasure Isle Time' radio show on RJR where his signature tune was Tab Smith's sentimental instrumental rendering of 'My Mother's Eyes' originally sung by George Jessel in the 1929 film 'Lucky Boy'.

"His trademark was Tab Smith's 'My Mother's Eyes' then you'd hear 'Treasure Isle Time' for fifteen minutes or half an hour and that became a way of life on the radio 'cause people used to listen out for it."

Bunny 'Striker' Lee

"'Duke' Reid popularised rhythm & blues on his radio programme on RJR 'Treasure Isle Time' from 1953 onwards and with Reid's Sound System."

'The Birth Of Ska'

In 1958 the Duke and Duchess opened larger premises on Bond Street, "every Saturday Duke's wife, the late Mrs Lucille Reid, would cook and sell crab from the famous Treasure Isle Liquor Store at 33 Bond Street on the corner of Charles Street", and his radio show would promote not only his liquor store and rum bar but also Reid's Sound System. Through his knowledge and love of music, the many connections made during his time in the constabulary and his fearsome reputation his sound rapidly rose to become one of the foremost sound systems in Kingston.

"When I was growing up the sounds used to play rhythm & blues and we used to copy the Americans when we started making our own music. Duke Reid used to go abroad and bring in rhythm & blues records like Lester Williams, Rosco Gordon, Smiley Lewis, Louis Jordan and Wynonie Harris... all them cats! They were some wicked blues singers and when they brought in the records they'd scratch off the name. King Edwards The Giant used to bring in some good tunes too 'cause these guys used to go abroad and do farm work and things.

Everybody used to be kinda scared of Duke... but him was alright. He was a no-nonsense man... a kinda wealthy man through he was a policeman... and when they come and go with the 78's they scratched off the names and the deejays would give them their own names. Duke Reid's deejay at the time was Leroy 'Cuttings' Cole. I saw him the other day (2005). He's 'Stranger' Cole's brother. These deejays used to lick up the place. Those guys were great! They could have run Jamaica!"

Bunny 'Striker' Lee

Although he was not one of the first sound system operators Duke Reid was undoubtedly one of the most forward thinking and his record buying trips to the USA were legendary. He continued to consolidate his reputation, playing out alongside his deejay/selector and right hand man, Leroy 'Cuttings' Cole, and another deejay called Clifford at venues such as the Success Club and Forresters Hall and, for three years in a row (1956, 1957 & 1958), he was crowned Kingston's undisputed 'King Of Sound And Blues'.

"There was a great rivalry going on at that time between Coxsone and Duke Reid. I don't know if you know this Delroy Wilson song called 'Spit In The Sky' or 'The Duke, The King & The Sir'? Those were the people that dominated... Duke Reid, Sir Coxsone and King Edwards. Then, later on, Buster joined the queue because Buster did some work for Coxsone and then he came with Prince Buster The Voice Of The People and Buster was producing his own hit songs so it was a big competition. When Buster started his label he was lucky... he had some really good hits to match Duke Reid and Coxsone... Edwards wasn't doing so much producing. So it was a sound war... who can dominate dance halls at that time and Coxsone, Duke Reid, King Edwards and Buster they were the dominant force. Then you had people like Count Bells, you had Tom The Great Sebastian... he was even before them... he used to play at a club called The Silver Slipper. You had Lord Koos... not the Koos from England... you had V Rocket but the greatest sounds at those times was Sir Mike The Musical Dragon, Sir Percy The Welterweight, Sir George The Atomic... the greatest sounds. A whole heap of sounds..."

Dennis AlCapone

ON THE RADIO

RADIO JAMAICA
BROADCAST BAND (A.M.)
720 Kc/s, 560 Kc/s, 1180 Kc/s,
SHORT WAVE: 4.95 Megs.
F.M. 88 6 Megs. and 94 6 Megs.
REDIFFUSION SPECIAL: 4.30 Sign On 5 00 Sunrise Service. 5 15 The Greatest Story Ever Told. 5 30 Weather Forecast

5 54 Radio Sign On 5 55 New Every Morning

6 00 Time Signal, Sacred Heart; 6 15 Weather Forecast — Wake Up Jamaica. 6.45 Fun at Breakfast. 6 50 Toast of the Town. 6 55 Calypso Corner

7 00 Time Signal, Local News. 7 08 Weather Forecast, 7 10 Morning Melody. 7 15 Time Signal, Breakfast Club 7 30 News Headlines. 7 34 Weather Forecast, 7 40 Breakfast Club

8 00 Time Signal BBC News. 8 10 Lift Up Your Hearts, 8 15 Breakfast Club 9 00 Time Signal, Music At Nine 9 30 Life with the Lyons

10 00 Time Signal Solo Spot 10.15 Freddy Martin 10 30 Housewives Choice

11 00 Time Signal BBC News, 11 10 Hit o' the Day. 11 15 Housewives Choice

12 00 Time Signal, Luncheon Date 12 30 Local News, 12 39 Weather Forecast 12 41 Luncheon Date

1 00 Time Signal Luncheon Date

2 00 Time Signal Educating Archie, 2 30 Anything Goes

3 00 Time Signal BBC News 3 10 Anything Goes

4 00 Time Signal Old New Orleans 4 15 Birthday Club, 4 45 Treasure Isle Time

5 00 Time Signal Music by Roth, 5 30 Ivory Interlude 5 45 Bing Sings

6 00 Time Signal BBC News, 6 10 Local News 6 19 Weather Forecast 6 20 Art Baker's Notebook 6 25 Musical Interlude

Stakes, 4 15 BBC Northern Orchestra

5.15 Scottish Magazine, 5 45 Sports Round-up and Programme Parade

6 00 The News, 6 03 Home News from Britain

16.80 M (17.86 Megs)
19.9. M (15.07 Megs)
16.77 M (17.89 Megs)

6 15 Commentary Reflecting West Indian Viewpoint.

16.77 M (17.89 Megs)
19.91 M (15 07 Megs)

6 45 Sports Review, 7 15 Radio Newsreel 7 25 Interlude

16 77 M (17.89 Megs)
19.91 M (15.07 Megs)
25 53 M (11 75 Megs)

7 30 Radio Theatre presents 'Landfall', 9 00 The News, 9 09 Commentary, 9 15 Encore, 10 00 Close Down

CLUB HAVANA
"Jamaica's Latin Quarter"
TONIGHT
AND EVERY NIGHT
Dance to Havana's Orchestra Celebrate your Birthday anniversary here and enjoy unlimited fun!

HAVANA FRUIT STORE
SPECIALISING IN ...

"Duke Reid still looks back on the sound system days and is ready to say that his colleagues in this field have been greatly responsible for the success of our vocalists. He speaks favourably of V Rocket, a sound which started about the same time as himself and was one of the top of its kind. V Rocket he says 'has been a great influence in promoting rhythm & blues and was and is always one of the leading sounds.'"

'Greatest Jamaican Beat'

"'Cuttings' worked for Duke Reid. Cuttings was like a deejay for Duke Reid's sound system, and he was, I suppose you could call him Duke Reid's assistant. He was the guy who used to come down and get the dubs on a Friday... he was the one who used to gather up the artists and make sure they're all there. He was sort of like Duke Reid's major-dom."

Graeme Goodall

The epithet Duke Reid 'The Trojan' was acquired from the truck, a UK built Bedford Trojan, "quite a smallish pickup apparently", that was used to transport Duke Reid's sound system and, on his arrival to string up the sound, he would invariably be met with shouts of "here comes the Trojan!". Duke's initial release, a 78rpm mento recording, came out on the Trojan label in 1958: 'Penny Reel' backed with 'Chambolina' by Lord Power & The Calypso Quintet. As Keith 'Scotty' Scott recalled "Duke really liked the Jamaican mento bands that played the hotel circuit".

Other mento 78's "Pressed Exclusively For Reid's Sound System", including 'Strip Tease' backed with 'Let's Do It' by Lord Power with The Trenton Spence Quartet and 'Matty Belly' by Roy Shurland with The Trenton Spence Quartet backed with 'One Baggie' by Lord Power with The Trenton Spence Quartet, appeared on the Hi-Lite label. But from 1959 onwards Duke Reid's productions were built around hard driving shuffle and boogie based on American rhythm & blues. These might, perhaps, have lacked some of the wild and spontaneous excitement that characterised a number of the other sound men's early forays into the studio. But, rather than any absence of inspiration, the reason behind this was a constant search for perfection that would continue throughout his recording career.

"Coxsone knew the type of sound he wanted from his musicians and singers from the start whereas Duke Reid was from an older generation... he was certainly no 'hep cat'." **Steve Barrow**

"In 1959 when Duke saw Dodd's successes with tunes like 'Easy Snapping' by Theophilus Beckford, 'My Baby' by Jackie Estick, 'Muriel' by Alton (Ellis) and Eddy (Perkins) and 'Shufflin' Jug' by Clue J and his Blues Blasters, he decided to venture into recording on a wider scale. The tune that Jamaicans really related to was 'Easy Snapping' for Dodd... he made so much money off of the record he didn't have a hand to count the money! At first he'd kept it for his sound system and the only way to hear it was you'd have to go to a dance. Smith's 'Fat Man' (by Derrick Morgan) was almost as big as 'Easy Snapping' on the sound systems so Dodd put the record out.

Jamaicans at that time were impressed with the fact that they could make their own music and Duke wanted a piece of the action. He recorded 'Duke's Cookies' at Federal in 1959, however, at that same session other recordings were also made: Laurel Aitken's 'Judgement Day', 'Parapinto Boogie' by Lloyd Clarke, 'Lollipop Girl' by The Jiving Juniors and 'Lover Boy' by Derrick Morgan were recorded but released a little later. The Jamaican public went to the record shops in droves to buy these records... they'd line up outside to buy them." **Keith 'Scotty' Scott**

Occasionally Duke Reid would take the vocals himself and other Kingston characters and a variety of musicians would be brought in on his recording sessions too.

"Duke Reid sang about three or four songs you know? Like 'Hill & Gully Ride' (credited to Duke Reid & His Group) and all that... 'Hill & Gully Ride' Duke sang it himself man! Duke sang 'Tend To Your Business And Leave My Affairs Alone', 'Can't Wear Two Face Under One Hat'... Duke sing them himself man! Sometimes in a competition they'd play the foreign 'Tend To Your Business' (by James 'Wee Willie' Waynes on the Sittin' In With label) and then play Duke's own." **Bunny 'Striker' Lee**

"Duke Reid? We came to an agreement, you know, and I went and made the tunes. I made 'Let George Do It', 'Blackberry Brandy' and quite a few more tunes. They wanted the shuffle and boogie but I was drawing in my 'boof boof' beat... the ska... into the thing." **Prince Buster**

"Them guys did great in the sound world and then Prince Buster used to make tunes for Duke Reid... tunes like 'Shake A Leg' (Derrick Morgan) and 'Humpty Dumpty' (Eric 'Monty' Morris) and all of those tunes there were Buster's tunes. And on 'Let George Do It' (Duke Reid's Group) with Rico they credited Don Drummond on it. That was the first stepping tune... listen to it! No bass inna it... just drums with a guy named 'Drumbago' (Arkland Parks) 'doof, doof, doof' with the stepping drum right through it. Drumbago's bass drum carries the tune. Those guys died and they don't get any recognition but Drumbago was a godfather for the music."

Bunny 'Striker' Lee

A number of Duke Reid's early shuffle and boogie recordings were credited to Drumbago And His Harmonisers, Drumbago And His Orchestra and, on one occasion, 'In And Out The Window' by Monty And Roy, as Lumbago And His Orchestra. One of the biggest and brightest stars of early Jamaican music, Derrick Morgan, made his recording debut for Duke Reid only to discover that his songs were destined to be retained for exclusive play on Duke's sound system and radio show.

"I hear Duke Reid was doing auditions for singers to record. So I went to him to do some recording and sang four songs... he picked two which we then recorded. The first song was 'Lover Boy', which got the alias of 'S (South) Corner Rock' then 'Oh My'... the first song I heard on the radio was 'Oh My' on Treasure Isle Time... which was Duke Reid's radio programme. I recorded the song Wednesday and Saturday I heard it on the radio. You can imagine the first time I heard it on the radio... I was so excited I started jumping around all over the place. It was so nice, you know... but he wouldn't release them until I recorded for Little Wonder in 1960."

Derrick Morgan

'Fat Man', the bolero based song that Derrick recorded for Little Wonder was released on Simeon L Smith's label, Smiths, in Kingston and Blue Beat in London. It was a massive hit and "immediately a Number One song in the charts" and Duke Reid promptly released 'Oh My' and 'Lover Boy'/'S (South) Corner Rock' back to back on his Duke Reid's label. Derrick later reminisced "then I started recording for anybody and everybody" with releases that included the double sided 'Leave Earth' and 'Wigger Wee Shuffle' for Clement 'Coxsone' Dodd's All Stars label, also released on Blue Beat in the UK, but after "I record about six songs Duke demand me back so I started recording for him with Millicent Todd as Derrick & Patsy".

Derrick also helped out with the arrangements and production on a number of Duke's recording sessions.

"Even with Duke Reid a lot of the times I used to guide the artists and musicians how to go into it". **Derrick Morgan**

Millicent 'Patsy' Todd, "the teen star of ska", had left school aged fourteen when her sole ambition was "to marry Frankie Lymon whether he liked it or not... I didn't have a career in mind". Her mother approached Derrick Morgan and proudly told him that "her daughter could sing" so Derrick asked Patsy to record with him. They enjoyed a number of huge hits for Duke Reid and their most popular song, 'Love Not To Brag', was released on the Duke's Dutchess label in Kingston credited to Derrick Morgan & Patsy and as Derrick & Patsy with the Drumbago All Stars on Blue Beat in London. But Derrick decided to leave Duke Reid and moved on to record with Prince Buster.

"Then I met Prince Buster on Orange Street and he asked me to help him out on some recording sessions so we get together and I started to record for Buster" and their work would consolidate Derrick Morgan's reputation as the island's most popular and prolific performer. As Jamaican shuffle and boogie transformed into the hypnotic rhythms of ska Derrick became the only artist to simultaneously hold the One to Seven positions on the Jamaican charts.

"So I went with him and do songs like 'Shake A Leg' for him (released on the Buster Wild Bells label) and it got to Number One again. Around 1960/1961 I scored seven times in the Top Ten on the radio station... from Seven to Number One pure Derrick Morgan. I still hold that record up until now. No-one break it!" **Derrick Morgan**

As the Sixties progressed business down on Bond Street began to go awry and Bunny 'Striker' Lee recalled how Duke's fortunes were allegedly turned around with a fortuitous win by the Duchess in The Irish Hospitals' Sweepstake. Tickets were sold internationally for this sweepstake, established in the Irish Free State in 1930 to finance hospitals and usually known as the Irish Sweeps or Irish Sweep, although "Lucille Reid denied ever winning a lottery or sweepstakes... but this was common talk".

"Like all people with a dream things got tough for 'Duke' Reid and he could do no more recording until 1962. Today it is his wife Mrs Reid who backs his dream, owns the family business 'Treasure Isle Liquor Store' and finances the recordings..." **'The Birth Of Ska'**

"Duke had a whole heap of trucks and he did bankrupt. Him and Mrs Reid was having problems. Then all of a sudden you heard that Mrs Reid won the Irish Sweep... the Irish Sweep was the thing... and she and Mr Reid get back together. Everything was in Mrs Reid's name after that. Duke wouldn't allow you to talk to Mrs Reid unless he'd sent you to her... you understand? If you talked to Mrs Reid the Duke would tell you not to come back to his place... and Duke used to have his guns them. You couldn't just go to Mrs Reid... Mrs Reid never talked to you." **Bunny 'Striker' Lee**

In 1962, in partnership with the Duchess, the Duke released the epochal, and unmistakably Jamaican, 'Rough And Tough' credited to 'The Stranger' (Wilburn 'Stranger' Cole) and The Duke Reid Band and allegedly written by Lee 'Scratch' Perry. 'Little Lee' had recently arrived in Kingston from Kendal in the rural parish of Hanover as a dance champion and, using his prowess on the dance floor as a calling card, had introduced himself to the Duke as a prospective singer and songwriter. Duke Reid was unimpressed with his vocal abilities but was sufficiently taken with Lee's song writing to give one of his best songs to Stranger Cole without obtaining the author's permission... although Stranger later insisted that he wrote 'Rough And Tough'. When the diminutive Lee remonstrated with Duke Reid he was summarily dismissed and, according to Joe Higgs, "Duke flattened him with a hefty punch". It was paradoxical that Duke, a highly respected ex-law enforcement officer, "Duke Reid and his wife were honoured members of the community and, in formal recognition, he would later be appointed a Justice Of The Peace", would return to prominence with a record with such a pronounced anti-establishment stance. However, this would certainly not be the only time that Duke Reid would confound convention.

"The Duke Reid produced single 'Rough And Tough', by Stranger Cole, was said to be the first rude boy anthem, representing a brewing atmosphere in Kingston as Jamaica gained independence in 1962. It brought a new self confidence, reflected by young men looking up to the bad boy figure in Hollywood who was invincible and wore his smart suit as a uniform...

Mrs Lucille Reid/David Rodigan

Duke Reid's

Herbie Miller, curator of the Jamaica Music Museum, told the New York Times; 'Any early rude boys were seen as strugglers who turned to violence and crime'. It was the 'idea of liberation for the common man: if you can't get jobs, if education and healthcare is poor, you resist by turning against the system... with language, how one wore clothes or challenged the traditional European style of dress.'" **Caroline Young**

"Most of the time in Duke Reid's Liquor Store... it full of police. He administrate like police as well. He has this rifle that he walks with. His hip gun. His hand grenade." **Dennis AlCapone**

"In 1962 'Duke' put out the song that everyone was singing... the still popular 'Rough And Tough'. After this came 'When You Call My Name'. 'River Bank', 'Musical Communion' and many others. Duke's beat was here to stay! In the light splashed night streets of Kingston bodies twisted and whirled to the joy of the rhythm & blues beat...

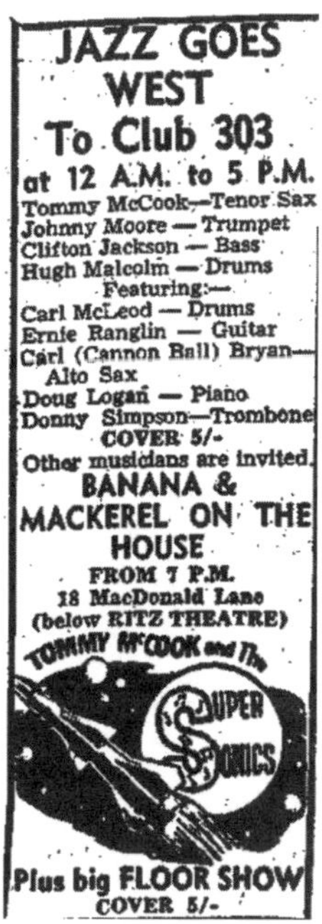

Ska and it's here to stay... but let's get it straight 'Duke' was there first for the ska is rhythm & blues grown up!

Let's set the record straight. It was 'Duke' Reid from Western Kingston who developed this beat based on the indigenous music of Jamaica. It was way back in 1952 and then the 'Duke' called it 'rhythm & blues'. Exciting, hypnotic... a mixture of Jamaican folk music and rock 'n' roll. Goes like this 'Duke' Reid, lover of music and the deep rolling rhythms of his Jamaican people heard the beat develop from watching his people dance. He got himself an amplified 'sound system' and while hiring it out for dances, he listened and he watched, on so many Saturday nights when the back streets and dance halls of Kingston come alive... and his dream was born... music sprung from the basic beat of Jamaica with all the USA influences and the power and beauty and joy of the earth." **'The Birth Of Ska'**

The runaway success of 'Rough And Tough' in 1963 was emulated the following year by 'Carry Go Bring Come', Justin Hinds & The Dominoes' debut recording, who had auditioned the song at Treasure Isle after "missing an appointment" with Coxsone at Studio One. The record, "made in one take", was an immediate hit and was followed by a number of releases that "immensely increased the stature of Duke Reid as a record producer".

'Greatest Jamaican Beat'

Tommy McCook at Treasure Isle

The Baba Brooks Orchestra/Band and 'Tommy McCook & His Ska-talite' had provided the majority of the music for Treasure Isle's ska recordings and, when The Skatalites ceased playing together in the summer of 1965, Tommy took over arranging the horn parts for society band Kes Chin and The Souvenirs. He soon moved on to become Treasure Isle's musical director and leader of the Bond Street house band: Tommy McCook & The Supersonics.

"Duke Reid came to me about playing for him. I said I needed a rest because with The Skatalites I did every damn thing. I was the manager, I did the advertising, rehearsed the group. Reid told me 'You don't have to do anything but deal with the music' and then he said 'name your salary'. All I had to do was play. This was August, September 1965."

Tommy McCook

"He had Tommy McCook & The Supersonics when The Skatalites broke up. Half of them went to Duke and some stayed with Coxsone and became The Soul Brothers." **Bunny 'Striker' Lee**

"Duke Reid started with Tommy and Roland (Alphonso) was with Coxsone. Roland was Coxsone's fancy and Tommy was Duke Reid's fancy."
Lloyd Brevett

"I was fortunate. I had the ideas that the guys needed on their sessions and they respected my compositional skills to put music to the rhythms."
Tommy McCook

Tommy McCook had already established himself as one of the island's most accomplished jazz musicians and, after some persuasion, changed his allegiance to ska. He would go on to play a pivotal, if still undervalued and largely unrecognised, role in the development of Jamaican music. Born Thomas Matthew McCook 3rd March 1927 in Havana, Cuba to Jamaican parents, "their father had taken a job to work at the Panama Canal and established a family home in Havana". The family returned to Jamaica in 1933 where, at the age of eleven, his mother "approached Alpha to see if there was room for Tommy with the school band" and the school told her "they needed a sax player". Alpha Boys' School on South Camp Road, a noted charitable institution established in 1880, had been running their own Alpha Band since the 1890's. His mother entrusted Tommy to the Roman Catholic nuns at Alpha, who had developed a formidable reputation for both their music and their discipline, and Tommy studied music theory, flute and tenor saxophone at Alpha for four years.

'The Birth Of Ska'

Tommy McCook and The Skatalites

"It was a Catholic school for the poorest kids of Jamaica. I grew up without a father and it was tough on my mum. I attended this school because of that and to learn music."
Tommy McCook

Owen Gray, "Jamaica's First Home Grown Star", was adamant that the pupils at Alpha were not necessarily all "wayward boys".

"I went to Alpha when I was very young but I never stayed there for no period of time. I wasn't a bad boy! It's not bad boys went to Alpha School... it was kids whose parents couldn't afford to give them the education that they wanted to give them. If you hear differently it's not true! The gates of Alpha were open... open like the gates of Heaven. You'd learn a trade there. If you were rude or naughty they'd send you to Stony Hill (an Approved School on the northern outskirts of Kingston... a former industrial school designed to inculcate work habits and skills in delinquent adolescents) if you skipped school you'd be picked up by the school police and taken there."
Owen Gray

Dave Hendley

33 Bond Street

Dave Hendley

33 Bond Street

At Alpha great emphasis was placed on musical tuition and many of Jamaica's foremost jazz musicians including Don Drummond, who often returned to help out at the school, Bobby Ellis, Vincent 'Don D Junior' Gordon, Johnny 'Dizzy' Moore and Rico Rodriguez all studied at South Camp Road under the guidance of band master Lennie Hibbert and the watchful eye of Sister Mary Ignatius Davies.

"The first thing you learnt at Alpha was the rudiments of music: lines, spaces and scales. Theory was a must. You were asked questions on a blackboard and you gave your answers verbally. You didn't start to play just so. You had to know what you were doing so our upbringing was very enlightening." **Rico Rodriguez**

So prodigious were young Tommy McCook's talents that he began to play with the Eric Deans Orchestra while still at Alpha. Eric Deans was also an instructor at the school and he enrolled the most promising pupils, including Roland Alphonso, Baba Brooks, Don Drummond and Ernest Ranglin, who all played with his Orchestra. "With Eric Deans Tommy learned to play the music he loved... jazz" before moving on to Don Hitchman's sextet and then Roy Coburn's Blu Flames who were voted Jamaica's second most popular band in Ivory magazine's 1952 annual popularity poll.

"Jazz was my first love. I love jazz music." **Tommy McCook**

Due to the lack of musical opportunities at home a number of Jamaica's jazz musicians, including Wilton Gaynair, Noel Gillespie, Joe Harriott and Harold McNair, left the island during the Fifties to seek their fortunes overseas. In 1954 Tommy McCook joined this exodus and left for the Bahamas for a long term engagement with a dance band at the Zanzibar Club in Nassau.

"We used to play orchestrated music from the USA from the big band era. I started in big band music. In 1943 I was playing American orchestrations: Count Basie, Glenn Miller, Woody Herman, Duke Ellington and later Stan Kenton, Gene Krupa... the whole thing. But in the dance bands I played in, especially in the Bahamas, the tourists didn't want to hear any jazz at all. They wanted to hear island music: rumbas, calypsos, whatever. The minute we started an American standard they would say 'We don't want no American music. We just left that at home. We don't want that here.' But it was fine by me. By 1963 I was tired of it."

Tommy McCook

When he returned to Jamaica in 1962 Tommy began playing alongside pianist Aubrey Adams at the Courtleigh Manor Hotel, where he was approached by Coxsone Dodd, "I listened to the music but I was playing jazz at the time", and he took some convincing that this burgeoning new music could be anywhere near as serious as his beloved jazz.

"Coxsone asked me if I would do some local recordings for him. I never really thought about it as I was really concentrating on the jazz scene."

Tommy McCook

Jazz in Jamaica had always been a minority interest yet the "twenty or so studio musicians who played on nearly all early Jamaican records" were usually jazz men and Coxsone and Lloyd Knibb eventually persuaded Tommy to organise this loose collective of musicians into a cohesive unit. He not only gave The Skatalites an added dimension through his arranging and organisational abilities and his melodious tenor saxophone but also their name... although he was careful to point out that he had nothing to do with the naming of ska.

"The term ska was invented before my time. It was introduced by Clue 'Clue J' Johnson the leader of The Blues Blasters. His nickname was

Duke Reid
DUKE REID
GREATEST Hits
D.R. Enterprises B.M.I.
33 Bond Street, Kingston, Ja.
Tel: 25629 27594
Teach The Children
DENNIS AL CAPONE
With Tommy McCook All Stars
RECORDED AT TREASURE ISLE RECORDING STUDIO
Treasure Isle
33 Bond St. Kgn., Ja.
Tel. 25629 27594
YOU HAVE CAUGHT ME BABE
THE MELODIANS
With Tommy McCook & The Supersonics
RECORDED AT TREASURE ISLE RECORDING STUDIO
PARAGONS MEDLEY
JOHN HOLT
With Tommy McCook All Stars
BARON'S
Dist. By THE BARON'S RECORD CENTER
94 Molynes Rd., Kgn. 10
Prod. By B. SMITH
MOSQUITO 1
EL PASSO
With Tommy McCook & The Supersonics
Treasure Isle
DRIVE HER HOME
SURE-SHOT
WILLOW TREE
ALTON ELLIS
SIDE 1
D. R. ENTERPRISES B.M.I.
I'M A LOVING PAUPER
DOBBY DOBSON
DUTCHESS
33 Bond St., Kgn., Ja.
Tel. 25629
YOU ARE MY LOVE
FLASHING MY WHIP
HUGH ROY
With Tommy McCook & the Supersonics
WOMAN COME
MAGUREITA
BABA BROOKS
MANUFACTURED BY FEDERAL RECORD MFG. CO. LTD. JA.
Every Day Is Just a Holiday
The Sensations
BARONS LABEL
94 Molynes Road
BARBWIRE
Nora Dean
33 BOND STREET
KINGSTON, JAMAICA
GOLDFINGER
TOMMY McCOOK
Trojan
Tel. 25629 27594
THINGS YOU SAY YOU LOVE
THE JAMAICANS
With Tommy McCook and the Supersonics Band
RECORDED AT TREASURE ISLE RECORDING STUDIO KGN. JA. W.I.

'Skavoovee'. That's the way he would greet everyone 'What's happenin' Skavoovee?' and since he was instrumental in creating the music that's the way it had to be called." **Tommy McCook**

"Satellites was the thing happening at the time. It was 1964. America was trying to go to the moon. These satellites were always orbiting the earth but I thought it shouldn't be satellites but Skatalites because we were playing ska...

Somebody had suggested 'The Satellites'. It was 'Dizzy', Lloyd Knibb or one of the brothers. But I said 'No. 'The Skatalites' since the ska was what we played." **Tommy McCook**

"One day in the studio Tommy McCook said 'Gentlemen we should give ourselves a name because people hear us backing all these records and are asking to see us perform live'. All agreed it was a good idea. But what would they name it? The Russians (sic) had just launched the Telstar satellite into space so Lord Tanamo suggested The Satellites. Almost as a joke Tommy said 'No. Let's call it The Skatalites and the name stuck."

Lloyd Brevett

"Then, after we decided to form a group, we had a meeting at the Globe Theatre near Cross Roads... But by this time some hot instrumentals were out there and people were going crazy over the recordings! So the group was formed, we went down the road and everything looked rosy for fourteen months." **Tommy McCook**

And The Skatalites, comprising Tommy McCook and Roland Alphonso on tenor saxophone, Lester Sterling on alto saxophone, Don Drummond on trombone, Johnny 'Dizzy' Moore on trumpet, Jackie Mittoo on piano, Jerome 'Jah Jerry' Haynes on guitar, Lloyd Knibb on drums, Lloyd Brevett on bass and vocalists Doreen Schaeffer, Tony Da Costa, Jackie Opel and Lloyd Tanamo, played their first engagement shortly afterwards on 16th May 1964 at the Hi Hat Club in Rae Town. The band played their farewell show in August of the following year at a police dance held at the Runaway Bay Hotel. Their break up was due to a combination of personal

'Greatest Jamaican Beat'

Byron Smith

'Independence Jump Up Calypso'

Well designed and boasting the modern recording studio equipment (sic) in the island is Treasure Isle Recording Stuido and financial problems but the loss of Don Drummond had been a major setback when he was convicted of the murder of his girlfriend, Anita 'Margarita' Mahfood, in January 1965. He was found criminally insane the following year and confined to Kingston's Bellevue Mental Hospital where he died three years later.

"We never used a substitute for Don... we left his space open. There was nobody around who could fit his space." **Tommy McCook**

The Skatalites only remained together for fourteen months but, during that brief period, they established many of the rules and set the precedents for all that was to follow. But, amid rumours of discontent amongst the band members with the musicians complaining they were not earning enough to support their families and with Coxsone allegedly playing off Roland Alphonso against Tommy McCook, The Skatalites ceased to play together. The component members formed into smaller studio based ensembles. As 1966 dawned the ska beat gradually gave way to rock steady and Tommy McCook began to play a defining role in creating the signature sound of Treasure Isle and in establishing Duke Reid's Recording Studio.

Lindon Pottinger, together with his wife Sonia, played a significant part in the story of Treasure Isle. His productions by artists including Dobby Dobson, Lord Tanamo, The Maytals, The Mellowlarks, Jimmy James and Winston Samuels were issued on seven inch releases on his Gaydisc, Golden Arrow and SEP (for Sonia Eloise Pottinger) labels during the early Sixties. He also released gospel recordings on the Glad Tidings label and the only Gaydisc long playing release was Lord Tanamo's 'Festival Jump Up' in 1965. One of his earliest and biggest hits, 'Come To Me Softly' by Jimmy James, was also released on WIRL (West Indies Records Limited), on Dice, a Melodisc subsidiary, in London and in Miami, USA too on the Sundown label in 1963.

"Motta's and Chin's they were the big guys at the time then Mr Pottinger came in... they were the calypso specialists... he was in the business before Sonia Pottinger who was his wife. He recorded Jimmy James, who is in London now, on a record called 'Come To Me Softly' which was done at the State Theatre with his equipment and released on WIRL. Mr Pottinger built his studio at Sundown Crescent... I don't remember the direct address... and did a lot of songs with Lord Tanamo like 'You Belong To My Heart'. He also worked with a guy called Winston Samuels... he used to make a lot of hits too! His labels were Gay Disc and SEP. He was the first black man to have a studio in Jamaica and he was one of the first men to have a pressing plant in Jamaica." **Bunny 'Striker' Lee**

However, Mr Pottinger did not continue with his own productions for long although he remained in the record manufacturing business with Disc Pressers Ltd initially at 103 and then 37 Orange Street. Mrs Pottinger began to produce records for her Excel, Gay Feet, Pep, Rainbow and High Note labels (gospel recordings were released on her Glory subsidiary) through the Tip Top Record Centre, also situated at 37 Orange Street. The first Gay Feet release, a lachrymose ballad 'Every Night' by Joe White & Chuck (Joseph), was a massive hit in 1965 and the record's popularity was further consolidated by the b-side: the equally popular ska track '1st Session' by Baba Brooks & His Recording Band.

It would be too simplistic to categorise Mrs Pottinger, also known as Miss Potts or Mrs P, as Jamaica's first and foremost female record producer for, in this male dominated arena, there are very few rivals to the title. The youngest of three children she was born Sonia Eloise Durrant 21st June 1931 in Leith Hall in the parish of St Thomas and moved to the capital to attend the island's only all girls' primary and infant school: St George's Girls' Primary and Infant School on Duke Street in downtown Kingston. On leaving school she took accountancy and secretarial courses before marrying Lindon O Pottinger in 1952. They set up a number of businesses together, including a bicycle store and a shop selling her home cooked patties, before she ventured into record production when the Pottingers separated in 1965. Sonia recalled that, with three children to support, she "needed to work and not work for someone and so I invested in the music industry". 'Every Night' remained on the Jamaican Hit Parade for month after month and established her as a serious contender in this highly competitive profession. Her reputation as a consistently creative record producer was always backed by her insightful business acumen and her hit making career would continue unabated until 1985 when she retired from music making.

"My first release was 'Every Night' by Joe White and Chuck (Joseph) and I got an award for this and went from strength to strength from there..."
Sonia Pottinger

Treasure Isle
33 Bond St. Kgn., Ja.
Tel. 25629 27594
FESTIVAL SONG 1967
BABA BOOM
THE JAMAICANS
With Tommy McCook & The Supersonics
RECORDED AT TREASURE ISLE RECORDING STUDIO
DUTCHESS
BLESSING OF LOVE
SUPERSONICS
LA LA MEAN
(I LOVE YOU)
Alton Ellis & the Flames
RECORDED AT TREASURE ISLE RECORDING STUDIO KGN. JA. W.I.
TROJAN
TR-634 A
LOVE UP KISS UP
TERMITES
treasure isle
TI-7004 A
ROCK STEADY
ALTON ELLIS and THE FLAMES
with TOMMY McCOOK and THE SUPERSONICS BAND
BLUE BEAT
45/BB 65
LET THE GOOD TIMES ROLL
DERRICK AND PATSY
DRUMBAGO AND HIS HARMONISERS
I CAN'T STAND IT
(A. ELLIS)
NU BEAT
45 RPM
NB.010A
ALTON ELLIS
(C. Bough)
DISTRIBUTED BY PAMA RECORDS LTD. LONDON, ENGLAND
Treasure Isle
BOND STREET SPECIAL
Treasure Isle
CARRY GO BRING COME
JUSTIN HINES WITH THE DOMINOES
TOMMY McCOOK & HIS SKA-TALITE
MANUFACTURED BY FEDERAL RECORD MFG. CO. LTD.
Treasure Isle
33 Bond St. Kgn., Ja.
Tel. 25629 27594
DRINK MILK
Justin Hinds & The Waves
Duke Reid
DUKE REID
PRESENT
One Life To Live, One Life To Give
(T. Randazzo-V. Pike)
Phyllis Dillon
Tommy McCook
RECORDED AT TREASURE ISLE RECORDING STUDIO
TEENAGE SKA
45 R.P.M.
WI-241
BABA BROOKS
℗ 1965
DUKE REID
DR-2515 A
VERSION GALORE
HUGH ROY
TROJAN
TR-641 A
MOONLIGHT LOVER
JOYA LANDIS
DOCTOR BIRD
DB 1059 A
A Treasure Isle Production
I'VE GOT A DATE
ALTON ELLIS AND THE FLAMES

"Mr Pottinger was a record distributor… Mr Pottinger now is in Miami… he started or still has recording business, pressing plants… everything like that. He used to distribute foreign records, local records. He was one of the guys who start the business." **Brent Dowe**

"Mr Pottinger was over the other side of Orange Street with his Gayfeet and Tip Top and so on… Mr Pottinger used to have a studio down at Sundown Crescent and Duke Reid purchased his equipment and opened Treasure Isle studio. He didn't come out the business. He sold the studio but he never left the business. He had his pressing plant and stamper cutting facilities and he used to export records all round the (Caribbean) islands. My brother Don Lee used to work for him and they kept in touch… he had a pressing plant in Suriname (the Republic of Suriname in northern South America).Then he set up in Miami with the new automatic presses. Tapper Zukie inherited this press and then Tapper sold it to King Jammy and those presses are still running!" **Bunny 'Striker' Lee**

'Greater Jamaica Moon Walk Reggay'

Clifton 'Jackie' Jackson

Prior to opening the Treasure Isle Recording Studio at 33 Bond Street Duke Reid had usually produced his recordings at Federal and Studio One and, as Keith 'Scotty' Scott recalled, "when Duke left Federal the Khouri's didn't even know that Duke was building a studio… they were surprised when it opened and he took Byron Smith with him… but Duke Reid did not achieve the sound he really wanted until 1967 and 1968".

"At the same time, the small (Federal) studio was being handled by Byron 'Baron'/'Smithy'/'Smitty' Smith, an engineer I had trained at RJR. I have to admit that when it came to laying down ska and rock steady tracks he beat me hands down. Isn't that the way it should be....the student excels the teacher? He eventually went on to work for Duke Reid at Treasure Isle Studios down on Bond Street. He was responsible for all the great Treasure Isle material." **Graeme Goodall**

"Having his own studio, not to mention a group of first class in-house musicians that would go firstly by the name of The Skatalites before evolving into The Soul Brothers, The Soul Vendors and The Sound Dimension during the Sixties, gave Coxsone Dodd an edge over his old rival, and for that matter, everybody else. Well, anything Dodd could do Reid was sure he could do too. So it was that in late 1965 that the Treasure Isle Recording Studio opened at 33 Bond Street, five blocks west of the main music thoroughfare of Orange Street and above the Reid's liquor store that was always a major provider of their regular bread and butter. The construction of his own studio meant that Reid would soon be able to match the output of Dodd by recording as and when he wanted to rather than having to book time at other studios. Thanks to a succession of excellent engineers, who included Byron Smith, Errol Brown and Carlton Hamil, the Treasure Isle sound soon became as distinctive as the one that Dodd's engineers were getting over at Studio One." **Tony Rounce**

"Duke Reid had a dream, and that dream was to have his own studio. That dream came through two years ago and it is in the form of Treasure Isle Recording Studio equipped with the most modern recording equipment in Jamaica. And it is Treasure Isle Recording Studio, with its excellent facilities and its knowledgeable engineer Byron Smith, that is partly responsible for ... the wildly acclaimed rock steady beat presented in all its glory." **'Greatest Jamaican Beat'**

"Byron Smith and Duke Reid decided to open their own studio mainly because he couldn't do with one day a week (at Federal)... so he built a studio, up on the roof." **Graeme Goodall**

'Alton Ellis Greatest Hits'

Alton Ellis

According to Bunny 'Striker' Lee, an argument with Clement 'Coxsone' Dodd at Studio One was another important catalyst in persuading the Duke to set up his own studio when, during a Treasure Isle recording session with The Silvertones at Brentford Road, Coxsone attempted to inveigle the group to record for his Studio One label.

"But Duke now... his studio was upstairs. I want to tell you how Coxsone make Duke Reid build his studio. After Coxsone built his studio Duke Reid started to support it too but it was Coxsone made Duke build his studio! Before Coxsone built his studio everybody else was still at Federal or Dynamic... or WIRL as they called it in those days. Duke Reid had his own sound but, before he built his own studio, he started to use Coxsone's studio and he voiced The Silvertones down there. One day Coxsone said to The Silvertones 'Jackson...' Coxsone used to call everyone Jackson...

'I want you to come and voice some tunes for me' and Duke got vexed because Coxsone started to check The Silvertones and they were singing for Duke Reid. You have plenty of people stay like that you know! You go to their studio and you have a singer and they start to check the singer behind your back. They tell the singer all kinda cr*p and some of these singers lose their heads but The Silvertones really reached places with Duke Reid so Duke just paid off Coxsone for the studio time with his bag of silver. He was a man who never paid in paper money… he always had this bag of silver. If it was ten thousand he'd give you some work to do! And Duke said 'I nah check none of your singers' and him just up and get his own equipment from L O Pottinger… Mrs Pottinger's husband… down Sundown Crescent.

Before you could buy fridges in Jamaica you used to go to the ice factory and buy a hundred blocks of ice and people used to make their ice box and go to the sawmill and stuff it with sawdust to keep it. So the ice would take time to melt. Then the first set of fridges that came into Jamaica you used to use kerosene oil to light it and it worked instead of the electric motor! I don't know if you guys know about that? People come a long way since then.

Duke Reid… him know what he wanted. He just took over the equipment and built his studio on top of the place! One day Derrick Morgan pass remarks (spoke disparagingly) and say 'Duke Reid's studio favour (looks like) a big ice box and Duke hold Derrick and say 'hear the sound that come out of the ice box though'. Heh, heh, heh! Duke Reid was a great man. He knew what he wanted…" **Bunny 'Striker' Lee**

According to Duke Reid's musicians and singers the wooden construction of the studio and the inherent acoustic qualities gave the Treasure Isle recordings an added warmth and richness that many of the competition's recordings lacked. Resident engineer Byron Smith had previously worked with Graeme Goodall at both RJR and Federal and ensured that the records made at Treasure Isle were as immediately recognisable as those made on Brentford Road at Duke Reid's arch rival's Clement 'Coxsone' Dodd's Studio One.

"But the Studio One sound is different to the Treasure Isle sound! The people have to know! Duke Reid made his own things and Duke was one of the greatest producers we had. He had his own style and everything."

Bunny 'Striker' Lee

The slower rhythms of rock steady not only allowed vocalists to shine but the soloists too as they no longer needed to blast their way through the "zinc fence wall of sound". It has been said that the advent of rock steady heralded the demise of Kingston's horn sections and, while there is a certain amount of truth in this, the players remained on the scene and took on the roles of featured instrumentalists and musical arrangers. Far sighted musicians, such as Tommy McCook, saw the limitless potential and open ended nature of this new form and, as musical arranger and tenor saxophonist for Treasure Isle's house band, he was, once again, at the forefront of another Jamaican musical revolution.

"But I'm based at Treasure Isle where I supervise the sessions and help with the mixing of tapes and cutting of the masters." **Tommy McCook**

On occasions Duke Reid would persuade other musicians and singers to play down on Bond Street and Bunny 'Striker' Lee recalled an occasion when Roland Alphonso, who was employed at Coxsone's Studio One, and another when Lloyd 'Tin Leg' Adams played on Treasure Isle sessions. Both ended rather ignominiously.

"Duke Reid had Roland Alphonso play some tunes for him one time… he was blowing over some rhythms upstairs at Treasure Isle and Coxsone got wind of it and he went straight down there. He just said 'Hello Mr Reid' and he took away Roland's horn and put it in his car!

Duke Reid's musicians them didn't come so Duke decide to use the musicians I use. But every minute Tin Leg drop the timing and thing. He was on a session and Duke Reid fired two shots over him head in the drum booth … heh, heh, heh… and he went to the bathroom… or toilet as we say in Jamaica… and him don't come back. Duke Reid say 'where you get that drummer?' The next thing I heard Tin Leg's living in the States."

Bunny 'Striker' Lee

But Striker, as ever, then gave credit where credit was due to guitarist Lorraine 'Ranny Bop' Williams an often overlooked member of The Supersonics.

"That guy now… people don't talk about him… but we call him Ranny Bop. He was a very good musician. He played on the Duke Reid tunes… if it's not Hux Brown it's him… he was part of Tommy McCook's band. So he used to play with The Supersonics and he was an Aggrovator. He's the

TOP TWENTY

LIST OF OUR LATEST RECORDS

1. BREAKING UP Alton Ellis Side 2 ABC Rega
2. TONIGHT . The Paragons Side 2 O How It Hurts
3. LOVE WAS ALL I HAD . . Phyllis Dillon Side 2 Girls And Boys
4. RAGA REGA . . Tommy McCook & Supersonics
5. TRUE TRUE . . . . Ken Parker
6. I'LL BE LONELY . . . . Jay and Joya
7. KANSAS CITY . . . . Joya Landis
8. MARY POPPINS . Tommy McCook & Supersonics
9. THERE COMES A TIME . . The Techniques
10. I WISH IT WOULD RAIN . . . The Techniques
11. ANGEL OF THE MORNING . . . Joya Landis
12. WILLOW TREE . . . . Alton Ellis
13. THOSE GUYS . . . . The Sensations
14. PEACE AND LOVE . . . . . The Jamaicans
15. LONELY STREET Tommy McCook & Supersonics
16. **MOONLIGHT LOVER Joya Landis New Release**
17. **DARLING FORGIVE ME Colonel and the Eternals New Release**
18. DON'T SAY NO . . . . Lloyd Charmers
19. SILVER BIRD . . . . The Paragons
20. LOVING PAUPER . . . . Dobby Dobson
21 WEAR YOU TO THE BALL . . . The Paragons
22. SOUL FOR SALE Tommy McCook & Supersonics
23. LAST TRAIN TO EXPO . . . The Melodians
24. HAPPY GO LUCKY . . . . . The Paragons
25. PERFIDIA . . . . Phyllis Dillon
26 MERCY, MERCY, MERCY . . . The Paragons
27. YOU DON'T CARE FOR ME . . The Techniques
28. WISE BIRD . . . . Alton Ellis

LATEST LPs

1. COME ROCK WITH ME IN JAMAICA
2. GREATEST JAMAICAN BEAT
3. ON THE BEACH
4. ROCK STEADY
5. REGAY BEAT

'Regay Rock Steady Soul Music For Sale'

guy who used to tell Reggie (Alva Lewis) and Glen (Adams) and Family Man (Aston Barrett) the chords. I don't know how they leave him out but through him go to Canada people tend to forget him but he made some great tunes." **Bunny 'Striker' Lee**

And he also gave credit to Duke Reid's generosity in giving him his first break as a record producer in 1967 after Striker had successfully promoted The Jamaicans' 'Baba Boom':

"Incidentally it was Duke Reid started me in the business. He gave me my first studio time for free so that I could I start doing my own sessions. I had twenty pounds and Lynn Taitt and Gladdy (Gladstone Anderson) took it and Duke Reid gave me the studio time because Duke was so pleased with what I'd done with 'Baba Boom'. It won the Festival Song Competition because Desmond Dekker should have won and 'Baba Boom' won so Duke was pleased and he gave me the studio time and that was when I left KIG (Kingston Industrial Garage)." **Bunny 'Striker' Lee**

In rock steady the rhythmic focus shifted to the bass and the drums where it has remained ever since and, although it only lasted for a brief period, its significance to the subsequent development of Jamaican music is incalculable. The rock steady beat that emanated from Duke Reid's studio defined the era and, for a while, no other producer could hope to match his supremacy: Treasure Isle was the epitome of this cool, sophisticated music and countless classic records were produced down on Bond Street. This pre-eminence was due to the musical majesty of Tommy McCook and The Supersonics with Tommy alongside Herman Marquis (who also arranged the sessions) on saxophones, Ernest Ranglin, Lynn Taitt and Ranny Bop on guitars, organists Neville Hinds and Winston Wright, Gladstone 'Gladdy' Anderson on piano, drummers Hugh Malcolm and Arkland 'Drumbago' Parks and Clifton 'Jackie' Jackson on bass. The ethereal gypsy flavoured violin of Raymond 'Paganilli' ('Paganini') Young, known as 'White Rum Raymond' would put in an occasional haunting appearance, featuring prominently on The Paragons' 'The Tide Is High', while Hopeton Lewis working un-credited (because he was contracted to Federal Records) coached singers, worked out vocal arrangements and sang backing vocals. The Supersonics were one the greatest Jamaican session bands ever and together with vocal groups such as The Jamaicans with 'Things You Say You Love', The Melodians with 'Come On Little Girl',

The Paragons with 'Only A Smile', The Sensations with 'Every Day Is A Holiday, The Techniques with 'Queen Majesty' and 'Love Is Not A Gamble' and solo singers including Phyllis Dillon with ''Don't Stay Away', Dobby Dobson with 'I'm A Loving Pauper' and Alton Ellis with 'Rock Steady' they "crafted some enduring classics that epitomised the best that the rock steady genre had to offer".

Lynn Taitt explained in an interview with Robert Schoenfeld how integral the bass guitar was to rock steady because it no longer gave equal emphasis to every beat but instead played a repeated pattern that syncopated the rhythm.

"For that tempo the tempo is very slow with the bass and guitar line playing the same thing. You used to use two guitars. Hux Brown and myself or another guitarist and myself. And it was very slow but with a definite bass line going straight through the song..." **Lynn Taitt**

"Backing all the cuts on this LP is (sic) Tommy McCook and the Supersonics, by far the most explosive sounding band where rock steady is concerned. Tenor saxophonist Tommy has been recording for Duke Reid since 1962. Duke says of Tommy McCook that he is one of Jamaica's greatest resident musicians. Tommy's band is without a doubt the greatest exponent of the rock steady beat, which is to music what three dimension is to vision." **'Greatest Jamaican Beat'**

"Tommy McCook is no newcomer to the local music scene. He has been in recent years one of the leading exponents of rock steady, ska and soul music generally. Tommy McCook's band The 'Supersonics' is regarded as one of the most explosive sound where rock steady is concerned."
'Come Rock With Me In Jamaica'

Every aspiring youngster yearned to record for Duke Reid and both Roy Cousins of The Royals and Tommy Cowan of The Jamaicans recalled trembling with trepidation before, and during, their groups' auditions for Treasure Isle.

"Gladstone 'Gladdy' Anderson was the one who played the piano and he said to us we were to come down to Treasure Isle on Sunday... come to audition 'cause he was the one who did the auditions for Duke Reid. So the Sunday we went down there he selected us and that's how come you hear that track 'We Are In The Mood' but that was never sung properly either because The Royals was always a four man group. Them days I didn't have the experience that I have now and, because Trevor didn't come, only the three of us sing it... if you listen to the harmonies you can hear there's something missing... which was a voice missing. 'Cause if I was singing it now I would have closed the gap but when we was voicing at the time them days you never had modern technology so you had to rehearse for weeks so when you go to the studio you sing exactly how you rehearsed. And, if a man didn't come, you'd have to sing the identical way. Now, if a man don't come, you know we can adjust the harmony and fix it if you understand me... " **Roy Cousins**

"Duke Reid walked with two guns on his waist and his shotgun but he became my hero after he rescued me a couple of times from the bad boys on the street. King Sporty (the deejay) and a guy called Cuttings were running the auditions. You had to creep in under the door to the rehearsal and, after Sporty and Cuttings had seen you, then you had to face the Duke! But I had a lot of fun with Duke Reid. When we recorded the song 'Baba Boom' he gave us a crate of soft drinks. This was a big thing and we thought the Duke must really like us. We never knew about royalties. We just wanted girls!" **Tommy Cowan**

Everything that followed in the story of Jamaican music owes a huge debt to the intense creativity of rock steady, and to Treasure Isle in particular as the leading exponents of the style, although Duke Reid's unorthodox production techniques might sometimes have been at odds with the final, unfailingly polished, results. For "although he had left the force, he still retained a passion for that job and continued to wear his guns at all times: .45 and .22 calibre pistols, tucked in his waist band, with a rifle at his side, during recording sessions".

"...and Smithy eventually went on to go and work for Duke Reid when Duke Reid built his own studio on top of the liquor store, the Treasure Isle Liquor Store downtown... which was incredible. It was right up on the roof of this place, built out of wood, with pigeons and God knows what up there. Duke Reid was unbelievable. He was again, deep down inside, one of the nicest men in the world but remember niceness you could not show. Too much niceness to a lot of the people there in the music business would be seen as a sign of weakness." **Graeme Goodall**

Euwart/Ewart 'U Roy' Beckford

"Duke made his own things and Duke was one of the greatest producers we had. He had his own style and everything. Duke would come in and sit down and look at the bass man and say 'I want you to play this Bassie. Dam. Dam. Dam' and the bassie would play 'Tam. Tam. Tam' and Duke would say no 'Dam. Dam. Dam' and Duke would take out his gun and fire it 'Dam. Dam. Dam!' He had three guns but he was a very nice man!

Byron 'Baron' Smith was Duke Reid's engineer... another great engineer. We used to call him Smithy. He was the man who, when every man said 'the tune gone!', and Duke would fire two shots in the air and say 'Smithy, what you talking about? Play it back like this!' and he'd stand up and everybody would listen... he used to have a man who was like his technical director. He'd hear if a man a sing off key and thing... a good musician named Marquis (Herman Marquis) who used to play a baritone saxophone after Tommy McCook did leave. Marquis would jump up and say 'quiet gentlemen. Yes. Yes. The boss was right. It needs a seventh'. So I started to tease him and call him 'Seventh'. Duke would tell the man what he wanted and then go back down to his liquor store and, if they made a mistake, he'd come back up. He knew what he wanted. Yeah man. That was Duke.

And as a producer... there was a speaker box downstairs in the liquor store (and) when him not in the studio him downstairs with him box listening to what's happening in the studio... him have a box come right down inna the liquor store where he was with his wife. And if he heard something he didn't like Duke would a come up with him cow cod... it come from cow and they used it to beat people. Them cure it and it have enough end... like a cat o' nine tails. Fire two shot in the air! 'Smithy what's going on? You don't hear the man them? It's stupidness the man them playing'.

I remember one day we were in the studio with my little crew of musicians and everybody a say 'bwoy Duke! This gone!' Byron 'Smithy' Smith was the engineer and Duke came up. So Duke always have him cow cod and him gun and him come up and fire shots up in the ceiling when everyone a say the tune gone. Him say 'Smithy? What's gone? What's all the fuss about? You'll have to do the tune over man. You understand?' And the place just go silent because Duke had fired him gun up in the air and everybody listened and Duke said 'play back this...'

Duke Reid had a ring on all his ten fingers and he used to have two guns on him side, one down him foot if you look good... but his pants were drawn over it... and a long shotgun. You understand? So plenty of people... if you don't understand Duke... if you went in his studio he'd say 'what you come in here for man? You have any business?' And he'd fire a shot over your head so the people did run!

But Duke would come to you as the bass man and say 'I want you to do this' and he'd say 'bop bop' and then say 'no! Listen again... be bop boof'. Him say yes! And they'd say 'Duke it nah go fit the chords' and Duke would say 'try it... you try it and make I see!' and then he'd fire two more shots. The men got busy! He used to get the best out of them... that's why he had so much hits. **Bunny 'Striker' Lee**

And Winston Blake, of Merritone Sound System, recalled another, far friendlier, side to Duke Reid's character when he was buying records for the sound on his way home from school.

"I was like Duke Reid's son... I was this little boy going to buy records in his school uniform. He'd say 'come here little boy...' and he'd give me back the money that I'd paid for the record! I was buying it for my Dad but he thought I'd bought it out of my savings. So I've been blessed to be a part of this great movement..." **Winston 'Merritone' Blake**

Many stories have been told of Duke Reid's stern stance and the tight hold he exercised over both his employees and his competitors that emphasise his background in law enforcement and his willingness to use any means necessary to create classic recordings. But the other side of the coin was that Duke Reid's reputation was second to none when it came to actually paying his musicians and artists. He had realised the value very early on of the public having one or two easily identifiable names to associate with and, apart from Treasure Isle, Duke Reid's and Dutchess (sic), his recordings were only ever released on a handful of subsidiary labels, Duke Reid Greatest Hits, Supersonics, Soul Shot, Sure Shot & Trojan, while his competitors' output was invariably issued on a plethora of different imprints. He exercised strict quality control on all aspects of the record making process and the amount of alternate versions subsequently showcased on later reissues stand as testament to his insistence on only the best at all times.

"And if you do a record for him, you know you're going to get recognised because his label was top. A man would go into a shop, he would always ask if they have anything new on Treasure Isle, Duke Reid's or Dutchess label." **Dennis AlCapone**

"This album was recorded at Treasure Isle Studios under the personal supervision of Duke Reid." **'Don Drummond Greatest Hits'**

"But a man like Duke Reid, he's one who'll cut five or six stampers for one record just to get it perfect". **Dennis AlCapone**

"Duke wouldn't let a bad song go on the road..." **Clive 'Azul' Hunt**

This ceaseless search for perfection was driven by more than mere imperiousness and the Duke continued to keep up with the bewildering changes in musical direction and constantly evolving styles and fashions. Towards the end of 1968 the pace of rock steady began to move towards the faster, more aggressive reggae rhythms and a new generation of producers, including Clancy Eccles, Bunny 'Striker' Lee and Lee 'Scratch' Perry, started to rise to prominence.

"Four of these numbers are currently in the JBC Top Twenty chart including Duke's latest sound, the 'raggae' (sic), which will sweep the West Indian market in the UK like the rock steady of last year."

'Here Comes The Duke'

"The Duke has done it again. Probably the foremost promoter of rock steady and the ska, Duke has played a great part in the present popularity the regay (sic) now enjoys."

'Regay Rock Steady Music Soul For Sale'

Treasure Isle continued to hold its own against the newcomers by releasing some of the biggest hits of the period including 'Lock Jaw', created in 1969 with the assistance of Lee Perry, now known as Scratch or The Upsetter, and successful enough in his own right to put his past disagreements with Duke Reid behind him. The record was particularly important as it was not reggae as it had been previously understood but one of the first to point in the direction that the music would next take, dub and deejays, and, once again, Duke would defy convention. It was a

Number One hit in Jamaica and a huge hit in England, where it was released on Trojan Records, and remained on the UK reggae charts for months. 'Lock Jaw' showcased the talents of Dave Barker, a seriously underrated singer but a deejay on this riveting release. Dave had previously, but unsuccessfully, auditioned at Treasure Isle singing Billy Bland's 1960 hit 'Let The Little Girl Dance' which was a big hit when covered by Hopeton Lewis for Federal in 1967.

"Tommy is the leader… 'everybody ready'… when I come in I start to sing… but nothing came. Roll again. Tommy asked 'are you alright?'… I think it was the shock of being amongst all them guys. Three… four takes. After that when we left the studio and began to walk home I felt terrible..."

Dave Barker

But, after this inauspicious start, a chance meeting outside Randy's Record Mart on North Parade proved to be Dave Barker's big break and the stupendous 'Shocks Of Mighty' became a notable early addition to the canon of foundation deejay records.

"One night myself and Glenmore (Glen Brown) were walking past Randy's and this green and black Jaguar drew up in front. 'It's Scratch… Lee Perry' and everyone was all excited boosting the man so myself and Glenmore followed them upstairs. I found the darkest corner of the studio to sit. They were recording 'Slip Away' with Busty Brown but Busty couldn't get the vibe. Scratch said 'make we done now 'cause Busty can't get into the song' and someone said 'try Dave, man!' and, of course, they said 'who's Dave?' So Scratch came out and said 'you feel you can handle the track?' It was 'Prisoner Of Love' and when I finished voicing the track Scratch was jumping up and down in the air and asking where did I come from. Vincent 'Randy's' Chin said 'Dave… are you from the States?'"

Dave Barker

The assembled cognoscenti were not only amazed at Dave's incredible voice and powerful delivery but, as Dave recalled, "I tend to stutter when I speak. It's all gone when I sing." He now teamed up with Scratch for a number of releases where he alternated between singing and deejaying although Dave is adamant that his deejaying happened by accident.

"'Dave can you deejay?' (and Scratch replied) 'Dave can do any damn thing man!' so I said... 'this is upsetting! Shocks of mighty! Hit me back!' It just came out...

Bunny Lee and Scratch used to share rhythms. 'Shocks Of Mighty' was made by Striker Lee... Scratch was short of rhythm so he passed it on to Scratch and he's a guy who moves spontaneously so that night he said 'make we go to Randy's and do some work'. Errol Thompson ran the track and I go up to the mic and couldn't get the vibe at all. Scratch get vexed, take off the tape and start to cuss. I was vexed too but he stormed out of the studio. The next week he decided to go back into the studio with me and Jimmy Riley. Errol Thompson ran the tape and from he span it I moved right up to the mic with 'it seems I was born to love you!' and Scratch draw off him hat! I can't believe it was the same Scratch."

Dave Barker

"Me and Scratch were such good friends that we ran sessions 'pon the same tape... same set of musicians... they didn't know if it was my thing or Scratch's thing. For instance you know 'Shocks Of Mighty' with Dave Barker? It's me who gave Lee Perry a cut of that rhythm. It was a tune named 'Hook Buttoo' but we call it 'Buttoo Girl' and some other tunes go on that rhythm... 'Prisoner Of Love' with Dave Barker... and Lester Sterling blew an instrumental on it."

Bunny 'Striker' Lee

Dave Barker recorded a number of tunes for Scratch including 'Don't Let The Sun Catch You Crying' with The Wailers on harmonies and two deejay interpretations of Wailers tracks, 'Upsetting Station' a version to 'Duppy Conqueror' and the self explanatory 'Small Axe v/s 2'. He recalled travelling down to Bond Street with Lee Perry to voice 'Lock Jaw'.

"We passed by Duke Reid's studio and we go upstairs... I was a bit on the shy side. Duke Reid and Scratch start talking. Duke Reid said 'I have a tune and I want a deejay to do it but I don't want a Jamaican deejay. He must have a Yankee feel'. Scratch said 'I have the right man here' and Duke couldn't believe it. Duke say 'Dave'... he was armed to the teeth... 'Dave'. The engineer played the track and him start to say how him would like me to do the track... 'this sound have to cover all over the place'. Duke stood right beside me... 'from coast to coast... the sound of now!' Byron Smith was engineering and Duke would nudge me when he wanted me to shout. Every time Duke Reid wanted me to say 'move it... groove it!' he tapped me and I'd do it! I did 'Funkey (sic) Reggae' a couple of months later. After 'Lock Jaw' Duke started to bloom again...

Every time I went to see Duke with Techniques (Winston Riley) as I would go through the door Duke would hand me a big bottle of Wincarnis Tonic Wine. Tommy McCook told me 'stick with Duke Reid. Him love you like a son'. Duke treated me nice. One time after 'Lock Jaw' he said 'Dave... don't move' and he went behind his desk in the liquor store and gave me a bundle... this thick... of pure five shilling notes and he wanted me to do a next tune." **Dave Barker**

Chris Lane

It is a tragedy, a travesty even, that Dave (whose real name is Dave Crooks), despite being a dynamic deejay and one of the most gifted, impassioned singers to ever come out of Jamaica, never attained the heights that his talents deserved. He should have become a household name but, instead, his name was omitted or mis-titled on the label copy of his hit records: 'Lock Jaw' was credited to 'Upsetter, Tommy McCook & The Supersonics' on Treasure Isle in Jamaica and on Trojan in England to 'Tommy & The Upsetters'. 'Shocks Of Mighty' was credited to 'The Upsetters' in Jamaica and again when it was released in the UK through Trojan on Scratch's Upsetter imprint although the Palmer Brothers UK release of the tune on their Punch subsidiary, 'Shock Of Might (Hit Me Back)', was actually credited to 'Dave Barker'. Worse was to come...

"When you went into a recording studio your problems just vanished away... for that time. Even when you finished and went home what went on kept you on a high... until you discover that your throat is being sliced."

Dave Barker

In 1968 Winston Riley of The Techniques had taken the then unprecedented step of forming his own label "let me just try a thing... first of all I mentioned it to the guys and everybody refused" so he borrowed money from his mother and set up the Techniques label with his brother Buster. He asked Dave, who he thought "had a sound just like an American... Dave Barker was more like a Yankee and he reminded me of a soul singer", to deejay over a rhythm track produced by Ansel Collins and Sly Dunbar inspired by two American records 'The Funkie Moon' by Smokey Johnson & Company on Intrepid and 'Party Time' by Ramsey Lewis on Cadet. The resulting release, 'Double Barrel', was credited to 'Dave & Ansil Collins' on Winston's Wind label in Jamaica and on his recently established Techniques outlet with Trojan Records in London in August 1970. In the spring of 1971, after over six months of exposure in English clubs, youth clubs and dance halls, 'Double Barrel' became the second Jamaican recording, the first by a Jamaican deejay, to top the UK National Charts. 'Double Barrel' also reached just outside the Top Twenty on the USA Billboard Hot 100 and went on to top the Canadian and Mexican Charts later that year. A rapidly recorded follow up single, 'Monkey Spanner', was released featuring Ansel on the Hammond organ, a dash of wah wah guitar and Dave proclaiming "this is the heavy, heavy monster sound" reached Number Seven in the UK National Charts in the summer

of 1971. Even Winston Riley was taken by surprise. "The follow up was something similar but in a different style... as long as you had an idea!"
Winston Riley

Dave Barker will be forever regarded as one of the greatest ever popularisers of the Jamaican deejay genre but, to his lasting regret, he never ever returned to record with Duke Reid at Treasure Isle...

"I never deejayed on a sound system. Deejays... I'm not keen on some of it... not keen on slackness or 'kick boy face'. U Roy, Dennis AlCapone, Scotty...brilliant! I was always a homely person. I do not go and see shows. One of the reasons I wasn't successful was because I locked myself away too much.

When we came to England with 'Double Barrel' we toured.... I went to Jamaica for three weeks. I drove down Bond Street in a cab and when it passed his shop he (Duke Reid) shouted me! 'Dave! Give me one more! Just one more!' but it never happened. Sometimes I think of him and what might have happened..." **Dave Barker**

Throughout the Sixties Jamaican deejays had begun to develop a highly individual style of 'toasting' where, instead of just introducing the records and exhorting sound system patrons to dance and enjoy themselves, they began to "ride the rhythm" and "talk over" the records. A number of enterprising record producers took the next step and began to transfer some of the excitement that the deejays were generating live every night on the mic in a dance onto record. The deejays' contributions, previously lost in the balmy Jamaican nights, were now captured for posterity in the recording studio. Winston 'King Stitt' Sparkes was the first to consistently make his presence felt as a recording deejay with a superb string of hits in 1969 for Clancy Eccles, including 'Fire Corner' and 'Herb Man', but the recordsthat Euwart/Ewart Asman Beckford made with Duke Reid as 'U Roy' in 1970 and 1971 would irrevocably alter the nature of the entire Jamaican recording industry. U Roy had deejayed on "sounds like Dickie (Wong)'s Dynamic, Sir George The Atomic and Coxsone Dodd's Downbeat (Number Two Set)". He had already recorded for Keith Hudson, Bunny 'Striker' Lee, Lloyd 'Matador' Daley and Lee 'Scratch' Perry prior to the 'Deejay Daddy' travelling down to Bond Street where his recordings "woke the town and told the people" in no uncertain terms, and legitimised an entirely new musical form. The Duke and U Roy made musical history together by using some of Treasure Isle's greatest and most popular rock steady recordings as their starting point and the influence of their work together has forever afterwards dominated reggae music. The impact of their innovations still reverberates, not only in Jamaica but also all around the world, although U Roy, in an interview years later in Kingston, mused "I thought that with the money I got for these records I might be able to buy a shirt…".

The contributions of the deejays who followed U Roy, including Dennis AlCapone and Lizzy, breathed a new lease of life into Duke Reid's rock steady classics and ever since few people of a certain age have been unable to hear those songs without joining in with the deejays' contributions and additions. But it wasn't always like this and a young Dennis Smith, later to find fame as Dennis AlCapone, recalled his first visit to the recording studio in 1970 to record 'Macka Version' with Keith Hudson.

"But I never think about putting out a record... that was brand new to me so when I made my first record I told someone:
'I've made a record.'
'So what do you do? Did you sing?'
'No.'
'Did you play an instrument?'
'No.'
'So what did you do?'
'Well… I kinda talk.'
'Man can talk 'pon record? Heh, heh, heh...'
'Well we call it deejay... you know I deejayed the record... it's a form of talk.'
And he laughed after me.
'You're a singer or you play instruments. You can't talk 'pon a record'."

Dennis AlCapone

But, less than eighteen months later, Dennis could proudly boast, on one of his best ever records, that his voice was insured for half a million dollars demonstrating just how far "talking 'pon records" had advanced.

"I'm sure that no-one needs to be told how good The Techniques' 'Queen Majesty' is; while the title is one of those few swell headed titles that actually lives up to its promise and, at the time (end of '72/beginning of '73), Dennis' voice was worth at least half a million dollars. " **Chris Lane**

"I'm the hottest deejay in radio land... I'm your main man
My voice is insured for over half a million dollars..."
'My Voice Is Insured For ½ Million Dollars' Dennis AlCapone

"As every student of Jamaican music knows (U Roy's) first Treasure Isle records were unbelievably popular. 'Wake The Town', 'Rule The Nation' and 'Wear You To The Ball' held the top three positions on both Jamaican radio station charts for twelve weeks (in 1970). As a result not only Roy's career but also those of Dennis AlCapone, Lizzy, King Sporty, King Stitt and all the rest, blossomed. Within a year deejay tunes were taken off the airwaves in order to give the ordinary singers a chance of surviving. The demand for toasting music was that strong." **Chris Lane**

"And then there was so much different deejays now... even producers... even drummers. Leroy 'Horse Mouth' Wallace he come on a track as Mad Roy. Sometimes people will ask about 'who was that deejay on that record?' but they were not deejays. It was people who'd have an idea and just go into the studio and just do something. They wasn't name deejays... it's three of us that did come and talk... U Roy, myself, I Roy (then) Dillinger, Jazzbo, Big Youth even Scotty... but Scotty was a singer in a group called The Federals and then he joined The Chosen Few later. He did some deejay tracks for Derrick Harriott and they went crazy about it... 'Sesame Street' and 'Draw Your Brakes' right? But everybody wanted to get in on the act. I'm sure there's a lot of nameless singers on record as singers couldn't get a look in at the time...

Well... at the beginning you had people like Count Matchuki and Sir Lord Comic, King Stitt, Prince Ruff and deejays like those... you have Little Wicked who used to play Ruddy's sound... Mango was another deejay on Ruddy's sound. But those guys just introduced the records, you know, and announce the dances to come... 'next Saturday night all roads lead to Port Henderson Beach you'll be dancing to the sound of Sir Coxsone The Downbeat'. That was the deejays thing at the time and on the records they'd be going 'chicka chicka chick a chick' and them kind of sounds but when U Roy come now… U Roy came with lyrics that went right through. One of the biggest selling tunes before U Roy came was a King Stitt tune called 'Fire Corner'... he did that for Clancy Eccles. You know the record! But he wasn't telling a story, right, he was just jive talking and that was mostly the deejay thing at that time. That was their trade... to boost up the dance.

But when U Roy came he came with a story and the lyrics flowing through the entire record not just the little bits. Sir Lord Comic did 'Ska-ing West'... 'Adam and Eve went up my sleeve and never came back down until Christmas Eve'... that's all he would say but U Roy would go right through and he changed the whole thing again. When he started with the big tune 'Wake The Town (And Tell The People)'... it was on Alton Ellis' 'Girl I Got A Date' rhythm… right... and he ride that rhythm right through and that's when the whole thing started. So what had gone before didn't actually kick off the deejay style... it was U Roy who done that. He really did wake the town and tell the people and then he followed it up with '(This Station) Rule The Nation' and 'Wear You To The Ball' and the whole of Jamaican music industry get a big boost because records were selling like hot bread. Duke Reid couldn't press (enough of) those records... Randy's was ordering them day by day and the records were just coming in and selling like hot bread. It was really a change... so much of a change that some of the singers wanted to be deejays because singers weren't selling at that time. And one of the great things (for the producers) was that Duke Reid or Coxsone didn't have to invest more money... they'd just go back and draw up the rock steady rhythms and put down new deejays 'pon them."

Dennis AlCapone

"'Wear You To The Ball' was special. It inspired an entire generation of toasters, boasters, and rappers locally and internationally" and, beyond any doubt, U Roy's 'Version Galore' album for Treasure Isle (and subsequently Trojan in the UK) will stand as one of the most influential records ever made.

"This is the man who has the town on its ears overnight. Few other recording artistes locally have managed to pull off one like having the top three records in the Top Ten for several weeks in a row. The U Roy craze has swept the island. Even staid swingers know about 'Wear You To The Ball' not to mention 'Wake The Town' and 'Rule The Nation'.

These are the three top records which have hung on the Hit Parade for weeks now and for once both radio stations seem to be in agreement as far as the top three places are concerned. U Roy is not a singer. He plays no musical instruments. He just deejays. Makes the sounds which create excitement when the music goes round. His comments are dubbed on to tapes of versions... instrumental arrangements of tunes.

All of a sudden Jamaica awoke one morning and U Roy was everywhere. When you met him, you'd never imagine he was the man who screams and shrieks and shouts, getting people all together. U Roy is a quiet looking guy of the Rastafarian faith, a subject which he says he 'don't joke about. It is a serious business. I believe that I man must know himself.'

His real name, by the way, is not Hugh Roy, as some fans think. He's Ewart Beckford; he was named U Roy by a younger cousin. He's twenty eight years old now and father of four children. He's happy for his success he says because 'they can live little better'." **'Version Galore'**

'Talkover', toasting or deejay records became the order of the day and began to form an integral part of Jamaican music. This combination of the familiar and the unfamiliar hit home then and has stayed there ever since. Byron Smith's technical prowess, and understanding of the recording process, meant that the music was able to accept radical modifications and make this truly startling and totally original mix actually work.

"The Treasure Isle sound was partly a product of the acoustics of the purpose built studio and, even more so the result of Reid's hiring of a genius engineer in Byron 'Smitty' Smith whose total mastery of Treasure Isle's two track board made the masters he engineered sound clean, fresh and vibrant and put the label ahead of Studio One in the rock steady race in terms of audio quality. Studio One had gone to two track too but their early rock steady records frequently lacked the fidelity of Treasure Isle as their engineers had not yet fully grasped that overdubbing and 'bouncing' to mono resulted in the loss of a generation of fidelity and frequently made it sound like the studio band was playing in one room while the singer was in a different part of the building. Byron Smith kept the overdubbing to a minimum and thus was able to create a clean backing track for one channel of the two tracks leaving the singer, group or leading instrumentalist to come in and put their contribution on the other track. These two track masters, with very little 'microphone bleed' onto the rhythms, were to prove priceless to Reid in the late Sixties when deejay music became all the rage and he was able to bring U Roy, Dennis AlCapone and Lizzy into Bond Street to ride those peerless rhythms all the way back to the top of the Jamaican charts." **Tony Rounce**

The deejays would strut their stuff and do their thing over instrumental versions of already popular records and, unsurprisingly, there are a number of versions of how this actually came about for, as Willie Williams once memorably commented, "there's more mystery than history" in the story of Jamaican music. However there can be no disputing that Duke Reid's Treasure Isle rhythms, featuring the subtle brilliance of Tommy McCook & The Supersonics, provided the solid musical cornerstone for the groundbreaking sonic experiments of both the deejays and the remix engineers.

Osbourne 'King Tubby' Ruddock had built his first sound system in 1957 and, after years of playing out at weddings and birthday parties in the Waterhouse district, was eventually crowned local 'King of the Dance Hall'. However, Tubby felt that King Tubby's Home Town Hi Fi only really got going in 1968 when he took on U Roy as his deejay. As tales of Tubby's renown began to make waves outside of the Waterhouse area he obtained employment with Duke Reid maintaining his studio equipment, dub cutting lathe and amplifiers. However, he was never the cutting engineer at Treasure Isle studio.

"No. It's not true! What Tubby's used to do, he used to repair Duke Reid's amplifiers so he used to go down there a lot. Byron Smith, The Baron, used to cut the dub." **Lloyd 'King Jammy' James**

'Versioning', 'doing over' or simply copying another producer's tune had been a feature of Kingston's musical maelstrom since its inception and a precedent had long been set for releasing instrumental or alternative vocal versions of popular rhythms often for pragmatic economic, as opposed to artistic, reasons.

"We couldn't afford for every song to get a different set of musician so we started using the same rhythm over again. It took off and then the people started wanting it on their records." **Bunny 'Striker' Lee**

"In the early part dubs used to sell for twelve pounds... you would get four tunes on a dub plate for about twelve pounds because in those days it was still pounds, shillings and pence in Jamaica. I can remember the first ever dub I bought from Duke Reid was 'Everybody Bawling', 'Travelling Man', 'Ali Baba' and a John Holt song called 'I Will Come To You Darling'. Wicked dub! These were not released... the tracks with vocals were released but not the rhythms. Rhythms didn't come on record in those days. I can remember the first song, as a sound man, that I hear with just the rhythm track on it. Duke Reid put it out and it was 'Stealing, Stealing' by John Holt. He just put pure rhythm track on it and it was like Christmas come early for us to buy a forty five with pure rhythm. I think Winston Wright did play a bit on it but that was the first one.

When you hear people talking about (rhythm) records being released Duke Reid was the man that put out the first one... because of the demand for dubs. In those days it was so exciting... it was unbelievable 'cause we were playing vocals in the dancehall so you can imagine one night you just go to the dance and you hear John Holt (sings) 'I'm gonna wear you to the ball tonight...' then, all of a sudden the deejay would say 'pull up that... now I'll play you version two' but nobody don't know what version two is. Not yet! It's a brand new era... this is not something that is established. When he jerked the needle 'pon the record and you hear (sings) 'bam pa ba bam...' 'where's the voice?' You understand? It sound so sweet... it nearly blow your head off! Especially when we played the 'Everybody Bawling' dub (sings) 'toom toom de toom toom...' and you're hearing that for the first time.

Normal people don't go to studios and hear a raw rhythm so listening to that in the dance hall... it just blow you away. And you hear that as a deejay and it's your playground now! You'd jump on the rhythm and say anything! And when you come on as a deejay now you'd lift the dance and the people would go crazy. You know you'd just find lyrics and while you're there chanting another man would be in the corner and another man round here... you know people who'd just come to the dance... but they're in such good spirits you'd hear them saying something and you'd say 'that sounds good' so I'd put that in my lyrics as well. And another one is saying something and that's how the vibes build up and that's how you get inspiration... in the dancehall. Everybody have a certain amount of vibes... that's why you have so much entertainers in Jamaica. We have people come to the dance 'cause them love it and they'll vibe with you. So you build up lyrics like that…" **Dennis AlCapone**

The importance of the rhythm, or version, to the subsequent history of reggae can never be overstated. King Tubby, in an interview with Carl Gayle, recalled that he had invented versions while cutting test plates for Duke Reid but Bunny 'Striker' Lee is insistent that Rudolph 'Ruddy' Redwood was the first man to actually play versions. The stories of Tubby or Ruddy taking out the vocals for special mixes of 'You Don't Care' or 'On The Beach' have been repeated many times but there are no arguments about the fact that it was a Treasure Isle rhythm that gave birth to the dub phenomenon.

"… but Tubby and me had really met upstairs at Duke Reid's one day when the version thing came in. It was a mistake made up at Duke's studio. Now Ruddy was really the man that started playing versions. We called it version not drum and bass. Ruddy was a big businessman and he had a club by the seaside too. When Ruddy from Spanish Town came to Coxsone's or Duke Reid's studio they gave him the keys to the city and allowed him to use any tape because his sound was like a big radio station in Spanish Town… anything that Ruddy played the other sound men wanted it and then the record buying people too. Ruddy was cutting a dub and Smithy forgot to put in the voice through we were talking and he was going to stop it and Ruddy said 'no, make it run'. So when it finished they cut it back on the other side and put in the voice. I never took any notice of it. Me and Tubby were just sitting there...

I used to go over and listen to Ruddy's and Stereo in Spanish Town and on the Monday I came in and said 'Tubby… you know the mistake we made up at Duke's studio? It's a serious mistake, you know, because the people them love it'. It mash up Spanish Town! I don't remember whose tune it was but it was Alton Ellis or John Holt they were playing. They played the singing version and then they said they're going to play part two… and those times you never had any versions… so when they played part two the people just caught the song and sang it over the rhythm. They must have played it about five or ten times and it brought down the house and, as we say in Jamaica, it mashed up the place!" **Bunny 'Striker' Lee**

Tubby's Home Town Hi Fi with U Roy on the mic were at the forefront of the fashion for playing versions where only snatches of the original lyrics remained and the added space gave U Roy, and every other deejay, the space to actually talk, question and then answer lines from the song's lyrics. U Roy, who was originally known as I Roy, became a fully fledged ghetto celebrity and many more followed in his footsteps including I Roy who stated unequivocally "me name Roy Reid... U Roy name Ewart Beckford… EWART. Me name ROY", U Roy Junior (Roy Bailey), Mad Roy (Leroy 'Horse Mouth' Wallace) and U Brown (Huford Brown) despite U Roy's on record admonishments on 'Things You Love'… "do not imitate 'cause I originate".

"But growing up older I realised that I was tuning into some of the wickedest sounds coming out and me gradually get to know the Studio One tunes… the Treasure Isle tunes. Through we used to live on Honour Street we used to pass Treasure Isle (on Bond Street) and Duke Reid had two guns 'pon him side so he was like a scary man and he always put me in the picture of a man like a cowboy in a movie. So me always ask who he is and me get to realise that was Duke Reid from the Duke Reid label. So then when I Roy… no U Roy… started to mash up the place he was I Roy when he started!

Make I tell you now when we as kids used to realise it was U Roy pass by our yard we used to shout out 'U Roy!' and always put up him hand and shout 'I Roy!'. You understand? That's why I gathered from that time that U Roy was never happy with the advent of a man who come up and call himself I Roy! 'Cause U Roy used to call himself I Roy! 'Cause him love Rasta so him always have little picky picky… him wasn't dread at the time. He'd say 'I Roy!' You know what I mean? So we loved those days as kids 'cause we used to have fun, you know?"

Ossie 'Black Solidarity' Thomas

"People who owned record shops in those days licked their fingers. On a weekend they knew they could sell ten thousand U Roy. It was something new…

And when I was working for Coxsone Duke Reid called me... no it wasn't Duke it was the engineer Byron Smith. He had a tune named 'Barbwire' with Nora Dean and he called me and said he wanted me to do the version so I went there and did that version ('Mosquito 1') but he put me out as El Paso (Dennis' sound system) 'cause he didn't want to upset Coxsone by putting Dennis AlCapone on it. Yeah! He put my name as El Paso so from that now Duke Reid hear what's going on and that I was the new sensation... U Roy was kinda on the wane 'cause U Roy did come to England with Bunny Lee and Roy Shirley. They were up here at the time and Bunny had U Roy do a tune 'my name is not Al Capone but I can keep up them tone and crack them bones!'

So that time I was running Jamaica and Duke sent for me again and said he wanted to do 'Teacher Teacher' and that tune mashed up the place. In less than no time it was Number One on both radio stations and from then on I just started working with Treasure Isle on a weekly basis. I'd get paid every week and sometimes Duke would ask me to go and do a few errands for him. Like when foreign guys would come in from America I would go and pick them up at the airport... and take them to Tivoli Gardens to some of their rude boy friends. But me and Duke were cool at the time... he put money in my pocket. People ask who is your favourite producer? And I'd always say Duke Reid... Duke Reid used to pay me money. Heh, heh, heh... a man have to live." **Dennis AlCapone**

Despite building the foundations for the next critical phase in Jamaica's musical development, Rastafarian influenced roots rock reggae, rebel music meant very little to the Duke as the insurrectionist role ran contrary to all that he believed in. Ironically some of his biggest hits over the years, Stranger Cole's 'Rough And Tough', Justin Hinds & The Dominoes' 'Carry Go Bring Come' and 'Lion Of Judah' and U Roy's 'Way Back Home'/'Behold' were imbued with rude boy and, later, Rastafarian references. But Duke Reid was never a man who could be accused of following fashions and had once refused to allow Dennis AlCapone to record a Rasta lyric by telling him "myself, I am Babylon".

In 1972 Duke Reid purchased the eight track equipment from Byron Lee when Dynamic Sounds upgraded to sixteen track recording. Not long afterwards Byron Smith followed in Duke's footsteps and opened a liquor store on Molynes Road but not before Duke's nephew, Errol Brown, had been shown how to run in the studio.

"I went down to Jamaica to help Duke Reid out... put a new console in (his studio)." **Graeme Goodall**

"Duke started with his little two track thing and then he moved up to four track… in the meantime Duke just bought the eight track and the rest is history…" **Bunny 'Striker' Lee**

"Errol Brown was born 1950 in Kingston; his father was a butcher, his mother worked in a shop. As a child, along with his sister and two brothers, he was taken by his parents to visit his uncle Arthur 'Duke' Reid…

After leaving school he attended Kingston Technical High School where he received training in electronics. He began working for the international telecommunications company Cable & Wireless… at that time actually owned by the British government. While working at Cable & Wireless he received a visit from his uncle, who arrived outside in his Pontiac GTO, which he had parked on the pavement. Duke informed his nephew to prepare for work at the studio and to carry on after the Duke's retirement replacing his first engineer Byron Smith." **Steve Barrow**

"It was hard work; the key thing was to have good ears. The balance (of instruments) was the most important thing, 'cause if a musician come in and don't hear his instrument you're in hot water. I proud of what I did at Treasure Isle 'cause everything had to be right; horns, kick drum, bass...Uncle was fussy 'bout them things. Him wouldn't put it out if it never sound right." **Errol Brown**

"When Byron Smith opened his own liquor store on Molynes Road, circa 1973, Errol was ready to take over. Indeed, when Smithy was not available Errol had been mixing dub plates for various sound systems... he remembers that King Tubby often visited the studio to buy dubs for his sound system and the future dub master would watch the younger man at the console. At this time the equipment was an Ampex two track tape machine, going into a twelve track mixing desk, according to Errol, of German manufacture. Outboard consisted of a Roland RE-201 Space Echo unit (new in 1973) along with a Fisher Reverb unit and Pultec equalisers." **Steve Barrow**

Byron Smith's also ran his own Baron's label, based in Molynes Road, on which he released a number of records between 1969 and 1971, the majority of which using rhythms that he had engineered for Duke Reid. Nora Dean's 'Barbwire' was a massive hit in the UK during the 'skinhead' era when it was released on Trojan.

"His biggest success as a producer in his own right came very early on in 1969 with Nora Dean's saucy tale of the boy with 'barbwire in his underpants' which Dean voiced over the original 1967 rock steady rhythm of the Techniques' You Don't Care'. Smitty got good value from said rhythm by also recycling it for 'Brubeck's' (Winston Wright) organ version 'Meshwire' and later, 'Mosquito 1', the first of a few cuts that Dennis AlCapone would commit to tape of his famous 'El Paso' lyrics."

Tony Rounce

Duke Reid's premature demise denied him the opportunity to become one of Jamaican music's elder statesmen and he was never able to impart his great wealth of musical experience to the younger generation. To the best of our knowledge the Duke was never actually interviewed although a young Chris Lane, now a highly respected record producer, musician and music historian and a young Tony Rounce, also a highly respected author and music historian, both met the Duke in 1974.

"When I was In Jamaica in January 1974 I went to the Treasure Isle premises on Bond Street with the intention of interviewing Duke Reid and anyone else who may have been available. I found the Duke standing behind the counter of the shop, and, after I'd introduced myself to him, he introduced me to Ernest Ranglin who he had just been chatting to. Unfortunately this was about as far as it got, although Duke was polite, he wasn't exactly welcoming and showed absolutely no interest in being interviewed. I think he told me he was 'too busy' and so I took a business card as consolation and trudged back along Charles Street to Orange Street. It was one of very few disappointments in that trip...." **Chris Lane**

"Arthur 'Duke' Reid was active in the recording business until cancer ended his life in 1976. He was never interviewed to the best of this writer's knowledge and, thus all the information we have on him, comes largely from the mouths of others. I was privileged to meet him briefly in the summer of 1974 when I visited the Bond Street premises one early morning in June. At first curmudgeonly to the point almost of hostility the Duke warmed slightly to the presence of this young, skinny white boy in his store when I started asking him about some of his recordings.

While I will not pretend that he was the most friendly and accommodating individual I met during my six week sojourn that summer I at least had the honour of being served by the man in his full regalia, guns and all. He seemed to be moving slowly, which I took to be a sign of old age. Ironically, he was younger then than I am now. It may well have been the beginnings of the cancer that would take his life less than a two years later. I did not try to interview him, as he did not look like a man who wished to be interviewed. He would have probably provided many answers to questions I did not yet then have..." **Tony Rounce**

After a long and protracted illness the Duke died of cancer 26th September 1976 in St Joseph's Hospital, Deanery Road, Kingston. The Treasure Isle Recording Studio and back catalogue had become the property of Mrs Sonia Pottinger when she took over the mortgage on Duke Reid's studio and purchased all the studio equipment towards the end of 1974.

"When it became known that Duke Reid was dying from cancer Errol Brown attempted to persuade Duke to let him take over. However, Duke decided to sell out to record producer Mrs Pottinger and her partner, radio programmer & deejay Holford 'Hol' Plummer. Following discussions between the three Mrs Pottinger decided to continue using Errol as studio engineer paying him the same weekly wage as he earned latterly with Duke Reid. Errol was earning a wage of Jamaican $100 a week... equivalent to approximately US$70 during this period." **Steve Barrow**

"Mrs Pottinger did get Duke Reid's studio. Mrs Pottinger's baby father was Hol Plummer the operator from RJR. He was a nice man. He resigned last year (2005) from RJR... he was a student there and he became the senior operator. They acquired the Treasure Isle studio when Duke got sick... you understand?" **Bunny 'Striker' Lee**

Errol worked alongside Horace 'BB' Seaton, lead singer with The Gaylads also a renowned songwriter and record producer and a key figure in the development of Jamaican music.

"... I was running the studio at the time along with Duke Reid's nephew Errol Brown. And then we got Willie Lindo in, Karl Pitterson. So I was running Treasure Isle for about two or three years in 1975 to 1977."

Horace 'BB' Seaton

By this time Sonia Pottinger had progressed from strength to strength since her breakthrough with 'Every Night' and her standing within the Kingston music business was more than assured. Her catalogue of rock steady recordings from 1966 onwards, using Lynn Taitt and The Jets and The Fugitives as her house bands, is exemplary and includes the perennially popular 'Won't You Come Home' from The Conquerors, 'Swing & Dine' and 'Little Nut Tree' from The Melodians, 'The Whip' by The Ethiopians, 'It's Hard To Confess' and 'ABC Rock Steady' from The Gaylads, Ken Boothe's 'Lady With the Starlight', the 1967 Festival Song entry 'Move Up' by Al & The Vibrators, the transcendental double sided 'Let's Get Together' and 'Cross My Heart' from Johnny & The Attractions and the not so well known but equally faultless Webber Sisters' charming 'Stars Above'. Many of these recordings were also released on Graeme Goodall's Doctor Bird label in London.

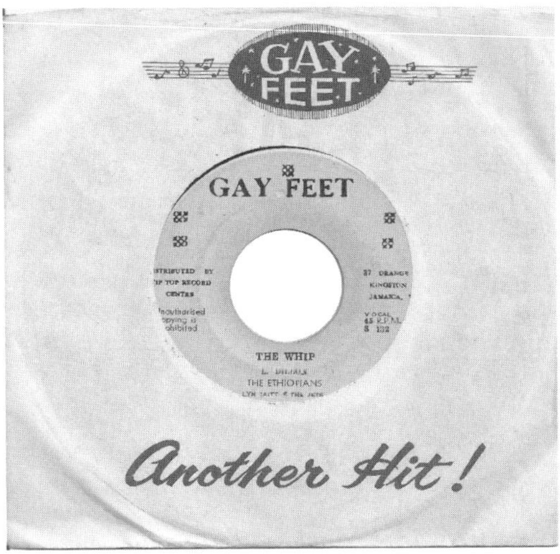

Steve Barrow

Towards the close of 1968 as the pace of rock steady speeded up into reggae, Mrs Pottinger put her foot on the accelerator too, and began using The Hippy Boys to build her High Note rhythms. The pressure never eased up with the more aggressive reggae rhythms and Mrs Pottinger continued to hit with 'Dance With Me' and 'That's Life' from Delano Stewart and instrumentals, including 'Doctor No Go' and 'Reggae Pressure' from The Hippy Boys, added to her redoubtable reputation. Younger producers such as Bunny 'Striker' Lee and Lee 'Scratch' Perry would give their productions to her Tip Top Record Centre to press and distribute and two of Striker's best ever records with Slim Smith, 'Everybody Needs Love' and 'The Time Has Come', were released on Sonia Pottinger's High Note label and given airplay on her 'Sounds Everlasting' radio show on RJR.

"Mrs Pottinger put out some big hit tunes for me too! They were my tunes but through Mrs Pottinger could get radio play… when you wanted to break an artist you gave Mrs Pottinger the tune. And then Hol Plummer used to back him (Duke Reid). That's why Hol Plummer did get his things when Duke got sick. Hol Plummer used to set up airplay for Duke and Mrs Pottinger. Nobody in Jamaica could get airplay on RJR, which was the main station, more than Mrs Pottinger and Duke Reid. Coxsone's tunes used to come out and nobody even hear about them! So the sound systems had to build it up. At this time Mrs Pottinger used to control the radio station and we were not interested in money in those days. We just wanted our artists to get the promotion and the air play for the records because then you could get the stage shows. We just want was to live. You understand?"

Bunny 'Striker' Lee

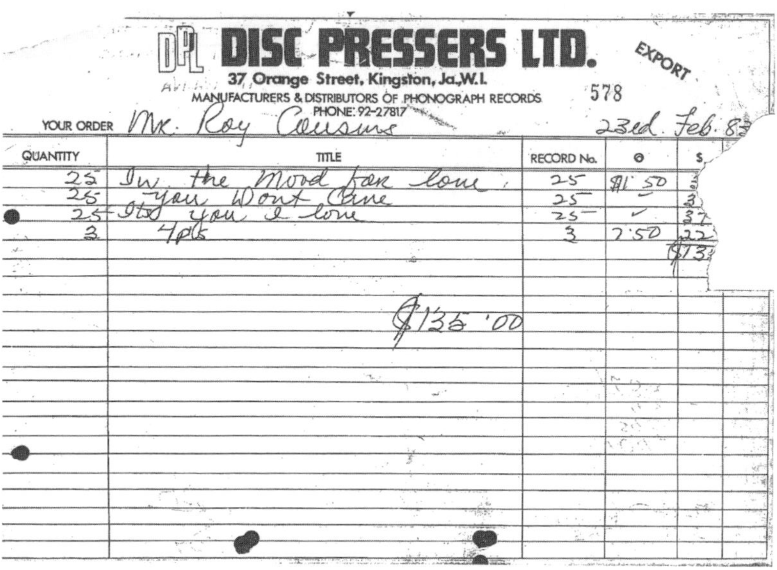
DPL DISC PRESSERS LTD.
EXPORT
37 Orange Street, Kingston, Ja.,W.I.
MANUFACTURERS & DISTRIBUTORS OF PHONOGRAPH RECORDS
PHONE: 92-27817
578

YOUR ORDER Mr. Roy Cousins 23rd. Feb. 8

QUANTITY	TITLE	RECORD No.	@	$
25	In the Mood for love	25	$1.50	3
25	You Wont Care	25	✓	3
25	Its you I love	25	✓	37
3	4 pls	3	7.50	22
				$13
	$135.00			

Roy Cousins

Sonia Pottinger now began a comprehensive reissue programme of Treasure Isle music through Disc Pressers Limited. Among her first releases were the faultless 'Hottest Hits Volumes One & Two' compilation albums featuring 'A Variety Of Local Hits By Various Artists' both of which were instrumental in keeping the Treasure Isle sound, and its place in Jamaica's musical history, alive and kicking.

DISC PRESSERS LTD.
37 ORANGE STREET
KINGSTON, JA., W.I.
TELEPHONE 27817

"Errol began working on reissuing material from the Duke Reid catalogue, beginning with the 'Hottest Hits' compilations and the dub albums, which included 'Treasure Dub' (Volumes 1 & 2), and 'Pleasure Dub'. These latter sets utilised rhythms made in the rock steady period originally produced by Arthur 'Duke' Reid, whereas 'Medley Dub', the fourth dub set mixed at the studio by Errol, utilised rhythms produced, with one exception, by Mrs Sonia Pottinger during the period 1968 to 1971. He also produced a series of twelve inch mixes from 1977 that featured deejay Jah Walton (aka Joseph Cotton) on versions of classic rock steady cuts from the Duke Reid & Sonia Pottinger catalogues." **Steve Barrow**

The roots rock reggae revolution of the mid-Seventies when 'conscious' themes came to the fore left a number of Kingston's established producers perplexed; after ten years of upgrading and updating their recording technology the music had now gone back to basics and many now had to re-trace their steps in order to move with the times. Mrs Pottinger, a devout Christian, "had also recorded an extensive catalogue of gospel music, releasing the results on her Glory label, including titles by leading singers Claudelle Clarke, The Creary Sisters & Otis Wright" but she rarely faltered in her output of secular music either. By carefully blending raw roots ire with a sophisticated rock steady sensibility, she continued to produce a profusion of superb singles including Marcia Griffiths' 'Stepping Out Of Babylon' and 'Peaceful Woman' and the dignified 'Steppin' album. And, as the decade drew towards a close, Mrs Pottinger came forward with a copious catalogue of High Note seven inch hits with Joseph Hill's Culture, devout exponents of the Rastafarian faith, and their 'Harder Than The Rest' and 'Cumbolo' albums too.

"Errol Brown who was, in effect, joint producer in the studio; as he told *The Gleaner* in November 2010: "She (Mrs Pottinger) loved the music ... loved it too much. She knew what she wanted in the studio, and had a lot of respect for the musicians." **Steve Barrow**

In 1977 Bob Andy produced and recorded his essential 'Lots Of Love & I' album in its entirety in Treasure Isle which was released on Sonia Pottinger's High Note label and, many years later, he recalled how pleasurable it had been to work with Errol.

"Errol Brown was a young engineer… we were all learning the business together. He was learning his engineering and I was learning how to put a project together outside of Studio One which was the first facility I worked in and put a project together and the place that allowed me to do that. So I was learning a lot of things… how to co-ordinate… and Errol was learning about me and how to engineer me but I guess all of us were a part of his engineering tapestry. When I worked with him he was very receptive to me and essential in accommodating and passing on whatever he knew." **Bob Andy**

Culture's seven inch High Note release, 'Natty Never Get Weary', was a huge hit in 1978 as a young Ossie Thomas, then working as a salesman for Mrs Pottinger, recalled.

"And I said to myself I have to play some part in this music business! 'Cause when you're in the music every day it become life so our love for this became stronger. My cousin started to work with Niney and then he said he'll get a work for me so he carried me down to Bunny Lee's shop and I get a work with Bunny Lee. That time Blackbeard was running the shop… but the shop kinda get mashed up on we and I go down a Niney's shop. Niney's shop nah really run like a business 'cause Niney a fly out and gone to England so the shop just get scanty so… Mrs Pottinger was more organised so me just go down to Mrs Pottinger and talk my way into the job. I told her I was the best salesman in town so she gave me a go and said 'prove yourself!'… so me just prove meself! The rest is history you know…" **Ossie 'Black Solidarity' Thomas**

GAY FEET
EVERY NIGHT
JOE WHITE & CHUCK
High Note
37 Orange Street
Pub: Push Music
Prod. by:
S. E. Pottinger
(Adapted)
BOBBY ELLIS
THE REVOLUTIONARES
GAY FEET
FESTIVAL 1967
LONESOME LOVER
AL & THE VIBRATORS
37 ORANGE STREET
KINGSTON JAMAICA, W.I.
WIRE
RECORDS
45 R.P.M.
G17
COME TO ME SOFTLY
JIMMY JAMES
SEP
RECORDS
Unauthorised
Copying is
Prohibited
45 R.P.M.
VOCAL
G74
JERICHO WALL
BY
WINSTON SAMUELS
GAYDISC
SPANISH LACE
JIMMY JAMES
MY HAPPY HOME
ROY AND PATSY
SEP
RECORDS
MOTHERS LOVE
GAY FEET
A LITTLE NUT TREE
SUN PLUM
MERRY GO ROUND
HUGH ROY
GAY FEET
WON'T YOU COME HOME
THE CONQUERERS
High Note
STOP THE FIGHTING
(Culture)
THE CULTURE
S. P. 143
RECORDS
Bird Music
DB-1138A
DELARNO STEWART

And Ossie certainly did prove himself by promoting Culture's 'Natty Never Get Weary'.

" ...and this tune end up selling two, three, four thousand a day! Sell like hot bread! The whole of Jamaica you'd hear 'weary, natty never get weary...'" **Ossie 'Black Solidarity' Thomas**

Two High Note instrumentals from Bobby Ellis, 'Stormy Weather' and an update of Baba Brooks' 'Shank I Sheck', went on to become staples of the dance hall era but, despite instigating the eponymous Dancehall record label with a handful of releases from rising stars Lee Van Cliff and Tony Tuff she retired from music making in the early Eighties. Errol Brown left Mrs Pottinger's employ in 1979 to take up engineering duties at Bob Marley's Tuff Gong studio.

"Mrs Pottinger continued in the music business until the early 1980s (1985). She started a ceramic business; when this writer met her in Jamaica in 1995, it was at her house in New Kingston where she had a kiln and several people working for her; she also taught flower arranging and told me she had visited many gardens in stately homes in England, in which she was particularly interested. However, these somewhat genteel activities of her later life should never obscure the fact that she was one of the most successful producers in the golden age of Jamaican music and fully deserving of her place alongside her male counterparts."

Steve Barrow

The ownership of the Treasure Isle catalogue has been a source of much contention over the years and in 2003 "She (Mrs Sonia Pottinger) won a lengthy court battle over the rights to Reid's catalogue... It has now been made legally official that Sonia Pottinger is the rightful owner of the Treasure Isle's recording catalogue, previously owned by its late founder, the legendary record producer Duke Reid".

"As of September 1975, Sonia Pottinger was and remains the legal and beneficial owner of master recordings, music publishing rights, all copyrights and related rights as well as the exclusive rights to administer, manufacture, release, distribute and license all publishing rights and master recordings owned by Arthur Stanley 'Duke' Reid." **Basil Walters**

In October 2004 she was awarded the title of the Honourable Sonia Pottinger OD (Order of Distinction) for her contribution to the music, arts and culture of Jamaica but, six years later, she died aged 79 at her New Kingston home on 3rd November 2010. A thanksgiving service in Sonia Pottinger's honour was held on 19th November 2010 attended by Minister of Culture Olivia 'Babsy' Grange and representatives from the Jamaican music industry.

Although, according to Bunny 'Striker' Lee, Mrs Pottinger's original intention had been to rebuild the Treasure Isle studio, "she pulled it all down to move it because it was in a bad area but she never fixed it back up again", the studio gradually fell into disrepair. The legend continued to grow with the premises described as "a musical shrine" where "stars on the sidewalk with the names of popular Jamaican artistes, including Horace Andy's, are testament to those days". In 2007 Horace Andy, "a Studio One alumnus", established his own Higher Grades Studio upstairs at 33 Bond Street. Horace told Mel Cooke at *The Sunday Gleaner* that his facility "is a studio for myself and all the youths in all the communities, not just West Kingston. Youths come from everywhere… Jones Town, Seaview, Papine, Southside, Portmore".

"I'm now working with Donovan Germain at Penthouse and I have my own studio downstairs in the old Treasure Isle premises on Bond Street although I never recorded at Treasure Isle... only Studio One. It's called Highest Grade."

Horace Andy

Arthur Stanley 'Duke' Reid had been a champion marksman during his time in the Jamaica Constabulary Force; he was rarely off target for his entire subsequent musical career and would never cease scoring hit after hit with his 'hands on' and finger on the trigger approach. His music was, smooth, soulful and sophisticated, clear and uncluttered. The music from Coxsone's Studio One influenced the sound and feel of reggae but Duke Reid's Treasure Isle studio completely changed its direction and was the starting point for the breakthrough of dub and deejays… the two most important musical movements to come out of Jamaica and which would, subsequently, influence the direction and content of popular music all over the world.

Over the ensuing decades Duke Reid's music has been made available on a bewildering range of compilations and reissues on a variety of different formats and labels. Much of the material has been duplicated but Charlie Reggae's indispensable 'Treasure Isle Time' discography should, hopefully, help to guide the listener through this particular minefield. Many of the Heartbeat albums are of particular interest due to the company's access to the original Treasure Isle master tapes and many of their releases feature alternate takes to classic recordings in addition to a wealth of previously unreleased obscurities. But whatever the format or label the name and the music of Duke Reid and Treasure Isle will live on forever.

"Although the Duke is gone his music lives on and sounds better with each passing year." **Chris 'Peckings' Price**

Tommy McCook died, aged 71, of pneumonia and heart failure on 5th May 1998. His considerable contribution to the development of Jamaican music and the Jamaican music industry was officially recognised in 1975 when he became "the first Skatalite, of seven, (to be) awarded the Order of Distinction".

On 15th October 2007 the Jamaican government posthumously awarded the Order of Distinction in the rank of Commander to Arthur 'Duke' Reid for service to the Jamaican music industry and the Order of Distinction in the rank of Officer to Euwart/Ewart 'U Roy' Beckford for his contribution to the development of Jamaican music for over forty years.

Postscript
Trojan Records

Duke Reid's Treasure Isle and associated imprints could always be relied on for musical quality but it was one of his less well known subsidiary labels that gave the name to, and helped build the foundation of, an entirely new London based musical empire whose influence would prove to be profound.

Chris Blackwell had been licensing Jamaican product for release in the UK on his Island label since 1962 and, five years later, started to release the Duke's productions on the Treasure Isle and Trojan labels in London. Both labels became casualties when Island changed its allegiance to British based 'progressive' rock and in 1968 Jamaican music was transferred to a new company, jointly owned by Island and Beat & Commercial, named Trojan Records.

"In the late 1960's Lee Gopthal and David Betteridge decided to merge our Jamaican music interests into a new company, to be called Trojan, which would focus purely on Jamaican artists. Though initially not that keen on the idea, I agreed because Island was now expanding so much into rock and other British music, and I wanted to be sure Jamaican music got the attention it deserved. The rest, of course, is history."

Chris Blackwell

"Between its formation in 1968 and the demise of reggae music in the public consciousness in 1975, prior to Bob Marley's assault on the bastions of white rock, Trojan led the way."

Michael De Koningh & Laurence Cane-Honeysett

And, in the same way that Emil Shalit's Blue Beat label had given its name to Jamaican rhythm & blues, shuffle and boogie and ska in the UK in the early Sixties, the Trojan name would become synonymous with reggae at the beginning of the next decade.

The importance of their 'Tighten Up' series of albums as catalysts for the crossing over of Jamaican music to a wider public can never be overstated. Paul McCartney referred to reggae as "tighten up music" after the Trojan compilations had provided the accompaniment to his DIY endeavours at his remote Scottish farmhouse on the Mull of Kintyre.

"He scaled a ladder and climbed on to the roof to fix its hole, Linda soundtracking his handiwork by spinning the newly released 'Tighten Up' reggae compilation LPs." **Tom Doyle**

Trojan was the parent label for every producer and label of importance in the reggae explosion and the company would grow to dominate a hitherto unimagined market where its beginnings as a Treasure Isle subsidiary were all but forgotten. But, as they say, that's another story and one that has been comprehensively covered in Laurence Cane-Honeysett's excellent and highly recommended book 'The Story Of Trojan Records'.

Treasure Isle Recording Studio
33 Bond Street
Kingston

Producers:
Arthur 'Duke' Reid & Byron 'Baron'/'Smithy'/'Smitty' Smith

Arrangers:
Arthur 'Duke' Reid, Gladstone 'Gladdy' Anderson, Clive 'Azul' Hunt, Herman 'Seventh' Marquis, Tommy McCook
& Harris/Horace 'BB'/'Bibby' Seaton

Engineers:
Byron 'Baron'/'Smithy'/'Smitty' Smith, Errol Brown,
Michael 'Mikey Dread' Campbell, Carlton Hamil, Sylvan Morris,
Karl Pitterson & Harris/Horace 'BB'/Bibby' Seaton

Labels: Cool Soul (USA), Discolite, Dutchess, Duke Reid Greatest Hits, Duke Reid's, Hi-Lite, Soul Shot, Supersonics, Sure Shot, Treasure Isle & Trojan

Gospel: Masters Time

Affiliated Labels:
Baron's (Byron 'Baron'/Smithy/Smitty' Smith)

Musicians:
Drumbago All Stars
Drumbago and His Harmonisers
Drumbago's Orchestra
Lumbago (sic) and His Orchestra
Drums: Arkland 'Drumbago' Parks
Bass: Cluett 'Clue J' Johnson
Guitar: Jerome 'Jah Jerry' Haynes & Ernest Ranglin
Piano: Aubrey Adams & Theophilus 'Easy Snapping'' Beckford
Alto Saxophone: Lester Sterling
Tenor Saxophone: Roland Alphonso
Tenor & Baritone Saxophone: Dennis 'Ska' Campbell
Trombone: Emmanuel 'Rico' Rodriguez

The Baba Brooks Band
Musicians include:
Drums: Aston 'Wackie' Henry
Saxophone: Roland Alphonso
Trumpet: Oswald 'Baba' Brooks
Trombone: Don Drummond & Emmanuel 'Rico' Rodriguez

Tommy McCook & His Skatalite (sic)
Drums: Lloyd Knibb
Bass: Lloyd Brevett & Lloyd Spence
Guitar: Jerome 'Jah Jerry' Haynes, Harold McKenzie & Ernest Ranglin
Piano: Jackie Mittoo
Alto Saxophone: Lester Sterling
Lead Tenor Saxophone: Tommy McCook
Tenor Saxophone: Roland Alphonso
Tenor & Baritone Saxophone: Dennis 'Ska' Campbell
Trombone: Don Drummond
Trumpet: Reverend Billy Cooke, Percival Dillon, Raymond Harper & Johnny 'Dizzy' Moore
Flute: Tommy McCook
Vocals: Tony DaCosta, Doreen Schaeffer & Lord Tanamo

Lynn Taitt & The Boys

Tommy McCook & The Supersonics
Drums: Paul Douglas, Winston Grennan, Lloyd Knibb, Hugh Malcolm, Arkland 'Drumbago' Parks & Wade Hampton "from Los Caballeros"
Bass: Clifton 'Jackie' Jackson
Guitar: Lynford 'Hux' Brown, Ernest Ranglin, Nearlin 'Lynn' Taitt, George 'Cowboy' Tucker & Lorraine 'Ranny Bop' Williams
Piano: Gladstone 'Gladdy' Anderson
Organ: Aubrey Adams, Lloyd DelPratt, Neville Hinds & Winston Wright
Alto & Baritone Saxophone: Herman 'Seventh' Marquis
Alto Saxophone: Mark West
Tenor Saxophone: Herman 'Seventh' Marquis & Tommy McCook
Trombone: Vincent 'Don D Junior'/'Trommie' Gordon & Danny Simpson
Trumpet: Rupert Dillon, Winston Graham, Johnny 'Dizzy' Moore, 'Spinners', Mark West & Lester Williams
Vocalists: Kes Chin, Roy Panton & Jackie Opel

Gaydisc Recording Studio
Sundown Crescent
Kingston 10

Producer, Arranger & Engineer:
Lindon O Pottinger

Labels: Gay Disc, Golden Arrow & SEP (Sonia Eloise Pottinger)
Gospel: Glad Tidings

"Disc Pressers Limited... Tip Top... one on each side of Orange Street."
Bunny 'Striker' Lee

Tip Top Record Centre & Disc Pressers Ltd
23, 37 & 103 Orange Street
Kingston

Producer:
Sonia E Pottinger

Labels: Excel, Dance Hall, Gay Feet, High Note, PEP, Tip Top, Sun Plum & Rainbow
Gospel: Glory

Musicians:

The Baba Brooks Band
Musicians include:
Drums: Aston 'Wackie' Henry
Saxophone: Roland Alphonso
Trumpet: Oswald 'Baba' Brooks
Trombone: Don Drummond & Emmanuel 'Rico' Rodriguez

Lynn Taitt & The Jets
Drums: Joe Isaacs & Lloyd Knibb
Bass: Bryan Atkinson & Clifton 'Jackie' Jackson
Guitar: Lynford 'Hux' Brown & Nearlin 'Lynn' Taitt
Piano: Gladstone 'Gladdy' Anderson
Alto Saxophone: Felix 'Deadly Hedley' Bennett

Tenor Saxophone: Carlton Samuels
Trumpet: Bobby Ellis
Trombone: Ron 'Willow' Wilson

The Fugitives
Musicians include:
Piano & Organ: Leslie Butler
Trumpet: Jo Jo Bennett

The Hippy Boys
Drums: Carlton 'Carlie' Barrett
Bass: Aston 'Family Man' Barrett
Rhythm Guitar: Alva 'Reggie' Lewis
Lead Guitar: Lorraine 'Ranny Bop' Williams
Organ: Glen 'Capo' Adams & Lloyd 'Charmers' Tyrell
Piano: Lloyd 'Charmers' Tyrell
Percussion: Lloyd 'Charmers' Tyrell
Vocalists; Max Romeo & Lloyd 'Charmers' Tyrell

The Revolutionaries
Drums: Stanley 'Barnabas' Bryan, Carlton 'Santa' Davis,
Lowell 'Sly' Dunbar & Leroy 'Horse Mouth' Wallace
Bass: Bertram 'Ranchie' McLean, Lloyd 'Sparks' Parks
& Robert 'Robbie' Shakespeare
Lead Guitar: Radcliffe 'Duggie' Bryan & Earl 'Chinna' Smith
Rhythm Guitar: Winston 'Bo Peep' Bowen, Albert Valentine 'Tony' Chin,
& Robert 'Robbie' Shakespeare
Keyboards: Ansel 'Pinkie' Collins, Bernard 'Touter' Harvey,
Oswald 'Ossie'/'No Go' Hibbert, Robert 'Robbie' Lyn & Errol 'Tarzan' Nelson
Tenor Saxophone: Tommy McCook
Trombone: Vincent 'Don D Junior'/'Trommie' Gordon
Percussion: Noel 'Scully' Simms & Uzziah 'Sticky' Thompson

DOCTOR BIRD
FESTIVAL WINNER—1966
DB-1038 A
Island Music
A BMN
Production
Bam-Bam
(Hibbert—McCarthy—Gordon)
The Maytals with Byron Lee &
The Dragonaires

ATLANTIC
45 R P M
AT 4003
JAMAICA SKA
(Lee)
THE SKA KINGS

BMN - 23101
THE MAYTALS
BMN
DADDY
(HIBBERT - HENRY - McCARTHY)

TIGER
A
DYNAMIC
SOUNDS
PRODUCTION
POP A TOP
(Lynford Anderson)
ANDY CAPP

WIRL
RECORDS
WIRL
RECORDS
NUMBER
203
PRETTY BABY
HIGGS & WILSON

DYNAMIC
A DYNAMIC SOUNDS PRODUCTION
Instrumental
Arranged by
Neville Hinds
Produced by
Byron Lee
ELIZABETH SERENADE
(Binge)
BYRON LEE &
THE DRAGONAIRES

Noel Hawks

Chapter 2

The Heavy Sounds Are On Dynamic:
WIRL (West Indies Records Limited) & Dynamic Sounds

"Out of many, one people..." **Jamaican National Motto**

"It's a thought that's encouraged by the scale of the racial diversity in Jamaica. In England when you say Jamaican you're usually thinking about someone of African descent. In Jamaica you're confronted immediately with a collection of races." **Mike Phillips**

There are usually more than two sides to every Jamaican record for, in addition to the a-side and the b-side, then later the version side, one has to take into account selling records and selling out, uptown and downtown, dreadlocks and baldheads, society and sufferers and authenticity and commercialism too. It is never simply black and white and, the closer the story is examined, the more complex and contradictory the narrative becomes. The initial two sides become increasingly multi-faceted when recounting the particularly Jamaican success story of Byron Lee's Dynamic Sounds.

"Embedded in the high/mass cultural distinction is the assumption that while high art meaning is derived from the artists themselves – from their intentions, experience and genius – mass cultural meaning lies in its function (to make money/to reproduce the social order)."

Simon Frith & Howard Horne

The perception of WIRL, and later Dynamic Sounds, as an 'uptown' corporate company that promoted 'foreign' music over 'local' product appears to have become the accepted wisdom regarding their role in the history of Jamaican music. There might be a certain amount of truth in this but their story has already been the subject of much historical revisionism and is nowhere near that simple or straightforward. The over simplified and highly romanticised view of reggae as the "music of the ghetto" was never strictly true. Dynamic's proprietor Byron Lee, as "a member of Jamaica's middle class, was able to gain credibility (for the music) with the wealthier members of Jamaica's population" and in doing so he not only "helped to build the careers of dozens of the island's most talented vocalists" but also built "Jamaica's first multi track recording facility". Innumerable important records were recorded, manufactured and distributed at Bell Road during what is now considered to be the era of Jamaican music's greatest creativity.

The history of these two closely linked companies has been too readily dismissed by later chroniclers of Jamaican music as one of rich, fair skinned, uptown, 'society' people of privilege exploiting poor, dark skinned, downtown, often dreadlocked, disadvantaged 'sufferers'. Every struggling artist's life story supposedly runs along these lines and their own personal plot is lifted straight from Perry Henzell's 'The Harder They Come'. In this1972 film Jimmy Cliff, as country boy turned ghetto struggler and singer Ivanhoe Martin, fearlessly fights a fierce but ultimately futile battle against the corrupt hierarchy of Kingston's music business. The big corporations work in collusion with the radio stations and record promoters to retain their dominance and keep the sufferers firmly in their place. This one dimensional viewpoint is mostly untrue and usually unfair not only to the creativity, resourcefulness and resilience of the ghetto artists and musicians but also to the business acumen of the uptown musicians and entrepreneurs.

Mr Hilton, the fictional Mr Big played by Bob Charlton in 'The Harder They Come', declares that "everything have to pass through me..." and, for over four decades, thousands upon thousands of artists, musicians, producers, engineers and entrepreneurs all passed through Bell Road to make, master and manufacture marvellous music at WIRL and Dynamic Sounds. The real life story of Jimmy Cliff, not Ivanhoe Martin, demonstrates that the reality was often a long way away from the screenplay as Byron's wife, Mrs Sheila Lee, reminisced "Byron laid a foundation for these artists to step off. The first time Jimmy Cliff got an encore was when he was singing with The Dragonaires in the early Sixties at Lake George Inn (New York State) where wealthy American families would go for their summer vacations. Jimmy had already left the stage area and gone back upstairs. He almost broke his neck falling down the stairs to get back on stage!"

Yet, even when they achieve a measure of success, the role of the outsider artist is so entrenched that the performers are still expected to conform to the same, clichéd conventions.

"I want to suggest that the aesthetic priorities of Jamaican producers and music makers do not readily match the expected Western stereotypes. That is, the common image of reggae artists as dreadlocked revolutionaries against a ghetto zinc fence backdrop appears to be typical more of an outsider's romantic view than the preferred vision of Jamaicans themselves. Attempts at accessing the international market, 'cosmopolitan' considerations of style and sexuality, are as common in reggae as elsewhere in popular music, but have been deemed 'inauthentic' by those who would prefer their Jamaican artists to remain, if not 'noble savages', then at least 'pure' and bold revolutionaries, ever ready to burn down the Babylon of Western dreams." **Hasse Huss**

In fact the beginnings of WIRL and Dynamic Sounds actually delved far deeper into the real, raw roots of Jamaican music than many of the supposed "bold revolutionary" releases produced during the Seventies heyday of roots rock reggae and its consequent crossover success in the international market place.

Edward Seaga was born 28th May 1930 in Boston, Massachusetts, USA to Jamaican parents: his father was Philip Seaga "a business man of Lebanese descent and his wife, Erna (nee Maxwell) (was) of mixed European and African heritage". The family returned to Jamaica when he was three months old where he attended Kingston's prestigious Wolmer's Boys' School whose motto is "whatever you do, do it to the best of your abilities". He returned to the USA to study at Harvard University and graduated in 1952 with a degree in Social Sciences for his research into the Jamaican cults of kumina (a religious dance ceremony), pocomania (a folk religion combining revivalism with ancestor worship and spirit possession) and obeah (the practice of malignant magic). Although he trained as an anthropologist Edward Seaga was also an astute businessman who had many interests, including clubs and bars, around the island. He would go on to become head of the JLP (Jamaican Labour Party) and eventually Prime Minister of Jamaica from 1980 to 1989 but he was originally "a music man".

On his return to Jamaica he began to conduct in depth research into the roots of Jamaican music for his doctorate studies. His first recording sessions in 1955 were of various different forms of secular and religious cult music for the New York based Ethnic Folkways label that he recorded "in the field". A selection of Edward Seaga's field recordings featuring 'Kumina, Ring Play and Pukkumania' songs were released, through the USA based Ethnic Folkways Library in 1956, on an album entitled 'Folk Music Of Jamaica'.

"This album includes both secular and religious music. All selections were collected in the process of a two year study of religious cults in Jamaica. The recordings were all made during the natural proceedings of festivities held by the participants for their own purposes."

'Folk Music Of Jamaica Recorded by Edward Seaga'

But, while conducting his research, Edward Seaga came to appreciate that the type of music he had recorded in the field was far more than a country mile away from what the downtown audiences were listening and dancing to in the ghetto.

"On the other side of the coin there had also been recordings of cult music. I myself have done considerable research and have produced two albums of music actually recorded at meetings of various cult groups in the country. These recordings, however, by their very nature, have had a limited appeal as they represent what is of greater interest to serious students of indigenous folk cultures than the public at large."

Edward Seaga

This was not the music that the people of Kingston's ghettos wanted to hear on record and, while trying to sell copies of his 'Folk Music Of Jamaica' to the record departments in Stanley Motta's and KG's stores Edward Seaga was asked by both if he could obtain the type of records that the customers actually wanted. This was neither a new, nor even a local, phenomenon and had been one of the most important criteria behind Harry Smith's selections for the hugely influential 'The Anthology Of American Folk Music' which he compiled in 1952.

"Smith's definition of 'American Folk Music' would have satisfied no-one else. He ignored all field recordings, Library of Congress archives, anything validated only by scholarship or carrying the must of a museum. He wanted music to which people really had responded; records put on sale that at least somebody thought were worth paying for."

Anthony Seeger & Amy Horowitz

Consequently Edward Seaga established a link with Savoy Records in Manhattan, New York and began importing records from artists such as "Fats Domino, Wilbert Harrison..." and other uptempo rhythm & blues releases that were being played out on the island's sound systems and juke boxes.

"In trying to sell the album in order to expose music that had never been recorded before, the response was weak but there were repeated requests for other recordings, mostly by uptown pop favourites like Pat Boone and Johnny Mathis, so called 'soft tunes'. This path took him into the recording business as an importer. But soon he had to become a producer and manufacturer, because the government began to restrict competing imports to assist record sales by local manufacturers. Edward Seaga did not indulge in removing the labels on the special imported records. He tried to discover their true identities. He was successful in many cases which allowed him to import quantities of the original commercially produced recordings where possible at much lower prices.

One such notable success was very rewarding. A record which was given the suggestive blank label title 'Beardman Shuffle' was very popular and in great demand. He came across a copy and detected a tiny piece of the original label still attached with the tell-tale Imperial Records colours. With knowledge of the label he soon discovered the real title 'Live It Up' by Ernie Freeman on Imperial Records. This was a lively record with an infectious rhythm. He imported a large quantity and flooded the market. The record was adopted by Teenage Dance Party as its signature tune, in a version form." **Daddy Lionel Chandell, Donald Clive Davison & Roy Black**

"Do you know Ernie Freeman's 'Live It Up'? They cut off the label when it came and named it 'Beardman Shuffle' 'cause the Rasta man used to like it. So plenty of these tunes from Jamaica have different names so sometimes when you see the original you won't know what it is... they just gave it their own name. A lot of tunes in Jamaica came off of that rhythm..." **Bunny 'Striker' Lee**

Striker is not exaggerating and "a lot of tunes" does not begin to describe how far reaching the influence of Ernie Freeman's 1959 release, 'Live It Up', would eventually prove to be. Although Edward Seaga had "flooded the market" with imported copies the Tropical Recording Company would go on to license and press 'Live It Up' as a 78rpm on the Imperial label in Kingston.

***Appendix 2: Page 140**
'Live It Up' Ernie Freeman

In 1958 Edward Seaga opened WIRL (West Indian Records Limited) at 13 Bell Road, Kingston 11 and began manufacturing records under licence from a number of American companies. He also started to sponsor talented local youngsters through his Chocomo Lawn Youth Club in Western Kingston and his next steps were recording these indigenous artists at the RJR studios and promoting their records. 'Manny, Oh', the debut release from (Joe) Higgs & (Roy) Wilson on WIRL, was a huge hit in 1960.

"My first time in the studio was with Mr Edward Seaga. He was our manager... the first person to put us on record. He was the best manager we ever had... we always got paid! He went into politics after this. He saw us at Ward Theatre. We tore down the place... and we made our first record 'Manny, Oh'. We were his only act. The song jumped from Number Forty Three to Number Three and then spent a couple of weeks at Number One. Sold plenty... he had thought of putting some money into building a studio so he built West Indies Records..." **Joe Higgs**

"Plenty of them were involved with the Chocomo Lawn Youth Club like The Techniques and all those youths. It's Edward Seaga who gave Dennis Brown, Slim Smith, The Techniques all those youths a break. They were all from Edward Seaga's Youth Club. He gave them all instruments and the lawn where they could practise ..." **Bunny 'Striker' Lee**

Edward Seaga would go on to build a small recording studio, using Ampex two track equipment, in 1962 and, the following year, WIRL began mastering records on the Bell Road site.

"So I met Bunny Rae and George Benson, who had started WIRL, West Indies Records Limited, with Eddie Seaga and on a couple of trips back to Jamaica (luckily enough my wife worked for an airline so it wasn't too expensive) I helped them out with their studio. It was a little smaller than the original Federal one." **Graeme Goodall**

Ronnie Nasralla and Byron Lee had recorded sessions for their BMN, Follow The Stars On Starline (aka Starline), Gala, Kentone, Soul, and Sunshine labels ("Boasy's (Phillip 'Boasy' James from The Blues Busters) daughter was called Sunshine so we called the label Sunshine") at Federal Studios with Byron Lee & The Dragonaires providing the backing. They enjoyed hit after hit with a variety of top local artists but, up until this point, Byron Lee had recorded in Ken Khouri's Federal Studio. He now began to use the new WIRL recording studio.

"I recorded at Ken Khouri's then onto WIRL once we'd built the studio with The Maytals, The Blues Busters and The Techniques. Graeme Goodall, an Australian, set up the studio... he was the technician that put the WIRL studio together.

You have to listen to the artists… they know better than us. I asked The Blues Busters to sing 'Wings Of A Dove' and it was Number One in Jamaica and all over the Caribbean. At another session there was only a bit of tape left… enough for one song. So I went off for lunch and The Maytals recorded 'Daddy'. Those days you had to put out a hit single to promote the LP so we put 'Daddy' on the b-side of 'It's You'. Tony Verity played the wrong side, 'Daddy', on the radio and it became a big hit. So I had two Number Ones with one record! It was big error and I lost money on that!"

Ronnie Nasralla

"Federal was the place until WIRL set up a little studio… and the work start to share. Federal had a few record presses then WIRL came in and WIRL had some big guys in it… WIRL Records had George Benson and Bunny Rae… but George Benson left later and went to Record Specialists."

Bunny 'Striker' Lee

"Edward Seaga was very, very interested in the entertainment business, and the people involved in it, and tried to get in. Now Edward Seaga was a very, very, very good friend of Byron Lee's and I think he was probably more influential, in a way, of convincing Byron Lee that this was the way to go."

Graeme Goodall

Byron Aloysius Lee was born in Christiana in the parish of Manchester on 27th June 1935; his mother was Jamaican and Byron's Chinese father came from Hong Kong. Byron attended St Joseph's Convent School in Mandeville, where he learned to play the piano, and continued his schooling at Campion Hall and St George's College after moving to Mountain View Gardens in Kingston when he was eight years old. St George's was situated on North Street, Kingston and "was run by Jesuit priests from the United States". Byron was an excellent footballer and, together with his fellow players in St George's Old Boys football team, would celebrate their many victories with impromptu musical sessions in the dressing room after the match.

In 1956 the band asked the authorities at St George's College if they could play at the club's Annual Dinner and they assented. The football team was known as The Dragons after St George the dragon slayer. Byron added "aires… a musical term… that's how he got Dragonaires" (an air is a tune or short melodious composition) and named the band Byron Lee

& The Dragonaires. On their first ever engagement Ronnie Nasralla, "a soccer mate" of Byron's, played percussion.

"It was always percussion. I used to also play an iron rim as one of The Dragonaires… like the one they used to make calypsos."

Ronnie Nasralla

Ronald Victor Nasralla was born in Kingston on 28th November 1930 to Jamaican parents; his father was Lebanese and his mother of Scottish and Jewish descent. Ronnie's first school was "Miss Atte in Vineyard Town" and he attended a number of schools before moving on St Aloysius, "a Catholic Government school downtown", then on to Huntsden High School in Kencot and eventually St George's College. When Ronnie graduated from St George's he began his own advertising agency, "I was in advertising and marketing", and, after a few more appearances with the band, he decided to become their manager. Ronnie already knew Ken Khouri whose father was Lebanese and whose mother was born in Jamaica of Cuban parents. Ken Khouri had established Records Limited, and began to manufacture "the first locally pressed records on the island" in 1954. In addition to pressing his own local mento productions Ken Khouri also secured the franchise to press and distribute Mercury Records in Jamaica.

"I was in advertising in an office at 129 King Street and Ken Khouri was in an alcove below me. He said 'come and listen to my first record'. 'Skokiaan' (August Msarurgwa/Musarurwa & The Bulawayo Sweet Rhythm Band)) was the first record they made. Before that we used to import records and there were only three stores that sold them: Depass Enterprises, Times Store and Stanley Motta's. Ken would get hit records from overseas and produce them in Jamaica and Byron later did the same thing."

Ronnie Nasralla

Ronnie wholeheartedly threw himself into the task of management and used all of the resources at his disposal to promote, push and plug Byron Lee & The Dragonaires.

"There was a lot of competition from Carlos Malcolm, Kes Chin and Sonny Bradshaw but I was able to use my own advertising agency and I made sure Byron Lee's band was very prominent … their picture appeared in all the ads!"

Ronnie Nasralla

Byron Lee & The Dragonaires' standards of performance and appearance were always consummately professional with smart stage outfits and "properly organised routines" and they soon became "household names" throughout the island by giving the public exactly what they wanted.

"It was Byron's policy to have the people dancing in front of the band, no lights on the audience but with the lights on the band and every band member dressed smartly. Carlos Malcolm was his biggest rival... he liked jazz and played it well but the people didn't like jazz! If a tune was popular Byron would learn it. If a tune came out he'd rehearse it at his home on Third Avenue until he got it right... his formula was to play the tunes that were popular. He'd have the people going wild." **Ronnie Nasralla**

Ronnie Nasralla was often accompanied by Sheila Khouri, who would later become Byron Lee's wife and business manager, to the Dragonaires' engagements. Sheila recalled that she would attend functions although she was very young and Ronnie Nasralla "was a family friend and he'd take me... like an older brother... to attend these dance parties" at Emmett Park (a sports stadium) where "Byron and the boys began the band after football matches on the school ground. Ronnie loved dancing and I loved dancing! This was before ska and the band played everything: rock 'n' roll, American music... Bill Haley, Fats Domino... but calypso was not popular with the uptown crowd".

Sheila's grandfather and Ken Khouri's father were brothers. "We were Lebanese so we did not mix socially as Byron was Chinese and not of our culture but I used to dance to his band". Sheila first met Byron in 1964 when he came to the World's Fair in New York although "she knew of him" before this. They were married on 6th September 1967 but Sheila stated that Byron "always counted from when we began our relationship so, for instance, if someone asked how long we were married he counted from 1964 instead of 1967 and I just went along with it. You can't fight young love and my parents couldn't fight our love... it came back to the race thing. Eventually my father and Byron became very close friends..."

In 1960 Edward Seaga produced Byron Lee & The Dragonaires' first record, 'Dumplin's', an update of Ernie Freeman's 1957 USA rhythm & blues smash on Imperial which was also a hit for Doc Bagby.

"I cut 'Dumplin's', my first song, in 1960 for Eddie Seaga at RJR. It was two mics they had: one forty four bass (a big one) and another little one. We used to get a piece of chalk and get tape and mark and balance it and this is how we sound now and start to play. And when you want a guitar solo the guitarist walks two steps and plays the solo and then back..." **Byron Lee**

"He started off playing mento tunes and foreign blues like 'Dumplin's'... and Byron Lee is still known for that tune 'Dumplin's' in Jamaica."
Bunny 'Striker' Lee

'Dumplin's' was released on the Dragon's Breath label in Jamaica and was the second release on Emil E Shalit's Blue Beat label, a subsidiary of Melodisc Records, in the UK; the third Blue Beat release was another Edward Seaga production Higgs & Wilson's 'Manny, Oh'. Emil Shalit, "an Austrian born American" had very little interest in music and saw it primarily as a business "selling records was the same as selling potatoes". However, his decision to release records with the "blues beat" that expatriate Jamaican customers were requesting in London, Birmingham, Nottingham and Bristol record shops was instrumental in moving Jamaican music into the UK mainstream where, for the remainder of the decade, all music of Jamaican origin would usually be referred to as blue beat. Melodisc continued to license Jamaican records for UK release on their Blue Beat label and, together with Chris Blackwell's Island organisation, became directly responsible for popularising Jamaican music outside of its immediate, intended audience.

"When the early ska records began to get recognition by markets outside Jamaica, mainly through the need of the massive numbers of Jamaican immigrants to the UK who craved the sounds of their home country, and Chris Blackwell releasing them on Island which, incidentally stopped the pirating that had already started and Emil Shalit, who owned Melodisc, created the Blue Beat label a name that was eventually tagged onto ska records by the non Jamaican population." **Graeme Goodall**

Prince Buster forged particularly close links with Emil Shalit which would later lead to a decidedly difficult situation for Derrick Morgan and Edward Seaga would have to be asked to mediate on his behalf before Derrick could continue his recording career. Prior to this the Prince and Derrick had been involved in an on record feud after Derrick had begun to work with Chinese Jamaican Leslie Kong who, alongside his brothers Cecil and Lloyd, ran Beverley's Record Shop and Ice Cream Parlour at 135A Orange Street.

"Then I met Prince Buster and we get together and I started to record for Buster. Prince Buster and I were good friends until I left him for Beverley's... owned by Chinese Jamaican Leslie Kong... and after 'Forward March' in 1962 he write a song about me called 'Black Head Chinaman'...

Anyway Prince Buster and I were going on until about 1962 when Jimmy Cliff met me and told me that Beverley's wanted to do some records. He had a song and he said that Beverley's had sent him to me although I didn't work for Beverley's at the time. I listened to the song he had... it was a soul song 'Dearest Beverley'. So then he took me to this place called Beverley's and, when we went there, they'd never done any recordings before. That was how Jimmy Cliff founded Beverley's because they liked what he was singing but they confided that if he couldn't find me they'd pass on the song. So... so said and so done... and we went and recorded the song. I also did recordings for them, 'Be Still' and 'Sunday Morning', while Jimmy Cliff did 'Hurricane Hattie'. From there Beverley's started and I stuck with Beverley's for a while because Beverley's paid better than the rest.

Prince Buster and I were good friends until I left him for Beverley's... then in 1962, when Jamaica got independence, I made this song called 'Forward March'. Prince Buster heard the song and said that part of it came off his song called 'They Got To Come' and he said I was taking his belongings to the Chinaman. He write a song about me called 'Black Head Chinaman'."

Derrick Morgan

"You done stole my belongings and give to your Chineyman
God in heaven knows, he knows, that you are wrong
Are you a Chinaman? Are you a black man?
It don't need no eye glasses to see that your skin is black..."

'Black Head Chinaman' Prince Buster

Derrick later clarified that the "belongings" which Buster had accused him of appropriating were actually alto saxophonist Felix 'Deadly' Headley Bennett and trumpeter Lester Sterling who had blown the solos in 'Forward

March'. Derrick then answered Buster with 'The Blazing Fire' for Beverley's which he introduced in Chinese and sung "be still and know I'm your superior". Buster retaliated with 'Praise Without Raise (Watch It Blackhead)' and matters continued to escalate.

"That's what caused the disruption... then he and I started a musical war... it was 'Blackhead Chiney' and 'Blazing Fire' time. We were stepping right up to the line and he and I kept doing it right on and on and creating a lot of history in Jamaica. People were fighting over the both of us... some said Buster was better... some said Derrick was better. It caused such a big thing that the government had to come in and stop us. We had to go in the paper and hug up and say that we were the best of friends and so on and stop the dispute." **Derrick Morgan**

And so Buster and Derrick began to work together again...

"(Buster) rang this man called Emil Shalit at Melodisc or Blue Beat who came down to Jamaica and signed me (to) a contract. I was singing for Beverley's and Buster got me out by signing a contract for Melodisc."
Derrick Morgan

In 1963 Derrick Morgan travelled to London with Emil Shalit "for live appearances and to record a few tracks" where, "backed by Georgie Fame", he recorded 'Telephone' and '(Never Too Late For A) Shower Of Rain'. Buster sang 'Wash Wash' at the same session. But Derrick "didn't like the weather" and, after six months, returned to Kingston and recorded 'Meekly Wait' with his cousin Yvonne for Lloyd Bell's The President label and 'Poison Ivy' as a solo singer for Prince Buster. The contract Derrick had signed stipulated that he could work only with producers who had contracts with his Blue Beat label. Leslie Kong's productions were released in the UK on Chris Blackwell's Island label and, consequently, Leslie Kong could not work with Derrick. However, Edward Seaga, who had by now relinquished his interests in WIRL and was Minister for Finance, intervened personally and wrote to Emil Shalit in London asking for Derrick to be released from the contract.

"Well I eased off recording because of my contract with Melodisc. Beverley's didn't want to touch me because the contract was so binding. Then Edward Seaga... he is the one who got it cleared. He was always in music in Jamaica... he used to have a studio... WIRL... West Indies Records Ltd... before he became a politician. So then I could record back with Beverley's and I also did a few songs for Coxsone."

Derrick Morgan

Edward Seaga's formal political career began in 1959 when he was nominated by Sir Alexander Bustamante, founder of the Jamaican Labour Party, to serve in the Upper House of the Jamaican Legislature. Three years later, in April 1962, he was elected as the Member of Parliament for Western Kingston. He was re-elected for the following thirty seven years and would become the longest serving member of Jamaica's parliament. Although he may have been one of the first Jamaican politicians to appreciate the importance and persuasive power of music with the electorate he was certainly not the last. Sound system entrepreneur Vincent 'King Edwards The Giant' Edwards later entered politics and was elected as a Member of Parliament for the PNP (People's National Party) and PJ Patterson (also of the PNP), "who managed the legendary Skatalites", became the first Jamaican Prime Minister to have been born of two black parents when he succeeded Michael Manley in 1993.

"Most of the politicians used music...

You had Edward Seaga, a music man himself, who was part owner of WIRL. When he became Jamaican Prime Minister he built up free access and that's why those guys stayed in power in Western Kingston for so long... 'cause they looked after the people them who put them there. Don't care about whether the other people don't like them. The people in their constituency put them in the House of Representatives.

Ken Lack from the Caltone label was the man who managed The Skatalites band one time along with PJ Patterson, who later became Jamaican Prime Minister, and PJ Patterson was a music man too. Patterson became the Prime Minister and Edward Seaga used to manage Higgs & Wilson and do a lot of sessions. Most of these politicians are musical people and they reach the people through music.

When PJ Patterson ran (for office) he couldn't lose because he took care of all his constituency people. But you have some people when they're in power you don't see them until the next election and they come with a truck load of flour! And they start dishing out food and they go round kissing all the babies and all that in the hills and gullies until voting time but when they get in then you don't see them for four or five years time.

In 1971 when Michael Manley was campaigning the PNP used my tune 'Better Must Come' by Delroy Wilson and Maxie Romeo's 'Let The Power Fall On I'… but Derrick Morgan did produce that… and the music reached the people and won the election. The music would speak for itself with all the artists of the time on the Bandwagon. So you find in every era if you have a good tune a politician will take it up. They even used 'Double Barrel' in America…

But remember who put you in power! You must keep them!"

Bunny 'Striker' Lee

In the early Sixties an entirely new genre was born as Jamaican rhythm & blues and shuffle and boogie developed into ska. A number of enterprising entrepreneurs, including Edward Seaga, were not slow in realising the "exciting possibilities of this innovative music" and Sheila Lee recalled that Byron Lee and Carlos Malcolm were commissioned to look for "a national sound for Jamaica" by Edward Seaga. "Byron went down to Chocomo Lawn and Carlos came back with mento… Byron came back with ska. This would have been 1960 or 1961" and Sheila was unequivocal that "Byron never claimed to have invented ska… he packaged it and made it acceptable uptown."

"Eddie Seaga was my good friend and he called me and said 'there's a music in Western Kingston that I'd like you to promote and he organised a dance at Chocomo Lawn. It was the best musical experience of my life! I moved around the dancers and studied their moves…"

Ronnie Nasralla

"Eddie Seaga sent us to the ghettos of western Kingston to learn how to play this new ska music. This learning process took approximately six months even though the band could easily play soul and rock 'n' roll music. Then we brought the ska from downtown to uptown Kingston. The middle and upper classes didn't know anything about this new type of music. It was, clearly enough, for the more underprivileged people..."

Byron Lee

"My close friend, Eddie Seaga, who was the Minister for that area, asked me if I could promote this very infectious music uptown to the elite Jamaicans. I suggested that Byron Lee & The Dragonaires was the best way to do this and he should get the band to perform in the West to capture the true feeling of the ska. Seaga organised a dance at the Chocomo Lawn in the heart of Western Kingston and Byron Lee & The Dragonaires and all the popular ska singers performed at what turned out to be the most exciting musical experience of my life. The Dragonaires along with Jimmy Cliff, Eric 'Monty' Morris, Derrick Morgan, The Charmers, The Maytals, Prince Buster, The Blues Busters and more had this open air ballroom swinging all night.

'Dance The Ska'

BASIC JAMAICA SKA STEP

● **1A, 1B –** The upper half of the body (waist up) keeps the beat by bowing forward with a straight back and a slight bend in both knees, similar to 1b. At the first bow the arms extend to the sides (1a & 1b). At the second bow the arms cross in front (1c & 1d). The body straightens up in between the change of arms from one position to the other. You continue in this way for the Basic Ska Step done on the spot.

● The Basic Ska with a Side Step is done as follows: First to the right by moving the right leg on the extension of the arms (1a) then bringing up the left leg on the closing of the arms (1c), then to the left by moving the left leg on the extension of the arms and by bringing up the right leg on the closing of the arms. Remember the basic body beat described in the first paragraph is performed during movements to right and left.

SKA–ING & SKA–RIDING

● **SKA–ING 3A, 3B –** This dance step is similar to the action of skiing and is done rapidly to the beat of the guitar. You start out by leaning forward at the waist with the hands in front and straight legs (3A.) In the second position (3B) the hands are brought down to the sides and at the same time the knees are bent. Both 3A and 3B are repeated simultaneously to the fast Ska beat of the guitar.

● **SKA–RIDING 3C, 3D –** Ska-riding is the step usually done immediately after Ska-ing and is similar to the action of riding a horse. Both dancers pretend to be riding a horse giving a pumping action of the hands in front of the body and at the same time bending the knees (3C). The bend of the knees and the push out of the hands are done together on the fast guitar beat. Occasionally, as seen in 3D, you use one hand to "whip your horse".

The Ska steps on this album are executed by the couple who taught New York the Ska
RONNIE NASRALLA and JANETTE PHILLIPS

During the heat of this Eddie Seaga came to me and asked me to move around and try and capture all the different dance steps and for me to come up with an official format on how to dance the ska. Well, I did just that, also danced with some of the girls and took in every move.

A week later I presented the Minister with a brochure with Seven Jamaica Ska Steps illustrated by Janette Phillips (a close dancer friend of my sister Jeanette) and yours truly with complete instructions on how to DANCE THE JAMAICA SKA." **Ronnie Nasralla**

In 1962 Byron Lee & The Dragonaires featured fleetingly in 'Dr No', the first James Bond film, which starred Sean Connery. Set in Jamaica the film was not only a showcase for the island's beautiful scenery but also gave some very early, if very brief, international exposure to its music.

"I got associated with 'Dr No' when they asked me to arrange the night club scene... that scene was all my work! Dancers and everything... I auditioned Bob Marley for the 'Dr No' movie but he was too untidy so I turned him down!" **Ronnie Nasralla**

"Unquestionably Byron Lee is responsible for the rebirth of the big dance band in Jamaica and, if you are a crowd counter by habit, you'll know the Dragonaires are still keeping up the pace they set back in '57. For six years they have led all the opinion polls by playing the most danceable music around. And, although the secret of success lies in keeping their Jamaican fans happy, Byron and the band have proven that their appeal is international with their sensational tour of the Eastern Caribbean in February 1963. 'You've got to live your music in the Dragonaires' says Byron. 'This way, and only this way, can a band have soul.' And Byron Lee and the Dragonaires have it... ask any Jamaican between fifteen and fifty." **'Let's Have A Red Stripe Party'**

After touring the West Indies the band then went even further afield when "the 'Byron Lee Show' went on for three successful months at the Peppermint Lounge in Miami Beach" in 1964. Although they had experienced a degree of prejudice in Jamaica outright racism became all too real when Byron Lee & The Dragonaires travelled to the USA. They might have been treated with a measure of suspicion in the land of their birth but were still able to fill the Glass Bucket club, however, they hit the glass ceiling when the band discovered they were not allowed to eat in the 'Whites Only' restaurants in the deep south of America.

"The uptown people would not have mixed with the musicians forty years ago! They shied away from them... the colour thing was a big thing back in the day. But when The Dragonaires were touring in Florida they couldn't get served in restaurants. Keith Lyn and Byron used to have to go in to get the food for them..."
Sheila Lee

That same year Edward Seaga, now Minister of Development and Welfare/Head of Social Welfare and Economic Development, organised a showcase for ska at the World's Fair at Flushing Meadows Park in Queens, New York USA to promote Jamaica and showcase its talent. The theme for the World's Fair was "Peace Through Understanding" and he enlisted Byron Lee & The Dragonaires to back The Blues Busters, Jimmy Cliff, Monty Morris, Millie Small and a troupe of ska dancers for this incredibly important promotion for the sound of young Jamaica. Ronnie Nasralla's liner notes for 'Byron Lee & The Dragonaires Plays Jamaica Ska' from 1964 succinctly sum up the story...

"Since 1959 the west end of Kingston, Jamaica has throbbed with a musical beat – a hypnotic sound of surging excitement and power. People hearing it became caught up in a mood of frenzy and could not help moving to the tempo of this pulsating, almost religious, beat.

This is ska, original and indigenous... the sound of a people almost primitive and elemental in its musical idiom... a music of guitar, drum, trumpet, saxophone and bass – playing a monotonic, grass roots rhythm.

Until 1961 ska never left its home. Instead it remained with Jamaica's lower classes, providing them with relaxation and entertainment, through the medium of the many 'sound systems' which operate in Jamaica's capital city. In 1961, with the migration of many Jamaicans to England, the sound of ska went over there and an imitation of ska started a slow but certain growth among the West Indian community. Because of the promotion of this imitation ska on a Blue Beat label the sound became known in England as 'blue beat' instead of ska. It grew in popularity and by 1963 it was strongly taken up by the English public.

Meanwhile, back in Jamaica, the beat continued to be more or less restricted to the lower classes. Then Byron Lee, leader of Jamaica's Number One band Byron Lee & The Dragonaires, heard the beat and was fascinated by it. Anxious to learn more about it, and to promote it, he took his band to the birthplace of ska. There, in the teeming dance halls of Western Kingston, he studied and played the music... with the people who had created it. The front line boys of the band studied the various steps of the ska dance which had been evolved by the people. The singers of the band studied the special sound effects peculiar to ska.

After many months of research and practice Byron and his boys presented ska to Jamaican society. As Byron expected it was a tremendous success. At nightclubs and in theatres the new sound took on: ska was doing in Kingston what the twist did in New York. It was an overnight sensation.

But Byron Lee was not the one to take the credit for himself. Proving himself to be a musical godfather he encouraged the leading ska singers by presenting them in shows throughout the island. Due largely to his efforts ska has become widely recognised and accepted in Jamaica. Indeed, so universal is its acceptance among all sections of Jamaican society today, that it is being hailed as the new national sound."

'Byron Lee & The Dragonaires Plays Jamaica Ska'

There was a concerted effort to promote ska in America that echoed the short lived calypso craze of the Fifties when Harry Belafonte's 'Calypso' long player achieved the accolade of the first album ever by a solo singer to sell in excess of a million copies. Sheila Lee recalled demonstrating the ska dances on American television and ska was primarily promoted as a dance rather than a music. However, despite ex-Mousketeer Annette Funicello singing and dancing 'Jamaica Ska' with host Bob Hope on his eponymous television show, it would be another twenty years before ska finally took hold and took off in America.

Sheila Lee moved to New York where her parents owned a night club and Edward Seaga's friend and lawyer, Paul Marshall (a music business attorney), was trying to promote the dance moves from Jamaica and, through her friendship with Ronnie Nasralla, Sheila became one of the dancers. She was "one of the six trying to get the ska to take hold as a dance and we'd go all over the eastern seaboard on American Bandstand television show. Sheila reminisced "every weekend we'd be on a show with Dick Clark and Arthur Murray so when Byron Lee & The Dragonaires came to the World's Fair we were in the front line demonstrating the ska. Needless to say it never took off despite Annette Funicello using it in her movie 'Annette At Bikini Beach'."

Annette Funicello's very successful 1963 'Beach Party' film for American International Pictures was followed by 'Muscle Beach Party' and then 'Bikini Beach' which was released in 1964. The soundtrack album, 'Annette At Bikini Beach', featured various dance themed numbers such as 'The Bossa Nova', 'The Watusi', 'The Twist' and '(The) Jamaica Ska'.

And, to this day, arguments continue to rage because, instead of The Skatalites, Edward Seaga enlisted the services of Byron Lee & The Dragonaires to showcase ska at the World's Fair. Sheila Lee was adamant that "Byron never projected himself and he always projected the music and he never claimed to have invented ska. Byron packaged it and made it acceptable uptown. Yet the ghetto people resented that this 'chinee man' represented Jamaica at the World's Fair... but the band had fifteen impeccably dressed, well behaved men and it worked because of Byron's charisma. He was very talented and very humble."

"Our principle was to play the music that the people want! The Skatalites played the type of music that people liked but they didn't play a variety! They had this one niche..." **Ronnie Nasralla**

However, with over fifty years of hindsight, it is too easy and probably misguided to criticise Byron Lee and Edward Seaga for 'commercialising' ska and, over the years, many have. But did Stanley Motta, Ivan Chin and Ken Khouri 'sell out' mento music? Does 'selling' have to mean 'selling out'? Many people at the early stages of Jamaican music's development worked tirelessly to make the inaccessible as accessible as possible. Who could have predicted, especially considering Edward Seaga's early experiences with his 'Folk Music Of Jamaica' album, that it would be the raw, unpolished and most uncompromising aspects of Jamaican music that, over a decade later, would play a major part in its eventual worldwide acceptance?

While Byron Lee was in New York he was introduced to Ahmet Ertegun by Edward Seaga and Paul Marshall. The Ertegun brothers, Ahmet and Nesuhi, were the sons of Turkey's ambassador to Washington and the far sighted proprietors of Atlantic Records. They were not slow in realising the potential of Jamaican music and the importance of the Jamaican market for their own extensive catalogue of releases. Atlantic Records contracted Byron Lee and the band to record a number of sides in Kingston and the resulting 'Jamaica Ska' album, released on Atlantic in the USA and the UK in 1964, was credited to Byron Lee & The Ska Kings and featured vocals from The Blues Busters, The Charmers and The Maytals.

"The Ertegun brothers thought that there may be a market for ska in the USA.... Federal was the only recording studio of any quality available and Eddie Seaga and Ken 'Poppa Koo' Khouri were not exactly on the best of terms. Nothing daunted, Atlantic sent Tom Dowd down to explore the situation and record some tracks. This was a major turning point in my life as this was the start of my lifelong friendship with Tommy, my mentor. Tommy was more of a producer with the artists and musicians corralled by Ken, Eddie and the staff at both (Federal and WIRL) record companies.

Engineering was handled by myself and Byron Smith.....believe me, what we both learned from Tommy, who was, unlike most in the recording industry in those days, only too eager to share his knowledge and tricks with anyone who was eager to learn. One idiosyncrasy that Tommy had (which I rejected as being excusable as part of genius), he reversed the straight line faders on his boards. The explanation that he gave was that if he wanted more of a particular channel, track or microphone he pulled it toward him, not away from him." **Graeme Goodall**

The meeting in New York marked the beginning of a long lasting business relationship between Byron Lee and the Ertegun brothers. Ken Khouri's Federal Records had previously controlled the franchise to manufacture and distribute Atlantic Records in Jamaica but their licence was due to expire in 1965 and when "he met the Ertegun brothers from Atlantic Records and, first of all, they did a contract with the band" Sheila Lee stated "Neshui looked at Byron and said you're going to be a dynamic force in the Caribbean and when our contract with Ken Khouri expires I'm going to give you the contract. We thought he was just making fun of us but he then got the call from Neshui 'OK… the label is yours for the entire Caribbean'."

On his return to Kingston Byron Lee had formed a production company with Victor Sampson and Ronnie Nasralla, Lee Enterprises Limited, to promote live shows around Jamaica; these concerts were also intended to showcase a variety of local talent backed by Byron Lee & The Dragonaires. They brought over American artists including Chuck Berry, Sam Cooke and The Drifters to headline Jamaican shows and another company, Lee Enterprises Holding Limited, was set up to handle recordings.

George Benson and Clifford 'Bunny' Rae bought out Edward Seaga in 1964. West Indies Records Limited remained at 13 Bell Road, Kingston 11 and the new incarnation of WIRL would begin to challenge Federal Records' "virtual monopoly" on the Jamaican recording industry.

"George Benson came to work for Ken Khouri originally selling records throughout the West Indies. And then he went out and bought West Indies Records Limited with Clifford 'Bunny' Rae…

Edward Seaga sold it to Bunny Rae and George Benson. Bunny Rae I think had an electronics company, very nice guy. I believe George Benson was Trinidadian originally and came up there. They bought West Indies from Edward Seaga and it was not doing very well at all." **Graeme Goodall**

The operation would move onto entirely new levels when Byron Lee and Ronnie Nasralla approached Clifford 'Bunny' Rae and George Benson and the four formed a partnership with Sheila Lee as business manager. The two track WIRL recording studio was rebuilt and refurbished with a new mixing desk and equipment and Graeme Goodall was installed as chief engineer.

"It's the same Dynamics studio that Byron and Ronnie built to this day! This is where I stepped in and took over the managing side of the business. By this time we had a share in the WIRL studios on Bell Road. Byron Lee owned 25%, Ronnie Nasralla 25%, WIRL 25% & British American Insurance held the other 25% and there was a rental agreement between WIRL Records and WIRL Studios." **Sheila Lee**

"Ronnie Nasralla and myself built a little studio in 1965 which was called West Indies Studio and later became Dynamic Studio." **Byron Lee**

"Byron Lee was a part of WIRL too and he brought in the Atlantic label. Byron Lee used to have the Atlantic label in Jamaica and WIRL was distributing it... so Byron Lee started to climb the ladder. Last year (2005) he celebrated fifty years in the business.

Mr Rae... Bunny Rae... was the man. They had a sister company in Barbados but WIRL Jamaica was the headquarters. They used to have a whole heap of calypso those days like Lord Brynner... plenty of them. The biggest one up to now was Sparrow... Sparrow and Byron Lee did two albums together.

They built a little studio first... it was like the one 'Baba'/'Dada' Tewari had... over the office but it couldn't hold everybody so they decided to build a big studio down the bottom. Even now if you go in that studio... when Byron Lee acquired the place he didn't change anything in the studio. It stayed the same way! He didn't even paint it! All he did was modernise the control room. He didn't want to lose that sound because that Dynamic sound have a bass sound that no matter how high you put it or amplified it... it never distorted. So Byron never troubled it. One of their best engineers was Linford Anderson... 'Andy Capp'".

Bunny 'Striker' Lee

The original WIRL two track recording studio was rebuilt with a new mixing desk and refurbished by Graeme Goodall and a German named Lutz H Meyer. Sylvan Morris, who began his career at WIRL in 1965, recalled that, initially, a three track recorder had been installed at Bell Road but "three wasn't feasible". Lutz Meyer had spent four years living and working in Peru and would go on to become Vice President of Marketing for MCI and then Operations Manager of Dynamic Sounds in the Seventies. Graeme Goodall now became WIRL's chief engineer.

"You must remember that WIRL went through several different permutations during the Sixties. Eddie Seaga started it but between politics and his more profitable business interests such as the travel agency... Seaga Travel was the leader in writing tickets and chartering boats and planes for the massive emigration of Jamaicans to the UK... the record business never really did develop. Remember too that there was this tremendous animosity toward Ken Khouri and Federal Records, who held a virtual monopoly.

... Also, George Benson and Bunny Rae they saw what was going on and they wanted me to start up Doctor Bird. They just wanted to start a record company because they had the access to the artists. By this time we'd built the West Indies Records big studio which I designed and we put in this German gear sold to us by Lutz Meyer, who was I think working in Lima in Peru... working for Neumann microphones, and he was a technical guy. And so we put this equipment in and at that time, it was well before Carlton Lee was working for them. I forget who Bunny Rae and George Benson had working for them but, anyway, we started making some records at WIRL."

Graeme Goodall

Doctor Bird, Graeme Goodall's London based record label, began to license Jamaican recordings for release in the UK in late 1965 in direct competition with Blue Beat and Island and Graeme returned to the UK in 1966 to oversee the Doctor Bird and Pyramid record labels. His Pyramid label, inaugurated in 1967, would achieve UK National Chart success with Leslie Kong's productions of Desmond Dekker's '007' that year, '(Poor Me) Israelites' in 1969 (the first ever UK National Chart Number One for a Jamaican produced record) and 'It Mek' in 1970.

"Graeme Goodall, who came from Australia and used to have the Doctor Bird label in the UK was the man who set up Federal and West Indies Records Limited. He did a lot of music too because when West Indies did anything Doctor Bird used to release it in the UK. If a thing came out on WIRL in Jamaica then Doctor Bird would automatically pick it up. He was the chief engineer there for a while then he left.... All of these people are the unsung heroes of Jamaican music. They are coming from the mento, come right down... " **Bunny 'Striker' Lee**

Many of Kingston's greatest technical talents, Striker's "unsung heroes", also worked at WIRL. Errol 'ET'/'Errol T' Thompson was trained there by Graeme Goodall. Bill Garnett, who had worked with Graeme at Federal, now moved to WIRL as a technician and engineer and would later go on to install the electronics at Randy's, Joe Gibbs' first studio in Duhaney Park, Harry J's and Channel One.

"Another engineer was a guy named Barry Lambert; those guys used to work at WIRL and then Dynamic Sounds...Barry Lambert and a guy called Bill Garnett. Bill Garnett used to be in America at Harry Belafonte's studio and then he came down to Jamaica." **Bunny 'Striker' Lee**

Sylvan Morris also began his career at WIRL with Graeme Goodall and would return to Bell Road in the Eighties to "supervise cassette manufacture for Dynamics".

"I started at Dynamic... roughly about fifteen years ago... at that time the name of it was West Indies Recording Studio (WIRL). I knew an engineer there... Graeme Goodall. He invited me down there. He wanted a technician to help start fixing up Dynamic Studio. So this is where I started... I was by WIRL for about two years and when I left WIRL I went immediately to Studio One. That would be about 1968." **Sylvan Morris**

After working at both RJR and WIRL "learning how to use the two track Ampex board" Linford 'Andy Capp' Anderson left the radio station and became a key figure in the WIRL organisation where he demonstrated his prowess as an engineer and at the mastering lathe.

"Andy Capp, as he was affectionately called by many" was born Linford Anderson 8th July 1941 in Clarendon and grew up in Kingston where he graduated from Buxton High School in 1959.

"Andy had an early chance introduction to the radio, television, and recording industry in 1961 when a total stranger encouraged him to apply for a position at the local radio station, Radio Jamaica Rediffusion (RJR). He was hired as a log keeper and was responsible for recording the commercials played and the order in which they were being played. His good fortune continued when a second position presented at RJR for an audio engineer. Andy applied and was able to complete a required three month training course in less than three weeks.

Andy's talent was immediately recognised as he went on to receive five Production Awards at RJR for Special Radio Programmes over a three year span (1961to1963). His radio broadcasting career at RJR was interrupted by his desire to venture into music recording. Andy's transition to recording studio engineering was aided by Byron Lee of The Dragonaires Group. Byron Lee hired Andy as his Chief Recording Engineer at West Indies Records in 1963." **'Andy Capp' Obituary**

"When they started off at WIRL it was just two tracks. Linford Anderson was the chief engineer. He used to work both places: RJR in the daytime and in his spare time in the night time and any time he got a chance he'd come to WIRL and cut masters and run the sessions. Some of my Slim Smith sessions it's Linford who do them like 'My Conversation' and all that... so he used to share himself between the two places." **Bunny 'Striker' Lee**

"I used to record and I used to master, almost a hundred songs a day for foreign and local..." **Linford 'Andy Capp' Anderson**

"Federal was the major studio in the beginning of the rock steady era until WIRL got the first four track recording machine and all of the producers left Federal for WIRL. Records were manufactured at Federal but recording

was done at WIRL. By 1967 Leslie Kong, Sonia Pottinger and Prince Buster had all moved to WIRL."
Keith 'Scotty' Scott

Now equipped with its own sophisticated studio, mastering facilities and pressing plant WIRL began to challenge Federal's hold over Kingston's musical scene and began employing up and coming producers from downtown to keep them in touch with the local grass roots happenings. The management set up an arrangement with Lee 'Scratch' Perry after he had left Studio One to "record now and pay later" while also acting as an A&R man and supervising other recording sessions at WIRL. His position was subsequently taken over by Bunny 'Striker' Lee who takes over the story here... the ins and outs of which should be more than sufficient to demonstrate just how important a part WIRL was playing in the frenetic, frenzied "war, musical war..." then taking place in Kingston.

"There was a great man at WIRL but he's dead now. Nobody talks about him. His right name was Clifford Rae but we used to call him Bunny Rae... an old army man. He always gave the little man a chance: he used to look out for us, gave us little producers studio time, cut our stampers and put out the records then they'd draw back their money. WIRL's sister company was in Barbados (Applethwaites Estate at St Thomas) so Mr Rae gave all of us a lot of chances.

I did about four tunes on my first session (at Treasure Isle) but I didn't have the money to put them out. I had given 'Do It To Me Baby' by Lloyd & The Groovers to Ken Lack because I didn't have no money to put out the records. I couldn't even cut the stamper. My brother was working at WIRL as a salesman and he went to Mr Rae, Bunny Rae, and Mr Rae took 'Music Field' by Roy Shirley and put it out. It came out on Lee... I made a label named Lee first.

And then Mr Rae called me to do some more production because their in house producer wasn't doing well. At that time it was Lee Perry so I went down there and I had money to hire people because the company was paying for it so I got Lynn Taitt and Tommy McCook and we did this session... 'Let Me Go Girl' with Slim Smith. So when the session started we did a tune first with a girl named Beverley Simmons but I don't remember the song now. Then, when we did the Slim Smith tune, Lee Perry came and set about the musicians: 'I'm the producer for the house and I don't know about it!' so the musicians started to panic and everybody started looking at me. They came up to me as a newcomer and said 'how come you called us in the studio and Lee Perry and them don't know about it?' and I said 'the boss asked me to do it. I don't know because Lee Perry used to work between WIRL and Coxsone's studio and I'm just doing my work' so they followed me, the whole set of musicians, up with me to the boss' office and Mr Rae said 'what is this gentlemen? A strike?' and they said 'no... this youth here come and say he's recording for West Indies Records and Lee Perry say him know nothing about it. We've done two songs already and we don't know if we're going to get paid' so Mr Rae said 'I authorised with Bunny to go and do some things for us because anything we're doing with Scratch we're not making any money. Bunny's song 'Music Field' is Number Five in the chart.'

So after that now Mr Rae said 'alright gentlemen?' and they decided to carry on with the session but I said 'no… you see how the vibe's gone? And we're going to call it a day' and Mr Rae paid them and (the next time) I went down to voice a tune that's how The Uniques started. Because Slim Smith was a part of a group with Winston Riley named The Techniques and I said I'm going to form my own group named The Uniques. Linford Anderson mixed and mastered it and when it came out it was the biggest tune in Jamaica for 1967 you know (sings) "girl you hold me trying to control me…" it was the baddest tune… everywhere in Jamaica!"

Bunny 'Striker' Lee

Striker then became the in house producer at WIRL but, as he said, "I no come to count cow. I came here to drink milk… that's a saying" meaning "mind your own business and enjoy what you are entitled to. Don't worry about details which do not concern you" and he continued to help out Scratch by giving him after hours studio time at Bell Road.

"And Mr Rae fired Lee Perry for that. Fired Lee Perry 'pon the spot because he never made any hits. I don't know if Roy Shirley had a hand in it too because he told them that any time anyone did a tune at WIRL Lee Perry carried it up to Coxsone to let Coxsone hear it… so Lee Perry was a spy! Roy said Lee Perry took away my tune ('Hold Them' by Roy Shirley for Joe Gibbs) and went to Coxsone and Coxsone copied it (as 'Feel Good') with Ken Boothe.

So after Mr Rae fired Scratch I became the house producer at WIRL. Me and Scratch started to move because Scratch never have no money now. Coxsone and him never got on and that's why he left for West Indies Records and now he was nowhere. So then the studio... he used to come in the night time and make his things. I used to let Lee Perry come back and work at night time and do his own things so we became good friends. We were inseparable: you see me... you see Lee Perry!"

Bunny 'Striker' Lee

And, through these connections, WIRL continued to promote the music of the ghetto, which by now had transformed into rock steady, to uptown music enthusiasts, tourists and to the international market.

"WIRL Records have done it again – on one block buster LP record the fantastic INTENSIFIED sounds of the Jamaican Rock Steady Beat. The new, big beat now INTENSIFIED, will send you for days and extra days!!

This new rhythm and dance form, originating in Western Kingston, has now spread to the tourist and resort areas of Jamaica's Gold Coast..."

'Rock Steady Intensified'

Unfortunately, behind the scenes, business was far from rock steady and the partnership was dissolved in 1968. Sheila Lee detailed the tangled web that had to be untangled before business could be resumed. "We were paying Atlantic all the royalties quarterly and Byron kept on doing this even though he was receiving no money from WIRL. They were responsible for paying the rental to satisfy the agreement... they were supposed to pay the studio bills but they defaulted on the studio contracts by not paying the rents. They were supposed to pay the rental to the owner of the property but they didn't pay... which meant that WIRL Records could swoop in and take control of the studio. Byron and Ronnie were locked out of the studio and things were getting really rough. The only option was to force them into liquidation so we filed an injunction against WIRL Records, forced them into bankruptcy, and the place burned down!"

The fire destroyed the main building at 13 Bell Road and WIRL went into liquidation but the studio was left intact and interested parties began to bid for what remained of the company and its assets. In addition to the recording studio, mastering facilities and pressing plant WIRL also owned a chain of record shops around the island. "West Indies Records had places named Disco Land. They had about ten different shops all over… they used to have Disco Land shops all over Jamaica". Bunny Rae gave the Disco Land shop at 101 Orange Street to Bunny 'Striker' Lee which Striker renamed 'Bunny Lee's Record City' and, along with Bob Gray, Mr Rae "then set up with two of WIRL's record presses on Chancery Lane by the side of Randy's in downtown Kingston".

"When WIRL burned down Mr Rae and a guy named Bob Gray, two army guys, kept two of the presses and set up in downtown Kingston on Chancery Lane by the side of Randy's. He used to have a set of shops called Disco Land and he wanted to give me the pressing plant but I couldn't do two things at the same time so I made him sell it to Jo Jo Hoo Kim who later became Channel One. I couldn't manage (the pressing plant) because I could barely pay rent for this shop when I took it over even though Mr Rae gave it to me well stocked. So I stayed there and made myself a man out of the shop.

Pama (the Palmer Brothers London based record company) was there too and recorded at WIRL. The price at the liquidation sale was £15,000 and Pama was going to come up with the money and be a part of it or take over all of West Indies Records which would have been good for Pama Records at the time. But Graeme Goodall and Byron were good friends and Graeme Goodall discouraged Pama from buying it."

Bunny 'Striker' Lee

Mrs Sheila Lee

Byron Lee at the controls

"Then they got into financial difficulties, one way or another, the factory burned which was a pressing plant... burnt but not the offices, strangely enough, and not the studio because that was a separate building... separate and remote. And I went down there and, I think, to see Leslie Kong 'cause Leslie's in a panic now because, you know, he was using West Indies Records studio which was a better sounding studio than Federal's big one because I'd learnt that the Federal studio was too big and we had to get more intimate, you know, for the musicians. I knew a lot more about acoustics... I learnt a lot more about acoustics being in England and watching... and listening and learning which is what a good engineer is supposed to do.

When Byron bought West Indies Records and had the studio it was then he decided 'well hell. I'll get the record plant going as well'. Through a lot of contacts he had... he managed to get the Atlantic franchise, he managed to get the Motown franchise and stuff like that... that enabled him to press records." **Graeme Goodall**

Sheila Lee harked back to this turbulent time "I had bought a piece of property on Hagley Park Road where we intended to build studios, mastering and pressing plants but, in the meantime we'd set up Lee Enterprises Holdings and our bid was accepted by the receivers. I was running Lee Holdings but we ended up owning Bell Road so I sold the property on Hagley Park Road. Byron changed the number from 13 to 15 Bell Road because 13 Bell Road had a bad feeling because it was WIRL where the fire began. But of course we now had to do everything the way big business was done... board meetings and everything... but Byron was always centred on the band and his music. Byron had tunnel vision... he just saw the music. He was never much interested in the business."

"Byron and Linford 'Andy Capp' Anderson went up to New York and got a custom built board from Atlantic Records and turned it into a four track studio. I was down there producing too and it became Dynamic Sounds..."
Bunny 'Striker' Lee

After purchasing WIRL from the receivers Byron Lee formed the 'Dynamic Sounds Recording Company Limited' on 1st May 1969. Its name was a direct echo of Nesuhi Ertegun's prophetic words from five years previously and the 15 Bell Road complex would became known amongst Kingston's musical fraternity as 'Dynamics'. Byron recruited Sam 'Mitch' Mitchell and Keith 'Scotty' Scott, two 'press men' who had produced and arranged a string of rock steady hits at Federal for Winston Blake's Merritone label during 1967 and 1968, to look after the pressing plant.

"We worked at Federal until 1968... we were young but experienced and we had a falling out with the Khouris. We left Federal and went to Byron Lee. He wanted people with experience to work in the pressing plant and studio. They had just opened up their factory but Byron Lee paid us to stay at home until the plant was ready for operation in 1969. We got paid and we stayed home and we would go to Byron's house every week to collect a cheque. I worked at Dynamics until I came to the USA. My girlfriend's mum took her to America and I decided I wasn't going to let her get away so I chased her to New York!" **Keith 'Scotty' Scott**

Dynamic rapidly established itself as the island's leading recording and manufacturing company and, as the year drew to a close, Byron Lee began again to promote stage shows with foreign artists including "a Miami teenager named Betty Wright".

"Stage shows featuring foreign artists are back with a rush. Chuck Jackson followed fast on the heels of Joe Simon and now Byron Lee is lining up an all star production for January... his first in over a year. It seems that there is still enough money and good feeling left after the Christmas festivities to make a big name event profitable.

On Byron's bill are expected to be Eddie Floyd (whose 'Consider Me' and 'Knock On Wood' attracted plenty of attention on the island), saxman King Curtis, Betty Wright, a Miami teenager who has already established herself on Atlantic Records with rhythm & blues hits like 'Girls Can't Do What Guys Can Do' and The Robert Patterson Singers, an up and coming US gospel group with a growing international reputation. Incidentally Byron negotiated heavily with Aretha Franklin (who was here on holiday at the Hilton not long ago) but she just couldn't make it.

A full roster of local entertainers will be on hand plus, naturally, The Dragonaires, who will have just completed their usual exhausting Christmas schedule. This year, once more the boys are demonstrating their political impartiality by playing for both Mr Seaga's Western Kingston

Benefit Ball and the Drumblair dance... (Drumblair was the home of the founder of the People's National Party Norman Washington Manley)."

Merry Go Round *The Daily Gleaner*

The Dynamic production of Boris Gardiner's 'Elizabethan Reggae' on Trojan's Duke subsidiary (initial copies credited Byron Lee as the artist) scaled the heights of the UK National Charts in January 1970 when it made the Number Fourteen position. The following year Byron Lee & The Dragonaires "played at the Ally Pally" (Alexandra Palace in London) and Byron, after meeting 'Jeep' Harned in Miami and being "inspired by Criteria", then decided to upgrade the WIRL studio.

"The studio wasn't burned down in the fire so we started work (on upgrading the studio) and everything was up to date because of Graeme Goodall. Byron saw that he could make more money if he opened his own studio and we eventually became competitors with the Khouris... but we never fell out." **Ronnie Nasralla**

"The problem was that people wanted to earn easy money but they didn't want to invest money in the music." **Byron Lee**

While in London managing his Doctor Bird and Pyramid labels Graeme Goodall had also expanded into record retailing with three shops named Record Plaza but "of all things I wasn't a retailer..." and Byron persuaded Graeme to return to Kingston.

"Doctor Bird didn't succeed, because I was not a retailer, I was not a shopkeeper. You know, England the land of shopkeepers... I was a misfit but anyway... we had a good time doing it but it just didn't work...

I have always believed that every country has a different 'atmosphere' that affects how the human ear perceives sound. This probably includes culture. When Jamaican records were released in the UK they were mastered direct disc to disc. It was virtually impossible to get copy tapes from Jamaica. Doctor Bird used John Hassell Recordings in Barnes... a suburb of London. I think that many of my competitors used Derek Strickland at Pye. It was difficult to get the UK mastering engineers to understand why we wanted a certain eq (equalisation) in the process. If you get the chance to compare a Jamaican pressing, a UK pressing and a USA pressing of the same 'tune' on 45's, you will notice the difference. I figured that the only way that I could cope with this was to escort John Hassell (who was, to all intents and purposes, blind due to an incredible incident that he survived during World War 2) to New York & Jamaica. His incredible Golden Ears quickly picked up on the differences.

I was fighting to try and keep Doctor Bird, Pyramid, everything going and Byron came up and said 'listen. There are bigger things'. I said 'like what?' He said 'well you're having a tough time here.' He said 'I'm building a new studio… I'm going to go four track. I'm going with this new equipment called MCI.' He said 'I've met this guy in Fort Lauderdale and I want you to get it together so we're going to design this stuff, put new equipment in the studio… redo it'.

And so I went out there… I decided OK we'll go back and I virtually just left everything. I literally closed down Doctor Bird Records as such, went back to Jamaica, re-built the Dynamic Studios using this new equipment MCI…

Around that time Byron Lee was rebuilding Dynamic Sounds, wanted to build it up into a venue for his own product, increase the technology and also around that time Eddie Seaga was heading up towards being Prime Minister… they wanted to build a Caribbean wide radio broadcasting network. And they asked me if I would come down and do the consulting for that and at the same time work for Dynamic Sounds… to install the new equipment… the new MCI equipment that he'd ordered. So I said I'll do that. I'll go back to the engineering… I'd had the hit records, I'd gotten them on the charts, I'd done virtually everything and it wasn't going anywhere."

Graeme Goodall

Grover C Harned, known as 'Jeep', had supervised the installation of a 'muzak' system at Fort Lauderdale Airport while running a hi-fi shop in Miami and was approached by Mack Emerman, the owner of Criteria Studios, who needed advice about distortion on their console. Mack then asked Jeep to design and build a new console for Criteria's Studio C and, from this, Jeep would go on to develop and expand Music Centers Inc. His company would become world famous and, as the Seventies progressed, MCI became "one of the foremost manufacturers of

Linford 'Andy Capp' Anderson

professional recording equipment" working at the cutting edge of American recording technology. MCI's first ever complete operation of mixer and recorder was installed at Byron Lee's new Dynamic Sounds Recording Studio. Their "custom built console", together with their latest equipment, was proudly detailed on the sleeve of their first long playing foray into the brand new 'Reggay' (sic) beat.

"This album was skillfully produced in the STUDIOS of DYNAMIC SOUNDS RECORDING CO BYRON LEE personally supervised the mixing of DYNAMIC'S New Sophisticated Console with Visible Electronic Computed Equalization.

Mics used were: Telefunken, Neumann, 87 Sony Condensers EV's, AKG's RCA 77DX, Senheiser feeding a custom built console. The programme was recorded on an Ampex AG440 employing the Haeco Equalization System.

'Jamaica and Caribbean's Number One Band' - Byron Lee & The Dragonaires introduces to you the sensational new Jamaican dance beat that's crashing all over the world – Reggay! Reggay has literally blasted its way like a turbulent Musical Hurricane throughout Jamaica and the Caribbean to all the Continents of the world. It's pulsating dance beat, which provokes most stimulating dance steps, has completely monopolised the Pop Music Scene reaching its peak with the world's greatest group The Beatles recording their great Reggay hit 'Ob La Di Ob La Da' and Jamaica's own Desmond Dekker & The Aces making Number One in Great Britain with '(Poor Me) Israelites'." **'Reggay'**

"The best people are Duke Reid, Ken Khouri and especially Byron Lee who runs the Dynamic Studio. They're all nice people. You can deal with them and feel happy with them." **Gladstone 'Gladdy' Anderson**

"This album compiles the greatest Reggay hits ever created – exciting and naughty and presents to you the liveliest Party Record in the true Byron Lee & The Dragonaires spirit. If you cannot be with Byron Lee & The Dragonaires on the dance floors of Jamaica, then take them home with you in this. One of their most exciting albums ever produced – Reggay!"
'Reggay'

Lik it back - Hawk it to the very last drop - Pop a Top - Sip a Sip - These are the genuine phrases of Jamaica's ethnic beat REGGAY Spawned in the embryo of Rock Steady and Ska, REGGAY has now matured. Hold Me Tight and Israelite invaded the International charts with such great force that they influenced the Beatles who recorded Ob-La-Di and Give Peace a Chance, both REGGAY. Now BYRON LEE and the DRAGONAIRES introduce an extension of the REGGAY - the "MOON WALK", and if you are curious, turn your record player on and get ready for - " REGGAY BLAST OFF "

Andy Capp

As the reggae beat progressed Dynamics became the studio of choice for freelance producers and artists who wanted to use the talents of the undisputed top session band of the era. Between 1969 and 1972 Dynamic Sounds provided a facility where almost anyone in the business could have their song arranged and backed by the best musicians on the island. Their house band played together every day and it has been argued that many of the freelance producers actually achieved far better results with the ensemble than Dynamic's own producers. When Clancy Eccles was in the producer's role he called them The Dynamites.

"To me the group of musicians I worked with sounded like something was going to explode. Well to get a strong explosion you need dynamite! At that time it proved to be the number one recording group in Jamaica. Everybody wanted to work with them: Duke Reid, Leslie Kong... and Dynamic Sounds." **Clancy Eccles**

"Winston Wright's organ was spot on. Hux Brown's lead guitar added special texture to the rhythm and the rest of The Dynamites chugged away..." **Chris Lane**

At this time their Bell Road studio was also the home of some unprecedented advances in sonic and technical innovation with Linford 'Andy Capp' Anderson numbering among the Dynamic engineers playing an incisive, if still largely unrecognised, role in the creation of dub.

"Linford 'Andy Capp' Anderson was an engineer at the radio station. First of all he used to work at RJR studio and he got a part time job at WIRL studio. I took Linford Anderson to Byron Lee's house and Byron gave him a permanent job. They went to America to get some equipment… Byron and Linford went up to New York and got a custom built board from Atlantic Records and turned it into a four track studio. The board they came back with is the board that Tubby used. Tubby had started with a little board that he made but Byron later sold him the four track board… I was down there producing too and it became Dynamic Sounds."

Bunny 'Striker' Lee

Andy Capp had worked with Lee Perry on the Upset label, founded with Barrington 'Barry' Lambert in 1967, and a number of releases on Upset, such as 'Noisy Village' credited to The Engineers, had been seriously experimental. The first chapter of Andy Capp's 'Pop A Top' saga, an entire series of "sound collage" records, combined updated versions of Derrick Morgan's 'Fat Man' with Bop A Loos' rhythm & blues instrumental 'South Parkway Mambo' (originally released on Mercury in 1955), deejay interjections and a reworking of radio advert for Canada Dry, was released on Dynamic's Tiger subsidiary towards the end of 1969.

"His passion for recording evolved into some playful and creative experimentation that led to the recording of several songs of his own, to include 'Pop A Top' and 'The Law'." **'Andy Capp' Obituary**

Further versions included 'Poppy Show', 'Pop A Top (Ver 2)' and a pre-release reverb vocal version of 'Fat Man' backed with a stripped back "music only" version. These records caused a sensation at the start of the Seventies and presaged the beginnings of dub and sampling but were initially dismissed by some of the Dynamic management as "that foolishness" and their importance and prescience has now been largely forgotten.

"Andy Capp was very great engineer… very creative engineer. He brought in a thing called 'Pop A Top' (sings) 'Pop a top, sip a sip…' He had about twenty different versions of 'Pop A Top' and all those tunes like 'Dr No Go' that Mrs Pottinger put out were Andy Capp's tunes. Linford experimented with those funny sounds… them great sounds… he was a great engineer and very creative." **Bunny 'Striker' Lee**

"The 'Pop A Top'? It was a big joke, you know. It was nothing to be taken seriously. Just frigging around and see what became of it..."

Jackie Jackson

During 1970 one of the enterprising engineers at Dynamics, possibly Andy Capp, Carlton Lee or Sid Bucknor, masterminded some of the first ever drum and bass records including 'Phantom' a minimal version to 'Herb Man'. The thrilling 'Ease Up'/'Squeeze Up' also known as 'Short Wave' and Part Two of 'Don't Call Me N*****r Whitey' from the same period, both credited to Byron Lee & The Dragonaires, showcased a very early airing on record of the sound effect that would become known as King Tubby's legendary 'big knob'. There has been some serious subsequent debate as to whether the effect on these records was actually created by the high pass filter on Dynamic's MCI board in Studio B but, it would appear, that King Tubby achieved his unique sound by patching it into the mixer differently, and using it in a more subtle and controlled manner that actually accentuated the effect.

"On the Dynamics tunes it sounds more like a sweep equaliser or a wah wah pedal because they're sending the track straight through it and then twisting the knob quite quickly. But if you listen to the way it's used at Tubby's you can hear there's more resonance (because of the way he's connected the unit to the mixer) and he'll go through the frequencies notch by notch. Tubby's will often turn the knob slowly, sometimes just leaving it on one setting for a while and really digging into that altered sound and the resonance rather than just using it as a gimmick ." **Chris Lane**

These were some of the first intimations of the music that would become known as dub although any details, apart from the vinyl releases of this remarkable step forward in recorded sound, went un-recorded and un-remarked upon at the time. Even the engineers, when subsequently interviewed by Chris Lane, had no recollections of their pioneering dub mixes.

Bunny 'Striker' Lee had continued to work at 'Dynamics' both as an independent producer and as one of their in house team.

"Then we leave and go to Dynamic. It's like I was a cricketer then Dynamic was my home ground. It's still the best studio in the whole Caribbean when it comes to the bass part. It holds the bass and it doesn't distort if you turn up the bass on the record or in the studio. Byron Lee do everything in the control room… but him never trouble inside of the studio because him don't want to lose that sound. Even now that studio exists."

Bunny 'Striker' Lee

The musicians, including master drummer Winston Grennan, self-styled creator of the 'one drop' drum pattern, and Striker's often unorthodox production techniques would, on occasion, offend Dynamic's studio engineers.

"Mr Winston Grennan was the master on the one drop but we used to call it the 'cow sh*t splash'. Excuse my language! It's like when the cow pass its faeces and it used to drop and make that 'plow' sound and I used to say 'Winston I want you to play the cow sh*t splash! Heh, heh, heh.' Right but later they started to call it the one drop. It came like the sound that the cow's sh*t makes when it drops on the road… in those days the cows used to walk plenty in Jamaica and you'd hear the cow dung splash. He was the master at that, man… when he dropped and his foot heavy and Linford 'Andy Capp' Anderson used to bawl 'bwoy you a mash up me needle!' and I'd say 'just take the tune same way. You understand?' Because Linford Anderson was good engineer and he used to watch the needles! But when Winston's drum dropped they'd go badly into the red! That was the cow sh*t splash man!" **Bunny 'Striker' Lee**

And, in 1971, Bunny 'Striker' Lee gave Dynamic Sounds their first ever gold record when Eric Donaldson's Festival winner 'Cherry Oh Baby', structured around Striker's new 'broken beat', was released on their Jaguar subsidiary. The Jamaican Cultural Development Commission Annual Festival Of The Arts had been established in 1963 after the island's independence in order to "develop and promote the creative talents and cultural expressions of the Jamaican people... also to ensure that the nation's cultural heritage is preserved for the benefit of future generations" and, since its inception in 1966, the Song Contest had been the most popular aspect of the Festival.

"I had a label with Dynamic, they still use it now, named Jaguar. Anything on Jaguar you know it's me who made it! One named Lion through Dynamic. Dynamic had the animal labels!

'Cherry Oh Baby'... heh, heh, heh... Well, one night the Festival eliminations were on and I went along with Delroy Wilson and some of the other artists. When this guy (Eric Donaldson) sung the tune Delroy bring it to me and I decided to record it the next day. At that time I was producing things for Dynamic. Sid Bucknor was working with Eric Donaldson before this and, because Sid was the engineer at Dynamic, Eric didn't want to do it. So that morning I reached early and put Eric in a chair at Dynamic. Neville Lee (Byron's brother) came in and said 'what's that ugly boy doing in my chair?' and Tommy Cowan said... 'no, no, Neville this guy have a tune that a go mash up the place man and Striker Lee did bring him come!' and they okayed the session.

I did that song about five times. Lloyd Charmers did a version of it too... you remember one of the first versions that came out the b-side was called 'Sir Charmers Special'? We did it in a studio that Byron Lee fixed up for me and Charmers but they didn't like the sound. They're using it for mastering now and for a tape room for making cassettes. I did 'Rain From The Skies' and all those songs there though. It had a different sound but the really big 'Cherry Oh Baby' was one Saturday morning ...

I went back in and brought in Denzil Laing and the band that I used was an outside band with my drummer Lloyd Adams who we called 'Tin Leg'. That band was The Inner Circle and later half of it became Third World... the Lewis brothers went to America and 'Touter' used to play organ with The Aggrovators. 'Ibo' Cooper and 'Cat' Coore they went off with Third World so Third World was a part of 'Cherry Oh Baby' too."

Bunny 'Striker' Lee

Acknowledged as Jamaica's biggest selling record ever the song was so successful that, for years afterwards, the Festival judges would invariably complain there were far too many 'Cherry Oh Baby' sound-alikes. In 1972 Dynamic Sounds released 'From 'Bam Bam' To 'Cherry Oh! Baby'', a compilation of Festival Song Contest Winners in a striking gatefold sleeve, that included their own 'Cherry Oh Baby' and 'Bam Bam' from The Maytals (Festival Song Winner in 1966) and other top producers' winning entries including Duke Reid's 'Boom Sha Ka Lacka' from Hopeton Lewis and Leslie Kong's 'Intensified' by Desmond Dekker and 'Sweet & Dandy' from The Maytals. 'Cherry Oh Baby' would be covered five years later by The Rolling Stones on their 'Black & Blue' album and again by UB40 in 1983 on their 'Labour Of Love' long player.

TROJAN RECORDS
TR 7731 B
SQUEEZE UP (Part 2)
BYRON LEE & THE DRAGONAIRES
Gala
GALA 4001
THE TECHNIQUES
I'M SO IN LOVE WITH YOU
Kentone RECORDS
OIL IN THE LAMP
Eric "Monty" Morris
Byron Lee
AND
The Dragonaires
MANUFACTURED BY FEDERAL RECORD MFG. CO. LTD. JAMAICA W.I.
Panther
P—01
JOHNNY (TOO) BAD
(The Slicker)
THE SLICKER
MANUFACTURED BY DYNAMIC SOUNDS, 15 BELL RD. KGN. JA.
afrik
STEREO
SIDE A
WIDE AWAKE IN A DREAM
(Wallace)
BARRY BIGGS
DUKE RECORDS
DU 69 A
THE LAW (Part 1)
ANDY CAPP
Trans-world
TWS-1731
STEREO
THE LAW
(Lee/Anderson)
BYRON LEE &
THE DRAGONAIRES
JAGUAR
J—08
Produced by:
B. Lee &
T. Cowan
CHERRY OH BABY
(Eric Donaldson)
ERIC DONALDSON
MANUFACTURED BY DYNAMIC SOUNDS, 15 BELL RD. KGN. JA.
TIGER
A
DYNAMIC
SOUNDS
PRODUCTION
POPPY SHOW
ANDY CAPP with
Val Bennett
SUNSHINE
VOCAL
BEHOLD
BLUES BUSTERS
WIRL records
Island
Records
Release
45-931
KEEP ON RUNNING
JACKIE EDWARDS
FOLLOW THE STARS ON
STARLINE

Byron Lee, "Your Man In The Sun", now became MCI's representative in Jamaica:

"Words could not express what it means to be MCI's first dealer..."

Byron Lee

"And then they put in the eight track at Dynamic and Byron did become like the agent for MCI because he did travel so much and then the big sixteen track tape did come..."

Bunny 'Striker' Lee

In 1972 Duke Reid purchased the eight track equipment from Dynamic for his Treasure Isle Studio and a deal was brokered between Osbourne 'King Tubby' Ruddock and Byron Lee where Tubby purchased the four track equipment from Dynamic's Studio B. The package included the MCI console that Tubby would go on to make world famous when he established his own studio on Dromilly Avenue, "the undisputed mecca of dub", deep in the heart of the Waterhouse ghetto.

"Studio A in Dynamics was the bigger studio... Studio A was eight track and Studio B was four track. In my time Karl Pitterson was the engineer in Studio A and Carlton Lee was the engineer in the B Studio. They were in two separate buildings... you went through a big gate at the front... all the buildings were on the left. The first bigger building was the office where you made the bookings... Byron Lee had his office in there... and the pressing plant was behind the office.

Then there was a canteen for the workers and then Studio A. Whoever did a cook at the canteen was a good cook... I did eat a lot of food at Dynamics and never complained! You came to the big studio first and the next building was Studio B with Carlton Lee and Linford 'Andy Capp' Anderson and all them man there. But Karl Pitterson was the main man in Studio A... he was also a musician... a guitarist.

Dynamics was a good studio with good equipment... it's where I first saw a grand piano. But the four track was what we could afford...none of we flat foot hustlers used eight track... only four track. It's one hour me used to book at Dynamics... enough for two rhythms. Then I'd book another hour to voice them.

They were good days...when you finished recording you'd go to the control room and listen to the playback. Dynamics was one of the best built studios in Jamaica... and a vast amount of reggae came out of Dynamic before Randy's and Channel One came on the scene. Dynamic and Federal were properly built studios... in them days they used to make them properly and the ceilings were eighteen feet high... but later on it all changed. If you saw a red light, you knew a session was going on. It was proper, proper, proper and when me come into the business Dynamic was one of the main studios... all roads lead to Federal or Dynamics."

Roy Cousins

Linford 'Andy Capp' Anderson returned to RJR in 1971...

"Andy Capp's studio recording ended in 1971 when he returned to RJR to serve as their Chief Broadcast Engineer for the next six years. Andy migrated to the United States in 1977 and lived in Bronx, New York. He drove a taxi cab before he was hired as an Audio Engineer by B Eichwald & Company to work at the United Nations Headquarters in New York. Andy recorded and broadcasted many world leaders and dignitaries to include former President George HW Bush and Bishop Desmond Tutu over his twenty six year career as an Audio Engineer at the United Nations Headquarters. Andy retired in June 2004. Andy's retirement led him to Charlotte, North Carolina where he fulfilled his dream of owning and operating a restaurant and bar establishment appropriately named Pop A

Top. His lengthy illness over the past four months led him to Austell, Georgia where he passed away on 16th March 2020."

'Andy Capp' Obituary

"So I went back to Jamaica and worked for Dynamic Sounds and round about that time because we brought the technology up we introduced sixteen and then later twenty four track recording and it made it a professional world class studio. Then we started getting the English rock and roll bands down there then it became fun again." **Graeme Goodall**

Graeme Goodall was not the only person to fly down to Jamaica. After nearly a decade of exporting the sound of young Jamaica all over the world a number of international artists now decided to "make a hit in the sun" and come to Kingston to record at Dynamic. The new upgraded sixteen track Dynamic Sounds studio began to attract "the English rock and roll bands" and artists including Eric Clapton, Joe Cocker, Elton John, Cat Stevens, "who recorded the 'Foreigner' LP in the B room using a 22x16 channel Sound Techniques System 12 console", and The Rolling Stones. Mick Jagger had come to Dynamic on the advice of Ahmet Ertegun and the band recorded a number of tracks for their 'Goats Head Soup' album on Bell Road in late 1972.

"The album itself didn't take that long but we recorded an awful lot of tracks. There were not only Jamaicans involved but also percussion players, who came from places like Guyana, a travelling pool of guys who worked in the studios. It was interesting to be playing in this totally different atmosphere. Geoffrey Chung the engineer at Dynamic, for example, was a Chinese man… you realise how much Jamaica is a multi-ethnic environment." **Keith Richards**

"We finished our new Studio B just in time for the Stones and we also got specific equipment they requested: a grand piano and Hammond B3 organ as well as special microphones and headphones (which Jamaican musicians never use in the studio) an investment of nearly $100,000."

Byron Lee

American artists Stevie Wonder and Paul Simon also recorded at Dynamic and The Dynamites supplied the rhythm for Paul Simon's 'Mother And Child Reunion' a Number Five hit in the UK National Charts in early 1972. Apparently Paul Simon wanted to record at Dynamic after hearing Jimmy Cliff's protest song 'Vietnam'. A studio was set up specifically for Roberta

Flack's use, again through Byron Lee's Atlantic Records connection, where she recorded the haunting 'Killing Me Softly With His Song' with Jackie Jackson, Hux Brown & Gladstone Anderson. Jackie later recalled "but the one that's out now, the one that you hear and that's on the record, that's not us".

"I liked the B Studio at Dynamic. It had been built for Roberta Flack to use but that never came off and so it became popular with local Jamaican producers. It was more for us than A Studio." **Jimmy Radway**

"This is the studio of choice for foreigners (Stevie Wonder, The Rolling Stones, Joe Cocker) who choose to record in Jamaica... very clean, clinical, precise and without much funk: but Dynamic has a wonderful aura of spaciousness, especially when Geoffrey Chung is at the board, that no other studio seems to get." **Stephen Davis**

"We took it up to sixteen track. We recorded the Rolling Stones, Cat Stevens, Elton John, Stevie Wonder... all these big bands, you know. Dynamic was now found as a recreational type studio. I was the Director of Engineering. We had our own disc cutting studio for which I built a lot of the equipment. We had our own stamper plant, we had our own label printing, shrink wrapping, cassette duplicating. We did cassettes as well so I took over the engineering of that and I loved Byron...I had a great time with him and we were very good friends. I was working with this guy, Jeep Harned, who was making MCI recording equipment in Fort Lauderdale, so we used to fly up there and talk to Jeep Harned about recording and find out from him and Tommy Dowd what was going on."

Graeme Goodall

Graeme Goodall continued to work for Dynamic Sounds until 1981 when he moved to the USA where "eventually I ended up working for the owner of MCI Recording Equipment". Jamaican Prime Minister Michael Manley's experiment in democratic socialism and his close links with Fidel Castro's communist regime in Cuba had convinced many, including Graeme, that Jamaica was heading for its own people's revolution.

"But the political situation in Jamaica got untenable... by this time I had two children, a son and a daughter, and I did not think it was a very good atmosphere in which to bring my children up so we came up to Miami. I was working on the broadcasting project with Eddie Seaga called Jamaica Information Services, JIS, who were the broadcasting arm of the Jamaica Federal Government..."

Graeme Goodall

His technical skills and empathy with Jamaican music were beyond compare and Graeme Goodall's role in the development of recorded music in Jamaica, and its subsequent UK crossover success, are worthy of a book of their own. His contribution was pivotal and his name is justifiably revered by everyone who was fortunate enough to work with him.

"Graeme Goodall was a great engineer and a very nice person. He set up Federal Records, WIRL and Dynamic Records too. He was from Australia originally. Byron brought him back in at Dynamic as an engineer and he fixed up the studio. Graeme Goodall set up Dynamic brilliantly. He was out of sight; he could do everything, wireless, studio, do everything! He used to work at RJR and his son came and got himself in the studio business too. Graeme Goodall was a brilliant engineer.

In those days I had a John Holt tune with only one verse and when he spliced it and put back a solo you'd think John had sung the song straight through. Play it! It's called 'A Little Love' but not the one that Jimmy London sang. John Holt sang two tunes on it and Stranger Cole has a tune on that rhythm too... 'a little love to make the heart grow fonder'... Graeme spliced on the drum roll and put the solo in the rhythm long before the computer thing came in! He was way ahead of his time and he taught plenty of the engineers in Jamaica too." **Bunny 'Striker' Lee**

In addition to working for Sony Graeme Goodall participated in many other projects and remained active as a consulting engineer up until his death, aged 82, of natural causes at his home in Atlanta, USA on December 4th 2014.

As the sound of reggae became increasingly popular worldwide Dynamic Sounds continued to lead where others followed and the visiting artists helped to convince local producers and artists the importance of Dynamic's insistence on professional recording standards.

"Is so much music that I work on, I tell you the truth, I can't remember them. Is a thousand and one music. But at that time man never too conscious 'bout sound on a whole so a engineer never too important at that time there... but now man start get conscious to the sound..." **Karl Pitterson**

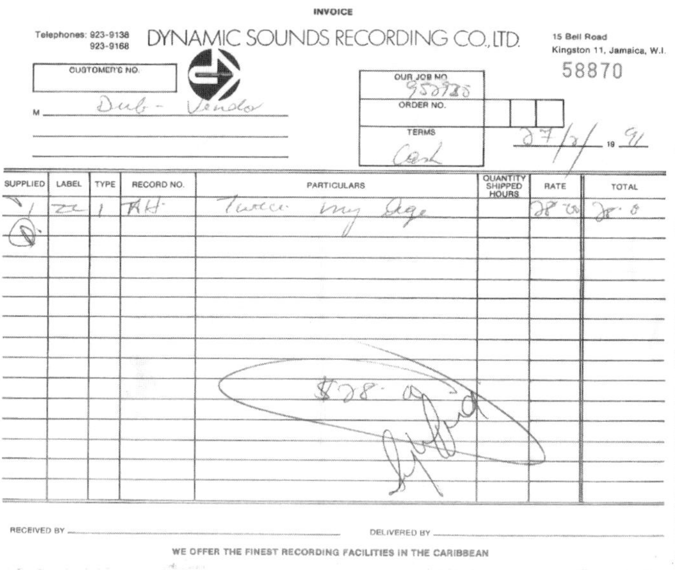
INVOICE

Telephones: 923-9138 / 923-9168 DYNAMIC SOUNDS RECORDING CO., LTD. 15 Bell Road, Kingston 11, Jamaica, W.I.

58870

CUSTOMER'S NO.

M Dub - Vendo

OUR JOB NO 950985

ORDER NO.

TERMS Cash

27/8/ 19 91

SUPPLIED	LABEL	TYPE	RECORD NO.	PARTICULARS	QUANTITY SHIPPED HOURS	RATE	TOTAL
1		1	AH	Twice my Age		28.00	28.00

$28.00

RECEIVED BY ______ DELIVERED BY ______

WE OFFER THE FINEST RECORDING FACILITIES IN THE CARIBBEAN

Noel Hawks

"Byron was very deeply involved in the studio and, where others were investing in real estate etc, he was pouring hundreds of thousands of US dollars constantly into upgrading equipment. He even built Studio B in the third building but it never had the success of the original studio. Through our recording studios we exposed local artists to people like Eric Clapton and Elton John... we brought all these guys in to meet them."

Sheila Lee

The Dynamic studios continued to turn out countless local hits with Byron in control musically while Sheila Lee continued to take care of the business as she recounted "Byron was always very, very hands on with the production because he was an artist himself. If he was out of the studio they would always come to him because he had to approve what had been done (in his absence). All the artists and musicians had a deep respect for Byron". Sheila laughingly recalled just how carefully she took care of business: "Over the years he didn't care about money and finances were a bother... I said to Byron 'you must call the shots and so on and so forth'. I was known as the bitch! I was out of the office for six weeks when I was hospitalised and having surgery and when I returned there was big sign on my desk 'The Bitch Is Back'! I was never musically inclined... I was all finance."

Dynamic Sounds had it covered on all fronts: they had become the first choice for visiting artists "from foreign" and their recording, mastering and pressing facilities were in constant demand from local producers and artists.

"You'd build the rhythm at Dynamic, voice at Tubby's, go to Lloyd (Campbell) to get the labels printed then back to Dynamics to master and press. Pre-release used to be a weekly thing and it had to be fresh. You could press twenty five of a record... sell it and then come back and press twenty five more. So when you come with a box of records from Dynamic you nah go home! You'd head for Randy's (to sell the records)..."

Roy Cousins

However, to some insiders, the directors at Dynamic were beginning to perceive Jamaican music as secondary to overseas product. They were accused of putting foreign performers in front of local talent which they were able to counter with sound financial, rather than creative, arguments.

"The companies that released foreign music in Jamaica stifled reggae music. Byron Lee told me 'when I release a record from abroad I pay nothing until I'm at the point of cutting a stamper... it's different with a local record.'" **Pete Weston**

When Island Records' Chris Blackwell made the previously unheard of move of advancing Bob Marley & The Wailers £4000 to record an album in late 1972 the repercussions were far, far greater than anyone could ever have anticipated. Tracks for what was to become 'Catch A Fire' were recorded at Dynamic Sounds with Carlton Lee engineering and the album proved to be the critical, if not commercial, breakthrough that Jamaican music had been waiting for.

"Listening to the playbacks Chris (Blackwell) compliments Carlton (Lee) on the drum sound he's getting... Carlton replies that it's the natural sound of the room and it's the reason he hasn't ever built a conventional sealed off drum booth." **Richard Williams**

Paradoxically it was the massive, and lasting, international success of Bob Marley & The Wailers that would eventually contribute towards the undermining of Dynamic Sounds' supremacy. Their business oriented approach was not necessarily considered to be part of the 'authentic' reggae experience that the new international audience had now come to expect as Sheila Lee wryly remarked "Ganja smoking? People nowadays think it's a mark of achievement to roll a spliff but Byron never allowed a cigarette on the bandstand!"

The most difficult and uncompromising, raw and rugged, 'mystical' and rebellious aspects of the music were now seen as a vital part of its attraction. This was exactly the kind of thing that WIRL and Dynamic had been working to get away from ever since Edward Seaga had been asked for the type of records that Motta's customers actually wanted and Byron Lee had imported "the first Fender bass here in Jamaica" and stepped on stage with his band dressed in smart outfits with "properly organised routines".

'Sparrow Meets The Dragon'

Byron Lee being presented to Her Majesty Queen Elizabeth II at the 8th Commonwealth Games Ball held at the Kingston Sheraton Hotel (August 1966).
Sir Herbert MacDonald does the Introduction

From 1975 onwards the worldwide popularity of Bob Marley & The Wailers brought Jamaican music to an entirely unprecedented level of popularity and reggae finally had to be taken seriously both at home and abroad. Many jumped on what Max Romeo tellingly termed the "Rasta bandwagon" but there had been very few on board before the music hit the big time. Promoters now looked to expand the possibilities of raw roots music and to manufacture and promote it to a standard that the international market would find acceptable. The demarcation lines between uptown and downtown codes of conduct and practice would no longer be so rigidly marked or observed. The music no longer needed translators but facilitators who could pass it on to the rest of the world without altering, diluting or interfering with its "raw roots" content.

In 1972 while the Dynamic Studio was being refurbished The Dynamites had taken advantage of the break from session work and undertaken World Tours backing Jimmy Cliff, immediately after his breakthrough success with 'The Harder They Come', and Toots & The Maytals. Some of the musicians decided not to return including Winston Grennan who stayed in the USA "to study jazz and pursue a career as a session musician" and would, along with August Darnell, become a founding member of Kid Creole and The Coconuts in the early Eighties. By the time the rest of The Dynamites returned to Jamaica Kingston's session scene had moved on, "in Jamaica out of sight... out of mind", and The Dynamites sounded out of step with the times. Through their work with Leslie Kong's Beverley's label and the UK hits of Jimmy Cliff, The Maytals and The Pioneers, they were now regarded as the crossover sound of 1969/1970 'pop' flavoured reggae. By 1974 Dennis Brown and The Soul Syndicate with Niney The Observer's new sound were everywhere and The Aggrovators with Bunny 'Striker' Lee's flying cymbals and The Revolutionaries with Sly Dunbar's 'militant' double drumming were just around the corner. The Dynamites were now considered to be passé.

Yet, ironically and inevitably, there is an alternative version to this narrative and Barry Biggs, former Astronauts band member now vocalist with The Dragonaires and producer and arranger at Dynamic Sounds too, enjoyed a year long run, through 1976 and 1977, of sustained crossover success in the UK National Charts.

"Unlike many of his contemporaries, Biggs avoided the political and Rasta themes then popular in Jamaica eschewing the standard image of the dreadlocked rebel for the pop style and fine clothes of the club singer."

Steve Leggett

"I was at the Creole offices in London and some guys from Holland came to interview me... they thought I must be a Rasta! But I was always interested in American music... it suits my voice... and in the Sixties I was a Beatles fan. I had Beatle boots and a Beatle hair style... I was a Jamaican Beatle!" **Barry Biggs**

'Work All Day' reached Number Thirty Eight in summer 1976, 'Sideshow' hit Number Three in December, 'You're My Life' made Number Thirty Six the following spring and, that summer, 'Three Ring Circus' hit the Number Twenty Two spot. All were classic examples of smooth crossover reggae at its very best and Barry's soothing, honeyed tones would be heard again on the international stage in 1982 with his superb interpretation of 'Wide Awake In A Dream'.

The dub explosion, largely inspired by King Tubby on equipment considered obsolete by Dynamic, now managed to make their go ahead approach seem positively old fashioned. Some of the Dynamic staff took advantage of this shift in attitude including Warwick Lyn, who had first worked as a sound engineer and A&R man for Leslie Kong's Beverley's Records and "helped shape some of Toots & The Maytals finest work", and Tommy Cowan who, as lead singer of The Jamaicans, recorded for Coxsone Dodd and Duke Reid and had won the 1966 Festival Song Contest with 'Baba Boom' for Treasure Isle.

"We were rehearsing at a place off Molynes Road and this guy (Aston McEchron) heard us and sent for us. He was from the United States, drove his own Cadillac, and he told us: 'you guys have talent. You could go far. I can get you on the Johnny Carson Show!' But we'd never heard of Johnny Carson!"

Tommy Cowan

Tommy Cowan and The Jamaicans went on to release records through both WIRL and Dynamic and, while touring the USA and Canada with Byron Lee & The Dragonaires, Byron Lee realised that, in addition to his obvious gifts as a singer, Tommy had a lot more to offer.

"Byron Lee first asked me to go to WIRL as he owned the distribution rights for Atlantic Records and he asked me to look into what was happening with Atlantic. He felt that he needed someone with a passion for the music so he took the label to his house and I was working from his garage. Not long after that WIRL burned down and Byron Lee bought it and called it Dynamic Sounds. Then we got Columbia, Motown and Polygram and I became the Sales & Marketing Manager." **Tommy Cowan**

Dealing with the major labels was only part of Tommy's job at Dynamic. He also organised concerts and stage shows for visiting American superstars including The Drifters, Aretha Franklin, Ben E King, Percy Sledge and The Temptations while he continued to sing with The Jamaicans and produce records for the company too.

"We did a whole Jamaicans album, some of the Christmas albums that came out with Byron Lee, 'Folk Song' the first Black Uhuru record, a blind singer named Adinah Edwards who had a big hit with 'Don't Forget To Remember' (released on Dynamic in 1972) and I helped to produce the Toots & The Maytals album 'Slatyam Stoot'. The recordings that came out on the Top Cat label were usually my productions...

My job with all the companies I worked with was to get records to hit. The last year before I left Dynamic (1973) we had the Number One record every month of the year... most of which were soul sounds."

Tommy Cowan

Tommy felt that the music of Jamaica should be given the same level of support and promotion as the music coming from overseas for he believed it was every bit as important. With Byron Lee's full support he branched out in 1974 and started releasing records on his own Starapple label. The following year he set up The Talent Corporation with Gayman Alberga and Warwick Lyn. The Talent Corporation based at "Tommy's sprawling Kingston yard" at 1C Oxford Road was described by Tommy as "an inspiration centre".

"The Talent Corporation came out of a belief about Jamaican music... just like the guy Aston McEchron had said years ago!" **Tommy Cowan**

There was a feeling that, by this stage, Dynamic was busy courting overseas rock stars and foreign label pressing and distribution deals. But Dynamic knew their market and, reputedly, their biggest selling album ever was Marty Robbins' 'Gunfighter Ballads And Trail Songs', licensed from Columbia in the USA where it was first released on in 1959. Marty Robbins' songs of "hard working, hard playing men… their days spent in dry deserts under blazing suns, their nights in exhausted rest or wild carousing" struck a resounding chord with Jamaican record buyers. Dynamic's methodical, business oriented approach provided an invaluable template for a new generation of entrepreneurs. Tommy Cowan's Talent Corporation, Pete Weston's Micron Music and Byron's brother Neville Lee's Sonic Sounds began to present roots based Jamaican music to the rest of the world using the many valuable lessons learnt from the Dynamic Sounds modus operandi.

The Jamaican Government awarded the Order of Distinction to Byron Lee in 1982 in recognition of his "contribution in the fields of music and entertainment both locally and internationally" which would be elevated to Commander status in October 2007. As the Eighties progressed Byron Lee & The Dragonaires began to move away from reggae and concentrate on a soulful update of calypso known as soca that they had first encountered twenty years previously in Trinidad.

"On the early Caribbean tours we covered all the islands and Byron picked up soca in Trinidad. Every time Byron's band played soca the crowd went wild but the Trinidadian bands didn't like them playing soca better than them! One time Byron started with the opening lines from 'Colonel Bogie', the crowd erupted and bottles started flying! Tony Verity had to hide behind the drums…" **Ronnie Nasralla**

Byron Lee & The Dragonaires achieved one of the biggest hits of their career in 1985 with what would become the soca anthem, 'Tiney Winey', and, in 1989, Byron and Sheila established 'Jamaica Carnival Limited' a company that brought carnival to Kingston, "introducing the 'Mas Camp' concept to Jamaicans", at an annual event based on the Trinidadian tradition.

In the early Sixties Byron Lee had worked towards expanding the audience for ska to include Jamaica's upper and middle classes and he now worked on taking soca in the opposite direction. He popularised a music that had previously only been enjoyed by Jamaica's upper and middle classes with everyone as Sheila Lee stated. "Carnival still exists today... everything in the parties is all soca. The dance floor is empty until a soca song comes on and a soca event will always be well attended in an acceptable venue. In the Sixties Byron took ska uptown and in the Nineties he took soca downtown for a period of time. The proof of the pudding is in the eating but the downtown people are still embracing soca music..."

Byron Lee Junior and Edward Lee, Byron & Sheila's two sons, took over much of the day to day running of Dynamic Sounds but Byron Lee & The Dragonaires never stopped touring. In October 2008, after receiving treatment for cancer in Florida, Byron Lee returned to spend his last days in Jamaica. Later that month in a ceremony by his hospital bed at the University Hospital of the West Indies, Kingston he was awarded the Order of Jamaica. The Hon Byron Lee OJ, CD died on 4th November 2008 aged 73. On the day of his death, Bruce Golding, then Prime Minister of Jamaica, stated "Jamaica, and indeed the world, has lost another great music pioneer with the passing this morning of Byron Lee one of the greatest band leaders ever to grace the entertainment stages of the world."

However, he was not only a "music pioneer" and "one of the greatest band leaders" as Byron Lee's Dynamic Sounds Recording Company also produced innumerable classic records under their own auspices while simultaneously enabling a plethora of producers, artists and musicians to make and manufacture their own records using Dynamic's world class resources. His contribution to the development and dissemination of the recorded music of Jamaica is immeasurable.

***Appendix 1**
Sonic Sounds Record Manufacturing Co Ltd
14 & 25 Retirement Road
Kingston 5

Byron and his younger brother by two years, Neville, "were close just like most brothers. They played on the St George's College football teams that won the schoolboy Manning Cup in 1956 and 1957 and shared a passion for music." After leaving high school Neville Lee emigrated to the UK where he served in the Royal Air Force and, in 1969, returned to Jamaica to work with Byron at Dynamic Sounds. Neville played a significant role in Dynamic's development and success but left in 1978 to start up his own manufacturing and distribution company, Sonic Sounds, and 'Sonics' would become "the biggest Caribbean rival to Byron's Dynamic Sounds in terms of record distribution".

"Byron brought him from England to be the managing director of Dynamic Sounds. However, a conflict of interest made Dad move on and start his own company. We were competitive rivals wanting our companies to have the hit songs."
Jason Lee

"Mr MacDonald who owned Total Sounds was selling out and Neville did buy it up and then they changed the name to Sonic Sounds and they never looked back until they had a monster building down the road... it was a rented place at first. So we all rallied round Neville and that's why Sonic Sounds put out so much music because we used to bring music and give it to him. Yeah!"
Bunny 'Striker' Lee

POWER HOUSE
Produced By
George Phang
Tel: 61204/62036
Sonic Sounds
Side 1
GREETINGS
(L. Roberts)
HALF PINT
DISTRIBUTED BY SONIC SOUNDS … RETIREMENT ROAD, KINGSTON 5

TAXI
PRODUCED BY
SLY AND ROBBIE
Dist. by
Sonic Sounds
P
ALL RIGHTS RESERVED - MADE IN JAMAICA
UNMETERED TAXI
(SLY)
SLY DUNBAR

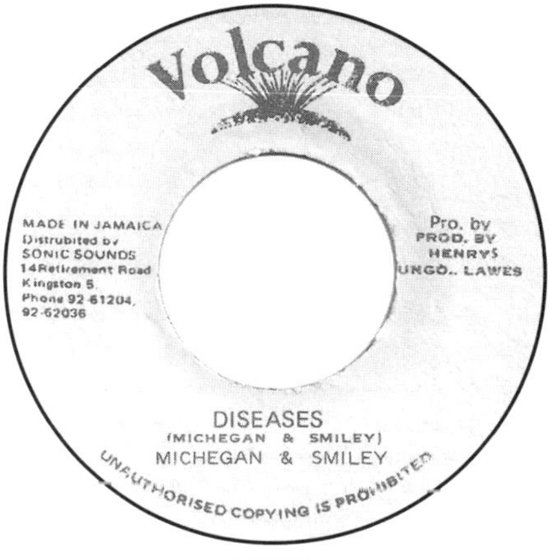
Volcano
MADE IN JAMAICA
Distrubited by
SONIC SOUNDS
14 Retirement Road
Kingston 5
Phone 92-61204,
92-62036
Pro. by
PROD. BY
HENRYS
JUNGO.. LAWES
DISEASES
(MICHEGAN & SMILEY)
MICHEGAN & SMILEY
UNAUTHORISED COPYING IS PROHIBITED

African Museum
Prod by:
G. ISAACS
Dist. by:
African
Museum
Side 1
2 Chancery Ln.
Corner of
North Parade
Kingston,
Jamaica.
Ph: 92-253
NIGHT NURSE
(G. ISAACS)
GREGORY ISAACS

TAXI
Produced by
SLY & ROBBIE
Distributed by
SONIC SOUNDS
25 Retirement Rd.
Kingston 5
SIDE A
TXI - 0874
MURDER SHE WROTE
(S. Dunbar/L. Willis/J. Taylor)
Chaka Demus/Pliers
All Rights Reserved

Winner
SIDE A
(C) 1985
GIRLIE GIRLIE
A. Davis
SOPHIA GEORGE

Based on Retirement Road, Kingston, initially in the former Total Sounds premises, Sonic Sounds became the company of choice for Kingston's local producers and artists throughout the Eighties and the Nineties.

"In direct contrast to his brother Byron Lee whose Dynamic Sounds is in charge of eighty percent of the foreign records pressed and distributed in Jamaica Neville Lee's Sonic Sounds controls seventy percent of the local labels. However Sonic Sounds always worked to develop foreign markets and also in distributing overseas labels in Jamaica... but their first commitment was to 'our own local music'."

Howard Johnson & Jim Pines

Sonic Sounds were "Jamaican distributors for major American record companies including RCA/EMI/Capitol, Sony/BMG and the BMG Music conglomerate" and Neville's children, Stephen, Gordon, Jason and Susan all worked together on Retirement Road.

"The company hit its stride during the Eighties by releasing some of that decade's biggest hit songs including the instrumental 'Unmetered Taxi' on Sly & Robbie's Taxi label, 'Diseases' by Michigan and Smiley, 'Night Nurse' by Gregory Isaacs, 'Girlie Girlie' by Sophia George, 'Stealing Love' by Carlene Davis, 'Greetings' by Half Pint and 'Murder She Wrote' by Chaka Demus and Pliers. In terms of overseas song 'Lady in Red' by British singer Chris de Burgh, Whitney Houston's 'Greatest Love Of All' and 'Lady' by Kenny Rogers were the biggest sellers for Sonic Sounds." **Jason Lee**

A visitor to Sonic Sounds headquarters during this period would invariably be met by a succession of ghetto celebrities, artists, musicians and producers all involved in the hectic day to day business of making, manufacturing and marketing their music. Jason Lee, Managing Director of Sonic Sounds, recounted:

"We release an average of twenty or thirty titles every week with a first press of usually five hundred copies. Depending on how it sounds and if the public like it we press a further five hundred the following week. If a record breaks it will sell for the next three months or more and we'll continue pressing between four and six hundred copies a week. A good seller can achieve sales of ten thousand in total." **Jason Lee**

On any given day everyone who was anyone in the Kingston reggae business would pass through Sonic's gate and, for two decades, their Retirement Crescent headquarters was the grass roots of the reggae business and a star struck autograph hunters' dream.

Neville Lee died 31st July 2018 in Kingston aged eighty after operating Sonic Sounds for over thirty years. Entertainment Minister Olivia Babsy' Grange paid tribute to Neville stating that "his contribution to the local music industry was monumental".

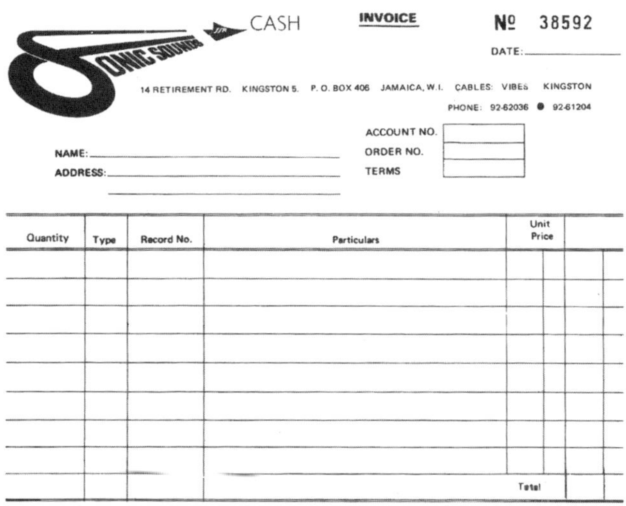
SONIC SOUNDS CASH INVOICE Nº 38592

DATE:

14 RETIREMENT RD. KINGSTON 5. P. O. BOX 406 JAMAICA, W.I. CABLES: VIBES KINGSTON

PHONE: 92-62036 ● 92-61204

NAME:

ADDRESS:

ACCOUNT NO.

ORDER NO.

TERMS

Quantity	Type	Record No.	Particulars	Unit Price	
				Total	

*Appendix 2
'Live It Up' Ernie Freeman

"Do you know Ernie Freeman's 'Live It Up'? A lot of tunes in Jamaica came off of that rhythm..." **Bunny 'Striker' Lee**

A 'beardman' or 'locksman' were names for the dreadlocked Rastafarians and Roland (Alphonso) & The Studio One Orchestra's 1965 ska update of 'Live It Up' was entitled, naturally enough, 'Beardman Ska'. In 1969 up and coming producer Clancy Eccles versioned the tune over with the Number One deejay from Coxsone's Number One Downbeat sound system alongside innovative recording engineer Linford 'Andy Capp' Anderson as 'Herb Man' or 'Herbsman'. Rastafarians refer to marijuana as herb and their interpretation was a celebration of ganja… "smoking is a habit" The record was not only a massive hit in Jamaica but also in the UK where it struck a chord with the young white 'skinhead' audience even though the majority, like myself, were blissfully unaware of either its genealogy or connotations at the time. It proved so popular that it inspired the London recorded 'Bush Beat' cover version.

"Whether you're white… whether you're black
Let's be friendly
Dig this beat
Bush Beat…" **'Bush Beat' Lloyd & The Prophets**

'Herb Man' was one of the earliest talking, or deejay, records, a style that would eventually travel back to the USA and give birth to the rap phenomenon. It was followed by 'Phantom', an incredibly innovative record credited to The Dynamites, where 'Herb Man' was minimally mixed down so that little remained apart from the drum and bass core and haunting organ refrain. This groundbreaking record was years ahead of its time and, six years later, it would be immediately recognised as dub which would lead to another leap forward, or backwards, for popular music: the remix. Yet when Andy Capp, then working at the United Nations in New York in the Nineties, was interviewed by Chris Lane he had no recollection whatsoever of mixing the tune.

Two years later Lee 'Scratch' Perry used the bass line for the sole release on his very attractive Scratch label for 'Puss See Hole' a politically incorrect mix of nursery rhymes and sly 'slackness'. In 1976 Scratch returned to the rhythm with Max Romeo for the far more serious 'Sipple Out Deh' which was released in the UK as 'War In A Babylon' and yet again the following year for the twelve inch release of 'Rastaman Shuffle' from The Upsetters. That same year Bob Marley & The Wailers' also appropriated the 'Live It Up'/'Herb Man' bass line for 'Three Little Birds' on their 'Exodus' long player which, in 1999, was named by Time magazine as "the best album of the 20th century".

1964 to 1969
WIRL (West Indies Records Limited)
13 Bell Road
Kingston 11

Labels: Bata, BRA, BMN, Dragon's Breath, Follow The Stars On Starline, Gala, Kentone, Pussy Cat, Soul, Sunshine & WIRL

1969
Dynamic Sounds Recording Company Limited
15 Bell Road
Kingston 11

Producers & Arrangers include:
Byron Lee, Linford 'Andy Capp' Anderson, Peter Ashbourne, U Belfast, Barry Biggs, Winston Blake, Geoffrey Chung, Junior Chung (Elizabethan Reggae), Tommy Cowan, Alty East, Boris Gardiner, Junior Gray, Gary Hall, Neville Hinds, Keith Jackson, Bunny 'Striker' Lee, Carlton Lee, Warwick Lyn, Ronnie Nasralla, Lee 'Scratch' Perry, Ted Pouder, Clifford 'Bunny' Rae, Edward Seaga & Lloyd 'Charmers' Tyrell

Engineers include:
Byron Lee, Richard Alderson, Linford 'Andy Capp' Anderson, Barry Biggs, Sid Bucknor, Geoffrey Chung, Jerome Francis, Bill Garnett, Graeme Goodall, Barrington 'Barry' Lambert, Carlton Lee, Ronnie Logan, Warwick Lyn, Sylvan Morris, George Philpotts, Karl Pitterson, Miley Riley, Byron 'Baron' Smith, Glen Witter, Philip Ziadie & 'Spider Man'

"Spider Man? Every man had an alias... me no know Spider Man's real name. It's only when me come a England you have to know that... you never know a man's full name... we just call a man a name!"

Roy Cousins

Labels: Afrik, Arrival, Dynamic, Jaguar, Lion, Melrose, Panther, Tiger, Top Cat & Weed Beat

Musicians:

Byron Lee & The Dragonaires (1963 to 1966):

Musicians include:
Drums: Paul Douglas, Esmond Jarrett & Barry Lloyd
Bass: Boris Gardiner & Byron Lee
Acoustic Guitar: Rupert Bent
Rhythm Guitar: Ken Lazarus & Wallace Wilson
Rhythm & Lead Guitar: Lynford 'Hux' Brown
Piano & Organ: Leslie Butler, Neville Hinds Joe Johnson, Felix Roach & Dorothy Wong
Saxophone: Sammy Ismay & Ossie Scott
Trumpet: Frank Anderson, Oswald 'Baba' Brooks, Chester Power, Lester Sterling & Norris Ridguard
Trombone: Sammy Johnson, Vernon Muller & Felix Taylor
Percussion: Carl Brady, Victor Chung & Junior Gray
Vocals: Jimmy Cliff, Ken Lazarus, Keith Lyn, Eric 'Monty' Morris, Yvonne Sterling & Roy Willis

The Dynamites (1969 to 1972):

Drums: Paul Douglas, Winston Grennan & Hugh Malcolm
Bass: Clifton 'Jackie' Jackson
Guitar: Lynford 'Hux' Brown, Radcliffe 'Duggie' Bryan & Lorraine 'Ranny Bop' Williams
Organ: Neville Hinds & Winston 'Brubeck' Wright
Piano: Gladstone 'Gladdy' Anderson
Percussion: Denzil 'Pops' Laing & Uzziah 'Sticky' Thompson

Musicland
DIST. BY RANDY'S
17 NORTH PARADE
Recorded at
Studio 17
Party Time — Part 1
HONEYMOON
BIM, BAM AND CLOVER
Recorded live at Studio 17

IMPACT!
JAVA
(C. Chin)
Agustus Pablo
Kingston, Jamaica.
COPYING OF THIS RECORD IS STRICTLY PROHIBITED ©

Randy's
MADE IN JAMAICA.
COPYING OF
THIS RECORD
IS PROHIBITED
45 RPM
Vocal
MY LOVE DIVINE
(Alton & Eddy)
ALTON AND EDDY
with The All Stars
MANUFACTURED BY CARIBBEAN RECORDING CO. LTD., JAMAICA, W.I.

DISTRIBUTED BY:
RANDY'S
7 NORTH PARADE
INGSTON JAMAICA
PHONE: 24859
SIDE (2)
RE BURN
I ROY
All Rights of the manufacturer and of the owner of the recorded work reserved.

CHECKER
SOUND

ISLAND RECORDS LTD., 108, CAMBRIDGE ROAD, LONDON, N.W.6.
HE'S THE GREATEST
Island Music
Randys
45 R.P.M.
island RECORDS
WI-130
(A)
THE FLAMES
RECORDING FIRST PUBLISHED 1964
ALL RIGHTS OF THE MANUFACTURER AND OF THE OWNER OF THE RECORDED WORK RESERVED · UNAUTHORISED COPYING OF THIS RECORD PROHIBITED

Noel Hawks

Chapter 3

You Name It We Have It: Randy's Studio 17

"Introducing...
The man called Tommy McCook on tenor saxophone,
Man called Errol T in console from sixteen track to two track
The man called I Roy at the microphone
Man called Dennis Thompson in the cutting room in Studio 17..."

'Fire Burn' Roy 'I Roy' Reid

For eight tumultuous years, between 1969 and 1977, everyone and anyone of note in the teeming Kingston musical scene recorded at Randy's Studio 17 above Randy's Record Mart on Kingston's North Parade.

"CB was the gateman at Randy's... sometimes it was murder to get past him to get up the stairs." **Roy Cousins**

The music from the studio became synonymous with the roots rock rebel sound that gained worldwide attention during this time and the producers and artists who worked at Randy's included legendary figures such as Glen Brown, Winston 'Niney The Observer' Holness, Bunny 'Striker' Lee, Bob Marley & The Wailers, Augustus Pablo and Lee 'Scratch' Perry before he established the Black Ark. The list for whom Randy's was the first choice studio goes on and on and on and its importance to the international development of reggae during its Seventies crossover period is considerable. Many of the new generation of rebel rock producers and musicians could have been held back by financial constraints but Randy's gave them their chance to record. This was often facilitated through deals that involved exchanging studio time for records and/or licensing contracts.

"When we started (the studio) at 17 North Parade Striker and Lee Perry were there all the while..." **Patricia 'Miss Pat' Chin**

"It was mostly my product and Lee Perry's product. We used to give Vincent our productions to release in America and in turn he'd give us back studio time." **Bunny 'Striker' Lee**

Vincent 'Randy' Chin was born in Kingston 3rd October 1937. His father, a carpenter by trade, came to Jamaica from mainland China "after a brief stopover in Cuba" in the Twenties. In the early Fifties Vincent began working for Isaac Issa, a prominent local Syrian-Jamaican business man, stocking and maintaining Mr Issa's juke boxes, collecting the money and regularly changing the records to ensure that the selections were kept up to date. Very few people could afford radios and the pivotal role played by juke boxes in Jamaica in the Fifties can never be overstated; they were omnipresent in bars, rum shops, ice cream parlours and clubs all over the island. Vincent's eldest son, Clive, born 14th May 1954 "under the sign of Taurus", recalled that his father's garage at their home in Vineyard Town was "full of tons and tons of records" that he had kept after he had replaced them with new discs in the juke boxes. And, instead of discarding these records, he bought them from Mr Issa "for a small price" and "he kept them... and that was the springboard of his business".

The popularity of the music inspired Vincent to open a small shop in 1959 in a "little grocery store" owned by his father on the corner of East Street and Tower Street in downtown Kingston where he began retailing these discarded records to a Jamaican public gripped by rhythm & blues fervour. Vincent continued working with Mr Issa, "travelling all over the island and making many stops between Kingston and Montego Bay" while his wife, Patricia better known to the musical fraternity as 'Miss Pat', ran the shop. Patricia was born 20th September 1937 and the pair had first met when Vincent was employed as the driver of Miss Pat's grandparents' bread van. They were married on 15th March 1957 and Miss Pat gave up her nursing studies at the University College Hospital of the West Indies to play a vital role in the growth of Randy's.

"Striker Lee and myself grew up in Greenwich Farm... he's about the same age as my sister... they went to the same school... so I knew him long before he became a record producer. I was going to Government school... if you were late the gate would be closed and you'd have to hold out your hand to get a slap.

My mother is Chinese and my father is Indian and they kept a little Chinese shop selling pots and pans. They couldn't speak English and they used to have a little piece of board and a nail in the shop so when people bought goods on credit they'd write it down in Chinese on a piece of paper and stick it on the nail. When it was time to settle up at the end of the month the customers would ask 'how do you know who's who?' and my parents would say 'we know all your faces' ...so they were doing 'facial recognition' years ago!

Marbles... all different sizes and colours... and rubber bands were a big thing at school so I used to get some from the shop and take them to school to sell and get lunch money. It's about the wants and needs of the people... my father used to say you have to do for others if they can't do it for themselves." **Patricia 'Miss Pat' Chin**

"This was the early Sixties and until moving to North Parade from East Street and Tower Street... which was a very tiny store... he was still working with Mr Issa. He didn't leave until he left East Street." **Clive Chin**

The shop was named in recognition of Randy's Record Shop in Gallatin, Tennessee run by 'Randy' Wood, the founder of Dot Records, also based in Gallatin, and co-owner of a local radio station "WHIN out of Nashville, Tennessee", whose broadcasts could be picked up on short wave radio in Jamaica. Their rhythm & blues selections exerted a huge influence on local music lovers and many of the island's leading sound systems would send to Randy's, "the world's largest mail order record store in the Fifties and Sixties", for their records.

"'You had to push people out of the way to get to the counter on a Friday' recalled one former customer." **Mike Atherton**

The small premises soon proved too constricting for Vincent and Pat's rapidly expanding business and, in 1961, they rented space in Charlie

Moo's restaurant at 17 North Parade in the heart of Kingston's commercial district where the buses from the countryside terminated. They then purchased the restaurant and entire building from Mr Moo and, for a while, kept the food side of the business running too. They also sold "automobile accessories and pots and pans" and Randy's Record Mart would gradually establish itself as Jamaica's premier retail and wholesale record outlet.

"You have to respect Vincent and Pat for what they built up."

Bunny 'Striker' Lee

"One key to the Chins' success was their decision to stock records from many different labels as singer Wilburn 'Stranger' Cole explains: 'Randy's was the place where you could go and get a Coxsone record, Clancy Eccles record, Beverley's record, anybody record, while if you went to Coxsone's he might only be selling Coxsone records'." **Mike Atherton**

Vincent also began to produce some of the earliest shuffle and boogie records for his Randy's label such as 'Rico's Special' from Emmanuel 'Rico' Rodriguez, recorded at RJR, and he continued hitting in 1962 with 'My Love Divine' from Alton (Ellis) & Eddie (Perkins) and Basil Gabbidon's 'Our Melody'. That year Jamaica celebrated its independence to the sound of Lord Creator's 'Independent Jamaica' produced by Vincent for his Creative Calypso label. The record was the Number One tune for the year in Jamaica and the first release on Chris Blackwell's Island label in the UK.

Kentrick 'Lord Creator' Patrick had come Jamaica from Trinidad with "some people from Guyana" and Vincent first heard him singing in January 1962 at The Havana club on Windward Road in East Kingston… "he had talent!", "Accompanying him that evening was journalist Raymond Sharpe. After the show, Lord Creator recalls Chin and Sharpe coming backstage with a business proposition that would benefit both of them. 'He asked if I could compose a song for him about Jamaica's Independence. I didn't know the details (of Independence) but I said yes' Lord Creator recalled in a 2003 interview with the *Jamaica Observer.* His nationalistic ode, 'Independent Jamaica', was written one week later on the porch of Chin's east Kingston home" **Howard Campbell**

Lord Creator decided to stay in Jamaica and, "because he had no family there", lived in the Chin's home where Clive recalls him also writing 'We

Will Be Lovers' on their porch which he subsequently recorded "as a duet with a young girl from the country named Norma Fraser". Lord Creator recorded 'King And Queen', his touching tribute to his adopted home, for Vincent which, as 'Kingston Town', which would become a huge reggae hit when Creator sang it again for singer/producer Clancy Eccles in 1970 and an even bigger international hit when UB40 covered the song twenty years later.

Independence would signal the beginnings of Jamaica placing itself in a premier position on the world's musical stage and, as it left its colonial past behind, the island's music began to take on its very own instantly recognisable characteristics as shuffle and boogie turned into ska. Vincent continued to hit with a plethora of records including 'Malcolm X' from The Skatalites, The Maytals' 'He's The Greatest', an electrifying paean of praise to Cassius Clay (Muhammad Ali) and Lord Creator again (as Kentrick Patrick) with the timeless 'Don't Stay Out Late'. Many of his productions were released in London on Emil Shalit's Blue Beat and Chris Blackwell's Island, Jump Up and Black Swan labels. However, after this burst of concentrated creativity, Vincent eased away from production to concentrate on his and Miss Pat's juke box, retail and distribution interests and Randy's continued to consolidate their position as Jamaica's foremost purveyor of music throughout the decade.

"Randy's was like the Jamaican Motown… we released people's tunes right, left and centre. If your tune's not distributed by Randy's it ain't going nowhere!"
Clive Chin

"Randy's chart is the most accurate barometer of what Jamaicans, the planet's most discriminating reggae audience, are listening to."
Stephen Davis

And, with their keen commercial acumen, the Chins realised that, although Kingston was not short of artists, musicians and record producers, studio facilities were scarce and costly to rent.

"There were only these main studios at the time: Duke Reid's studio (Treasure Isle), Federal, WIRL, Coxsone's Studio One and JBC/RJR and a lot of other independent producers had started to come on board…"
Clive Chin

Patricia 'Miss Pat' Chin

Patricia 'Miss Pat' Chin & Vincent 'Randy's' Chin

"When Coxsone and Duke Reid had opened their studios in the mid Sixties my father had a great interest in recording and he had connections abroad because his brother had started his own record shop in Brooklyn, New York. He told him he could get whatever equipment he needed for a studio in Kingston but I think my Dad had a vision to see a broader spectrum in the music because... the whole top level of the store was empty so he decided to lick it down and build the studio. But he had to get help from outside and the help that he had was his brother in Brooklyn and he also met a gentleman by the name of Bill Garnett who was working as an engineer and technician for WIRL at the time.

After WIRL burned down he spoke to Bill and he agreed to come to the premises and do all the acoustics... basically Bill was the engineer. The studio was actually commissioned in 1967 and the work started in 1968... that's why we didn't have any rock steady productions during that time. The only rock steady production that we were able to record was when Lord Creator came out of prison in 1968 and dad picked up Creator from Tambrin Farm Prison and went straight to Bond Street...Treasure Isle... commissioned Tommy McCook who was the in house musician with The

Supersonics... and the recording came out 'Such Is Life' and 'Come Down '68' ... 'come down 1968, let me through those iron gates, I'm longing to be with my woman...'."

Clive Chin

"...and a next guy named Bill Garnett. He put up Randy's studio and Channel One studio. We used to call him Billy Neat and I hear he passed away. He was great! He was in Harry Belafonte's studio in the early days... somewhere in New York. Bill Garnett built it up and worked on it when he left Jamaica but he used to go backwards and forwards."

Bunny 'Striker' Lee

Bill Garnett was born in Jamaica and raised in New York where he became an accomplished electronics expert. He began his career in Kingston working with Graeme Goodall at Federal before moving on to WIRL and then worked closely with Vincent setting up a four track recording facility. Randy's Studio 17 opened above the shop on North Parade in the spring of 1969. Although Clive recalled that the studio was originally intended solely for Randy's use it would soon become one of Kingston's leading studios when Vincent gave in to the overwhelming demands for studio time and opened the door to Kingston's music business with Harris 'BB'/'Bibby' Seaton of The Gaylads occasionally assisting at the early sessions. Ironically the first producer to use the studio was Danny Sims from the USA who block booked it for two months and not only worked with a number of American artists but also recorded Bob Marley & The Wailers.

"Bill Garnett was the first engineer. Dad had commissioned him to build the console, everything was custom made: we had Ampex half inch four track, Ampex quarter inch two track to mix down and the rest of the board was all, you know, outboard equipment: Ampex equaliser, Pultec and Soundcraft equalisers. But Bill, having worked at West Indies Records, had a relationship with a company called JAD... Danny Sims, Arthur Jenkins and Johnny Nash... so when West Indies was out of commission it had to move to another studio and Bill invited Danny Sims and Arthur Jenkins up to Randy's. That's where the relationship with JAD blossomed... Dad gave them a massive amount of studio time. They could come in the morning, in the afternoon... at midnight. Any time they wanted to come the time was there! That's where I met guys like Quincy Jones, Hugh Masekela (from South Africa), Cissie Houston (Whitney Houston's aunt), Arthur

Prysock, Jimmy Norman a songwriter... a massive amount of Americans. This was the first time I saw guys come down with dashikis and bell bottom pants, afros and some sunglasses... I mean it was out of this world! I saw Johnny Nash peeling a cane with his hands one time. I said 'no man! You peel it with your teeth... you don't peel it with your hands!" **Clive Chin**

"But the type of tune they wanted to record was saying nothing. Bob's (Bob Marley) was the cream of the crop." **Clive Chin**

"But it was a real good experience and it brought Bob, Bunny, Peter and Rita down to the studio. Apparently they had some kind of deal where they were involved in song writing for Johnny Nash... it was the start of a five year relationship but I didn't really know what kind of deal they had until long after... but during the '69 period Dad had actually built a relationship with Peter and Peter used to come down with his guitar... he'd do rehearsals with my father through Peter was very talented. He could play the piano, could play the guitar, could play bass, he could blow the melodica... he could do everything. A very innovative musician but we used to get a lot of foreign records from my uncle in Brooklyn. So this record 'Sugar Sugar' from The Archies was sent down from the States and Dad commissioned Bob, Peter & Rita ('cause I think at that time Bunny was serving some prison time for herb) and the song was recorded for Randy's in 1969. It didn't really come out as a release because there was a little bit of friction between JAD and them... but Peter's stuff...numerous tracks after tracks... 'Little Green Apples' the OC Smith song was recorded there, 'Whistling Jane', 'Apollo 11'... all these songs were recorded during that time." **Clive Chin**

The first local hit to come out of the new studio was 'Them A Laugh And A Ki Ki', credited to The Soul Mates for producer Joe Gibbs, but Bill Garnett did not remain very long as the engineer at Studio 17 and Errol Thompson took over the controls later that year. Also known as Errol T or simply ET, born 29th December 1948, he remains one of the great unsung heroes of Jamaican music; destined always to remain in the background although his technical and musical innovations were at the forefront of reggae's artistic and commercial thrust in the Seventies.

Leonard 'Santic' Chin

Leonard 'Santic' Chin & Errol Thompson

'This Is Augustus Pablo'

Dennis Thompson, Errol Thompson, Clive Chin & Augustus Pablo

He spent much of his youth at the home of one of his relations, an electronics engineer and amplifier builder, in Harbour View, Kingston. The El Don Sound System operated out of the same premises and, from a very early age, Errol was given valuable insights on the importance of how music should sound and the vital role of electronics. His first engineering job was as apprentice at Studio One on Brentford Road where one of his earliest sessions was for Bunny 'Striker' Lee when Max Romeo voiced his infamous 'Wet Dream'... much to Mr Dodd's disgust.

"ET used to work at Coxsone's too, you know, and the first tune he ever took was 'Wet Dream'. That's just come to show you! This is a serious joke... I put it on the 'Hold You Jack' rhythm. 'Hold You Jack' was done at Duke Reid's studio. It was Derrick Morgan's rhythm and he'd sung a different tune 'pon the rhythm and I said to Derrick: 'I want you to sing 'Wet Dream'' but Derrick said 'no... I want to sing this tune called 'I Love You Down To My Liver'' or something like that 'pon it. I asked Pat Kelly and all those man to voice it and they said 'no... we nah go voice that slack tune'. All the big names at the time... nobody wanted to sing it and Maxie (Max Romeo) was the last man now... he was working for me as a salesman. So I turned to Maxie and I said 'every day you want to voice a tune... even on a flipside... so as you can play it to your girlfriend'. He said 'boy... Striker I don't want to sing it' and I said 'if you don't sing this tune then don't come to work tomorrow!'

So I said 'come Maxie... make we go inna the studio' and we voiced it up at Coxsone's studio. Coxsone had gone out to the bathroom to wash his face and Sylvan Morris was in the studio. He said to ET 'you take the tune'. Glen (Adams) said to Maxie 'come round here and do this! One cut!' and Maxie started (sings) "every night me go to sleep me have wet dream..." and as the tune finished Glen shouted 'in deh!' and Coxsone said 'no!' He came back and raised Cain! 'no Jack... you have to just wipe off that because you can't do those kind of tunes in my studio... I don't want that tune recorded here!' and I said 'no Beat... you can't wipe it off' but he said the session had to stop." **Bunny 'Striker' Lee**

'Wet Dream' spent twenty five weeks in the UK National Charts in 1969 "coming like Frank Sinatra and 'My Way'" with no radio play: the BBC banned it and Alan Freeman used to describe it as "a record by Max Romeo' on the Sunday afternoon weekly chart run down on Radio One. Mecca Ballrooms also banned the record. Max attempted to explain to the

UK music press that the song was not at all slack but referred to his leaking roof: he was asking his girlfriend to move out of the way as he tried to push a broom up into the hole to stop said leak "lie down girl let me push it up, push it up. Lie down…".

"Striker was very comical! No-one wanted to sing 'Wet Dream'… but you must never underrate the song. It's the people make the hits."

Patricia 'Miss Pat' Chin

"Well after Bill Garnett left to go to the States to work we had to employ another engineer and we were scouting around. Several guys came on board, a few guys from RJR, but we weren't satisfied. So along came Errol… why Errol really got involved was through a guy having to tune up the Hammond B3 organ so Errol came down to the studio to help him. Errol was very into electronics and he had just left Studio One where he was an apprentice under Sylvan Morris. I met him and said 'Errol… I know you, you know! We used to go to school together' and Errol said 'right… right' but he was an older guy than me… a couple of years older. My dad asked the organ tuner what he thought of this young man and he said 'he's good! He has a good sense of electronics and he has a good ear' and, being as he was unemployed at the time, we hired him. And he came on board…"

Clive Chin

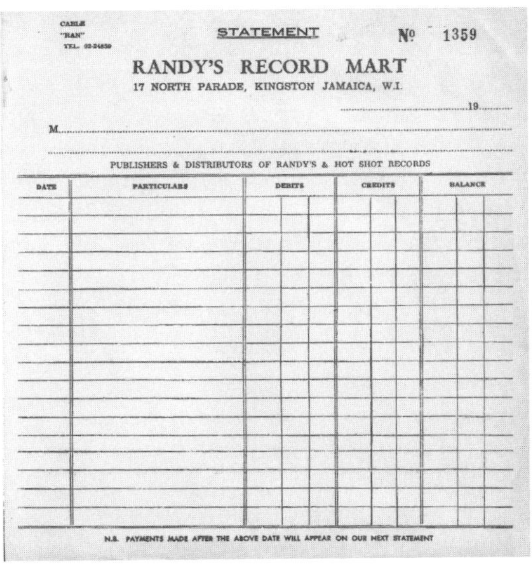
CABLE "RAN" TEL. 92-24859

STATEMENT   № 1359

RANDY'S RECORD MART
17 NORTH PARADE, KINGSTON JAMAICA, W.I.

……………………19……

M……………………

PUBLISHERS & DISTRIBUTORS OF RANDY'S & HOT SHOT RECORDS

DATE	PARTICULARS	DEBITS	CREDITS	BALANCE

N.B. PAYMENTS MADE AFTER THE ABOVE DATE WILL APPEAR ON OUR NEXT STATEMENT

Noel Hawks

With Errol Thompson at the controls Studio 17 would become one of the most important focal points for the Jamaican music business during the first half of the Seventies as it established itself as the studio of choice for the up and coming rebel rock producers and musicians. From the outset the studio had its own unique sound and ambience that many tried to emulate, but no-one ever came close, and many of reggae music's most enduring classics from this period were recorded upstairs at Studio 17. Artists and musicians would congregate outside the shop and in Chancery Lane at the side of the shop waiting for the chance of a session, selling their records, waiting for their time in the studio or checking to see if their records were being played in the shop. Chancery Lane became such a well known and popular meeting place among Kingston's musical fraternity that it was known as 'Idler's Rest'.

"...on the street called North Parade. Chatting to his mates, the session musicians and the producers who hang around there outside Randy's and Joe Gibbs respective shops, discussing the events of the day, their latest hits or their latest flops."

Chris Lane

"What happened was that Errol came and saw the equipment and everything and said 'let's just play around and ship around certain things... you know.' Then bam! The main thing... the most significant thing... that we got was the bass and the warmness of the drums. He had to do some modifications obviously and when he got that patterned I think the first recording that we did that proved that the sound was perfect was Lee 'Scratch' Perry recording Bob Marley & The Wailers... the first 'Soul Rebels' album and tracks like 'Soul Rebel', 'My Cup', 'Sun Is Shining'... every single track that was recorded there proved that we had the sound that people were hungry for. There were other studios... like Studio One... that had their sound. Treasure Isle had a beautiful middle range... the organ and the whole horn section at Treasure Isle was good. But we had a sound that was just unique and so in demand."

Clive Chin

"Lee Perry loved the studio... he turned Randy's into the studio it was."

Clive Chin

"So I told him to come downtown to Randy's 'cause in those days it was like the studio was there and you could always get some time. It was busy but if you wanted to get there early you could say to Miss Pat 'I need a couple of hours' and the musicians were always around..."

Lloyd 'Spiderman' Campbell

"I like to have Errol Thompson operating the controls. He's the best studio engineer on the island." **Winston 'Niney The Observer' Holness**

"If the producer didn't have enough money to pay for the session we'd tell them we'll hold the tape until you can pay us and Niney once took an old tape box to the studio and left that with us!

Vincent once said to Niney: 'Niney! Come here. How come you make so much hits in one hour's studio time?' and Niney said 'studio time is twenty dollars an hour so I practise one thousand times at home already before we come to the studio. I laid the groundwork for 'Cassandra' with Dennis Brown but Dennis got sick and I had to steal him out of the hospital, take him to Studio 17 to record the song and then take him back to the hospital!' So the struggle is there but the sense of humour is part of the struggle..." **Patricia 'Miss Pat' Chin**

"Randy's was the main studio because it was downtown and that's where all the artists hang out, so it was close by for them to make a minute's step, and it became the key studio really." **Wilburn 'Stranger' Cole**

And Bunny 'Striker' Lee is insistent that Studio 17 was responsible for a musical genre he named the John Crow Skank (in Jamaica a turkey buzzard is referred to as a John Crow) that he feels has been unjustly overlooked in the many histories of reggae.

"But we moved from mento and calypso to soca... we had a part of that with Byron Lee... to ska. From ska we went to rock steady; from rock steady we came with a music called John Crow Skank like 'Better Must Come' from Delroy Wilson and 'Duppy Conqueror' from Bob Marley & The Wailers. They were not reggae or rock steady 'cause they had the creep organ like how the crow flies. In Jamaica we call them John Crows and so you had the John Crow Skank. Listen to 'Stick By Me' by John Holt and you'll hear the creep organ! Randy's studio used to give you the best creep organ but Dynamics was a bit too refined 'cause in Randy's the organ was out of tune and you just had to touch it and... creep! The historians of this music don't talk about it because they don't know! You understand? Yeah man! 'Duppy Conqueror' and all those tunes... they're the John Crow Skank.

It was the creep organ at Randy's studio… not the creak… the creep. It was off tune and if you couldn't shuffle… you couldn't play the reggae. So you have to touch it and you get the creeping sound like on Bob Marley's 'Duppy Conqueror', '(Who Is) Mr Brown' and all those tunes there are John Crow Skank. So we had to start doing it at Dynamic too 'cause Randy's studio was known for the best creep. We called it the John Crow Skank and a man would say 'play John Crow Skank!' and it reached Dynamic too. Dynamic had a good Hammond organ so all them Hopeton Lewis tunes 'Grooving Out On Life' is all shuffle and creep… 'Better Must Come', 'Stick By Me', 'Cool Operator'… all them tune is the John Crow Skank too. You just touch the organ.

Once you hit with a sound you know everybody follows but in Randy's studio the organ was out of tune so it was distinct. It was a Hammond organ too but you couldn't shuffle 'pon it. You could play an intro but it was a semitone out. But people didn't used to watch that! The man in a dance wanted to hear this new sound… shuffle… it threw the rhythm right out of place so that's how the John Crow Skank did come in and eventually it stayed with the reggae but the creep was more refined on Byron Lee's organ. It did come like salt! You have coarse salt and fine salt! You understand? So the reggae is really the organ shuffle you know…"

Bunny 'Striker' Lee

Studio 17, now upgraded to eight tracks, became known as the studio where the hits were made and, when Clive Chin entered the family business, Randy's began to produce the hits there too. After leaving Glenmore Road Elementary School, "I met all the roughneck boy them there!", Clive had studied at Kingston College where he numbered Alan 'Skill' Cole, Tyrone 'Organ D' Downie and Horace 'Augustus Pablo' Swaby among his classmates. Vincent had wanted Clive to further his studies at the University Of The West Indies but on graduating from KC he went straight into the family business; his earliest productions were with his old friends, Tyrone Downie and Augustus Pablo, from Kingston College.

"Augustus Pablo? We both went to Kingston College on North Street. You know Pablo…I called him Swaby 'cause that's his right name… he always used to come to me and say 'introduce me to the studio now!' It's like once they knew who you were and who your family is… I had over a dozen guys

SANTIC
PABLO IN DUB
AGUSTOS PABLO
WAMBESI
PRODUCED BY R. COUSINS
PROMISE LAND
(R Cousins)
THE ROYALS
LEO
RECORDS
45 RPM
ML-5051-A
NO JESTERING
CARL MALCOLM
SOUNDS OF JAMAICA
IMPACT!
CHEATER
(R. Chin)
Dennis Brown
CHAPPY
CARL MALCOLM
FATTIE BUM-BUM
A
UK
RECORDS
TUFF GONG
45 RPM
CURFEW
Bob Marley & The Wailers
RANDY'S
RANDY'S
IMPACT!
NOTTY NO JESTER
Big Youth
GIANT
ORDINARY MAN
LLOYD PARKS
Randy's
MADE IN JAMAICA
Dont Stay Out Late
(R. Chin)
LORD CREATOR
Hot Shot!
MU-3919-A
GIVE ME THE RIGHT
(LET'S GET IT ON)
HEPTONES
DEMON
RECORDS
HOLD TIGHT
(W. Morris)
AFRICAN BROTHERS
UPSETTER
DUPPY CONQUEROR
BOB MARLEY & THE WAILERS
KEITH'S
KR-200-B
RIGHTEOUS RULER
HUGH ROY & PETER TOUCH
GUIDANCE
Prod. by
H. Laws
HAMMER
Barrington Levy
FOX
Producer
L. Lindo
Ruby's Record
1 James St.
Ocho Rios
MARCUS GARVEY
(B Spear)
BURNING SPEAR
Ordinary version

tracking me down. You had Tyrone Downie… Organ D… you had Harold Butler who was much younger but all of them who went to Kingston College knew who I was and the connection with me and Randy's. They'd all come to me at some point during lunch time and say 'give me a little jook now man! Interject me into certain things'.

But Pablo made his headway down there by doing sessions for Scratch and Herman Chin-Loy because Pablo was an uptown guy. He used to take the bus to Half Way Tree and just stand up at Aquarius and Herman saw him with this plastic thing underneath his arm and said 'wha' happen? You can play that?' and he said 'yeah man!' because once you can play keyboards you know the chords and stuff but you have to blow into it so you have to have a good sense of the key. And they're all minor keys so that kinda manifested into a thing called…the first recording that he did for him (Herman Chin-Loy) was a thing called 'Iggy Iggy' (a version to The Heptones' 'Why Did You Leave') and that was a track that was actually bought from Glen Adams and Pablo overdubbed on it." **Clive Chin**

Clive's first hit record was 'Java', a melodica outing from Augustus Pablo with harmonies from The Chosen Few and guitar from Jackson Jones, released on the Impact! label in 1972. 'Java' had been intended as a vehicle for a vocalist but Pablo was brought in because the original singer was allegedly unable to fit the vocal to the rhythm track. It was voted 'Top Instrumental Record' for that year and introduced the type of music that Pablo had been pioneering with Herman Chin-Loy to the more mainstream audience. It would go on to dominate the direction of reggae for the rest of the decade.

"Pablo was only sixteen when he first came to the studio… he was a breath of fresh air. It was beautiful to add instruments to dub. It was a turning point for the music. He was very quiet… they were just kids doing it for fun. We never knew it would be as big as it is today or know how much history it would make…" **Patricia 'Miss Pat' Chin**

Further versions of 'Java' followed including 'Jaro' from Tommy McCook, 'Maro' a keyboard cut, 'Java Passion' a different melodica cut with Nyahbinghi style percussion on the b-side of 'Mava', Dennis AlCapone's talking version, and a later I Roy deejay cut entitled 'Hospital Trolley'. And, in late 1973, Clive and Pablo followed these with one of the tightest long playing instrumental sets ever assembled in Jamaica: 'This Is Augustus Pablo'.

"Over the past years reggae has generated a trend in and 'round Jamaica and other parts of the world. Today the type of sound which the younger generation digs is the rebel rock music which is here now." 'This Is Augustus Pablo'

"After I recorded Pablo's 'Java'... it was a massive, massive instrumental. When I say massive it sold over fifty thousand copies. It was voted the Number One Instrumental in 1972. Pat, my stepmother, said to me 'Clive we have to record this guy some more!' and I said sure. At that time I'd got a little bit cocky, you know, and I said I can get him to do some recording. I had an Alton Ellis track called 'Too Late To Turn Back Now' that I decided I was going to use on the album. Then I had 'Ordinary Man' from Lloyd Parks, I had The Heptones' 'Guiding Star'... I remember three or four tracks I had already recorded that I could use and then we recorded six original tracks. No! 'Foot Of The Mountain' was 'Point Blank' and then we did 'Please Sunrise Please' which was a Young Holt Unlimited tune... beautiful tune... and, after he played the piano, he did the melodica as a harmony. 'Skateland Rock'... 'Pretty Baby' was a Heptones tune. 'Dub Organiser' now we got off of Lee Perry." **Clive Chin**

Leonard 'Santic' Chin (no relation) recorded a number of hit records for his fledgling Santic label upstairs at Randy's and described in great detail how things worked at Studio 17 and the importance of being able to work spontaneously. Leonard's production of 'Pablo In Dub' was included on the 'This Is Augustus Pablo' album. He recalled that the legendary musician, Theophilus Beckford, known as 'Snappin'' after his massive early Sixties rhythm & blues/shuffle and boogie breakthrough record 'Easy Snapping' was one of the musicians he employed. But, at the time, Leonard knew nothing of his illustrious lineage...

"Like I said when I went in the studio how old was I? Sixteen? So I was just working with those guys but I didn't know their history... as the years went by I got to understand more and, being in the business, I learnt more and more. A lot of people my age in Jamaica wouldn't know those things so that's how I get to know. Anyway, 'Snappin'' played the piano. The organ player was Ossie Hibbert. I did a mix for the Jah Mojo record, 'Jacamma Rock', and everybody loved the rhythm. One time Leroy Sibbles and some other people were standing up in Randy's and Leroy said 'this rhythm a bad! It's like the bass carry the melody by itself' and then I decided to do a next mix of it.

Eventually… things just happen sometimes when they're supposed to happen. I went up to Randy's and mixed the tune and for some reason Pablo just walked into the studio that evening and said 'that rhythm there sound good!' So I said 'blow a thing on it now then, man!' I was into Pablo from 'Java' and was always asking him to do a tune for me and he used to smile and say I couldn't afford to pay him and all those things there. He said 'you'll have to ask my manager Paul' and his manager said 'alright… do you have any weed?' My brethren, Carl Prehay, was there and he said 'yeah man… we have the boom!' And we bought a few Red Stripe beers, took the next two hours in the studio, set up the tape and he just blew through the tune a couple of times. The next one was a take and I said 'this is 'Pablo In Dub''.

After 'Pablo In Dub' got on the Top Five it went to Number One for a week and then dropped back to Number Two and I asked Horace Andy if he could sing a tune on it for me. He loved the rhythm from time too… the Pablo version was so popular! Horace just came in the studio… it was a Friday morning. The day before I'd got Leroy Sibbles to put in the rhythm guitar because 'Pablo In Dub' never had a rhythm guitar in it. So it was Leroy Sibbles who actually chopped the rhythm guitar in it and then, the following day, I got Horace to sing on the rhythm. We played the rhythm track and Horace ad-libbed and said 'Errol! Rewind back the tape there' and he sang 'Children Of Israel' and went through it once, wrote some more lyrics, went through it again and half way through he said 'now run the tape Errol. And take it too!' We did 'Children Of Israel' and 'Problems' both at the same time. We didn't spend two hours to do all that! The lyrics were written and voiced at that moment… there and then.

Looking back now I'm thinking, in the Eighties and Nineties, people would spend these relentless hours voicing, dropping in, voicing, dropping in. And nobody's happy! Doing that you have no soul! You're just like a mechanical thing. When you hear sweet things and think it can be sweeter… but it's sweet enough already! You become over technical and everybody wants to be greater than they really can be. It doesn't really happen like that. You can only be the best you can be… "

Leonard 'Santic' Chin

For many of his self productions Pablo worked closely with Errol Thompson and the version side of 'El Rocker's', Pablo's interpretation of The Soul Vendors' 'Reel/Real Rock', featured some startlingly original echoed clavinet overdubs and tape rewinds.

"That was Errol Thompson! I and I used to try a lot of things even before King Tubby's time. Most of the ideas I come up with it's just vibes… a certain feel... you know. Always me is a man who just try and do something new… me don't do things that people follow. So you can check the whole selection of my music. Me no follow nothing! It's the same way Tubbys stay and Errol Thompson stay too... him was great part of the industry in that period. Bringing up the youths and showing them...

Errol Thompson was the first man who tell me I'm supposed to get money for publishing! Him and Keith Hudson. So... me and him used to move through him loved instrumentals too… and that's the key to it. When Errol Thompson take my melodica he take it a way that... I don't know... he just do it different. Him and Tubbys always have that special touch.... they just took the melodica a special way... I don't know. It's through Errol Thompson that I get the experience mostly 'cause him was the first person who really have the experience of the melodica... there was so much music done in the studio that time I can't remember them. A whole heap of works me and Errol do in that studio." **Augustus Pablo**

Leonard 'Santic' Chin

Leonard 'Santic' Chin

In 1973 Clive produced one of the first ever dub albums 'Java, Java, Java, Java', also known as 'Java Dub', which was mixed in ground breaking, trend setting fashion by Errol. Originally released in a limited pressing of one hundred and fifty copies, without sleeves, credits or liner notes, the album opened, naturally enough, with a further dubwise version to 'Java' and moved through dubs of Dennis Brown's 'Meet Me At The Corner' and 'Cheater', Leroy Sibbles' 'My Guiding Star', a recut of The Soul Vendors' 'Fiddler On The Roof'/'Swing Easy' before culminating in an extraordinary version to Lloyd Parks' 'Ordinary Man' entitled 'Dun-Kirk' also released on a seven inch single as 'Ordinary Version'.

"That tune there now. Lloyd Parks couldn't put it out for himself so I paid for the session… I was in charge of the 'Ordinary Versions'". **Clive Chin**

This astonishing cut to Lloyd Parks' 'Ordinary Man' was built around a humorous spoken exchange, "listen everything now", featuring Errol T as an established engineer with Eric 'Bingy Bunny' Lamont playing a young hopeful who, although he did not know how to operate, was willing to co-operate.

"Hold on just a little…
Right now I man a go show you how fe operate…right?
Watch the bass now… you hear the bass how it sound round?
Just listen the bass… you see how it make the girl them wiggle their waist?
Alright?" **'Ordinary Version' Impact All Stars**

"Coming back to this dub argument... I used to play out you know. I had a sound called Black Moses and what I used to do, rather than playing the straight instrumentals, I used to cut dubs with stripped down rhythms. So what I used to do in the studio with Errol I used to take out the rhythm tracks and then the snare and the hi hat we'd put with the reverb... sometimes we used to echo the guitar track because at that time we had a flexibility of not only four tracks but eight tracks to play with. So... we can play around with the tracks, strip them down, bring them back up. You know. Play with them!

We never really had those pretty effects like Tubbys... we had a Scully cutting lathe and I had the opportunity to cut the plates with Dennis (Thompson). And when I played them out I used to get 'nough forwards! And I said it looks like this thing could a sell! So the whole idea to do a dub LP was... Errol said 'let's just take some of the popular rhythm tracks that came out on singles... just combine ten tracks... master the ten tracks and just test them out'. Mark this! We don't have no covers, we don't have no liner notes, we don't have no credits. When we did that we did a hundred and fifty copies... pre-release... and put it on the market!

This was in 1973 and... mark you... after that happened the rest of the business saw that there was a demand for dubs. So right after that Herman came out with 'Aquarius Dub'... Lee Perry came with 'Blackboard Jungle' ('Upsetters 14 Dub Blackboard Jungle'). You must remember that all eyes were focused on Randy's because we were one of the main distributors of records... not only were we the main distributors you had guys by Slipe Road by the Carib Theatre (KG's). When those hundred and fifty copies were gone now my stepmother... she's a business woman... and if she sees something that's going to move she's going to just say 'hey... commission another thing! Quick! Don't hesitate!' And that's how the whole idea of other producers and labels got going, you know."

Clive Chin

Errol T's engineering innovations began to shape and form the early sound of dub and the switches on the Randy's board, as opposed to King Tubby's faders, gave his music a unique and highly individual sound. Errol was always keen to experiment with new ideas.

"An innovative producer. You see Errol is the history of certain music in the Seventies... (he put) a microphone in the toilet and flush it just to get the sound effect." **Clive Chin**

Clive recounted that, in 1973, the studio was upgraded to sixteen tracks as a result of attempting to do his old school, Kingston College, a favour but, what could have been a total disaster, was fortuitously turned around to Randy's advantage. KC's musical director, Barry Gordon, commissioned a recording of the Kingston College Choir in honour of the Bishop of Kingston with half the recording to be done at Studio 17 and the other half at a chapel on Camp Road near the military camp. The studio equipment, except for the board, was moved to the chapel but when it was returned to the studio Clive and Errol were unable to retrieve the proper sound and could not recover the bass depth and top end. This resulted in the purchase of brand new sixteen track recording equipment... every cloud has a silver lining.

Randy's was at the centre of Kingston's musical scene and making music in Studio 17 was Clive Chin's occupation. He had hit with records such as Alton Ellis' reworking of the Cornelius Brothers & Sister Rose's 'Too Late To Turn Back Now' which proved to be one of Alton's biggest ever hits.
"Alton wanted to record originals but I wanted this one (because) I knew the soul original. I arranged the rhythm...

We gravitated towards a lot of the American music. I for one... why do you think I called my sound system Black Moses? I used to love Isaac Hayes... I loved The Meters... I loved The Bar-Kays, Booker T & The MGs. That was what was going on at the time." **Clive Chin**

Clive identified and empathised with the aspirations of the local artists and musicians having been "born and grown in music... the artists were there and they had nobody to listen to them" and he recorded countless classic records with The Gladiators, The African Brothers, Dennis Brown, Gregory Isaacs and many, many more. Clive persuaded Donovan Carless, who sang in The Soul Syndicate, to sing William De Vaughn's 'Be Thankful For What You Got', "I love that song and I gave it to him to cover it", and Gregory Isaacs' version of Mike Williams' 'Lonely Soldier'... "I found the tune and I knew he could do it." He was also the first to record the original Black Uhuru.

"Duckie (Derrick Simpson) came up with the name 'Black Sounds Of Uhuru'! Big name! (We) just called them Uhuru but nah put it out."

Clive Chin

Randy's updated to twenty four track in 1974 and, for his sessions, Clive had the pick of Kingston's musicians and would use Skin, Flesh & Bones, The Soul Syndicate, and the Barrett brothers (Carlton and Aston) in various permutations and combinations who were usually billed as the Impact All Stars. He could always get the best musicians because he was willing to pay "top dollars" and because of Randy's reputation and location.

"If you don't love what you're doing you're a hypocrite. You have to do something in life and the inspiration for the music just flow. I work off a feeling. I was never limited in terms of time but if I had something to do I went straight ahead and did it. When you do a thing (if) it's not right you cool off until the time is ready and try again." **Clive Chin**

Carl Malcolm gave Randy's an uncharacteristic crossover hit in the autumn of 1975 when he reached Number Eight in the UK National Charts with 'Fattie Bum Bum'. Earlier that year Carl's gentle, pleading voice had been perfect for the role of a lovelorn suitor attempting to impress the parents of "a girl called Jean" on 'No Jestering'. The record was a huge local hit and inspired versions from Big Youth with 'Notty No Jester', Augustus Pablo with 'Pablo No Jester'/'The Last Of Jestering' (for Leonard Chin) and many more. Carl followed it up with 'Miss Wire Waist', released in the UK on Pama's Camel label and the Birmingham based Black Wax label too, which proved to be every bit as popular.

"I arranged an audition with young Clive Chin at Randy's Records on North Parade in the heart of the city. He liked 'No Jestering' and it was recorded, mixed and mastered upstairs..." **Carl Malcolm**

"Skin, Flesh & Bones, Al Brown's band, laid the record's compulsive music track. Fellows like Lloyd Parks on bass guitar, Ranchie McLean on guitar and Charlie (sic) Dunbar on drums. An instant hit starting a local phrase 'No Jestering'. It sold about fifty thousand locally in Jamaica. A lot of versions inspired by the song have been recorded and released: 'Notty No Jester' by Big Youth, 'Ten To Ten (aka 'Jestering)' by Shorty The President and 'Pablo No Jester' from melodica player Augustus Pablo...

Carl's second hit for Randy's, 'Miss Wire Waist', was a slow rocking soulful roots one with a haunting rhythmic melodica riff from Augustus Pablo stepping in the background. It has sold well in Britain and New York."

Andell Forgie

And the third, and perhaps least innovative, record that Carl and Clive made together, 'Fattie Bum Bum' a version to Derrick Morgan's timeless 'Red Bumb Ball' rhythm, proved to be the biggest hit of all when it was licensed in London by the now disgraced Jonathan King for release on his opportunistic UK label.

"It was really amazing. I just thought it ('Fattie Bum Bum') was average music." **Clive Chin**

"We never dreamt of having an artist with a hit in England..."

Patricia 'Miss Pat' Chin

Unfortunately this unexpected crossover success did little more than add to the public's perception of reggae as novelty music and that winter, when 'Miss Wire Waist' was re-released on UK as the 'follow up', it failed to chart despite Carl Gayle's hopeful prediction in *Black Music* magazine. "Sounds a little jaded now having been almost forgotten in West Indian circles since its popularity three months ago. For dancing it's just as good as Carl's hit and, perhaps, a better record all round. Could be another pop hit." **Carl Gayle**

But releasing, distributing and selling records worldwide was not a new phenomenon for Randy's who also operated a mail order service from their North Parade premises. From 1970 to 1973 Trojan Records in London operated their own Randy's subsidiary dedicated to Vincent's and Clive's productions. Vincent's brother, Victor, owned an electronics shop on Schenectady Avenue in Brooklyn, New York and Vincent convinced him to stock some imported Jamaican singles in the shop. Victor soon began to press and distribute Jamaican recordings for the American market before moving from his cramped shop to "the corner of Schenectady and St John". Another brother, Keith who ran Keith's Records at 1394 St John's Place, also released records on his Keith's label. Keith and Victor also ran Chin Randy's Records at 1342 St John's Place while Vincent's sister, Molly Feliciano, was in charge of Music Land at 317 Utica Avenue, Brooklyn.

I can personally vouch for the first rate quality of her service and the incredible selection of 'American and Jamaican Oldies' stocked by Ms Feliciano and spent hundreds of dollars (literally) with Music Land's excellent mail order operation.

"Vincent's brother used to release records in New York… he called himself Chin Randy's and when Vincent used to take the tunes from us he'd give them to his brother to put out…

Jim Silles

Randy's

PRE-RELEASE RECORDS

AS COMPILED BY RANDY'S RECORD MART, 17 NORTH PARADE, KINGSTON.PH.24859

PRE-RELEASE RECORDS $1.25¢ EACH.

1. ENDUST Vaa 1 & 2..........................YOUNG ONES
2. AMAL JAMAL..........................NORA DEAN
CENSUS TAKER..........................SUCCESS
4. ARTIBELLE..........................KEN BOOTHE
5. MESH WIRE..........................T/McCOOK & W. WRIGHT
6. HIT ME BACK..........................DAVE BARKER
7. FUNKEY REGGAE TIME..........................INST.
8. DANCE OF LOVE..........................ROY SHIRLEY
9. SINGER MAN..........................DERRICK HARRIOT
10. TAKE A LITTEE TRIP..........................."HEATHER"
11. OVER TAKER..........................DERRICK HARRIOT
12. L.S.D..........................YOUNG ONES

****

MRS ROBINSON..........
CUTE MAN..........
LAND LORD..........
LASH- LA- RUE..........
GANJA PLANT..........
SAY ME SAY..........
SATAN GAL..........
RUN COME..........
STRANGER IN TOWN..........
GOT TO BE MELLOW..........
BOWIE BOWIE..........
WH[illegible] A BOY FALLS IN LOVE....
OH BABE..........
GIVE AND TAKE..........
JUMBO TET..........
SO YOU LOOK PON IT..........
SEPREANO..........
DARLING DARLING..........
I CANT HIDE..........
PRESSURE PROOF..........
CHAPTER THREE..........
BOSS..........
MY CUP RUNNETH OVER....
PHANTOM..........
GIVE ME A TICKET.....
GOOD GIRL..........
EXPOSURE..........
OPEN JAW VERI.......
SPY THIRTEEN.......
TELL THE CHILDREN..
SON OF THUNDER....
A COUSIN OF MINE..
SET ME FREE......
BABYLON........
LAUGH IT OFF....
MUSIC POLICE....
MESSAGE FROM A B
RAT TRAP......
PSYCHEDELIC TRA
BLACK ORGAN..
SOUNDS MIGHTY.
DONT CALL ME
NO TIME.....

Nick Hodgson/Ken Smith

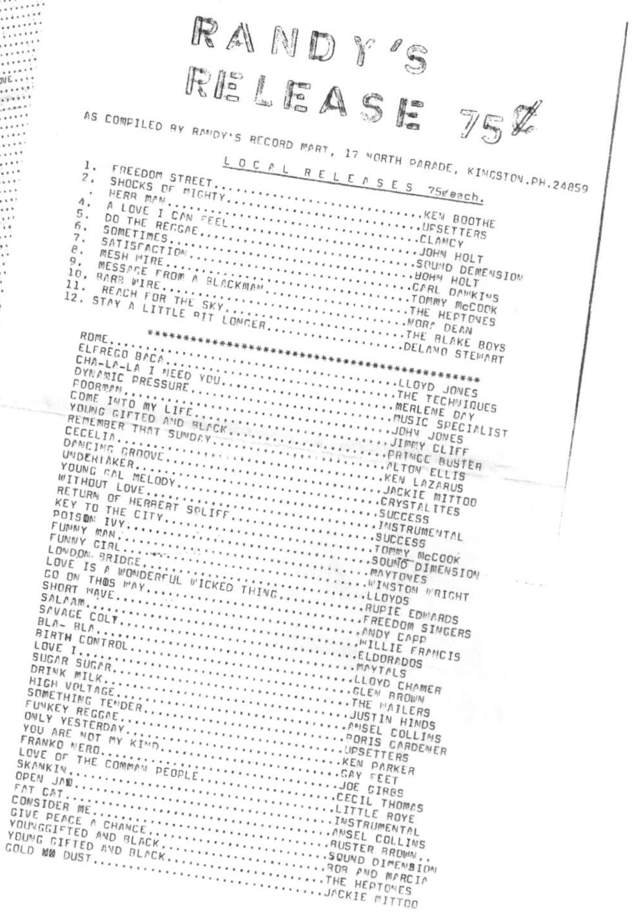

RANDY'S RELEASE 75¢

AS COMPILED BY RANDY'S RECORD MART, 17 NORTH PARADE, KINGSTON.PH.24859

LOCAL RELEASES 75¢each.

1. FREEDOM STREET..........................KEN BOOTHE
2. SHOCKS OF MIGHTY..........................UPSETTERS
. HERB MAN..........................CLANCY
4. A LOVE I CAN FEEL..........................JOHN HOLT
5. DO THE REGGAE..........................SOUND DEMENSION
6. SOMETIMES..........................JOHN HOLT
7. SATISFACTION..........................CARL DAWKINS
8. MESH WIRE..........................TOMMY McCOOK
9. MESSAGE FROM A BLACKMAN..........................THE HEPTONES
10. BARB WIRE..........................NORA DEAN
11. REACH FOR THE SKY..........................THE BLAKE BOYS
12. STAY A LITTLE BIT LONGER..........................DELANO STEWART

****

ROME..........................LLOYD JONES
ELFREGO BACA..........................THE TECHNIQUES
CHA-LA-LA I NEED YOU..........................MERLENE DAY
DYNAMIC PRESSURE..........................MUSIC SPECIALIST
POORMAN..........................JOHN JONES
COME INTO MY LIFE..........................JIMMY CLIFF
YOUNG GIFTED AND BLACK..........................PRINCE BUSTER
REMEMBER THAT SUNDAY..........................ALTON ELLIS
CECELIA..........................KEN LAZARUS
DANCING GROOVE..........................JACKIE MITTOO
UNDERTAKER..........................CRYSTALITES
YOUNG GAL MELODY..........................SUCCESS
WITHOUT LOVE..........................INSTRUMENTAL
RETURN OF HERBERT SPLIFF..........................SUCCESS
KEY TO THE CITY..........................TOMMY McCOOK
POISON IVY..........................SOUND DIMENSION
FUNNY MAN..........................MAYTONES
FUNNY GIRL..........................WINSTON WRIGHT
LONDON BRIDGE..........................LLOYDS
LOVE IS A WONDERFUL WICKED THING..........................RUPIE EDWARDS
GO ON THIS WAY..........................FREEDOM SINGERS
SHORT WAVE..........................ANDY CAPP
SALAAM..........................WILLIE FRANCIS
SAVAGE COLT..........................ELDORADOS
BLA- BLA..........................MAYTALS
BIRTH CONTROL..........................LLOYD CHAMER
LOVE I..........................GLEN BROWN
SUGAR SUGAR..........................THE WAILERS
DRINK MILK..........................JUSTIN HINDS
HIGH VOLTAGE..........................ANSEL COLLINS
SOMETHING TENDER..........................BORIS GARDENER
FUNKEY REGGAE..........................UPSETTERS
ONLY YESTERDAY..........................KEN PARKER
YOU ARE NOT MY KIND..........................GAY FEET
FRANKO NERO..........................JOE GIBBS
LOVE OF THE COMMAN PEOPLE..........................CECIL THOMAS
SKANKIN..........................LITTLE ROYE
OPEN JAM..........................INSTRUMENTAL
FAT CAT..........................ANSEL COLLINS
CONSIDER ME..........................BUSTER BROWN..
GIVE PEACE A CHANCE..........................SOUND DIMENSION
YOUNGGIFTED AND BLACK..........................BOB AND MARCIA
YOUNG GIFTED AND BLACK..........................THE HEPTONES
GOLD DUST..........................JACKIE MITTOO

Nick Hodgson/Ken Smith

When I used to leave for England, the market wasn't small like it is now, then I'd come to Canada and New York. We were just trying to get the music out to the people and most of the people who left Jamaica came to live and work in England and then Canada and America so we used to try and get the music to them. So we kinda start that market too with the same Chin Randy's in New York until Chin Randy's owned a whole block! They later became VP… VP stands for Vincent and Pat Chin his wife.

Bunny 'Striker' Lee

"The customers would prefer to buy a record than a loaf of bread."

Patricia 'Miss Pat' Chin

If your record was not played regularly in Randy's shop on North Parade it was unlikely to be a hit and the store played a vital role in the promotion of local "domestic and ethnic" product throughout the Sixties and Seventies. Augustus Pablo recalled how the support of Randy's had proved instrumental to his career.

"Through Randy's Miss Pat she gave me all the freedom. I became like a little son. Even clavinet! It's me order the clavinet and put it in the studio. The only person who had one that time was Stevie Wonder so you see it's right after that I get my clavinet! Through Miss Pat had relations in America she had a catalogue and we just send for it. Anything we want she just send for it. Yeah! Get a xylophone too... all kinda things.

Them days me nah have a whole heap of money to press so me just press one hundred, one hundred, two hundred, two hundred or three hundred, three hundred. Sometimes with Miss Pat now it would be a big order. She really helped me sell a lot of my tunes... especially in America too you know. Randy's had a deal where she'd help me press it and she just worked out a terms and she'd pay off all the money 'cause she had the money to pay! I never had no money to pay and she just carried it to America and sell it... slowly but surely." **Augustus Pablo**

And Randy's helped out the "flat foot hustlers" as Roy Cousins termed himself and the other impecunious producers.

"The four track was what we could afford! I only ever had one eight track tape… for 'Promised Land'. When Errol Thompson was at Randy's he just give me the tape!" **Roy Cousins**

Randy's also offered a record mastering service supervised by a young engineer, Dennis Thompson (no relation), whose official role was to cut the masters in Randy's cutting room. However, Dennis would add extra effects utilising "a parametric eq in 'emulations' of King Tubby's high pass filter" and remix the version sides of the records live as the acetates were being cut on the lathe.

"The b-sides of the records were usually mixed at Randy's. The person who did it was Dennis Thompson who used to do the mastering while Errol was engineering in the studio. He had a different kind of equalising thing. It was all done during the mastering!" **Leonard 'Santic' Chin**

"Yes. It was Dennis Thompson who was the cutting engineer at Randy's...he was a good engineer. There was another guy used to do the cutting at Randy's too but I can't remember his name. Dennis was one of the main cutters but ET used to cut too. They fiddled with the version when they were mastering and, if you wanted that effect, you have to get it off of the record because it was done in the control room when Randy's were mastering so it's not there on the direct master. When you mastered something you just played with the controls and the man say 'bwoy! Any part of it gets spoiled it's not my fault and we'll have to tell the boss it was you who troubled it now!'" **Bunny 'Striker' Lee**

"Dennis came on board after the whole studio initiative had started to blossom... when I say blossom I mean we had so many outside independent producers coming into the studio like Bunny 'Striker' Lee, Niney, Phil Pratt, Success... Rupie Edwards, Clancy Eccles, Derrick Harriott all those guys were coming into the studio. We started to run 24/7 now and that's when I started to get involved. Not only helping Errol to set up the mics but I used to run sessions as well. Dennis, no relation to Errol, was involved with Merritone (Winston Blake's sound system) buying records and so forth. Winston Blake introduced him to Aunt Pat, saying he had a little bit of knowledge in the music, and he learned the mastering. He came down and started to master... now, mark you, the lathe that we used to master on was a Scully... Grampian head... and we could only cut in mono. We couldn't cut stereo... but when you're putting out forty fives you don't really cut stereo forty fives!

So if you record and mix your session there it goes from one department to another so Dad made a little room right by the control room and employed Dennis… but the overabundance of work that Errol was on we needed help… Dennis knew a lot of club owners in St Andrew and he had a close relationship with a guy named Dickie Wong who had a club called the Tit For Tat. He had a relationship with a band called Skin, Flesh & Bones and he was also the band manager for The Fabulous Five. You know we used to do a lot of recording with these guys. The song that Dickie Wong produced with Skin, Flesh & Bones called 'Here I Am Baby Come And Take Me' (sung by Al Brown)… a cover of the Al Green song… Dennis took that session, Dennis mixed that session and Dennis mastered that recording. And that's how Dennis became involved in the production… and also 'Shaving Cream' with Fabulous Five and 'Sixpence' by Max Romeo." **Clive Chin**

Dennis and Errol were also part of the team that ensured the success of Niney The Observer's 'Live At The Turntable' project, "the first 'live' recording emanating from the very popular Turntable Club", with Marie Garth, the "queen of Jamaican radio" from RJR, in charge of the introductions of "all your favourite selections…"

"A very good evening to you. This is Marie Garth welcoming you to the Turntable Club and the Observer explosion. Tonight you'll be part of a live album…" **Marie Garth**

"On this cool December Sunday evening engineers Errol Thompson and Dennis Thompson got to work on their equipment well in advance of the stampeding crowd that soon filled the club..." **Johnny Golding**

"It's the first ever recording done outside of a studio in Jamaica. Dennis Thompson supersedes friendship… he's like a family member… and he sometimes played with us on the sound. Dennis Thompson carried in the mixing board and they set it up at the Turntable Club and we did the live show... Part One and Part Two with a band. It was awesome… it's become a classic album and people ask me about it all the time."

Winston 'Merritone' Blake

His work on cutting the stamper for the Bob Marley & The Wailers' Tuff Gong seven inch of 'Curfew' (aka 'Burnin' And Lootin') backed with 'Chant I' (aka 'Rastaman Chant') in 1974 so impressed Bob that he offered Dennis a job and he would later move on to work with Tuff Gong where he became an integral part of the organisation.

Many artists and musicians came "from foreign" to Kingston hoping that some of the laid back charm of Jamaican's recording studios would work for them. Joe Cocker came to Jamaica in 1976 to record at Dynamic but he wanted to use The Wailers on certain tracks and Lee Jaffe took him to Randy's where, late one night, he recorded Bob Dylan's 'The Man In Me' with The Wailers line up apart from Bob Marley and Bunny Livingston. The song was included on Joe's 'Stingray' album but the rest of the set was recorded at Byron Lee's Dynamic Sounds.

"I also worked with some exceptional overseas artists you know... Joe Cocker from Sheffield... some tracks on his album that came out in 1976. He actually worked out of Dynamics to do the basics, you know, but he wanted to get the Randy's sound for particular tracks... it was Bob Dylan's 'The Man In Me'. And I tell you that night was out of this world! They came to the studio about midnight... some of the musicians thought it was Dynamics they were going to. They veered down Bell Road and realised it wasn't down Bell Road! It was North Parade...

Beth Lesser/Blood & Fire

CLIVE CHIN - RANDY'S

PHOTO CREDIT: BETH LESSER

Blood and Fire

I set up mics and everything ready for them... there were some 'boasy' musicians... a guy named Cornell Dupree a guitarist for Atlantic Records, Richard Tee on keyboards to name a few! But the main rhythm section was Carlie Barrett on drums, Tyrone Downie on keyboards, Aston 'Family Man' Barrett on bass and Peter Tosh on rhythm guitar. I tell you man! What a session! I set up a mic for Joe Cocker and the man was smoking a big spliff and him just knocked out you know... because he did drink before! He was a man who drunk a little whisky and stuff and when he smoked this thing...

Of course I have out takes of the session but you can't touch them! Brilliant session man. You know. Brilliant!" **Clive Chin**

Niney The Observer had introduced Errol Thompson to Joe Gibbs when Errol was first working at Randy's, "Gibbo you want engineer?", and Joe and Errol established a close rapport which developed into a working relationship in 1975. Errol moved to 24 Retirement Crescent to work with Joe in his new sixteen track studio where they became 'The Mighty Two'. Joe Gibbs recalled it "was like putting one over on Randy's" and it proved very difficult to replace Errol; Clive's praise for Errol Thompson's contribution to Randy's Studio 17 was unequivocal.

"Not saying we have a whole heap of secrets and technology or anything like that but it was like you take away a part of us...

If I could turn back the hands of time Errol would never leave Randy's. He was the innovative one. I felt like something left me when he left."

Clive Chin

"I used to do my own productions, my personal self, but when it came to outside producers they would have preferred Errol because Errol was the man. He was recognised and he was so recognised that Mr Joe Gibbs decided that he needed an engineer and... the main culprit was Niney. Niney was the one who whispered into Joe Gibbs' ear 'you want to tap up Errol'. Errol mixed a couple of dub albums for Mr Gibbs... the 'African Dub' series... and they had a relationship going. When Errol left in '74/'75 the whole momentum of the studio kinda... it didn't really collapse because we still had a sound... but I came in full force at that time." **Clive Chin**

Vocalist Pat Kelly, also a highly accomplished and fully qualified recording engineer who would also work at King Tubby's, Dynamic and Joe Gibbs studios, was employed as Randy's engineer for a while but he had many other commitments and did not stay very long.

"He was good but then he was an artist not only an engineer..."

Clive Chin

George Philpott was then drafted in from Dynamic Sounds and, together with Clive, engineered Burning Spear's epochal 'Marcus Garvey' sessions at Randy's. Clive was bitterly disappointed when the tapes were then taken to Joe Gibbs' Retirement Road studio for Errol T to mix.

"We had a first engineer from Dynamics called George Philpott... George had the technique of the board because the same board that we had was the same kind that George use to work at Dynamic... the Sound Techniques... "

Clive Chin

"I also worked with Burning Spear on 'Marcus Garvey'... a landmark album... I knew that working with Winston (Rodney) was... there were going to be great moments. The element that Winston brought to recording was that he brought back the horns into reggae music which was lacking from the rock steady time. Not many musicians used horns because the less musicians that you used is the better for them because of the money. But I knew working with Winston was going to be enjoyable... it wasn't hard for me to work with him because he left everything up to the engineer that knew what he wanted, you know. And it wasn't something that was hard for me to do because of the experience I'd had working in the studio before. It brought a lot of exposure for me because it opened a door that wasn't there before and, when the album came out on Island. Bam! It was really brilliant... 'Marcus Garvey' was a very special album."

Clive Chin

But George Philpott only "stayed with us for a couple of months" and Trevor 'Leggo' Lambert told Clive "about Karl Pitterson" who had also previously worked at Dynamic. Karl then replaced George and worked with Clive for eighteen months at Randy's before returning to Dynamic. The pair put together the 'Randy's Dub' album which was released in 1975 in a very limited pressing of only two hundred copies. And Randy's continued to be the place where the hits were made including Keith Hudson's 'Rasta Communication' another key album of the Seventies.

"I worked with Keith Hudson... Keith was a person who was very difficult to work with! You had to understand him... bwoy I tell you! He's not the greatest vocalist but he knew what he wanted and he got what he wanted. He had a presence! It was 'Rasta Communication'... wicked album! I recorded it... took all the overdubs and everything." **Clive Chin**

There are still "tunes right now in Randy's never been released" including a Dennis Brown cut to Augustus Pablo's 'Point Blank', "a Dennis Brown vocal at his best. Fresh! Never released", and "one album's worth of material with Black Uhuru" but Studio 17 was closed down in 1978. Clive recently (2019) starred in a film 'Studio 17 The Lost Reggae Tapes' that tells the story of this unreleased treasure trove of music left behind in Randy's: "I unravelled pretty close to six hundred odd tapes that were buried in the studio".

The shop on 17 North Parade continued to prosper and Miss Pat, remaining resolute in living up to Randy's proud 'You Name It - We Have It' slogan, would often send someone into Joe Gibbs shop at 20 North Parade to buy a few copies over the counter of the latest releases on his label because "Joe Gibbs refused to sell to us because we were right next door". The Chin family moved to New York in 1975 and, after "briefly using the 328 Utica Avenue address of Vincent's sister", they moved on to "a small rental store" at 17-03 Jamaica Avenue in Queens and inaugurated VP Records. In 1979 Vincent & Patricia purchased Raymar House Of Oldies from Mr Kleinholt, a one stop distribution that dated back to the early Thirties, at 170-21 Jamaica Avenue. Miss Pat recalled that Mr Kleinholt's former secretary, Rhoda Bernstein, made "their transition into New York life easier" and VP Record Distributors & Retail Store, "Specializing in Reggae Music, Master Cutting & Dub", would become the world's largest independent label and distributor of Caribbean music.

"All we had were instincts, experience and the music..."
Patricia 'Miss Pat' Chin

Clive Chin subsequently became involved with a number of other projects including running the J&C Kitchen, an 'ital food' store, in the Bronx. Over the years he has released a number of classic Randy's recordings through the VP 17 North Parade imprint, his own Impact! and Above Rock labels and through re-issue specialists including Blood & Fire, Pressure Sounds and Soul Jazz.

"I try my upmost best to keep the authenticity of the label Randy's."

Clive Chin

Clive has "always been at pains to point out other people's contributions to his works and to place his own achievements in the context of Randy's and his father's place, in particular, in Jamaican musical history". Jamaican music had needed a constant, fixed focal point with all the attendant creativity that Randy's Record Store and Studio 17 had provided but this essential role has never been replaced.

"Up to this day certain producers ask me why did you close the studio?"

Clive Chin

After a series of strokes Errol Thompson died on 13th November 2004. Errol always avoided the limelight and reggae researchers and historians, including myself, tell of trying to get Errol to sit down for an interview only for him to be called away on "other business". Arguably the most gifted and distinctive recording engineer in the history of Jamaican music Errol's contribution to the sound of reggae can never, ever be overstated.

"Errol Thompson died in the University Hospital of the West Indies following a stroke. Joe Gibbs said Thompson complained that he felt like 'something burst' inside his head after the session and was hospitalised."

Vincent 'Randy' Chin moved to Miami "to establish a wing of VP" in Miami, Florida but died of diabetes aged 65 on 2nd February 2003 in Fort Lauderdale. Truly "a giant of the Jamaican record industry" his legacy lives on through his wife, Miss Pat, his children and grandchildren. On 6th October 2006 the Jamaican government awarded the Order of Distinction Rank of Officer to Patricia Chin for her contribution to the development of Jamaican music. And, in 2015, she was honoured with the American Association Of Independent Music Lifetime Achievement Award but, in characteristic Chin family style, she modestly recalled.

"My husband would let them practise upstairs in the studio... his contribution will never be forgotten. Some of the artists didn't have shoes but we loved them for who they are... and we're still doing it sixty years later and giving back to our community." **Patricia 'Miss Pat' Chin**

It is a family affair and Vincent and Patricia's sons, Christopher and Randy, are currently at the helm of VP Records in Jamaica, New York where Chris Chin is "well known as something of a mastering master". Daughter, Angela Chung, is in charge of the Miami operation and the "shipping and distribution". Miss Pat "now in her eighties still lives and works in New York an extraordinary woman who today mentors the latest risqué dancehall acts on the VP label".

"I don't go in every day and my two sons and grandchildren do most of the work. Randy looks after the business side and Chris looks after artists and production. My grandson, Stephen, looks after the digital side and my granddaughter, Stephanie, looks after our art and design. But I still keep my ears to the street!" **Patricia 'Miss Pat' Chin**

The company have released more than three thousand titles over four decades "with a catalog of 25,000 recordings, VP is the largest reggae label in the world and has one of the largest catalogs among independent labels in any genre".

"By staying true to their roots VP Records became a crucial link between reggae music and culture and an ever growing market of reggae enthusiasts around the world." **VP Press Release**

"My journey has been full of laughter, struggle and pain but I wouldn't change a thing. I didn't realise how rich our culture was until I travelled to Alaska, Cuba, Mexico, Spain and France and I could see how much people love our music..." **Patricia 'Miss Pat' Chin**

According to 'Reggae The Rough Guide' over 100,000 records were made in Jamaica between 1952 and 1997 and, in an oft repeated fact, more Jamaicans have made a record per head of population than anywhere else in the world. The majority of these records would have passed over the counter at Randy's in downtown Kingston and at VP Records Retail Store in Jamaica, New York. Who would have thought, as Vincent and Pat Chin surveyed the racks of records in their newly opened store on North Parade that, before the century came to a close, every record shop in every town and city all around the world would have its own reggae section expressly dedicated to the music of Jamaica?

Randy's Studio 17
17 North Parade
Kingston

Producers:
Clive Chin, Keith Chin, Patricia 'Miss Pat' Chin, Vincent Chin
& Errol 'Errol T'/'ET' Thompson

Engineers:
Clive Chin, Pat Kelly, George Philpott, Karl Pitterson, Dennis Thompson
& Errol 'Errol T'/'ET' Thompson

Labels: Above Rock, Arrival, Big Hit! (USA), Chappy, Checker Sound, Creative Calypso, Demon, Giant, Hot Shot, Impact!, Jah Guidance, Kaya, Leo, Love, Music Land, Pat's Record, One Way Sounds, Randy's, Roots, Roots From The Yard, Soulful, Tanya, Voice Voice, VP
& Wisdom Sounds Inc

Musicians:

Skin, Flesh & Bones

"I have my own band too called Skin, Flesh & Bones." **Lloyd Parks**

Drums: Lowell 'Sly' Dunbar
Bass: Lloyd 'Sparks' Parks
Guitar: Bertram 'Ranchie' McLean
Organ: Ansel 'Pinkie' Collins & Errol 'Tarzan' Nelson
Percussion: 'Pat'
Vocals: Al Brown

The Soul Syndicate

"The credit belong to Bunny Lee because he was the first one that took us into the studio." **Tony Chin**

Drums: Carlton 'Santa' Davis
(originally Max Edwards & Leroy 'Horse Mouth' Wallace)
Bass: George 'Fully' Fullwood

Rhythm Guitar: Albert Valentine 'Tony' Chin
Lead Guitar: Earl 'Chinna' Smith (originally Alva 'Reggie' Lewis)
Keyboards: Bernard 'Touter' Harvey, Keith Sterling & Oswald 'Ossie'/No Go' Hibbert (originally Glen 'Capo' Adams, Tyrone 'Organ D' Downie & Eric 'Bingy Bunny' Lamont)
Vocalists: Dennis Brown, Donovan Carless, Freddie McGregor & Earl Zero

Randy's All Stars

Musicians include:
Drums: Lloyd 'Tin Leg' Adams, Carlton 'Carlie' Barrett & Michael 'Mikey Boo' Richards
Bass: Aston 'Family Man' Barrett, Val Douglas & Lloyd 'Sparks' Parks
Guitar: Aston 'Family Man' Barrett, Mikey Chung, Alva 'Reggie' Lewis, Errol 'Tarzan' Nelson & Karl Pitterson
Keyboards: Glen 'Capo' Adams, Ansel 'Pinkie' Collins, Tyrone 'Organ D' Downie, Earl 'Wire' Lindo & Robert 'Robbie' Lyn
Tenor Saxophone: Tommy McCook
Trombone: Vincent 'Don D Junior' Gordon & Ron 'Willow' Wilson
Percussion: Eric 'Bingy Bunny' Lamont & Errol 'Errol T'/'ET' Thompson

Paul Coote

HARRY J
HJ 6605-A
YOUNG, GIFTED AND BLACK
BOB AND MARCIA

HARRY J
LIQUIDATOR

HARRY J.
NO MORE HEARTACHES
(The Belltones)
THE BELLTONES
RECORDED BY HARRY J. RECORD-DUHANEY PARK BOULEVARD

Cass Cass
81

HARRY J. RECORD

HARRU
Recorded at
Harry J. Studio
Ja W.I.
Eng. S. Bucknor
Arranged by
SCOTTY
A HARRY J.
Production
Kingston 6.
Produced by
Chung &
Harvey
S KANK IN BED
(D.Scott)
SCOTTY

Noel Hawks

Chapter 4

Young, Gifted And Black
Harry 'Harry J' Johnson

"Harry J? Great producer. Great, great, great producer. One of the best studios... Harry J's studio."
Bunny 'Striker' Lee

Harry Zephaniah Johnson, born 6th July 1945 in the parish of Westmoreland, first entered the music business in the late Sixties. He originally worked both as a warehouse manager and insurance salesman and, consequently, adhered to a strict business oriented approach when he started to make music.

"Harry J was a top salesman in insurance. He was really an educated man who know a lot of things before we. It's I did bring him up here (to the UK) amongst Pama them and him and I is friends all now."
Bunny 'Striker' Lee

One of the first Jamaican record producers to have international hits Harry J would go on to capitalise on his overseas connections. His state of the art recording complex at 10 Roosevelt Avenue was the studio of choice throughout the Seventies for numerous musicians and artists, including Bob Marley & The Wailers, who followed his lead in taking the music out of the Kingston ghettos and onto the worldwide stage.

He was always interested in music from his schooldays onwards and, after watching Byron Lee & The Dragonaires perform, Harry started a band named The Virtues in which he played the bass guitar. The Virtues used to store their equipment at Studio One on Brentford Road and Mr Dodd's musicians would often use their instruments.

"... Coxsone used to borrow my equipment because we didn't have anywhere to keep the instruments so they just stay in Coxsone's studio and make Roland Alphonso and those guys use them. But I was a youth and didn't understand what was going on." **Harry Johnson**

Harry J did not make any recordings with The Virtues, "just experiment", and it was not long before they got into financial difficulties. In addition to his full time job as a warehouse manager he also began work as a salesman for Confederation Life (a Canadian insurance company). As the Sixties drew to a close the rock steady beat that had captivated Jamaica began to speed up and the faster, more aggressive reggae rhythms began to take over. He was one of the first to record this new style of music.

Beth Lesser/Kingston

Harry 'Harry J' Johnson

"Those guys used to come to me and I would say 'look I'm saving money. When I come back I'm going straight into the recording business instead of going with the band'. So these guys used to know me from seeing me at Coxsone...

At the time you had the rock steady and I used to watch Byron Lee when he used to come with his band and people used to say: 'people used to dance like that long ago. In the ghetto they are doing a new dance named reggae'. And you watch the dance and you say 'for them to dance like that you have to have the music going like that.' And I saw my big opportunity there and I produce about three songs..." **Harry Johnson**

All three songs were recorded at Studio One, the first was with Bob Andy, although Harry "didn't bother to release the song" but the second, 'No More Heartaches' by The Beltones who had already hit with 'Dancing Time' and 'Smile Like An Angel' for Coxsone, eventually became a huge hit.

"To get the movement in the recording we had to follow a heavy organ beat. I called Winston Wright into the studio and we develop this organ beat to go with the dance craze and that was the first reggae hit."

Harry Johnson

"The driving sound on 'No More Heartaches' was totally different; we were like outsiders starting something new but didn't know it at the time. The song was Number One on the Jamaican charts for about four weeks which was no easy feat in those days." **Trevor Shields (The Beltones)**

But it was an uphill struggle and, when he was first trying to sell his record, Harry J had to use the experience and persuasive powers he had gained selling insurance as he trod the rounds of Kingston's record shops and distributors trying to interest them in the music with the brand new beat.

"... I used to go out in jacket and tie. And I remember when I put out this record... I took it first to KGs (an influential shop and distributor with premises at Half Way Tree and Cross Roads) and KG said 'we don't want any'. So I said 'okay... just hold twenty five of it and I will come back'. Then I went to another shop and I ask them to take six and they didn't want to buy it so I ask the lady to play it. She played it and I was dancing.

Them think I'm a madman dancing in the sun in a jacket and tie… and it's so hot. A lady saw me in the shop and said 'let me buy one of those records'. And I said 'well I can't sell them. I'm trying to give the store six on consignment' (sale or return). So I said 'see the lady want to buy one.' So the lady said 'leave six with me.' I was glad to see somebody bought one of my records." **Harry Johnson**

Powered by his own unstoppable enthusiasm and the record's frantic beat it was not long before 'No More Heartaches' caught on with the public and Harry vividly recalled the first time his first record was ever played on the radio.

"Then one day somebody said they were going to play the record at the radio station and I was passing Half Way Tree at the bus stop so I stopped like the car break down and turn up the radio and there was this record playing… The Beltones." **Harry Johnson**

'No More Heartaches' hit the Number One spot in Jamaica in late 1968 heralding a new and highly significant phase in the development of the music. Harry J followed this up with 'Cuss Cuss' with Lloyd Robinson, again recorded at Studio One on Brentford Road, and propelled by the unmistakable sound of Coxsone's then current house band The Sound Dimension. This dense, churning song went on to become one of the most popular (and most versioned) rhythms in the history of Jamaican music. And, with his first two releases, Harry J was immediately recognised as a producer to watch.

For his next release, an organ instrumental entitled 'Liquidator', instead of laying a new rhythm track Harry purchased a "cut of the rhythm" of Tony Scott's 'What Am I To Do Now' previously released on the Estick Records label.

"'Liquidator'? Is a man sell Harry J that cut of the rhythm and sell me a cut of the rhythm too. You know him… Sowell who played with The Roots Radics… him is a good guitarist. Harry J put Winston Wright 'pon it and (you had) Tony Scott with 'What Am I To Do Now'. But we never knew about publishing in those days." **Bunny 'Striker' Lee**

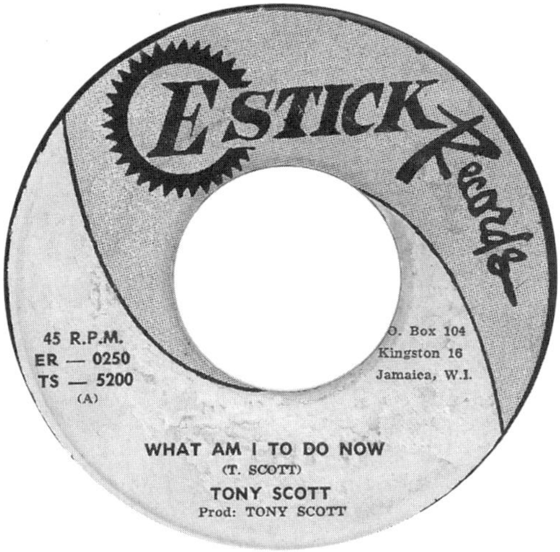

Released through Trojan Records in London on Harry J's UK subsidiary 'Liquidator' was credited to the Harry J All Stars although the record showcased the keyboard talents of the criminally under rated Winston 'Brubeck' Wright. It was largely due to the white 'skinhead' interest in the music at this time that it became one of the first records with a reggae rhythm to enter the UK National Charts reaching Number Nine in the autumn of 1969.

"Winston Wright... not even his name (was) on the label for composing that most famous of reggae tunes: 'Liquidator'." **Chris Lane**

"You see recording you never know what will happen you know. You can't know... Winston Wright just went and just played ('Liquidator') and nobody thought anything of it and then Harry J must have given him $500 and it was a whole heap of money in them times and it was cool."
Jackie Jackson

In addition to Noel 'Sowell Radics' Bailey, "my first session", Lorraine 'Ranny Bop' Williams recalled that he played lead guitar while the other musicians included Lloyd 'Tin Leg' Adams on drums, Aston 'Family Man' Barrett on bass guitar and Jackson Jones on rhythm guitar.
Winston Wright's haunting Hammond organ refrain has ensured its enduring status as a 'golden oldie' on UK radio. 'Liquidator' also achieved

a striking cultural cross over after being adopted by Chelsea, West Bromwich Albion, Wolverhampton Wanderers and a number of other football clubs as an unofficial anthem to play over the PA system as their fans "clapped the players onto the pitch". The bass line from 'Liquidator' (although similar to Alton Ellis' Treasure Isle classic 'Girl I've Got A Date') and its distinctive introduction became the subject of a protracted legal battle when USA gospel group, The Staple Singers, sang 'I'll Take You There' for Stax in 1972.

"The Staple Singers did 'I'll Take You There'. Like I said we never know about publishing them times there... them dispute that all the while."

Bunny 'Striker' Lee

***Appendix 1: Page 200**
'Liquidator' Harry J All Stars

Although he was a relative newcomer to the music business Harry Johnson's understanding of its nuances and what the public wanted to

Pekka Vuorinen

Sylvan Morris at Harry J's

hear were remarkable and, in the spring of the following year, he broke into the UK charts again. Early in 1970 he recorded the talented duo of Bob Andy and Marcia Griffiths, who had previously enjoyed solo success for Studio One, on an upbeat version of 'To Be Young, Gifted And Black'.

"We see Studio One as Jamaica's Motown. Because, any great singer that you can think of that came out of Jamaica, they all pass through Studio One. That's where you graduate...

I didn't actually leave Studio One but I went to Harry J. He actually came to Studio One and talked to myself and Bob Andy and we went to the studio and that's when we recorded 'Young Gifted And Black'."

Marcia Griffiths

When Nina Simone had performed the song there was an underlying bitter irony but Bob and Marcia sounded as if they were truly celebrating being young, gifted and black and transformed the song into an ovation. The original Jamaican release was straight ahead soul influenced reggae but Harry then took the two track tapes to Trojan in London where Johnny Arthey "sweetened the recording" by adding a sympathetic string arrangement.

"I was the first producer to put strings on reggae music... I took up the two track tape with the voice and everything, transfer it to an eight track, and do the strings there..." **Harry Johnson**

Released in the UK on Trojan's Harry J outlet it soared to Number Five in the UK National Charts in March 1970 again largely due to the allegedly racist 'skinhead' audience for reggae. No irony there then. The record was also released in the UK on Pama's Escort subsidiary without the string accompaniment and Bob and Marcia travelled to London to promote the record. 'Young Gifted And Black' "earned a Silver Disc" and was one of the first, and biggest, crossover hits from the period when Jamaican music was first insinuating itself into the UK National Charts and international consciousness. Marcia was already in Europe where she "did two recordings at Philips Records in Berlin in the German language and in English" and, after Bob had flown to England, the duo joined a package tour of the UK and Europe with "other new pop stars of the day including Elton John". Bob later recorded a version of Elton's 'Border Song (Holy Moses)' and, incidentally, Elton covered Bob & Marcia's version of 'Young Gifted

& Black' anonymously for a cut price compilation album of current hits which enjoyed great, if not necessarily lasting, popularity. It was later released on the '16 Legendary Covers As Sung By Elton John' compilation CD.

After the tour had run its course the pair returned to Jamaica and recorded the tracks for the 'Young, Gifted And Black' album with Harry J before flying back to London where they recorded 'Pied Piper', the follow up album, with Bob Andy handling production duties. The title track, a cover of The Changin' Times' recording 'The Pied Piper' (a UK hit for Crispian St Peters five years previously), was another crossover hit stalling just outside the Top Ten on the UK National Charts. The pair toured again and went on to sign to CBS but, as a result of "poor management" and the company's "apathy about promoting reggae", there were no more crossover hits and the association did not last. At that time no one really knew how to manage or promote either reggae music or reggae artists and, with no further crossover hits forthcoming, Bob and Marcia "decided to go their separate ways, at least for now". 'Young, Gifted And Black' was a huge hit all over Europe but, surprisingly, not in America despite a proposed licensing arrangement with Motown in Detroit.

"Motown actually took the record from Trojan and released it in the States. They said they pressed up twenty thousand copies for promotion. So I don't know really. It kinda get tied up in some advance money and all of that. We didn't know what the true facts were behind it..."

Harry Johnson

The Harry J Record Shop in the Kingston Arcade at 79 King Street prospered for a while but Harry sold up in 1971 when "somebody made me an offer" to open up a jewellery store on the premises. The following year he opened his recording studio on Roosevelt Avenue in uptown Kingston.

"When we (Bob & Marcia) left Jamaica, Harry J did not have a studio. When we came back, he had a studio... and a brand new Benz."

Bob Andy

"Back then, we were recording two track and four track sessions so it took great foresight for someone to go all the way to sixteen tracks which brought us on par with the rest of the world... because he had the latest in technology Harry J attracted the best artists of the day."

Stephen Stewart

The equipment was installed by Bill Garnett who had begun his career working with Graeme Goodall at Federal before moving to WIRL as a technician and engineer; he had previously installed the electronics at Randy's and Joe Gibbs' first studio in Duhaney Park. Harry Johnson's sixteen track recording studio was facilitated through Chris Blackwell of Island Records and its opening was another giant step towards Jamaican music becoming a serious commercial proposition.

"He said to me, just at the time the Bob Marley thing was going to launch, if I could get all those things organised for him. I didn't know that Chris had a company that was making consoles and I gave him these records and I went up to England to get a board. And I was thinking of getting an eight track and then he said 'boy, why not get a sixteen track?' and he could get credit for me he said... and that's where it started...

He assist me in selecting the board in terms I would let Bob Marley and all these artists use the studio and then I would take it up to Island Records studio (in London) and mix it...

Johnny Nash came to my studio here and did 'I Can See Clearly Now' with The Fabulous Five Band (in 1972) and took it to England. Bob (Marley) went with him and I was there... Bob was doing harmony for him. He did some Bob Marley tunes and he wanted some back up harmony. The master tape was up there and Bob Andy and Lloyd Charmers and we went into the studio..."

Harry Johnson

Texan Johnny Nash, who played a still undervalued role in the international dissemination of Jamaican music, hit internationally with his cover versions of Bob Marley's 'Stir It Up' and 'Guava Jelly' both recorded on Roosevelt Avenue. Harry J's studio was "committed to maintaining and promoting the essential and unique qualities of Jamaican music while having to come to terms with the demands and prejudices of the worldwide market place" and reggae could no longer be accused of sounding monotonous or crude. The music that emanated from 10 Roosevelt Avenue, with Sid Bucknor as its first engineer, was equal to anything that the rest of the world could offer.

"It might use more sophisticated recording techniques... but the same basic feel remains." **Harry Johnson**

Never losing sight of the roots of the music Harry J rented out the studio to other producers who were shaping the sound of the future of Jamaican music and, inevitably, the ubiquitous Bunny 'Striker' Lee was the first producer to use its facilities... and in doing so made one of the biggest hits of his career.

RECORD RETAILER TOP 40 CHART

WEEK ENDING 4th SEPTEMBER 1971

This Week				Last Week
1.	Stick By Me	John Holt	Agro	2
2.	Teach The Children	Dennis Alcapone	Treasure Isle	1
3.	Trench Town Rock	The Wailers	Tuff Gong	4
4.	Draw Your Brakes	Scotty	Move & Groove	3
5.	Cry To Me	Julian	Gay Feet	5
6.	A Little Love	Jimmy London	Impact	15
*7.	Three In One	Errol Dunkley	Success	20
8.	Black And White	The Greyhound	Majestic	13
9.	Baby Make It Soon	Dobby Dobson	Success	10
10.	Well Dread	Dennis Alcapone	Upsetter	11
11.	It May Sound Silly	John Holt	Moodisc	14
12.	I Love Jamaica	Neville Willoughby	V. & N.	12
13.	Hot Pants	James Brown	Polydor	19
14.	Deep Meditation	Errol Dunkley	Success	9
15	Sunday Morning	Ernie Smith	London	18
16.	Picture On The Wall	Freddie McKay	Money Disc	6
17.	Cool Operator	Delroy Wilson	Agro	7
18.	Peace To You Brother	Hopeton Lewis	Treasure Isle	22
19.	Bridge Over Troubled Water	Jimmy London	Impact	8
*20.	Staga Lee	John Holt	London	34
*21.	Linger A While	John Holt	Syndicate	-
22.	Romp In This Room	Rupie Edwards All Stars	Success	29
*23.	Love Of The Common People	Eric Donaldson	Jaguar	33
24.	I Wanna Be Loved	Ken Parker	Success	30
*25.	Six In One	Ken Boothe	Aquarius	39
26.	Mother Oh Mother	Max Romeo	Opportunity	31
27.	Little Boy Blue	Sidney Elliott	Columbia	32
28.	Rod Of Correction	Clancy Eccles	Clandisc	26
29.	Thinking	Ken Boothe	Aquarius	16
30.	Freedom To The People	The Hepstones	Jo Gib	21
31.	Satta Version	The Abbysinians	Clinch	17
32.	Upsetter Version	Dennis Alcapone	Jo Gib	27
33.	Oh Fari	Bongo Herman & Bunny	Move & Groove	36
34.	Walk With Love	The Maytals	Beverley's	25
35.	Black And White	Gregory Isaacs	Success	-
36.	Chirpy Chirpy	-	-	-
37.	Drums Of Passion	Tony's All Stars	Tony's	-
38.	That Special One	Pat Kelly	Sun Shot	38
39.	Spanish Harlem	Aretha Franklin	Atlantic	-
40.	Tip Of My Tongue	Hortense Ellis	Upsetter	-

*********** Sure Shots

NEW COMERS

1.	God Bless Who Ever Sent You	Heptones	Money Disc
2.	Boy Blue	-	G.G.
3.	Half Past Nine	Righteous Flames	Success
4.	Mother Radio	Joe Higgs	Success
5.	Harbour Shark	The Pipers	Tuff Gong
6.	Seeing The Right Love	Keith Lyn	Dynamic
7.	Black And White	The Maytones	G.G.
8.	I Am A Believer	The Ethiopians	J.J.
9.	Sing Along	Lyric	Lyric
10.	Original Six	Ken Boothe	Studio 1

LA-FUD-DEL RECORDS PRESENTS

CHAPTER ONE TO SIX

"ILL NEVER FALL IN LOVE"

Also available

1. Chapter Six.....Fud Christian
2. Butterfly........Oswald & Calvin
3. Dying Love......The Linkers
4. Bye Bye Love....The Invaders

"La - Fud - Del Records"
187 Spanish Town Rd. Kingston 13. Open Until 8 p.m.

Noel Hawks

"… 'Stick By Me' that was the first tune voiced at Harry J's studio. When a studio opened in Jamaica and they wanted to test it out they always send for me so I'd always travel with a two track version of the tape. John Holt and myself was driving… and John voiced his version of the tune. When I did 'Cherry Oh Baby' a guy called Huey Meaux sent for me… they were trying to blend the soul and the reggae together. So I went to Texas and he asked me to bring some of the tunes that I'd done. And as him hear 'Stick By Me' he said 'this guy's singing flat… but this tune is going to be a hit!' He said 'who wrote the tune?' and I said 'it's a Shep & The Limelites tune. Why you say so Mr Meaux?' He said any tune you can wake up shaving and hum it and sing it when you've heard it once then it's a hit… (sings) 'stick by me… I'll stick by you'. So I came back to Jamaica and just dropped the tune and I have the record now for the longest selling Number One in Jamaica with John Holt. It was the biggest tune in Jamaica for that year… John Holt's biggest local hit. Yeah…

I used to open every studio! Harry J's studio… we used to use it a lot when we couldn't get Channel One. Most of my things were done at Channel One but 'Stick By Me' was the first tune done when Harry J fix up him studio. But me is a man who'd find all the musicians lunch money and then carry them home. Sometimes my car had twenty men in it coming from Harry J's studio with some 'pon the top because I didn't leave anybody on the street. I even bought Robbie Shakespeare a bike."

Bunny 'Striker' Lee

Striker's 'Stick By Me' gained the record for the longest consecutive period at the Number One position in the Jamaican Charts and established the template for Harry J's studio over the ensuing decade as a place where hits, and there were innumerable hits, were created by other producers. Harry Johnson was usually content to ensure that all ran smoothly and efficiently.

"The studio vibes are very relaxing and the place itself is a nice hangout especially when the boss, Harry Johnson, is around." **Stephen Davis**

When Sid Bucknor left in 1974 Sylvan Morris, "ace engineer of simple but powerful dub mixes without electronic effects", took over his position. He had begun his apprenticeship at WIRL with Graeme Goodall and, at the age of nineteen, after a few brief months at Treasure Isle, Sylvan took over from Sid Bucknor at Studio One. He stayed at Brentford Road for six years before moving on to Roosevelt Avenue.

"Sylvan Morris was at Coxsone's studio before moving to Harry J. Plenty of people don't talk about that engineer. And Sylvan Morris was an engineer and technician all in one. You understand? Is he teach Errol Thompson…"

Bunny 'Striker' Lee

The combination of Sylvan Morris' prowess on the board and some of the best equipment on the island ensured Harry J's leading role in Kingston's recording studio hierarchy. Countless classic and internationally successful Jamaican albums from the Seventies, including Bob Marley & The Wailers' 'Burnin'' and 'Natty Dread' and Bunny Wailer's 'Protest' were voiced and mixed at 10 Roosevelt Avenue.

"In Harry J's Studio, though, the group (Bob Marley & The Wailers) is preparing something which might well shake the world. They're laying down overdubs on the rhythm tracks for an album which ought to awaken everyone to the power of this island's music." **Richard Williams**

"Bunny Wailer and Bob Marley them… when Chris Blackwell gave them the money to make the music Harry J's studio them use! Harry J was a sympathetic man and he gave them a bligh." **Bunny 'Striker' Lee**

"When Bob Marley was breaking we join together. It was an organised effort to let Bob Marley carry the weight… we were all enthused and interested. We never even think about making money. We were just thinking about the reggae music and the pride and the satisfaction we get out of it. If we guys was thinking about the money we'd be rich!"

Harry Johnson

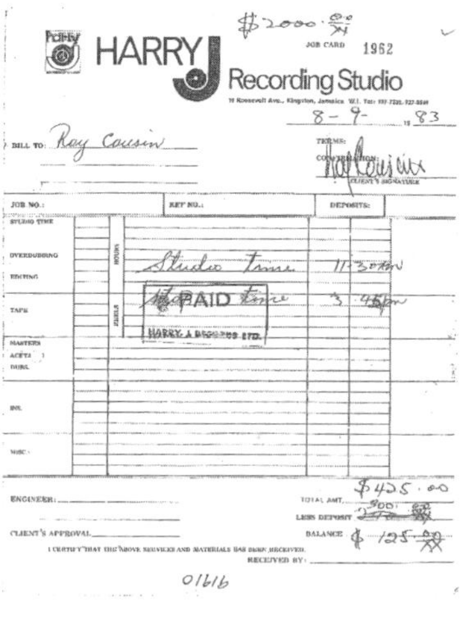
$2000.00
HARRY J Recording Studio
JOB CARD 1962
8-9- 19 83
BILL TO: Roy Cousin
TERMS:
CONFIRMATION: Roy Cousins
CLIENT'S SIGNATURE
JOB NO.: REF NO.: DEPOSITS:
STUDIO TIME
OVERDUBBING
EDITING
TAPE
MASTERS
ACETA
DUBS.
INS.
MISC.
HOURS
REELS
Studio time 11:30 am
PAID time 3:45 pm
HARRY J RECORDS LTD.
ENGINEER:
CLIENT'S APPROVAL
I CERTIFY THAT THE ABOVE SERVICES AND MATERIALS HAS BEEN RECEIVED.
RECEIVED BY:
TOTAL AMT. $425.00
LESS DEPOSIT 300.00
BALANCE $125.00
01616

Roy Cousins

Harry J had come from a business background and saw the value in treating reggae as a business, and although the nature of the business changed as the Seventies progressed, he maintained his position and produced and released a number of classic records. These included 'The Wave Of War', 'World Upside Down' and 'Lay A Foundation' with the inestimable Joe Higgs in 1972 and the same high standards were maintained with 'This Is Reggae Music' from Zap Pow, despite some critics claiming it was not actually reggae music. The subtle mastery of Bob Andy's 'Life' and 'You Don't Know' and The Heptones' acerbic 'Country Boy' were tempered with less serious releases such as a charming version of 'Breakfast In Bed'. Lorna Bennett achieved a worldwide hit in 1972 with her version of Dusty Springfield's 'Breakfast In Bed' written for Dusty's celebrated Memphis sessions. Lorna's outing, produced by Harry J, inspired a memorable deejay version from Scotty entitled 'Skank In Bed'. She became the first female artist to top the Jamaican charts for five years and went on to repeat the feat with 'Going To The Chapel' her cover of The Dixie Cups' 'Chapel Of Love'. Lorna gave up singing to study law and opened a legal practice in the Parish of St Elizabeth but returned to music in the New Millennium when she performed at Christmas Vintage shows and Heineken Startime concerts. The Scotty cut entitled 'Skank In Bed'..."excuse me Lorna"... stopped two thirds of the way through to give an insight into what was occurring in the studio.

"Cut. Cut. Cut. Cut...
Tell me something? What you a doing in my studio?
Want to play something on your tune sir
Tell me something. What the little boy just like ting ting so?
You can play bass?
No sir
You can play drums?
No sir
Eh?
As a matter of fact tell me something...
You can play organ?
Eh?
No sir. You can give me a chance?
Give you a chance?
Leave the studio man. You understand? Leave the studio man. Leave the studio I don't want you inside here. Leave the studio Watch a...
Rhythm come forward!" **'Skank In Bed' Scotty**

Stick By Me
JOHN HOLT
HARRY J.
45 RPM
Harry J. Record
Kingston, Ja.
COWBOY LIFE
(H. Johnson)
WINSTON SINCLAIR
ZAP-POW
DJ
COPY
ONLY
WIP 6277-A
THIS IS REGGAE MUSIC
HARRY
Recorded at
Harry J. Studio
Ja. W.I.
A HARRY J.
Production
COUNTRY BOY
THE HEPTONES
SIOUX
RECORDS
SI 021
SIDE A
Ⓟ 1972
45 RPM
Tulip Music
(M. Johnson)
DISTRIBUTED BY
HARRY J. RECORD
KINGSTON ARCADE
79 KING ST. PHONE 24956
RELEASE
7/6
You Don't Know
Bob Andy
MADE IN GT.BRITAIN
I'LL TAKE YOU THERE
(Alvertis Isbell)
MCPS
2025-110 A
Ⓟ 1972
THE STAPLE SINGERS
Produced & Arranged by Al Bell
GREEN DOOR
Made in England
GD-4047 A
Ⓟ 1972
LIFE
BOB ANDY
Roosevelt
HARRY J
RECORDING
STUDIO
10 Roosevelt Ave.
Kingston 6
Jamaica W.I.
THE WORLD UPSIDE DOWN
JOE HIGGS
HARRY J PRODUCTION Unauthorised Copying Prohibited
NATTY DREAD
Produced by CHRIS BLACKWELL AND THE WAILERS
BOB
MARLEY
& THE
WAILERS
WIP 6212-A
ISLAND
10 ROOSEVELT AVE.
Side B
45 RPM
VERSION
YELLOWMAN, ASHMAN &
WELTON IRE
SUNSET RECORDS
JAYWAX
Producer:
Sheila Hylton
Arranged by:
Sly & Robbie
(The Taxi Team)
THE BEDS TOO BIG
WITHOUT YOU
(STING)
SHEILA HYLTON
HARRY J PRODUCTION Unauthorised Copying Prohibited
Killamanjaro
PROTECTION
Ninja Man & Courtney Melody
ALL RIGHTS RESERVED

Lorna Bennett's album for Harry J, 'This Is Lorna' was the multi talented Clive 'Azul' Hunt's initial introduction to a glittering career in reggae music although, at the time, Clive was still playing trumpet in the 1st Battalion Jamaica Regiment Band.

"Then I was introduced to Geoffrey Chung who wanted me to work on the Lorna Bennett LP after she'd had a big hit with her version of 'Breakfast In Bed'. My first official session was with Lorna Bennett... she's Protégé's mother! It was the same pay for two minutes work as I'd get for two weeks in the army! And I wasn't even aware I was working with the best band in reggae at the time... The Now Generation.

And Geoffrey asked me to come back tomorrow! I was already an accomplished musician... I could read scores and do arrangements so reggae was a very easy thing for me! And I was still in the army! But I now became a regular studio musician... I'd be there whether I was hired or not because I knew chords and arrangements. I played piano, trumpet and bass..." **Clive 'Azul' Hunt**

"I always wanted to have international hits, like hit the British charts and influence the work..." **Harry Johnson**

After producing two excellent albums with The Heptones, 'Book Of Rules' in 1973 and 'Cool Rasta' in 1976, Harry J stepped aside and Danny Holloway was in the producer's chair for their 'Night Food' set which was given heavyweight international promotion by Island Records that same year. And, for the most part, Harry appeared content to be a facilitator, to take care of business, to rent out the studio to other producers and artists and allow them to make their music. The Roosevelt Avenue studios were featured prominently in the film Rockers', directed by Theodoros Bafaloukos, "in a scene that spotlights singer Kiddus I recording 'Graduation In Zion'". The next year Harry enjoyed further international acclaim when Sheila Hylton's update of 'Breakfast In Bed' reached Number Fifty Seven in the UK National Charts and her sultry cover of The Police's 'The Bed's Too Big Without You' went on to reach Number Thirty Five early in 1981.

"Drummer Sly Dunbar and his longtime music partner, bassist Robbie Shakespeare, played on 'The Bed's Too Big Without You'. Dunbar said Johnson was 'steady as a producer, wasn't afraid to tell you what he wanted'."

As the dance hall boom of the early Eighties got under way Harry made a return to producing records and came up with a seemingly unstoppable series of seven inch releases featuring artists including vocalists Echo Minott and Frankie Paul and deejays Yellowman and Welton Irie.

"... for a few years little was heard from him but suddenly, in 1984, the Harry J label began to reappear along with new labels Sunset and 10 Roosevelt Avenue." **Beth Lesser/Kingston**

A number of Ninjaman's earliest records, including 'Protection' with Courtney Melody, were also released on his Killamanjaro subsidiary. These records proved hugely popular and epitomised the more raucous dance hall style, their content somewhat at odds with the refined perfection that Harry J had always championed, and were very, very popular in Jamaica and all around the Caribbean. He explained at the time to Beth Lesser/Kingston:

"It's from a pride thing.... I'm back in the business big and strong."
Harry Johnson

As one of the first Jamaican producers to break the music internationally Harry Johnson went on to use his crossover success to build something lasting and permanent. Harry J's Studio with Sylvan Morris at the controls and the sophisticated roots sound of Roosevelt Avenue, neither Dynamic nor Channel One, defined the sound of crossover reggae. His astute business acumen and licensing arrangements with overseas companies ensured that his recordings reached millions of music lovers all around the world.

"I think the other problem is when artists start doing their own producing. They start hustling now. They give it to somebody in New York, somebody press it in Washington, somebody press it in Toronto, somebody press it in London. You have the same record coming to you in five different packages and that is what's mashing up the business... In my days I used to give it to Trojan. I wait on them to make all the deals... I give it to Island and wait on them to make all the deals." **Harry Johnson**

After a long battle with diabetes Harry Johnson died at the Savanna la Mar Hospital in his native Westmoreland on 3rd April 2013. His very early understanding of how the rest of the world could and would take to reggae music, if it was presented in a palatable yet uncompromised manner, is a testament to his insight and longevity in the business. His groundbreaking work in the late Sixties and Seventies, and the recordings emanating from his superior uptown studio complex, stand forever as Harry J's lasting legacy to Jamaican music.

"Harry J is an A1 producer too. I don't think they've started looking 'pon him for the whole heap of product that he made... some Heptones songs like 'Book Of Rules'... some great Bob Andy songs... Harry J."

Bunny 'Striker' Lee

'Don't Ask My Neighbours' Island Records

Sheila Hylton

Postscript

"In 2000, after seven years of inactivity, Stephen Stewart (Engineer, Producer, Musician), who worked in the early years alongside Sylvan Morris, refurbished, re-equipped and reopened Harry J Studio. Since then under the management of Stephen Stewart the studio has seen the return of people like Burning Spear, Toots, Shaggy, Sly & Robbie and newer projects of Shakira, Papa Sam/Kirk Franklyn, Luciano and Sizzla...

'Harry J pushed the business aspect of the industry, putting deals together and cataloguing his songs (including releases on the Jaywax, Roosevelt, 10 Roosevelt Avenue and Sunset subsidiaries) which were separate from the studio operations... the legacy of the musicianship that has come through here makes Harry J studios really special; it's part of the vision Harry brought to Jamaican music. People come here to capture that live session chemistry where recording is more than just one person using a computer program'."

Stephen Stewart

*Appendix 1
'Liquidator' Harry J All Stars

There are, inevitably, a number of conflicting accounts regarding 'Liquidator' and 'I'll Take You There' and, many years later, Harry J recounted some of the story and the difficulties he had encountered to Beth Lesser/Kingston.

"This guy came over. I think his name was Al Jackson from Muscle Shoals... they used to be down there doing Booker T & The MGs. They used to play with them and they were here just to see what reggae was like. Apparently what he did he was trying instrumentals and he just lay the rhythm and get The Staple Singers to voice it, to just try it, because it was an instrumental. We tried in court but we just didn't get through because he claimed he didn't know anything about it. He said it was just a coincidence."

Harry Johnson

And again to Kingston's *Gleaner* as reported in the *Jamaica Observer*...

"One of the stops Jackson made during his stay in Kingston was the recording studio of producer Harry 'Harry J' Johnson who recalled meeting Jackson and giving him two copies of his label's latest production. The name of the song was 'Liquidator', an instrumental done by (Harry) Johnson's house band, the Harry J All Stars. Built around organist Winston Wright's brilliant soloing, 'Liquidator', was a strong seller in the United Kingdom in 1969. It was the biggest success for Johnson, a former insurance salesman, who started producing in 1968. Three years after his meeting with Jackson, (Harry) Johnson got the shock of his life when he heard a song by gospel group, The Staple Singers, named I'll Take You There'. Its intro was eerily similar to 'Liquidator'...

'I had no doubt it was our song. I couldn't believe it when I first heard it' (Harry) Johnson said.

Noel Hawks

Just Off Spanish Town Road, Kingston

The Staple Singers were signed to Stax Records, a Memphis, Tennessee record company that helped make Otis Redding and Isaac Hayes famous. Booker T and the MGs were the house band at Stax. 'I'll Take You There' was a monster hit and became a rallying cry for the black power movement in the United States. (Harry) Johnson said he took aggressive steps to collect royalties from Stax but made little headway with the company which folded in 1975."

In Rob Bowman's 'The Story Of Stax Records' the Memphis musician, Jimmy Johnson, is credited with taking 'I'll Take You There' to the studio.

"...Island owner Chris Blackwell had given Jimmy Johnson a paid vacation in Jamaica. Johnson took some time to visit local recording studios and record stores, picking up a slew of current Jamaican records along the way. Upon his return he distributed the records to all the members of the Muscle Shoals rhythm section...

In actuality the record's introduction, bass line, and general groove were lifted directly from a 1969 Jamaican instrumental recording by The Harry J All Stars entitled 'Liquidator'... this was probably one of the records Jimmy Johnson had brought back from Jamaica..." **Rob Bowman**

And Tony Rounce has kindly contributed the following...

"I interviewed several members of the Muscle Shoals Rhythm Section at length between 2009 and 2013, and David Hood, who played bass, became a pretty good friend of mine. I asked him what he recalled about the creation of the track for 'I'll Take You There' and David, who has an exceptional memory backed up by copious diary notes dating back to the mid Sixties, said that Al Bell pitched up at Muscle Shoals Sound Studio with a copy of 'Liquidator' (possibly the USA release on A&M) and got him and drummer Roger Hawkins to play along with the record over and over again until he got the riff perfected and Rog' had worked out the drum pattern he was going to use.

The guitarists on the record, the late Jimmy Johnson (who played rhythm) and the late Eddie Hinton (who played lead), worked their parts out as the session progressed. Eddie was filling in for 'Pops' Staples who was supposed to overdub his own solo when The Staple Singers arrived later. The rhythm track was complete before the group even hit town although Mavis Staples was there to put down a guide vocal that was actually used on the finished track which is why she's calling her 'Daddy' to 'play your guitar' over Eddie's solo..." **Tony Rounce**

And, as always, Bunny 'Striker' Lee proffered a more pragmatic approach to what might constitute an 'original' composition, melody or bass line.

"It come like Derrick Morgan and Prince Buster with 'They Got To Come' and 'Forward March' with Harry J's 'Liquidator' when The Staple Singers did 'I'll Take You There'. They disputed that all the while. 'Liquidator' is close to 'Girl I Got A Date'... near to it. You see if I like 'Girl I Got A Date' and I used a couple of bars you wouldn't recognise it because I'd put a swinging bridge in the tune. Make the bass player go right back inna that, then solo, then bridge again, and come back so when you hear it it's a totally different tune. Or you make the bass player play it back ways so you create a new sound. With 'Bongo Natty' that Owen Gray sung for me it was like 'Girl I've Got A Date' with a different intro and it sound like so..."

Bunny 'Striker' Lee

During the 2008 United States presidential election Senator Barack Obama regularly played 'I'll Take You There' on the campaign trail...

Harry J Recording Studio
10 Roosevelt Avenue
Kingston 6

Producer:
Harry 'Harry J' Johnson

Arrangers include:
Bob Andy, Chris Blackwell, Geoffrey Chung, Oswald 'Ossie' Harvey, Danny Holloway & David 'Scotty' Scott

Engineers:
Sid Bucknor, Sylvan Morris & Stephen Stewart

Labels: 10 Roosevelt Avenue, Cancer, Harry J, Jaywax, Killamanjaro, Roosevelt & Sunset

Musicians:

The Harry J All Stars & The Jay Boys
Musicians include
Drums: Paul Douglas & Winston Grennan
Bass: Boris Gardiner & Clifton 'Jackie' Jackson
Guitar: Lynford 'Hux' Brown, Radcliffe 'Duggie' Bryan & Lorraine 'Ranny Bop' Williams
Organ: Winston 'Brubeck' Wright
Piano: Gladstone 'Gladdy' Anderson

The Now Generation
Musicians include
Drums: Martin 'Largie' Sinclair & Leighton 'Sparrow' Thompson later Michael 'Mikey Boo' Richards
Bass: Valentine 'Val' Douglas
Lead Guitar: Radcliffe 'Duggie' Bryan & Michael 'Mikey'/'Mao' Chung
Rhythm Guitar: Geoffrey Chung
Organ: Neville Hinds, Earl 'Wia'/'Wire' Lindo & later Robert 'Robbie' Lyn
Keyboards: Geoffrey Chung, Val Douglas, Earl 'Wire'/'Wia' Lindo later Robert 'Robbie' Lyn
Percussion: Michael 'Mikey Boo' Richards

AMALGAMATED RECORDS
℗ 1968
Island Music
AMG 808
(AMGMX.608A)
THE UPSETTER
LEE PERRY
Producer: J. A. Gibson

AMALGAMATED RECORDS
℗ 1968
B. & C. Mus.
AMG 822
(AMGMX.622 A)
(Amalgamated Records Jamaica)
PEOPLE GRUDGEFUL
SIR GIBBS
Producer J. A. Gibson

DOCTOR BIRD
Amalgamated Records
DB-1068 A
HOLD THEM
(R. Shirley)
ROY SHIRLEY with LYNN TAITT & HIS BAND

PRETTY GIRL
J. GIBSON — L. WINT
DELROY WILSON

AMALGAMATED RECORDS
NEW YORK RECORD MART 11 SOUTH PARADE KGN., JA., W.I. PHONE 22386
arty
MAMA LOOK DEH
(J. Gibson)
THE REGGAY BOYS
With the Blenders

HERE COMES THE JUDGE
(P. Touch)
PETER TOUCH

Noel Hawks

Chapter 5
The Golden Sound Of The West Indies: Joe Gibbs

"There was one man, however, who although starting a little after the others, exercised extreme longevity and success in the music production business..."

Roy Black

"A man who has used his head better than any other single producer since the legendary Clement 'Coxsone' Dodd." **Carl Gayle**

Born Joel Arthur Gibson in Salt Spring, Hanover on 14th October 1942 Joe Gibbs grew up in the resort town of Montego Bay but, in the Fifties and early Sixties, he felt "Mobay was always very quiet and Kingston was the place that had much more excitement". After studying to gain his qualifications in electronic engineering through a Correspondence Course with the National Electronic School in Amercia he worked at the now notorious US naval base at Guantanamo Bay in Cuba. Joe proved to be an excellent technician, in constant demand, and returned to Jamaica to work for a Canadian company who were supervising the island wide conversion to a single electrical frequency.

"I was an electronic technician, specialising in sound and picture, with Stone and Webster, a frequency converter company in Montego Bay. Previously, for example, Kingston was on sixty and Mo Bay was on forty so when the island all moved to one frequency I was busy as a technician running around sorting out the conversion work. Then I came to Kingston (in 1962) and realised that it was much faster than MoBay and decided to stay." **Joe Gibbs**

But, like so many before him, Joe found that the streets of Kingston were not paved with gold and that the living was not particularly easy.

"Joe Gibbs? You have to rate Joe Gibbs so it's not anything bad I'm talking now! When he first came to Kingston Joe Gibbs lived down Gretna Green Road in one little room with just him, a stereo and a single bed. Two people couldn't pass in there!" **Bunny 'Striker' Lee**

Four years later Joe opened his first electronics shop at 32 Beeston Street in downtown Kingston where he sold and repaired radio and television sets and began to sell records too as a way of drawing customers into the shop. Leslie Kong's Beverley's Ice Cream Parlour and Record Shop was situated just over the road in Orange Street and Joe had watched how people were drawn into the Kong brothers' shop to buy music. His background in electronics gave him the confidence to move into music production as he had always been "fascinated by the different frequencies that he heard in the music". Although Joe had no formal musical training he did have a few piano lessons during this time and "around 1967" the legendary drummer Arkland 'Drumbago' Parks gave him some informal lessons too.

"I had a service department at 32 Beeston Street but I wanted something to sell too and, at the time it was difficult to get around the importation of spare parts, so I say let's start selling records. We did that but I always have to buy, buy, buy from these people and I have nothing to sell them. So I said I'll invest some of my money so people can buy from me too. I start going round listening to bands and I find one that I liked. Now because of my radio knowledge I have a good ear for sound so it wasn't difficult to adapt myself to say what would sound good. The first session we had a big hit and hits thereafter." **Joe Gibbs**

Dave Hendley

20 North Parade

For his first recording session Joe recruited Lee 'Scratch' Perry to supervise proceedings, the legendary Lynn Taitt And The Jets and vocalist extraordinaire Roy Shirley. Together they produced 'Hold Them', a Number One hit in 1967 "recorded in one take" in the groundbreaking rock steady style, one of the first, many say the first, rock steady releases. Roy had been inspired to build the rhythm around the sound of a Salvation Army marching band and the record was promptly versioned by Ken Boothe as 'Feel Good' for Studio One; Ken later alleged that he was originally supposed to sing the song with Roy at Studio One. It was through Roy Shirley that Joe got to know Bunny 'Striker' Lee and he "always loved Bunny's vibes". Lee 'Scratch' Perry was also working as an in-house producer and arranger for West Indies Records Limited but, after Striker had helped Joe to promote 'Hold Them', he took over Scratch's role at WIRL. Scratch now became the musical arranger for Joe Gibbs as bass player Jackie Jackson recalled:

"He's like the producer… he's not a musician but he can relate to you what he wants that kind of way." **Jackie Jackson**

Stranger & Gladdy (Wilburn 'Stranger' Cole & Gladstone 'Gladdy' Anderson) gave Joe two of their self produced songs 'Just Like A River (La La La)' and 'Seeing Is Knowing' to release on his Amalgamated label. Both records proved to be huge hits.

"Lee Perry decided to take me to Joe Gibbs with the songs. Joe Gibbs like them and decided to release them for me and Gladdy."

Wilburn 'Stranger' Cole

Joe's first label was named Amalgamated after his electronics company even though "people always had difficulty pronouncing it" and "coming from country" he was often made to feel like an outsider. It was difficult to break into Kingston's relatively closed musical scene and Joe reckoned that you had to be tough to be able to deal with some of the more menacing characters. He often felt excluded and referred to the "clannish vibe" surrounding the studios and producers and, in an attempt to consolidate his reputation, Joe always paid all the artists and musicians he worked with in cash. He recorded extensively in 1968 hitting again with Errol Dunkley's 'Please Stop Your Lying' and again with Hugh Malcolm's 'Good Time Rock' and, perhaps most significantly, with The Pioneers who released a number of important records on Amalgamated as Luddy of The Pioneers recalled.

"Scratch used to move very good with Joe Gibbs and all of us..."

Sidney 'Luddy' Crooks

The group's hits with Joe included 'Jackpot', 'Mama Look Deh', 'Catch The Beat' and 'Long Shot' and The Pioneers proceeded to hit internationally for Leslie Kong's Beverley's label with 'Long Shot Kick The/De Bucket' the following year.

"Scratch was a freelance producer... he's got a good hearing for sound. Joe Gibbs, at the time, he was just the guy who's spending the money. Lee Perry's the guy who could compare with the musicians" **Errol Dunkley**

The b-side to the The Pioneers' 'Jackpot' proved to be one of forerunners for the direction that the music would take over the following decade. Credited to The Creators 'Kimble', a version to 'Seeing Is Knowing', featured Scratch accompanied by various sound effects including breaking bottles and cracking whips acting out the part of Dr Richard Kimble from the popular American television series, 'The Fugitive', starring David Janssen. Scratch then became 'The Upsetter' on one of his best ever records, also known as 'I Am The Upsetter', which was a forceful musical attack on his former employer Clement 'Coxsone' Dodd. The always inspirational Lynn Taitt was double tracked playing two different guitar lines and the record gave Scratch the name for his own label when he left Joe Gibbs the following year. According to Scratch he left Joe because he felt that he was receiving neither the proper financial credit nor his rightful recognition. But, after their bitter parting, they began again to enjoy a great rapport despite Scratch's musical riposte to Joe Gibbs, 'People Funny Boy', released on his own Upsetter label soon after leaving Joe's employ. It was one of the first records with the faster reggae beat where, to the melody of 'Jackpot', Scratch adopted the same vindictive, vengeful stance against Joe that he had previously taken against Coxsone. Joe replied by versioning the tune as 'People Grudgeful' where 'Sir Gibbs', in turn, admonished Scratch.

Joe Gibbs' first recording studio, "a simple but effective two track studio modelled on the studio at Federal Records", was installed by Bill Garnett on Burns Avenue in the Duhaney Park district of Kingston towards the end of 1968 although Joe had already done some basic recording at the rear of his retail premises.

"I started off in 1967 with my two track studio in the back of the shop here… " **Joe Gibbs**

Following Lee Perry's departure Winston Holness, a young record salesman and freelance producer known as 'Niney' after he lost a thumb in an accident at work, began to work for Joe on a freelance basis in 1969. Niney was already a well known character on Orange Street and Joe laughed as he recalled that "Niney liked working for me because I always paid cash".

"That was just my night time work because I used to work for Bunny Lee during the days and Scratch. Night time was like my hustling with Joe Gibbs, earn some extra money." **Winston 'Niney' Holness**

"Niney was a salesman for me and so Niney became one of the best salesmen for Pama and myself in Jamaica. I bought him a bike and he'd go to every dance promoting the tune them until every sound man in Jamaica knew Niney." **Bunny 'Striker' Lee**

Working with Niney was another way of keeping up with Kingston's musical in-crowd and together they helped to set the pace in 1969 with two very early prototype dub records featuring radical mixing techniques:

'Navado Joe'/'Straight To The Head' and 'News Flash Version 1'/'News Flash Version 2' were both credited to Joe Gibbs & The Destroyers.

"I did name Destroyer before. When I decide to start out on my own I remember Lee Perry come down and said to me 'I am The Upsetter so you can't destroy me…'" **Winston 'Niney' Holness**

'Spaghetti Western' films were very popular and innumerable records with themes inspired by these films were produced. The Destroyers hit with their tribute to Franco Nero, 'Franco Nero (Versions 1 & 2) whose breakthrough role as the title character in Sergio Corbucci's 'Django' in 1966 had made an indelible impression in Jamaica. Niney would go on to an impressive, inventive career with his innovative dubs being "among the first to feature sound effects and disruptive false starts and breaks". The style would later become commonplace but was practically unheard of in 1969 and these releases, along with the aforementioned 'Kimble', were early indications of how dub would gradually develop.

Joel 'Joe Gibbs' Gibson

Noel Hawks

At the beginning of 1972 an album entitled 'Dub Sequeldo' was advertised through Joe Gibbs' Mail Order Service at the astonishing price of fifty dollars. At the time a vocal album would have cost approximately four dollars and the astronomical price indicated just how exclusive the music was. Unfortunately a copy of 'Dub Sequeldo' has yet to be located. Perhaps no-one could afford it? Towards the end of the year Joe Gibbs was one of the first Kingston producers to release a full length dub album: the subtle and obscure 'Dub Serial' which was probably mixed by Joe... who remarked "why would I want to employ an engineer?". Pressed in very limited numbers with a cover featuring a moody shot of foundation deejay Johnny Lover it is now one of the rarest, and consequently one of the most expensive, dub albums. At the time dub was still a strictly underground phenomenon and interest in it was restricted to sound systems and their followers. The set included primal drum and bass versions to one of the earliest versions of The Abyssinians' 'Satta A Massa Gana', (which Joe used for Peter Tosh's denunciation of European colonialists on 'Here Comes The Judge') and Burning Spear's 'He Prayed'. Big Youth would transform 'He Prayed' into 'Joe Frazier' on two records celebrating the 'Sunshine Showdown' in Kingston when George Foreman fought Joe Frazier the following year.

"In the early days the music came out on seven inch records with an a-side and a b-side and dub plate was for the sound man alone. The majority of the early dubs we did make were made for the sound systems. Me did never believe in it at the beginning but the public became interested and it brought the sound system business into the record business." **Roy Cousins**

Joe's first record shop, the Parade Record Shack, was situated on the corner of South and West Parade but in 1969 he opened the New York Record Mart at 11 South Parade with Cecil 'Nicky' Thomas running errands and working behind the counter for a while as a salesman before he scored a hit in 1970 in the UK National Charts when his version of 'Love Of The Common People'. The record reached the Number Nine position and was one of the earliest Jamaican records to cross over and enjoy mainstream success and Nicky moved to London to capitalise on his hit. The Pioneers had already made the move but "because they enjoyed considerable UK success they are now unjustly overlooked..." yet their early international success should not be so readily written off. For countless thousands of record buyers these hits were their first experience of "the sound of young Jamaica".

"... and, through the years, I've made people like The Pioneers and Nicky Thomas what they are today. They're still my favourite artists although, of course, I don't produce them now." **Joe Gibbs**

The shop was a success from the outset, "it was in a great location and people would come off the buses straight into the shop" and, when the lease expired, Joe moved to 20 North Parade "right next door to Randy's". Joe's record production also continued from strength to strength hitting with early deejay records such as Sir Lord Comic's 'Jack Of My Trade', Winston Scotland's 'Skanky Dog' (credited to Bunny Flip) and Dennis AlCapone's 'Upsetter Version'. Peter Tosh's updates of 'Maga Dog' and 'Them A, Fi Get A Beaten' and the sublime 'Here Comes The Judge' were all recorded at the Duhaney Park studio.

In 1971 Joe started work on a new studio complex and pressing plant at 24 Retirement Crescent, Cross Roads, Kingston 5. It would take another two years to complete.

"When you have a hit you're always having problems. If a pressing plant have one or two hits going and your record seems to be standing in the

Al Fingers

Bunny 'Striker' Lee's Recording Studio, Duhaney Park

way all them have to do is just don't give you your record. So I needed a pressing plant... and I realised that the recording scene was getting a bit sophisticated so two track wasn't going to do this thing no more. So I decided to build a new studio and consolidate everything with the factory and form a company instead of just operating as a sole trader. So I acquired sixteen track recording facilities..." **Joe Gibbs**

"Joe Gibbs' sixteen track Sound Techniques console was purchased from Dynamic." **Clive Chin**

The Duhaney Park studio was sold to Bunny 'Striker' Lee whose humorous recollections of purchasing the premises demonstrated just how much Joe's business acumen had developed since he first arrived in Kingston.

"And then when he moved out to build a new studio he decided to sell me his old one... at a price. We agreed the price but he moved out all the things into the other one. I got the empty building and after he had raised the price too! I didn't know at the time that him and the neighbours were not getting on and that the area wasn't a commercial area... not like the sort of place you'd put a studio. So after I did buy it I decided to fix it up and I put King Tubby's sound in it. And the amount of police that did turn up and cordon off the area! It's a good thing I did know some of them!

So after I'd bought it from him I had to lock it up! I had it locked up for about fourteen years and continued using Harry J's and Tubby's studios until a long time after when I put in my things and me and the local people work. They got to know me so they didn't bother to report me. Some had died off and some had gone to foreign. It was a good studio because when Joe Gibbs did have it... he did 'Maga Dog' there with Peter Tosh. It was a strong PNP area but Joe Gibbs was a Labour man (JLP) 'pon the other side and when I came they said 'we've got rid of one and now another one come back with a sound system'. So..."

Bunny 'Striker' Lee

Errol 'Errol T'/'ET' Thompson had been introduced to Joe Gibbs by Niney when Errol was working at Randy's... 'Gibbo you want engineer?'... and they rapidly established a rapport. Errol would often work on Joe's sessions at Randy's and also 'moonlighted' at Duhaney Park and Retirement Crescent after finishing work at Randy's. This developed into a full time working relationship in 1975 when Errol moved on from Randy's to work with Joe in his new studio which "took reggae to another level through complex productions expertly mixed by ET". Joe Gibbs and Errol Thompson became known as 'The Mighty Two' and the pair worked closely together for the rest of their careers. Joe remarked that "teamwork and fun" were the key elements in putting their productions together.

"Many players say that, in terms of engineers and layout, Joe Gibbs is the most pleasant studio to work at." **Stephen Davis**

"Errol T was a great engineer. I think he was the best engineer. He learnt his trade up at Coxsone's with Sylvan Morris." **Bunny 'Striker' Lee**

The 'African Dub All Mighty' series, produced by The Mighty Two, brought together many of the elements of Jamaica's mid-Seventies dread and dub drenched music and made it into a wholly complete and readily accessible musical form. As the series progressed Errol T increased and amplified the electronic trickery and sound effects. It speaks volumes for Joe and Errol's musical and technical expertise that they were able to take so much of the cutting edge and quite seriously avant-garde to fashion and produce a package that was able to cross over to the rest of the world in such an explosive manner. Very few producers could hope to approach the success of The Mighty Two and their willingness to experiment gave their records an indefinable edge. "Errol T was instrumental in capturing and crafting the sound of recorded reggae as the style developed" and nothing was excluded if Errol and Joe, together with the aptly named Joe Gibbs & The Professionals house band, thought it would help to make another hit record.

"... cuckoo clocks, low flying space ships, doorbells, dentist's drills, telephones, babies crying, flies being swatted and all the other Errol T sound effects." **Dave Hendley**

Joe and Errol introduced some of Kingston's more innovative artists to the latest recording techniques and fashioned a commercial form that proved every bit as popular abroad as it did in Jamaica. This "creative incongruity" was achieved by seriously hard work. The Mighty Two would usually mix the dubs together and Joe's background in electronics proved very useful as he contributed ideas for the quirky noises although, by his own admission, he never had great rhythmic sense and was never much of a dancer. The other members of the team would tease him mercilessly, "if Gibbo danced then the tune caan hit"," but he had a great feel for music and The Mighty Two would demand take after take until the feel was right.

"Often we would cut a tune three or four times. The last cut would be mine and the one with the best feel." **Joe Gibbs**

In 1977 Culture, fronted by the charismatic Joseph Hill, found crossover success with the music they created for The Mighty Two with an audience who had decided that there was more to this music than Bob Marley & The Wailers. Their apocalyptical dread sermonising on the 'Two Sevens Clash' single captured the mood of the times perfectly. The power of their earnest seriousness persuaded many Jamaicans to take the prophecy, Marcus Garvey's warning of dread catastrophe that would befall the country in 1977, quite literally.

"People thought something was going to happen in 1977... but sometimes people misunderstand songs and put the wrong meaning on them. They were looking for something but I don't think Joe felt it was going to be taken that far..." **Pauline Hill**

'Two Sevens Clash', the album that followed, thrust Culture to the musical forefront internationally and forever afterwards it has been cited in innumerable influential 'Best Ever Albums' lists. It might well have been fashionable to sing about 'reality' at this time but, despite the ever changing styles and fashions in Jamaican music, Culture never ever deviated from the straight and narrow way over the next three decades.

"The songs that Joe played in his time... people looked at them very seriously... they're not just ordinary songs. People will listen and feel that they're in church....

We need to listen to the words of the songs of Bob Marley, Burning Spear, Dennis Brown, Garnet Silk, Luciano... and Culture. Their songs have to live on so we can stop the fussing and fighting. We need more educational songs... songs that put you into a meditation. We have to be careful what we teach our children..." **Pauline Hill**

'Two Sevens Clash' was "a major influence on London's emerging punk scene" and the cover of Joe Gibbs & The Professionals' 'State Of Emergency' album, portraying the Jamaican security forces apprehending suspects, was appropriated by The Clash for their 1977 'White Riot' seven inch picture sleeve.

The Mighty Two's recordings were full of hook lines and melodies yet remained dynamic and aggressive and it was these contradictory elements that helped to give their music its edge. One of the most prevalent and popular fashions from the mid-Seventies was the adaptation of Sixties rock steady and reggae songs to the then current 'rockers' rhythms as exemplified by the Hoo Kims at Channel One. The Mighty Two, alongside the Hoo Kim brothers, were responsible for many of the biggest hits of this genre. Many of their updates or 'do-overs' eventually became far better known than the originals: The Gaylads' 'Joy In The Morning' became Bobby Melody's 'Jah Bring I Joy' and The Heptones' 'I've Got A Feeling' was transformed by Culture into 'I'm Not Ashamed'.

"But the floodgate was opened in 1976/77 when a new youth audience on the UK and Kingston lapped up rejuvenated Studio One and Treasure Isle rhythms..." **Steve Barrow & Peter Dalton**

IRON SIDE
DISC
JOE FRAZIER
(Scorcher)
Burning spears
MORRIS TUFFEST
Ultra Sound
LOVE HAS FOUND ITS WAY
DENNIS BROWN
PRESSURE BEAT
NEW YORK RECORD MART 11 SOUTH PARADE KGN., JA., W.I. PHONE 22386
JACK OF MY TRADE
(The Whip)-J. Gibson
SIR LORD COMIC
GIBBS
RECORD
GLOBE
Foreman vs Frazier
J. GIBSON
BIG YOUTH
PRESSURE BEAT
GOOD TIME ROCK
HUGH MALCOLM
JOGIBS
RECORD GLOBE
Straight To The Head
J. Gibson
Johnnie Lover
GIBBS
RECORD
GLOBE
CHUKY NO LUCKY
BIG YOUTH
TROJAN RECORDS
TR-7750 A
LOVE OF THE COMMON PEOPLE
NICKY THOMAS
AMALGAMATED RECORDS
JUST LIKE A RIVER
JOGIB
RECORDS
NEW YORK RECORD MART 11 SOUTH PARADE KGN., JA., W.I. PHONE 22386
A JOE GIBBS PRODUCTION
NAVADO JOE
(J. Gibson)
JOE GIBBS & THE DESTROYERS
ERROL T
CREATED BY THE FATHER
(D. Brown)
DENNIS BROWN
TOWN-N-COUNTRY
RECORD
KNOTTY KNOTS
(Joe Gibbs)
I ROY
MADE IN JAMAICA
UNAUTHORISED COPYING PROHIBITED
JOE GIBBS ROOTS SOUND
BIG IRON
(M. ROBBINS)
NIGGER KOJAK
Belmont
BURN BABYLON
SILFORD WALKER
CRAZY JOE
NO CHILDREN DON'T CRY
(A. CAMPBELL)
AL CAMPBELL
MADE IN JAMAICA
UNAUTHORISED COPY OF THIS RECORDING IS STRICTLY PROHIBITED
CRAZY
JOE
PRODUCERS TROPHY
Joe Gibbs
MR. BOJANGLES
MADE IN JAMAICA

The success story of 'Uptown Top Ranking' provides an illustration of how popular, and populist, their work could be. In 1977 Joe and Errol had decided that the time was right for updating the legendary Alton Ellis' classic 'I'm Still In Love' originally recorded ten years previously for Studio One. Alton Ellis had written many of his greatest ever songs while trying to come to terms with the breakup of his marriage and his enduring love for his wife, Pearl, was translated into the aching, heartbreaking 'I'm Still In Love'. Marcia Aitken sang the song for The Mighty Two as 'I'm Still In Love With You Boy' and Joe and Errol followed this with a version from Wade 'Trinity' Brammer the deejay currently carrying the swing. Trinity's unashamedly sexist boast, 'Three Piece Suit', detailed, down to his "earthman shoes" and "diamond socks and t'ing", just what a dapper dresser he was and how irresistible all the girls found him. 'Three Piece Suit' was a massive hit and an album of the same name from Trinity followed soon after.

The Mighty Diamonds sang a much slower, yearning version of the song for the Hoo Kims on a Channel One 'Economic Package' seven inch release which segued into an uncredited I Roy version. Ranking Trevor then deejayed over The Mighty Diamonds version hitting back at Trinity with 'Three Piece Chicken And Chips'. Coxsone dusted down his stampers and re-released Alton's original while Doreen Schaeffer sang a further version on Coxsone's original rhythm coupled with a 'duet' with Alton entitled 'Still In Love Part Two'. Trinity's younger brother, Robert Brammer, also a highly accomplished deejay under the nom de mic of Clint Eastwood, then announced he was "tougher than Trinity, harder than Dillinger…" on 'Badder Than You'. Bunny 'Striker' Lee, inevitably, got in on the act with Alton's sister Hortense Ellis deejaying as Queen Tiney on 'Natty Dread Time', "more cut, different fashion", while Hortense sang the song as 'I'm Still In Love With You Boy' too. Alton also returned to the song with a self produced version of 'I'm Still In Love With You' for the London based Bam Bam label. The rhythm was running hot! The Mighty Two gave the ladies a voice too with Althea & Donna's 'Uptown Top Ranking' whose lyrics were a direct response to Trinity's macho bragging. It was a moderate seller in the reggae market where the jokes made perfect sense if you knew the records that had led up to its release but it did not stop there. In fact it was only the beginning.

"While on the subject of the khaki suited sisters there was a pretty funny article in *Sounds* the other week that probed into the social significance of 'Up Town Top Ranking' and Althea and Donna's relevance to women's rights in the distinctly male dominated isle of Jamaica." **Dave Hendley**

Towards the end of the year it was played on UK National Radio by John Peel, a reggae aficionado, who was in on all the jokes. The infectiousness of Althea and Donna's innocence and the power of Joe Gibbs & The Professionals' cut of the rhythm touched a chord with the listeners and Radio One playlisted the record. It shot to Number One in the UK National Charts in January 1978.

"... they were the first female deejays to appear on the scene and they completely displaced all their male counterparts. They even displaced Paul McCartney & Wings' 'Mull Of Kintyre' in their climb to the top of the British Charts where they remained for four weeks! Althea and Donna's style was very unique and everyone could relate to their lyrics. They were saying 'although we are from uptown and we are top ranking we can relate to the happenings of the downtown people'." **T 'Boots' Harris**

'Uptown Top Ranking' had begun as an answer record: a reply to a record that the people who were now purchasing it were probably unfamiliar with which, in turn, had been released in response to a Seventies version of a Sixties Jamaican classic that they had definitely never heard of. The duo's appearance on BBC Television's 'Top Of The Pops' was unforgettable for all the wrong reasons as the session band tried unsuccessfully to recreate the feel and the drive of the Jamaican rhythm. And, although Althea & Donna failed to follow up the record, they are still fondly remembered.

Dennis Brown, who Joe described as "a unique talent... in a class by himself", was "the most consistently successful solo performer to record for The Mighty Two" and many of the greatest recordings of Dennis' illustrious career were recorded under their auspices.

"'Niney brought Dennis Brown to me about 1970/71, and told me he had potential and that I should take care of him. We became very close.' The rest was history. Brown was undoubtedly Gibbs' most successful act, putting out hit after hit, too numerous to mention." **Roy Black**

Dennis had worked with Joe and Niney on the original version of 'Money In My Pocket' at Duhaney Park in 1972 and, the following year, Niney recorded a series of records for his own Observer label with Dennis Brown and The Soul Syndicate that took the Jamaican musical scene by storm. Their string of hits included 'Africa', 'I Am The Conqueror', 'No More Will I Roam', 'Tribulation' and 'Westbound Train'.

"Niney was a great producer and Dennis was young and learning as he sung..." **Yvonne Brown**

The depth of expression and feeling in Dennis Brown's music with The Mighty Two touched a chord, in 1978, their 'Visions Of Dennis Brown' album set musical and lyrical standards that have rarely been bettered. Initially the LP was only available in the UK as an expensive 'pre-release' import but, despite the prohibitive price, it went straight to the top of the UK reggae charts and stayed there. It was voted reggae album of the year by two leading UK music papers, *Black Echoes and Melody Maker,* before it was released in London through Lightning Records. Dennis' update of 'Money In My Pocket' went on to reach Number Fourteen in the UK National Charts in the spring of 1979.

"Through his appointed field: music, he has realised its potential of communication/education and the role it should assume in this age as an expression for self definition and self determination." **Patrick Griffith**

A version to Clive 'Azul' Hunt's (as The In Crowd) 'Milk And Honey' was one of the standout tracks on 'Visions Of' and Clive was instrumental in the creation of Dennis Brown's 'Foul Play' follow up album, which he produced with Joe Gibbs. Clive also wrote two songs, 'On The Rocks' and 'Come On Baby', for the set which was released internationally through A&M Records in 1981.

"Errol Thompson approached me when I was working with The Abyssinians at Joe Gibbs studio (on the group's essential debut album 'Forward On To Zion'/'Satta') and asked me if he could use 'Milk And Honey' on Dennis Brown's 'Visions' album and he wanted to use my (original) rhythm. But there was no space left on the original eight track tape...

Noel Hawks

The 'Foul Play' album was another significant album for me... I'd sing the guide vocals for the musicians although Dennis was in the studio every day... often playing cards or dominoes while we put everything together. I moved the gambling table inside the studio! Joe Gibbs wasn't sure if some of the songs I'd worked on were really Dennis' type of song but the next thing I knew Dennis Brown was signed to A&M on the strength of those songs." **Clive 'Azul' Hunt**

The following year saw the release of 'Love Has Found Its Way' on A&M co-produced by Willie Lindo, Joe Gibbs and Dennis Brown. This soul influenced album was a big hit and the smooth, sophisticated title track touched the lower reaches of the UK National Charts and attracted

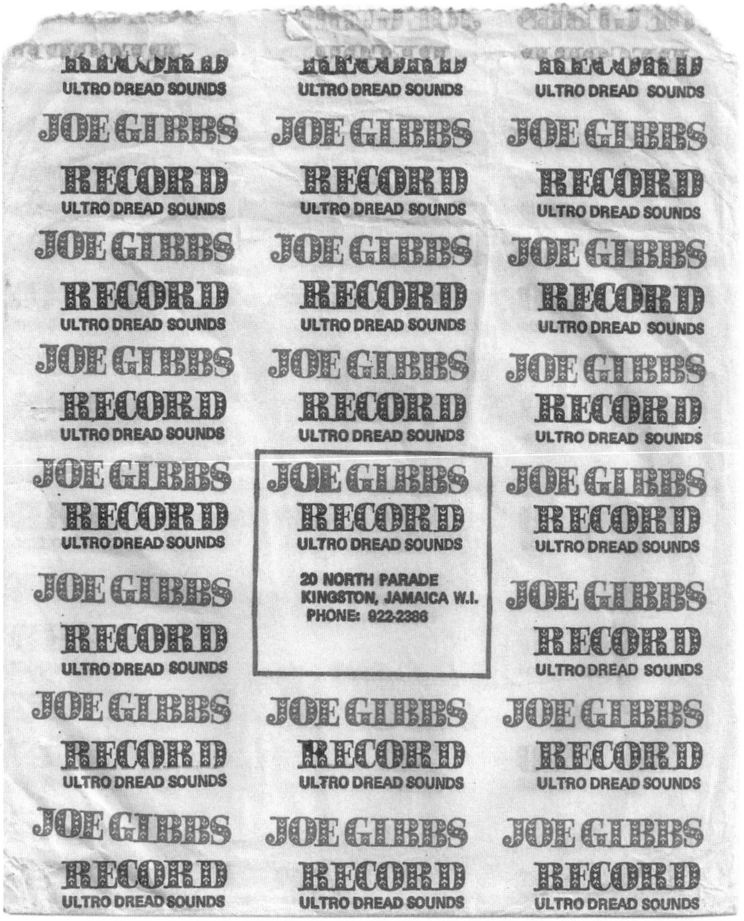

Noel Hawks

a great deal of interest in the USA. It was described in 'Reggae The Rough Guide' as "the nearest a reggae album can get to the international pop audience without losing something very vital in the process".

The pair ran regular auditions together searching for new talent to work with and, from the beginning, Joe would handle the ones with a more 'gimmicky' feel while Errol T would deal with the ones with a more roots based content. If Joe heard a conscious song "I would a say... boy you better make sure Mr T like it". Nothing ever succeeds quite like success and, during the latter half of the Seventies, few producers came near to succeeding like the success of the productions of The Mighty Two. "The duo worked on over one hundred Jamaican Number One hits" and were inevitably accused of over reliance on previously popular formats. Their work together was at the forefront of roots reggae's big breakthrough and captured the mood of the times perfectly yet the pointed 'commercial dread' epithet has somehow become the accepted, but wholly erroneous, view of their productions.

"Often we would cut a tune three or four times. The last cut would be mine and the one with the best feel." **Joe Gibbs**

A number of characters from Kingston's musical frontline assisted The Mighty Two including deejay Prince Far I who "was the security guard at Joe Gibbs Studio". Vocalist Enos McLeod was also the gateman at Joe Gibbs' Retirement Crescent studio and "all strangers who come to Gibbo's HQ must pass him before they can enter the studio." Another vocalist, Ruddy Thomas, often engineered there too.

"Ruddy Thomas is the same as Flick Wilson. He started as Flick Wilson… you had an American comedian named Flip Wilson… so you know. ET taught him and he was an engineer at Joe Gibbs and he started to sing. He was the curtain raiser for Dennis when Dennis came to England for the first time…" **Bunny 'Striker' Lee**

Ossie Hibbert, another stalwart on the scene, worked closely with The Mighty Two and gave two of his albums to The Mighty Two to release on the Joe Gibbs Record Globe label in a rather unorthodox licensing deal which probably tells you more about the history of the Kingston recording business than an entire library of scholarly tomes.

"Errol Thompson was driving this car! So I gave Joe Gibbs two albums, 'United Dreadlocks' and 'Earthquake Dub', and Errol T gave me the car. Flick (Ruddy Thomas) was there learning the job… he used to carry youths to Errol and Gibbo." **Ossie Hibbert**

"'Earthquake Dub'… best seen as a more militant extension of the second and third sets in the 'African Dub' series." **Steve Barrow & Peter Dalton**

Dave Hendley

Joseph 'Big Joe' Spalding

Dave Hendley

Herman 'Bongo Herman' Davis

Dave Hendley

Left to right: Lloyd 'Sparks' Parks (obscured), Winston 'Bo Peep' Bowen, Eric 'Bingy Bunny' Lamont, Bernard 'Jah Satta' Collins, Maurice 'Blacka Morwell' Wellington, Ruddy 'Flick Wilson' Thomas seated in foreground (studying the paper), Franklyn 'Bubbler' Waul in doorway and Chris Lane standing to the right

But the level of success that Joe and Errol enjoyed will always attract jealous criticism and their popularity with reggae's crossover market led one seasoned, if rather cynical, observer to complain about everyone "...singing the praises of anything else that appears on the Joe Gibbs label". Sly Dunbar recalled being bawled out on stage "you think it's Channel One and Joe Gibbs tunes we a play?" by Peter Tosh.

Joe recalled that "teamwork and fun" were the key elements in their productions together and the Retirement Crescent premises were one of the most popular and in demand studios in Jamaica and, on occasion, even Dennis Brown found it hard to book studio time for productions for his DEB label.

"At the moment I use Joe Gibbs' to cut the rhythm, you get a nice sound down there, you know. Then I usually take the tapes over to Tubby's for the mix and some of the voicing although I sometimes do vocals at Joe's.

Well you know how it goes with Errol... he's always got a lot of work on you know... like he's always pretty busy that if I waited for him to find time to do my thing I'd... well I'd sort of be waiting for ever." **Dennis Brown**

In the early Eighties Joe established a record distribution outlet in Florida, USA and The Mighty Two began to work in the dance hall style. Rising stars, including Barrington Levy on 'My Woman', and established luminaries such as Dennis Brown, with 'Let Me Love You' and 'A Little Bit More', ensured their continued presence in the upper reaches of the hit parade.

"Remaining active for a long time in this competitive market was not an easy task, bearing in mind the myriad changes the music went through and the accompanying readjustments to technique that would have been necessary to keep abreast of the music. Many either slacked off or retired after about a decade..." **Roy Black**

In a more sentimental style The Mighty Two recorded a version of 'Someone Loves You Honey' with JC Lodge which would not only become their biggest ever international hit but would also "result in the closure of his studio".

"We were trying to promote my boyfriend Errol O'Meally's song writing, not my singing, and, after it had been auditioned by several music industry characters, we ended up at Joe Gibbs Recording Studio.

There was always a line of hopefuls but they took our cassette and told us to come back, come back, come back. It took months but we stuck with it, returning week after week, after week, after week. Finally we were asked 'who's singing on the tape?'... they were more interested in me than the songs!"

JC Lodge

And, for the first time, JC entered the studio to voice for The Mighty Two who recommended a cover version of Captain & Tennille's then current hit 'Do That To Me One More Time'.

"That track was like a test run and didn't cause much of a stir. As far as I know Joe Gibbs only released it in the Bahamas. In retrospect it seemed they were still searching for the song, they believed, would be the right launching single which turned out to be 'Someone Loves You Honey'."

JC Lodge

Written by Don Devaney the song had been a huge hit for Charley Pride in 1977 and was the first of JC's "tracks to be released in Jamaica and other territories around the world". In 1980 her interpretation, produced by Joe, ET and Willie Lindo, was released on a Belmont seven inch single in Kingston and on a Joe Gibbs Music twelve inch disco in Miami in combination with a deejay version, 'One Time Daughter', from George Nooks as Prince Mohammed . The record was a massive reggae hit:

the seven inch release topped the Jamaican charts and the twelve inch version was huge in the American reggae market. The record then went on to even greater success in Europe reaching Number One in Belgium and the Netherlands too where it earned gold and platinum discs before going on to become the top selling single of 1982.

"We did an album which included a couple of Errol's (O'Meally) songs and I was offered a lot of work but I wasn't ready. I hadn't planned on pursuing a career as a singer... and I was petrified. I liked acting... I was in a number of Louis Marriott plays and revues as well as playing a role in the popular TV soap 'Royal Palm Estate'... but acting and singing are two different things. I think now maybe I could have done more in the early stages. Errol did his best to coach me and ensured that the 'wolves' were kept at bay." **JC Lodge**

But, as JC's popularity increased, Joe Gibbs' fortunes came to an abrupt halt when "an improper song writing credit" for 'Someone Loves You Honey' landed him in copyright problems. The ensuing commotion allegedly bankrupted the producer and also "resulted in the closure of his studio" which remained inoperative until 1993.

"I thought Joe had an endearing, gentle fatherliness about him when we spoke privately that made you feel he had your interests at heart. I wish this had followed through in his business dealings. Some people thought that I sued Joe and others thought I'd been sued along with him but I hadn't done anything wrong! And, when it came to money, we got something but nowhere near what it should've been. " **JC Lodge**

The Mighty Two now concentrated on Joe's Kingston supermarket, which was managed by Errol, and "for the better part of a decade Joe Gibbs was chiefly concerned with his downtown Kingston grocery store". Joe's son, Carl 'Rocky' Gibbs, continued the family's musical tradition by re-releasing many of his The Mighty Two's biggest hits and producing his own hits too. In 1993 the Retirement Crescent studio was re-opened and The Mighty Two began again to record occasionally with Sydney 'Luddy' Crooks of The Pioneers working on the arrangements. These recordings "proved popular in Brazil where Joe Gibbs began spending increasing periods of time". It is their incredibly impressive collection of recordings from the late Sixties, Seventies and early Eighties that are Joe Gibbs' and Errol Thompson's lasting legacy and that consolidate their central role in the history of Jamaican music.

After a series of strokes Errol Thompson died on 13th November 2004. Joe Gibbs died of a heart attack after a short illness on 22nd February 2008.

"An engineer and producer of real merit..." **Carl Gayle**

The name of Joe Gibbs & Errol Thompson will forever be associated with the now legendary 'African Dub Chapter Three', a "vital catalyst in breaking dub music outside of the reggae market", but amongst aficionados of the genre the importance of 'Dub Serial' can never be forgotten. They were also behind many crossover international successes which seems to have somehow tarnished their name in critical circles where selling hundreds of thousands of records apparently equates to "selling out". In consequence much of The Mighty Two's Two's formidable body of work has subsequently been overlooked yet it remains inexplicable how their reputation has been subsequently "tainted by success".

"Joel Gibson is not normally spoken of as an outstanding Jamaican record producer. As comparisons go Gibbo isn't half as renowned outside the business as Lee Perry or Bunny Lee, for instance, even though he is an engineer and producer of real merit and has made several very big hits. Yet Gibbo is far wealthier than the two put together..." **Carl Gayle**

Joe Gibbs certainly did not personally suffer from being successful and, as early as 1972 had moved into in a "Beverly Hills mansion with swimming pool" high above Kingston. However, his work with Errol Thompson is long overdue some serious critical reassessment and reaffirmation that their name, The Mighty Two, was much, much more than an idle boast.

JC Lodge

JC Lodge and Desi Roots

Joe Gibbs Recording Studio

17 Burns Avenue
Duhaney Park
Kingston 20

Joe Gibbs Recording Studio
24 Retirement Crescent
Cross Roads
Kingston 5

Producers:
Joel 'Joe Gibbs' Gibson, 'The Mighty Two': Joe Gibbs & Errol 'Errol T''ET' Thompson

Arrangers include:
'The Mighty Two': Joel 'Joe Gibbs' Gibson, Errol 'Errol T'/'ET' Thompson, Clive 'Azul' Hunt, Oswald 'Ossie'/'No Go' Hibbert, Winston 'Niney' Holness, Pat Kelly, Oswald 'Trini' Palmer, Lee 'Scratch' Perry, Ruddy 'Flick Wilson' Thomas & Maurice 'Blacka Morwell' Wellington

Engineers include:
'The Mighty Two': Joel 'Joe Gibbs' Gibson & Errol 'Errol T''ET' Thompson & Oswald 'Trini' Palmer

Labels: Amalgamated, Belmont, Crazy Joe, Errol T, Heavy Duty, JG Ultra Sound, Joe Gibbs, Joe Gibbs Music, Joe Gibbs Record Globe, Joe Gibbs Roots Sound, Jogib, Jogibs, Jogibs Record Globe, Preassure (sic) Beat, Pressure Beat, Reflections, Rocky One, Shock & Town 'n' Country

Gospel Labels: Calvary Temple, Help The Blind, Resurrection & Testimony

Musicians:
Lynn Taitt & The Jets
Drums: Joe Isaacs & Arkland 'Drumbago' Parks
Bass: Bryan Atkinson & Clifton 'Jackie' Jackson
Guitars: Nearlin 'Lynn' Taitt & Lynford 'Hux' Brown
Keyboards: Gladstone 'Gladdy' Anderson, Theophilus 'Easy Snappin'' Beckford & Winston 'Brubeck' Wright

Alto Saxophone: Karl 'Cannonball' Bryan
Tenor Saxophone: Tommy McCook

The Hippy Boys
Drums: Carlton 'Carlie' Barrett
Bass: Aston 'Family Man' Barrett
Rhythm Guitar: Alva 'Reggie' Lewis
Lead Guitar: Lorraine 'Ranny Bop' Williams
Organ: Glen 'Capo' Adams & Lloyd 'Charmers' Tyrell
Piano: Lloyd 'Charmers' Tyrell
Percussion: Lloyd 'Charmers' Tyrell

Third & Fourth Generation & Love Generation (The Now Generation)
Musicians include
Drums: Martin 'Largie' Sinclair & Leighton 'Sparrow' Thompson & later Michael 'Mikey Boo' Richards
Bass: Valentine 'Val' Douglas
Lead Guitar: Radcliffe 'Duggie' Bryan & Michael 'Mikey'/'Mao' Chung
Rhythm Guitar: Geoffrey Chung
Organ: Neville Hinds, Earl 'Wia'/'Wire' Lindo & later Robert 'Robbie' Lyn
Keyboards: Geoffrey Chung, Val Douglas, Earl 'Wire' Lindo & later Robert 'Robbie' Lyn
Percussion: Michael 'Mikey Boo' Richards

The Soul Syndicate

"One of our best dub albums that we ever did was with this guy Joe Gibbs… the first one named 'African Dub Chapter One' and then the second one named 'African Dub Chapter Two'. Now on the second album there's a hit rhythm that he took off that album called 'Uptown Top Ranking' with these girls named Althea & Donna." **Tony Chin**

Drums: Carlton 'Santa' Davis
(originally Max Edwards & Leroy 'Horse Mouth' Wallace)
Bass: George 'Fully' Fullwood
Rhythm Guitar: Albert Valentine 'Tony' Chin
Lead Guitar: Albert Valentine 'Tony' Chin & Earl 'Chinna' Smith
(originally Alva 'Reggie' Lewis)
Keyboards: Bernard 'Touter' Harvey & Keith Sterling
(originally Glen Adams, Tyrone Downie & Eric 'Bingy Bunny' Lamont)
Tenor Saxophone: Richard 'Dirty Harry' Hall & Tommy McCook
Trumpet: Bobby Ellis
Vocalists include: Dennis Brown, Freddie McGregor & Earl Zero

Noel Hawks

Joe Gibbs & The Professionals

"You used to have Joe Gibbs & The Professionals and the people don't know who played the music. Joe Gibbs, like myself, couldn't play a note!"

Bunny 'Striker' Lee

Drums: Basil 'Benbow' Creary, Carlton 'Santa' Davis,
Lowell 'Sly' Dunbar & Leroy 'Horse Mouth' Wallace
Bass: George 'Fully' Fullwood, Lloyd 'Sparks' Parks
& Robert 'Robbie' Shakespeare
Rhythm Guitar: Winston 'Bo Peep' Bowen, Tony Chin, Lennox Gordon
& Eric 'Bingy Bunny' Lamont
Piano: Oswald 'Ossie'/'Nogo' Hibbert, Errol 'Tarzan' Nelson
& Franklyn 'Bubbler' Waul
Organ: Harold Butler, Errol 'Tarzan' Nelson, Leroy 'Horse Mouth' Wallace
& Franklyn 'Bubbler' Waul
Alto Saxophone: Herman 'Seventh' Marquis
Tenor Saxophone: Richard 'Dirty Harry' Hall & Tommy McCook
Trumpet: Bobby Ellis
Trombone: Vincent 'Don D Junior'/'Trommie' Gordon
Percussion: Ruddy 'Flick Wilson' Thomas & Uzziah 'Sticky' Thompson

Noel Hawks

PRODUCED
AND DIRECTED BY
UPSETTER
WONDER
MAN
JUSTICE
LEAGUE
DUB ORGANISER
(L. PERRY)
UPSETTERS

INTERNATIONAL
PABLO
STEREO
ROCKERS
PRODUCTION
Produced &
Arranged By
A.PABLO
TUBBY DUB SONG
(H. Swaby)
AUGUSTUS PABLO

PANTOMINE
King Street
45 RPM
Produced by
G. L. Brown
M. Miller
ONE STOP
86 KING ST.
KINGSTON,
JAMAICA.
TUBBY'S AT THE CONTROL
(G. L. BROWN)
UNAUTHORISED COPYING OF THIS RECORD PROHIBITED

Dist.
In U.K. By
Dub Vendors.
Prod. by
W. Thompson
Root's Roots
Shoe House
129 Orange St
Kingston
An I.S.D.A.
Prod. Ja. W.I.
DUB VENDORS MEETS
ALIMANTADO AT
KING TUBBY'S
With Jammy at The Controls

ROSIE
℗ 1975
KING TUBBY'S IN
FINE STILE
UNAUTHORISED COPYING PROHIBITED

INTERNATIONAL
STEREO
ROCKERS
PRODUCTION
45 RPM
Produced &
Arranged By
A.PABLO
King Tubbys Meet Rockers
Up Town
(H. Swaby)
AUGUSTUS PABLO

Naoki Ienaga

Chapter 6

The Dub Master Presents
The Roots Of Dub & Dub From The Roots
King Tubby

"Tubby's love affair with 'sounds' started in a very basic manner – building amplifiers and repairing radios. This was the grounding of a man who eventually became a leader and possibly the leader of 'roots' music in Jamaica. Tubby first made a name for himself playing other people's music through his increasingly popular 'hi fi' sound system, 'Tubby's Home Town Hi Fi', at a time when the giants of sound system dances towered over the scene Tubby gradually built up quite a large following of his own and held his place among the best. This naturally led to his own record productions and this was where Tubby was to make his greatest mark. He pioneered the deejay records through Hugh Roy then brought in the 'version' flip side styling. His own unique engineering skills produced the almighty 'dub' which has now evolved into the very latest – 'the now sound' – styling symbols (sic) on simply flyers. This album is a showcase of the latest Tubby sound featuring 'dubs' and 'flyers' of original Bunny Lee hits. Tubby will always be at the roots of Jamaican Sounds… "

'King Tubby The Dub Master Presents The Roots Of Dub'

The significance of Osbourne 'King Tubby' Ruddock and his tiny Dromilly Avenue recording studio can never, ever be overstated and so many legends have grown up around him that much of the truth has been obscured by the subsequent myth making. It is as if people are unable to believe that such extraordinary innovation could come from such a down to earth, modest and retiring person. Although he irretrievably changed the way we listen to, make and understand music in the latter half of the twentieth century Tubby was at his most content when rewinding transformers, fixing a neighbour's television set or hair dryer. He was a retiring, introspective family man and renowned as someone who would prefer to listen rather than talk.

"Me know Tubbys more than anyone else and he was always a loner. He got on well with Striker, I Roy and me… it's only them type of man… the talkative type… could sit down with Tubbys." **Roy Cousins**

"The fame that was thrust upon him rested as uneasily as the cardboard crown he sometimes wore in photos…" **Dave Hendley**

A producer has been defined as "someone who doesn't write the songs or play them… but he is in charge. The real skill of producing music is how to arbitrate, how to keep people together with a common purpose" yet, throughout the Seventies, Tubby worked exclusively on other peoples' productions. At the height of his fame Tubby never actually 'produced' records, not even in the way that Kingston's artists and musicians had come to understand the term, and never ran his own record label.

His role was to encourage and promote not only his studio apprentices and sound system deejays but also the record producers whose work he remodelled and remade into something very, very special. This was not "new age noodling" but the "music of the ghetto" underpinned by rock solid drum and bass where the recording studio transcended its traditional role and the mixing desk became an instrument in its own right. In a remarkably prescient 1976 *Melody Maker* article Richard Williams stated:

"How can I persuade you not to laugh when I say that the technique of dub may well be the most interesting new abstract concept to appear in modern music since Ornette Coleman undermined the dictatorship of Western Harmony almost two decades ago?

It strikes me that there are possibilities inherent in this aberrant form which could perhaps resonate through other musics in the years to come; this may seem wild prophecy, but it could change the nature of some areas, and the nature of the ways in which we both play and apprehend music."

Richard Williams

Osbourne Ruddock was born in Kingston on 28th January 1941 to Winston Ruddock and Thelma Tubman and grew up in the High Holborn Street area of downtown Kingston close to the harbour. His Tubby epithet appears to have been adapted from his mother's maiden name for he was a slim youth who could not be described as 'tubby'. His large family included three brothers Leslie, Rouel (known as Stagga) and Lloyd (known as Scunna who would go on to sing with The Jayes and as a solo singer for Roy Cousins) and four sisters Margaret, Pat, Diane and Doreen. The family moved to 18 Dromilly Avenue, part of a new working class housing development in Western Kingston named Waterhouse, in the early Fifties. On leaving Calabar Elementary School he enrolled on an electronics course at Kingston's National Technical College and also studied electronics through two American correspondence courses. By the age of sixteen Osbourne 'King Tubby' Ruddock had starting to define his destiny, and his dynasty, as he cycled from Waterhouse into downtown Kingston on his old fashioned delivery bicycle to collect scraps of electrical equipment from the radio shops which he would then repair and recycle to build radios and amplifiers.

After he had completed his college course Tubby began repairing radios and other electrical appliances in a shack in the back yard of his mother's home and, as he took on more work, he employed an experienced technician called Barry Williams. Lloyd 'Jammy' James, a young neighbour and close friend of Tubby's who would go on to find worldwide renown as Prince Jammy, and later King Jammy, spent much of his time at the Ruddock's yard at 18 Dromilly Avenue too and would later become Tubby's apprentice. The work in those days was mainly repairing domestic appliances, winding transformers and building amplifiers for Kingston sound systems such as Arrows, Emperor Faith and El Toro. Bunny 'Striker' Lee recalled that Barry was a renowned electronics expert on Kingston's sound system circuit.

"King Edwards The Giant now he built an amplifier in about 1962 with a guy named Barry Williams. He ruled the roost! He brought down Coxsone and Duke Reid at the Lodge Hall on Independence Night with an amplifier named 'Hercules Unchained'. That time the 'Hercules' film did a gwaan… the man a feel that amp man… he pumped down everything the sound was so heavy!" **Bunny 'Striker' Lee**

Both Roy Cousins and Dennis AlCapone recalled another "electronics genius" at work on Dromilly Avenue who helped Dennis build the El Paso sound system.

"Irwin at Tubbys was a big black man like me! He was an electronics genius and, when Tubbys was building an amp, he used to send for Irwin. He always walked with an electronics book under his arm and any problems Tubbs had Irwin would sort them out for him. But he never worked there… he was more of an adviser." **Roy Cousins**

"One of my friends was working with Irwin, this great engineer, who later worked with Tubbys and he was teaching Winston the trade. So I said 'Winston why don't you ask Irwin to help you build an amplifier? I'll buy the records and get the speakers'. When we started to play my pre-amp was on a sardine tin with one tube! Can you imagine it?

I was in the sound with my landlord's son... his name was Winston Cameron. Me and him started it... he was the one learning a trade with Irwin so I told him to actually get Irwin to help him so Irwin would get him things like transformers and tubes 'cause at that time we couldn't afford it… Irwin had those things so Irwin would let him have them. But any time him and Irwin would fall out Irwin would take all his transformers and tubes back so we can't play. No dance tonight!" **Dennis AlCapone**

Tubby built his first sound system in 1957 playing jazz and rhythm & blues from the USA at local weddings and birthday parties. He particularly liked Fats Domino and Wynonie Harris, however, Bunny 'Striker' Lee recalled that one of Tubby's top tunes for 1963 was Herb Alpert's mournful 'Lonely Bull'. During a dance held by a man named Jack Lloyd at Reedie's Lawn, 32 Antigua Road, Waterhouse he was crowned as local King Of The Dance Hall but felt that his sound's reputation increased exponentially in 1968 when he enrolled Euwart/Ewart 'U Roy' Beckford as his deejay.

Noel Hawks

Waterhouse, Kingston 11

Noel Hawks

Waterhouse, Kingston 11

U Roy had worked for Doctor Dickie's Dynamic in Jones Town, "Dickie's was a Chinese guy", and, on leaving Dickie's, he went to Sir George before he began deejaying on Coxsone's Number Two set. King Stitt was the deejay on Downbeat's Number One set. U Roy was recruited for King Tubby's Home Town Hi Fi with the assistance of Lloyd 'King Jammy' James, who was serving his apprenticeship in electronics with Ivan Chin at Chin's Radio Service. On completing his training on Church Street he started to work at Tubby's workshop repairing domestic appliances, winding transformers and building amplifiers for Kingston sound systems as well as running his own sound system, he would also "go with Tubbys sound".

King Jammy recalled that, as well as running his own sound system, he would also go with Tubby's sound to lift the boxes and help them string up. Tubbs "was a guidance" but never a selector although he would be at the forefront and tell the selector "to put this tune on and direct them what to do." Tubby "had a lot of people before U Roy like Skeewee and Scotty". And, through Jammy's many connections in Jones Town, "I happened to know a lot of people in Jones Town", he sent him to "check U Roy and say that he could come and talk to Tubby". And "from then him and U Roy link up".

"We never really get famous until May 1968 but even in 1964 I fool around with sound system but it was only a hobby. Coxsone and Duke Reid was still there but they was losing them name those times. Top sounds those times was Sir Mike, Sir George Kelly and Stereo from Spanish Town. Then we come on as Tubby's Home Town Hi Fi, we just say we wasn't going in it that big, just play in we home town which was the Waterhouse area. But eventually we get big." **Osbourne 'King Tubby' Ruddock**

His reputation as a man who knew both music and electronics grew steadily and it was his expertise in both areas that made Tubby's own sound system so special. He built reverb into his amplifiers and decorated the fronts with rows of lights that flashed and flickered on and off in time to the rhythm. It was said that people at his dances would stand near the 'control tower' just to admire its beauty.

"I design my amplifier from top to bottom and I arrive at a certain equalisation, a standard sound for the local scene. Most people that build amplifiers them try to copy the foreign principle. They can't get the sound I get because there's a lot more to it than just getting a transformer. I make my own transformer and all the necessary little things for it."

Osbourne 'King Tubby' Ruddock

"Trust me. I'd never heard a sound like Tubbys sound... the greatest without a doubt. Respect to every other sound that was in Jamaica at the time but when Tubbys came into being it was a whole new world of sound systems.

When Tubbys sound came along it was a new revelation in the sound system world. Sound quality at the time was of a high standard but Tubbys came on and made it to a higher standard. Tubbys introduced a thing called echo in the dance hall... he introduced reverb and those wasn't heard before so we'd say 'what? This sounds good...' Like when U Roy would talk and say 'this coming Saturday night, night night all roads lead to Copacabana Beach, Beach, Beach' and it sounded really impressive. You know the reverb sound quality it wasn't just coming through the horns it was coming through the heavyweight speakers too so the whole, complete sound changed. Sweet! You know in Jamaica in the night when the breeze was blowing... you know Jamaica is a warm place... and you'd hear Tubbys playing and I tell you it's like paradise... like you're in heaven!

Imagine yourself in a studio listening to music and the engineers are displayed with all the necessary knobs well that's how Tubbys was playing. He brought that in and, you know, changed the whole sound system culture in Jamaica. And then Jammys... who was Prince Jammy at the time... had the same effect as well. But not as big as Tubbys...Tubby's sound was too sweet... too sweet.

The rude boys them they used to just mash up the dance 'cause the music was too nice. They couldn't believe it... trust me! Too nice... couple of beers inna my head, couple of spliffs and Tubbys playing like that and the thing that they call the salute with the people running all over the place. You understand? 'Cause Tubbys blow their minds... it was that good."

Dennis AlCapone

Towards the close of the Sixties he purchased his own basic two track recording equipment which Tubby installed alongside his lathe for cutting acetates (dubs), a home-made mixing console and his impressive collection of jazz albums in the back bedroom of his home at 18 Dromilly Avenue which he christened his music room.

"I was there with Tubbys before he bought Studio B from Dynamic. He had a reel to reel tape recorder in a suitcase and a series of Sony amps in his bedroom in his mother's house where he started from. The house was expanded and Tubbys then had the end room before he bought the house over Duhaney Park. The room in front of the carport was Tubbys' bedroom where he did have a wall full of jazz records... he was a John Coltrane collector. "
Roy Cousins

"I remember once Tubby took me into his inner sanctum, that one room that was always locked at the studio, and inside was this huge collection of jazz albums. It was just amazing! And suddenly I realised that this was where all Tubby's inspiration came from. When he was mixing he must have been playing jazz in his head. It was the same improvisational thing... if you think about it... of leaving the main theme, taking it somewhere totally different and then bringing it back. It was that thing of how you put a bit of what you really love into whatever you're doing. "
David Rodigan

As well as cutting dubs for his own Home Town Hi Fi he also cut for other sound systems including an upcoming set named Rockers Hi Fi controlled by two brothers Garth and Horace Swaby. Horace was later renamed Augustus Pablo by record salesman and producer Herman Chin Loy and the music that Pablo and Tubby made together would go on to play a definitive part in Tubby's musical revolution. Stories of Tubby's prowess began to make waves outside his home town area and he was employed by Duke Reid to maintain his studio equipment, dub cutting lathe and amplifiers. He was never the cutting engineer at Duke's Treasure Isle studio and King Jammy, who was by now operating the dub cutting lathe at Dromilly Avenue, stated that Tubby used to repair Duke Reid's amplifiers "so he used to go down there a lot" but "Byron Smith, The Baron, used to cut the dub".

However, in 1970, Iris, who was then Jammy's girlfriend and is now his wife, emigrated to live with her mother in Toronto; he also flew to Canada initially intending to stay for a short while. When he left Kingston he had told Tubby to expect him back "after two weeks" but, instead, King Jammy settled in Toronto and the pair kept in constant touch through letters.

Although it wasn't "really my bag" Jammy was prepared "to give this thing a try… try to do something different" and "that try went on for five years". He not only did "technician work serving television sets" but also worked "in a factory where they built swimming pool equipment".

In a 1976 interview with Carl Gayle Tubby reminisced that he invented 'versions' when cutting test plates for Duke Reid but Bunny 'Striker' Lee is insistent that Rudolph 'Ruddy' Redwood from Spanish Town was the first man to actually play 'versions'. He remembered being in Duke Reid's Treasure Isle studio with Tubby when engineer, Byron 'Baron'/'Smithy' Smith, was cutting acetates for Ruddy.

"… but Tubby and me had really met upstairs at Duke Reid's one day when the version thing came in. It was a mistake made up at Duke's studio. Now Ruddy was really the man that started playing versions. We called it version not drum and bass. Ruddy was a big businessman and he had a club by the seaside too. When Ruddy from Spanish Town came to Coxsone's or Duke Reid's studio they gave him the keys to the city and allowed him to use any tape because his sound was like a big radio station in Spanish Town… anything that Ruddy played the other sound men wanted it and then the record buying people too. Ruddy was cutting a dub and Smithy forgot to put in the voice through we were talking and he was going to stop it and Ruddy said 'no… make it run'. So when it finished they cut it back on the other side and put in the voice. I never took any notice of it. Me and Tubbys were just sitting there. Now Tubbys wanted some rhythms to play on his sound of 'Ain't Too Proud To Beg' and we drove over to Greenwich Farm to pick up the tapes…

I used to go over and listen to Ruddys and Stereo in Spanish Town and on the Monday I came in and said 'Tubby… you know the mistake we made up at Duke's studio? It's a serious mistake, you know, because the people them love it'. It mash up Spanish Town! I don't remember whose tune it was but it was Alton Ellis or John Holt they were playing. They played the singing version and then they said they're going to play part two… and those times you never had any versions… so when they played part two the people just caught the song and sang it over the rhythm. They must have played it about five or ten times and it brought down the house and, as we say in Jamaica, it mashed up the place! When Tubby started doing it he left a little bit of the voice in and then he dropped it out. The people started going round saying 'bwoy! Tubbys have an amplifier that is the greatest. It takes out the voice and leaves the pure rhythm'. We started putting in some voice, taking it out, and then putting back some little voice in the middle. People started asking me about it. Even Vincent Chin from Randy's! So I said 'Vincent. It's a gow (untrue) but I don't know how you got to hear about it'. So I told him 'you just start off with the voice and bring in the rhythm and then bring back the voice... sometimes you bring in the voice with no rhythm and you just hear the singer on the soft wax' . And I had to tell Vincent it was little thing we did; we just took the voice out of the record and put it in back on the dub plate but the people believed it was the amplifier that did it. We couldn't afford for every song to get a different set of musician so we started using the same rhythm over again. It took off and then the people started wanting it on their records."

Bunny 'Striker' Lee

Paul Coote

There is "a well known phrase or saying" in Jamaica "every spoil make a style" meaning "if something goes wrong do not fret; use this mishap to your advantage to create something new. The use of serendipity with creativity is wonderful advice". These acetates, with most of the vocal track left off and the rhythm allowed to run, were the beginnings of the creation of dub. Do-overs of another producer's rhythm or song had always been prevalent in Kingston's musical rat race and a precedent had long been set where instrumental or alternative vocal versions of popular songs were part of the scene. But the importance of the rhythm in reggae can never be overstated and a straightforward 'rhythm only' version was not really a leap too far from what was already happening.

Justice
A DANCE IN A GREENWICH FARM
Cornell Campbell
Black & White
Produced by
C Patterson
45 R.P.M.
PSALMS OF DUB
KING TUBBY'S
ATTACK
Straight to I Roy's Big Mouth
King Tubby & the Aggrovators
Produced &
Arranged By
A.PABLO
45 R.P.M.
PHILLIP'S SHOWCASE
(H. Swaby)
Pablo all Stars
DUB
PRODUCED BY
RUPIE EDWARDS
STUDIO 1
SO - 0091A
OH MR. D.C.
(S. Minott & C. Dodd)
Sugar Minott
UPSETTER
FREAK
OUT
SKANK
40 LEG
MICKEY DREAD &
THE INSTIGATORS
DREAD
AFRICAN ANTHEM
DREAD ALL THE WAY
Love
B
45
ROOTES DUB
I.ROY
LIKE
RECORDS
45 RPM
High Fidelity
SOCK IT TO 'EM J. B. - Part 2
REX GARVIN
AND THE MIGHTY CRAVERS
301-B
Randy's
RECORDS
45 RPM
2007A
IVAN ITLA THE CONQUER
TUBY AND FAMILY MAN
Hot Shot!
MC-4011-A
IT'S A SHAME
DELROY WILSON
Beserkley
Home of the Hits
STEREO
BZZ2
a
Egyptian Reggae
Jonathan Richman and the
Modern Lovers

"One day Niney went to U Roy and U Roy said 'another version of it again?' and, as I told you Niney is a quick man, and he told me 'Striker! The new name is version! U Roy just told me about it!' and I said 'bwoy it sound good'...and from that day they did name it version. Before that they used to say part one and part two of a tune but from that everybody said we play version until U Roy come and start saying 'Version Galore' with Duke Reid. This is how the version thing really start with U Roy when him come to play the part two and him call it version two."

Bunny 'Striker' Lee

"Yes... it's the drop out and drop in thing that create that effect when the raw rhythm is being played and you get the different versions. You'd get version one, version two, version three, version four until nowadays you can see just how far version has gone. Version one would be pure rhythm with all the instruments in it... then version two they would drop out all the rhythm section just leaving the drum and bass. People would react to it and that's how it got popular..." **Dennis AlCapone**

Tubby was instrumental in the next move in transforming versions into what would become known as dub. Beginning by cutting his own instrumental versions to popular rhythms, using two track tapes on loan from Treasure Isle, he would drop the vocal track out but always leaving enough for the crowd to immediately recognise the song.

"So I said 'Tubbs we're going to have to start to do something like that...' and Tubbs was a man who improvised. On Slim Smith's tune you'd hear Slim Smith start to sing and then he'd just take out Slim Smith's voice and bring in the (sings bass line to) 'Ain't Too Proud To Beg' and we had about five or six different cuts of that tune. Some U Roy... and Slim Smith sing a next tune 'pon it 'Keep That Light' with Lester Sterling, Roland Alphonso. Well the next Saturday night now when Tubby strung up down the Farm and U Roy said he's going to play part two but Tubby did it different now. He started with the voice then dropped it out and let the rhythm run and then he brought in the voice in the middle." **Bunny 'Striker' Lee**

Tubby's Home Town Hi Fi with U Roy on the mic popularised the fashion for playing versions where the added space gave U Roy, and every other deejay that followed, the space to actually talk and to answer and question lines from the song's lyrics. Jamaican deejays no longer sounded like USA radio disc jockeys but gradually developed their own style of 'toasting' and "rode the rhythm" right through the proceedings. The next logical step was for U Roy to transfer his work live on the mic in the dance to the recording studio. King Stitt had preceded U Roy as a hit making recording deejay and Duke Reid was not the first to record U Roy but this further emphasises that being first is not necessarily what it is all about. Keith Hudson, Bunny 'Striker' Lee & Lee 'Scratch' Perry had all taken U Roy to the recording studio before he travelled down to Bond Street...

"I recorded U Roy before Duke Reid, you know, with a song named 'King Of The Road' and a song named 'Organarang'. I just made him introduce 'Bangarang' with Lennox Brown and then another tune with Lester Sterling... 'Reggae/Blowing In The Wind'. When he did it U Roy even started in the middle and I got Jeff Barnes from the radio station to come down and talk 'The heights by great men reached and kept were not attained by sudden flight... this brother's been in the musical fight' till U Roy came in and then you hear the brother with 'let love shine bright along the way...' those were U Roy's first set of tunes."

Bunny 'Striker' Lee

Perhaps the records that U Roy had made with Striker, Keith Hudson ('Dynamic Fashion Way') and Lee 'Scratch' Perry ('Earth Rightful Ruler'), were just too different to what had gone before? Perhaps deejay records needed the more familiar touch of a tried and trusted Treasure Isle rock steady rhythm track in order for this new genre to hit home with the record buying public? For when this mix of the familiar and totally unfamiliar hit home it most certainly did and in 1970 U Roy's first three records for Treasure Isle, 'Wake The Town', 'Wear You To The Ball' and 'Rule The Nation', held the top three spots in the Jamaican Hit Parade.

"U Roy is not a singer. He plays no musical instruments. He just deejays. Makes the sounds which create excitement when the music goes round. His comments are dubbed on to tapes of versions – instrumental arrangements of tunes."

'Version Galore'

U Roy continued to work live on the mic for King Tubby but the popularity of his records in the UK led to his first international tour with Roy Shirley and Max Romeo in 1972. A deejay of the same calibre as U Roy was urgently needed to fill the gap on Tubby's Home Town Hi Fi and Bunny 'Striker' Lee, a man who can always make things happen, introduced I Roy to King Tubby.

"So Tubbys a fret now because Big Youth and Jah Wise have Tippertone Sound and them challenge him. Them supposed to have a contest over a dancehall 'cross the water' at Port Henderson a little distance out of town. I said 'well Tubbs no bother fret. Me have a deejay called I Roy... him sound the same like U Roy. Me a go bring him in. Him up a Spanish Town. Sometime he play a sound called Wasp, Ruddys or Stereo'. I bring him in now and it was an honour for him to come and play Tubbys sound. Everybody a back Tippertone now..." **Bunny 'Striker' Lee**

Bunny then left for London to co-ordinate the U Roy tour but he made sure that he kept up with all the news from Kingston.

"I hear Tubby just beat Tippertone and I Roy beat Big Youth. I wasn't there but I Roy on Tubbys sound just get popular now because U Roy was on tour. Them never look back and I start to do a lot of recording with I Roy too and I Roy becomes like one of the most famous deejays. They used to say him is the most intelligent deejay. The man used to have some great lyrics!" **Bunny 'Striker' Lee**

Naturally enough Big Youth tells a different story...

"I Roy? Me just mash him up every time!" **Big Youth**

I Roy went on record to propagate deejaying for Tubby in the highly amusing introduction to 'Black Man Time' where he neatly sidesteps producer Gussie Clarke (for it is he) playing the part of a youth first praising him and then begging for money. I Roy's incredulous "Ten cents...?" is worth the price of the record alone.

I Roy: Wow!
Gussie: Hail star. The man name I Roy?
I Roy: Sight, sight, sight...
Gussie: I man sight the man. I hear the man a play King Tubbys Hi Fi more time.
The man's sound hard y'know star.
I Roy: Yeah, Well. King Tubbys have a sound that really wild me a tell you, y'know youth.
Yeah. You know...
Gussie: I man a beg the man a ten cents. Y'know.

I Roy: Ten cents…?
Gussie: Yeah y'know. I man want to buy a stick of iley y'know.
I Roy: Well right now I man a support that, you know I, but if it's food I man give food for thought.
You hear Sir?"
Gussie: I Love. Hear? Forward. More time. Y'hear?
I Roy: Love youth… **'Black Man Time' I Roy**

And Striker was also responsible for encouraging Tubby that his 'music room' already had all that it took to be a 'proper' recording studio.

"Striker was the man who come and saw Tubbs with his little mixing board and said 'let's start a studio'. They didn't even have no proper voicing facilities but Striker say 'yes… we can do it here' so they hook up a microphone and just work like that." **Lloyd 'King Jammy' James**

Byron Lee upgraded to sixteen track in 1972 and that man again, Bunny 'Striker' Lee, brokered a deal between Tubby and Byron where Tubby purchased the old four track equipment from Dynamic's Studio B, including the MCI console, which had which had been used for Dynamic's own prototype experiments in dub. The studio started coming together when Tubby converted the toilet adjoining the music room into a voicing booth.

"He took the bowl out of the outside toilet and padded it with egg boxes and the toilet became his voicing booth when him buy the equipment from Dynamics… two quarter inch machines and two four track machines… so you could transfer from four track to four track. Tubbys bought the four track board from Studio B, two half inch tape machines and two quarter inch tape machines. He got two Tannoy Gold Studio Monitor speakers and he had them hanging on chains from the ceiling…

That facility was perfect for us because them days you'd record four track rhythm at Dynamics and leave a track for the voice. But you couldn't see the singer… and the toilet was so small! Imagine three men in there voicing! So if a man say 'it was voiced in the toilet' then you know it come from Tubbys! When you come out you were wet like you'd been in a bath but them days were good days. Now they've taken all the joy out of recording." **Roy Cousins**

"Well... Tubbys had started out as an amplifier builder, you know, he used to build amplifiers for all the sound systems until he started his own little thing cutting dubs for sound men. He wasn't actually cutting dubs for producers... just sound men. He would make his living by ordering the dubs from Duke Reid or Coxsone and then the sound men would come and order dubs from him... so he'd cut dubs and make his money from that.

And people heard about him with the studio and when he got the Dynamics board Bunny Lee, Scratch, Niney and everybody start go there and do their thing. Because what the sound system culture and what the sound system at the dance required... Tubbys knew that! He knew how to mix the dubs to make them sound good in the dance hall... and that's what people were hearing and they flocked to him to mix some of their stuff. He knew what specialities the sound system required and that's why the sound men flocked to him as well. He had the sound and his sound was tops over anything else. So if a man wanted a piece of the action they would come to Tubbys and Tubbys would know what they were looking for... mixing all those dubs. And that's how Tubbys established himself.

How Tubbys had his sound and when U Roy played the sound... he started out on the mic and the echo effect he had and the reverb and he'd see the reaction of the crowd to those kind of effects... he'd take them into the studio now and realise that we've got something here to go on record. Then Tubbys would play with the instruments 'cause he would get the master tape with different, different tracks then reverb, echo and whatever effects he felt would make it sound better. Well those things now when they reach places like England and people like it and now you have sound boys here who play mainly dubs..." **Dennis AlCapone**

The four tracks on his new board gave Tubby far wider scope to work with as he began to create the music that would become known as dub. The bass and drum parts were brought to the fore and the four faders allowed him to ease the vocal and rhythm in and out of the mix. It has been suggested that Tubby had to make modifications to the board to get the sound he achieved but King Jammy insists that any work that was done was because the board needed repairing and that the sounds that Tubby coaxed from it were due to his technical abilities rather than any modifications.

"Well to be frank the board wasn't that much different from when it used to be at Dynamic Sounds but they never used it in the way King Tubby used to use it. It had all those features from time but as they never did so much roots reggae music they just didn't know what to do with it. Now that Tubby got his hands on it he knew exactly what those things were for... like all those quirky sounds it have like the high pass filter."

Lloyd 'King Jammy' James

"High pass filter: the effect has variously been described as a phase shifter and an equaliser but it is, in fact, a sophisticated high pass filter... a type of tone control designed to remove whole portions of unwanted bass frequencies from material sent through it. The control has several notches, so that you can hear the separate frequencies disappearing when the knob is being twisted."

Chris Lane

"Through he knew the value of the board and what it could do when it came down to dub. Man! It changed the whole thing..."

Bunny 'Striker' Lee

In addition to being a technical virtuoso Tubby possessed an innate understanding of music although he had no formal musical training. Augustus Pablo, whose music is indelibly linked with the development of dub, recalled that it was Tubby who first advised him that his music was at its most haunting when played in minor keys. Tubby was a major player in the development of Pablo's 'Far East' signature sound and their relationship had begun before Pablo started creating his own music.

"Tubbys a my brother! Him buy xylophone for me... him did show me certain things and him come like the man who pass the music... 'just stay inna them type of key there!'.

I had a sound before I started playing music... them days we used to play soul music and reggae but after a time we decide to call it Rockers Sound System and through we called it Rockers we nah bother playing any more soul music! We'd play dub and dub plate... my set was always playing dub plates. I cut dub at Tubbys... there was no choice!

When me started working with Tubbys he didn't have the board that he had later... it was a board he'd built himself. I was the only person who used to blow on that board... he never used to cut specials. All Tubbys used to do that time was cut dubs but we were the first to cut specials at Tubbys. Yeah. We called it dub plate so when you hear a tune like 'AP Special' it was Tubbys come up with those ideas.

I see dub different to how everybody else see dub, you know. Everybody have their own view about dub. Some people say to me in an interview that me invent dub. But me no invent dub! You understand? 'Cause I don't want it to look like some swell headed thing or I look some title! It was a whole class of us together... dub is really drawing out the rhythm. Right? That's what them call dub and you echo it. But some people give a different meaning for dub..." **Augustus Pablo**

And Augustus Pablo, Augustus 'Gussie' Clarke and Leonard 'Santic' Chin all recalled the easy going and open nature of how things worked down on Dromilly Avenue.

"Gussie (Clarke) was the person who carried me round Tubbys... I don't remember which rhythm or what but I know that's how we get there!"

Augustus Pablo

On graduating from Kingston College in 1971 Augustus 'Gussie' Clarke established his own home studio at 81½ Church Street where he cut dubs for local sound systems on a lathe he had purchased from the Treasure Isle studio down on Bond Street.

"Here's a couple of interesting things. I used to import foreign records and sell them to soul sounds like Soul Tone, Sanatone, Gemini, Afrique etc so everybody came to me to buy foreign records. Jamaican record producers would give me a lot tapes and I bought eight tracks which I'd run through to two tracks and start cutting specials from the versions on the eight tracks. All the sound men were coming to me because I could create dub specials that no-one else had.

A lot of producers like Channel One (Jo Jo Hoo Kim), Phil Pratt and Lee 'Scratch' Perry and a host of other producers gave me their rhythms on two track to expose their music for them and I'd add effects to make unique versions.

I learnt engineering at King Tubbys.... I worked as an engineer at Tubbys the same time as Phillip Smart. Tubbys and me had a perfect relationship. That's how I got further into the studio business. I loved it! "

Augustus 'Gussie' Clarke

And Leonard Chin recalled Gussie working at Tubby's studio...

"I always used to go to King Tubby to cut dubs. I voiced the 'Chalice Blaze' album with Jah Woosh down there but Gussie Clarke did the mix. It was a night at Tubbys when he was working on a television so he asked Gussie to do it for him!" **Leonard 'Santic' Chin**

"It all depended on who was working or not... who wanted to work. Them days I used to do a lot of overdubbing at Tubbys. Nobody never used it more than so but I and I make Tubbys get popular you know! Between me, Bunny Lee and Lee Perry... Tubby's was a place to cut dub. Nobody never used it as a studio... we made it a studio just for us. He had the four track machine and he did buy Dynamics board... and everyone loved how Tubbys mixed. Most times you'd just say 'Tubbys you want to work?' And he'd say alright him ready... and just gwaan.

I'll tell you the truth... when you're doing works like that you never plan fe think about it say twenty years later. I just do a work and just go through..."

Augustus Pablo

Before long every young, and often not so young but forward thinking, record producer in Kingston found their way to Dromilly Avenue despite the forbidding reputation of the Waterhouse district. Leonard Chin spoke of his determination to overcome any obstacles in the way of his entry into Kingston's music scene:

"... I just wanted to get in there. I didn't have any fear. I would leave out places like Tubbys at eleven o'clock at night and walk back to Eastern Kingston." **Leonard 'Santic' Chin**

There were other advantages as well as Tubby's mixing and musical skills, "studio time means money", and, because of its downtown location and relatively cheap rates, Tubby's reputation as studio for the ghetto artists and producers continued to grow. Many who would go on to achieve international fame and fortune would not have been able to make their first recordings without the favourable rates and ambience of King Tubby's studio. All that was needed was a large degree of inspiration, a singer or a deejay, a cut of a rhythm (as Tubby's studio did not have sufficient space to build rhythms), often begged or borrowed from another producer and history could be made.

"King Tubby always said that if the original engineer didn't do his job properly and the first take wasn't spot on then no engineer could get nothing from it."
Roy Cousins

As Tubby's reputation grew it was only a matter of time before his dubplate experiments started to be transfered onto vinyl. The first record to (possibly) name King Tubby as an 'artist' was a Bunny 'Striker' Lee production in 1970. 'Ivan Itla The Conquer'(sic), a version to Slim Smith's 'Everybody Needs Love' and/or Roland Alphonso's 'One Thousand Tons Of Megaton' was credited to 'Tuby & Family Man' on a seven inch Randy's USA release. However the UK pressing on Pama's Unity label, 'Ivan Itler The Conqueror', was more prosaically credited to the Bunny Lee All Stars.

Many artists and producers celebrated their work at Tubby's not only through making music but also by naming their records in tribute to the King: Glen Brown with 'Tubby's At The Control' and 'Number One In The World' from U Roy, Rupie Edwards with 'Dr Satan Echo Chamber', Lee Perry with Dillinger's 'Dub Organiser' and Augustus Pablo with 'Tubby's Dub Song'. Bunny 'Striker' Lee made countless records at Dromilly Avenue referencing King Tubby but possibly the best of all was Cornell Campbell's 'Dance In A Greenwich Farm' which effortlessly evoked all the thrills, spills and atmosphere of a ghetto dance.

***Appendix 1: Page 273**

Over And Over Over And Over And Over...

"And from there Tubby started to get really popular. Then everybody started coming to Tubby's studio. It was a little room and a bathroom set up..."
Bunny 'Striker' Lee

Producers would leave their tapes at Dromilly Avenue for Tubby to cut 'specials', exclusive dub mixes, for Kingston's leading sound systems and the importance of King Tubby's studio and the Home Town Hi Fi to the development of Jamaican music during this period can never be overstated.

"I often used Tubbys for voicing and mixing. Tubby was a brilliant guy. Brilliant in his work and Tubby would always do the mixing on my tunes. Tubbys was a bit cheap (for studio time) and he'd take them (Winston's recordings for his Techniques label) and put them on his sound. When his sound play it... it sell. Them was like the radio station in those times."

Winston Riley

"Tubbys was the place now and I used to keep all of my tapes up there and all the guys used to come to Tubby... so the sound men started flocking to Tubbys for a different cut... their style...every man!"

Bunny 'Striker' Lee

"Those days Tubbys was the chief dub cutter and all the man them used to leave their tapes there. None of those tapes belonged to Tubbys... the vast amount of tunes were Yabby You (Vivian Jackson), Striker Lee and Scratch. Tubbys never produced them... he just a cut them." **Roy Cousins**

"Most people used to give Tubbys their tapes you know... through he used my rhythms and make specials for him sound. Certain specials him did have him make certain sounds get it who a go promote it...

Them days dub was more like you'd go to a dance and that's where you'd hear the dub plate but... commercial... when it start to get upfront through the different producers... 'cause some man used to do that. It's like a trend start and it's just really working... it's like when they hear Tubbys mix some dub every producer from over there so start come a Tubbys too. It's a craze did start now so everybody just into this dub thing... everybody want mix some dub. But dub was a part of the whole thing them times...it became like you feature the musicians!" **Augustus Pablo**

Jammy recalled that "Bunny Lee was the most prominent producer that used Tubbys studio" and gave him credit for the idea of Tubby opening his studio. Other early Dromilly Avenue regulars included "Niney and Lee Perry" and "occasionally you used to find Derrick Harriott... then Yabby You came along later..." A number of astute, older producers were not slow to realise Tubby's potential. Derrick Harriott was one of the first of the established producers when, in 1972, he featured some very subtle Tubby's dubs on Dennis Brown's 'Super Reggae And Soul Hits' album. The following year Derrick introduced Augustus Pablo's version to 'Silhouettes', 'Bass & Drum Version', with "from Tubby's studio we bring you dubwise 'Silhouettes' featuring the man Augustus Pablo. Wow!".

After three break-ins in 1973 Derrick Harriott had been forced to vacate his downtown King Street retail premises. On one occasion Derrick was actually in the shop... "I was in the back of the shop when a guy came in to hold up the place. I came out and the guy ran! No violence was created". But after moving uptown to Constant Spring Road he continued to travel downtown to Dromilly Avenue.

"...amazing for an uptown producer to use Tubbys. What on earth gave him the great idea of using a couple of Tubby's dubs on Dennis Brown's vocal LP 'Super Soul & Reggae Hits'? He had just opened a shop in uptown Twin Gates Plaza at about the same time he was getting music mixed in Waterhouse!" **Chris Lane**

And Derrick later recalled:

"Tubbys was the thing. If he touch your tune it can't miss. We had a real good thing... I used to leave all my tapes at King Tubbys. I said to Pablo 'you're a wicked man 'pon your instrument'. We used to go to Tubby regularly. He mashed up the rhythms... the twelve inch version (to 'Slave' by Derrick Harriott) was a Channel One mix that sound like Tubbys and Tubby had about thirteen different versions. So did Arrows and Jack Ruby. 'Slave' was a big thing then." **Derrick Harriott**

Many of Tubby's experiments in sound from this period can never, ever be matched. With the King at the controls recordings were transformed and changed into something that could, on occasion, be totally at odds to the original through the power of Tubby's "musical imagination and engineering ingenuity". Even Niney, who had been involved in some very early examples of dub experimentation, recounted that when King Tubby had completed remixing his 'Dubbing With The Observer' album he had difficulty in recognising some of the tracks. Much of the music that Lee 'Scratch' Perry made with King Tubby still sounds as unsettling now as it did when it was first released. Tubby's 1973 mix of Lee Perry & The Upsetters' 'Jungle Lion' had started as an odd enough instrumental interpretation of Al Green's 'Love & Happiness' (a hugely popular song in Jamaica versioned vocally by both Leroy Smart and Big Youth) with vocal interjections from Scratch. Tubby refashioned the b-side as 'Freak Out Skank' with cavernous echo and liberal use of the MCI board's high pass filter, now known as 'Tubby's big knob', to make the type of music that can never be assimilated into the mainstream.

"Either he'd put more echo or more of the squawking effect 'swwwt, swwwt, swwwt…' the high pass filter you know. First time we do that Tubbys said 'it's madness' and then they listened it back and he couldn't believe it when they tried it on the sound system crowd! So they started using it… the high pass filter." **Bunny 'Striker' Lee**

There had been 'experimental' music in Kingston before but, as had happened previously with deejay records, it was mixing the well known with the unknown that made dub so appealing. Towards the end of that same year Lee Perry released his subversive and challenging 'Black Board Jungle' (also known as 'Upsetters 14 Dub Black Board Jungle') LP mixed at King Tubby's. Utilising some of the greatest Upsetter rhythm tracks of the time it was one of the earliest dub albums and remains one of the best ever. Although only three hundred copes were initially pressed it has subsequently attained legendary status through various reissues and it stands today as a monument to musical daring when Jamaica led the world with its breathtaking, groundbreaking work. Their partnership came to an end when Lee Perry's dream of owning his own studio, The Black Ark, finally became a reality.

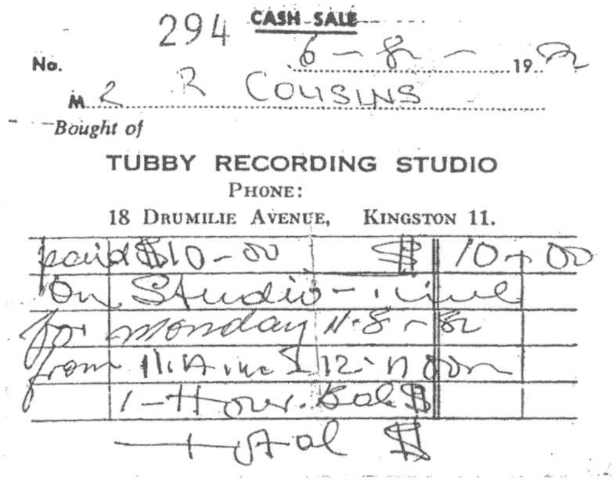
294 CASH SALE

No. 6-8-1982

M R Cousins

Bought of

TUBBY RECORDING STUDIO

PHONE:

18 DRUMILIE AVENUE, KINGSTON 11.

paid $10-00 $ 10-00

On Studio-time

for Monday 11-8-82

from 11 AM to 12 noon

1-Hour. Bal $

total $

Roy Cousins

"'Black Board Jungle' showed the very power of dub to transform a piece of music, to radically alter any given composition through creative mixing and spatial representation." **David Katz**

Tony Rounce

In late 1973 the workload in the studio increased to such a degree that Tubby employed Phillip Smart as his apprentice engineer.

*Appendix 2: Page 275
Phillip 'Prince Phillip' Smart

Bunny 'Striker' Lee, together with Soul Syndicate drummer Carlton 'Santa' Davis, now popularised a new style of rhythm based around the Philadelphia Disco or 'Philly Bump' style, the sound of an open and closed hi-hat, termed 'flying cymbals', that would become known as 'flyers'.

"Santa was a great drummer. He started with The Soul Syndicate. He wore size fourteen shoes and that's why when he licked the drum it sound! Sly played the drums so brilliant but he played different from Santa...

Yeah… I used to eat the chicken wings and I said 'Santa I want something that sound like it's come from outer space!' Sly played the flying cymbals. I said to Sly 'you played it first on the Delroy Wilson tune for Channel One named 'It's A Shame' and Sly played it with Skin, Flesh & Bones on 'Here I Am Baby Come And Take Me' (the Al Green tune) when Al Brown sung it (on Tit For Tat in 1973 for Dickie Wong) with the 'tsk, tsk, tsk' sound on the hi-hat. But he never realised what he had and because I loved my chicken wings we just named it flyers (sings) 'tsk, tsk, tsk, tsk…' We carried it to Tubbys to mix the tune and passed it through the high pass filter on his machine where he pushed up one of the things on his board and it thinned it out. Styled it out man! (sings) 'tsk, tsk, tsk, tsk…' it took on!"

Bunny 'Striker' Lee

One of the first records in this new style was with Striker's protégé, Johnny Clarke (at the time known as 'Studio Idler') on his rendition of Earl Zero's song 'None Shall Escape The Judgement'. Striker gave it to Tubby for 'exclusive' play on the Home Town Hi Fi where it rapidly became his most in demand dub.

***Appendix 3: Page 276**
'None Shall Escape The Judgement' Johnny Clarke

Striker's 'flyers' rhythms went on to totally dominate the reggae scene throughout 1974 and on into 1975 and every Kingston producer would follow suit with their own variations of flying cymbals.

"I named it 'flyers' but they didn't know what flyers was! It's not the right name really. I used to get Kentucky Fried Chicken and when it came they'd say 'put up the flyers for Striker' meaning the wings, which I loved, and they used to say 'Striker. When you a go fly?' And everybody started to get puzzled when Johnny Clarke hit with this 'flyers' now."

Bunny 'Striker' Lee

Bunny's two dub albums showcasing his new style rhythms, 'King Tubby The Dub Master Presents The Roots Of Dub' and 'King Tubby The Dub Master Presents Dub From The Roots', came with fabulous photographs of the King wearing his crown on the front cover. The album 'Brass Rockers: Bunny Lee & King Tubby Present Tommy McCook & The Aggravatars' (sic) displayed Tommy McCook and his tenor saxophone resplendent on the front and the entire Aggrovators band photographed and named with their respective instruments on the back cover. Striker had long championed the naming of artists and musicians who had previously remained in the background.

"I started to put the musicians' names on the LP sleeves because people never used to put on their names. I was the first to start that. Give Caesar what him due! Who play organ. Who play what. And that's why these men made a name for themselves because now you could know 'Sly on drums' or 'Santa on drums'". **Bunny 'Striker' Lee**

All three albums were released through Total Sounds and helped to promote the name of King Tubby with music lovers in Jamaica and internationally too. Much to Striker's displeasure a plethora of 'King Tubby' albums followed in their wake. King Tubby's name on an album was guaranteed to sell the set although the King's involvement with many of them was minimal, to say the least, and a number of long players credited to the King were released with neither his approval nor his knowledge.

"Now every producer on the island wanted to jump on the bandwagon and there was a flood of inferior dub albums whose only claim to fame was the fact that they mixed at Tubby's. No matter how good a mix is if the music is hopeless there's very little you can do. Anyway, it was Tubby's name that sold these records..." **Dave Hendley**

"All of those 'Tubby' albums that you see out on the street... most of them are frauds as it was only three albums that Tubby did: 'Dub From The Roots', 'The Roots Of Dub' and perhaps one named 'Shalom Dub'. You could call that Tubbys too because he mixed the versions but they were versions off of forty fives. Klik took it and put it out but the third is 'Brass Rockers' with Tommy McCook 'pon the flying cymbals where he mixed it with the horn going in and out in a kind of dub way but all the others a man just get something and say it's King Tubbys. Me and Tubby used to do a whole heap of different forty fives too. They can get put together and we can call it 'Unreleased Tubbys'." **Bunny 'Striker' Lee**

"...but it was Tubby's 'Roots Of Dub' that set a precedent. Because it was distributed by Total Sounds, Jamaica's leading record distributor at the time, the music reached many people who were previously unfamiliar with this new development in reggae." **Beth Lesser/Kingston**

"Bunny has made or been a part of Jamaica's transition from VERSION the strictly rhythm b-side of our local 45's then dub (the bass and drum with a little rhythm popping through) that is now popular. Now his current flying symbols (sic) is being copied by all. Bunny has lead the field for many a year and possibly one man more than any other has been at his side. Osbourne Ruddock or King Tubby as his fans know him."

'Bunny Lee Then'

Record buyers had become accustomed to an instrumental or dub version accompaniment to the vocal side and now knew to ask record salesmen to play the b-sides of records first because that was often where the most exciting music was to be found.

"When the version thing come out now we start putting the rhythm on the back and the sound men start playing it... it was a much cheaper way. For I used to say I give the people them value for money... two strong sides... but when a man want to hear the rhythm and turn it over he'd bypass it! It would have to be exceptionally good before he'd take it without the version... 'cause in the dance now we'd start play the rhythm and man start sing or deejay over it and that's how those things come in...

Because the first time I stood up in Randy's and a man played 'Queen Of The Minstrel' with Cornell (Campbell) and turned it over... no version! I always gave the people value for money... two big sides... but it never go like that now. Them no want that. The man them wanted the version 'cause when they no hear the version they'd walk and leave it so from that we just started to deal with the version and put it behind the record."

Bunny 'Striker' Lee

Rupie Edwards' 'Irie/Ire Feelings', one of the strangest ever dub records, even made it to Number Nine in the UK National Charts in the winter of 1974. Rupie had been an early visitor to Dromilly Avenue and had worked with Tubby on a number of his records including 'Dr Satan Echo Chamber Water House', a deconstruction of The Uniques' 'My Conversation' released on Rupie's Peaceful Road label in 1972. On this release Johnny Clarke's 'Every Day You Wondering' was totally taken to pieces as Rupie's voice impersonated and approximated the instruments that had been excised from the mix.

"Of course we must mention the hit single 'Ire Feelings'; this one Ire is a totally new creation in sound and may very well go down in musical history as one of the most unusual records. Note how Rupie uses his voice to imitate sounds of instruments like the guitar Skenga Skanga, and the organ Ku Chucku, Ku Chucku, then onto the drums Ka Chicka Ka Chicka etc." **'Ire Feelings'**

Dub music had finally arrived and articles on its significance and its 'meaning' belatedly began to appear in mainstream music papers and magazines and records, singles and albums credited to King Tubby now began to flood the record shops.

"Without stretching the point too far we could say that dub alienates the listener from the prevailing aesthetic of unobtrusive naturalism (ie the polished product). It leaves the studio door open." **Dick Hebdige**

"Oh, and I've heard some interesting new music from Jamaica… a sort of hybrid between electronic music and reggae. It's a fascinating study in the new musical forms generated when a largely pre-technological culture is given access to modern recording techniques without the technological preconceptions that we've allowed to accumulate, limiting our vision. It's called dub music. You'd like it I'm sure." **Alan Moore & Dave Gibbons**

Chris Blackwell's Island Records helped to introduce the concept to a wider audience in 1975 with the release of Jacob Miller's version to Augustus Pablo's 'Cassava Piece' rhythm, 'Baby I Love You So', in the UK. The Island release elevated the original International label b-side, 'King Tubbys Meet Rockers Uptown', to the a-side, modified the title to 'King Tubby Meets The Rockers Uptown' and promoted it heavily in the 'rock press'. Pablo followed up the single with one of the definitive dub albums, 'King Tubbys Meets Rockers Uptown', initially released in New York on Brad Osborne's Clocktower label in 1976.

"Well... most of the mixing on them dubs through we used to use echo a lot them days (was) me and Phillip Smart. When we decide to do this dub LP it's the first LP I did put out but me want it mixed in stereo and that's what I was showing Tubbys . I used to do it with Errol Thompson before that... you understand. Me and ET sometime we'd try and mix some dub and experiment... we'd be there in the studio and nobody nah book in the studio so we'd be trying out some echo kinda style and sound. So when I went to Tubbys I said I want to mix a dub LP in stereo and him say 'yeah' and we just start doing it..." **Augustus Pablo**

Every seven inch single, and, as ever, there were countless releases, now came with its own version and it was next to impossible to keep up with the bewildering amount of dub albums that appeared in the shops one week, often on blank, white labels without sleeves with rubber stamped and/or hand written titles (usually at seriously inflated prices) never to be seen, heard or heard of again. In order to cope with the increased workload Tubby employed Pat Kelly the lead singer from The Techniques. Pat also freelanced as a recording engineer at Dynamics, Randy's, Joe Gibbs, Channel One and, most famously, at King Tubby's. As Tubby's 'temporary' replacement for 'Prince' Phillip Smart he would remain with the King until the beginning of 1976.

"After Phillip Smart Pat Kelly came along... Pat studied electronics... he did a course in Jamaica. Both of us used to learn together at Chin's Radio Service." **Lloyd 'King Jammy' James**

***Appendix 4: Page 279**
Pat Kelly

Tubby's letters to King Jammy had kept him informed of all the latest news from Waterhouse but he always wanted to know when Jammy was going to return to work with him. When Phillip Smart left for New York Tubby's requests for Jammy to return to Kingston became even more pressing. However, by this time Jammy felt properly settled in Toronto and, after studying electronics at George Brown Technical College, had built his own recording studio in the basement of a house in Lakeshore Boulevard, Toronto and released some self produced sides but, as 1975 came to a close, Jammy decided to visit Jamaica. Once again his original intention was to stay for a couple of weeks...

"When I came home I saw my mother and my brothers and I saw the studio Tubby had built and realised all this was everything I ever wanted."
Lloyd 'King Jammy' James

And so he remained in Kingston and took over as engineer at 18 Dromilly Avenue where he put into practice all that he had learnt in Canada. Tubby and Jammy had started together in the early days and Tubby had faith in Jammy's abilities so, consequently, allowed him to get on with the studio work while he concentrated on the electronics side of the business.

"King Jammy? Jammy alright! I'll be seeing him later today... Jammys is one of the men when he was in Canada he used to send down mics and things for Tubby and when he came back to Jamaica he went straight to Tubbys. He used to work in a little studio in Canada...

When Jammy came back to Jamaica the rest is history. We did a lot of work together because when Jammy came Tubby kinda handed over the studio to him and Jammy ran it." **Bunny 'Striker' Lee**

"He (Tubby) was comfortable with me there and he would have more time to do other things because he was doing other business; electronics business and winding transformers...

I used to work non-stop. I was so interested to learn that I would be there early in the morning, long before Tubbys arrive, practising. He used to give me my own key. I never got tired because I loved the work.

In a way to me he was a great teacher... somebody who taught me what I know today... Many of us learn from him and he was so cool and nice... . very cool. And he was a scientist to me because he always invents."

Lloyd 'King Jammy' James

Jammy rapidly established his own identity in Tubby's studio and his first session on his return was with that man again... Bunny 'Striker' Lee.

"I think it was Cornell Campbell... a very good artist in his time. Bunny Lee used to have some wicked rhythms: flying cymbals, some one drop and horns. I used to love horns and harmonies. He was a great vibes man. Always boosting you up. He would make anyone work wonders. It was Striker who first give me the name 'Prince Jammy'".

Lloyd 'King Jammy' James

Tubby's Home Town Hi Fi reached a peak in 1975 and its reputation was supposedly sealed as the top Jamaican sound system after playing out with Bob Marley & The Wailers at Kingston's National Arena that autumn. Differing sources have subsequently dated the concert in August, September and October but Carl Gayle's liner notes remain as a definitive description of the marathon, although perhaps, apocryphal session.

"On the 26th September 1975 at the National Arena, Kingston, Jamaica, King Tubby's Sound System entertained the excited audience there to listen

to the almighty live sound of The Wailers on stage and the overpowering dub music that Tubby has made world famous. Before the concert followers of other sound systems in Jamaica from Admiral Fate, Black Harmony and Soul Attorney were claiming that King Tubby was no longer king. Tubbs had not been playing regularly and U Roy, the live deejay king, had left him for Soul Attorney. But on this particular night Tubby proved that he is still the king because he played from 6pm to 6am. The dreads hail the king. He continues to be the king of the dub rock at his musical chamber."
'King Tubby Surrounded By The Dreads At The National Arena'

In spring 1994 Robert 'Nasty Love' Allen, pirate radio deejay and selector for Nasty Love Sound, caused a sensation when he returned to London after a jaunt to Jamaica with an hour long cassette tape of Tubby's Hi Fi in full swing in 1975 with U Roy on the mic.

***Appendix 5: Page 283**
King Tubby's Home Town Hi-Fi Live & Direct 1975

Noel Hawks/Fashion Records

Augustus Pablo

But, later that year in the last of a long line of similar attacks, the police destroyed the sound system at a rural dance in St Thomas. King Jammy recalled that Tubby's sound was not shot up but broken up by police at Gold Coast Lawn. Apparently Tubby intended to rebuild it but "was awaiting a writ to be filed against the police... he was supposed to get some money back." The forces of authority had decided that because of its Waterhouse connections and alleged criminal followers that the Home Town Hi Fi had to be taught a lesson. Dennis AlCapone takes up the story:

"Tubbys sound... bad men in Jamaica they love the best things. Bad man want the best woman, they want the best outfit, they drink the best drink, they want the best ganja to smoke... that's the rude boys in Jamaica... and they listen to the best sound. So King Tubbys was the best sound and plenty bad man follow Tubbys sound and the police didn't like that so they will interrupt the dance from time to time looking for wanted men and things like that, you know. And sometimes gangs would meet up at the dance and kick off... all hell broke loose and the dance finished. Police informers would tell the police them 'that man was at that dance' and the police don't like to hear that Tubbys was harbouring that man at his dance. So they picked up a dislike for Tubbys 'cause too much bad men follow the sound. One particular night Tubbys was playing in St Thomas and the police mash up the sound.

They'd done it before and Tubbys persevered but that particular time Tubbys just lose interest and decide he doesn't want to carry on. But if your sound is good bad man are going to follow it and that's how the police come and intimidate you. Sometimes you'd string up the sound and, before the dance start, they'll come and tell you to pull it down. Jamaica reached a stage one time when dance just could not go on... you'd go to a dance, string up the sound and, when you start playing, if it's not rude boys mash up the dance it's police and, if it's not police it's soldiers. That was going on all the time when I left Jamaica because dances were constantly being interrupted by the law and the rude boys were killing in the dance too. Because how it works in Jamaica if you and somebody have something... they will see the dance hall as the place to commit his crime. You understand? If he's going to hurt you he will do it in the dance hall... because there's so much people around no-one's going to know who committed the crime. So they'd just take it to the dance hall on a regular basis..."

Dennis AlCapone

Although Tubby's had left the majority of the running of the sound to the crew and the deejays he took this final assault very badly. Two years later, in April 1977, Dave Hendley made his first visit to Dromilly Avenue where King Tubby told Dave that he was still fighting his unsettled claim against the Jamaican constabulary and working on plans to come back with a bigger and better sound system. The broken speaker boxes were stacked in the yard at 18 Dromilly Avenue where they provided makeshift seating for the singers and deejays waiting their time to voice. King Tubby's Home Town Hi Fi never played out again. ...

"... and on to Dromilly Avenue. The area was a mixture of run down concrete bungalows and zinc fence yards. It was unsettling and quiet compared to other parts of town and this just added to what was either a real or imagined atmosphere of tension.

The studio came as something of a shock. Number 18 Dromilly Avenue was just another anonymous bungalow on this quiet crescent shaped road. Unlike the neighbouring dwellings there were a couple of cars parked outside including an immaculate white Triumph 2000 that I later found out to belong to resident engineer Lloyd 'Prince Jammy' James... it was somehow surreal to see such a beautifully preserved vehicle in this distinctly Third World landscape.

Aside from the sound of a muffled bass line pounding from within the CCTV camera and an electronically operated security gate were the only other pieces of evidence that Number 18 was anything out of the ordinary.

Entry to the studio was via a steel barred cage that ran along the left hand side of the building into a dusty back yard through a back door and down a narrow corridor into Tubby's inner sanctum.

There was no evidence of the cutting edge technology that had produced spectacular records like 'King Tubbys Meet Rockers Uptown' and 'King Tubby's In Fine Stile (sic)' instead squeezed into what had once been a small back bedroom were a couple of four track machines, various other pieces of studio hardware, amplifiers, compressors, a dub cutting lathe and an antiquated mixing console that looked like a prop from a Fifties science fiction film. Two big Tannoy monitors were suspended from the ceiling by chains while the brown velvet curtains, pale blue walls and ornate brass light fittings gave the room a relaxed and homely feel."

Dave Hendley

The demise of his sound system heralded the all round recognition of King Tubby as 'The Dub Inventor' as the music emanating from his Waterhouse studio became an international phenomenon. Although Tubby had stepped back from engineering and dub cutting and was concentrating on the more lucrative electronics side of the business the studio, with Jammy at the controls, entered a new phase and demand for studio time was greater than ever… especially when Bunny 'Striker' Lee was in town.

"… and it was a common sight to see Striker arrive at eight in the evening with a suitcase full of tapes and an entourage of singers and deejays ready to begin an all night session. Jammy remembers working long hours at this time with shifts that began in the mid morning and ended in the early hours of the next day." **Dave Hendley**

"Tubbys studio became so in demand that not even me could get studio time now! I'd have to wait until late at night because everybody was coming and wanted Tubbys to mix their tunes until Pablo bring Phillip Smart down there and Phillip Smart started work… then Jammys then Scientist and then Professor…" **Bunny 'Striker' Lee**

"We worked at Tubbys through the Sturgav connection because U Roy and Tubby were close and Sturgav sound played like Tubbys. Tubby would mix specials for us… he used to take a special interest in us and he supported me as a young man in the rub a dub business. We used to book hours and hours mixing dub…

King Tubby was mixing for me and he was my mentor. I'm a rub a dub specialist and he taught me a little bit of mixing. His board was easy to work on as it was only four tracks and we'd get the ideas and make these dubs." **Paul 'Jah Screw' Love**

Tubby continued to work with his own particular favourites such as Vivian 'Yabby You' Jackson who Tubby had given free studio time in 1972 to record his first single 'Conquering Lion' and the pair had remained firm friends ever since. Yabby's singular stance as a 'Jesus Dread' had set him apart from his contemporaries but his deep religious beliefs were as thoughtful and considered as his music and Tubby's empathetic mixing added yet more mystery and depth to his ethereal songs.

"Yabby You… Tubby used to do most of Yabby You's work personally and then I took over." **Lloyd 'King Jammy' James**

Towards the end of the decade Tubby began to work regularly with Greenwich Farm producer Bertram Brown's Freedom Sounds label and radio deejay Michael 'Mikey Dread' Campbell initially assisting Mikey Dread on his groundbreaking 'Dread At The Controls' radio show and later when Mikey began producing records for his label of the same name. Their work together on the Dread At The Controls and Forty Leg releases 'Parrot Jungle', 'African Anthem' and 'Robber's Roost', proved to be the final anthemic recordings with King Tubby at the controls.

Jammy had gradually begun to move away from engineering and now worked extensively on his own recordings. His first Kingston production was voicing fellow Waterhouse resident Michael Rose, later lead singer of Black Uhuru, on a Vivian 'Yabby You' Jackson rhythm known as 'Prayer To Jah' in 1976: 'Born Free' was released in the UK by the Mighty Fatman (Ken Gordon) on his 'pre-release' Boss label. He then began building his own rhythms and the first release on his own Jammy's label was an updating of the Baba Brooks/King Edwards ska classic 'Shank I Sheck' entitled 'Zambia' credited to Jammy's & King Tubby's. Tubby now employed two new apprentice engineers: Hopeton Overton 'Scientist' Browne in 1977 and Winston 'Professor' Brown the following year.

Dave Hendley

Osbourne 'King Tubby' Ruddock

"I took Scientist up there too you know. Scientist came up there to fix amplifiers and Pat Kelly used to mix the singing so they said 'Scientist... you practise on the dub.' And he made some extraordinary dub! I gave him the name because of his experiments...

Jammys caught him one day licking (striking) the reverb unit! And Tubby said 'Bunny Lee! How come you're making the man mash down my studio?' And I said 'No Tubbs. Scientist a just experiment! Scientist have to do his thing you know!'" **Bunny 'Striker' Lee**

"Scientist came to Tubbys in 1977. He was to learn technician work, electronics but he got interested in the engineering. He came to me and started to ask me questions... if I can teach him. I took him under my wing. Professor was here. He came on a little later after Scientist and I started teaching him. Professor becomes almost the resident engineer and then he migrated abroad." **Lloyd 'King Jammy' James**

"When I came to work here my brother used to deal with transformers and stuff. Him left and leave me to work here. And from then, with the experience and encouragement from Tubbs now, well, I give all the credit to Tubbs. I learn everything from him. Everything."

Winston 'Professor' Brown

"Then he had another one named Professor... we used to call him Mad Crazy Professor. He's in America now... 'Laser Beam' and all those Don Carlos tunes... it's him mixed them you know. The youths all had their different ideas because when Professor used to mix a tune, all of a sudden, he'd just drop out the rhythm. Everybody had their different style! Sometimes you have to let a man do his own thing you know! 'Cause everybody has their different sound." **Bunny 'Striker' Lee**

As the decade came to a close the musical emphasis gradually shifted away from roots based records towards what would become known as the dance hall style. Among the newcomers whose work helped to define this brash new music were up and coming producer Henry 'Junjo' Lawes, deejay now producer Nkrumah 'Jah Thomas' Thomas and singer now producer Linval Thompson. By this time Jammy was busy developing his own studio at his mother's house where he had installed a two track tape machine for basic editing.

"When I formed my own studio now... I couldn't be at Tubbys twenty four hours go and come from mine to Tubbys". **Lloyd 'King Jammy' James**

In 1982 Tubby began work on upgrading his studio.

"Tubby's little four track studio has played a major role in the evolution of reggae music. Other studios have more modern facilities, but Tubby has the history and the sound. Now Tubby is embarking on a new project of updating his equipment and workshop. Behind the present location stands the skeleton of what is to be a complete sixteen track recording and mixing studio. He and his engineer apprentices are wiring and building it. When finished in early 1984 it will not only ease the pressure on the overbooked studios of Kingston but probably emerge as the people's first choice."

Beth Lesser/Kingston

Although King Tubby's work from the Eighties is nowhere near as well documented, well regarded or compiled as yet, in its own way, it would prove to be every bit as inventive as his incredible output from the preceding decade. This story is detailed in 'Tempo: King Tubby In The Digital Age' in Part Three of 'A History Of The Jamaican Recording Industry' series entitled 'The Upsetter To The Computer'. In the same way that Studio One on Brentford Road is regarded as the spiritual home of reggae so the Dromilly Avenue studio of Osbourne 'King Tubby' Ruddock and his sorcerer's apprentices will be known forever as the spiritual home of dub.

"In was in these humble surroundings using outdated but imaginatively modified second hand studio equipment that King Tubby redefined the role of the recording engineer in modern music. While no one man could truly claim to have invented dub (experimenting with studio engineered effects had already taken place on USA soul recordings such as Rex Garvin & The Mighty Cravers' 'Sock It To 'Em JB' Part 2 1966 on Like) it was Tubby above all others who advanced the concept of remix engineering to the point where it became an art form all of its own."

Dave Hendley

The concept that a piece of work that had been created in a recording studio by musicians and singers could be later released in a totally altered form is nothing short of unbelievable. Take a step back and try to imagine a dub mix in any other form of artistic endeavour. How would an author feel if, after handing in a finished manuscript to their publishers, their book was then printed with only a handful of the chapters remaining? Or a playwright seated in the stalls discovering that the actors introduced themselves in echoed snatches of their speeches as the curtain rose then left the stage and the majority of scenes from Acts Two, Three and Four had been excised and their characters did not speak again until the closing scene? Or if a painter discovered that three quarters of their completed creation had been cut away from the canvas during the journey from the garret to the gallery? This has led to protracted legal battles over the authorship and ownership of the music which have yet to be rightfully resolved. Perhaps they never will be? Who does own the rights to a dub mix? The songwriter? The composer? The arranger? The musicians? The producer? The recording engineer? The remix engineer? Or the company that released the recordings?

"Its evanescence and randomness make it perhaps the most existential of musics, and its most stunning implication comes with the realisation that no dub track is ever 'correct' or 'finished': it can always be done again a thousand different ways, each one as 'correct' as any other."

Richard Williams

Who could ever have predicted that a technique that some would claim was born out of economic necessity to fill up a b-side at little cost would become one of the most profound influences on music making in the last quarter of the Twentieth Century and beyond? In many ways the story of dub echoes the history of many other groundbreaking artistic movements, not necessarily musical, where radical new forms of expression are assimilated into the mainstream where their presence eventually, from starting out as truly startling, becomes commonplace. What was once regarded as a revolution is inexorably turned into a style.

"Distorting hackneyed words in hackneyed songs
He turns revolt into a style, prolongs
The impulse to a habit of the time."

'Elvis Presley' Thom Gunn

Ken 'Fatman' Gordon

First, Second & Third Generation Of Dub: Scientist, Prince Jammy & King Tubby

Dub has refused to fade away and its revolutionary reverberations continue to echo all around the world. King Tubby, 'The Dub Master', transformed not only the music making process but also the way that we listen to and appreciate music in the latter half of the Twentieth Century. In his hands the mixing desk became an instrument in its own right and music would never sound the same again.

*Appendix 1
Over And Over Over And Over And Over...

The b-side of Bobby Day's 1958 rhythm & blues smash hit 'Rockin' Robin' entitled 'Over And Over' had long been a sound system favourite and one of the first 78's to be pressed in Jamaica through a licensing agreement with Dada Tewari's Kingston based Caribbean Recording Company with Class in California. Coxsone Dodd released a shuffle and boogie version that he called 'Sweeter And Sweeter' in 1961 on his Worldisc label credited to Fay (Abrahams) & Gabby (Basil Gabbidon) with 'Orch By Roland Alphonso & His Alley Cats' backed by an adaptation of Shirley & Lee's 'That's What I'm Gonna Do' entitled 'I'm Still In Love With You'. Five years later The Clarendonians, whose original line up featured Peter Austin, Fitzroy 'Ernest' Wilson and, later, a very young Freddie McGregor, sang it for Coxsone Dodd's Studio One label as 'The Jerk' and the song was given a new lease of life as a classic of the late ska period.

Forward on another nine years and Bunny 'Striker' Lee transferred the excitement of a rhythm & blues jump up turned ska rave up into a celebration of the very roots of dub and King Tubby's Home Town Hi Fi when he wrote a song with Cornell Campbell. The Clarendonians had already moved the action from California to Kingston and Cornell now took it way downtown to 'A Dance In A Greenwich Farm'.

"So we go a Tubbys... Tubbys had a contest that night... him a play at Greenwich Farm and I passed and see the dance full. So I see some guys up there and I said 'Cornell... the tune that John Holt was going to sing 'pon it. You know the Bobby Day tune? (sings) 'well I went to a dance the other night and everybody was there... over and over and over' and this idea hit me so I said 'Cornell... write this tune here (sings) well I went to a dance in Greenwich Farm King Tubbys and the dreads were there... there was dread, dread, dread and dread and natty roots everywhere'. I finished write it and Chinna sing harmony. 'But when I man take a stock it was just a baldhead informer just a try a thing'. Right? But the dread them come back to the dance and dub to King Tubbys beat. That was one of the first sound system specials that go 'pon the road. 'Cause by the Monday morning I had it out man!" **Bunny 'Striker' Lee**

On the b-side of Cornell's celebration of all things dread, 'A Dancing Roots Version' credited to King Tubbys & The Agrovators, King Tubby took the rhythm to pieces and put it together again in the style that was still usually referred to as version. And version after version followed with tenor sax man Tommy McCook bringing a jazz sensibility to 'A Dancing Dub' on the opening track of Striker's 'Brass Rockers' album. Coxsone Dodd at Studio One stepped back into the arena with foundation musician William 'Sugar Belly' Walker playing his home made bamboo saxophone on 'Over Dub A' with the aptly titled 'Over Dub B' on, naturally enough, the b-side. Dr Alimantado voiced 'The Challis Blaze' and 'Dread Lock's Music' a sustained variation on the same theme for the At It label.

*Appendix 2
Phillip 'Prince Phillip' Smart

Born 9th April 1952 in St Andrew parish Phillip Smart was a record collector with a love of both music and electronics and, naturally enough, became involved in a local Havendale sound system. While living at Harbour View he became friendly with Errol Thompson when he was working at Studio One and Errol encouraged Phillip to pursue a career in sound recording. Phillip recalled trying to get into Randy's studio to see how recordings were made and, after working with Karl Pitterson in a Kingston electronics shop, he moved on to work in a car repair workshop "just around the corner" from Tubby's studio where he began to spend all of his spare time and "hang out there every night".

He was originally originally introduced to King Tubby by his childhood friend Horace 'Augustus Pablo' Swaby in 1971 and, in addition to working on some of Pablo's original home recorded two track mixes, Phillip was involved in Pablo's first self production for his Hot Stuff label, 'Skanking Easy', an update of the Soul Vendors' 'Swing Easy' for Studio One. Phillip began to cut dubs regularly at Tubby's and became firm friends with the King.

"Well Phillip Smart is my brethren. We all grew up in the same area Havendale... we used to work together. I used to share dub with him. He had a sound. I had a sound, you know. We just loved it...

He used to work at a company that deal with Ford cars on Spanish Town Road nearby Tubbys. It was like Tubbys was just round the corner. He used to come there lunch time and evening through him want to learn the thing." **Augustus Pablo**

Dubbed 'Prince Phillip' by Bunny Lee he rapidly found his feet and it was not long before the apprentice became a Dromilly Avenue dub master whose name started to appear on the b-side of records such as Pablo's 'Far East' ('Phillip's Showcase') credited to the Pablo All Stars. As the resident engineer at King Tubby's he would take charge of the mixing while Tubbs was winding transformers... "the big hotels needed the transformers to maintain the steady currents for their air conditioners". But

Phillip Smart soon graduated from Tubby's and emigrated to America at the beginning of 1975 to continue his electronics studies where he would later mastermind the influential HC&F Studios in Long Island "New York's most notable reggae recording facility". King Jammy recalled Prince Phillip's time at Dromilly Avenue:"Phillip Smart was there from about 1973 to 1975 then he left to migrate to America. He was a good engineer... a wicked engineer."

***Appendix 3**
'None Shall Escape The Judgement' Johnny Clarke

"This tune now, 'None Shall Escape The Judgement', I was going home one night and I heard Chinna and Earl Zero playing this tune and Earl Zero was singing 'none shall escape the judgement in this time...' I come and I listened and I said 'I like the tune, you know, Chinna' and Earl Zero said 'Mr Lee. Come tomorrow down to Duke Reid's studio. I think I'm going to record it.' They had 'dum, dum, dum... dum dum dum...dum dum dum dum dum dum dum' and the beat of it...

So I asked Johnny Clarke to sing it with Earl Zero ... they rehearsed it the whole day... but Earl Zero could only sing the front part so that night I asked Siddy (Bucknor) to run off a cut of the rhythm... 'I a go try something'. That night me and Johnny Clarke... we were always around together... we were up at Tubbys and Tubbys said 'this guy can't manage the song' and I said 'Johnny. Do you think you could a do it?' and Johnny went into Tubby's studio. One cut! One cut! No error or nothing... 'cause he'd been rehearsing it with Earl Zero the whole day."

Bunny 'Striker' Lee

"At the time Tubby had 'None Shall Escape The Judgement' by Johnny Clarke as his number one dub and every sound man had to have a copy of it."

Ivanhoe 'Lloydie Slim' Smith

Lloydie Slim was "minding the store" for Striker when Cornell Campbell "Bunny's top singer recorded 'Natty Don't Go' for Downbeat". Lloydie heard on the grapevine: "your guy gone work with a different producer" so Lloydie was keen to release 'None Shall Escape The Judgement' as soon as possible in order to counteract Cornell's Studio One recording.

"The whole thing then was to get Johnny Clarke on a stage show and one time we were coming from Tubbys and I asked Byron Lee 'is Johnny Clarke getting on stage?' and I asked Marie Garth from JBC 'can she put Johnny on the show?' They said 'no... he hasn't rehearsed' and so I told the band the chords and the rhythm and while we were playing it someone shouted 'I hear this tune at a dance!' So they put Johnny on during what should have been the band break and him mash up the show!"

Ivanhoe 'Lloydie Slim' Smith

"So Tubbys had it on the sound system for a while and the people them forced me to release it. I did leave and go to England and I was going to give it to Delroy Wilson. I bring it for Delroy to sing it and Delroy said 'Striker... the youth sing it good! Give the youth a break man. Let the youth sing it... if you want I will sing it but I figure you should give the youth a bligh'. So I said 'alright Delroy. If you say so...' That time Delroy was in England so we didn't bother voice it... we voiced some other tune. So when we went back to Jamaica I said to Johnny Clarke 'you have to like Delroy because I was going to make him sing over the tune in England'."

Bunny 'Striker' Lee

And another of Striker's protégés, David 'Tappa Zukie' Sinclair, told Striker about the burgeoning popularity of 'None Shall Escape The Judgement'.

"Tapper Zukie came to me and said 'Striker? You have a tune there on Tubbys sound. It a mad! Every time it plays the dance catch a fire'. I said 'which tune?' so Tapper told me 'the tune that the new youth a sing… Studio Idler'. Studio Idler is what we used to call Johnny Clarke because he was always around the studio…" **Bunny 'Striker' Lee**

Phillip Smart also informed Striker of the urgent necessity to release the song on record but they met with some unexpected opposition.

"Then Phillip Smart come and he said 'Mr Lee… I'm tired of cutting dubs of this tune. You have to put out the tune' so I said to Phillip 'take a mix off this tune…' so when Phillip was mixing it Tubbys a fly in and said 'what's happening? I've cut 'nough dub with people and you can't put out this now because the dub people will come back…' So I said 'Tubbs we're mixing this tune to go send to England for Fatman. We're not going to put it out' and Tapper and Tubbys started to quarrel. Tapper said to Tubbys 'let the new tune go out on the road' and Tubbys said 'no man!' So I didn't bother row. We just took a rough cut of the master and mixed the version. Tubbs said 'where are you sending the version? I'll send it…' and I said 'no… I have somebody going to England this evening and by the time you mix it yourself and send it they'll be gone. It's just Fatman's sound it's for'.

So at the same time I just went down to Federal to master it with the version and everything and when the tune came out it had the 'swwwt, swwwt, swwwt…' Phillip Smart mixed the first version that went out on the road… not Tubbys! And Tubbys was vexed… but everybody started flocking to Tubbys then and I said 'it's better you put out the tune because now everybody wants different dub cuts'. Sound men started to line up at Tubbys gate for different pieces and different cuts with their sound's name in it and things. So it was a feather in his cap… but he didn't want it released! But from Tubbs put out that tune there was no turning back 'cause every tune we put out we put the rhythm behind it. But flyers is not the right name really and everybody started to get puzzled when Johnny Clarke hit with this flyers now." **Bunny 'Striker' Lee**

Released in the spring of 1974 on Justice and Jackpot in Kingston, on Explosion in London and on Clocktower in New York backed with Phillip Smart's mix, 'This A The Best Version', the record was a spectacular hit throughout the reggae world. Striker, true to form, went on to release a plethora of alternative versions including 'Give (Me) A Helping Hand' from Owen Gray, 'Gun Court Law' by Cornell Campbell and Johnny

Clarke in combination with Dillinger on the heavyweight 'Jah Jah Dub'. Johnny demonstrated his songwriting skills on two more cuts to the rhythm, 'Jah Jah Bless Joshua' and 'Joshua's Word', which echoed the dread mood of those troubled times.

The American 'proto-punk' group, Jonathan Richman & The Modern Lovers, hit the Number Five spot in the UK National Charts with 'Egyptian Reggae', their instrumental interpretation of 'None Shall Escape The Judgement', in the autumn of 1977. Striker ruefully recalled.

"Then they copied 'None Shall Escape The Judgement'. Yeah man... 'cause we didn't know nothing about publishing at that time so Larry Sevitt and a guy named Tony Seddon dealt with it. When 'Egyptian Reggae' came out the bass line was Chinna's and the other part belongs to Family Man. He played guitar on that session... where the change is 'arise black man'... that's Family Man. It was giving them trouble so him and Chinna worked out the chords and that was it. And Chinna played a brilliant solo... something like Santana... it kinda introduced guitar solos into reggae. You understand?

So when these people copied the tune Larry and them had to fight it 'cause Larry was my good friend. I think Johnny Clarke did register it at one time but they said no. If anybody it's Earl Zero and Chinna Smith... you only sing it so you can't do that... you might get a percentage of part of it but you can't register the tune. So I did clear up that so everybody got a piece of the action. I think I did get a piece of the action as the producer and the man who spent the money to make the rhythm and everything like that."

Bunny 'Striker' Lee

*Appendix 4
Pat Kelly

Horatious Adolphus Pat Kelly, born Kingston 6th August 1944, recalled gaining his first experience of recording, engineering and voicing for King Tubby in his "music room" as early as 1969 after having served his electronics apprenticeship working part time at Chin's Radios in downtown Kingston alongside Jammy in the early Sixties. After studying Electrical Engineering at Kingston Technical High School he was awarded a scholarship which took him to the Massachusetts College Of Technology in the USA for three years where he graduated with a degree in Advanced Electronics.

He was not only a highly accomplished recording engineer when he took over Tubby's board from Phillip Smart but also lead singer in one of Jamaica's greatest close harmony groups The Techniques. A naturally gifted vocalist with a fine soulful falsetto Pat formed a group called The Sheridans alongside Winston Francis, Owen Roberts and Edwin Brown who recorded for Carlos Malcolm's Up Beat label and, when the group broke up, Pat joined The Techniques as a replacement for Slim Smith. Their adaptation of The Impressions' 'You'll Want Me Back' re-titled 'You Don't Care' was a huge hit on the Treasure Isle label and the Curtis Mayfield songbook was turned to again as The Techniques sang over The Impressions' 'Minstrel & Queen' as 'Queen Majesty'. Both records have assumed legendary status in the annals of Jamaican music and are rightly regarded as bona fide rock steady classics to be versioned over time and time again. Pat later sang with The Uniques and enjoyed a highly successful solo career which took off in a big way when he recorded 'How Long Will It Take' for Bunny 'Striker' Lee.

"A return to the Striker Lee stable gave Pat a taste of international success with 'How Long Will It Take' one of the biggest reggae hits of 1969/70. In the UK the song was one of the last great anthems of the skinhead era eventually breaking out of this niche market to become a minor pop hit."

Dave Hendley

When he toured the UK in late 1969 The Beatles allegedly tried to sign him to their newly formed Apple label, "planning to re-launch his career as a pop artist", but Pat was unable to do so because of previous contractual obligations and "no deal was ever materialised". Pat returned to Kingston and went on to work as an engineer at Dynamic, Joe Gibbs, Randy's and King Tubby's recording studios.

Chris Lane has fond memories of Pat Kelly's kindness and self deprecation recalling, in particular, a 1985 recording session at Hillside Studio in Streatham, South London. Pat stayed behind after everyone else had left and helped to dismantle and pack up the drum kit remarking: "I know what it's like! I've worked at every studio in Kingston apart from Tuff Gong."

"Pat Kelly remains perhaps the most underrated of all the engineers to have sat in the chair at Tubby's studio. By nature a shy and retiring man Pat never captured the limelight in the way of his contemporaries, Prince

Jammy and Scientist. Although his engineering style was less flamboyant than others in the Dromilly Avenue dynasty he was a highly accomplished technician and his dub mixes from the mid to late Seventies remain some of the most enduring of the roots era. A bonus was the fact that he was also one of Jamaica's most gifted singers which added another dimension to his skill on the board when it came to laying vocal tracks.

Sunshot Records

Pat Kelly

Pat had his own unique techniques and timing. He used a more considered, almost ponderous, mixing style to great effect and was at his best on rhythms featuring unrelenting bass lines. A good showcase for Pat Kelly's skills can be found on the superb dub side of Ricky 'I Kong' Storme's 1976 underground roots classic 'Trod Along Zion Pathway' where the engineer is credited as 'I Pat'. On this mix Pat adds even more ballast to the already considerable weight of the track by drenching the bass in reverb to create one of the very heaviest dubs of the Seventies.

The late Seventies saw Pat's singing career enjoy something of a renaissance in part boosted by the huge UK demand for the softer sounds of lovers rock... a new form of reggae. Outside of Jamaica twelve inch singles (universally known as discos) ruled the market and Pat scored huge hits with releases such as 'It's A Good Day' for young producer Ossie Hibbert and the recut of 'They Talk About Love' a recording that saw the singer reunited with Phil Pratt.

Pat continued to work informally at Tubby's right into the early Eighties and his first class mix of Don Carlos' 'Late Night Blues' is a particularly fine example of how easily he adapted his craft to the heavy duty rhythms typical of the dance hall."
Dave Hendley

Pat Kelly died on 16th July 2019, aged 74, from complications of kidney disease.

"He and I go back a long way to our days at Chocomo Lawn, a place where so many of our artistes and musicians got their start, thanks to Edward Seaga. I was the president of the Victor's Youth Club at Chocomo Lawn and Pat was a member. It was there that he began developing his talent, which has seen him become a great Jamaican singer and outstanding audio engineer. I have been very proud of his success with The Techniques and in his solo career, and satisfied with his contribution to our music. I offer sincerest condolences to his family, friends and colleagues at this time."
Minister of Culture and Entertainment Olivia 'Babsy' Grange

Bunny 'Striker' Lee

King Tubby

*Appendix 5
King Tubby's Home Town Hi Fi 1975

It would be difficult to overestimate the impact of Robert Allen discovering and disseminating this tape. Apparently, he had had to bother one of Kingston's numerous street vendors on a daily basis until he came up with the cassette as his customers were usually only interested in the latest sound tapes. It was a revelation and respect and gratitude goes to Robert for his perseverance...

Although it had been rumoured to exist for years it was, to the best of our knowledge, the first tape that anyone had ever heard of King Tubby's Home Town Hi Fi. The sixty minute tape, dating from 1975, starred U Roy and shook London's reggae world to its very foundations. Although it was very basically recorded live and direct in the dance it was still one of the most exciting finds of the decade and it still sounds amazing. Seriously...

Side One:
Foundation Version
b-side to 'Foundation Scank' - Hugh Roy - Rebel 7"
Federal cover of 'Sweet Talking' - The Heptones

"Horace Andy selection..."
Something On My Mind – Horace Andy – Money Disc (Studio One)
I'll Be Gone – Horace Andy – Skylarking – Studio One LP
Love Of A Woman – Horace Andy – Skylarking – Studio One LP
(It's) Gonna Be Dread – Horace Andy – Dub Plate

"Kinda scratchy. Very, very scratchy..." U Roy
Spangler's Clap – King Tubby's Dub Plate
Tubby's dub to 'To Be A Lover' – George Earl (George Faith)/
'Have Some Mercy' – Delroy Wilson

A Dance In A Greenwich Farm – Cornell Campbell – Justice
A Dance In A Greenwich Farm Version – The Aggrovators
So Jah Seh – Bob Marley & The Wailers – Island (UK)
Satisfy My Soul Jah Jah – Bob Marley & The Wailers – Tuff Gong
*cuts out...
Ethiopians Live It Out – Burning Spear – Coxsone

Side Two:
Ethiopians Live It Out – Burning Spear – Coxsone
Everyday You Wondering Version – Johnny Clarke – Success
Satta Amassa Gana Version – The Abyssinians – Clinch
Ain't No Sunshine – Horace Andy – Earth Quake
False Rasta – Jacob Miller – Thompson Sound
Ain't No Sunshine Version
Queen Of The Minstrells (sic) – The Eternals – Supreme (Studio One)
Stars – The Eternals – Supreme (Studio One)
Heptones Gonna Fight (Fight It To The Top) Version –
The Heptones – Studio One
Party Time Version – The Heptones – Studio One
Pretty Looks Isn't All Version – The Heptones – Studio One
And back to Foundation Version...

Three further King Tubby's tapes have subsequently surfaced (East Queen Street, University of the West Indies Student Union & South Side) all from 1975 and they are all good (of course they are) but not as good as this slice of audio dynamite.

***Appendix 6**
Hopeton Overton 'Scientist' Browne

Greensleeves Records

Scientist at King Tubby's

Hopeton Overton 'Scientist' Browne was born18th April 1960 in Kingston. His father was an electronics engineer and television and radio repair technician and, as a very young man, Hopeton, who had been drawn to music through an interest in electronics, began building amplifiers for sound systems. He tested his amplifiers by playing King Tubby's mixes "to ensure that the amplifiers would not break down under extreme conditions". He used to buy transformers from King Tubby and was soon doing "odds and ends jobs" repairing television sets and amplifiers and, in 1977, Tubby employed him help wind transformers at Dromilly Avenue.

During 1979 Scientist worked briefly at Studio One to learn live recording as Tubby's studio only had facilities for mixing and voicing. His early mixes at Brentford Road coincided with Mr Dodd's first forays into the dance hall style and Sugar Minott's translation of The Tennors' 'Pressure And (The) Slide' into 'Oh Mr DC' is cited as one of the first ever Scientist mixes. But, after disagreements about how to record, Scientist returned to the Dromilly Avenue studio where his first big break came with Henry 'Junjo' Lawes when he recorded and mixed Barrington Levy's 'Collie Weed' for Randy's Roots From The Yard subsidiary when Jammy had been unable to make it to the session. His unorthodox dub mixing techniques began to make their mark as he breathed new life into a genre that some commentators had written off as being past its best.

The Roots Radics were the top session band of the period bridging the gap between the roots dominated Seventies and the digital rhythms that followed and Scientist's approach to their sparse, spare, pared down rhythms ushered in a new period of popularity for dub music.

"Most of the time I used the Roots Radics. I'd pay them before a session so they'd work better with money in their pockets! In one session we made ten different rhythms and seven of them were hits... " **Jah Thomas**

In 1980 Greensleeves Records in London began what would become long and close working relationships with Henry 'Junjo' Lawes and Linval Thompson when their 'Scientist vs Prince Jammy' dub album pitted the mixing skills of Scientist against his mentor Prince Jammy. The set, sequenced like a sound system battle with each mixer taking a turn at the controls, came in a superb eye catching sleeve by designer and illustrator Tony McDermott. The two opponents, portrayed as boxers, faced each other from opposite corners of the ring/dance hall; Tony recalled the difficulties that he encountered in getting a likeness for Scientist.

"It's true… the only photo we had was an out of focus print which I had to interpret as best as I could. Jah Thomas helped us out by making suggestions… he was looking over Chris Cracknell's shoulder while Chris was talking to me on the 'phone. It was bit like putting one of those photo-fits together!" **Tony McDermott**

The album proved to be very popular and Greensleeves' next Roots Radics dub album, which followed later that year, was credited solely to Scientist and entitled 'Heavyweight Dub Champion'. The release of 'Scientist Meets The Space Invaders' the following year signalled the beginning of Scientist's international fame. Over the next two years a series of imaginatively titled dub albums, all with excellent artwork from Tony McDermott, were released in the UK where after Meeting The Space Invaders Scientist Encountered Pac Man and then Rid The World Of The Evil Curse Of The Vampires before Winning The World Cup. These albums were among the last Jamaican dub albums to achieve classic status among the cognoscenti. And, as they had done with King Tubby in the previous decade, every other producer in the reggae business also began releasing dub sets with Scientist's name emblazoned across the cover.

Scientist's work on the mixing desk backed dub music out of its late Seventies cul de sac and played an important role in expanding the popularity of reggae music when, in 2001, five of the tracks from 'Scientist Rids The World Of The Evil Curse Of The Vampires' album featured on the K-Jah radio station in the 'Grand Theft Auto 3' video/computer game.

ROCKERS INTERNATIONAL
Myrie & Pablo Skanking
ROCKERS ALL STARS
MICRON
Tubby's Vengeance
SONS OF JAH
PROD. BY V. Jackson
JACKPOT
A RUFFER VERSION
THE AGGROVATORS
HOT CITY
PHILLIP SMART
All Copyrights Reserved)
FREEDOM SOUNDS
GRATE STONE
King Tubby's
SANTIC
Santic Meet King Tubbys
KING TUBBYS
& The Santic all Stars
MOVE & GROOVE
"ACID VERSION"
CRYSTALITES
PANTOMINE
NUMBER ONE IN THE WORLD
U – ROY
ARAB
KING TUBBY'S VERSION
PRODUCED AND DIRECTED BY UPSETTER
JUSTICE LEAGUE
French Connection
Lee Perry
ROCKERS
555 CROWN STREET
(H. Swaby)
Agustos Pablo
ROCK - OVER
45 R.P.M.
TUBBY
King Tubbs At His Best
Rockers All Stars
Success
Irie Feelings
Rupie Edwards
VERSION
PRODUCED BY RUPIE EDWARDS
45 RPM
VERSION
Rupie Edwards all Stars
PROPHET
King Tubby's
SPECIAL
Black & White
KING AT THE CONTROL
KING TUBBYS
MICRON
CONFERENCE AT WATERHOUSE
Jah Stitch
Jah Stitch

*Appendix 7
A Selection Of King Tubby's Seven Inch Releases

Many of the original King Tubby's seven inch records are now very hard to find (many were hard enough to find at the time) and this Top Thirty listing is designed to point the listener in the direction of some of the very, very best Dromilly Avenue singles. This is neither a definitive list nor an exercise in wilful obscurity for the majority of the following records have been subsequently re-released or compiled on the many dub sets that are now readily available. In no particular order:

'King Tubby's In Fine Stile' (sic) Rosie 1975
'Power Of Love' Ronnie Davis
Producer: Ivanhoe 'Lloydie Slim' Smith
The undisputed top Tubby's mix of all time? Ronnie Davis emotes soulfully over Horace Andy's thundering 'You Are My Angel' rhythm while Tubby goes for it like there's no tomorrow.

'King Tubbys Meet Rockers Uptown'
Augustus Pablo International 1975
'Baby I Love You So' Jacob Miller
('Cassava Piece' Augustus Pablo)
Producer: Horace 'Augustus Pablo' Swaby
When Island released the Jamaican b-side of Jacob Miller singing over Pablo's 'Cassava Piece' as the UK a-side it helped to introduce the concept of dub to mainstream attention. Later that summer Bob Marley announced on stage at The Lyceum, London "So we return to the rockers…" and dub had truly arrived.

'Freak Out Skank' The Upsetters Justice League 1973
'Jungle Lion' The Upsetters
Producer: Lee 'Scratch' Perry
An early King Tubby/Upsetter collaboration of Scratch's interpretation of Al Green's 'Love & Happiness' burnished with copious use of the high pass filter on the Dromilly Avenue MCI board.

'Tubby's Vengeance' Sons Of Jah Micron/Prophets 1975
'Jah Vengeance' Vivian Jackson & The Sons Of Jah
Producer: Vivian 'Yabby You' Jackson

'Tommy & King Tubbys Greetings' Prophet 1976
'Revenge' Tommy McCook
Producer: Vivian 'Yabby You' Jackson

Originally built at Lee Perry's Black Ark the 'Jah Vengeance' rhythm was undoubtedly one of Yabby's most powerful ever. "Tubby's treatment (on both the vocal and its instrumental counterpart) shows both the open ended nature of Yabby's music and Tubbs' inventiveness with the endless possibilities within it".

'Park Lane Special' Pablo All Stars Pablo International 1976
'Africans Must Be Free' Hugh Mundell
Producer: Horace 'Augustus Pablo' Swaby

This song defined Hugh Mundell's unwavering stance and would give the title to his debut album at the close of the decade. Uncluttered and unadorned the message really hits home…

'A Ruffer Version' The Aggrovators Jackpot 1976
'Don't Trouble Trouble' Johnny Clarke
Producer: Bunny 'Striker' Lee

The dub with everything thrown into the mix as Johnny Clarke, Bunny 'Striker' Lee and King Tubby assert their ascendancy on the Kingston musical scene. No-one could come near them… never forget that "trouble is very dangerous".

'This A The Best Version' The Agrovators (sic) Justice 1974
(Engineer: Phillip 'Prince Phillip' Smart)
'None Shall Escape The Judgement' Jonnie (sic) Clarke
Producer: Bunny 'Striker' Lee

Phillip Smart's debut release, the record that made Johnny Clarke a superstar, introduced Striker's flying cymbals sound and eventually became a worldwide hit in 1977 as 'Egyptian Reggae' for Jonathan Richman & The Modern Lovers.

'King Tubby's Version' Talent Crew Arab 1975
'Please Officer' Earl Zero
Producers: Ian & Roger Lewis

"Brutalisation… that's what we get from Babylon" as Tubby racks up the tension on Earl Zero's legendary plea for tolerance and understanding.

'Acid Version' The Crystalites Move & Groove 1972
'He Can't Spell' Dennis Brown
Producer: Derrick Harriott

Oddly enough the version in question is a spare, sparse cut to Dennis' beautiful 'I Didn't Know' and not 'He Can't Spell'. The dub is minimal in the extreme but all the lovelier for it. Derrick Harriott was one of the first uptown producers to regularly use the services of King Tubby's downtown studio and he gave the Tubby's dubs to 'I Didn't Know' and 'Concentration' equal billing to the vocal cuts on Dennis' 'Super Reggae & Soul Hits' album.

'Dread Version' Bar Bell/Micron 1976
(Engineer: Phillip 'Prince Phillip' Smart)
'Satta Dread' Wayne Jarrett
Producer: Robbie Shakespeare

Threatening, full of foreboding and further proof that less is definitely more. Jah Stitch introduced his equally awesome deejay version to the rhythm, 'Conference At Waterhouse', with "Your destination King Tubby's studio..."

'Irie Feelings' Rupie Edwards/'Feeling High'
Rupie All Stars Success 1974
'Everyday Wondering' Johnny Clarke Circle
Producer: Rupie Edwards

The criminally under rated Rupie Edwards hit the UK National Charts in 1974 by impersonating a selection of instruments over a Tubby's deconstruction of Johnny Clarke's 'Every Day You Wondering'. Regarded as a 'novelty', but actually straight from Dr Satan's Echo Chamber, the record was years ahead of its time.

'Santic Meet King Tubbys'
King Tubby & The Santic All Stars Santic 1975
'I Don't Want To Lose You' Paul Whiteman
Producer: Leonard 'Santic' Chin

One of the youngest producers of the era, Leonard 'Santic' Chin, fully understood the power and the weight that a King Tubby's remix could add to an already superb rhythm and song.

'Tubby Dub Song' Augustus Pablo Pablo International 1975
'Pablo's Theme Song' Augustus Pablo
Producer: Horace 'Augustus Pablo' Swaby
The records King Tubby worked on with Pablo always emphasised the spiritual qualities of his music and unfailingly brought out higher heights and deeper depths.

'Chapter 2' Upsetters Justice League 1972
'French Connection' Lee Perry
Producer: Lee 'Scratch' Perry
Scratch introduces this primal dub as "a must for your selection..." and who are we to argue?

'Myrie & Pablo Skanking'
Rockers All Stars Rockers International 1979
(Engineer: Overton 'Scientist' Browne)
'Humble Yourself' Asher & Trimble
Producer: Michael 'Myrie' Taylor
No apologies for the preponderance of Augustus Pablo music here but this one is actually a Michael 'Myrie' Taylor production for Rockers featuring an early sparse and spare Scientist mix. All the trademark signatures are here...

'Gorgon Version' The Aggrovators Attack 1975
'The Gorgon' Cornell Campbell
Producer: Bunny 'Striker' Lee
Cornell Campbell's 'The Gorgon' was the starting point for version upon version as his fragile voice soared high above a barrage of flying cymbals. Back then this was the sound of now.

'A Useful Version' Prince Jammy &
The Aggrovators Jackpot Revive 45 (UK) 1990
(Engineer: Lloyd 'Prince Jammy' James)
'Don't Try To Use Me' Horace Andy
Producer: Bunny 'Striker' Lee
A Nineties press of Prince Jammy's dubwise interpretation of Horace Andy's melancholy, misogynist 'Don't Try To Use Me' memorably versioned by Jah Stitch as 'Greedy Girl'.

'Grate (sic) Stone' King Tubby's Freedom Sounds 1976
'Stone' Prince Allah
Producer: Bertram Brown
Tone signals, swirling organ, militant drumming, snatches of Prince Allah's impassioned vocal mixed into oblivion by the King and, like the Biblical trumpets and the wall of Jericho, this really does sound as if it could mash down Babylon.

'African Anthem' Mikey Dread Dread All The Way
Dread At The Controls 1978
'His Imperial Majesty' Rod Taylor
Producer: Michael 'Mikey Dread' Campbell
"Please would you mind saying that again?" ... straight from the rule breaking DATC radio extravaganza via Dromilly Avenue the radical roots rhythm powers ahead embellished with Mikey Dread's jingles and random sound effects.

'A Noise Place' The Aggrovators Jackpot 1975
'A Quiet Place' Horace Andy
Producer: Bunny 'Striker' Lee
Tubby takes the songs subject matter literally here and the "pots and pans" clatter and crash against the wall as Horace Andy sings over The Paragons classic 'Quiet Place'.

'Rootes (sic) Dub' Well Charge 1975
'Roots Man' I Roy/'Fade Away' Junior Byles
Producer Earl 'Chinna' Smith/Jo Jo Hoo Kim
Channel One usually kept their mixing in-house down on Maxfield Avenue but, perhaps due to Chinna's influence, this all time classic made it over to Tubby's where the b-side of I Roy's deejay cut was given the Waterhouse treatment.

'Psalms Of Dub' Black & White 1974
'Not Responsible' Carlton & Leroy
Producer Carlton Pitterson
One of the first b-sides actually credited to King Tubby: a restrained and subtle drum and bass workout of Carlton & Leroy's 'Not Responsible'.

'A Good Version' Clocktower 1974
'Shirley Come Back To Me' Derrick Morgan & Hortense Ellis
Producer: Bunny 'Striker' Lee

A seriously under rated mix of a Shirley & Lee song from 1953 interpreted by Derrick and Hortense for Striker Lee over twenty years later and then taken to the cleaners by Tubby putting in some serious overtime on the board.

'Watergate Rock' Black & White 1975
'I Admire You' Larry Marshall
Producer: Carlton Patterson

Another beautifully understated mix from the King of Larry Marshall's fragile love song for Carlton Patterson.

'1 Ruthland Close' Rockers All Star Rockers 1974
'555 Crown Street' Augustus Pablo International
Producer Horace 'Augustus Pablo' Swaby

So minimal it's hardly there at all but proving, once again, that less can sometimes be much, much more as Tubby shreds Pablo's ethereal melodica version to Jacob Miller's accusatory 'False Rasta'.

'Tubby's At The Control' Pantomine 1974
'Number One In The World' U Roy/'Get Up' Ron Wilson
Producer Glen Brown

Two superb sides: U Roy extols the virtues of King Tubby on the a-side and the King returns the compliment by taking over the proceedings on the b-side with Tubby's 'secret weapon', the high pass filter, put to full use.

'Tribulation Dub' Soul Syndicate Scorpio/MCM 1977
'Tribulation' Bim 'Bim Man' Sherman
Producer: Bim Sherman

Simply beautiful.. a subtle, restrained remix of a subtle, restrained rhythm.

'Jah Jah Dub' Dillinger, King Tubby & The Aggrovators Attack 1975
'None Shall Escape The Judgement' Jonnie (sic) Clarke
Producer Bunny 'Striker' Lee

Johnny Clarke sings as Dillinger chants his way through a run down all the necessary ingredients required for a truly dread version... "ital dub, vital dub..." over a next Tubby's mix of 'None Shall Escape The Judgement'.

'Version' King Tubby's & The Intimidates (sic) Stars 1976
'Bosrah' Ras Allah
Producer: Tappa Zukie
A roots classic from Prince Ras Allah and Tapper Zukie replete with blazing horns and dread, dreader than dread, sermonising.

And it would be every bit as easy to showcase another thirty… and another thirty… and another thirty…

As the years go by the records sound better and better and their iconoclastic techniques sound more and more unbelievably startling. In the era of playing safe it is difficult to imagine a time when the more daring the music was then the more popular a record would be. These records demonstrate the incredible range of King Tubby's dub techniques and show that even the most unlikely candidates could end up in the UK Charts…

*In late 1978 King Tubby produced a searing critique of Kingston's trigger happy gunmen… 'Pure Rankin'' by Horace Andy. The rhythm track was recorded by Prince Jammy at Harry J's studio and voiced at Dromilly Avenue and, after being extensively played out on dub, the record was released as a twelve inch 'discomix' on Carlton Patterson's Black & White label in Jamaica and on Dave Hendley's Sufferer's Heights outlet in the UK in 1979.

Compiled by Paul Coote, Noel Hawks, Dave Hendley, Chris Lane & Ian McCann

*Appendix 8
Blood & Fire Records

Some twenty years after their first sonic experiments King Tubby and Bunny 'Striker' Lee reached an entirely new audience through Steve Barrow's Blood & Fire organisation.

"The cost of recording had stunted the growth of the music for years but the four track tape gave an artistic (and financial) impetus and producers like Bunny Lee took full advantage of it!

But if you packaged it correctly and annotated it properly then it opened up a whole world of dub to a potentially new audience... a younger audience... which was the audience we wanted to make this music available to. That is, people who hadn't been immersed in it for years. We were lucky that no-one had done it before to the standards we tried to do it to... dub albums were bashed out quickly because the companies didn't want to spend money on them.

So we went to Striker's studio (at Duhaney Park) every day with Garth the engineer. He just ran the tapes... but he couldn't switch on the air conditioning... and we managed to copy one hundred and fifty or so tracks... it may have been a few more... on to DAT (Digital Audio Tape). I then compiled the first two releases on Blood & Fire into 'Dub Gone Crazy' which did very well then 'Dub Gone Crazy Two'. We had a photo of the tapes strewn all over the floor so we called the third one 'Dub Like Dirt'. A lot of the dubs didn't have names so I named them... except for 'Dub Fi Gwaan'... which was Garth. We were running the tape of Jackie Mittoo's do over of 'Totally Together' which was based on a deejay track that wasn't finished. The deejay stopped chatting half way through and Garth said 'dub fi gwaan...' so we took that title! It had an easy rolling momentum...

A lot of the tracks were taken from seven inch singles where they were labelled 'version'... singers like Johnny Clarke, Horace Andy, Cornell Campbell... and a lot of Bunny's artists from that time. But they had to be given proper titles in order to secure the publishing... actually I quite liked giving them titles. It probably took me half a day to compile from the DATs, run it to cassette, shuffle it a couple of times. It was extraordinarily successful!

Rob Partridge and Gaylene Martin were our press agents and they sent it to one of the deejays headlining at Glastonbury that year (1994)… I think it was Andy Weatherall… and he created a real interest in it. We ended up selling over forty thousand copies… even Bunny said he didn't think you could sell that many of a dub album." **Steve Barrow**

David Hendley 30th July 1952 to 19th July 2016

This chapter is respectfully dedicated to the memory of Dave Hendley. Dave was a true and generous friend for nearly forty years, an internationally acclaimed photographer and acknowledged expert on reggae music. I have shamelessly (but with his full permission) used his two King Tubby 1977 articles from *Blues & Soul* magazine and Dave's definitive article, 'King Tubby Mr Dub', originally published in *'Natty Dread'* magazine in 2003 as the template for this chapter. Dave's accounts of Tubby's studio come from first-hand experience and I am forever indebted to him for his kindness in allowing me to use his work. The only excuse I can offer is that the *'Natty Dread'* article appeared in French only and that Dave's account deserved some sort of English translation. Thank you Dave… as always.

Noel Hawks/Fashion Records

Johnny Clarke

King Tubby's
Tubby Recording Studio
18 Dromilly Avenue
Kingston 11

Producers:
Osbourne 'King Tubby' Ruddock & Lloyd 'Prince Jammy' James

Engineers:
Osbourne 'King Tubby' Ruddock
Winston 'Professor' Brown, Overton 'Scientist' Browne, Augustus 'Gussie' Clarke, Lloyd 'Prince Jammy' James, Pat Kelly & Phillip 'Prince Phillip' Smart

Musicians:
There was no 'live room' so the bands never actually built rhythms at King Tubby's studio. There was only ever space for voicing and mixing but I have listed two bands because Bunny 'Striker' Lee's Aggrovators' rhythms were instrumental in the creation of dub and The Roots Radics were similarly influential in the birth of the dance hall style.

The Aggrovators
Musicians include
Drums: Lloyd 'Tin Leg' Adams, Carlton 'Carlie' Barrett, Basil 'Brother Benbow' Creary, Carlton 'Santa' Davis & Lowell 'Sly' Dunbar
Bass: Aston 'Family Man' Barrett, George 'Fully' Fullwood, Bertram 'Ranchie' McLean, Lloyd 'Sparks' Parks, Robert 'Robbie' Shakespeare Earl 'Bagga' Walker (Cornell Campbell occasionally)
Lead Guitar: Radcliffe 'Duggie' Bryan, Jerome 'Jah Jerry' Haynes & Earl 'Chinna' Smith
Rhythm Guitar: Aston 'Family Man' Barrett, Winston 'Bo Peep' Bowen, Radcliffe 'Duggie' Bryan, Albert Valentine 'Tony' Chin, Alva 'Reggie' Lewis & Lorraine 'Ranny Bop' Williams
(Horace Andy & Cornell Campbell occasionally)
Piano: Gladstone 'Gladdy' Anderson, Ansel 'Pinkie' Collins, Bernard 'Touter' Harvey, Oswald 'Ossie' 'Nogo' Hibbert, Bobby Kalphat, Errol 'Tarzan' Nelson & Keith Sterling
(Johnny 'Studio Idler' Clarke occasionally)
Organ: Glen 'Capo' Adams, Ansel 'Pinkie' Collins, Tyrone 'Organ D' Downie, Bernard 'Touter' Harvey, Oswald 'Ossie'/'Nogo' Hibbert,

Earl 'Wire' Lindo, Jackie Mittoo, Lloyd 'Charmers' Tyrell, Ian Winter & Winston 'Brubeck' Wright (Horace 'Augustus Pablo' Swaby occasionally)
Tenor Saxophone: Roland Alphonso, Val Bennett, Karl 'King Cannon' Bryan, Richard 'Dirty Harry' Hall, Tommy McCook & Lester Sterling
Alto Saxophone: Felix 'Deadly' Hedley Bennett, Lennox Brown, Dean 'Youth Sax' Fraser, Alphanso Henry & Herman 'Seventh' Marquis
Trumpet: Bobby Ellis, Mark Lewis, David Madden & Lester Sterling
Trombone: Vincent 'Don D Junior'/'Trommie' Gordon, Dave Parks & Ron 'Willow' Wilson
Harmonica: Charles 'Charlie Organaire' Cameron
Percussion: 'Barnabus', Denzil 'Pops' Laing, Noel 'Zoot'/'Scully' Simms & Uzziah 'Sticky' Thompson

The Roots Radics
Musicians include
Drums: Eric 'Fish' Clarke, Carlton 'Santa' Davis & Lincoln Valentine 'Style' Scott
Bass: Errol 'Flabba' Holt
Lead Guitar: Noel 'Sowell' Bailey, Roy Hamilton, Dwight Pinkney & Earl 'Chinna' Smith
Rhythm Guitar: Winston 'Bo Peep' Bowen, Eric 'Bingy Bunny' Lamont & Dwight Pinkney
Keyboards: Gladstone 'Gladdy' Anderson, Ansel 'Pinkie' Collins, Wycliffe 'Steely' Johnson,Errol 'Tarzan' Nelson & Winston 'Brubeck' Wright
Saxophone: Felix 'Deadly' Headley Bennett & Dean 'Youth Sax' Fraser
Trombone: Val Bennett & Ronald 'Nambo' Robinson
Trumpet: Chico Chin & Bobby Ellis
Percussion: Christopher 'Sky Juice' Blake

CHANNEL 1
Channel 1
29 Maxfield Ave.
Kgn. 13, Jamaica
45 R.P.M.
UNAUTHORISED PUBLIC PERFORMANCE BROADCASTING AND COPYING OF THIS RECORD IS PROHIBITED

CHANNEL ONE
Economic Package
MADE
IN JAMAICA
Unauthorised
Copying is
Prohibited
33⅓
R.P.M.
FIRST ISSUED
29 Maxfield Ave.
Kingston 13
Phone: 92-38792
BADNESS DON'T PAY
L. SMART & T. PALMER
SMART

UNAUTHORISED
COPYING
IS PROHIBITED
45 R.P.M.
NIGHT TIME
MIGHTY DIAMOND

PRODUCED BY
CHANNEL ONE
REVOLUTIONARIES
MADE
IN JAMAICA
45 R.P.M.
Unauthorised
Copying is
Prohibited
℗ 1977
RECORDDING
FIRST ISSUED
29 Maxfield Ave.
Kingston 13
ANSWER ME QUESTION
RANKING TREVOR

DISCO MIX
UNAUTHORISED
COPYING
IS PROHIBITED
DILLINGER

CORD
MADE IN
JAMAICA
L. McKenzie
Kingston 13
Jamaica W.I.
℗ 1978
Unauthorised
Copying
Prohibited
TELL ME WHAT IS WRONG
DIAMONDS

Noel Hawks

Chapter 7

The Revolutionary Sound : Channel One

"No other Jamaican studio was to have quite the same impact in 1975 to 1976 or exert as much influence on the direction of the music."
Steve Barrow & Peter Dalton

The "revolutionary sound of Channel One" achieved worldwide prominence during the mid-Seventies reggae boom. It was no overnight sensation or flash in the pan but the result of copious amounts of hard work and dedication but, perhaps most importantly of all, its origins were based on the Hoo Kim brothers' lifelong love of music and their fascination with the way it was made and recorded.

"In the Seventies Maxfield Avenue was one of Kingston's happening communities. Journalists from around the world flocked the area for stories on its people, politicians and music." **Howard Campbell**

The Hoo Kim brothers' father was from China, "he was going to Panama in 1926 and he stopped off in Jamaica", and their mother was Jamaican of "half Jewish half Chinese" heritage; their four sons were born in St Andrew, Kingston and all grew up in the Greenwich Farm area: Joseph, known as Jo Jo, was the eldest born on 10th December 1942, then Paulie who repaired bicycles, followed by Ernest who was a technician and then the youngest brother Kenneth. All four were involved in music and sound systems from an early age and Jo Jo recalled how important music was because "it was one of the few forms of entertainment available to the people before television arrived in Jamaica". They were all rhythm & blues devotees, particularly the music of Louis Jordan, but, as much as they loved music, they were even more fascinated with the way it was made and were always attempting to obtain amplifiers and similarly hard to find pieces of equipment.

"It was from birth that the whole Hoo Kim family love music..."

Kenneth Hoo Kim

The family ran "an ice cream parlour and rum bar at the corner of Maxfield Avenue and Spanish Town Road" and "moved to 29 Maxfield Avenue in 1966" in the heart of the Kingston 13 ghetto. In "about 1960" the Hoo Kim brothers had started in the entertainment industry operating juke boxes in rum bars and ice cream parlours that they purchased from Isaac Issa a prominent Syrian-Jamaican entrepreneur. They also controlled coin operated slot machines, or "one armed bandits", and Jo Jo "took care of business while his brother, Ernest, repaired and serviced the machines", but in 1970 the Jamaican government declared gaming machines illegal. Although their juke box operation and ice cream parlour were lucrative the income was not enough for the Hoo Kims to live on and "Channel One became their most profitable venture". However...

"If you don't know what you're doing you're going to get burnt..."

Jo Jo Hoo Kim

"The juke box and sound system that them own enhanced them desire to build a studio." **Franklin 'Ben Up' Irving**

"When WIRL went bankrupt Mr Rae started a thing with his partner, Bob Gray, in Chancery Lane but I don't remember the name. Jo Jo Hoo Kim bought the presses, built the studio and the rest is history. Jo Jo will tell you it was me and John Holt made him get interested in a studio. Jo Jo was a juke box man and he got interested through buying records at the pressing plant." **Bunny 'Striker' Lee**

The brothers ran a sound system called Dynamic Sound Disco before

Paulie established the Well Charge sound system and, in 1973, they opened the Channel One Recording Studio at their 29 Maxfield Avenue premises. The four track studio was originally intended solely for the Hoo Kim's use and the brothers had no intention of renting it out to other producers. An inordinate amount of time was spent discussing various mixing boards before coming to the decision that an API desk, "one of the most expensive on the market", would best suit their purposes as it "did not need a lot of outboard gear. The console was cutting edge at the time. It was responsible for the unique sound on Channel One recordings". A further $12,000 was invested in two tape machines and they hired Bill Garnett, then living in New York, to install the board and he spent two weeks in Kingston ensuring that the sound was right.

"Bill Garnett was the man who wired up the studio for Jo Jo. He was a freelance man but he was a recording engineer and a very good technician at WIRL and Dynamic for years… he built Channel One up and worked on it then he left Jamaica but he used to go backwards and forwards." **Bunny 'Striker' Lee**

The sound of Channel One was of crucial importance to the Hoo Kim brothers and the best quality equipment, including microphones such as Neumann, Sony and AKG and "big Urei 813 monitors" were purchased and the Hoo Kims strove to get the required amount of separation in order to give them complete flexibility on every one of the four tracks.

The brothers received assistance and advice from a number of luminaries on the Kingston musical scene including Ivanhoe 'Lloydie Slim' Smith who, although he was "amongst Bunny Lee", also worked at Channel One "taking orders, go to the bank, buy food, clear the juke boxes". He told the Hoo Kims that the only way an artist will stay with you is if you pay them… "if an artist gets $10,000 from Studio One another guy will give him $15,000!" and Alton Ellis and John Holt were called in as the first two Channel One artists:

"I don't keep secret when it come to music. I'll help any and any man!"
Ivanhoe 'Lloydie Slim' Smith

Lloydie continued to help out the Hoo Kims and later gave them 'Welding' by I Roy to put out "I done it at Tubby's but I gave it to Channel One" and foundation deejay Roy 'I Roy' Reid encouraged the Hoo Kims to visit King

Tubby's studio as "the sound of their studio was not right… the equipment was not being used to its full potential…"

Jo Jo gave foundation deejay, I Roy, great deal of credit for his contribution to their success not only for his hit recordings for Channel One but also for his tireless enthusiasm and help on the early sessions. "We had no experience… he'd get the artists together but (although) he never ran a proper session he was able to turn a session round through his charismatic personality. He would vibe up the musicians and help us coax more out of the players".

Veteran Norman 'Sid'/'Siddie' Bucknor who had previously worked at Studio One and Federal, was the first engineer employed at Channel One. He was an old school perfectionist whose precise approach was often at odds with what became known as Striker's "every spoil is a style" way of working. According to guitarist Cecil Smith "he was a great studio engineer, producer and songwriter… he helped to shape the sound of the music alongside the musicians of the time and pioneered new ways and techniques of capturing the feel and spirit of the music".

"But I said 'no Siddie it can't work so... when we're up at Tubbys we bring in the voice anywhere it come'. The first Channel One sound never did sound like how it ended up. I got Siddie Bucknor the job down there and Jo Jo used to ask him 'how that board sound so?' because Jo Jo recorded a whole Alton Ellis LP but it never came out. I don't know if they can find the tape.

So Jo Jo got his brother Ernest and Barnabas (Stanley Bryan)… they said 'Siddy. Come listen now… we've got the sound we were looking for!' So I went down there with them and there was a big difference and the next thing Jo Jo got rid of Siddy. That's why I brought Sid Bucknor to London… he was working over at Chalk Farm Studios." **Bunny 'Striker' Lee**

Although the album was abandoned Alton's version of Jerry Butler's 'I Dig You Baby' from these sessions was released on a Well Charge seven inch single and Lloydie Coxsone's London based sound system obtained another of the tracks, 'Tell Me', that they played out on dub. A further dub version to the track, entitled 'Energy', was released in the UK on the 'Revolutionary Sounds Volume 2' album through Ballistic Records towards the end of the decade. I have to say that they all sound magnificent to my cloth ears.

One album was released in the UK while Sid Bucknor was engineering on Maxfield Avenue: 'Dancing Shoes' by BB Seaton on Caroline Records, a Virgin subsidiary, in 1974. BB Seaton recalled in '60 Years After' that "it holds the status of being the first album ever recorded at the legendary Channel One Studios and also the first reggae LP to be released by Virgin Records."

When Ernest took over at the mixing desk he picked up the required skills "as he went along" and Jo Jo described him as "the most hands on in terms of the studio". The brothers referred to the manual supplied by API to carry out any repairs that were required and their perseverance gradually paid off and, in late1973, the first two releases on a Channel One label, using Lloyd Campbell's standard 'readymade' label templates, were Bunny 'Striker' Lee productions.

"The first tunes voiced at Channel One studio to test it out were Delroy Wilson and Dennis AlCapone and the first tune recorded at Channel One was Delroy Wilson with 'Can I Change My Mind'... same day we did 'Cassius Clay' with Dennis AlCapone. Dennis will tell you that. The two of them were voiced on the same day. The rhythms were done at Harry J but they were voiced at Channel One. The first Channel One label was mine. I was the first to use it but it was a favour to Jo Jo... I used it for Delroy Wilson on 'Can I Change My Mind' and 'Cassius Clay' with Dennis AlCapone." **Bunny 'Striker' Lee**

The first release on the Hoo Kim's Channel One label, 'Don't Give Up The Fight' by 'Stranger' Cole and Gladstone 'Gladdy' Anderson with production credited to Channel One and arrangement to Glady (sic), sold a respectable two thousand copies. Jo Jo laughed when he recalled that the records were relatively easy to dispose of because of the Hoo Kim's juke boxes and that their cousin, Ramsey, was the only one of their customers to return any of the records. Other early Channel One productions, such as 'Stand Firm' by The Tidals, were made in conjunction with 'Mello' Williams.

"Yeah well... number one it has a lot to do with the equipment that you have to work with you know. Providing you know the sound you want and you have the equipment to really get the sound that you want... you get it." **Anthony 'Soldgie' Hamilton**

The Hoo Kims started to develop a sound of their own after they assembled their house band which, for reasons that would later become obvious, were named The Revolutionaries. Driven by the 'militant' drums of Lowell 'Sly' Dunbar the music of The Revolutionaries at Channel One would become one of the most influential and imitated Jamaican sounds ever. The drums were of vital importance to the signature Channel One sound and Ernest would often spend an entire day with Sly working on tuning the sound and learning how to perfect the art of recording drums. This would exasperate Jo Jo but the 'depth' of sound would prove pivotal in making "Sly's drums roll like thunder" and the close working relationship between the Channel One production team and their musicians helped to foster the long overdue rise of Jamaican musicians as stars in their own right.

"The Revolutionaries are to rockers music what The Skatalites were to ska. With their producer, Jo Jo Hoo Kim, and Channel One's engineer, Ernest Hoo Kim, they created a new era in sound which completely revitalised the music of Jamaica." **David Rodigan**

"Ernest and I often had an input into the patterns Sly would play. Ranchie (Bertram McLean) on bass was very influential too. The 'wah wah' guitar drop was provided by Duggie (Radcliffe Bryan)... I'm very proud of it as it was unique to Channel One..." **Jo Jo Hoo Kim**

Their hard work began to pay off in 1975 with the Well Charge release of 'Right Time' from a vocal harmony trio, The Mighty Diamonds (Lloyd 'Judge' Ferguson, Donald 'Tabby' Shaw and Fitzroy 'Bunny Diamond' Simpson), who had enjoyed a moderate hit the previous year with the yearning 'Shame And Pride' for Pat 'Jah Lloyd' Francis' Teem label. Later that year Jah Lloyd introduced The Mighty Diamonds to Jo Jo and together they recorded soulful cover versions of three Stylistics songs including the perennially popular 'Country Living' but 'Right Time' proved to be "the catalyst that started a revolution".

"We did songs for Stranger Cole, Rupie Edwards, Bunny 'Striker' Lee and 'Shame & Pride' for Jah Lloyd but the only thing that was a hit was 'Shame & Pride'...

Then with Channel One where we do 'Country Living', 'Hey Girl, 'Stoned Out Of My Mind'... they were all Stylistics songs (except 'Stoned Out Of My Mind' which was a Chi-Lites song). Then we moved on from The Stylistics to 'Right Time' and 'I Need A Roof'. What really happened was we started to write about happenings in Jamaica... everyday happenings.

Sly, Ranchie, Duggie and Lloyd Parks made all the rhythms. When them give we the rhythm we'd sit down and write... we'd sit down and imagine... paint pictures...and write songs like 'Right Time'. Sometimes me, sometimes Tabby... sometimes we'd collaborate."

Fitzroy 'Bunny Diamond' Simpson

"The disco thing started to come in 1975 and there was not a lot of work for live bands so I started to concentrate more on the studio work. The first session I played for Channel One was Delroy Wilson's version to The Spinners' 'It's A Shame'. It was a big hit for Jo Jo...

But I couldn't afford to do too many sessions for myself at this time and I remember one time there were four musicians on a session with Ernest engineering. He gave us time to do four tunes, one each, but we did five and gave him one." **Sly Dunbar**

Ernest voiced The Mighty Diamonds on the fifth rhythm track that Sly had generously donated and their prophetic 'Right Time' created the 'rockers' era. I remember the Saturday morning when 'Right Time' was released in the UK on the Birmingham based Locks label strolling round Brixton's Granville Arcade and hearing every record shop in the arcade, I think there were five at the time, playing the tune at full volume. Somehow simultaneously relaxed yet urgent their apocalyptic message was delivered in perfect three part harmonies backed by a rhythm that was as up to date as the Nine O' Clock News yet one that came knowingly imbued with years of Jamaican musical history. 'Right Time' provided a template that the reggae business would adhere to for the remainder of the decade and The Mighty Diamonds "would go on to be one of the most enduring harmony groups in reggae".

"Ernest Hoo Kim has never got the recognition. When he took over at Channel One he revolutionised the whole reggae sound and moved it twenty years forward! Ernest was a perfectionist and Jo Jo always made it his business to drive round and know what was going on." **Roy Cousins**

Lowell 'Sly' Dunbar had grown up in the Waterhouse area where he too had been captivated with music from a very early age.

"As a kid I used to listen to songs on the radio and when we had a free period at Trench Town School I'd play Skatalites songs in the class room. I was a Studio One fanatic! Ken Boothe and The Gaylads did a concert at our school and we used to spend our lunch money in the juke box instead of buying something to eat. I left school at fifteen. I was supposed to go on to Kingston College to continue my studies but I told my Mum I wanted to play music. She never tried to stop me and just allowed me to get on with it." **Sly Dunbar**

His mother died tragically the following year and was never able to see just how successful her son would become but Sly has never forgotten her early encouragement and still feels that "to this day I feel that everything I do is for my Mum." Incidentally the epithet 'Sly' has nothing to do with his character which has always been warm, open and friendly but was given to him because of his early admiration for the music of Sly & The Family Stone. His first recording session was for Ansel Collins in 1969.

"I checked Ranchie and Tin Leg (Lloyd Adams) and the first session I played on, age sixteen, was for Ansel Collins on 'Night Doctor'. He gave it to Lee Perry to put out and it was credited to The Upsetters. A little while after that I played with Ansel Collins again on 'Double Barrel' for Winston Riley. Ansel Collins was instrumental in taking me to the studio. We worked in The Invincibles together. He gave me the go-ahead to do it. My next band was Skin, Flesh & Bones, "we were trying to do a name like Earth, Wind & Fire", and we were the resident band at Dickie Wong's Tit For Tat Club on Red Hills Road. We'd be playing in the studio all day and in the club every night. Twenty four hours just playing, playing, playing..."

Sly Dunbar

Skin, Flesh & Bones consisted of Lloyd 'Sparks' Parks on bass, Sly on drums, Ranchie on guitar, Errol Nelson on organ and 'Pat' on percussion. Their smash hit, Al Brown's version to Al Green's 'Here I Am Baby' for Dickie Wong's Tit For Tat label with its instrumental counterparts 'Butter Fe Fish' and 'Bammie & Fish', was the sound of 1974.

"I really started looking at music... started to experiment on the drums... to see if we could make the drum dance by itself. I worked African rhythms in and, because I was recording so much, I could work on developing a sound for reggae. This is reggae. This is the sound. The double drum sound. Jo Jo gave me the freedom to create. I'd sit for hours with Ernest getting the drum sound right. They were really into it and they left me free to play whatever I wanted. We were like one family trying to move the music forward."

Sly Dunbar

While Sly was playing at the Tit For Tat Club on Red Hills Road Robbie Shakespeare was often to be found in the Evil People Club across the street on "the strip" playing bass with The Hippy Boys.

"The Turntable is situated on the Red Hills Road, north of the metropolis Kingston, capital city of the most beautiful little island in this whole world. The club is the third of fourteen night clubs stretching a half mile from south to north along the Red Hills Road. *Swing* magazine has titled the area 'the strip' and there is a lot of entertainment nightly on the strip."

Johnny Golding

During their breaks each would go to listen to the other one working and a mutual respect and admiration began to grow and, in 1974, they found themselves playing together for the first time on a session for the omnipresent Striker Lee on Maxfield Avenue.

"One Saturday I went to Channel One with four people. Me, Cornell Campbell, Horace Andy and somebody else I can't remember… it's the keyboard man I can't remember but a keyboard man was there with me. I said 'Sly I'd like you to play 'pon a tune for me'. He said 'what we a go make over?' and I said 'let's lick over 'Cherry Oh Baby' in your stepping style'. Cornell sang the 'The Stal A Wat' 'pon it. So Sly played the drums, Cornell played the bass and Horace played the guitar.

I went into the control room and said 'the drum is hard. It's the heart of this session' and so I asked Sly if he could do one more session for me 'but don't tell me no Sly! I have a John Holt session tomorrow. You'll be playing with Robbie.' The next day was Sunday. So I got up went to the studio and the musicians all came and it was first time Sly and Robbie played drum and bass together. Before that it was Sly and Ranchie or Lloyd Sparks. Robbie was my bass man but I said 'no matter… you can work with anybody.'" **Bunny 'Striker' Lee**

The pair began to play regularly at the Maxfield Avenue studio for the Hoo Kims and, from these humble beginnings, Drumbar & Basspeare or The Rhythm Twins would go on to establish their reputation as one of the world's most renowned and reliable rhythm sections.

"Jo Jo started to record a lot of sound that way and that's how the big change come about. The whole idea was musician's feel but nobody wanted to take a chance. The only way to prove it to them was to take some time and do it." **Sly Dunbar**

A recording made at Channel One in its heyday is unmistakable. Their exciting 'revolutionary' sound struck a chord with Kingston's musical fraternity and it soon became apparent that a trip downtown to Maxfield Avenue was essential for any producer who wanted to have a hit record. Musicians would tell stories of preferring to work through the night and leave the studio in the morning rather than risk leaving in the hours of darkness because of the insalubrious nature of the area… but it never stopped them from coming. I recall, after driving a friend home at night to his yard in Glen Road just off Maxfield Avenue, being advised for the journey back uptown to wind up the car windows, lock the doors and "nah stop at the traffic lights until you reach Half Way Tree... slow down and make sure there's nothing coming... then go!". Which I did... following his instructions to the letter.

"Yet, in spite of all this, most musicians say it's a lot of fun to play there. The sound they get on the playback is the best in Jamaica and the psychic vibrations in the studio are very comfortable. Despite its location in the heart of the ghetto Channel One is one of the nicest studios at which to hang out."

Stephen Davis

"If you're in the music business you have to check how things are down by Channel."

Dave Hendley

The overwhelming demand soon meant that there was very little time left for the Hoo Kim's own productions and, consequently, Sundays were set aside for the "select few".

"Sunday was the day at Channel One when we did not hire out the studio. We kept it for our own recordings. The rest of the week the studio was hired out to clients and everyone would arrive there with their own crew and time could be from a couple of hours to two days or so."

Jo Jo Hoo Kim

The Hoo Kim brothers' time in the juke box industry had given them valuable insights into what would make a record popular and they understood how to immediately connect with the record buying public. Jo Jo was proud of the way that the Channel One seven inch version sides were mixed expressly for the sound system audiences and every single release would have its own custom mixed dub side. He knew how important the first twenty seconds of a record were and personally re-arranged the beginning of The Mighty Diamonds' 'I Need A Roof' in order to make it more difficult to version. One thousand copies with the original arrangement were released before Jo Jo was able to stop the presses. He would regularly enlist the services of a group of youths who used to congregate outside the studio to come in and listen and decide whether the music should be taped or not. This would "drive the musicians crazy" but it was typical of a man who recalled being embarrassed

STEADY
PRODUCED BY STEADY RECORD CORP.
45 R.P.M. TIME:
PAD LOCK
LEROY
BLACK MAN
45 R.P.M. TIME 2.45
LEROY SMART
UNAUTHORISED COPYING IS PROHIBITED
Channel 1.
45 RPM
Produced by
Distributed by
Classius Clay
Dennis Alcophone
CHANNEL GET KNOCK OUT
Jammie and The Agrovators
Produced by BLACK BEARD 101 Orange St., Kgn.
CHANNEL CRASH
JIMMY RILEY
UNAUTHORISED COPYING IS PROHIBITED
CHANNEL ONE
Economic Package
MADE IN JAMAICA
Unauthorised Copying is Prohibited
$33\frac{1}{3}$ R.P.M.
(P) 1974
FIRST ISSUED
29 Maxfield Ave. Kingston 13
Phone: 92-38792
I'M STILL IN LOVE WITH YOU
THE MIGHTY DIAMOND
WINRO RECORDS
MADE IN JAMAICA
WOMAN SHADOW
(JOE STEAL)
SUGAR MINOTT
COXSONE RECORDS
1975
TUNNEL ONE
(T. McCOOK & C. DODD)
TOMMY McCOOK
& THE SOUND DIMENSION
HIT BOUND
MADE IN JAMAICA
45 R.P.M.
Unauthorised Copying is Prohibited
(P) 1974
RECORDING FIRST ISSUED
29 Maxfield Ave. Kingston 13
Phone: 92-38792
GIRL A LOVE YOU
H. Andy
PRODUCED BY
CHANNEL ONE
MADE IN JAMAICA
45 R.P.M.
Unauthorised Copying is Prohibited
(P) 1974
RECORDING FIRST ISSUED
29 Maxfield Ave. Kingston 13
Phone: 92-38792
DE. ALMANTADO
UNAUTHORISED
IS PROHIBITED
THINGS AND TIME
WAILING SOUL
Jail house
MIGHTY diamond
45 R.P.M. TIME 3:21
UNAUTHORISED COPYING IS PROHIBITED
STEADY
PRODUCED BY STEADY RECORD CORP.
45 R.P.M. TIME:
SUNSHINE FOR ME
GREGORY ISAACS
UNAUTHORISED COPYING IS PROHIBITED
made in Jamaica
IN TIME TO COME
UNAUTHORISED
IS PROHIBITED
RIDE ON MARCUS
THE ENFORCER

to see nine out of the top ten records on the JBC charts on his own Well Charge label. He did not like the limelight and Dave Hendley later wrote "I've not seen Jo Jo since 1979 but remember him to be a very modest and helpful man".

"I would prefer to have a Top Ten hit rather than a Number One."

Jo Jo Hoo Kim

Jo Jo recalled that their main rivals were Joe Gibbs and Bunny Lee and it had taken a seriously different sound to usurp Striker's dominance with his all conquering flyers beat... which Sly had unknowingly originated.

"I said to Sly 'You played it first on the Delroy Wilson tune for Channel One named 'It's A Shame' and played it with Skin, Flesh & Bones on 'Here I Am Baby Come And Take Me' when Al Brown sung it with the 'tsk, tsk, tsk' sound on the hi-hat'. But he never realised what he had..."

Bunny 'Striker' Lee

And the 'militant' double drum sound of Sly Dunbar would influence the entire Jamaican recording scene for the next three years with every producer stepping forward with their own variation.

"I'm going to tell you a story now! When Sly started playing and Channel One was sounding good I remember Herman Chin-Loy went down to Channel One and borrowed the drum kit. And when he carried it back to Aquarius he couldn't get the sound! He thought that it was the Channel One drum that sound so... I looked 'pon him and I said 'Herman! It's not the drums, you know. It's the man who plays them make it sound so good!'"

Bunny 'Striker' Lee

The updates of the Jamaican musical canon throughout 1976 on an entire series of insurrectionist instrumentals by The Revolutionaries meant that, nine times out of ten, the Channel One versions became better known than the Studio One originals. The Soul Vendors' 'Frozen Soul' became 'Leftist', Roy Richards' 'Freedom Blues' became 'MPLA' and Don Drummond's 'Addis Ababa' became 'PLA'. For many music lovers these releases on Well Charge and Disco Mix were their first introduction to innumerable songs and rhythms that are now regarded as reggae classics.

As always, success led to a degree of what the Irish term "begrudgery" but it usually went no further than musical name calling with Striker Lee giving his version sides titles such as 'Channel Get Knock Out', 'Channel One Feel It' and 'Straight To Channel One Head'. His protégé Rodguel 'Black Beard' Sinclair's production of Jimmy Riley singing 'Channel Crash' to the tune of The Ethiopians' 'Everything Crash' was backed with 'Big Nose Joe' which was all rather ironic when you consider Striker had helped to establish the Hoo Kim's studio.

Even Clement 'Coxsone' Dodd whose name, Studio One, and rhythms the Hoo Kims had adopted and adapted began overdubbing and re-releasing records from his extensive back catalogue with the double drum sound. Coxsone's horns update of Jackie Mittoo's 'Hot Milk' referred to Channel One as 'Tunnel One' and new recordings such 'Namibia', released on Forward Records and slyly credited to The Liberation Group, managed to somehow sound more like The Revolutionaries than The Revolutionaries. Their rivalry became so intense that, on one occasion, it broke out in a fist fight between Jo Jo and Coxsone that had to be broken up by singer Leroy Smart.

"In reply, Coxsone had The Gladiators utilise his original rhythm from The Cables' 1968 hit 'Baby Why' with a song called 'Re-Arrange'; a stinging rebuke to The Mighty Diamonds whose 'Have Mercy' had copied Coxsone's rhythm. The Mighty Diamonds' big hit, 'I Need a Roof', was likewise a version of Larry Marshall's 'Mean Girl' from 1969 and there were many more cut by the Channel One studio band The Revolutionaries.

But Coxsone still had a few tricks up his sleeve: he allowed Lincoln 'Sugar' Minott to work on his original late Sixties rhythms, often with new drum tracks added, and began releasing the results. One of the first was Sugar Minott's copy of The Mighty Diamonds' 'I Need A Roof', a Studio One cover version of the imitation, but using the original rhythm! Since then, recycling of Coxsone's original rhythms has continued virtually unabated almost up to the present day…" **Steve Barrow**

And, when Sugar Minott went on to cover one of Channel One's biggest hits, 'Woman Is Like A Shadow' by The Mediations, as 'Woman Shadow' Coxsone credited the song to 'Joe Steal' while the b-side, 'Shadow Version', was credited to 'Joe Rigger' by The Versionairs and published by 'Capture Music' on the Winro seven inch release.

Beth Lesser/Kingston

Lowell 'Sly' Dunbar

"Cover version of The Meditations' song 'Woman Is Like A Shadow'. Writer credits on label are clearly pranks directed at Coxsone's major rival at the time, Channel One's producer Jo Jo Hoo Kim, and are not to be taken literally. Real composer of the song credited above..." **discogs.com**

The line "a woman is like your shadow" comes from Chamforth, an Eighteenth Century playwright, but too much emphasis can be placed on the concept of 'originality'. The history of recorded music in Jamaica is based around adopting, adapting and improving on already existing musical forms: 'I Need A Roof' echoed a Louis Jordan song and 'Freedom Blues' was a Little Richard number. Reggae music has continued to work off a combination of the old and the new. Much criticism was directed at Channel One at the time of its greatest success due to an alleged lack of originality yet Jo Jo never denied the debt he owes to the history of Jamaican music and the Hoo Kims' updates undoubtedly "laid the foundation for the early dance hall sound".

"He gets a lot of heavy criticism for pinching so many of the rhythms of Studio One rock steady oldies... but Jo Jo isn't losing any sleep over it and he openly admits he's copied Coxsone rhythms." **Dave Hendley**

"Conscious and unconscious appropriation, borrowing, adapting, plagiarising and plain stealing have always been part and parcel of the process of artistic creation." **Charles Seeger**

Their recordings at Channel One made The Mighty Diamonds international stars and their debut album, 'I Need A Roof' on Well Charge, was signed by Virgin Records in the UK in 1976 and re-packaged in a gatefold sleeve and re-released as 'Right Time'. It was a big seller and the group headlined a stunning stage show at London's Lyceum Theatre to further promote the album.

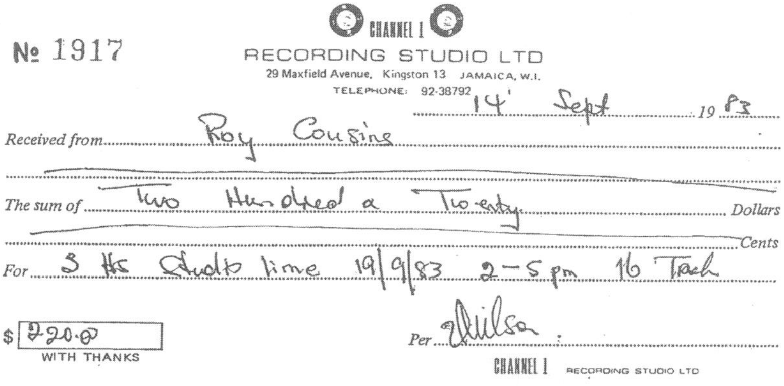
CHANNEL 1
№ 1917
RECORDING STUDIO LTD
29 Maxfield Avenue, Kingston 13 JAMAICA, W.I.
TELEPHONE: 92-38792
14' Sept 1983
Received from Roy Cousins
The sum of Two Hundred a Twenty Dollars
Cents
For 3 Hs Studio time 19/9/83 2-5 pm 16 Track
$ 220.00
WITH THANKS
Per Wilson
CHANNEL 1 RECORDING STUDIO LTD

Roy Cousins

"The Hoo Kim brothers were the first producers we get success with and we just keep on a high from those times at Channel One… we stay high! We first visited England in 1976… there was a riot at the gate! Me love the English people… even now it seems like 1976!"

Fitzroy 'Bunny Diamond' Simpson

But, the following year, acting on misguided advice from Virgin, the trio abruptly changed direction and recorded their all important follow up long player, 'Ice On Fire', at Sea-Saint studios in new Orleans with legendary rhythm & blues producer Allen Toussaint. It proved popular with no-one, including The Mighty Diamonds, and it was some time before they were able to regain their premier position at Channel One with recordings such as 'Tell Me What Is Wrong' and 'Stand Up To Your Judgement'.

"Virgin Records wanted to move us away to do soul… not reggae at Channel One. They wanted to try something different. The singing was alright but the beat wasn't like the Jamaican beat. They wanted us to try to move from Channel One and we took a nose dive. So we went back... we changed too quick... we shouldn't have made that u turn. But we still had the same strong stage show..."

Fitzroy 'Bunny Diamond' Simpson

Deejays Trinity with the wonderful 'School Days' and Ranking Trevor with 'Hotter Fire' became local stars through their releases for the Hoo Kims and many established vocalists and vocal groups also hit with Channel One including Junior Byles' chilling 'Fade Away', Leroy Smart with 'Ballistic Affair' and 'Black Man', The Wailing Souls with 'Things And Time' and 'Joy Within Your Heart', Ernest Wilson with 'I Know Myself', and newcomers Earth & Stone with 'In Time To Come' and The Enforcer with 'Pay Them'. Little Roy's 'Tribal War' sung by John Holt, an incisive critique of the Kingston ghettos' internecine strife originally sung by Little Roy for the Tafari label, became a huge hit and eventually outsold Little Roy's version.

"John Holt's Channel One produced 'Up Park Camp' remained in the charts week after week. He was able to follow it up with another very popular record... a recut of his Coxsone oldie 'Hooligan' also known as 'Change Your Style'."

Dave Hendley

Mo 'Mojo' Claridge/Mark 'Marcus' O'Connell

Joseph 'Jo Jo' Hoo Kim

Occasionally, as Jo Jo reminisced over twenty years later, it could become quite difficult...

"I try to be fair with the artists... it's tough to satisfy them. They don't care what you do! (Sometimes) it's never enough but records never sell enough to pay a heavy royalty and no-one considers the money it takes to put out the records. So you put out a hit record and it can't make money. The only one I would work with again was Leroy Smart..." **Jo Jo Hoo Kim**

An experienced Kingston musician, Oswald 'Ossie'/'No Go' Hibbert, despite initially informing me that he was holding back his best information for his own book with Sly & Robbie, went on to generously, and with good grace, recount stories regarding his time as an in-house musician, engineer and producer at Channel One. It should come as no surprise that it was Bunny 'Striker' Lee who first introduced Ossie to Jo Jo Hoo Kim.

"I don't want to put everything in this 'cause I'm doing my own book with Sly and Robbie. I'm going to call it 'The Sex Life In Reggae Music'! People must pick up the book…

Bunny Lee came to check me at Idler's Rest (Chancery Lane)… 'Ossie a Chinaman want see you! Him tell me to tell you to come!' and that's how I got with Jo Jo but the first Diamonds hit tune 'Right Time' was already on the road on dub so I don't know why he sent for me." **Ossie Hibbert**

But he was soon to find out and it was not long before the multi talented Ossie became a key player in the Maxfield Avenue team…

"I always used to select the artists for Jo Jo… I was working with Sly, Ranchie on bass and a guitarist named Duggie. Officially me and Sly used to make the tunes but Jo Jo was always named as the producer… we used to control the bookings book and Sly would look and write his name in the book. After a while Ernest said to me 'I need help… I'll show you the board.' And Ernest taught me the board… done showed me everything! Knowing what sound good is the thing. I done know what sound good so it was not hard for me. Jo Jo did have a sound and everything we did was good. "

The first tune that I engineered by myself was 'MPLA' in 1976 and I asked Robbie to come and play the piano. Trinity and Dillinger were singing the song to make sure the measurements were right! (The dub side was released as the a-side and 'the straight instrumental relegated to the b side'). The next song was a Festival song…'Big Heel Boot' with Freddie McKay ('Dance This Ya Festival')… Bobby Ellis arranged the horn section… he came with the horn section well prepared" **Ossie Hibbert**

Dillinger enjoyed deejay hit after deejay hit with 'Fire Bun', 'Caymanas Park', 'Natty A General', 'Ragnampaiza', 'Eastman Skank' and 'CB 200' his celebration of the Kingston cult of the motorbike… "hail Diamonds… ites Dillinger". For this record, an unabashed advertisement for Honda's CB 200 motorcycle, Dillinger sat as comfortably on the 'Salary Is Thin' rhythm,

Gregory Isaacs' reading of Bob Andy's sublime 'The Sun Shines For Me' produced by Ossie Hibbert, as he did on the saddle of his motorbike. It provided the title track for his Channel One album but, although the long playing set was never issued in Kingston, the 'CB 200' album achieved international crossover success through its release on Island's Black Swan and Mango subsidiaries reaching Number Seven in the Netherlands album charts. The uncharacteristic funk track, 'Cokane In My Brain', which bore no relation to Dillinger's usual style, became a Number One seven inch single in the Netherlands, reaching Number Two in Belgium and Number Thirty Five in Germany. The backing track (based on a riff from Philadelphia trio People's Choice's 1975 club hit 'Do It Anyway You Wanna)', was another rhythm gifted to the Hoo Kims by Sly Dunbar but the brothers did not release 'Cokane In My Brain' in Kingston either although Ossie Hibbert later issued it on Ossie Sounds as 'Coaine (sic) In My Brain'.

"Jo Jo gave me rhythm tracks for my first Virgin album that he'd already paid me for! 'Cokane In My Brain' was my rhythm track but I gave it to Jo Jo." **Sly Dunbar**

Island, Virgin and later Greensleeves all released Channel One records for the international market but it was not only one-way traffic. American influences, filtered through the Jamaican experience, continued to resonate in Kingston and, towards the end of 1976, Channel One released the first ever reggae twelve inch single or 'Disco 45'. This 45rpm single, running over the length of a 33⅓rpm album, provided wider spacing of the grooves which not only added dynamic range (distinction between loud and soft) and gave better treble response but also increased the all important bass frequencies. The format was wide open for all manner of experimentation too.

The one sided "for promotion only" USA release in 1971 of Swamp Dogg's 'Straight From My Heart' on his Swamp Dogg Presents label is generally acknowledged to be the first twelve inch single. The properties of the format were further investigated in New York by renowned American recording engineer, Tom Moulton, who is usually credited for its introduction to a wider audience.

"Most people thought I was from another planet anyway. I'd say: 'listen to that guitar! You don't hear the notes he's playing?' Some people... I felt like their nerves aren't connected to the brain." **Tom Moulton**

"Before certain record companies started to manufacture promotional twelve inch singles for 'disco play' most disco mixes were cut to ten inch or twelve inch 'dub plate' acetates and handed out or sent to a few choice deejay tastemakers. There's no doubt that the first ten inch or twelve inch was Tom Moulton's remix of Big Al Downing's 'I'll Be Holding On' which turned out to be cut to a ten inch plate just because the cutting engineer, who had a couple of ten inch plates lying around the studio, didn't think five minutes and thirty five seconds would sound good on a seven inch dub plate and so cut a reference ten inch dub for Moulton to audition.

Moulton liked the idea of a bigger size for better fidelity and had Jose Rodriguez (the cutting engineer) cut dub plates of his next few remixes as ten inchers and dubs were circulated to a limited number of deejays. South Shore Commission's 'Free Man' was one such item.

A few record companies started to show interest in servicing promotional copies of Moulton's remixes, notably Scepter Records for whom he did a fair bit of work in 1974 and early 1975 such as 'Free Man'. They started a line of limited (and immediately highly collectable) 'Disco Mix' promos but went with twelve inch singles rather than ten inch because there were already plenty of twelve inch presses around and hardly any ten inch ones." **Tony Rounce**

The first official promotional twelve inch was, allegedly, South Shore Commission's 'Train Called Freedom' but these releases remained the preserve of the deejays in the discotheques until demand proved overwhelming and, in 1976, Double Exposure's 'Ten Percent', released on Salsoul Records in the USA, became the first commercially available twelve inch single.

Kingston's record producers and vinyl manufacturers had always pushed levels of sound quality far beyond what were regarded as acceptable elsewhere and the bass beat, ideally experienced as a physical rather than aural force, had always been of integral importance to Jamaica's sound system operators. Jo Jo and Ernest were the first Jamaican record producers to take advantage of the boundless possibilities of a twelve inch single, "it actually made the productions sound more dynamic", with The Jayes' update of Marcia Griffiths' 1968 Studio One rock steady classic 'Truly' towards the close of 1976 which added new dimensions to an already beautiful song. The first twelve inch single to be recorded, manufactured and released in Kingston was released, naturally enough, on the Disco Mix label and, instead of the record fading out as The Jayes finished singing, Ranking Trevor stepped up to the mic to deliver a deejay version without a break in the proceedings. The effect was shattering. On the b-side The Jayes' rockers interpretation of 'Yaho', originally recorded by The Viceroys at Studio One, seamlessly segued into a dub workout which allowed sound system deejays to add their own talk over versions as the record played out.

The release met with mixed reactions, "a record that's not worth sixty five pence (the then current cost of a UK seven inch single) let alone the £6.50 some shops are asking". In Jamaica twelve inch records rarely reached past the novelty stage where prohibitive prices and recurrent vinyl shortages ensured the enduring ubiquity of the seven inch single. However, in the other two important overseas markets for Jamaican music, New York and London, the twelve inch single would become the only acceptable format for the reggae record buyer. The popularity of what were soon universally referred to as 'discos' on the UK and USA reggae scenes was all encompassing. Often featuring either alternate mixes to Jamaican releases, or music that had never been released in Jamaica, even hardcore music followers who had previously purchased 'strictly pre-release' were now obliged to buy released twelve inch records.

Further explorations of this new direction, where the vocal was followed immediately by a deejay or instrumental cut, ensued when the Hoo Kims attempted to reproduce the same formula on their 'Channel One

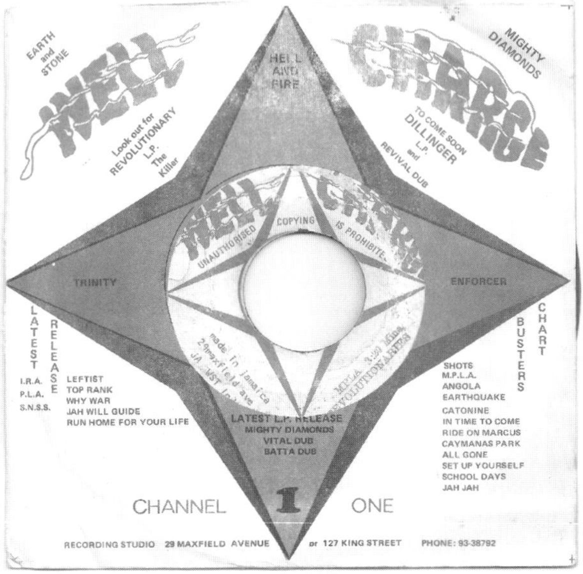

Economic Package' seven inch 33⅓ rpm singles. These were discontinued after two releases due to problems with the sound quality although the music on The Mighty Diamonds' (and an un-credited I Roy) interpretation of Alton Ellis' 'I'm Still In Love With You' and Leroy Smart's 'Badness No Pay' backed with an update of his signature tune, 'Pride And Ambition', was faultless.

The fashion for dub LPs had begun to fade towards the end of the decade but not before Channel One had added one classic long player, 'Vital Dub', to the canon of essential dub albums. At the time of its initial release at Christmas 1976 a copy would set you back upwards of £25.00 in one of the London record shops fortunate enough to have imported this in demand outing. I couldn't afford to buy one at the time. The Hoo Kims went on to release a series of twelve inch four track dub discos including 'Scanking Dub' which featured 'Jungle Scank', 'Tivoli Scank', 'Rema Scank' and 'Dunkirk' downtown ghetto areas scarred by political conflict. English 'punk rock' group, The Clash, later discovered just how dangerous the Kingston ghetto could be when they managed to only record one track at Channel One for their 'Sandinista!' album.

"I was supposed to produce the entire album (Sandinista!). Then we went to Jamaica and it was close to election time and the tension was too much.

We could only record a song called 'Junko Partner' at Channel One. They wanted to use Channel One for the same sound that I used to get on my records. But then, to me, taking them into the ghetto in the middle of election and working late nights, twelve hours a day for weeks, it was kinda risky because they're foreigners and it's like I'm taking them into a really trouble zone because of the tension with elections."

Michael 'Mikey Dread' Campbell

Channel One was now a complete independent, in-house operation with recording, mastering, label printing and pressing facilities all located at their Maxfield Avenue premises where "Paulie also ran a bicycle repair shop on the Maxfield Avenue side of the building".

"Eventually Jo Jo even had his own pressing plant organised downtown and even the labels were printed on his own machines." **Dave Hendley**

The Jamaican Weekly Gleaner

The close partnership between Sly & Robbie and the Hoo Kims lasted for a number of highly productive and creative years but, inevitably, a time came when the pair felt that they needed to move on.

"After a while the musicians start to produce for themselves and... we always figure they're holding back for us! When a singer start to sing and Robbie feel a nice bass line he's not going to play it... we can't hold them any further."

Jo Jo Hoo Kim

There was no rancour or acrimony at their parting from Channel One and they would continue to help each other out as and when the need arose. Theirs had always been a mutually beneficial relationship with everyone involved always ready, willing and able to help out everyone else and knowledge, music and favours were freely reciprocated. Sly & Robbie started to release their own productions on the Taxi imprint and hit records with Black Uhuru and 'General Penitentiary' and 'Shine Eye Gal', Junior Delgado with 'Fort Augustus', Gregory Isaacs with 'Soon Forward' and The Tamlins with 'Baltimore' would establish them as top flight producers by the close of the decade.

"Taxi was Ansel Collins label. Sly & Robbie did some tunes with Hortense Ellis and they asked Ansel could they use the label. Ansel said yes..."

Ossie Hibbert

Following Paulie's killing in 1977 Jo Jo relocated to New York although he continued to return to Kingston once a month to supervise recording sessions.

"Paulie got killed on the Greenwich Town beach playing dominoes at three in the morning around an oil drum table. A man emptied his gun in Paulie and he died on the spot. Much of the enjoyment (of the music business) went out of it for me." **Jo Jo Hoo Kim**

In 1979 the studio was upgraded to sixteen track facilities and the Hit Bound label was introduced. Ernest took charge in Jo Jo's absence and Kenneth was left to look after the new artists', gathering them together and getting everything ready for when Jo Jo arrived. He felt that this would help to build up Kenneth's experience so that he could go on to work with the established stars although Jo Jo still did the mixing and the final work.

"I make the tune them and then when Jo Jo comes he listens to them and says 'put horns in that one... put synthesiser in this one... mix it down."

Kenneth Hoo Kim

"People were bawling that the tracks were too small for them. Four track... that was too limiting to them and reggae music was advancing so they say if we don't become a sixteen track we're not going to have a business. So we bring in a sixteen (track) and it boost the music very much. "

Kenneth Hoo Kim

Jo Jo would then return to New York with the tapes and release them on albums, twelve inch discos and the new ten inch 'dub plate style' records initially designed for sound systems but eventually for the general public too.

Noel Hawks

"We moved to New York for financial reasons. It didn't make sense to keep putting out records in Jamaica...no profit at all. We started to press twelve inch records because they started to become very popular abroad and they actually made more money. The ten inch records were mastered on my own dub machine. They were lighter, smaller than a twelve inch... although you could fit no more on a twelve inch... less to manufacture and more profit." **Jo Jo Hoo Kim**

Jo Jo was responsible for another innovation at this time, "anything you see on record I have the idea", coming up with a series of 'Clash' albums where an established star was given one side and a new artist was introduced on the other side. Frankie Paul first came to prominence when he 'clashed' with Sugar Minott on one of the earliest 'Clash' releases and his 'Worries In The Dance' is one of the key records of the early Eighties.

The Maxfield Avenue studio also proved pivotal in the creation of the dance hall style with the musical talents of The Roots Radics and the sparse, stripped back to basics mixing techniques of Overton 'Scientist'

Browne who had moved on from King Tubby's studio to Channel One in 1983. However, he had been recording live sessions at Channel One as early as 1981 and Jo Jo recalled that "Scientist was the best mixer". His highly successful dub albums, for producers Prince Jammy, Linval Thompson and Henry 'Junjo' Lawes released on Greensleeves in London, consisted of rhythms recorded at Channel One and mixed at King Tubby's and Scientist became the most celebrated engineer of the dance hall period. Along with Barnabas (also drummer with The Gladiators and a deejay as Ranking Barnabas) and Soldgie the Channel One team helped to fashion a new style by returning the music to its beginnings in Kingston's dance halls. A bridge was built down on Maxfield Avenue between the roots based reggae of the Seventies and the digital assault of the mid-Eighties.

The Radics' core members were The Morwells' rhythm guitarist Eric 'Bingy Bunny' Lamont and bass guitarist Errol 'Flabba' Holt who had initially recruited Wycliffe 'Steely' Johnson on keyboards and Lincoln 'Style' Scott, who had learnt his craft while serving in the Jamaican Army and whose military training emphasised the band's relentless beat, on drums. To this already heavyweight aggregation they added veteran keyboard maestro Gladstone 'Gladdy' Anderson and Noel 'Sowell' Bailey and Dwight Pinkney on guitars. Initially working as a session band for various producers they really came into their own and began to define their sound when they began working for Henry 'Junjo' Lawes, Linval Thompson, Nkrumah 'Jah Thomas' Thomas and the Hoo Kim brothers at Channel One.

"Channel One with Barnabas, Peter Chemist, Soldgie and Maxie too... Bunny Tom Tom mixed my first tune." **Jah Thomas**

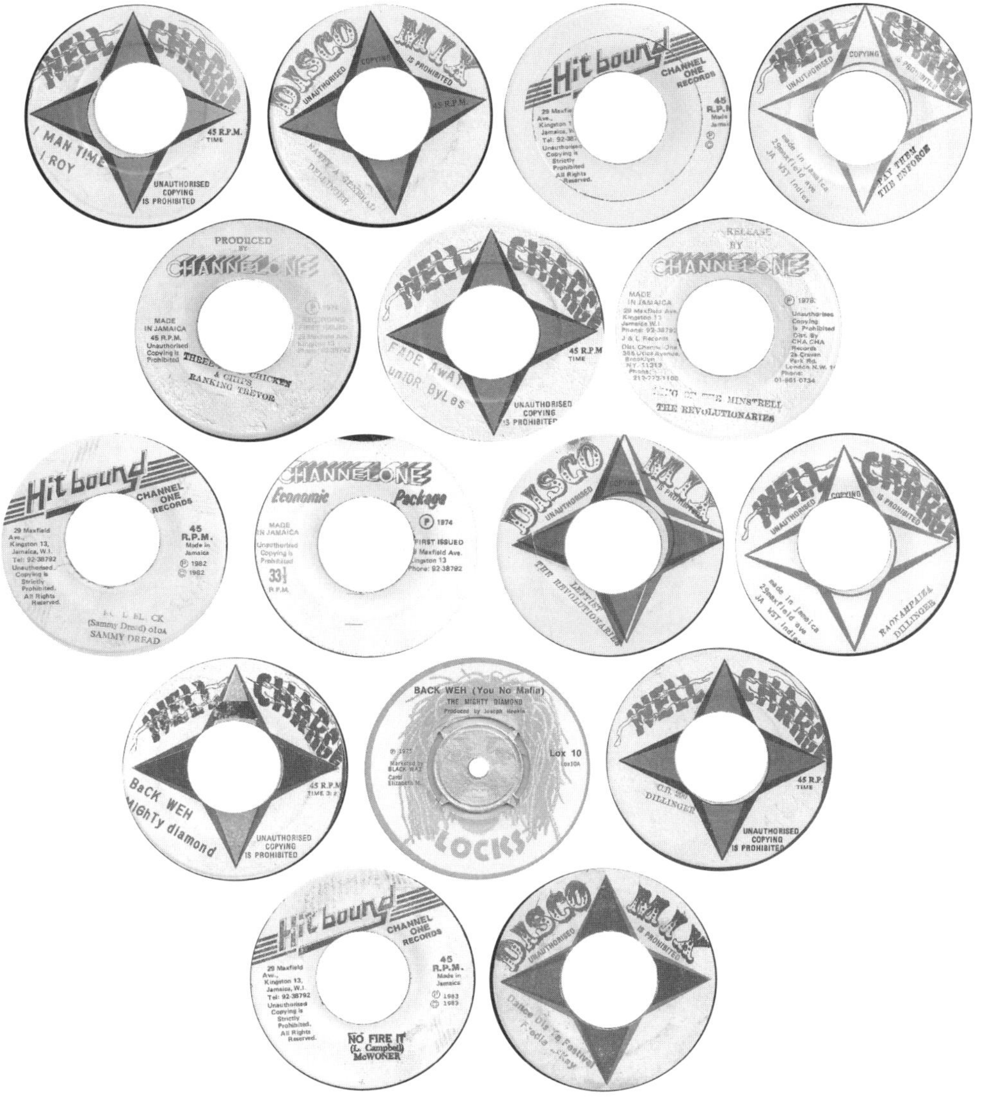
WELL CHARGE
I MAN TIME
I ROY
45 R.P.M.
UNAUTHORISED COPYING IS PROHIBITED
DISCO MIX
UNAUTHORISED COPYING IS PROHIBITED
Hit bound
CHANNEL ONE RECORDS
29 Maxfield Ave., Kingston 13, Jamaica, W.I.
Unauthorised Copying is Strictly Prohibited All Rights Reserved.
PAY THEM
THE ENFORCE
made in Jamaica 29maxfield ave JA WST indies
PRODUCED BY
CHANNEL ONE
MADE IN JAMAICA
45 R.P.M.
Unauthorised Copying is Prohibited
THREE PIECE CHICKEN & CHIPS
RANKING TREVOR
FADE AWAY
JUNIOR BYLES
45 R.P.M.
UNAUTHORISED COPYING IS PROHIBITED
RELEASE BY
CHANNEL ONE
MADE IN JAMAICA
THE REVOLUTIONARIES
Hit bound
CHANNEL ONE RECORDS
45 R.P.M.
29 Maxfield Ave., Kingston 13, Jamaica, W.I. Tel: 92-38792
(Sammy Dread)
SAMMY DREAD
CHANNEL ONE
Economic Package
MADE IN JAMAICA
FIRST ISSUED
29 Maxfield Ave. Kingston 13 Phone: 92-38792
33⅓ R.P.M.
DISCO MIX
LEFTIST
THE REVOLUTIONARIES
WELL CHARGE
made in Jamaica 29maxfield ave JA WST indies
DILLINGER
WELL CHARGE
BACK WEH
MIGHTY DIAMOND
45 R.P.M.
UNAUTHORISED COPYING IS PROHIBITED
BACK WEH (You No Mafia)
THE MIGHTY DIAMOND
Produced by Joseph Hoo Kim
Lox 10
LOCKS
WELL CHARGE
DILLINGER
45 R.P.M.
UNAUTHORISED COPYING IS PROHIBITED
Hit bound
CHANNEL ONE RECORDS
45 R.P.M.
29 Maxfield Ave., Kingston 13, Jamaica, W.I. Tel: 92-38792
Unauthorised Copying is Strictly Prohibited. All Rights Reserved.
NO FIRE IT
(L. Campbell)
McWONER
DISCO MIX
UNAUTHORISED IS PROHIBITED

Innumerable Channel One albums defined the music of the era including Barry Brown's 'Far East', Sammy Dread's 'Road Block', The Lone Ranger's 'M16' and their hugely successful early Yellowman recordings 'One Yellowman' and 'Them A Mad Over Me' which were supervised by Niney The Observer in his role as in-house producer. But Channel One still remained very much a family business and Kenneth's son, Wayne Hoo Kim, was appointed as studio manager in 1983.

"People like the vibes at Channel and the sound they can get. A constant flow of artists, musicians, producers and their supporters pass through all day long. Kenneth doesn't mind the crowd though as he feels it gives Channel a friendly atmosphere that is easier to work in."

Beth Lesser/Kingston

"Well yes... Channel One is one of the most up to date studios that can be found in Jamaica right now. You find out that a lot of the top musicians and singers work here. We have the quality sound here... we have the type of equipment that is needed... that can get an original sound. You find the musicians enjoy working here. They work in comfort..."

Wayne Hoo Kim

Jo Jo continued to press records at the Hit Bound Manufacturing Inc in New York (which had opened in 1982 in Long Island and later relocated to Brooklyn) but the Maxfield Avenue premises were shut down and, as the Eighties drew to a close, the Hoo Kims gradually withdrew from making music. They continued to press albums at Hit Bound and license releases from their extensive back catalogue and, in

Dave Hendley

Ossie 'Black Solidarity' Thomas at Channel One

2005, Jo Jo began work on a brand new state of the art recording facility in uptown Kingston. However, five years later the work was still uncompleted.

"I've been waiting on Channel One to set up for four and a half years. Their new uptown studio is a masterpiece! They've tested the sound already and any time the studio's done I'll go back to Jamaica because when they launch it they're going to take the reggae world by storm.

There's 'nough talented artists there! It's on West Kings House Road about a hundred... hundred and fifty yards from the corner of Constant Spring Road near the Canadian Embassy. You can't miss it! The sound is going to be a different set of sound.

I'm a big man now and I know everything about the business! Me and Jo Jo have an understanding already. I always used to select the artists for Jo Jo and we've come to a general understanding: my name goes on it and Executive Producer Jo Jo Hoo Kim." **Ossie Hibbert**

But it was not to be. Ossie Hibbert died of a heart attack 1st July 2012, Kenneth Hoo Kim died from lung cancer 1st October 2013 and Jo Jo Hoo Kim died in New York on 20th September 2018 after suffering from liver cancer. When I last spoke to Jo Jo he was keen to emphasise how much fun was had when Channel One was in its heyday and how much love the music was made with. He was aware of how influential they had been and this gave him "a lot of satisfaction". The history of Jamaican music abounds with men of vision like the Hoo Kim brothers whose knowledge, vision and understanding made Channel One happen. Although countless other producers used the studio, often with the same musicians and engineers, the magic they created was impossible to reproduce and no-one ever managed to emulate the Hoo Kim's exclusive sound.

*Appendix 1
Oswald 'Ossie'/'No Go' Hibbert

Ossie Hibbert played a vital role in the story of Channel One...

"I was born in Jones Town, Kingston on January 16th 1951 and I grew up in Jones Town... there were no musical influences in my family but my mother used to send me to lessons to learn the piano.

When I was only eleven or twelve I used to listen to Coxsone's Number Two set... the deejay was big and fat and we called him Red Man... he lives in London now. Coxsone's Number One set sometimes played in the neighbourhood especially on a Monday night... the deejay for the Number One set was always King Stitt. Coxsone generally played his own music but a popular Trench Town sound called Sir Nyah used to play in Jones Town and he used to play Duke Reid's music and records by Monty Morris and The Maytals...

I was seventeen or eighteen when I first played in a band... it was around the time 'Monkey Man' by The Maytals came out (1969). They were the resident band at The Stables Club. Lloyd Parks was on bass... I grew up with Lloyd Parks... Bobby Aitken on guitar and Winston Grennan on drums. To tell the truth Bobby's band was called the Caribeats but we were just called The Stables Band. But I'd started to record before I started in a band... I used to get sessions... Bunny Lee was the first producer I ever worked for but I used to play a couple of tunes for Mrs Pottinger too. I used to play the piano or the organ but whenever I played with 'Snappin'' (Theophilus 'Easy Snappin'' Beckford) it was organ. 'Snappin'' was not an organ man. Strictly a piano man! When I played with a next musician I'd play piano...Bunny Lee always used to love the organ shuffle.

When I became a full time musician the song that really broke me was 'S90 Skank' (Big Youth)... before that nobody really knew me. It was only Bunny Lee and some of the other producers who knew me. The rhythm was on one track... and we just took it away! When Big Youth came on that rhythm that made me famous and then people like Duke Reid used to use me. I played with The Soul Syndicate: Fully (George 'Fully' Fullwood on bass), Chinna (Earl 'Chinna' Smith on lead guitar), Tony (Albert Valentine 'Tony' Chin on rhythm guitar) and Santa (Carlton 'Santa' Davis on drums) ... we played on all of Bunny Lee's and Niney's earlier songs... Dennis Brown's 'No More Will I Roam' and 'Cassandra'. They played Bob Marley's 'Sun Is Shining' at Randy's... but the Soul Syndicate don't get the recognition they deserve." **Ossie Hibbert**

Ossie Hibbert died 1st July 2012 in New York following a heart attack.

CHANNEL ONE

RECORDING STUDIO
29 Maxfield Avenue, Kingston 13, Jamaica.

Channel One Recording Studio
29 Maxfield Avenue
Kingston 13

Producers:
Ernest Hoo Kim, Joseph 'Jo Jo' Hoo Kim & Kenneth Hoo Kim

Arrangers include:
Ernest Hoo Kim, Joseph 'Jo Jo' Hoo Kim, Kenneth Hoo Kim, Gladstone 'Gladdy' Anderson, Norman Syd'/'Siddie' Bucknor, Wilburn 'Stranger' Cole, Lowell 'Sly' Dunbar, Oswald 'Ossie'/'No Go' Hibbert, Winston 'Niney The Observer' Holness, , Lancelot 'Maxie' McKenzie, Roy 'I Roy' Reid & 'Mello' Williams

Engineers include:
Ernest Hoo Kim, Wayne 'Chiney Buru' Hoo Kim, Overton' 'Scientist' Browne, Stanley 'Barnabas' Bryan, Norman 'Syd'/'Siddie' Bucknor, Anthony 'Crucial Bunny'/'Bunny Tom Tom' Graham, Anthony 'Soldjie' /'Solgie' Hamilton, Oswald 'Ossie'/'No Go' Hibbert, Lancelot 'Maxie' McKenzie & Donovan 'Peter Chemist' Thompson

Labels: Channel One, Cord, Crown, Disco Mix, E&J, Hit Bound, Mellos, Nots, Revolutionaires, Steady & Well Charge

Musicians:

The Revolutionaries
Drums: Stanley 'Barnabas' Bryan, Carlton 'Santa' Davis,
Lowell 'Sly' Dunbar & Leroy 'Horse Mouth' Wallace
Bass: Bertram 'Ranchie' McLean, Lloyd 'Sparks' Parks
& Robert 'Robbie' Shakespeare
Lead Guitar: Radcliffe 'Duggie' Bryan & Earl 'Chinna' Smith
Rhythm Guitar: Winston 'Bo Peep' Bowen, Radcliffe 'Duggie' Bryan,
Albert Valentine 'Tony' Chin & Robert 'Robbie' Shakespeare
Keyboards: Ansel 'Pinkie' Collins, Tyrone 'Organ D' Downie,
Bernard 'Touter' Harvey, Robert 'Robbie' Lyn, Oswald 'Ossie'/
No Go' Hibbert & Errol 'Tarzan' Nelson
Tenor Saxophone: Tommy McCook
Alto Saxophone: Felix 'Deadly' Hedley Bennett
& Herman 'Seventh' Marquis
Trombone: Vincent 'Don D Junior'/'Trommie' Gordon
Flute: Tommy McCook
Percussion: Christopher 'Sky Juice' Blake, Noel 'Scully'/'Zoot' Simms
& Uzziah 'Sticky' Thompson

The Aggrovators & The Revolutionaries (courtesy Ossie Hibbert)
Drums: Carlton 'Santa' Davis & Lowell 'Sly' Dunbar
Bass: George 'Fully' Fullwood, Bertram 'Ranchie' McLean
& Robert 'Robbie' Shakespeare
Lead Guitar: Radcliffe 'Duggie' Bryan & Earl 'Chinna' Smith
Rhythm Guitar: Radcliffe 'Duggie' Bryan & Albert Valentine 'Tony' Chin
Keyboards: Ansel 'Pinkie' Collins, Oswald 'Ossie' Hibbert
& Winston 'Brubeck' Wright
Alto Saxophone: Dean 'Youth Sax' Fraser & Herman 'Seventh' Marquis
Tenor Saxophone: Tommy McCook
Trombone: Vincent 'Don D Junior'/'Trommie' Gordon
& Ron 'Willow' Wilson
Trumpet: Bobby Ellis & David Madden
Percussion: Noel 'Zoot'/'Scully' Simms & Uzziah 'Sticky' Thompson

The Roots Radics
Drums: Eric 'Fish' Clarke, Carlton 'Santa' Davis
& Lincoln Valentine 'Style' Scott
Bass: Errol 'Flabba' Holt
Lead Guitar: Noel 'Sowell' Bailey, Roy Hamilton, Dwight Pinkney
& Earl 'Chinna' Smith
Rhythm Guitar: Winston 'Bo Peep' Bowen, Eric 'Bingy Bunny' Lamont
& Dwight Pinkney
Keyboards: Gladstone 'Gladdy' Anderson, Ansel 'Pinkie' Collins,
Wycliffe 'Steely' Johnson, Errol 'Tarzan' Nelson & Winston 'Brubeck' Wright
Saxophone: Felix 'Deadly' Hedley Bennett & Dean 'Youth Sax' Fraser
Trombone: Val Bennett & Ronald 'Nambo' Robinson
Trumpet: Chico Chin & Bobby Ellis
Percussion: Christopher 'Sky Juice' Blake

Sources

Introduction
Interviews with Roy Cousins London/Liverpool UK 6th & 13th July 2004
Interview with Bob Andy London UK/Kingston Jamaica 9th November 2018
In conversation with John Peel Stowmarket UK 12th October 2003

Danny Baker: Going To Sea In A Sieve The Autobiography Weidenfield & Nicholson 2012
Roy Black: 'Unbreakable Joe Gibbs Produces Almost Unmatched String Of Hits'
The Gleaner 20th October 2013
David Cavanagh: Good Night And Good Riddance
How Thirty Five Years Of John Peel Helped To Shape Modern Life Faber & Faber Ltd 2015
Sebastian Clarke: Jah Music The Evolution Of The Popular Jamaican Song
Heinemann Educational Books Ltd 1980
Robin Halstead, Jason Hazeley, Alex Morris & Joel Morris:
'Williamson Tunnels' B******s To Alton Towers Uncommonly British Days Out Penguin Books 2006
Michael Hann: 'On Music' *The Guardian* 10th April 2009
Brian Jahn & Tom Weber: Reggae Island Jamaican Music In The Digital Age Kingston Publishers Ltd 1992
Ardella Jones: 'Gussie Clarke Music Works (In The Making)' More Axe Seven 1989
Chris Lane: 'Bob Marley Live At The Lyceum' *Blues & Soul* Number 167 19th August 1975
Colin McGlashan: 'The Sound System Reggae And The Culture Of The West Indians In London'
The Sunday Times Magazine 4th February 1973
Richard Osman: 'From Justin Bieber to Mrs Brown's Boys' *The Guardian* 1st February 2014

'The Roots Of Reggae' The Jamaican High Commission London 1975

Harry Hawking: Liner Notes Evolution Of Dub Box Four Natural Selection GRE 2028 2009
Harry Hawking: Liner Notes Evolution Of Dub Box Five The Missing Link Greensleeves/VP GRE 2061 2010
Harry Hawks: Liner Notes Bunny Wailer Dub D'sco Volume 1 Dub Store DSR CD/LP 027 2018
Ian McCann: Liner Notes This Is Dub The Original Dub Masters Union Square METRTCD830 2007

Rupie Edwards: 'Promoters Grouse' Opportunity 7" produced by Rupie Edwards 1969

Recommended Further Reading:
Steve Barrow & Peter Dalton: Reggae The Rough Guide Rough Guides Ltd 1997
Kevin O'Brien Chang & Wayne Chen: Reggae Routes The Story Of Jamaican Music
Ian Randle Publishers 1998

Chapter 1 Down On Bond Street
Treasure Isle
Interview with Winston Riley London UK 16th June 1997
Interview with Winston Riley London UK 7th April 1999
Interview with Derrick Morgan London UK/Kingston Jamaica 17th July 2003
Interviews with Roy Cousins London/Liverpool UK 6th & 13th July 2004
Interview with Tommy Cowan London UK/Kingston Jamaica 3rd August 2006
Interview with Bunny 'Striker' Lee London UK 17th August & 6th December 2006
Interview with Bunny 'Striker' Lee London UK 23rd October 2007
Interview with Bunny 'Striker' Lee London UK 17th September 2008
Interview with Winston 'Merritone' Blake London UK/New York USA 15th September 2011
Interview with Ossie 'Black Solidarity' Thomas London UK 30th October 2012
Interview with Bunny 'Striker' Lee London UK 30th October 2012
Interview with Roy Cousins Liverpool UK 24th March 2014
Interview with Bunny 'Striker' Lee London UK 9th November 2015
Interview with Bob Andy London UK/Kingston Jamaica 9th November 2018

Interview with Chris Lane London UK 18th February 2019
Interview with Clive 'Azul' Hunt London UK/Linstead Jamaica 7th April 2019
Interview with Keith 'Scotty' Scott London UK/Los Angeles USA 23rd May 2019
Interview with Owen Gray London/Bilston UK 25th October 2019

Laurence Cane-Honeysett: Interviews with Dave Barker London UK 26th & 27th November 1999
Laurence Cane Honeysett: Interview with Graeme Goodall London UK/Atlanta USA January 2000
Laurence Cane-Honeysett & Jim Silles: Interview with Derrick Morgan London UK 7th August 1991
Paul Coote: Interview with Lloyd 'King Jammy' James Kingston Jamaica 9th August 1996
Paul Coote: Interview with Euwart/Ewart 'U Roy' Beckford Kingston Jamaica November 1997
Paul Coote & Dave Hendley: Interview with Lloyd 'King Jammy' James
Kingston Jamaica 24th November 1998
Chris Lane & Noel Hawks: Interview with Dave Barker London UK 5th December 2000
Frank Malone & Noel Hawks: Interviews with Bunny 'Striker' Lee London UK
7th August & 6th December 2006
Frank Malone & Noel Hawks: Interview with Bunny 'Striker' Lee London UK 30th October 2012
Frank Malone & Noel Hawks: Interview with Dennis AlCapone London UK 9th November 2015
Frank Malone, Noel Hawks & Diggory Kenrick: Interview with Dennis AlCapone
London UK 9th November 2015
David Rodigan: Interview with Cecil 'Prince Buster' Campbell Capital Radio London UK 1984

Heather Augustyn: Don Drummond The Genius And Tragedy Of The World's Greatest Trombonist
McFarland & Company Inc 2013
Heather Augustyn & Adam Reeves: Alpha Boys' School Cradle Of Jamaican Music Half Pint Press 2017
Steve Barrow & Peter Dalton: Reggae The Rough Guide Rough Guides 1997
Roy Black: 'Duke Reid 'The Trojan' *The Gleaner* 9th November 2014
Patrick E Bryan: The Jamaican People 1880 to1902 Race Class And Social Control
University of the West Indies Press 2000
Howard Campbell: 'Chordially Speaking Errol Brown 'Still Mixing After 35 Years'
Jamaica Observer 24th October 2003
Laurence Cane-Honeysett: The Story Of Trojan Records Eye Books 2018
Mel Cooke: 'Horace Andy At Home On Bond Street' *The Sunday Gleaner* 4th March 2012
Michael De Koningh & Laurence Cane-Honeysett: Young Gifted And Black The Story Of Trojan Records
Sanctuary Publishing Limited 2003
Tom Doyle: Man On The Run Paul McCartney In The 1970s Polygon 2013
Chuck Foster: Roots Rock Reggae Billboard Books 1999
Carl Gayle: 'Straight To The Nation's Head' *Black Music* Volume 3 Issue 26 January 1976
Carl Gayle: 'Marcus Garvey Meets The Rockers Uptown' *Black Music* Volume 3 Issue 27 February 1976
Fernando Gonzalez: 'Reunited Jamaican Group Marks Year's End In Style'
The Miami Herald 30th December 1994
*reprinted in Chris Potash: Reggae, Rasta, Revolution Schirmer Books 1997
Mark Gorney: 'Doctor Bird Graeme Goodall' *Full Watts* Volume 3 Number 2 May 1999
Mark Gorney: 'Doctor Bird Graeme Goodall' *Full Watts* Volume 3 Number 3 Winter 1999
Noel Hawks & Jah Floyd: Reggae Going International 1967 to 1976 The Bunny 'Striker' Lee Story
Jamaican Recordings Publishing 2012
Dave Hendley: 'King Tubby Mr Dub' *Natty Dread Le Magazine Du Reggae* Number 19 June/July 2003
Hoagy:' Long Fashion Way' *Dub Catcher* Volume 1 Issue 4 June 1992
Ray Hurford & Geoff Sullivan: 'Dennis AlCapone The First DJ Cup Winner'
More Axe Muzik Tree/Black Star 1987
Shizuo Ishii & Tommy Far East: The Rocksteady Book Rittor Music Inc 2018
Howard Johnson & Jim Pines: Reggae Deep Roots Music Proteus Books 1982
Tero Kaski & Pekka Vuorinen: 'Brent Dowe' *Small Axe* 26 1988
David Katz: People Funny Boy The Genius Of Lee 'Scratch' Perry Payback Press 2000
David Katz: Solid Foundation An Oral History Of Reggae Bloomsbury Publishing 2003
David Katz: Sonia Pottinger 'Hit Making Jamaican Record Producer' Obituary
The Guardian 18th November 2010

Chris Lane: 'Tommy McCook' 'The Reggae Scene' *Blues & Soul* Number 127 29th January 1974
Chris Lane: 'Sufferer's Choice' *Pressure Drop* Issue 2 1977
Chris Lane: 'Versions Galore!' *Black Music & Jazz Review* Volume 2 Issue 10 February 1980
Beth Lesser/Kingston: 'U Roy' *Reggae Quarterly* Volume 1 Number 6 1985
Rich Opre Lowe: The Matador Lloyd Daley Sonic Pioneer Of Jamaican Music Jamaica Way Publishing 2018
Kevin O'Brien Chang & Wayne Chen: Reggae Routes The Story Of Jamaican Music
Ian Randle Publishers 1998
John Public & Miss Pat: 'BB Seaton' *Full Watts* Volume 5 Number 4 Spring 2004
Charlie Reggae: Treasure Time Treasure Isle Productions Discography Volume 1
Mad Dog Publications 2001
David Roberts (Managing Editor): British Hit Singles & Albums Guinness World Records Ltd 2005
Robert Schoenfeld: 'Interview with Lynn Taitt' *Dub Catcher* Volume 1 Issue 4 June 1992
BB Seaton: 60 Years After Metronome Music Publishing 2020
Michael Turner & Robert Schoenfeld: Roots Knotty Roots Nighthawk Records 2001
Rasbert Turner: 'White Rum Raymond Ska, Rock Steady, Reggae Violin'
Jamaica Star 9th June 2012 (thanks to Foundation SKA)
Micheal E Veal: Dub Soundscapes & Shattered Songs In Jamaican Reggae
Wesleyan University Press 2007
Basil Walters: 'Landmark Ruling In Treasure Isle Legal Battle' *Jamaica Observer* 30th October 2009
Caroline Young: Style Tribes The Fashion Of Subcultures Frances Lincoln Limited 2016

'Artists Presented With National Awards' *Jamaica Observer* 16th October 2007
Errol Brown 'De Treasure Isle A Tuff Gong'
Natty Dread Le Magazine Du Reggae Number 58 Decembre 2009/Janvier 2010

Steve Barrow: Liner Notes Medley Dub Backshot/Hydra CD BSCD 001 2012
Jackie Estick: Liner Notes Lord Tanamo Festival Jump Up Gaydisc LP 100 1965
Harry Hacks: Liner Notes Dave & Ansel Collins Double Barrel Doctor Bird DBCDD 016 2018
Harry Hacks: Liner Notes Various The Treasure Isle Ska Collection Doctor Bird DBCDD 031 2019
Harry Hawke: Liner Notes The Skatalites Guns Of Navarone (The Best Of) Trojan TJACD 078 2003
Harry Hawks: Liner Notes The Count Ossie Band featuring Millicent 'Patsy' Todd
Gay Feet Nyahbinghi The Call Of The Drums 1966 to 1970 Dub Store DSR CD/LP 029 (unreleased)
RG Johnson BSc & Desta Miriam Johnson: Liner Notes Love Was All I Had Phyllis Dillon
Rhino CD RNCD 2088 1994
Chris 'Peckings' Price: Liner Notes Various Treasure Isle Presents Tribute To Peckings Treasure Isle LP 2004
Tony Rounce: Liner Notes Various Gay Jamaica Independence Time BMG/Doctor Bird DBCDD 0028 2019
Tony Rounce: Liner Notes Various Greatest Jamaican Beat BMG/Doctor Bird DBCDD 033 2019
Harry Wise: Liner Notes Tommy McCook & The Supersonics Pleasure Dub
Pressure Sounds PSCD/LP 63 2009
Liner Notes: Various Independence Jump Up Calypso Treasure Isle LP DR 1001 1 circa 1965
Liner Notes: Various The Birth Of Ska Treasure Isle LP FDRL 200 1966
Liner Notes: Various Rock Steady Beat Treasure Isle's Greatest Hits Treasure Isle LP 101/2 1968
Liner Notes: Various Greatest Jamaican Beat Rock Steady Baba Boom Time Treasure Isle LP 102/3 1968
Liner Notes: Various Come Rock With Me In Jamaica Land Of The Sea And Sun Rock Steady Soul
Treasure Isle LP 101/4 1968
Liner Notes: Various Regay Rock Steady Soul Music For Sale Treasure Isle LP 101/5 1968
Liner Notes: Don Drummond Greatest Hits Treasure Isle LP 101/6 1969
Liner Notes: Various Greater Jamaica Moon Walk Reggay Treasure Isle LP 101/7 1969
Liner Notes: Various The Skatalite! Treasure Isle LP 101/8 1969
Liner Notes: Various Here Comes The Duke Trojan LP TRL6 1968
Liner Notes U Roy Version Galore Sound Of Now Treasure Isle LP TIS 079/Trojan LP TBL 161 1971

Hugh Roy: 'Wake The Town' Treasure Isle 7" produced by Arthur 'Duke' Reid 1970
U Roy: 'Things You Love' Version Galore Sound Of Now Treasure Isle LP TIS 079/Trojan LP TBL 161
produced by Arthur Duke Reid 1971

Dennis AlCapone & The Techniques: My Voice Is Insured For ½ Million/½ Million Dollars
Duke Reid Greatest Hits/High Note 7" produced by Arthur 'Duke' Reid 1972
U Roy: 'Treasure Isle Time' 'Duke Reid's Treasure Chest' Heartbeat CD HB 95/96 1992

https://www.discogs.com/

Recommended Further Reading:

Laurence Cane-Honeysett: The Story Of Trojan Records Eye Books 2018
Michael De Koningh & Laurence Cane-Honeysett: Young Gifted And Black The Story Of Trojan Records Sanctuary Publishing Limited 2003
Charlie Reggae: Treasure Isle Time Treasure Isle Productions Discography Volume 1 Mad Dog/Reggae Retro Publications 2001

Recommended Further Viewing:

Rude Boy The Story Of Trojan Records (Directed by Nicolas Jack Davies) Pulse Films 2018

Chapter 2
The Heavy Sounds Are On Dynamic
WIRL and Dynamic Sounds

Interview with Jason Lee London UK/Kingston Jamaica April 1996
Interview with Winston Riley London UK 16th June 1997
Interview with Winston Riley London UK 7th April 1999
Interview with Derrick Morgan London UK/Kingston Jamaica 17th July 2003
Interview with Tommy Cowan London UK/Kingston Jamaica 3rd August 2006
Interview with Bunny 'Striker' Lee London UK 23rd October 2007
Interview with Pete Weston London UK/Kingston Jamaica 27th March 2008
Interview with Bunny 'Striker' Lee London UK 17th September 2008
Interview with Paul Coote London UK 4th May 2009
Interviews with Ronnie Nasralla London UK/Atlanta USA 30th September & 27th October 2014
Interviews with Mrs Sheila Lee London UK/Florida USA 23rd September and 15th & 16th October 2014
Interview with Mrs Sheila Lee London UK/Florida USA 26th January 2015
Interview with Keith 'Scotty' Scott London UK/Los Angeles USA 23rd May 2019
Interview with Roy Cousins London/Liverpool UK 19th March 2020
Interview with Chris Lane London UK 29th July 2020
Interview with Barry Biggs London UK 17th October 2020

Laurence Cane-Honeysett: Interview with Graeme Goodall London UK/Atlanta USA January 2000
Laurence Cane-Honeysett & Jim Silles: Interview with Derrick Morgan London UK 7th August 1991
Paul Coote & Hasse Huss: Interview with Jimmy Radway St Mary Jamaica 4th December 1998
Pete Holdsworth: Interview with Tommy Cowan Granada Spain/Kentucky USA 17th August 2006
Pete Holdsworth: Interview with Pete Weston Tokyo Japan/Kingston Jamaica 25th March 2008
Naoki Ienaga: Interview with Llans Thelwell Fort Lauderdale USA April 2012
Naoki Ienaga: Interview with Ronnie Nasralla Fort Lauderdale USA April 2012
Frank Malone & Noel Hawks: Interviews with Bunny 'Striker' Lee London UK 17th August & 6th December 2006

Steve Barrow & Peter Dalton: Reggae The Rough Guide, Rough Guides Ltd 1997
Howard Campbell: 'Music Producer Warrick Lyn Dies' *The Daily Gleaner* May 16th 2009
Howard Campbell: 'Ska's Teen Star To Be Honoured Tonight ... 'Patsy' Todd Recalls Good Old Days' *The Gleaner* 30th July 2011
Howard Campbell: 'Looking Back At Neville Lee's Legacy' *Jamaica Observer* 8th August 2018
Cecelia Campbell-Livingston: 'Singer Patsy Todd Enjoying Retirement' *Jamaica Observer* 30th March 2012
FG Cassidy & RB Le Page: Dictionary Of Jamaican English University Of The West Indies Press 2002
Roger Dalke: Blue Beat A Reference Guide To Jamaican Music Version 4 TSI Publications 1996
Roger Dalke: Record Selector 17 (Fourth Edition) TSI Publications 1996
Stephen Davis & Peter Simon: Reggae International Thames & Hudson 1983

Carl Gayle: 'Getting My Share Of Humiliation, Just Like The Blackheart Man'
Black Music Volume 3 Issue 35 October 1976
Charlie Gillett: Making Tracks The History Of Atlantic Records Panther Books Ltd 1975
Mark Gorney: 'The Jackie Jackson Story' *Full Watts* Volume 3 Number 1 January 1999
Noel Hawks: 'Over & Over (R&B into Reggae)' *Record Collector* Issue 396 Christmas 2011
Noel Hawks & Jah Floyd: Reggae Going International The Bunny Striker Lee Story
Jamaican Recordings Publishing 2012
Dave Hendley: King Tubby In Fine Style More Axe Muzik Tree/Black Star 1987
Hasse Huss: The 'Zinc Fence Thing': When Will Reggae Album Covers Be Allowed Out Of the Ghetto?
Black Music Research Journal 2000
Howard Johnson & Jim Pines: Reggae Deep Roots Music Proteus Books 1982
David Katz: People Funny Boy The Genius Of Lee 'Scratch' Perry Payback Press 2000
David Katz: Solid Foundation An Oral History Of Reggae Bloomsbury Publishing Plc 2003
David Katz: Byron Lee Obituary *The Guardian* 12th December 2008
Chris Lane: 'Gladdy Adams' 'The Reggae Scene' *Blues & Soul* Number 123 23rd November 1973
Chris Lane: 'King Stitt The Ugly One' *Black Music & Jazz Review* Volume 2 Issue 12 April 1980
Steve Leggett: Barry Biggs Biography AllMusic *undated
Dora Loewenstein & Philip Dodd (Editors): According to the Rolling Stones Chronicle Books 2003
Peter Mason: Edward Seaga Obituary *The Guardian* 30th May 2019
Patricia Meschino: 'Island Records Co-Founder and Jamaican Music Engineer Graeme Goodall Dead at 82'
Billboard 12th December 2014
Steve Milne: 'The Return Of Winston Grennan' *Full Watts* Volume 1 Number 2 Spring 1997
Vivien Morris Brown: The Jamaica Hand Book Of Proverbs Island Heart Publishers 1993
Ronnie Nasralla: Lessons To Learn www.booksurge.com 2008
Kevin O'Brien Chang & Wayne Chen: Reggae Routes The Story Of Jamaican Music
Ian Randle Publishers 1998
Judy Pearsall (Editor) The New Oxford English Dictionary of English Oxford University Press 1998
Mike Phillips: 'Carifesta (Version)' *Black Music* Volume 3 Issue 36 November 1976
David Roberts (Managing Editor): British Hit Singles & Albums Guinness World Records Limited 2005
Michael Turner & Robert Schoenfeld: Roots Knotty Roots Nighthawk Records 2001
Michael E Veal: Dub Soundscapes & Shattered Songs In Jamaican Reggae Wesleyan University Press 2007
Richard Williams: 'Black Gold Of Jamaica' *Melody Maker* 30th September 1972

Merry Go Round *The Daily Gleaner* 31st October 1969
'Music Industry Needs Better Management - PJ Patterson' *The Daily Gleaner* 31st December 1969
'The Rolling Stones Recording In Jamaica' *Rolling Stone* 18th January 1973
'We Grew Together' *Billboard* 1st September 1979
'Neville Lee Of Sonic Sounds Dies' RJR News 1st August 2018
West Cobb Funeral Home & Crematory: Linford 'Andy Capp' Anderson Obituary March 2020

Aad Van der Hoek: Liner Notes Byron Lee & The Dragonaires Play Dynamite Ska Volume 1
Dr Buster Dynamite DBD LP 101 1992
Aad Van der Hoek: Liner Notes Byron Lee & The Dragonaires Play Dynamite Ska Volume 2
Dr Buster Dynamite DBD LP 102 1995
Andy Capp: Liner Notes Byron Lee & The Dragonaires Reggay Blast Off! Dynamic DYNA 3310 1969
Daddy Lionel Chandell, Donald Clive Davison & Roy Black:
Liner Notes Various Reggae Golden Jubilee 50th Anniversary VP Records VP 63 2012
JR Gonne: Liner Notes Derrick Morgan In London Burning Sounds BSRCD 920 2018
Harry Hawke: Liner Notes Various Red Bumb Ball Pressure Sounds PSLP/CD 40 2003
Harry Hawke: Liner Notes Various Life Goes In Circles Pressure Sounds PSLP/CD 52 2006
Harry Hawke: Liner Notes Various Micron Music Presents Every Mouth Must Be Fed
Pressure Sounds PSLP/CD 59 2008
Harry Hawke: Liner Notes Various Byron Lee & The Dragonaires Uptown Top Ranking VP VPRL 2496 2015
Chris Lane & Harry Hawking: Liner Notes A Brief History Of Dub Part Two
Evolution Of Dub Box Two The Great Leap Forward Greensleeves GRE 2018 2009

Ronnie Nasralla (VN): Liner Notes Byron Lee & The Dragonaires Plays Jamaica Ska Kentone LP 107 1964
Edward Seaga: Liner Notes Various Folk Music Of Jamaica Ethnic Folkways Library Album No 4453 1956
Edward Seaga: Liner Notes Various From The Grass Roots Of Jamaica Dynamic LP DY 3305 1969
Anthony Seeger Curator and Director and Amy Horowitz Deputy Director Smithsonian Folkway Recordings:
A Booklet Of Essays, Appreciations, and Annotations Pertaining To The Anthology Of American Folk Music
Edited by Harry Smith Smithsonian Folkways Recordings Washington DC SFW 40090 1997
Richard Williams: Liner Notes The Wailers Catch A Fire Tuff Gong/Island CD 314 548 635-2 27 2001
Harry Wise: Liner Notes King Tubby & The Clancy Eccles All Stars
Sound System International Dub LP Pressure Sounds PSLP/CD 65 2009
Harry Wise: Liner Notes Various Uptown Top Ranking Byron Lee & The Dragonaires VP VPCD 2496 2015

Liner Notes Various From 'Bam Bam' To 'Cherry Oh! Baby' Dynamic LP DY 3332 1972
Liner Notes: Various Let's Have A Red Stripe Party Premiere Records FLP 105 1963
Liner Notes: Various Byron Lee & The Dragonaires Liner Notes Reggay Dynamic LP BLP 012 1969
Liner Notes Various Rock Steady Intensified! WIRL LP 1060 1968

Prince Buster: 'Black Head Chinaman' Voice Of The People/Dice 45CC 11 7"
produced by Cecil 'Prince Buster' Campbell 1963
Lloyd & The Prophets: 'Bush Beat' Big Shot BI 553 7" A Grape production 1970

https://www.discogs.com/
http://www.reevesaudio.com/reevesimagesnds/jamaicasoundconsole.jpg

Chapter 3 You Name It We Have It
Randy's Studio 17

Interview with Clive Chin London UK /New York USA 6th & 7th November 1997
Interviews with Roy Cousins London/Liverpool UK 6th & 13th July 2004
Interview with Leonard 'Santic' Chin London UK 29th December 2004
Interview with Bunny 'Striker' Lee London UK 23rd October 2007
Interview with Bunny 'Striker' Lee London UK 17th September 2008
Interviews with Leonard 'Santic' Chin London UK 29th October & 16th November 2009
Interview with Winston 'Merritone' Blake London UK/New York USA 15th September 2011
Interview with Roy Cousins London/Liverpool UK 19th March 2020
Interview with Chris O'Brien London UK 29th April 2020
Interview with Mrs Patricia 'Miss Pat' Chin London UK/New York USA 30th April 2020

Steve Barker: Interview with Clive Chin "I've made a full circle…" Beijing China 6th November 2009
With kind permission of Steve Barker On The Wire BBC Radio Lancashire
Paul Coote, Noel Hawks, Dave Hendley & Chris Lane: Interview with Augustus Pablo
London UK 21st September 1996
Frank Malone & Noel Hawks: Interviews with Bunny 'Striker' Lee
London UK 17th August & 6th December 2006

Mike Atherton: 'Randy's Records' *Record Collector* Number 363 June 2009
Howard Campbell: 'Saluting Randy Chin' *Jamaica Observer* 20th July 2014
Steve Barrow & Peter Dalton: Reggae The Rough Guide Rough Guides 1997
Dorothy Patricia Chin OD: Miss Pat My Reggae Music Journey
From Mento, Ska, Rock Steady, Reggae to Dance Hall VP Music Group 2020
Stephen Davis & Peter Simon: Reggae Bloodlines Anchor Books 1977
Michael de Koningh & Laurence Cane-Honeysett:
Young, Gifted And Black The Story Of Trojan Records Sanctuary 2003
Andell Forgie: Carl Malcolm 'No Jestering' *Black Music* Volume 2 Issue 23 October 1975
Carl Gayle: 'Singles Hot Locks' *Black Music* Volume 3 Issue 26 January 1976
Noel Hawks & Jah Floyd: Reggae Going International The Bunny Striker Lee Story
Jamaican Recordings Publishing 2012

Balford Henry: 'Producer Errol ET Thompson Is Dead' *Jamaica Observer* 19th November 2004
Ray Hurford & Geoff Sullivan: 'Clive Chin And The Rebel Rockers'
More Axe Muzik Tree/Black Star 1987
David Katz: People Funny Boy The Genius Of Lee 'Scratch' Perry Payback Press 2000
David Katz: Solid Foundation An Oral History Of Reggae, Bloomsbury Publishing Plc 2003
David Katz: Vincent Chin Obituary *The Guardian* 22nd February 2003
David Katz: Errol Thompson Obituary *The Guardian* 9th December 2004
Chris Lane: 'Big Youth Chapter Three' *Blues & Soul* Number 136 4th June 1974
Chris Lane: 'Niney The Observer' 'Skanking' *Blues & Soul* Number 144 24th September 1974
Beth Lesser/Kingston: 'The Amazing Chins Of Jamaica' *Reggae Quarterly* Number 7 1986
Ian McCann & Harry Hawke: Bob Marley The Complete Guide To His Music Omnibus Press 2004
Steve Milne: 'Tony Chin The Master Of Reggae Rhythm Guitar' *Full Watts* Volume 1 Number 3 1997
Steve Milne: 'Clive Chin' *Full Watts* Volume 3 Number 1 January 1999
Steve Milne: 'Solid Rock: Lloyd 'Spiderman' Campbell Unmasked!'
Full Watts Volume 5 Number 3 Fall 2005
Rich Opre Lowe: The Matador Lloyd Daley Sonic Pioneer Of Jamaican Music
Jamaica Way Publishing 2018
Kevin O'Brien Chang & Wayne Chen: Reggae Routes The Story Of Jamaican Music Ian Randle Publishers 1998
John Public & Miss Pat: 'BB Seaton' *Full Watts* Volume 5 Number 4 Spring 2004
David Roberts (Managing Editor): British Hit Singles & Albums Guinness World Records Limited 2005
Michael Turner & Robert Schoenfeld: Roots Knotty Roots Nighthawk Records 2001
Carter Van Pelt: The Reggae Trail By VP Records 2019
Michael E Veal: Dub Soundscapes & Shattered Songs In Jamaican Reggae Wesleyan University Press 2007
Showtime: 'Lord Creator To Answer Roll Call' *The Gleaner* 25th March 1994

VP Records: For Immediate Release Vincent G Chin 8th February 2003

Steve Barrow: Liner Notes Impact! All Stars Forward The Bass Blood & Fire BAFCD 022 1998
Johnny Golding: Liner Notes Various Live At The Turntable Club, Kingston, Jamaica
Observers/Trojan TRLS 110 LP 1975
Harry Hawke: Liner Notes Various Seventeen North Parade Pressure Sounds PS 017 1997
Harry Wise: Liner Notes Various Out Of Many Fifty Years Of Reggae Music VPCD 1962 2012

Liner Notes Augustus Pablo This Is Augustus Pablo Kaya LP 1974

Marie Garth: Introductions Various 'Live At The Turntable Club, Kingston, Jamaica'
Observers/Trojan TRLS 110 LP produced by Winston 'Niney The Observer' Holness 1975
Impact All Stars: 'Ordinary Version' Giant 7" produced by Clive Chin1972
I Roy: 'Fire Burn' Errol T 7" produced by Errol 'ET' Thompson 1974

https://www.discogs.com/

Recommended Further Reading:

Dorothy Patricia Chin OD: Miss Pat My Reggae Music Journey
From Mento, Ska, Rock Steady, Reggae to Dance Hall VP Music Group 2020

Recommended Further Viewing:

Studio 17: The Lost Reggae Tapes (Directed by Mark James) BBC 4 2019

Chapter 4 Young, Gifted And Black
Harry 'Harry J' Johnson

Interview with Bunny 'Striker' Lee London UK 23rd October 2007
Interview with Bob Andy London UK/Kingston Jamaica 9th November 2018
Interviews with Clive 'Azul' Hunt London UK/Linstead Jamaica 20th March & 7th April 2019
Interview with Tony Rounce London/Surrey 4th January 2022

Paul Coote, Noel Hawks, Dave Hendley & Chris Lane:
Interview with Augustus Pablo London UK 21st September 1996
Frank Malone & Noel Hawks: Interviews with Bunny 'Striker' Lee
London UK 17th August & 6th December 2006

Steve Barrow & Peter Dalton: Reggae The Rough Guide Rough Guides 1997
Rob Bowman: Soulsville USA The Story of Stax Records Books With Attitude 1997
Howard Campbell: 'Marcia Griffiths To Receive Order Of Distinction' *Jamaica Observer* 6th August 2014
Mel Cooke: 'Bob Andy Talks Life, Love And Running Away' & 'Bob Andy Experiences Success And Exploitation'
The Gleaner 14th March 2014
Stephen Davis & Peter Simon: Reggae International Thames & Hudson 1983
Michael de Koningh & Laurence Cane-Honeysett:
Young, Gifted And Black The Story Of Trojan Records Sanctuary 2003
Mark Gorney: 'The Jackie Jackson Story' *Full Watts* Volume 3 Number 1 January 1999
Noel Hawks & Jah Floyd: Reggae Going International The Bunny Striker Lee Story
Jamaican Recordings Publishing 2012
Howard Johnson & Jim Pines: Reggae Deep Roots Music Proteus Books 1982
Tero Kaski: Sylvan Morris Tales Of Brentford Road More Axe 7 Muzik Tree/Black Star 1989
David Katz: Solid Foundation An Oral History Of Reggae Bloomsbury Publishing Plc 2003
Chris Lane: 'The Reggae Scene' *Blues & Soul* Number 126 15th January 1974
Beth Lesser/Kingston: Harry J *Reggae Quarterly* Volume 1 Number 6 1985
Patricia Meschino: 'Harry Johnson, Legendary Jamaican Producer of Harry J Studios Credited With First Reggae Single, Dead at 67' *Billboard* 4th August 2013
Steve Milne: 'Marcia Griffiths: Jamaica's First Lady Of Song On Her Life And Music'
Full Watts Volume 4 Number 1 Spring 2000
David Roberts (Managing Editor): British Hit Singles & Albums Guinness World Records Limited 2005
Roger Steffens & Leroy Jodie Pierson: Bob Marley & The Wailers The Definitive Discography LMH Publishing 2005
Michael Turner & Robert Schoenfeld: Roots Knotty Roots Nighthawk Records 2001
Michael E Veal: Dub Soundscapes & Shattered Songs In Jamaican Reggae Wesleyan University Press 2007
Richard Williams: 'Black Gold Of Jamaica' *Melody Maker* 30th September 1972
'Producer Harry J Dead At 68' *Jamaica Observer* 6th April 2013
Scotty: 'Skank In Bed' Harry J 7" produced by Geoffrey Chung & Oswald 'Ossie' Harvey 1972

http://www.jamaicaobserver.com/entertainment/Who-cashed-in-on-The-Liquidator
https://www.discogs.com/

Chapter 5 The Golden Sound Of The West Indies
Joe Gibbs

Interview with Clive Chin London UK/New York USA 6th/7th November 1997
Interviews with Roy Cousins London/Liverpool UK 6th & 13th July 2004
Interviews with Bunny 'Striker' Lee London UK 17th August & 6th December 2006
Interview with Bunny 'Striker' Lee London UK 23rd October 2007
Interview with Oswald 'Ossie'/'No Go' Hibbert London UK/New York USA 11th January 2010
Interview with Mrs Pauline Hill London UK/Kingston Jamaica 12th May 2012
Interview with Mrs Yvonne Brown London UK 30th December 2015
Interview with Clive 'Azul' Hunt London UK/Linstead Jamaica 4th January 2016
Interview with Clive 'Azul' Hunt London UK/Linstead Jamaica 20th March & 7th April 2019
Interview with June 'JC' Lodge London UK 10th February 2020
Interview with Chris Lane London UK 21st May 2020

Pete Holdsworth: Interview with Joe Gibbs London UK 11th August 2002
Frank Malone & Noel Hawks: Interviews with Bunny 'Striker' Lee
London UK 17th August & 6th December 2006
Steve Barker: Interview with Clive Chin "I've made a full circle..." Beijing China 6th November 2009
With kind permission of Steve Barker On The Wire BBC Radio Lancashire
Steve Barrow & Peter Dalton: Reggae The Rough Guide Rough Guides 1997
Roy Black: 'Unbreakable Joe Gibbs Produces Almost Unmatched String Of Hits' *The Gleaner* 20th October 2013
Rob Chapman: Never Grow Old Studio One Singles Listing & Rhythm Directory 4th Edition 1999
Stephen Davis & Peter Simon: Reggae International Thames & Hudson 1983
Carl Gayle: 'Niney The Observer' *Black Music* Volume 2 Issue 21 August 1975
Carl Gayle: 'Straight To The Nation's Head' *Black Music* Volume 3 Issue 26 January 1976
Carl Gayle: 'De Baldhead Bridge Is Burning Down' *Black Music* Volume 5 Issue 49 December 1977
T 'Boots' Harris: 'Creating New Dimensions In Jamaican Music'
Vibrations Volume 1 Number 1 Summer 1978
Noel Hawks & Jah Floyd: Reggae Going International 1967 to 1976 The Bunny 'Striker' Lee Story
Jamaican Recordings Publishing 2011
Dave Hendley: 'King Tubby King Tubby's In Fine Style' More Axe Muzik Tree/Black Star 1987
Dave Hendley: 'The Reggae Scene' *Blues & Soul* Number 229 5th to 18th July 1977
Dave Hendley: 'Rebel Music' *Blues & Soul* Number 242 3rd January 1978
Dave Hendley: 'Glen Brown As God Son: South East Rock' 'Rebel Music'
Blues & Soul Number 245 14th February 1978
Dave Hendley: 'In His Own Way An Interview With Dennis Brown' *Blues & Soul* Number 246 28th February 1978
David Katz: People Funny Boy The Genius Of Lee 'Scratch' Perry Payback Press 2000
David Katz: 'Joe Gibbs Celebrated Jamaican Record Producer' *The Guardian* 29th April 2008
Chris Lane: 'Joel Gibson' 'Skanking' *Blues & Soul* Number 145 8th October 1974
Steve Milne: 'Tony Chin The Master Of Reggae Rhythm Guitar' *Full Watts* Volume 1 Number 3 1997
David Roberts (Managing Editor): British Hit Singles & Albums Guinness World Records Limited 2005
Roger Steffens & Leroy Jodie Pierson: Bob Marley & The Wailers The Definitive Discography LMH Publishing 2005
Michael Turner & Robert Schoenfeld: Roots Knotty Roots Nighthawk Records 2001
Michael E Veal: Dub Soundscapes & Shattered Songs In Jamaican Reggae
Wesleyan University Press 2007

Steve Barrow: Liner Notes Impact! All Stars Forward The Bass Blood & Fire BAFCD 022 1998

Patrick Griffith: Liner Notes Dennis Brown Visions Of Joe Gibbs Record Globe LP 1978
Harry Hawking: Liner Notes Evolution Of Dub Box One The Origin Of The Species GRE 2007 2009
Noel Hawks: Liner Notes JC Lodge Telephone Love Storybook Revisited Burning Sounds BSRCD 897 2021
Harry Wise: Liner Notes Dennis Brown At Joe Gibbs VPCD 4174 2010

https://www.discogs.com/

Chapter 6 The Dub Master Presents The Roots Of Dub & Dub From The Roots
King Tubby

Interview with Derrick Harriott London UK 22nd May 1998
Interview with Derrick Harriott London UK/Kingston Jamaica 20th June 1998
Interview with Winston Riley London UK 16th June 1997
Interview with Winston Riley London UK 7th April 1999
Interviews with Roy Cousins London/Liverpool UK 6th & 13th July 2004
Interview with Leonard 'Santic' Chin London UK 29th December 2004
Interview with Lloyd 'King Jammy' James London UK/Kingston Jamaica 3rd August 2005
Interview with Bunny 'Striker' Lee London UK 23rd October 2007
Interview with Paul 'Jah Screw' Love London UK/Kingston Jamaica 18th March 2008
Interview with Nkrumah 'Jah Thomas' Thomas London/Kingston 26th March 2008
Interviews with Leonard 'Santic' Chin London UK 29th October & 16th November 2009
Interview with Bunny 'Striker' Lee London 30th October 2012
Interview with Roy Cousins London/Liverpool UK 19th March 2020

Interviews with Augustus 'Gussie' Clarke London UK/Kingston Jamaica 5th & 6th March 2014
*updated and amended Augustus 'Gussie' Clarke London UK/Kingston Jamaica 6th April 2014
Interview with Steve Barrow London/Somerset UK 13th January 2015
Interview with Roy Cousins London/Liverpool UK 19th March 2020
Interview with Tony McDermott London UK 17th April 2020
In conversation with Chris Lane London UK 2nd November 2020

Paul Coote: Interview with Lloyd 'King Jammy' James Kingston Jamaica 9th August 1996
Paul Coote & Dave Hendley: Interview with Lloyd 'King Jammy' James
Kingston Jamaica 24th November 1998
Paul Coote, Noel Hawks, Dave Hendley & Chris Lane:
Interview with Augustus Pablo London UK 21st September 1996
Noel Hawks, Diggory Kenrick & Frank Malone: Interview with Dennis AlCapone
London UK 9th November 2015
Noel Hawks & Frank Malone: Interview with Dennis AlCapone London UK 9th November 2015
Dave Hendley: Interview with Osbourne 'King Tubby' Ruddock Kingston Jamaica April 1977
Pete Holdsworth & Noel Hawks: Interview with Ivanhoe 'Lloydie Slim' Smith
London UK 13th February 2002
Frank Malone & Noel Hawks: Interviews with Bunny 'Striker' Lee London UK
17th August & 6th December 2006

Heather Augustyn & Adam Reeves: Alpha Boys' School Cradle Of Jamaican Music Half Pint Press 2017
Steve Barrow & Peter Dalton: Reggae The Rough Guide Rough Guides 1997
Roy Black: 'Remembering Singer Pat Kelly' *The Gleaner* 21st July 2019
Lol Bell Brown: 'Augustus Pablo For The Love Of Music' *Boom Shacka Lacka* Spring 1993
Rob Chapman: Never Grow Old Studio One Discography & Rhythm Directory (5th Edition) 2016
Carl Gayle: 'Marcus Garvey Meets The Rockers Uptown'
Black Music Volume 3 Issue 27 February 1976
Thom Gunn: 'Elvis Presley' The Sense Of Movement (1957) Faber & Faber 2001
Noel Hawks: 'Over & Over (R&B into Reggae)' *Record Collector* Issue 396 Christmas 2011
Noel Hawks & Jah Floyd: Reggae Going International The Bunny Striker Lee Story
Jamaican Recordings Publishing 2012
Dick Hebdige: Subculture The Meaning Of Style Methuen New Accents 1979
Dave Hendley 'The Story Of King Tubby' *Blues & Soul* Number 228 21st June to 4th July 1977
Dave Hendley 'King Tubby Continued' *Blues & Soul* Number 229 5th to 8th July 1977
Dave Hendley: 'King Tubby Mr Dub' *Natty Dread Le Magazine Du Reggae* Number 19 June/July 2003
Dave Hendley: Pat Kelly *undated
Ray Hurford & Colin Moore: Augustus Pablo Tales Of Pablo More Axe Muzik Tree/Black Star 1987
Richard Johnson: 'True Believer In Johnny Clarke' *Jamaica Observer* 11th February 2014
David Katz: People Funny Boy The Genius Of Lee 'Scratch' Perry Payback Press 2000
David Katz: Solid Foundation An Oral History Of Reggae Bloomsbury Publishing Plc 2003
Chris Lane: 'Bunny Lee The Agro Man' *Blues & Soul* Number 109 May 1973
Chris Lane: 'Big Youth' *Blues & Soul* Number 132 9th April 1974
Chris Lane: 'Big Youth Revisited' *Blues & Soul* Number 134 7thMay 1974
Chris Lane: 'Big Youth Chapter Three' *Blues & Soul* Number 135 21st May 1974
Chris Lane, Dave Hendley & Noel Hawks: 'Riddim Selection At The Dub Station'
Natty Dread Le Magazine Du Reggae Number 19 June/July 2003
Beth Lesser/Kingston: King Jammy Black Star/Muzik Tree 1989
Beth Lesser/Kingston: 'The Dubmasters King Tubby And The Apprentices'
Reggae Quarterly Volume 1 Number 3 1982
Beth Lesser/Kingston: 'Waterhouse Special Report' *Reggae Quarterly* Volume 1 Number 6 1985
Steve Milne: 'Johnny Clarke In His Own Words' *Full Watts* Volume 2 Number 3 1998
Alan Moore & Dave Gibbons: 'After The Masquerade Doug Roth Visits Antarctica To Interview Adrian Veidt'
Watchmen Titan Books 1986
Vivien Morris-Brown: The Jamaica Hand Book Of Proverbs Island Heart Publishers 1993
Mike Pawka: 'Scientist Scientology Sparring With The Dub Champion'
Full Watts Volume 3 Number 3 Winter 1999
Floyd 'N****r Kojak' Perch: The Roots Of Reggae '93 MX 3 Entertainment Centre 16th January 1993

David Roberts (Managing Editor): British Hit Singles & Albums Guinness World Records Limited 2005
Michael Turner & Robert Schoenfeld: Roots Knotty Roots Nighthawk Records 2001
Michael E Veal: Dub Soundscapes & Shattered Songs In Jamaican Reggae Wesleyan University Press 2007
Richard Williams: 'The Sound Of Surprise' *Melody Maker* 21st August 1976

Steve Barrow: Liner Notes Johnny Clarke Don't Trouble Trouble Attack LP ATLP 107 1989
Steve Barrow: Liner Notes Johnny Clarke Dreader Dread 1976 to 1978 Blood & Fire BAFCD 024 1998
Carl Gayle: Liner Notes King Tubby Surrounded By The Dreads At The National Arena
Fay Music Inc LP FMLP 307 1976
Harry Hawking: Liner Notes Evolution Of Dub Box Five The Missing Link
Greensleeves/VP GRE 2061 2010
Noel Hawks: Liner Notes Bunny Lee's Kingston Flying Cymbals 1974 to 1979
Jamaican Recordings JRLP 057 2015
Dave Hendley: Liner Notes Various The Crowning Of Prince Jammy
Pressure Sounds PSCD/LP 25 1999
Dave Hendley: Liner Notes Johnny Clarke At King Tubby's A Ruffer Version 1974 to 1978
Trojan CD TJACD 025 2002
Harry Wise: Liner Notes Evolution Of Dub Box Eight The Search For New Life
Greensleeves/VP VPGS CD 7012 2014
Harry Wise: Liner Notes Johnny Clarke Creation Rebel VPCD 4220 2018

Liner Notes King Tubby The Dub Master Presents Dub From The Roots Total Sounds LP 1975
Liner Notes King Tubby The Dub Master Presents The Roots Of Dub Total Sounds LP TSL 105 1975
Liner Notes Bunny Lee & King Tubby Present Tommy McCook And The Aggravators Brass Rockers
Total Sounds LP TSL 106 1975
Liner Notes Various Bunny Lee Then Total Sounds LP TSL 107 1975
Liner Notes: U Roy Version Galore Sound Of Now Treasure Isle LP TIS 079/Trojan LP TBL 161 1971
Liner Notes: Rupie Edwards Ire Feelings Cactus LP CTLP 106 1975

I Roy: 'Black Man Time' Gussie 7" produced by Augustus 'Gussie' Clarke 1973

https://www.discogs.com/
https://www.whocorkthedance.com/

Chapter 7 The Revolutionary Sound
Channel One

Interview with Joseph 'Jo Jo' Hoo Kim London UK /New York USA 31st August 1998
Interview with Lowell 'Sly' Dunbar London UK 12th March 2004
Interviews with Roy Cousins London/Liverpool UK 6th & 13th July 2004
Interview with Bunny 'Striker' Lee London U.K. 23rd October 2007
Interviews with Nkrumah 'Jah Thomas' Thomas London UK/Kingston Jamaica 26th March & 8th April 2008
Interview with Oswald 'Ossie'/'No Go' Hibbert London UK/New York USA 11th January 2010
Interview with Fitzroy 'Bunny Diamond' Simpson London UK/Kingston Jamaica 23rd December 2012
Interview with Joseph 'Jo Jo' Hoo Kim London UK/New York USA 18th February 2014
Interview with Chris Lane London 5th May 2020

Noel Hawks & Pete Holdsworth: Interview with Ivanhoe 'Lloydie Slim' Smith London UK 13th February 2002
Pete Holdsworth: Interview with Joseph 'Jo Jo' Hoo Kim London UK /New York USA 4th September 1996
Pete Holdsworth: Interview with Joseph 'Jo Jo' Hoo Kim London UK /New York USA 28th November 2000
Frank Malone & Noel Hawks: Interviews with Bunny 'Striker' Lee London UK 17th August & 6th December 2006

Stuart Baker & Steve Barrow: Clement 'Sir Coxsone' Dodd And The Rise Of Studio One Records
The Album Cover Art Of Studio One Records Soul Jazz Books 2011
Steve Barrow & Peter Dalton: Reggae The Rough Guide Rough Guides Ltd 1997
Howard Campbell: 'Joseph Hoo Kim's Legacy Lives On' *Jamaica Observer* 22nd September 2018
Howard Campbell: 'Norman 'Syd' Bucknor An Ear For Hit Songs' *Jamaica Observer* 21st February 2018

Sebastian Clarke: Jah Music The Evolution Of The Popular Jamaican Song
Heinemann Educational Books Ltd 1980
Stephen Davis & Peter Simon: Reggae International Thames & Hudson 1983
Noel Hawks & Jah Floyd: Reggae Going International The Bunny Striker Lee Story
Jamaican Recordings Publishing 2012
Dave Hendley: 'The Reggae Scene' *Blues & Soul* Number 216 28th December 1976 to 18th January 1977
Dave Hendley: 'Channel One: Vital Dub' *Blues & Soul* Number 238 8th to 21st November 1977
Ray Hurford: Sly Dunbar 'The Sly Factor' More Axe Muzik Tree/Black Star 1987
Ray Hurford & Colin Moore: 'Henry 'Junjo' Lawes And The Dance Hall Revolution' *Small Axe* Number 18 1984
Tero Kaski & Pekka Vuorinen: Reggae Inna Dance Hall Style Black Star 1984
Tero Kaski & Pekka Vuorinen: 'Channel One Soldgie & Wayne Hoo Kim' *Small Axe* Number 19 1984
David Katz: Solid Foundation An Oral History Of Reggae, Bloomsbury Publishing Plc 2003
Beth Lesser/Kingston: 'Inside Channel One' *Reggae Quarterly* Volume1 Number 5 1984
Steve Milne: 'Mikey Dread Come Fe Conquer' *Full Watts* Volume 3 Number 2 May 1999
Michael Turner & Robert Schoenfeld: Roots Knotty Roots Nighthawk Records 2001
Michael E Veal: Dub Soundscapes & Shattered Songs In Jamaican Reggae Wesleyan University Press 2007

Johnny Golding: Liner Notes Various Live At The Turntable Club, Kingston, Jamaica
Observers /Trojan TRLS 110 LP 1975
Harry Hawke: Liner Notes Various Well Charged Channel One Pressure Sounds PS CD/LP 14 1996
Harry Hawke: Liner Notes Various When The Dances Were Changing Pressure Sounds PS CD/LP 22 1998
Harry Hawke: Liner Notes Drum Sound More Gems From The Channel One Dub Room
Pressure Sounds PS CD/LP 55 2007
David Rodigan: Liner Notes The Revolutionaries Revolutionary Sounds Volume 2
Ballistic Records UAK 30237 1979

https://www.discogs.com/

Acknowledgements

With grateful thanks to:

Dennis AlCapone, Robert 'Nasty Love' Allen RIP, Bob Andy RIP, Horace Andy, Mike Atherton, Dave Barker, Steve Barker, Steve Barrow, Barry Biggs, Roy Black, Winston 'Merritone' Blake RIP, Bob Brooks, Mrs Yvonne Brown, Laurence Cane-Honeysett, David Cavanagh RIP, Sue Chambers RIP, Clive Chin, Leonard 'Santic' Chin RIP, Mrs Patricia 'Miss Pat' Chin OD, Augustus 'Gussie' Clarke, Paul Coote, Roy Cousins, Tommy Cowan, Roger Dalke, Peter Dalton, Michael De Koningh RIP, Carl 'Captain Sinbad' Dwyer, Dave Feneron, Carl Gayle, Graeme Goodall RIP, Ken 'Fatman' Gordon, Mark Gorney, Owen Gray, Lars Gredal, Maria Green, Marcia Griffiths, Gary Hall, Derrick Harriott, Manny Hawks, Dave Hendley RIP, Oswald 'Ossie'/'No Go' Hibbert RIP, Mrs Pauline Hill, Nick Hodgson, Pete Holdsworth, Joseph 'Jo Jo' Hoo Kim RIP, Clive 'Azul' Hunt, Ray Hurford, Hasse Huss, Naoki Ienaga, Lloyd 'King Jammy' James, Kaori Joma, Penny Jones RIP, Tero Kaski RIP, David Katz, Brian Keyo, Seija Kouva, Chris Lane, Bunny 'Striker' Lee OD RIP, Jason Lee, Mrs Sheila Lee, Beth Lesser/Kingston, June 'JC' Lodge, Paul 'Jah Screw' Love, Frank 'Jah Floyd' Malone, Ian McCann, Tony McDermott, Steve Milne, Dave Millar, Derrick Morgan, Ronnie Nasralla, Andrew Neale (Tradition Records), Al 'Fingers' Newman, Chris O'Brien, Mark 'Marcus' O'Connell, John Peel OBE RIP, Chris 'Peckings' Price, Janis Punford, Jimmy Radway, Pete Reilly, Winston Riley RIP, David Rodigan MBE OD, Tony Rounce, Keith 'Scotty' Scott, Karl Shale, Jim Silles, Fitzroy 'Bunny Diamond' Simpson, Aaron 'English' Smith, Ivanhoe 'Lloydie Slim' Smith, Ken Smith RIP, Martin Steibelt, Horace 'Augustus Pablo' Swaby, Karen Tate, Nkrumah 'Jah Thomas' Thomas, Ossie 'Black Solidarity' Thomas, Pekka Vuorinen, Derek Walmsley, Pete Weston, Olston Wiltshire and many, many more…

All interviewees were generous, gracious and patient although legendary producer Bunny 'Striker' Lee and singer/producer extraordinaire Roy Cousins of The Royals were both particularly unstinting in their co-operation and support and deserve my special thanks

Thank you to Aaron 'English' Smith for his never to be forgotten kindness in arranging for me (and my family) to go to Jamaica and to Carl 'Captain Sinbad' Dwyer and Ossie 'Black Solidarity' Thomas (and his brothers Howie & Chris)

for showing me how things run in Kingston. Without Dennis AlCapone's patience, insight and generosity the first chapter could never have been written Without Roy Cousins' patience, insight and generosity the second chapter could never have been written

"When me gone how many people from my era will be left to talk to?" **Roy Cousins**

Without Mrs Sheila Lee's patience, insight and generosity the second chapter could never have been written

Without Clive Chin's patience, insight and generosity and Steve Barker's generosity, "of course, welcome to use any of my stuff", the third chapter could never have been written

Without Mrs Patricia 'Miss Pat' Chin's kindness, humour and generosity the third chapter could not have been completed satisfactorily

Without Beth Lesser/Kingston's groundbreaking reporting, generosity and kind permission the fourth chapter could never have been written

Without June 'JC' Lodge's "balanced view" the fifth chapter could not have been concluded satisfactorily

A very special thank you to Lloyd 'King Jammy' James for his patience, insight and generosity; the sixth chapter could never have been written without his sterling contribution. The King granted Dave Hendley (RIP) and Paul Coote two extremely illuminating interviews for a proposed book project we were working on together (with Chris Lane) in the Nineties which, unfortunately, never came to fruition. However, with their kind permission, I have used a great deal of the invaluable information here. Thank you King

Respect is also due (to coin a cliché) to Dennis AlCapone and Roy Cousins for very kindly sharing their reminisces of King Tubby's sound system and studio and to Robert 'Nasty Love' Allen for his persistence in obtaining, and then sharing, the first, and best, cassette tape of King Tubby's Home Town Hi Fi with U Roy on the mic

Without Chris Lane's patience, in depth knowledge and attention to detail, the importance and role of the high pass filter could never have been resolved in the sixth chapter

Without Joseph 'Jo Jo' Hoo Kim's patience, insight and generosity the seventh chapter could never have been written

My grateful and sincere thanks to Steve Barrow, Laurence Cane-Honeysett, Paul Coote, Dave Hendley RIP, Ray Hurford, David Katz, Seija Kouva (for Tero Kaski RIP), Chris Lane, Beth Lesser/Kingston & Steve Milne for their kind permission in allowing me to quote from their works and to Steve Barrow, Chris Lane & Tony Rounce for generously reviewing the manuscript. Any errors that remain are mine alone...

My sincere apologies to anyone whose name I have inadvertently omitted

With sincere gratitude and love to Anna, Maria & Manny for their endless patience and unfailing support

About the authors

Noel Hawks

Noel 'Harry Hawke' Hawks is the author, with Jah Floyd, of 'Reggae Going International 1967-1976 The Bunny Striker Lee Story', 'Songs Of Freedom: Complete Lyrics of Bob Marley', co-author, with Ian McCann, of the 2004 edition of 'The Complete Guide To The Music Of Bob Marley', co-author with Stuart Baker & Steve Barrow of 'Reggae 45 Sound System The Label Art Of Reggae Singles' and helped to compile 'The Guinness Who's Who Of Reggae'. He has also contributed to 'Covers: Retracing Reggae Record Sleeves In London' by Alex Bartsch, 'Clarks In Jamaica' by Al Fingers, 'Reggae Deep Roots Music' by Howard Johnson & Jim Pines, 'Skinhead' by Nick Knight and 'The Story Of Trojan Records' by Laurence Cane-Honeysett.

Noel has written for Billboard, Music Week, Record Collector, Vox, The Wire and numerous other magazines and has compiled and written liner notes for over 350 reggae releases on Bear Family, Blood & Fire, Burning Sounds, Dub Store, Fashion, Greensleeves, Jamaican Recordings, Pressure Sounds, Secret Records, Soul Jazz, Trojan, Universal and VP.

Jah Floyd

Jah Floyd has compiled and released over 150 reggae re-releases for the Jamaican Recordings and Kingston Sounds labels.

Also available:
Reggae Going International
1967 to 1976
The Bunny 'Striker' Lee Story
Noel Hawks & Jah Floyd
Jamaican Recordings Publishing

In 2008 the Jamaican Government conferred the Order of Distinction on Bunny 'Striker' Lee for more than forty years of dedicated service to the music industry. Here, in Striker's own words, is the incredible story of how reggae went international...

"In a career that has lasted for over forty years Bunny 'Striker' Lee has faithfully met the needs of his audience for music that accurately reflected their concerns and, in the process, enjoyed huge hits and provided work for dozens of singers, musicians and studio technicians. His contribution to the story of Jamaican music has been as great, if not greater, than that of many, more celebrated, men."

Steve Barrow
Co-author of 'Reggae The Rough Guide'

Nominated for the 2012 Association for Recorded Sound Collections Awards for Excellence in Historical Recorded Sound Research

"Quite simply an incredibly important historical document"
David Rodigan MBE OD

"Here's the history of Jamaican music told in an utterly authentic way through the words of one man"
Ian McCann
Record Collector

"For any serious student of the music I urge a close reading of his autobiography 'Reggae Going International: 1967 to 1976' in which he details to Noel Hawks and Jah Floyd his contributions over time, as well as those of several artistes, sound system operators and producers...

His autobiography, in my view, represents the most comprehensive discussion of the development of Jamaica's popular music produced by anyone, foreign or local. I am particularly drawn to it because Bunny is able to speak from the perspective of someone who intimately knew the artistes, including instrumentalists, as well as rival producers and sound system operators.

I am particularly pleased that he found the time to put his reflections in writing, thus providing any serious student of Jamaican pop music with a reference masterpiece..."
Omar Davies Tribute to Bunny 'Striker' Lee
The Daily Observer Kingston Jamaica 13th November 2020

2012 Pop Music Books of the Year
Independent on Sunday
******Mojo*
******Record Collector*
******Riddim*

I AM THE GORGON DVD
BUNNY 'STRIKER' LEE & THE ROOTS OF REGGAE

Directed by musician and film maker, Diggory Kenrick, and narrated by legendary deejay, Dennis AlCapone, this acclaimed documentary tells the larger than life tale of legendary record producer, Bunny 'Striker' Lee charting his rise from motorcycle mechanic and record plugger to reggae's most successful record producer in the Seventies. Striker's story involves politics, arguments, gangs and guns as Jamaican music moved from ska to rock steady, from dub to dancehall, from the ghettos of Kingston to the world stage.

Featuring an amazing roll call including:
Singers: Horace Andy, Ken Boothe, Cornell Campbell, Johnny Clarke, Stranger Cole, Errol Dunkley, Winston Francis, John Holt, Derrick Morgan, Jimmy Riley, Max Romeo, BB Seaton, Roy Shirley & Linval Thompson Vocal Groups: The Blackstones & The Twinkle Brothers Deejays: Dennis AlCapone, Dr Alimantado, Dillinger, Prince Jazzbo, Jah Stitch, Trinity, U Roy & Tapper Zukie Musicians: Aston 'Family Man' Barrett, Carlton 'Santa' Davis, Sly Dunbar, Robbie Shakespeare & Earl 'Chinna' Smith Record Producers: King Jammy, Niney The Observer, Lee 'Scratch' Perry & Scientist And many, many more...

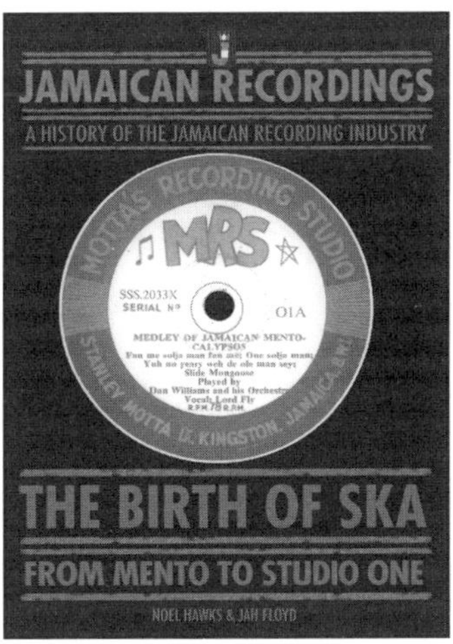

Out Now ...
Jamaican Recordings A History Of The Jamaican Recording Industry Part One
The Birth Of Ska: From Mento To Studio One
Stanley Motta, Ivan Chin, 'Baba'/'Dada' Tewari, RJR & JBC, Federal & Studio One

"The book speaks with multiple voices... the fruits of twenty years' worth of interviews with key music business figures are expertly woven into the text and bring the story to life.

It's an enthralling story which will continue in the next volume."
Mike Atherton
Record Collector

"The golden ages of Jamaican music, ska, rock steady, reggae, roots, dance hall, digital and ragga had all passed before the first serious attempts at documenting their impact and importance got underway...

This book is the first of a promised series that aims to provide a totally fresh approach to documenting the Jamaican recording industry as told through its most significant studios and the characters who inhabited them... with source material generated by interviews with many of the key artists, players, engineers and producers responsible for the music.

These stories are collated from quotes taken from a vast array of interviews conducted over the years by Hawks' connecting passages... overall these parts are folded into a flowing, rich conversational narrative..."
Steve Barker
The Wire

"This book is the first in a trilogy aimed at documenting the most important Jamaican recording studios and labels. Author Noel Hawks effortlessly mixes enthusiasm and knowledge as he details how a British colony, valued seemingly only for its agriculture and minerals, came very late to recording music yet, once given a taste, Jamaica passionately embraced making music and issuing records...

While primarily aimed at those with an interest in ska/reggae, this fine book is recommended to anyone with an interest in the music industry, the Caribbean and development studies."
Garth Cartwright
Songlines

"Volume One of 'Jamaican Recordings' provides a fascinating and immensely detailed insight into the origins of this amazing music. As an avid collector myself I was able to glean so much new information and for this I am indebted to Noel Hawks for his tireless journalistic enthusiasm."
David Rodigan MBE OD

****Record Collector*
*****Songlines*

Coming soon...

Jamaican Recordings A History Of The Jamaican Recording Industry Part Three
The Upsetter To The Computer:
From The Black Ark To Firehouse
The Black Ark, Aquarius, Tuff Gong, King Jammy, King Tubby In The Digital Age & A Brief History of Dub

Catalogue

CAT No: KSCD001/KSLP001 | CAT No: KSCD007/KSLP007 | CAT No: KSCD013/KSLP013 | CAT No: KSCD019/KSLP019 | CAT No: KSCD025/KSLP025 | CAT No: KSCD031/KSLP031 | CAT No: KSCD037/KSLP037

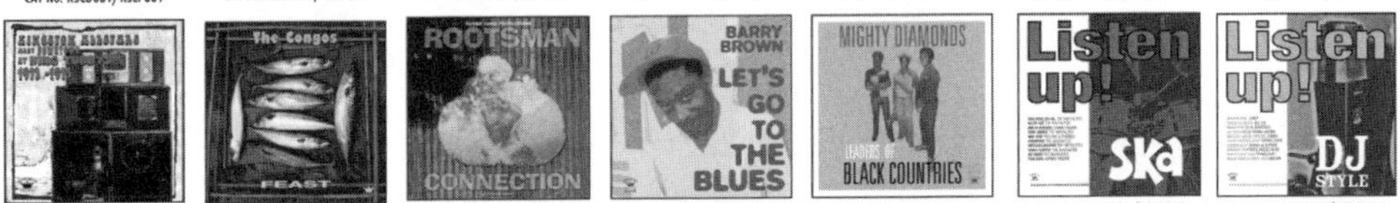

CAT No KSCD002/KSLP 002 | CAT No: KSCD008/KSLP008 | CAT No: KSCD014/KSLP013 | CAT No: KSCD020/KSLP020 | CAT No: KSCD026/KSLP026 | CAT No KSCD032/KSLP032 | CAT No KSCD038/KSLP038

CAT No KSCD003/KSLP003 | CAT No CD: KSCD009/KSLP009 | CAT No: KSCD015/KSLP015 | CAT No: KSCD021/KSLP021 | CAT No: KSCD027/KSLP027 | CAT No KSCD033/KSLP033 | CAT No KSCD039/KSLP039

CAT No KSCD004/KSLP004 | CAT No: KSCD010/KSLP010 | CAT No: KSCD016/KSLP016 | CAT No: KSCD022/KSLP022 | CAT No: KSCD028/KSLP028 | CAT No KSCD034/KSLP034 | CAT No KSCD040/KSLP040

CAT No KSCD005/KSLP005 | CAT No CD: KSCD011/KSLP011 | CAT No: KSCD017/KSLP017 | CAT No: KSCD 023 / KSLP 023 | CAT No: KSCD029/KSLP029 | CAT No KSCD 035/KSLP035 | CAT No KSCD041/KSLP041

CAT No: KSCD006/KSLP006 | CAT No KSCD012/KSLP012 | CAT No: KSCD018/KSLP018 | CAT No: KSCD024/KSLP024 | CAT No: KSCD030/KSLP 030 | CAT No: KSCD036/KSLP 036 | CAT No: KSCD042/KSLP042

CAT No: KSCD043/KSLP043 | CAT No: KSCD051/KSLP051 | CAT No: KSCD059/KSLP059 | CAT No: KSCD067/KSLP067 | CAT No: KSCD075/KSLP075 | CAT No: KSCD083/KSLP083

CAT No: KSCD044/KSLP044 | CAT No: KSCD052/KSLP052 | CAT No: KSCD060/KSLP060 | CAT No: KSCD068/KSLP068 | CAT No: KSCD076/KSLP076 | CAT No: KSCD084/KSLP084

CAT No CD: KSCD045/KSLP045 | CAT No: KSCD053/KSLP053 | CAT No: KSCD061/KSLP061 | CAT No: KSCD069/KSLP069 | CAT No: KSCD077/KSLP077 | CAT No: KSCD085/KSLP085

CAT No: KSCD046/KSLP046 | CAT No: KSCD054/KSLP054 | CAT No: KSCD062/KSLP062 | CAT No: KSCD070/KSLP070 | CAT No: KSCD078/KSLP078 | CAT No: KSCD086/KSLP086

CAT No CD: KSCD047/KSLP047 | CAT No: KSCD055/KSLP055 | CAT No: KSCD063/KSLP063 | CAT No: KSCD071/KSLP071 | CAT No: KSCD079/KSLP079 | CAT No: KSCD087/KSLP087

CAT No KSCD048/KSLP048 | CAT No: KSCD056/KSLP056 | CAT No: KSCD064/KSLP064 | CAT No: KSCD072/KSLP072 | CAT No: KSCD080/KSLP080 | CAT No: KSCD088/KSLP088

CAT No: KSCD049/KSLP049 | CAT No: KSCD057/KSLP057 | CAT No: KSCD065/KSLP065 | CAT No: KSCD073/KSLP073 | CAT No: KSCD081/KSLP081 | CAT No: KSCD089/KSLP089

CAT No: KSCD050/KSLP050 | CAT No: KSCD058/KSLP058 | CAT No: KSCD066/KSLP 066 | CAT No: KSCD074/KSLP074 | CAT No: KSCD082/KSLP082

JAMAICAN RECORDINGS

Catalogue

CAT No: JRCD001/JRLP001

CAT No: JRCD007/JRLP007

CAT No: JRCD013/JRLP0013

CAT No: JRCD019/JRLP019

CAT No: JRCD025/JRLP025

CAT No: JRCD031/JRLP031

CAT No: JRCD002/JRLP002

CAT No: JRCD008/JRLP008

CAT No: JRCD014/JRLP014

CAT No: JRCD020/JRLP020

CAT No: JRCD026/JRLP026

CAT No: JRCD032/JRLP032

CAT No: JRCD003/JRLP003

CAT No: JRCD009/JRLP009

CAT No: JRCD015/JRLP0015

CAT No: JRCD021/JRLP021

CAT No: JRCD027/JRLP027

CAT No: JRCD033/JRLP 033

CAT No: JRCD004/JRLP004

CAT No: JRCD010/JRLP0010

CAT No: JRCD016/JRLP0016

CAT No: JRCD022/JRLP022

CAT No: JRCD028/JRLP028

CAT No: JRCD034/JRLP034

CAT No: JRCD005/JRLP005

CAT No: JRCD 0011/JRLP0011

CAT No: JRCD017/JRLP0017

CAT No: JRCD023/JRLP023

CAT No: JRCD029/JRLP029

CAT No: JRCD035/JRLP035

CAT No: JRCD 006/JRLP006

CAT No: JRCD012/JRLP0012

CAT No: JRCD018/JRLP0018

CAT No: JRCD024/JRLP024

CAT No: JRCD030/JRLP030

CAT No: JRCD036/JRLP036

THE RADICAL VISION OF

EDWARD BURNE-JONES

The Radical Vision of
Edward Burne-Jones

Andrea Wolk Rager

Paul Mellon Centre for Studies in British Art
distributed by Yale University Press · New Haven and London

First published in 2022 by the Paul Mellon Centre for Studies in British Art
16 Bedford Square, London, WC1B 3JA
paul-mellon-centre.ac.uk

ISBN 978-1-913107-27-7 HB
Library of Congress Control Number: 2021948026

British Library Cataloguing-in-Publication Data
A catalogue record for this book is available from the British Library

Designed by Emily Lees
Origination by Evergreen Colour Management Ltd
Printed in Wales by Gomer Press

MIX
Paper from responsible sources
FSC® C114687

ENDPAPERS ∗ *The Nativity* window, 1896–98 (details of fig. 131)
PAGE I ∗ Study for *The Finding of Medusa*, 1885 (detail of fig. 107)
PAGES II–III ∗ *Perseus and the Graiae*, 1892 (detail of fig. 59)
FRONTISPIECE ∗ *The Baleful Head*, 1885–87 (detail of fig. 43)
PAGE VI ∗ *The Pelican in Her Piety*, 1880–81 (see fig. 122)

Contents

Acknowledgments

This book represents the work of many years. It originated with a seminar paper following a formative trip to Rome during graduate school, when Ashley Jones first introduced me to Edward Burne-Jones's mosaics in the church of St Paul's Within the Walls. That paper eventually developed into my doctoral dissertation, and, finally, into this volume. Over that long span of time, I have accrued far too many debts of gratitude to thank properly everyone who helped make this book possible. I would like to begin, therefore, with a thank you and an apology to anyone whom I have neglected to include here.

My greatest thanks go to Tim Barringer, who has provided invaluable mentorship and abiding support, helping me to believe in this project even when my own courage failed. His ground-breaking scholarship has served as a constant source of inspiration for my approach to the art and labor of Burne-Jones. I could not have asked for a better doctoral advisor, role model, colleague, and friend.

Given that this book is rooted in my doctoral studies at Yale University, I would like to thank Edward S. Cooke, Jr. and Angus Trumble, who served on my dissertation committee and offered indispensable guidance. I would also like to thank the Paul Mellon Centre for Studies in British Art for the support of a Junior Fellowship, which allowed me to fully immerse in the archives of institutions across London and beyond, providing the core foundation for my research on Burne-Jones. Although many librarians and archivists offered their support in this research, I would like to offer particular thanks to Nicholas Robinson, Senior Curatorial Assistant in the Department of Manuscripts and Printed Books at the Fitzwilliam Museum, for facilitating access to the Burne-Jones Papers. I am also grateful for the award of a Robert W. Wark Fellowship at the Huntington Library, Art Museum, and Botanical Gardens, as well as a John F. Enders Research Grant from Yale.

I continued to develop my scholarship on Burne-Jones during my time as a Postdoctoral Research Associate at the Yale Center for British Art, where I received vital feedback on work in progress from colleagues and visiting scholars, as well as benefitting from their tremendous institutional resources. I would particularly like to thank Amy Meyers, former Director of the YCBA, for serving as an unfailing advocate for junior scholars in the field of British art, as well as my outstanding colleagues Cassandra Albinson, Jo Briggs, Martina Droth, Gillian Forrester, Imogen Hart, and Alicia Weisberg-Roberts. I would also like to thank Angus for his continued mentorship, collaboration, and support during this time and in the years that have followed.

I am very grateful to the many conference organizers who facilitated the sharing of papers adapted from this book while it was in progress. I would also like to thank the brilliant scholars and curators who have shared their thoughts and offered crucial recommendations, including Caroline Arscott, Florence Boos, Roberto C. Ferrari, Pamela Fletcher, Kate Flint, Michael Hatt, Anne Helmreich, Jongwoo Jeremy Kim, Kristin Mahoney, Elizabeth Prettejohn, Romita Ray, Jason Rosenfeld, and Alison Smith. I would especially like to thank Morna O'Neill, whose intellectual generosity and friendship has helped to shape this project since our time together as fellow Victorianists in graduate school and has remained a tremendous source of inspiration.

I would also like to acknowledge my amazing colleagues at Case Western Reserve University. In particular, I would like to thank Elizabeth Bolman and Catherine Scallen for their mentorship and motivation as I negotiated balancing my teaching, service, and research responsibilities. I owe an enormous debt to Maggie Popkin, who not only provided expert editorial advice, but also kept me going during the most difficult stretch of writing. I would also like to thank Henry Adams, Erin Benay, Elina Gertsman, Peter Shulman, and Holly Witchey for their insights and guidance. My work would not be possible without the resources of the Cleveland Museum of Art, and I would like to thank my extraordinary colleagues there as well, including Heather Lemonedes Brown, Cory Korkow, and Barbara Tannenbaum. A very special thank you to my fantastic students, for continually challenging and inspiring me. I owe particular thanks to Victoria Hepburn, as well as Kate Heller, Julia LaPlaca, Ben Levy, Lauren Lovings-Gomez, Casey Monda, Reed O'Mara, and Bing Wang.

This book has benefitted immeasurably from the support of the Paul Mellon Centre for Studies in British Art. I would like to thank Mark Hallett and the Publications Committee for their guidance on improving the manuscript. I am also grateful to the three anonymous peer reviewers, who provided expert commentary and helped to transform this book in significant ways. I would like to thank my superb copy editor, Katharine Ridler, for her meticulous and expert work. I owe thanks as well to Catherine Osborne, who helped with copy-editing before the submission of my final manuscript. I would like to express my deepest thanks to Emily Lees, for her exceptional efforts in stewarding and shaping this volume, as well as her patience along the way. The book is far more beautiful than I could ever have hoped thanks to her.

Thank you to my friends and family, near and far, who helped to make this book a reality with their generosity and kindness. A special thank you to Amy Rogers, Kate Mrofcza, and the remarkable network of care-givers and educators who have made managing parenthood and a career possible. Above all, I can't begin to put into words my gratitude to Matthew and Lily. Thank you for your understanding during the many hours of writing late at night, the long conversations, the editing of innumerable drafts, the weeks of research away from home, and so very much more. Your love and support has meant more to me than you can ever know and this book is as much yours as mine.

Finally, I would like to dedicate this book to the memory of my father, Professor Robert M. Wolk (1949–2009), and my mother, Maureen A. Wolk (1948–2011). *Ars longa, vita brevis*.

"I mean by a picture"

REDISCOVERING EDWARD BURNE-JONES

In 1975, the scholar and curator John Christian organized the first substantial exhibition devoted to the Victorian painter and decorative artist Edward Burne-Jones (1833–1898) in more than four decades.[1] Sponsored by the Arts Council of Great Britain and debuting at the Hayward Gallery in London, the exhibition strove to bring new attention to the artist after a long period of critical disregard. Christian concluded his introduction with a quotation from one of the artist's letters that has now become the canonical description of the art and reputation of Burne-Jones:

> *It is often quoted but I cannot do better than repeat it here and let it find its own reaction: 'I mean by a picture a beautiful romantic dream of something that never was, never will be – in a light better than any light ever shone – in a land no one can define or remember, only desire – and the forms divinely beautiful.'*[2]

A little over twenty years later, Christian and Stephen Wildman curated an even more extensive international exhibition, *Edward Burne-Jones: Victorian Artist-Dreamer* (1998).[3] When the show opened at the Metropolitan Museum of Art, New York, this same quotation was transcribed directly onto the wall at the start of the exhibition. Moreover, Wildman and Christian reproduced the passage in their final catalogue essay. Questioning the recent revival of interest in the artist, the curators pondered whether his appeal was "primarily escapism, from the horrors of modern life into what Burne-Jones said he 'meant' by a picture – ' a beautiful romantic dream of something that never was, never will be – in a light better than any light ever shone... and the forms divinely beautiful'?"[4]

Seizing on these words, the reviewers of the exhibition frequently cited them as evidence of Burne-Jones's irrelevance to nineteenth-century avant-garde art.[5] More recently, the passage surfaced yet again in critical reviews of the monographic exhibition on the artist, *Edward Burne-Jones: Pre-Raphaelite Visionary*, curated by Alison Smith for Tate Britain in 2018.[6]

It is not difficult to see why the quotation appealed to Christian, as well as those seeking an economical way to encapsulate Burne-Jones's career and classify his work. Beginning with the overt statement "I mean by a picture," the passage promises a declaration of intent, an artist succinctly summarizing, in his own words, the aims of his artistic practice. Moreover, "a beautiful romantic dream" conforms to the superficial expectation of Burne-Jones's work, and arguably the fantasy genre more broadly. The assertion accords with the perception of Burne-Jones as an artist who eschewed modernity to depict a languid world of fairy tales and mythic heroes, adorned in the garments of the past. The source and accuracy of this quotation, as it has been circulated, is taken for granted as self-evident. However, taken out of its original context, these excerpted words belie the seriousness of purpose and dedication with which Burne-Jones pursued his artistic career, as well as the radical potential for his work to challenge viewers.

Tracing the origins of the passage reveals one of the ways that Burne-Jones's legacy and artistic practice have been subtly, but significantly, distorted over the years. The quotation most often appears in the shortened form used by Christian; however, it first emerged in print a year after Burne-Jones's death. In 1899, the Burlington Fine Arts Club organized a posthumous exhibition of his drawings and studies. In the introduction to the accompanying catalogue, the art critic Cosmo Monkhouse stated that Burne-Jones's art attests to his lifelong pursuit of a "noble ideal":

> *What this ideal was may be told in his own words, written to a friend: 'I mean by a picture a beautiful romantic dream of something that never was, never will be – in a light better than any light that ever shone – in a land no one can define or remember, only desire – and the forms divinely beautiful – and then I wake up, with the waking of Brynhild.'*[7]

This longer statement suggests that what Burne-Jones "meant by a picture" was much more complicated and nuanced than it later appeared in its truncated form.

The original passage derives from a letter to Helen Mary Gaskell, now held in the British Library.[8] The letter is undated, but Burne-Jones notes that it is a Sunday and describes his lifelong friend and colleague William Morris (1834–1896) drawing "an initial letter for the Chaucer," which locates it during the 1892–96 production of the Kelmscott Press edition of *The Works of Geoffrey Chaucer*. The surviving correspondence begins mid-letter, with Burne-Jones relating an episode from earlier in the day, when Morris was vehemently protesting about the destruction of an ancient hornbeam in Epping Forest to clear land for a golf course. Burne-Jones then responds to an apparent question from Gaskell about whether he likes to paint portraits. The artist replies that he only cares for portraits of those he loves. Otherwise, he perceives their value as "limited" to "private domestic use." The now famous statement follows directly on from this critique. Quoted here in full, Burne-Jones writes:

> *I mean by a picture a beautiful romantic dream of something that never was nor will be, in a light better than any light that ever shone, in a land no one can define or remember – only desire – and the forms divining [sic] beautiful + then I wake up – with the waking of Brynhild – and do you remember what she said when she woke up? I am sadly afraid you have forgotten what she said – so have I – only she said everything that was meet, when the byrnie was ripped and she stood on the hill + remembered and foresaw.*[9]

Two key elements were lost when this quotation was shortened and excerpted. First, Burne-Jones follows his description of "a picture" as "a beautiful romantic dream" with the declaration "then I wake up." In other words, artistic practice and experience may serve as a conduit to an ideal, utopian vision, but that dream state is understood as necessarily ephemeral.

The manner of waking is also imperative to parsing this statement, as Burne-Jones invokes the legend of Brynhild. Aware that his reference to a Norse character in the medieval Volsunga Saga might be obscure, even for Gaskell, Burne-Jones explains the circumstances of Brynhild's awakening. A shield-maiden cursed by Odin into a magic sleep, she is woken by the hero Sigurd, who frees her from a chain-mail shirt, or "byrnie." Brynhild then sits beside Sigurd, looking out over an expansive landscape, and reveals the prophetic vision that unfolded during her long slumber.[10]

Across the remaining four pages of the letter, Burne-Jones carefully transcribes the account of Brynhild's dream given by Morris in *The Story of Sigurd the Volsung and the Fall of the Niblungs* (1876).[11] Burne-Jones later provided two illustrations for the Kelmscott Press edition, published in 1898 two years after Morris's death (fig. 1). Filling the recto and verso of each sheet, Burne-Jones copied out a long stretch of Morris's text verbatim. This close attention to Morris's exact description of the episode demonstrates Burne-Jones's intimate familiarity with the work of his collaborator, as well as his sympathy with Brynhild's dream.[12] As Florence Boos has argued, Morris portrays Brynhild as a powerful, oracular figure, inflecting her vision with imagery evocative of the heavenly Jerusalem.[13] Through Brynhild, Morris offers the reader a sweeping description of heaven and earth, encompassing past, present, and future:

THE STORY OF SIGURD THE VOLSUNG AND THE FALL OF THE NIBLUNGS. BOOK I. SIGMUND

IN THIS BOOK IS TOLD OF THE EARLIER DAYS OF THE VOLSUNGS, AND OF SIGMUND THE FATHER OF SIGURD, AND OF HIS DEEDS, AND OF HOW HE DIED WHILE SIGURD WAS YET UNBORN IN HIS MOTHER'S WOMB

I. Of the dwelling of King Volsung, & the wedding of Signy his daughter.

THERE WAS A DWELLING OF KINGS ERE THE WORLD WAS WAXEN OLD; DUKES WERE THE DOOR-WARDS THERE, & THE ROOFS WERE THATCHED WITH GOLD; EARLS WERE THE WRIGHTS THAT WROUGHT IT, AND SILVER NAILED ITS DOORS; EARLS' WIVES WERE THE WEAVING-WOMEN, QUEENS' DAUGHTERS STREWED ITS FLOORS, And the masters of its song-craft were the mightiest men that cast
The sails of the storm of battle adown the bickering blast.
There dwelt men merry-hearted, and in hope exceeding great
Met the good days and the evil as they went the way of fate:
There the Gods were unforgotten, yea whiles they walked with men,
Though e'en in that world's beginning rose a murmur now and again
Of the midward time and the fading and the last of the latter days,
And the entering in of the terror, and the death of the People's Praise.
THUS was the dwelling of Volsung, the King of the Midworld's Mark,
As a rose in the winter season, a candle in the dark;
And as in all other matters 'twas all earthly houses' crown,
And the least of its wall-hung shields was a battle-world's renown,
So therein withal was a marvel and a glorious thing to see,
For amidst of its midmost hall-floor sprang up a mighty tree,
That reared its blessings roofward, and wreathed the roof-tree dear
With the glory of the summer and the garland of the year.
I know not how they called it ere Volsung changed his life,
But his dawning of fair promise, and his noontide of the strife,
His eve of the battle-reaping and the garnering of his fame,
Have bred us many a story and named us many a name;
And when men tell of Volsung, they call that war-duke's tree,
That crowned stem, the Branstock; and so was it told unto me.
SO there was the throne of Volsung beneath its blossoming bower,
But high o'er the roof-crest red it rose 'twixt tower and tower,
And therein were the wild hawks dwelling, abiding the dole of their lord;
And they wailed high over the wine, and laughed to the waking sword.
STILL were its boughs but for them, when lo on an even of May
Comes a man from Siggeir the King with a word for his mouth to say:
All hail to thee King Volsung, from the King of the Goths I come:
He hath heard of thy sword victorious and thine abundant home;
He hath heard of thy sons in the battle, the fillers of Odin's Hall;
And a word hath the west-wind blown him (full fruitful be its fall!),

1 ∗ Frontispiece and first page, William Morris, *The Story of Sigurd the Volsung*, 1898. Borders, initials, and Chaucer type by William Morris; illustrations by Edward Burne-Jones. Ink on paper, 34 × 47 cm. The Cleveland Museum of Art, Cleveland, Ohio, Collection of Ingalls Library, Gift of William H. Marlatt and Julia Morgan Marlatt

[S]he told of the hidden matters whereby the world is moved:
And she told of the framing of all Things and the houses of the heaven
+ She told of the star-worlds' courses, and how the winds be driven;
And she told of the Norns, + their names, and the fate that abideth the Earth.[14]

By invoking Brynhild's prophetic dream vision as a means of elucidating his concept of "a picture," Burne-Jones complicates his seemingly straightforward proclamation earlier in the letter. If his art is "a beautiful romantic dream," it is also a transitory, transformative state. "The forms divining beautiful" create a remove from the mundane, but only a temporary one. The immersive experience of the dream is vital, but equally crucial is the necessity of awakening and sharing that revelatory encounter. Like Brynhild, the dreamer must wake up, remember, and foresee.

What Burne-Jones "meant by a picture," then, was the creation of an alternative space indicting the status quo: not as an escape, but as a site of salvation. In *Slow Print: Literary Radicalism and Late Victorian Print Culture* (2013), Elizabeth C. Miller dedicates a chapter to the "utopian aestheticism" of Morris, which aligns closely with my own approach to Burne-Jones.[15] Miller explores Morris's contribution to radical print culture through the journal *The Commonweal*, where he first published both *A Dream of John Ball* (1886–87) and *News from Nowhere* (1890), and his work at the Kelmscott Press. She argues that Morris's "print ventures ... establish print literature as a utopian space in which one can imagine the possibility of a future detached from present conditions." In turn, she cites the postmodern theorist Fredric Jameson's *Archaeologies of the Future* (2005), which argues for utopian form as capable of generating a revolutionary "pocket of stasis" from which to disrupt dominant power structures and elicit the desire for revolutionary change.[16] Jameson describes "Utopian form" as "a representational meditation on radical difference, radical otherness."[17] Discussing Morris's *News from Nowhere* as a key example, he argues for the utopian form as positing a radical break with the present in order to depict a future that seems impossible.[18]

In an earlier text, *The Cultural Turn* (1998), Jameson suggested that, as deceptively familiar as Victorian society seems, the potent critique offered by the aesthetic protest against commodity culture and industrial mass-consumerism no longer appears as radical as it once did:

> *The final point I want to make has to do with beauty itself.... it only seems appropriate in the present context to recall beauty's subversive role in a society marred by nascent commodification. The* fin de siècle, *from Morris to Wilde, deployed beauty as a political weapon against a complacent materialist Victorian bourgeois society and dramatized its negative power as what rebukes commerce and money, and what generates a longing for personal and social transformation in the heart of an ugly industrial society.*[19]

Jameson claims that, since the image became so ubiquitous and commodified in the postmodern era, it is no longer possible to perceive beauty as a critique. Extending Jameson's theorization to Burne-Jones, his work can be acknowledged not as a series of escapist dreams, but as revolutionary calls for awakening and transformation.

Challenging the dominant characterization of Burne-Jones as an artist who withdrew from the Victorian world into imaginary realms of his own creation, this book will demonstrate that he was instead engaged in a fundamentally radical defiance of the artistic, social, and political hierarchies of the modern age.[20] For Burne-Jones, modernity was defined by utilitarianism, industrialization, imperialism, capitalist acquisitive materialism, and a pervasive disregard for the sanctity of the natural world and the suffering of collective humanity. As a young student at Oxford, Burne-Jones first began to rebel against these injustices, vowing to embark on what he termed his "crusade and Holy Warfare against the age, 'the heartless coldness of the times.'"[21] After declaring that he would abandon Christian ministry for the secular ministry of art, his protest "against the age" took the form of immersive, epiphanic aesthetic experiences. Adopting the medieval concept of dreams as visionary states of transformation, Burne-Jones hoped to reveal the utopian power of embodied aesthetic encounters, not as a retreat but as a vehicle for revolutionary awakening.

Dissatisfied with the London art market, which privileged the portable, easily commodified oil-on-canvas medium, Burne-Jones continually sought to exceed the established parameters of painting, either through executing colossal individual works or through expansive, multi-work cycles.[22] Moreover, he pursued opportunities not only to resist the established artistic supremacy of painting, but also to generate site-specific immersive environments through the decorative arts. Although it is often overshadowed by his painting practice, Burne-Jones was a prolific designer for the decorative arts, including book illustration, mosaic, stained glass, tapestry, and bas-relief sculpture. This book will re-center his work in the decorative arts, demonstrating that he consistently interrogated the boundaries of artistic media, in keeping with wider debates over the role of the arts in the nineteenth century. Each chapter investigates the use of different artistic media, introducing case studies in his experimentation with book illustration, the single monumental canvas, the multi-part painted series, mosaic, and, finally, stained glass, tapestry, and paintings in dialogue.

Crucial to my argument is a re-examination of Burne-Jones's supposed schism with Morris over socialism. I posit that their divergence was unequivocally one of methods, not beliefs, thereby returning their profound artistic and intellectual collaborative partnership to the core of Burne-Jones's career.[23] When Morris turned to socialist activism, Burne-Jones supported his radical ideological stance, but disapproved of his impatience and the tendentious factionalism that quickly embroiled his friend. For Burne-Jones, the petty bickering and bureaucratic haggling of politics was ephemeral. Unlike the politics of tracts and pamphlets, art could endure, speaking not only to the present, but to the future as well. Adhering to his calling as a painter and decorative artist, rather than a poet and orator, Burne-Jones expressed his deeply held convictions through the vital language of the visual arts.[24]

There is ample evidence to suggest that many of Burne-Jones's contemporaries perceived his work as operating in this radical and confrontational mode. The subversive qualities of his art were, for example, repeatedly noted by the art critic Julia Cartwright Ady, who began her monographic 1894 essay on Burne-Jones by elaborating his challenge to modernity: "[T]he most original and remarkable manifestation of art during this period has been due to a painter whose aims and achievements were in marked contrast to the leading characteristics of the age. The art of Burne-Jones from first to last has been a silent and unconscious protest against the most striking tendencies of the modern world."[25] Cartwright Ady continued:

> *His whole life has been one long search after loveliness, one long endeavour to lay hold of the fairest and the best. In this quest he has never faltered. He has helped us to rise out of the dust that blinds our eyes in this all too prosaic world, and to realise the enduring might of the things that are unseen. The appeal which he has addressed to the children of his generation has been the appeal of art, and he will not have lived in vain if he has spoken to the hearts of men through beauty, 'which is the other side of truth'.*[26]

Similarly, in his series of essays on Burne-Jones for *The Architectural Review* in 1897, Henry Wilson described the power of opposition in the artist's work as a catalyst for change. For Wilson, "Burne-Jones's work, like that of Watts and others, forces one to think, in despite of contracts and clients, in spite of haste and the consequent hideousness around, we might do much if only our energies were united."[27] The French critic Robert de la Sizeranne, writing on the state of English art in 1898, advocated a similar assessment:

> *[I]t is an immense error, made by realists in search of modern superficiality, to think that his works suggest fewer contemporary pictures, fewer existing interests, because they are farther apart from our daily life than the illustrations of the* Graphic, *and the* Illustrated News. *This is proved by the permanent impression they leave on anyone who has seen them. For myself, I never looked at some of his works without a revival of the anxieties and realities of the passing hour.*[28]

In the obituaries published in 1898, several authors noted Burne-Jones's dedication to critiquing modernity through his art, as well as the lasting impact his work would have for future generations. An anonymous author in *The Quarterly Review* predicted:

> *His art will be reckoned among the forces that have helped to regenerate the world in these latter days, and, with the music of Wagner, the poetry of Tennyson and Browning, and the painting of Watts and Rossetti, will be recognized as forming part of a movement which is the natural reaction from the materialism of the present century and the rationalism of the last.*[29]

The author observed that Burne-Jones sought to "make life beautiful... to keep alive the sense of a world that is out of sight, and to show how the troubled waves of human life may dimly reflect the beauty and mystery of God."[30] Finally Joseph Jacobs, a folklorist and literary scholar, attested not only to the remarkable erudition of his friend, but also to Burne-Jones's dedication to the more humble aspects of craft and labor, proclaiming:

> *Apart from his great works of imagination, there was what may be called the workmanly side of his character, the steadfast determination to do his day's work. Alive to all the great spiritual movements of his time, he was equally or perhaps more concerned with the daily life and surroundings of the people. His great complaint against modern civilisation was that a workman could not turn out honest work that would last. He was determined in his own life to give an example to the contrary.*[31]

The object of this book is neither to revert to an earlier view of Burne-Jones and his career, nor to assume a determinate intentionality on the part of the artist. Instead, I seek to strip away the accretions that have amassed around the figure of Burne-Jones and his work, obscuring the ability to perceive his artistic practice as a radical confrontation with modernity. Throughout, I seek to adopt a rigorously investigated period eye, with careful consultation of the archive and of primary source criticisms. These archival sources include collections of correspondence written by and exchanged with Edward Burne-Jones in the Fitzwilliam Museum, Cambridge; the British Library; the Huntington Library, San Marino, California; the Castle Howard Archives; and the Yale Center for British Art, New Haven, Connecticut, among others. In addition to Burne-Jones's extant correspondence, I have also examined the unpublished memoirs of his studio assistant, Thomas M. Rooke. Although I will frequently refer to this memoir, the conversations recorded there deserve some extra scrutiny, given that they were often transcribed after the fact and are inflected by Rooke's own opinions.[32] Finally, I have given careful consideration to Georgiana Burne-Jones's two-volume biography of her husband. Her *Memorials of Edward Burne-Jones* (1904) is an invaluable resource that not only transcribes key passages from Burne-Jones's correspondence (much of which survives in the Fitzwilliam), but also records conversations and personal insights into his working practice and relationship with William Morris.

Although these archival records and the recovery of primary source criticism is vital to this reexamination, the center of my study is devoted to close visual analysis, assessing as far as possible the unique experiential qualities of Burne-Jones's paintings, designs for the decorative arts, and monumental public works under their original conditions of display and reception. This approach has been informed, in particular, by the work of Tim Barringer and Elizabeth Prettejohn. Both scholars have persuasively articulated the need to adopt such a model of art historical inquiry for nineteenth-century British art.

This methodology remains attentive to the rigors of social art history, but asserts that the unique material and phenomenological qualities of the art object itself must remain at the core of the argument.[33]

The first chapter centers on *When Adam Delved and Eve Span*, Burne-Jones's iconic composition for the frontispiece to the 1892 Kelmscott Press edition of Morris's socialist novel *A Dream of John Ball*.[34] Although this woodcut was one of the most widely circulated and readily recognizable of Burne-Jones's works, even transformed into a socialist banner, it has generally been considered to belong more to Morris and his political ideology. I demonstrate that the composition did not originate in Morris's text, but represents a continuous iconographic thread that can be traced throughout the course of Burne-Jones's career to one of his very first designs, a stained-glass window executed in 1857 for James Powell & Sons depicting *Adam and Eve After the Fall*. Through an exploration of this nuanced image of egalitarianism and empowered labor, I elucidate Burne-Jones's personal relationship to socialism and radical politics, as well as detailing his involvement with the Eastern Question Association, and the conditions of his supposed schism with Morris over political activism. The Labors of Adam and Eve emerge from Burne-Jones's image not as a curse, but as a means of redemption: a mandate to the people of the nineteenth century to achieve salvation through a return to the kind of satisfying physical labor and pleasurable handicraft embodied by this icon of primitive humanity.

Burne-Jones's monumental painting *King Cophetua and the Beggar Maid* (1880–84), as seen at the Paris Universal Exposition of 1889, opens the second chapter. Set against the backdrop of this concentrated and frenzied microcosm of urban modernity, industrial consumerism, and imperialist propaganda, *King Cophetua* achieved a striking air of immediacy, proving confrontational and epiphanic. In the words of Sizeranne, "we [visitors] had come forth from the universal Exhibition of Wealth to see the symbolical expression of the Scorn of Wealth.... It was a dream – but a noble dream.... It was the revenge of art on life."[35] As a painting that blatantly overturned the social order, that employed an ancient legend to call attention to the modern obsession with materiality, and that proclaimed the nature of its making, *King Cophetua and the Beggar Maid* depicted a multilayered vision of what might be, of a world rooted in fellowship rather than acquisition, in which beauty can be set free for all. *King Cophetua*, I argue, functioned as a secular altarpiece that flouted the modern art market and exhibition system. Inviting the viewer to cross the threshold of the painting and enter an immersive and transformative encounter with decorative materiality, it was a potent disruption of the gallery space and a visual manifesto of craft practice as a rebellious act.

The third chapter examines the *Perseus* series as a revival of the Renaissance *paragone* for modernity, exploring the productive tension between sculpture and painting, the haptic and the optic, amid the debates over the nature of mimesis that arose in the nineteenth century. Commissioned by Arthur Balfour in 1875 for the music room of his London residence at 4 Carlton Gardens, the *Perseus* series was a significant project for Burne-Jones that was nevertheless left incomplete at the time of his death. Consequently, the series has struggled to take its proper place as perhaps the defining work of Burne-Jones's career, which occupied his mind, labor, and studio for well over twenty years. While the second chapter explores Burne-Jones's experimentations with the single monumental painted canvas, this chapter considers the distinctive qualities of the multipart painted series. Notably, I investigate the kinesthetic properties of the *Perseus* series, which exceed the individual boundaries of each painting to become an immersive site-specific experience.

Burne-Jones's expansive mosaic cycle for the American Episcopal Church of St. Paul's Within the Walls, Rome, is the subject of the fourth chapter. This vast decorative scheme presented Burne-Jones with an opportunity to create a prominent, public work in an adamantine medium that could not only speak to his own era, but also endure through the ravages of time to inspire future generations. Interpreted as a coherent, experiential whole, the Rome mosaics offer a vision of the redemption and salvation of humanity in terms of ecological rebirth. The mosaic cycle alludes to ancient Byzantine precedents, but Burne-Jones infused them with an environmental allegory that progresses from a bleak scene of the Annunciation set in a barren desert to the lush triumph of a verdant Tree of Life and at last to a vision of the heavenly Jerusalem as a flourishing paradise. This chapter elucidates Burne-Jones's contribution to nascent ecological thought and protest alongside John Ruskin and William Morris, illuminating his own reciprocal call for environmental rebirth from the natural devastation of the industrial revolution.

The concluding chapter adopts a thematic approach, tracing the subjects of the Nativity and the Adoration through key works across Burne-Jones's career and a range of media. Through stained glass, tapestry, oil on canvas painting, and colossal watercolor, Burne-Jones meditated on the theological doctrine of the Incarnation, which resides at the heart of the Nativity story, as the manifestation of the divine in collective humanity and the natural world. Despite his religious skepticism, I argue that Burne-Jones employed the Christian religious iconography of the Nativity and the Adoration in order to assert the intertwined concepts of manifestation, embodiment, and witness as analogous to the process of artistic labor, contemplation, and revelatory awakening. This chapter links *The Adoration of the Magi* tapestry for Exeter College Chapel, Oxford (designed 1887–88, executed 1888–90), and the vast *Star of Bethlehem* watercolor for the city of Birmingham (1887–91) with monumental pendant paintings created for the Church of St. John the Evangelist in Torquay, *The Nativity* and *The King and the Shepherd* (1888), and finally with *The Nativity* stained-glass windows for St. Deiniol's, Hawarden (1898) and St. Philip's,

Birmingham (1887). I argue that the concepts of manifestation, embodiment, and witness emerge as radical and revolutionary commentaries on art and society in modernity, through the alchemical alignment of medium and subject.

In her early monograph on Burne-Jones, published in 1904, Fortunée de Lisle simultaneously acknowledged that the artist was "an idealist, a dreamer," but also one who confronted the "materialistic age of mammon-worship."[36] She concluded by arguing that although he drew inspiration from the past, Burne-Jones should nonetheless be remembered as an artistic and political rebel who actively challenged the modern age:

> *A radical of the radicals, a hot Home-Ruler, a revolutionist against the social anarchy which appeared to him and to William Morris as the result of the capitalist system, he had that "sympathetic perception of the dominant under-current of progress" which enabled him to keep to the end the enthusiasms of his youth. He longed for progress in every direction, and, like his Briar Rose knight, would fain have been the one to "smite this sleeping world awake" to a new order of things.*[37]

The aim of this book is to reevaluate the art and career of Burne-Jones, shifting from the model of the somnambulist to the revolutionary. This reorientation will also enable a concurrent reassessment of the work of Morris. Recognizing the central importance of Morris's and Burne-Jones's collaborative partnership, this shift in the perception of both artists will facilitate new insights into their lifelong pursuit of transformative, utopian awakening through the visual arts.

Chapter One

"An ideal of the world"

REVIVING THE LABORS OF ADAM AND EVE

In the summer of 1855, Edward Burne-Jones and William Morris embarked on a tour of the medieval cathedrals of northern France, including Beauvais, Chartres, and Rouen. Morris and Burne-Jones had first met two years earlier as students at Exeter College, Oxford. Although they came from vastly different backgrounds, the two quickly formed a lifelong friendship. Morris was the wealthy son of a financier raised on the outskirts of London, while Burne-Jones was the only child of a frame-maker in industrial Birmingham. Both went to Oxford with the intention of taking clerical orders, but quickly became disillusioned with what they perceived as the hypocrisies of the Anglican Church and the Oxbridge educational system. They found inspiration instead in the writings of Thomas Carlyle and John Ruskin, as well as medieval literature, illuminated manuscripts, and the art of the Pre-Raphaelite Brotherhood, and their journey in France proved to be a crucial turning point in their lives and careers. Nearly forty years later, Burne-Jones recalled with reverence their shared epiphany when faced with Gothic architecture. Describing his experience at Beauvais cathedral, he writes of hearing "ancient singing" – so beautiful he thought Judgment Day had come – "and the roof & the long lights that are the most graceful things man has ever made what a day it was – & how alive I was, & young."[1]

Inspired by this transformative encounter, Burne-Jones and Morris swore together to turn away from a Christian ministry. Instead, they would dedicate themselves to a secular ministry through art, enabling others to experience this same revelatory awakening. Burne-Jones later wrote, "we resolved definitely that we would begin a life of art, and put off our decision no longer.... [It] was the most memorable night of my life."[2] For the two

young men, this was a call to arms, a shared "Crusade against the Age," that would bind their lives together, forever informing their faith in the revelatory power of art.[3] "If I took account of my life and the days in it that most went to make me," Burne-Jones recalled, "the Sunday at Beauvais would be the first day of creation."[4]

In 1857, not long after this fateful trip, the firm of James Powell & Sons commissioned Burne-Jones to design a three-light stained-glass window for St. Andrew's College, Bradfield (fig. 3).[5] His experimental approach to iconography and composition was evident from the outset, particularly in his design for the left-hand light, *Adam and Eve After the Fall* (fig. 2).[6] Rendered in vibrant, tessellated blocks of color, the figures of Adam, Eve, and an angel appear along a synchronic vertical axis. At the very bottom of the light, Adam kneels to tend a fertile garden, pulling weeds and thorns with his bare hands to allow the blooming lilies and stalks of grain to flourish. Directly above him, Eve sits nursing a baby at her breast, while her hands are occupied with a spindle and distaff, busy at work to clothe her growing family. A green wattle fence adorned with vibrant sunflowers encloses their simple home, demarcating the boundary between terrestrial and celestial realms. An angel with a flaming sword occupies the top third of the window, guarding the gates of heaven and the rivers of paradise, just visible between his outspread, polychromatic wings. Finally, the fruited branches of the Tree of Life fill the uppermost reaches of the window. Adam and Eve are barred from the vision of paradise unfolding just above their heads. However, they have begun to create their own Eden on earth, enabled by their productive labor in harmony with nature. In this early composition, Burne-Jones depicts the Labors of Adam and Eve not as a curse but as a means of redemption. *Adam and Eve After the Fall* proposes a new utopian model for salvation, achieved through a return to the kind of satisfying physical labor, pleasurable handicraft, and intimate familiarity with nature embodied by this image of the primigenial couple.

More than three decades later, in 1892, Burne-Jones adapted this composition into one of his most iconic and widely circulated designs, the woodcut *When Adam Delved and Eve Span* (fig. 4). This revolutionary emblem of egalitarianism served as the frontispiece

2 * Edward Burne-Jones, for James Powell & Sons, *Adam and Eve after the Fall*, 1857. Watercolor and Indian ink, 214.4 × 47.8 cm. Victoria and Albert Museum, London, E.1319-1970

3 * Edward Burne-Jones, for James Powell & Sons, *Adam and Eve after the Fall*, *Building the Tower of Babel*, and *Solomon and the Queen of Sheba*, 1857. Stained glass, St. Andrew's College, Bradfield

to the Kelmscott Press edition of Morris's socialist novel *A Dream of John Ball* (1892).[7] Consequently, the design and its import have largely been attributed to Morris's words, invention, and political beliefs.[8] This negation of Burne-Jones's agency in creating an indelible image of anti-capitalist protest arises from the false perception that he rejected Morris's socialist political views. To the contrary, this chapter demonstrates that their divergence over socialist activism arose from a disagreement about the best way to achieve the same revolutionary aims.[9] As Georgiana Burne-Jones incisively observed, "they only parted

WHEN ADAM DELVED
AND EVE SPAN
WHO WAS THEN THE
GENTLEMAN

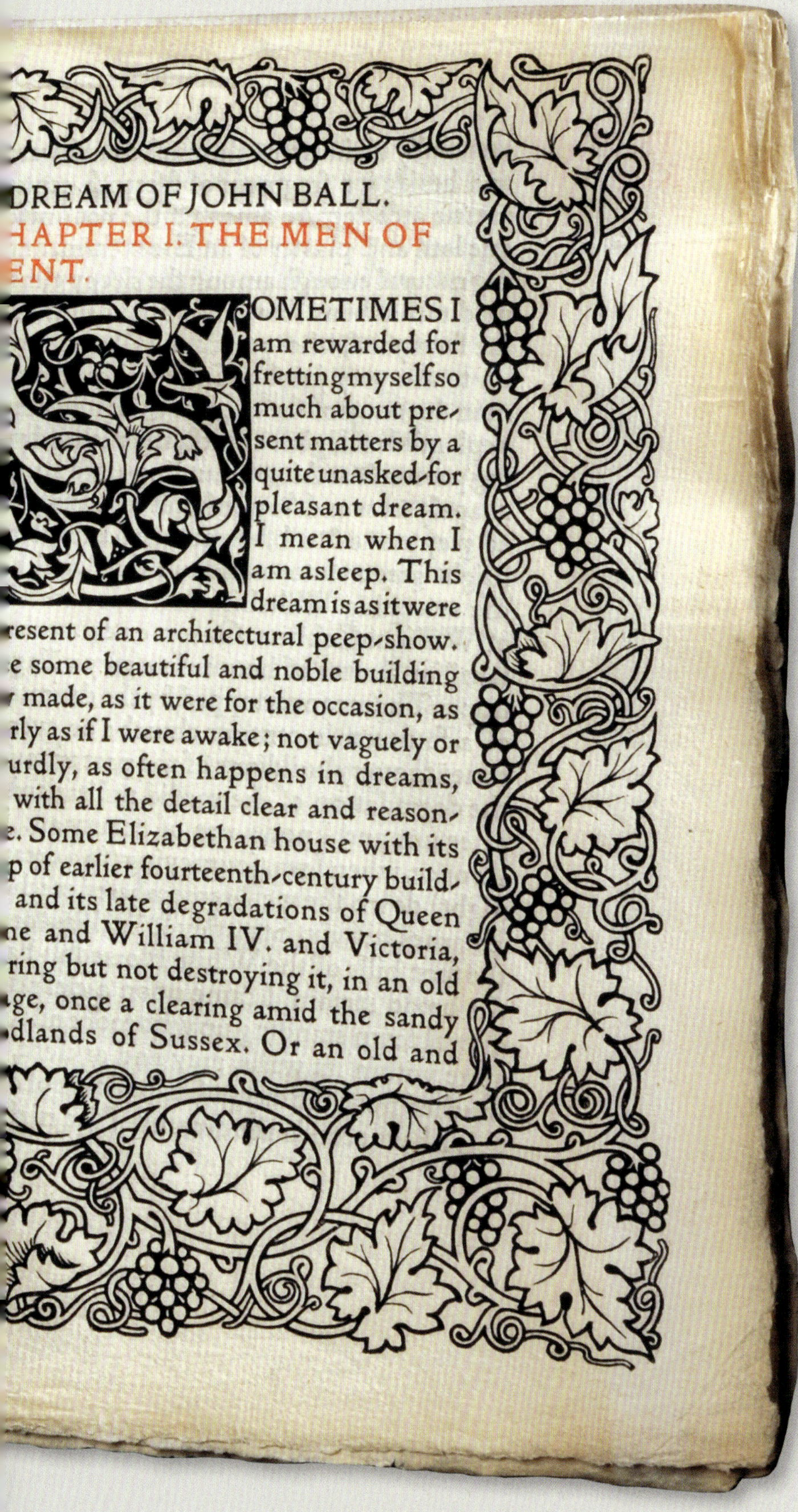

DREAM OF JOHN BALL.
HAPTER I. THE MEN OF
ENT.

SOMETIMES I am rewarded for fretting myself so much about present matters by a quite unasked-for pleasant dream. I mean when I am asleep. This dream is as it were resent of an architectural peep-show. e some beautiful and noble building made, as it were for the occasion, as rly as if I were awake; not vaguely or urdly, as often happens in dreams, with all the detail clear and reason-e. Some Elizabethan house with its p of earlier fourteenth-century build- and its late degradations of Queen ne and William IV. and Victoria, ring but not destroying it, in an old ge, once a clearing amid the sandy dlands of Sussex. Or an old and

4 ∗ Edward Burne-Jones, *When Adam Delved and Eve Span*, frontispiece for William Morris, *A Dream of John Ball*, Kelmscott Press, 1892. Woodcut, 37.5 × 31.8 cm. William Morris Gallery, London (K6)

company about the means to be employed for one and the same end."[10] Rather than a mere illustration to Morris's words, *When Adam Delved and Eve Span* embodies Burne-Jones's own radical artistic and political beliefs, testifying to his ongoing dedication to those ideals throughout his career.

"Perfect communion of thought and heart between them": Burne-Jones, Morris, and Socialism

In November 1883, Burne-Jones wrote to Mary Gladstone, the daughter of the Liberal Prime Minister William Gladstone, offering a rare articulation of his most deeply held political beliefs, while at the same time clarifying his divergence from Morris over socialist organizing. This letter provides yet another example of how the artist's words have often been excerpted and distorted, privileging his assertions of escape while omitting his declarations of protest. Although Mary Gladstone's half of the correspondence is no longer extant, she evidently had posed a question about Henry George's *Progress and Poverty* (1879), which argues that poverty is a direct result of the hoarding of profits by monopolists.[11] Burne-Jones replied:

> *Yes, I know* Progress & Poverty *– and admire greatly its nobility of temper and style – but its deductions, O I knew all that long ago – it is a book that couldn't more persuade me of a thing I believed already – and have patience with some of us who say things more strongly still. How can some men help having an ideal of the world they want, & feeling for it as for a religion – and sometimes being fanatical for it, & unwise – as men are too for the religion that they love. It must be – and Morris is quite right, only for my own sake I wish he could be out of it all and busy only for the things he used to be busy about – I shall never again make myself much unhappy about passing events – it would be easy to break oneself to bits with fruitless trouble – I shall try never again to leave the world that I can control to my hearts [sic] desire – the little world that has the walls of my workroom for its furthest horizon – & I want Morris back to it, & want him to write divine books and leave the rest – someday it will all change violently – & I hate & dread it but say beforehand it will thoroughly well serve everybody quite right – but I don't want to see it or foresee it or dwell upon it. . . . I want nothing else, but to paint and paint.*[12]

George likened the free market capitalist system to slavery, which rendered his views highly influential for the burgeoning socialist movement in the United States and Britain. Burne-Jones was clearly familiar with the book, while also insisting that George did not go far enough in his condemnation of the ills of capitalism ("have patience with some of us who say things more strongly still"). Writing several months after Morris had joined the board of the Social Democratic Federation, Burne-Jones emphasized that Morris was "quite right" in his political beliefs. But while he supported Morris's stance, he nonetheless lamented the loss of the undivided energies of his artistic partner and collaborator. A socialist uprising might be an inevitability, but rather than prophesying it, his response was to "paint and paint," creating art for that impending, post-apocalyptic world. What could be interpreted as a gesture of retreat was instead an assertion of the radical potential of art to serve as a utopian space, for the present and for future generations.

When Burne-Jones exchanged these letters with Mary Gladstone, she was not only the daughter of the prime minister but was also serving as his private secretary.[13] With her own office at 10 Downing Street, Mary Gladstone was a trusted adviser to her father and a political force in her own right. Despite his claim that he would "never again make myself much unhappy about passing events," Burne-Jones's frequent correspondence with the Gladstones during this time was not limited to personal or artistic matters. In letters to both father and daughter, he repeatedly urged against imperial aggression and in favor of self-governance, protesting the British role in the First Boer War of 1880–81 and the Anglo-Egyptian War of 1882, while adamantly supporting Irish Home Rule.[14] He also wrote to both Mary and William Gladstone in 1882 on behalf of the Jewish Committee to condemn the pogroms in Russia.[15] Although he was not offering public lectures or campaigning in the streets like Morris, Burne-Jones nonetheless pursued his own networks of political influence, quietly but consistently throughout his life. As he explained to the artist and politician George Howard (later the 9th Earl of Carlisle) in 1878, "Morris is very great these days and influences young men for their souls' good.... Of course I am sick and miserable to the heart about public things – and have ceased to talk but not to think of them."[16]

Burne-Jones's revulsion against the inefficacy of public political protest was the direct result of his participation alongside Morris in the Eastern Question Association (E.Q.A.) between 1876 and 1878, and his despair when this protest movement failed. The "Eastern Question" was the name given to the ongoing territorial disputes that occurred amid the decline of the Ottoman Empire. Motivated by imperial interests, Britain became embroiled in a series of conflicts in the region throughout the nineteenth and early twentieth centuries, including the Greek war of independence in the 1820s and the Crimean War (1853–56). With the route to India at stake, the British sought to preserve peaceful relations with the Turks and prevent Russian influence over the area. The E.Q.A. was formed during the Balkan crisis of 1875–78 (also known as the Russo-Turkish War), during which the Turks were rumored to be committing atrocities against the Christians of the Balkans.[17] When Russia invaded under the pretense of aiding the Christian populations of the region, the British public was roused into action. The Conservatives, led by Benjamin Disraeli, favored going to war on behalf of the Turks in order to curb Russian aggression. Countering this hawkish response was a coalition of Liberals and humanitarians headed by Gladstone who adopted a neutral stance in the conflict, with the hope that Russia would help stem violence against Christians and contain the Turks. The E.Q.A. was formed by this latter group, with the particular goal of rallying and organizing the working classes in protest against a war motivated by the financial interests of the upper classes.

Morris stressed the oppressive, class-based, imperialist motivations of the impending war in an open letter of May 1877. Addressing the working classes directly, he wrote:

> *Working-men of England, one word of warning yet: I doubt if you know the bitterness of hatred against freedom and progress that lies at the hearts of a certain part of the richer classes in this country.... these men, if they had the power... would thwart your just aspirations, would silence you, would deliver you bound hand and foot for ever to irresponsible capital – and these men, I say it deliberately, are the heart and soul of the party that is driving us to an unjust war.*[18]

Morris's statement elucidates the ties between this supposed matter of foreign affairs and the core beliefs of his later socialist politics. Both Morris and Burne-Jones became active members of the E.Q.A., with Morris signing on as treasurer. Burne-Jones attended meetings, participated in rallies, and wrote letters to influential friends, including John Ruskin, seeking support.[19] At the outset of the conflict, Burne-Jones expressed the vehemence of his stance in a private letter:

> *I never cared about any matter so much in all my life and felt so certain of anything, as to how I should decide rightly.... in my heart I know politics to be the one great subject of life, for which one should put aside all private matters and for which one should give up everything.... What I mean by politics – I do from my soul want my country to help mankind – to set aside its low interests that are base in the individual and shameful in the community – I want it dreadfully, so that if at this time we by indifference, folly, or selfishness lose our chance, I shall never in my life days recover from the disappointment of it.*[20]

Sadly, his words proved prophetic. Although he continued to adhere to his belief in the need to help humankind, Burne-Jones was forever disheartened by what he perceived as the futility of political protest after the collapse of the E.Q.A.

Morris's fears that the ruling classes would silence the collective demands of the working classes came to pass. As the tide of war began to turn in Russia's favor, the crisis reached its peak in early 1878. The E.Q.A., in an effort to stave off the imminent call for war by Parliament, organized a massive Workmen's Neutrality Demonstration at Exeter Hall in London on January 16, 1878. The moment was a triumphant one, with a passionate but peaceful gathering of protesters from all classes united in common purpose.[21] Morris wrote the rousing anthem "Wake, London Lads" for the occasion, which was sung by all in harmony, and Burne-Jones contributed an original design, titled *Blind War*, for the platform ticket.[22] This exultant moment of solidarity cruelly raised the hopes of Morris, Burne-Jones, and the E.Q.A., but they were dashed in the following days when British battleships were deployed over the objections of the people. In the end, the Balkan conflict was quickly resolved without the need for a prolonged military engagement. However, for Morris and Burne-Jones both, the damage had been done. They were deeply troubled by the fact that, in spite of their most fervent efforts and the successful mobilization of the working classes, they had failed to effect political change.

The disheartening experience of the E.Q.A. prompted Morris and Burne-Jones to opposite reactions, thus initiating the one critical divide of their careers. In the immediate aftermath, the two friends returned to their shared artistic labor with a renewed sense of purpose. Just over a month later, Morris expressed his lingering disillusionment:

> *I am that ashamed that I can scarcely look people in the face, though I did my best to keep the thing up.... There was a stormy meeting of the E.Q.A. yesterday, full of wretched little personalities, but I held my tongue – I am out of it now; I mean as to bothering my head about it: I shall give up reading the papers, and shall stick to my work.*[23]

However, this retreat from the world of politics was only temporary. After further contemplating the ramifications of this incident, Morris committed himself fully to the cause of radical socialist agitation throughout the next decade. History has tended to side with Morris in his decision to throw himself into political activism wholeheartedly, and perhaps even recklessly. In contrast, Burne-Jones has often been portrayed as retreating in silence to his studio, turning his back disapprovingly and abandoning modernity for fantastical visions of an imaginary past.[24]

This notion, and the corresponding implication that, of the pair, Morris was the true radical and Burne-Jones the reactionary, was entrenched in twentieth-century critical discourse by E. P. Thompson's influential biography, *William Morris: Romantic to Revolutionary* (1955).[25] Thompson persuasively argued for the centrality of Morris's socialism to his career, recasting him from poet and interior decorator to militant and committed political activist and redeeming much of his aesthetic practice by association. However, Thompson drastically marginalized Burne-Jones, minimizing his role in their shared artistic endeavors and apparently sacrificing Burne-Jones as a conservative, apolitical foil to the heroic Morris. For example, of Morris's decision to commit to the socialist cause in 1884, Thompson declares: "Of his old friends, only Philip Webb and Charlie Faulkner, both of whom knew his greatness, went with him. It was 'the only time when I failed Morris,' said Edward – soon to be Sir Edward – Burne-Jones many years later." Thompson indicted Burne-Jones with his own admission of "failure," paired with the pointed use of "soon to be Sir Edward," implicitly accusing the artist of aristocratic ambitions and elitism.[26]

Thompson, however, oversimplified and distorted Burne-Jones's choice not to participate in socialist political activism, falsely partitioning his career from Morris's and diminishing the strength of their commitment to art as a means of enacting change and prompting revelation.[27] Burne-Jones's decision to adopt art as a language of protest, rather than political haggling and bureaucratic committees, was a rebellious act. By contrast, it was Morris who lost faith in their original radical vision by betraying their sacred sworn vows to pursue a life of art, a path they had embarked on together under the soaring vaults of Beauvais Cathedral.[28] According to Georgiana Burne-Jones, herself a devoted socialist, Burne-Jones regretted Morris's denial of his true vocation and his abandonment of their shared quest to transform the world through art:

> *Morris was growing more and more restless and disturbed in mind by the conditions of modern life, and his conscience was dragging him towards some definite work for its amendment, while Edward held that it was always a mistake, if not a wrong thing, for a man to swerve from the exercise of his own special gift, or seek another way of helping the world.*[29]

Burne-Jones's critique of the age does not leap stridently off the page, as in Morris's lectures, but emerges instead through extended visual immersion and organically unfolding aesthetic awakening. This vital thread can be traced throughout his work, from beginning to end.

Despite Morris's deviation from a life solely dedicated to art, the two held fast to their friendship throughout the 1880s, as well as to their sacred Sunday ritual of working side by side on their collaborative projects without interruption. Several passages, from Burne-Jones's own letters and the recollections of their friends, provide insight into the continued commitment of both men to each other and to their shared cause of art as a vehicle of protest and change during this period. The Scottish socialist J. Bruce Glasier observed with curiosity Morris's enduring dedication to his partnership with Burne-Jones, as well as their steadfast custom of shared work every Sunday.[30] Unable to comprehend how Morris could accept his friend's reluctance to join in the movement, Glasier made the mistake of dismissing the value of Burne-Jones's work. Morris's response was shocking in its vehemence, as he immediately attacked the inability of society, and Glasier by implication, to appreciate the vital importance of art. Morris declared, "This infernal civilisation has no capacity to understand either nature or art. People have no eyes to see, no ears to hear. The only thing they understand is how to enslave their fellows or be enslaved by them."[31] Morris's quick and forceful defense of Burne-Jones's artistic practice attests not only to their persistent friendship, but also to his steadfast belief in art as a means of voicing dissent.

In 1885, Burne-Jones expressed his own understanding of this time in their friendship in a letter inviting a fellow artist, Ford Madox Brown, to dine with him:

> *I'll make a feast and Morris shall come and harangue us: I can't say I am altogether with him in his rebellion – nine tenths of the way or more perhaps: but I haven't his hopefulness and what seems to him already in sight is a thousand years off to me & so I go on painting and he is preaching every day.*[32]

Burne-Jones conceived of their work continuing along parallel paths: although he was with Morris "nine tenths of the way," they diverged in their approach. Morris preached, but Burne-Jones painted every day, with his eye on future generations. In his memoirs, the curator and art critic Sidney Colvin echoed this assessment:

> *When his oldest and closest friend of all, William Morris, with whom he had worked and thought and felt all their lives in the closest brotherly association, threw himself headlong into the cause of socialism, Burne-Jones would not follow him, holding that an artist's first and paramount duty was to his art.... But this partial sundering of their ways did not bring about the least jar or breach of friendship between the two.*[33]

Their work remained constant during this period, as did their mutual admiration, respect, and intimacy. Indeed, many of Burne-Jones's most important projects came to fruition in the decade of Morris's most active participation in socialist agitation. Close analysis of these works, across painting, mosaic, tapestry, stained glass, and book illustration, attest to Burne-Jones's sustained commitment to confronting the inequities of modernity through the immersive, epiphanic, and transformative capacity of aesthetic experience.

After Morris's death in 1896, Burne-Jones reflected on the interlude when his friend turned to socialist activism. Thomas Rooke, Burne-Jones's studio assistant, transcribed a conversation between Burne-Jones and the artist and former socialist Robert Catterson-Smith in his diary. The two discussed the failures of the socialist political movement, how it devolved through a lack of commitment and bickering among participants. Burne-Jones then clarified his choice not to join Morris's participation in political agitation, resulting in the shortened quotation later used by Thompson to censure his retreat from socialism:

> *All that I felt at the only time when I failed Mr Morris, the one thing upon which he and I did not stand together. I used to tell him that if a number of people were moved to throw themselves entirely into it that would give it a different aspect to me. And even as I said it I was afraid he might do it, and it would have been such an injury to him and to his work and to us all and to the world.*[34]

Burne-Jones here expresses not disappointment in himself, but regret that Morris could not hold fast to their mutually held belief that art, not political activism, could foster true ideological, social, and artistic change. In 1896, Julia Cartwright Ady similarly recorded Burne-Jones's thoughts on his lasting friendship and sympathy with Morris in the wake of his death:

> *He went back to the old days when the two shy boys of 18 met as Freshmen at Exeter College and how from that moment until now there had been perfect communion of thought and heart between them. . . . Only once he felt he had failed Morris – in his Socialism. To that my painter could not rise. He thought it a beautiful but impossible dream.*[35]

In the end, the "perfect communion of thought and heart between them" withstood this period of divergence. Their collaborative endeavors continued throughout the last two decades of their lives, as Burne-Jones committed to his paintings and decorative arts projects with renewed clarity of purpose and determination.

"An ideal of the world": The Labors of Adam and Eve as Revolutionary Iconography

In 1885, at the height of Morris's participation in socialist political activism, he and Burne-Jones worked concurrently on two interrelated projects that attest to their ongoing artistic and intellectual exchange. In this year, Burne-Jones returned to his early stained-glass window depicting the Labors of Adam and Eve and began to adapt the design into an expansive mosaic. Around the same time, Morris drafted his socialist dream-vision novel, *A Dream of John Ball*. Although the mosaic never came to fruition, the imagery appears in Morris's novel in the form of a banner held aloft by the followers of John Ball. Burne-Jones continued to revise the design until he settled on the composition that ultimately became the frontispiece to Morris's text, *When Adam Delved and Eve Span* (see fig. 4). Burne-Jones's investment in the revitalization of the medieval imagery of the

Labors of Adam and Eve did not originate with Morris's novel, but developed from his own commitment to the principles of unalienated labor, socioeconomic equality, and the sanctity of the natural world.

Derived from God's curse of Adam and Eve (Genesis 3:16–24), the Labors held a prominent place in Christian iconography throughout the medieval era. For disobeying God's commandment and eating the fruit of the Tree of Knowledge, Adam and Eve were expelled from Eden. God then charged each with a gender-specific punishment: Adam was ordered to till the soil, while Eve was condemned to bring forth children in pain. An illumination from the early fourteenth-century Holkham Bible (fig. 5) exemplifies the codified attributes of the Labors.[36] An angel bars the gates to a walled Paradise, while Adam and Eve are left to struggle in the rugged world beyond. Adam holds a spade and Eve a spindle and distaff, pointing not only toward their allotted share of God's curse, but also to the conditions of peasant labor. The spade was a particular and recognizable implement, associated with the lowly work of land cultivation and specifically the act of delving. It was a common tool, available to even the poorest serf, but it was also invaluable to the agrarian economy.[37] As for Eve's attributes, which can be traced back to as early as the fourth century, the task of spinning was synonymous not just with domestic labor, but femininity itself.[38] Moreover, Eve is often located within a cave when holding these implements of textile production, suggesting that her toil belongs in the interior, domestic space of the home, while Adam labors in the exterior, public sphere.[39]

Given the popularity of this iconographic tradition across the long Middle Ages, Burne-Jones may have encountered any number of examples during his travels in Britain, France, and Italy. He appears to have drawn particular inspiration from the twelfth-century stained-glass window *Adam Delving* in the great west window of Canterbury Cathedral (fig. 6).[40] Echoes of the muscular, almost classicizing form of the Canterbury *Adam*, as well as the prominently placed tree, can be found across the multiple incarnations of the Labors in Burne-Jones's oeuvre. During his time in Florence, Burne-Jones undoubtedly would have viewed, at Ruskin's urging, the marble bas-reliefs of the campanile of the Cathedral of Santa Maria del Fiore (c. 1343–8), then attributed to Giotto.[41] The third panel of this group depicts the Labors of Adam and Eve or, as Ruskin titled it, *Original Labour* (fig. 7).[42] Also at Ruskin's behest, Burne-Jones studied the mosaic cycle in the atrium of St. Mark's, Venice, which includes a prominent depiction of the Labors of Adam and Eve in the southernmost cupola. Moreover, Burne-Jones consulted early printed editions of the popular medieval theological text *Speculum Humanae Salvationis*, or *The Mirror of Salvation*, which incorporated woodcut illustrations of the Labors of Adam and Eve captioned "Here Adam with sweat on his brow delves the earth" (fig. 8). *The Mirror of Salvation* condensed complex theological concepts into vivid, intelligible visual emblems, which could

5 ∗ Holkham Bible, *Adam and Eve Being Expelled from the Garden of Eden*, c. 1320–30. Parchment, 28.6 × 21.2 cm. British Library, London, Add. 4682, fol. 4v2

6 ∗ *Adam Delving*, c. 1176. Stained glass, Canterbury Cathedral, Kent

communicate to erudite and illiterate populations alike. The bold simplicity and clarity of these woodcuts appealed to both Morris and Burne-Jones, inspiring their approach to book illustration, particularly evident in the Kelmscott Press publications.[43]

For the medieval agrarian worker, the Labors of Adam and Eve functioned as a reminder of their daily hardships, of the unremitting necessity of constant, backbreaking drudgery. This iconography also lent support and justification to the feudal system. As a result of their transgression against God, Adam and Eve were condemned to a life of arduous toil. The agrarian worker carried on their labors, as well as their suffering.[44] However, there was also hope to be found in the Labors. Adam and Eve were presented as crucial actors within the medieval economy of salvation. In keeping with the early Christian typological interpretive scheme, which paired New Testament with Old Testament antecedents or types, Adam and Eve were understood to prefigure Jesus and Mary. In their sin, Adam and Eve fell from grace, but in their labor upon the earth they enabled redemption.[45] According to Stephen Prickett, a literary and religious studies scholar, typological thought forged temporal connections across past, present, and future:

> *Typology eliminates both time and space. . . . To find in the Bible all things necessary for salvation, with the grand narrative of humanity beginning with the Creation in Genesis and concluding with the Apocalypse in*

7 ✶ Andrea Pisano, *First Labors of Adam and Eve*, hexagonal relief, panel from the west side of the Campanile, Florence Cathedral, c. 1337–48. Marble, 33.9 × 39.6 cm. Museo dell'Opera del Duomo, Florence

8 ✶ "Here Adam with sweat on his brow delves the earth"/ "The Ark of Noe," *Speculum humanae salvationis* (*The Mirror of Salvation*), c. 1474–75, from Utrecht, Netherlands. Woodcut on paper, 11 × 19 cm. Bodleian Library, Oxford, Arch. G d.56

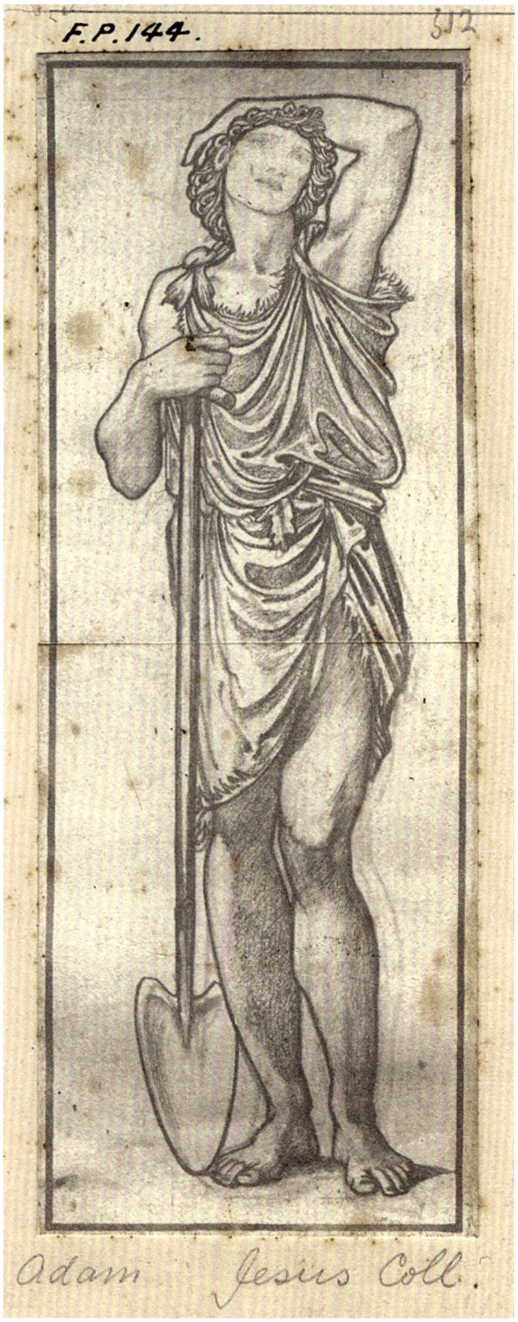

9 ∗ Edward Burne-Jones for Morris & Co., *Adam*, 1873–74. Photograph after original cartoon, 14.6 × 5.4 cm. William Morris Collection, Huntington Library, San Marino, California, 2000.5.1854h

10 ∗ Edward Burne-Jones for Morris & Co., *Eve Spinning/ Eve with Cain and Abel*, 1877. Photograph after original cartoon, 18.7 × 7.6 cm. William Morris Collection, Huntington Library, San Marino, California, 2000.5.1969a

11 ∗ Edward Burne-Jones for Morris & Co., *Adam*, 1874. Stained-glass window. Jesus College, Cambridge

ADAM PRIMO-
GENITOR

Revelation, is to see all history in a timeless present composed of separable incidents related less to their own immediate context than to their typological place in the whole.[46]

This mode of thought was a vital inspiration for Burne-Jones and part of the appeal of the Labors of Adam and Eve. With the fractured bonds between humanity and nature wrought by urbanization and industrialization, the perception of the Labors shifted from punishing toil to noble and fulfilling work in harmony with the organic world. Rather than calling for a return to medieval feudalism, Burne-Jones transformed the meaning of the Labors. The physical toil of Adam conveyed the importance of an innate connection with the earth, while Eve's spinning asserted the urgency of handicraft as part of daily life. The revived iconography of the Labors of Adam and Eve could thus play a new role in the modern economy of salvation.

Following the creation of his early stained-glass window *Adam and Eve After the Fall* for St. Andrew's College in 1857 (see figs. 2 and 3), Burne-Jones returned to the imagery of the Labors for two single-figure lights of Adam and Eve.[47] In 1874, Adam appears with a spade as part of a commission for Jesus College, Cambridge, strongly reminiscent of the Canterbury window (figs. 9 and 11). Shortly after, in 1877, he depicted Eve with a distaff and spindle in a window for Lamerton, Devon (fig. 10).[48] Both designs emphasize the sculptural qualities of the figures, while experimenting with the symbolic possibilities of the Labors in emblematic form. In 1885, Burne-Jones at last had the opportunity to return to the subject on a monumental scale in a design for mosaic. Earlier that year, his first mosaic, *Christ Enthroned in the Heavenly Jerusalem* (see fig. 126), was unveiled in the apsidal semi-dome of St. Paul's Within the Walls, Rome.[49] This project not only represented the culmination of a longstanding desire to work in mosaic, but also fulfilled his aspiration to carry out immersive decorative programs in dedicated, publicly accessible settings. Following the successful completion of *Christ Enthroned*, Burne-Jones began to execute a series of preparatory drawings for a vast mosaic cycle to fill the remaining surfaces of the church. These preliminary mosaic designs, including possible subjects for the entrance wall, choir arch, chancel arch, and choir wall, are preserved in an album that he referred to as "The 'Secret' Book of Designs."[50]

Tracing the development of the Labors of Adam and Eve as a mosaic panel in "The 'Secret' Book" not only demonstrates Burne-Jones's engagement with the subject independent of Morris's *A Dream of John Ball*, it also provides crucial insights into the elements of the topic that he found most compelling. As Burne-Jones began to experiment with different configurations for the mosaic scheme, he alternated between the Annunciation and a complementary composition of the Expulsion and the Labors.[51] The first designs to suggest this pairing appear on both sides of a single sheet early in the sketchbook (figs.

12a and b). The recto has two small inset rectangles depicting two versions of the Annunciation, the top set in an interior, the bottom in a landscape with the suggestion of a river. To the right is a large angel, dramatically highlighted in red and blue watercolor. On the verso, this same angel has been traced through the page, rendering the two sides as mirror images. The angel of the Annunciation becomes that of the Expulsion, standing with a flaming sword at the gates of heaven. Occupying the place of Mary on the opposite side is the figure of Eve, huddled at the feet of the angel, wearing ragged clothing, and clutching her children tightly about her – a forlorn and desolate scene. The implication of the pairing is that Mary is a "second Eve," redeeming the sin of her predecessor and enabling the salvation of humanity. The two women are connected in a cycle of fall and redemption, bound through the curse and miracle of childbirth.

Several pages later in "The 'Secret' Book," Burne-Jones returned to the Labors of Adam and Eve, here with a more fully realized design (fig. 13) that closely resembles his later frontispiece for *A Dream of John Ball*. On the left, Eve sits on a grassy, raised hill beneath a

12 a and b ∗ Edward Burne-Jones, "The 'Secret' Book of Designs," 1885–98, nos. 337 and 338.
Album, 37 × 29.4 cm. British Museum, London, 1899,0713.337-338 recto and verso

13 ✷ Edward Burne-Jones, "The 'Secret' Book of Designs," 1885–98, no. 396. Album, 37 × 29.4 cm.
British Museum, London, 1899,0713-396

small, cave-like structure comprised of stacked blocks of stone. Her two children cling to her, one holding onto her leg, the other resting against her breast; she also holds a distaff and spindle. On the right of the composition, turned away from Eve, Adam bends forward in a dynamic posture as he plunges his spade into the rocky ground. He is surrounded by arcing briars, suggesting the challenges posed by the wilderness left to conquer. However, at the center of the image, a large sheaf of grain rises out of the earth in a sign of hope for the survival of humanity. Three angels loom above, standing watch before the fortress-like gates of paradise, while also serving as guardians for the exiled figures below. The very top of the composition is filled with a dense canopy of tree branches.

The next design for the Labors of Adam and Eve, spread out across two sheets of the sketchbook, is the most elaborately realized (fig. 14). The long, rectangular format indicates that Burne-Jones was considering this design for the choir wall of St. Paul's, below the existing apse mosaic of *Christ Enthroned in the Heavenly Jerusalem*. In the background, tall stone walls are surmounted by imposing angelic forms with their backs turned to the viewer and their wings outspread. The angels keep a protective vigil over the lush paradise that lies beyond the wall, seemingly indifferent to the plight of humanity. Below this fortress-like enclosure, the earthly realm has been divided into feminine and masculine spheres. On the left, Eve stands at the threshold of a simple cave, a primeval domestic space sheltering the family. The distaff and spindle found in earlier designs is notably absent, although her long, draped garment suggests she has performed her allotted labors, creating textiles through spinning. Eve cradles one babe in her arms, while the other clings to her ragged dress. She is surrounded by suggestions of fertility, including flowers, fruit trees, and a small pool, pale echoes of the lost Eden. On the right, Adam occupies a much more rugged, barren, and unforgiving landscape. His back bends as he digs into the rocky soil, an active laborer attempting to tame the unforgiving earth. Behind him are the thorny brambles that God warned would impede his task and a bare, spindly tree that recalls both the Tree of Knowledge and the Tree of Life: a reminder of the Fall, but also perhaps a feeble cause for hope. This two-page sketch is the fullest expression of the Labors of Adam and Eve as a design for mosaic in "The 'Secret' Book." Several pages later, Burne-Jones returned to his composition of the Labors and began to adapt some of the key features into what became his final design for the choir arch, *The Tree of Life* (fig. 15). Here, Adam and Eve no longer toil in exile, but are returned to paradise alongside Christ, whose body is uplifted and sustained by a flourishing, generative tree.

Given that Morris wrote *A Dream of John Ball* in proximity to Burne-Jones's experimental designs for the Labors of Adam and Eve as a mosaic in 1885–86, it is perhaps not surprising that the composition found its way into the novel. At a crucial point early in the dream-vision narrative, set during the Peasants' Revolt of 1381, the followers of John Ball march toward a commons. The peasants carry with them a heraldic banner that closely aligns with Burne-Jones's designs of the Labors of Adam and Eve:

> *Above the heads of the crowd, and now slowly working towards the cross, was a banner on a high-raised cross-pole, a picture of a man and woman half-clad in skins of beasts seen against a background of green trees, the man holding a spade and the woman a*

FOLLOWING PAGES ∗ 14 ∗ Edward Burne-Jones, "The 'Secret' Book of Designs," 1885–98, nos. 398 and 399. Album, 37 × 29.4 cm. British Museum, London, 1899,0713-398 and 399

15 * Edward Burne-Jones, "The 'Secret' Book of Designs," 1885–98, no. 418. Album, 37 × 29.4 cm. British Museum, London, 1899,0713-418

distaff and spindle rudely done enough, but yet with a certain spirit and much meaning; and underneath this symbol of the early world and man's first contest with nature were written the words: When Adam delved and Eve span, Who was then the gentleman?[52]

The banner is then placed at the foot of "a tall cross of stone ... the head beautifully carved with a crucifix amidst leafage."[53] This living cross not only metonymically recalls the "green trees" of the banner itself, but also reaches beyond the text to invoke Burne-Jones's design for *The Tree of Life*. It is before this white stone cross and heraldic banner that the villagers gather to hear Ball's defiant speech. Morris's description of the banner has mistakenly been credited as the source of Burne-Jones's frontispiece design. Consequently, the enduring, radical connotations of the image have largely been credited to Morris's aims and philosophy alone, eliding Burne-Jones's role in its development.

Both Stephen F. Eisenman and Elizabeth C. Miller have recently contributed compelling, innovative scholarship on *A Dream of John Ball*, arguing for the radical nature of the book in the context of Morris's approach to print culture and socialist activism. However, both emphasize Morris's agency in the project, leaving Burne-Jones's contribution to the frontispiece ambiguous. While Eisenman acknowledges the complexity of the composition and its active dialogue with the text, as well as the similarities between the frontispiece and other works in Burne-Jones's oeuvre, he nonetheless identifies Morris as the driving force in their collaboration: "Burne-Jones's etching is largely faithful to the text that inspired it, even down to its interweaving...of several discrete historical moments..." Similarly, Miller identifies the active exchange between text and image as an essential aspect of the Kelmscott Press edition of the book, emphasizing the significant contribution of the frontispiece to the materiality of the volume. And yet, her discussion centers firmly on Morris's radical utopian project, leaving Burne-Jones's investment in it uncertain.[54] With its unequivocal union of art, nature, and revolutionary spirit, I assert that Burne-Jones's *When Adam Delved and Eve Span* was not dictated by Morris's novel, nor is it a discordant design superimposed on the book. Instead, the frontispiece condenses and extrapolates the core message of Morris's *A Dream of John Ball* into a single dynamic image that exists in active dialogue with the narrative it accompanies.

Although *A Dream of John Ball* was initially published as a serial in *The Commonweal* between November 1886 and January 1887, Burne-Jones's frontispiece did not appear with the text until it was compiled into a single volume by Reeves & Turner in 1888 (fig. 16). In 1892, the Reeves & Turner etching was adapted into a woodcut for the Kelmscott edition of *A Dream of John Ball* (see fig. 4). Since Morris and Burne-Jones controlled every step of the production process, the final incarnation of the frontispiece retains the same essential composition as the etching, but the bold, dark lines of the woodcut medium heighten the clarity and dynamism of the design. Significantly, rather than appearing on the preceding page, the frontispiece in the Kelmscott edition is positioned directly opposite the first page of text, with similar enveloping borders.[55] Comprising a signature interlacing pattern of sinuous leaves and flowers, the decorative borders assert Morris's presence as designer and author, guiding the reader toward the text itself. The eye is encouraged to linger on Burne-Jones's frontispiece, but the design of the page is such that the reader would inevitably, seamlessly, be drawn onward into the novel that follows. Indeed, nearly a quarter of the frontispiece itself is devoted to text, with the prominent inscription, "When Adam delved and Eve span, who was then the gentleman?" Indicative of the collaborative

16 * Edward Burne-Jones, *When Adam Delved and Eve Span*, 1888. Etching. Frontispiece for William Morris, *A Dream of John Ball and a King's Lesson* (London: Reeves & Turner, 1888)

creative partnership between their makers, the illustration and narrative form an almost symbiotic relationship, amplifying and enriching each other in turn.

The preparatory drawings for the frontispiece suggest the subtle alterations that occurred during the transformation from mosaic to printed illustration (figs. 17 and 18).[56] Adam and Eve now appear facing each other and in proximity, their echoing bodies curved to form an insular unit along with their infant children. The ground around their bare feet is covered in menacingly sharp briars and thorns, while the sparse trees behind them reveal the presence of a stone wall and a darkened, arched entryway in the background. Here, the original family is undoubtedly cast out of Eden, laboring on the periphery of paradise, keenly aware of what they have lost. In the final version of the frontispiece, Burne-Jones transformed the thin and rugged vegetation into a dense, enclosing wilderness of briars, branches, and leaves. A single tree, evocative of the Tree of Life, spreads its fruit-laden branches from one edge of the frame to the other, seemingly embracing, sheltering, and nourishing the first family, while completely obscuring any sign of the barrier to Eden. In contrast to the medieval iconographical tradition, Adam and Eve are not languishing under their earthly punishment. Instead, they evince a sense of pride, bodily strength, and innate nobility gained through their labor. Burne-Jones's reimagining of the Labors of Adam and Eve reminds the viewer that it was only through their Fall that the first couple found redemption, their toil at one with the elements allowing them once again to exist in paradise.

In the Kelmscott frontispiece, Adam's labor is arduous, but it also sustains his body and unites him with the natural world. Occupying the right side of the image, Adam is nearly doubled over as he leans forward, struggling at the task assigned him by God, to "till the ground from which he was taken" (Genesis 3:23). The whole composition is drawn in toward his idealized form with an almost gravitational pull. Every flexed muscle expresses his concentration on the work at hand as his spear-like spade pierces the rocky soil. The resemblance of his spade to a weapon recalls not Genesis, but the Book of Isaiah: "and they shall beat their swords into plowshares, and their spears into pruning hooks; nation shall not lift up sword against nation, neither shall they learn war any more; but they shall sit every man under his vine and under his fig tree, and none shall make them afraid" (Isaiah 4:3–4). Adam's physical power is tied to peaceful work, rather than violence, as he seeks to cultivate his own patch of earth. While he bends at his labor, he is not broken. On the contrary, his body is strengthened, his form ennobled, as he forges his way in the wilderness.

Gazing on her husband's work, Eve perches gracefully on a seat of stone to the left of the image, behind him, but also slightly raised above. Wearing a woven crown of vines, she, like Adam, is clothed in ragged furs. Her naked breast and the two babies at her feet

17 * Edward Burne-Jones, study for *When Adam Delved and Eve Span*, 1888. Black chalk over graphite on white paper, 25.2 × 17.5 cm. Ashmolean Museum, University of Oxford, WA1941.108.5

18 ✶ Edward Burne-Jones, *When Adam Delved and Eve Span*, c. 1888. Pen and ink, 19 × 14.5 cm. William Morris Gallery, London

signal her labor: the bearing and raising of children. Depicted in the pose of a Madonna enthroned, Eve embodies the unique procreative power of motherhood.[57] With distaff and spindle deftly grasped, Eve's act of spinning, synonymous with femininity itself, is in service of the clothing and protecting of her family. And yet Eve also functions as an allegorical representation of the artist, preserving the tradition of quotidian handicraft and safeguarding beauty. Further strengthening her symbolic power, Eve evokes the ancient archetype of the Three Fates, spinning, twisting, and cutting the thread of life and death in her fingers.[58]

When Adam Delved and Eve Span is the culmination of Burne-Jones's experimentation, over more than three decades, with a re-envisioning of the Labors of Adam and Eve as a revolutionary iconography for modernity. His imagery progressed from stained glass, to mosaic, and finally to book illustration. Notably, he chose not to create a painting of the Labors, which would probably have been kept locked away by the very wealthy "gentlemen" whom Burne-Jones wished to defy with the egalitarian message of the woodcut.[59]

The subsequent circulation of *When Adam Delved and Eve Span* independent of *A Dream of John Ball* must also necessarily be considered as part of Burne-Jones's endeavor to revive the Labors as a forceful message of equality and craft in harmony with nature. Shortly after its appearance as the frontispiece, Burne-Jones's woodcut was reprinted as part of a pamphlet produced on behalf of the Ancoats Brotherhood (figs. 19a and b). Founded by the socialist reformer Charles Rowley, this Manchester recreational society brought lectures, exhibitions, concerts, and other cultural activities to the working-class neighborhood of Ancoats.[60] Produced by the Kelmscott Press, the vellum-bound pamphlet served as a yearbook commemorating the activities of the Brotherhood for 1894–95. In addition to *When Adam Delved and Eve Span*, it contained two poems by Tennyson and an excerpt from Ruskin's fiery lecture on political economy, "Traffic."[61] Distributed to the members of the Ancoats Brotherhood, this pamphlet circulated as an object of exchange among the working-class laborers of industrial Manchester, expressing the radical ideals of Burne-Jones's woodcut beyond the framework of Morris's novel. *When Adam Delved and Eve Span* was published once again on February 11, 1895 in *The Daily Chronicle*, where the woodcut was re-drawn, enlarged, and given the unmistakable title *Labour*.[62]

Following the deaths of Morris and Burne-Jones, the novel and its frontispiece were widely circulated through inexpensive reprintings well into the twentieth century. In 1934, the socialist scholar Harold J. Laski described finding tattered copies of *A Dream of John Ball* in the homes of Cumberland coalminers.[63] Both in dialogue with Morris's text and as an independent printed image, Burne-Jones's re-envisioning of the Labors of Adam and Eve became a rousing popular emblem, raised in protest against the inequities of Victorian society. *When Adam Delved and Eve Span* demonstrated the possibility for art to

19 a and b ✱ First and last pages of unpaginated *Ancoats Brotherhood* pamphlet (Kelmscott Press, March 1894–March 1895) showing "When Adam Delved and Eve Span, Who was then the Gentleman" (woodcut). Each page 20.5 × 14.2 cm. Huntington Library, San Marino, California, Rare Books 607652

disrupt modernity, attesting to Burne-Jones's active engagement with the radical political ideals he held in common with Morris.

"A great pain filled my heart at the sight of all that beauty": Aesthetic Epiphany in *A Dream of John Ball*

In order to restore Burne-Jones's crafting of *When Adam Delved and Eve Span* in active and collaborative engagement with Morris's *A Dream of John Ball*, it is vital to consider the ways in which the novel itself foregrounds the role of aesthetic epiphany and the redemptive dream-vision model. In other words, rather than examine Burne-Jones's image for evidence of Morris's political philosophy, I will instead elucidate how the expression of Burne-Jones's belief in art as a means of catalyzing socio-political awakening appears in Morris's text. The novel proffers the radical rhetoric of the fourteenth-century priest

John Ball and the bravery of the stalwart peasantry rising up against tyranny as a model for a future working-class uprising.[64] However, it is the richly realized aesthetic of this dream world, the insistently detailed descriptions of the architecture and decorative arts, that leave the strongest impression on the reader.[65] Written during the period of Morris's active engagement with socialist political organizing, the novel nonetheless stands as a testament to his shared vow, made with Burne-Jones in the shadow of Beauvais Cathedral, to foster change through art.

A Dream of John Ball unfolds against the backdrop of the Peasants' Revolt, the populist uprising broadly motivated by the economic hardships that spread throughout Europe in the wake of the Black Death and threatened the stability of feudalism.[66] Morris turned to this event as an example of the vernacular tradition of socialism in the English countryside, with the aim of reviving its revolutionary spirit for the people of the nineteenth century. The Peasants' Revolt was sparked by resentment over economic inequality and fomented by the sermons of John Ball. Called the "mad priest of Kent" by the medieval chronicler Jean Froissart, the following passage attributed to Ball demonstrates that his incendiary speeches against villeinage were founded on the notion of Biblical equality:

> *My good friends, things cannot go on well in England, nor ever will until every thing shall be in common; when there shall neither be vassal nor lord, and all distinctions levelled; when the lords shall be no more masters than ourselves.... Are we not all descended from the same parents, Adam and Eve? and what can they show, or what reasons give, why they should be more the masters than ourselves? except, perhaps, in making us labour and work, for them to spend.*[67]

This theme of Edenic egalitarianism, of radicalism couched in Christian theology, found widespread appeal. The popular phrase integrated into Morris's text and Burne-Jones's image – "When Adam delved and Eve span, who was then the gentleman?" – which had been in use since at least the twelfth century, was adopted as a rallying cry for Ball and his followers.[68] Thus incited to action, the Peasants' Revolt began in the countryside under the leadership of Kentish rebel Wat Tyler and culminated in a violent and destructive siege of London.[69] Ultimately, the uprising was quelled, the leaders, including Ball and Tyler, put to death, and the peasantry dispersed with empty promises.

Over the succeeding years, the rebellion was recounted as a cautionary tale about the potential volatility of the feudal class system and the importance of keeping laborers in check. Froissart, for instance, openly condemned the peasants in his account, writing that this episode was meant to warn the nobility of Europe, "in order that gentlemen and others may take example, and correct wicked rebels."[70] His was a treasured medieval text for both Morris and Burne-Jones, a volume so much a part of their common intellectual heritage that Burne-Jones wished always to have it on hand throughout his life.[71] Accordingly, Froissart was probably Morris's primary historical source for *A Dream of John Ball*.[72] By reading against the grain and culling a radical socialist message from the unlikely pages of Froissart, Morris hoped to recast the perception of this episode in English history, seeking sympathy for the rebels and their cause and igniting working-class insurgency in his own time.[73]

The majority of *A Dream of John Ball* occurs in a medieval village in the idyllic countryside of Kent on the eve of the march of the rebels on London, as witnessed through the eyes of a narrator (implicitly, Morris) magically transported back in time from the nineteenth century in a dream. After surveying his new environment and becoming acquainted with several of the villagers, the dreamer finds himself swept up in the crowd gathering at the crossroads to witness a rousing sermon delivered by Ball. Standing beneath the banner of Adam and Eve, the "mad priest" rallies the villagers with a speech that closely echoes the account found in Froissart, but overlaid with much of Morris's own ideology. United by the words of Ball and his message of equality under God's fellowship, the peasants engage in a brief but bloody battle that heralds the start of the nascent rebellion, while the dreamer watches safely from the sidelines. Later that evening, within the village church where the bodies of the fallen have been laid out, the dreamer conducts a lengthy exchange with Ball over the state of labor, political economy, and the struggle for fellowship that binds together the medieval, the modern, and their vision of the world yet to come. At the breaking of dawn, the dreamer's reverie comes to an end, and he finds himself once again facing the bleak reality of Victorian London.

The novel begins not with the dream of the title, but with a different recurring dream, described as a kind of "architectural peep show."[74] This opening passage signals to the reader the centrality of immersive aesthetic encounters to the narrative. In such dreams, the narrator states that he sees "as clearly as if I were awake" a survey of English architecture, but particularly those exemplary Gothic and medieval buildings he most prizes, "untouched by the degradation of the sordid utilitarianism that cares not and knows not of beauty and history."[75] While brief, this prologue calls attention to the frequent architectural references throughout the story and, by extension, the importance of architecture as an immersive aesthetic space, as well as a memorial fabric recording the history and health of a society.

When the dream of the Peasants' Revolt that is the focus of the text commences, Morris persists within this aesthetic mode by closely observing the medieval countryside and the rural village. He is struck by "the garden-like neatness and trimness" of the orchards and common lands, before proceeding into the town, where he marvels at the buildings around him:

[T]he church... quite ravished my heart with its extreme beauty, elegance, and fitness. The chancel of this was so new that the dust of the stone still lay white on the midsummer grass beneath the carvings of the windows. The houses were almost all built of oak frame-work filled with cob or plaster well whitewashed.... There was much curious and inventive carving about most of them; and though some were old and much worn, there was the same look of deftness and trimness, and even beauty, about every detail in them which I noticed before in the field-work.[76]

Such descriptions of the "fitness" of the buildings indicate the comparative socioeconomic health of this rural village in Kent, in contrast to the urban dilapidation the narrator encounters in his own time. Oppressed as they may be by the enslavement of the feudal system, these laborers nonetheless retain their ties to nature and craft. They are allowed to exert creative freedom through the decoration and ornamentation of their humble homes.

This belief in the intimate relationship between the health of a society and its architecture was principally inspired by John Ruskin's seminal text "The Nature of Gothic" (1853). In this well-known chapter from *The Stones of Venice*, Ruskin credits the grandeur and magnificence of Gothic architecture to the freedom of imaginative and intellectual expression afforded medieval workers.[77] By contrast, Ruskin deemed modern English architecture to be not merely devoid of quality, but actively injurious to the health of a society. This destructive architecture was due in large part to an economic system that kept workers in a state of artistic, intellectual, and financial slavery. Ruskin writes:

And now, reader, look round this English room of yours.... Examine again all those accurate mouldings, and perfect polishings, and unerring adjustments of the seasoned wood and tempered steel. Many a time you have exulted over them, and thought how great England was, because her slightest work was done so thoroughly. Alas! if read rightly, these perfectnesses are signs of a slavery in our England a thousand times more bitter and more degrading than that of the scourged African, or helot Greek.... And, on the other hand, go forth again to gaze upon the old cathedral front, where you have smiled so often at the fantastic ignorance of the old sculptors... but do not mock at them, for they are signs of the life and liberty of every workman who struck the stone.[78]

According to Ruskin, one of the best indications of the servility or liberty of a building, and by extension of the society that produced it, is the care devoted to representations of the natural world in architectural ornamentation:

The affectionate observation of the grace and outward character of vegetation is the sure sign of a more tranquil and gentle existence, sustained by the gifts, and gladdened by the splendour, of the earth. In that careful distinction of species, and richness of delicate and undisturbed organization, which characterize the Gothic design, there is the history of rural and thoughtful life, influenced by habitual tenderness, and devoted to subtle inquiry.[79]

Thus, ideal architecture results from a profound and respectful relationship with the earth, as well as meaningfully productive labor. Finally, Ruskin urged the viewer to approach a building "on the same principles as that of a book," to "read" from the stones the richly illuminated collective history encoded on the architectural fabric.[80]

In his essay "The Prospects of Architecture in Civilisation" (1882), Morris similarly stresses the integration of nature and architecture in the medieval home of the rural peasant. In former days, he claims,

the new house indeed would have taken away a little piece of the flowery green sward, a few yards of the teeming hedge-row, but a new order, a new beauty would have taken the place of the old: the very flowers of the field would have but given place to flowers fashioned by man's hand and mind: the hedge-row oak would have blossomed into fresh beauty in roof-tree and lintel and door-post.[81]

Morris wished to demonstrate to the working classes of the nineteenth century that the cheap comforts and "sordid utilitarianism" of capitalism had limited, rather than augmented, their freedom and happiness. "Old and much worn" as these medieval houses may have been, the lives of agrarian laborers were not yet severed from the natural world. For Morris, it was better to live in poverty surrounded by natural beauty and meaningful work, than to possess comparative monetary wealth and live surrounded by meaningless industrial objects and barren, mechanical structures.

The importance of architecture in *A Dream of John Ball* as a source of epiphany and a testament to the vitality of a society also recalls the revelatory experience of Morris and Burne-Jones during their tour of the Gothic cathedrals of France in 1855. An echo of that transformative encounter, when Burne-Jones recalled "ancient singing" so beautiful he thought Judgment Day had come, can be found in the dreamer's account of the arrival of John Ball and his men into the Kent village. Morris describes hearing "a piece of the plain-song of the church, familiar enough to me to bring back to my mind the great arches of some cathedral in France and the canons singing in the choir."[82] Rife with personal meaning, the music signals a call to arms for the villagers, exhorting them to rise up against the feudal state. Perhaps it was also a veiled reminder for Morris to remain true to his pledge to live a life dedicated to art as a language of protest.

Later, after the brief battle, when the dreamer is confronted with violence, death, and tyranny, his spirits are nonetheless lifted by the vibrant beauty of the architecture and decorative arts of a simple parish church. The importance placed on visual ornamentation, even at the cost of human life, is made shockingly plain in the passage when Morris first encounters the bodies of the dead peasants laid out before the altar. Within this sepulchral setting, the narrator fixates on the decoration of the chancel rather than the corpses:

> *We went into the chancel; a light burned on the high altar before the host, and looked red and strange in the moonlight that came through the wide traceried windows unstained by the pictures and beflowerings of the glazing; there were new stalls for the priests and vicars where we entered, carved more abundantly and beautifully than any of the woodwork I had yet seen, and everywhere was rich and fair colour and delicate and dainty form. Our dead lay just before the high altar on low biers, their faces all covered with linen cloths.*[83]

The reader is, therefore, urged not to mourn for those who sacrificed their lives to the cause, but to admire the enduring splendor of what they were able to achieve, the eternal testament of art. The stone carvings and stained-glass windows will transcend human suffering to bear witness to the future. In a final striking passage before the dreamer is transported back to the nineteenth century, he is overwhelmed with a kaleidoscopic vision of the splendor of the church where he sits beside John Ball:

> *In a flash I saw all – the east crimson with sunrise through the white window on my right hand; the richly-carved stalls and gilded screen work, the pictures on the walls, the loveliness of the faultless colour of the mosaic window lights, the altar and the red light over it looking strange in the daylight, and the biers with the hidden dead men upon them that lay before the high altar. A great pain filled my heart at the sight of all that beauty...*[84]

When Morris abruptly awakens into a cold, gray dawn, he is assaulted by the view of a dirty and desolate modern London.[85]

With the memory of his vision still achingly clear in his mind, he finds himself tempted to turn away from the city and retreat into what semblance of the rural idyll still remains. But this untenable urge is shattered by the sound of the factory whistles and, just as the working classes are called to their duty, so too is Morris reminded of his: "I grinned surlily, and dressed and got ready for my day's 'work' as I call it, but which many a man besides John Ruskin (though not many in his position) would call 'play.'"[86] Morris's dream does not lull him into yearning for a state of eternal slumber, but instead strengthens his resolve to transform the waking world through his artistic labor. It is his hope that the reader will be inspired to do the same.

The structural model adopted by Morris for two of his most strongly political works of literary fiction, *A Dream of John Ball* and *News from Nowhere*, is that of the medieval dream vision. Morris's use of the dream vision not only implies a pointed ideological investment in the trope, but must, in turn, be viewed in conjunction with Burne-Jones's persistent imagery of dreaming and awakening throughout his oeuvre. According to Cynthia Hahn, the Augustinian model of the prophetic dream was prevalent throughout the Middle Ages. Hahn writes, "For Augustine dreams are a middle ground of mixed nature with the potential to reveal both the human and the divine. Made up of images, garnered from corporeal vision, they have the potential for 'prophetic insight.'"[87] Both Morris and Burne-Jones were strongly influenced from the beginning of their careers by a number of medieval texts that employ the dream vision conceit. These included the French courtly poem *Roman de la Rose* (c. 1230–75), William Langland's *Piers Plowman* (c. 1370–90), Geoffrey Chaucer's *House of Fame* (c. 1374–85) and *Legend of Good Women* (c. 1386–88), as well as Francesco Colonna's later Italian text, *Hypnerotomachia Poliphili* (1499), which would have been doubly significant for its abundant use of woodblock illustrations. Given the particularly widespread popularity of the dream vision genre during the English fourteenth century, the epoch of John Ball, the choice is also especially appropriate. *A Dream of John Ball* displays all the hallmarks of the medieval dream vision: the narrator drifts off to sleep and awakens in an idyllic, pastoral setting where he is guided and advised by a prophetic figure before returning to his own world.[88] By stressing the apple trees and "garden-like" qualities of the rural Kentish environs, Morris further conforms to the common motif of Edenic imagery within medieval dream texts, while simultaneously directly invoking the legend of Adam and Eve that is central to the message of the story.[89]

Rather than a depoliticized and detached stance, Morris employed the dream lens as a means of actively critiquing the nineteenth century, of reflecting the world back on itself within a new ideological framework. Despite E. P. Thompson's disapproval of Burne-Jones's fantastical imagery, he nonetheless defended Morris's use of the dream vision model. Thompson argued that the dream underlies not only *A Dream of John Ball* and *News from Nowhere*, but all of Morris's literary work:

> *From beginning to end, Morris's writing... partakes of the nature of dream. We are taken out of the world we know into a world having its existence only in the writer's imagination.... Into this world of dreams Morris was driven by his "hatred of civilization" during his youthful revolt: and ever after his imagination found natural expression in this form.*[90]

John Goode later contended that Thompson did not go far enough in aligning Morris's engagement with dreams as inherently political:

> *Art is ineluctably the creation of the individual – socialism is the recognition of collectivity. Such a recognition can only be registered through the transformation of individual epistemology, and the transformation has to take place within the individual through an entry into dream. Socialist art does not transcend alienation: it transforms it into revolutionary consciousness by the recognition of the collective possibilities of the mind's curves away from actuality. For Morris, in dreams begins responsibility.*[91]

It is not for the sake of lingering within a fantastical reverie that we are shown these dream worlds. Instead, it is the awakening that is the key, returning the reader to the modern world with new eyes and a mind troubled by the disparity.[92]

In the introduction to this book, I argued for the crucial importance of challenging our perception of Burne-Jones as an escapist artist-dreamer. Rather than the retreat of a reactionary, I contend that Burne-Jones, informed by the very same medieval tradition that inspired Morris, also found provocative power in the dream mode. That Morris selected the dream genre for his most blatantly political novels lends further credence to interpreting Burne-Jones's enactment of the dream vision as similarly confrontational. This liminal space of the dream, for Burne-Jones just as for Morris, was not meant as a space of hazy eternal reverie, or a psycho-sexual exploration of the unconscious mind, but as a critical stance from which to reflect back on the ills of the modern world and elicit a desire for change. The dream model functions, as Jameson argues, as a disruptive utopian space, a "pocket of stasis," where an alternate future can be imagined and then enacted.[93]

"A happiness to the maker and the user": The Kelmscott Press Edition of *A Dream of John Ball* as Immersive Aesthetic Experience

Both Morris's *A Dream of John Ball* and Burne-Jones's iconography of the Labors of Adam and Eve achieved their definitive form in the Kelmscott Press edition of the book, published in 1892. Founded in 1891, the Kelmscott Press allowed Morris and Burne-Jones to create the handmade and carefully crafted books they had envisioned since their youthful days in Oxford. The Kelmscott Press books express attention to every detail of production, including the paper, ink, type, binding, the arrangement of the text on the page, the borders, and the illustrations, as well as the texts themselves. If the narrative of *A Dream of John Ball* performed a literary dream vision, then the Kelmscott Press edition existed as a dream in material form. As Miller writes, "The Kelmscott books were artifacts from the future, material and aesthetic reminders that after the revolution labor and production would no longer be the alienating, repetitive industrial enterprise that mechanized mass print so neatly symbolized."[94] *A Dream of John Ball* describes a narrator from the nineteenth century who experiences a vision from the past. The material book, however, existed as a post-apocalyptic survival, an object that, in form and function, suggested the art of an ideal society after the ills of modernity have been overcome.[95]

The experience of reading the Kelmscott Press edition of *A Dream of John Ball* is embodied and tactile, engaging not just the eyes and the mind, but also the sense of touch.[96] As with all works published by Kelmscott, the book itself is a carefully crafted object. Bound in smooth vellum the color of ivory, with hand-dyed red silk ties and a gold-embossed title on the spine, the material qualities of the volume function as an ideological framework for the text and image found within. Its handmade paper testifies indexically to the traditional printing process, clearly displaying the impress of the woodblock and thereby lending the frontispiece and typeface a rich visual depth and tactility.[97] The volume fits comfortably in the hands, designed for ease in portability and exchange, a quality that stands in sharp contrast to the mammoth masterpiece of the press, *The Works of Geoffrey Chaucer* (1896). *A Dream of John Ball* was admittedly beyond the means of an average working-class reader to purchase, costing thirty shillings, or the equivalent of three weeks' salary for a housemaid.[98] The compactness of the volume, however, allowed it to exist as a communal object. As Miller suggests, the slim book could ideally be passed from hand to hand in solidarity, much like the pipe given to William Guest in *News from Nowhere*, which, if lost, "somebody is sure to find, and he will use it."[99] Produced through the employment of meticulous handicraft and traditional processes, the physical presence of this volume prompts the viewer to contemplate the possibility of another kind of world beyond the industrial, mass-consumer culture of the nineteenth century. The book seems to emerge from a time and place where such an object can provide "a happiness to the maker and the user."[100]

In elucidating their concept of the book arts, especially the production of the Kelmscott Press, Burne-Jones and Morris frequently employed architectural metaphors. Echoing the prominence of architectural encounters throughout *A Dream of John Ball*, Burne-Jones and Morris likened their approach to the creation of the Kelmscott books as akin to Gothic stonemasons constructing and decorating a cathedral. When describing the Kelmscott Chaucer to Julia Cartwright Ady, Burne-Jones explained, "It will be, thanks to Morris, something like a cathedral to stroll through and linger in, a kind of pocket Chartres in fact."[101] Similarly, Burne-Jones wrote to his friend and adviser Charles Eliot Norton, describing the intimacy and fluency of his collaborative working process with Morris on the Kelmscott Chaucer:

> *I am making the designs as much to fit the ornament & the printing as they are made to fit the little pictures – & I love to be snugly cased in the borders & buttressed up by the vast initials. . . . if you drag me out of my encasings it will be like tearing a statue out of*

its niche & putting it into a museum – indeed when the book is done, if we live to finish it, it will be a little pocket cathedral – so full of design.[102]

This implicit give and take, with Burne-Jones likening his illustrations to architectural sculpture and Morris's borders, initials, and type to niches and buttresses, attests to their commitment to the book arts. The two men were working together to craft volumes that would function as experiential, immersive aesthetic experiences, modeled after the communal, memorial fabric of Gothic architecture.

When Morris proclaimed that "the only work of art which surpasses a complete Mediaeval book is a complete Mediaeval building," he was speaking of the ability of each medium to convey, on multiple levels, through various means, and to a diverse audience, a coherent and communal artistic program.[103] In his mission statement for the Kelmscott Press, Morris echoed Burne-Jones's explanation of their holistic approach to book design:

I have always tried to keep in mind the necessity for making my decoration a part of the page of type. I may add that in designing the magnificent and inimitable woodcuts which have adorned several of my books... my friend Edward Burne-Jones has never lost sight of this important point, so that his work will not only give us a series of most beautiful and imaginative pictures, but form the most harmonious decoration possible to the printed book.[104]

Elsewhere, Morris elaborated on this organic conception of book design, classifying the art form as essentially "architectural":

The ornament must form as much a part of the page of type itself, or it will miss its mark, and in order to succeed, and to be ornament, it must submit to certain limitations, and become architectural... a book ornamented with pictures that are suitable for that, and that only, may become a work of art second to none, save a fine building duly decorated.[105]

It is striking that Burne-Jones and Morris inverted Ruskin's fiat to "read" architecture as a book, now urging readers to apply their knowledge of the construction and observation of Gothic architecture to the appreciation of a hand-printed volume. By rendering the text architectural, they were effectively defining their work at the Kelmscott Press as likewise collaborative and bound to the welfare of a society. Moreover, in the manner of their production, these texts effectively willed Ruskin's ideal society into existence by reviving, to the greatest extent possible, the working conditions of the Gothic craftsman.

Accordingly, the text and frontispiece of *A Dream of John Ball* should be interpreted as a kind of monumental and memorial ornamented fabric, constructed through the collaborative efforts of not only two interdependent craftsmen – Morris the "builder" and Burne-Jones the "sculptor" – but also a team of artisans working together. As Morris states in "On the Woodcuts of Gothic Books" (1892): "The designer of the picture-blocks, the designer of the ornamental blocks, the wood-engraver, and the printer, all of them thoughtful, painstaking artists, and all working in harmonious co-operation for the production of a work of art. This is the only possible way in which you can get beautiful books."[106] Burne-Jones was not, then, subservient to Morris's vision in his creation of the frontispiece *When Adam Delved and Eve Span*. Rather, the image and the text worked together to communicate the same radical message of egalitarianism in labor, performed through the creation of the printed book itself. This communal aspect was extended to the reader, as well as the workers who produced the volume. Much more than a solitary activity aimed solely at the mind, Morris and Burne-Jones sought to transform the nature of reading a book into a multisensory, mutual experience of collective cultural memory.[107] Hence, just as a building records the tenor of the age which created it on its stones to be read by later generations, so too do *A Dream of John Ball* and *When Adam Delved and Eve Span* reclaim and illuminate a lost, and specifically egalitarian, past, with the aim of eliciting change for the future, when a harmonious balance of art, labor, and human fellowship might be restored.

"The progress of all life must be not on the straight line, but on the spiral": Afterlives of *When Adam Delved and Eve Span*

In 1885, Morris published "The Manifesto of the Socialist League" in *The Commonweal*, the same journal where *A Dream of John Ball* appeared a year later. Setting forth his core philosophy of socialism, Morris emphasized a temporal progression along the curving arcs of a spiral. In this scheme an understanding of the past is essential to achieve the ideal future, and for every step forward, there must also be a look backward. As Morris writes:

> *The enemy will say, "This is retrogression not progress"; to which we answer, All progress, every distinctive stage of progress, involves a backward as well as a forward movement; the new development returns to a point which represents the older principle elevated to a higher plane; the old principle reappears transformed, purified, made stronger, and ready to advance on the fuller life it has gained.... The progress of all life must be not on the straight line, but on the spiral.*[108]

When he later published *A Dream of John Ball*, Morris was not calling for a return to the kind of bucolic rural community found under feudalism. Instead he was urging his readers, in particular the working classes, to heed the precedent and encouragement of the past in their efforts to forge a future of equality in life and pleasure in labor. Similarly, in

SOCIALISM
FELLOWSHIP
BROTHERHOOD
WHEN·ADAM·DELVED
AND·EVE·SPAN
WHO·WAS·THEN
THE·GENTLEMAN

reviving the medieval iconography of the Labors of Adam and Eve, Burne-Jones was not idealizing a fantastical vision of the past, but proclaiming a radical, utopian possibility for the future. *When Adam Delved and Eve Span* functioned as a potent emblem, an egalitarian vision condensed into a clarion call for transformation.

In 2009, the William Morris Gallery in Walthamstow acquired a late nineteenth-century embroidered and painted red silk protest banner that demonstrates the contemporary significance of Burne-Jones's design of the Labors of Adam and Eve, as well as its emblematic association with radical political and social protest (fig. 20). The banner is akin to that described in *A Dream of John Ball*, here brought vividly to life. At the center is a recreation of Burne-Jones's frontispiece, featuring Adam with his spade, Eve with her spindle and distaff, the two children at her feet, and the sinuous limbs of a fruit-laden apple tree filling the space above and behind. Below, in gold embroidery, are the words "WHEN ADAM DELVED AND EVE SPAN WHO WAS THEN THE GENTLEMAN"; to the left appears the word "FELLOWSHIP"; to the right, "BROTHERHOOD"; and across the top in even larger letters, "SOCIALISM." At the very base of the banner is a rising sun caught on the horizon line, evocative of the coming revolution. The banner, along with the imagery of the Labors of Adam and Eve, is inextricably bound to Morris's text of *A Dream of John Ball*, with its overt call for a socialist rebellion modeled on the fourteenth-century Peasants' Revolt. Yet this powerful message of egalitarianism, fellowship, and labor, of a paradise restored on earth, unequivocally belongs to Burne-Jones as well. The creation and circulation of this emblem, with its clarity of design and forcefulness of message, directly contradicts the perception of Burne-Jones as an aloof and elitist dreamer who turned his back on the world. As a persuasive and accessible visual emblem aimed at the working classes, *When Adam Delved and Eve Span* stands as a striking testament to Burne-Jones's radical investment in his artistic practice and its impact as a political utterance, communicating from the past into the future along the curves of the spiral of time.

20 * Socialist banner, c. 1890s. Painted and embroidered silk, 168 × 91 cm. William Morris Gallery, London Borough of Waltham Forest, F432. Presented by Mr Peter Jacobs, 2009. Conserved with the assistance of the Kathy Callow Trust, 2012

Chapter Two

"The Apotheosis of Poverty"

KING COPHETUA AND THE BEGGAR MAID

In 1889, Burne-Jones exhibited his monumental 1880–84 painting *King Cophetua and the Beggar Maid* (fig. 21) in the English Section of the Palais des Beaux Arts at the Paris Universal Exposition. Commemorating the centennial of the French Revolution, the exposition featured dizzying modern spectacles and feats of industrial manufacture.[1] These included Gustave Eiffel's controversial ironwork tower, fantastical electric light displays, the behemoth Galerie des Machines, and theatrical colonial tableaux. In contrast to this riotous atmosphere, visitors who wandered into the fine arts pavilion to stand before Burne-Jones's *King Cophetua* encountered a mesmerizing vision of quiet contemplation that poignantly rebuked the cacophonous crowds beyond. Soaring twelve feet in height, surrounded by an ornate gilded frame, the composition centers on an armored king who has removed his crown and sword in homage before a pale female figure in a thin grey gown. Rendered in richly saturated tones with a lush, shimmering surface, sumptuous details of jewels, textiles, and flowers give the painting an alluring tactility. The work, inspired by an old English ballad of a king who fell in love with an impoverished maiden and made her his queen, exceeds the bounds of its origins. It presents the viewer with a world turned upside down, where poverty rises above wealth, weakness above strength, woman above man. Amid the frenzied microcosm of industrialism, imperialism, and consumerism at the Universal Exposition, Burne-Jones's *King Cophetua* prompted a revelatory, near-religious experience for numerous visitors.[2]

According to the French art critic Robert de la Sizeranne, Burne-Jones's *King Cophetua and the Beggar Maid* appeared not as a retreat from the modern world, but as a direct cen-

sure of the inequities and excess epitomized by the exposition. Sizeranne recalled, "As we came out of the Gallery of Machinery, in which the rumble of wheels fatigued our ears, we felt as though everywhere else in the exhibition we had seen nothing but matter, and here we had come on the exhibition of the soul." Throughout the exposition he had seen celebrations of the great material wealth of the world and the triumphs of capitalism: but now "we had come forth from the universal Exhibition of Wealth to see the symbolical expression of the Scorn of Wealth.... It was a dream – but a noble dream.... It was the revenge of art on life."[3] Far from an escapist fantasy, *King Cophetua and the Beggar Maid* compellingly critiqued acquisitive, materialist capitalism and imperial aggression.

In her own assessment of *King Cophetua and the Beggar Maid*, Georgiana Burne-Jones illuminated the parallels between her husband's painting and the political activities of Morris:

> *I have always thought this picture contained more of Edward's own distinctive qualities than any other that he did.... It is noteworthy that he designed and carried it out during the divergence of opinion between himself and Morris on the subject of Socialism, bringing it to an end soon after Morris joined the Democratic Foundation. The thought of the King and the Beggar lay deep in both their minds.*[4]

As established in the previous chapter, when Morris turned toward political activism, Burne-Jones dedicated himself with renewed efforts to enact change in the world through the visual arts. In *When Adam Delved and Eve Span*, he forged an image of egalitarian and pleasurable labor that was accessible, legible, and easily circulated through print. *King Cophetua and the Beggar Maid*, which has striking compositional similarities to the woodcut illustration, exemplifies a complementary aspect of Burne-Jones's visual discourse and artistic practice. Exhibited first at the Grosvenor Gallery in 1884 and subsequently at the Universal Exposition in 1889, *King Cophetua*'s critique was aimed directly at the privileged classes. With this single, expansive canvas, Burne-Jones interrogated not only the possibilities of the painted surface, but also the capacity for art to challenge the perceptions of an audience. Emulating the form, proportions, and spiritual imperative of a Renaissance altarpiece, *King Cophetua* defied the nineteenth-century art market, protesting against the institutions that kept art, wealth, and visual beauty in captivity.

21 * Edward Burne-Jones, *King Cophetua and the Beggar Maid*, 1880–84.
Oil on canvas, 293.4 × 135.9 cm. Tate Gallery, London, N01771

"An exhibition of the soul": *King Cophetua and the Beggar Maid* as Secular Altarpiece

After his transformative encounter with *King Cophetua* at the Universal Exposition, Sizeranne traveled to London in order to meet Burne-Jones in person. As they discussed the origins of the painting, Burne-Jones described his process of consulting historical and literary sources as one of inspiration, not direct translation. Sizeranne writes: "We spoke of the subjects of his pictures, and I asked him where he found them. 'I do not find them,' said he; 'I make them – or, at least, I entirely re-make them from vague impressions left by poems which I have forgotten.' This was the origin of King Cophetua."[5] Burne-Jones's introduction to the story, a variant of the archetypal Cinderella narrative, was probably through Alfred Tennyson's poem "The Beggar Maid" (1842).[6] In this re-envisioning of the traditional English ballad, Tennyson fixated on the physical allure of the beggar maid who bewitches the king with her beauty. Burne-Jones may also have encountered a version of the story in Thomas Percy's *Reliques of Ancient English Poetry* (1765), which cites the appearance of King Cophetua in the writings of Shakespeare and Ben Jonson. There Cophetua is described as an African king who disdains love until he sees the impoverished Penelophon, "clad all in gray," and falls deeply in love. The two are soon married and live "a quiet life," so beloved by their subjects that the mourning over their deaths "did pierce the starry sky."[7] However, as with Burne-Jones's approach to the revival of the ancient iconography of the Labors of Adam and Eve, recovering the story of King Cophetua became an opportunity to explore the theme of the triumph of love over wealth, imparting a message of socioeconomic disruption in the guise of a medieval folktale.

The latent theme of radical class upheaval within *King Cophetua and the Beggar Maid* became more pronounced as Burne-Jones developed the composition over the span of nearly twenty-five years. His designs progressed through three distinct phases: an early painting begun in 1861 and abandoned, unfinished, in 1862 (fig. 22); a series of small but significant sketches dating to roughly 1875; and, between 1880 and 1884, a number of studies and preparatory works leading to the monumental final canvas. Apart from containing the most basic elements of the tale, Burne-Jones's first painting seemingly has little in common with the final version, save for the incongruous tightness of the pictorial space, hemmed in by the compositional conceit of the staircase. In this first composition the relative positions of the king and the beggar mirror their respective social standings, as Cophetua adopts an active and elevated pose, reaching down toward the object of his affection.[8]

After putting aside the subject for more than a decade, in 1875 Burne-Jones once again attempted to delineate the composition, through a series of pencil studies spread out across two pages of a sketchbook (figs. 23a and b). These schematic drawings are nota-

22 ∗ Edward Burne-Jones, *King Cophetua and the Beggar Maid*, 1862, unfinished. Oil on canvas, 76.2 × 63.5 cm. Tate Gallery, London, N03454

ble for the rapid evolution of the image from the left side to the right, marking the transition from an active and intimate relationship between the king and beggar maid, to one of physical separation, passive contemplation, and an inverse hierarchical arrangement of the two social classes.[9] On the far left, in a nude study, the king embraces the beggar maid, their bodies nearly entwined and made all the more sensual by the suggestion of bare skin. As the images progress from left to right, the beggar maid not only becomes removed from the king and heavily draped, but she also adopts an elevated, seated posture.[10] The figure of the king, meanwhile, shifts to one of seated adoration, gazing up in an attitude of increased emotional tension, his embrace of the maiden forever postponed

23 a and b * Edward Burne-Jones, sketch for *King Cophetua and the Beggar Maid*, c. 1875. Left and right side of a double sheet in sketchbook, No. 1085, 25.5 × 72.4 cm. Fitzwilliam Museum, Cambridge

and replaced instead with the cool grasp of his jeweled crown in his hands. When Burne-Jones returned to the subject five years later to create his final set of studies and the ultimate version on canvas, this figural arrangement remained essentially unchanged. By inverting the physical positions of the king and the beggar maid, Burne-Jones offers the viewer a vision of a world gone topsy-turvy, where poverty is elevated and adored by wealth. The dramatic verticality and nearly overwhelming scale of the finished painting reinforces this reversal of the expected hierarchies, allowing the beggar maid to tower over not only Cophetua but the viewer as well.

Burne-Jones's ultimate composition for *King Cophetua and the Beggar Maid* drew on two significant Italian Renaissance precedents, which strengthened this central theme of upheaval and inversion through the embrace of established, gendered stereotypes aligning

love with femininity and martial aggression with masculinity. The first, widely acknowledged referent is Andrea Mantegna's *Madonna della Vittoria* (1495–96; fig. 24), which entered the Louvre in 1798.[11] The other overt quotation is of Sandro Botticelli's *Venus and Mars* (c. 1485; fig. 25), in the National Gallery, London, from 1874. Both artists were of particular importance to Burne-Jones. As the critic M. H. Spielmann observed in a commemorative essay written shortly after Burne-Jones's death, "Mantegna and Botticelli . . . were his chief masters" when he looked to the past for inspiration.[12] More importantly, however, these two touchstones allowed Burne-Jones to adopt a syncretic iconographical approach, fusing Christian and classical symbolism. The beggar maid becomes a type of the Madonna enthroned and Venus triumphant, imbuing her with greater power and amplifying the central conceit of the painting as a secular altarpiece.[13]

The association of Mantegna with *King Cophetua and the Beggar Maid* was immediately evident; in 1885, the art critic Claude Phillips described "the noble figure of the king" as suggestive "of the art of Mantegna."[14] Nearly a century later, two separate studies noted

24 * Andrea Mantegna, *Madonna della Vittoria* (Madonna of Victory), 1495–96. Oil on canvas, 285 × 168 cm. Musée du Louvre, Paris, Département des Peintures, Inv. 369

a more specific correlation between *King Cophetua* and Mantegna's *Madonna della Vittoria*.[15] Subsequent discussions of the painting have reiterated this stance, rendering Mantegna's Renaissance altarpiece the definitive touchstone for *King Cophetua*, based largely on the similarities between the poses of the two principal male and female figures.[16] The *Madonna della Vittoria* was commissioned by Francesco II Gonzaga (Giovan Francesco III), the fourth Marchese of Mantua, in commemoration of his defeat of the French at the battle of Fornovo. Francesco himself appears on the left of the painting, kneeling in supplication to the enthroned Virgin and Child above him. Depicted in full armor and surrounded by the warrior saints Michael and George, the Marchese thanks the Virgin and Child for his recent triumphs. Just as Francesco has conquered his enemies through physical might, so too has the Virgin conquered Francesco through her divine grace. Thus, Mantegna's *Madonna della Vittoria* provides an apt model for conveying a sacred act of masculine homage.[17]

Although King Cophetua does not kneel in the manner of Francesco, his posture similarly honors the elevated and enthroned beggar maid. Burne-Jones was not looking to Mantegna merely for stylistic or compositional influence, but in order to reinforce the crucial theme of an armored knight bowing in supplication before a personification of sacred, maternal love and chaste femininity. By emulating a Christian altarpiece, Burne-Jones imbued his image with an air of worship that exceeds the narrative relationship of the primary figures. Infusing the painting with a religious aura, as well as symbolically transforming the beggar maid into a type of the Virgin Mary enthroned, Burne-Jones expanded the symbolic import of the archaic English legend, amplifying its themes through Christian allegory.[18]

Botticelli, like Mantegna, has long been recognized as an important source of inspiration for Burne-Jones. Indeed, Burne-Jones was at the vanguard of the nineteenth-century rediscovery of Botticelli.[19] As Elizabeth Prettejohn argues, not only did Burne-Jones emulate iconographical elements of Botticelli's work, but his acts of imitation were also a means of engaging with a "Botticellian sensibility." Describing allusions to both Mantegna and Botticelli in *The Golden Stairs* (1880), Prettejohn writes, "Since the early days of his career . . . Burne-Jones had been interested not merely in imitating specific artists but rather in revealing, or proposing, affinities and correspondences among them. . . . by the Grosvenor Gallery period he had become adept at combing his sources of inspiration so as to create new meaning as well as new form."[20] Just as Burne-Jones actively turned to Botticelli as a source of inspiration for his work, so too did his viewers apply their grow-

25 ✱ Sandro Botticelli, *Venus and Mars*, c. 1485. Tempera and oil on poplar, 69.2 × 173.4 cm. National Gallery, London, NG915

ing knowledge and opinions of Botticelli to their reception of Burne-Jones. The public perception of one artist bled into that of the other. Given the associative link between these two artists, those who encountered *King Cophetua* at the Grosvenor Gallery would have been heavily informed by their own increasing familiarity with Botticelli.

In 1869, Alexander Barker, a West End bootmaker and self-educated art collector, increased Botticelli's visibility among the London public by loaning a number of his paintings to the South Kensington Museum.[21] Botticelli's *Venus and Mars*, given the title *Mars Asleep* and attributed to an artist "under the influence of S. Botticelli," featured prominently in this temporary display.[22] Burne-Jones, a frequent visitor to the museum and already an established admirer of Botticelli, could hardly have failed to see and study these rare works. He had yet another opportunity to view the Barker collection, including *Venus and Mars*, when it was put up for auction in June 1874. Indeed, he attended the Christie's sale in the company of Frederic Burton, the Director of the National Gallery. It can reasonably be assumed, therefore, that Burne-Jones was instrumental in persuading Burton to acquire *Venus and Mars* for the nation.[23] In 1875, the following year, Burne-Jones executed the pivotal series of studies for *King Cophetua* that shifted it into the final configuration – a vertical reorientation of Botticelli's *Venus and Mars*.

The prominent act of disarming is the pivotal point of convergence. Just as Mars, the god of war, surrenders his weaponry and armor for the love of Venus, so too does Cophetua lay aside his lance, shield, and unsheathed sword in homage to the beggar maid. Running along the entire vertical length of the right-hand side of the painting, the conspicuously phallic lance creates a triangulated space within the painting that encompasses both Cophetua and the beggar maid. This lance functions as the base of the triangle, with the spear at the very top of the picture and the shield at the very bottom forming two of the vertices. Cophetua's sword that lies against his chest creates a sharp forty-five degree angle with the lance, serving as the second side of the triangle and pointing toward the head of the king at the apex. The beggar maid is securely enclosed within this geometric space, as the eye is drawn along Cophetua's devoted stare up toward her own penetrating gaze, then on to the point of the lance, down its shaft and back to the armored body of the king. Similarly, in Botticelli's *Venus and Mars*, a centrally featured lance stretches across the upper half of the horizontal panel. Here, the lance also creates a pyramidal shape within the painting, drawing the eye from the head of Venus, following her stare along the length of the lance to the head of Mars, and then dipping down and over the intermingled bodies of the lovers. As her playful satyrs carry off the lance, helmet, and breastplate of Mars, Venus reclines opposite the slumbering god of war, alert and triumphant in her conquest.

Patricia Rubin warns of the threat of emasculation in the Botticelli painting's act of disarmament: "The ascendancy of Venus over Mars ... could literally unman him."[24] And yet, in *King Cophetua*, the male protagonist seems to elude this fate. Cophetua was praised by contemporary critics for his masculine virility, contrasting with Burne-Jones's usual preference for androgyny in both his male and female figures. For example, a reviewer for *The Times*, writing shortly after the painting's debut in 1884, commented that the king's "form and the expression of his face are singularly noble; he is, in fact, every inch a man, a true king and knight, before whose arm and lance many an enemy has gone down."[25] This assessment was echoed by *The Art Journal* that year: "Can we in two lines tell of the high humility, the manliness, the chivalry of the noble figure, who, his crown in his hand, sits on the lowest step of the throne, on whose summit he has placed the beggar maid?"[26] The naked, slumbering, prostrate body of Botticelli's Mars, stripped of its armor, conveys a certain vulnerability in contrast with the suggestively draped, but nonetheless clothed and alert, Venus. In Burne-Jones's re-envisioning, the surrender of Cophetua's arms is offset by the encasement of his flesh in near impenetrable steel and leather. The beggar maid may be ascendant, but her thin gray garment, supposedly the modest garb of poverty, invites a masculine gaze on the readily apparent flesh beneath. By conjuring the image of *Venus and Mars*, Burne-Jones adds a subtly charged eroticism to an otherwise chaste painting, but in rendering this a moment of sexual anticipation and not consummation, he allows Cophetua to be simultaneously conquered and conqueror.

Moreover, by rendering Cophetua as a type of Mars, the god of war, under the influence of Venus, the goddess of love, the figure poses a rebuke to unchecked martial aggression. As established in the previous chapter, Burne-Jones's decision to join the Eastern Question Association (E.Q.A.) was an act of protest against the blatantly imperialist wartime motivations of the British government. Burne-Jones retained and asserted repeatedly his opposition to British imperial aggression through the succeeding years. For example, during the summer of 1882, he wrote to Mary Gladstone about his frustration over the developing Anglo-Egyptian War. When military action to suppress the Urabi Revolt became inevitable, he lamented,

> *I suppose what I want isn't possible [ever] & is outside practical politics – & I'm not a bad patriot for wanting our hands to be very clean – & for feeling shame when I see how carefully we avoid meddling with nations who are strong & how readily we meddle when they are weak – I know only of one war that could be justifiable.*[27]

Later, in January 1896, Burne-Jones reacted with disgust over the news of Jameson's Raid on the Transvaal, one of the sparks that ignited the Boer War: "Ours is only a material empire, and no material empire can last forever – ours'll have to go someday."[28] He developed this theme in another conversation shortly thereafter: "I've no sympathy with these material empires. We're known for overweening greed only too well.... Things will never be right at all until the same rule that governs individuals in a society in their behaviour towards each other is applied to nations."[29] For Burne-Jones, the insatiable greed of industrial capitalism and Britain's aggressive foreign policy of bullying and violence were both symptoms of the same disease. Cophetua is not only a chivalric knight willing to place his strength and weaponry in the service of the vulnerable and impoverished maiden, but also a figure identified in the traditional narrative as an African king. Thus, through Cophetua the painting poses a rebuke to British imperial militarism, which benefited the wealthy at the expense of the poor and powerless at home and abroad.

If Cophetua is a figure of the king and warrior, then the beggar maid is a figure of feminine virtue, poverty, and beauty. Echoing the posture of a Virgin Enthroned, she simultaneously adopts the guise of Venus disarming Mars, collapsing Christian and classical iconographic traditions in one body: both sacred and profane love. In this she is much like the female figure in *When Adam Delved and Eve Span*, where Burne-Jones collapsed the Sinner Eve and the Redeemer Mary into one body in keeping with medieval typological tradition. Transforming the beggar maid into a personification of Venus allows for the introduction of another compelling interpretative possibility. The art historians Caroline Arscott and Katie Scott argue that, "Since Venus is pre-eminent in beauty, as well as in sexual love, her presence in art triggers a meditation on the domain of the aesthetic.... Artistic allusions to Venus invite us to see art itself as cosubstantial with the body of the goddess: seductive in its contours, colour, texture or surface, irresistibly inciting feelings of pleasurable excitation." In other words, "the motif of Venus (whether explicit or implicit) triggers and facilitates an exploration of the gross materialism of art, without losing sight of its highest and purest aspects."[30] As an allegorical Venus figure, the beggar maid thus becomes a metaphor for the nature of art and aesthetics, forcing the viewer to examine the painting not just as a social commentary, but also as a meditation on the act of artistic creation.

This allegorical quality extends from the Venus-like pose of the figure to the very treatment of the body as painted surface. In sharp contrast to the richly crafted detail found in the rest of the painting, the body of the beggar maid is remarkable for its sheer ethereality, verging on the point of transparency. The paint is applied deceptively thickly across much of *King Cophetua*, with the patterning of the fabric and gilt decoration reaching an almost gesso-like effect. Burne-Jones frequently adopted this treatment of the painted surface, flattening the picture plane in order to allow for an emphasis on the detailed labor of the artist in applying pigment to canvas rather than the illusion of three-dimensional space. As Burne-Jones observed, "It may be certainly said that for each material there's a different way of laying on paint. That a dress ought to have a kind of warp and woof in it, that a face should have mystery in its texture and surface."[31] Accordingly, in *King Cophetua*, every fictive medium has its own experiential qualities, from the gilded metallic throne with its repoussé decorative schemes and shimmering reflective surfaces, to the tactile presence of the silks, leathers, and wools. The monochromatic beggar maid, however, is rendered in thin, smoothed strokes. Burne-Jones employed an intense *sfumato* technique, creating the "mystery" he described, while she is haloed by a light that seemingly separates her from the fictive world around.[32] She resembles a paper doll inserted within her ornately textured surroundings. Her fragile presence as thinly painted surface prompts a rupture in the visual schema of the work. The otherworldly but nonetheless jarring presence shatters the reverie of the scene, forcing the viewer to recognize that this golden treasure house is in fact a gilded cage.

This sense of instability, of profound tension between the material sumptuousness of the surface and the status of the painting as a physical object, was further heightened by Burne-Jones's integration of a specially made frame for his colossal canvas. Commissioned from the workshop of Andrew and Paul Vacani in 1884, this immense, gilded Italianate Revival frame was unsympathetically altered at an unknown point early in the twentieth century to accommodate a glazing window.[33] In 2011, when Tate Britain undertook the repair and restoration of the frame, the conservator Alastair Johnson discovered a photograph by Emery Walker of the painting with the frame in its original state (fig. 26). Documenting the memorial exhibition for Burne-Jones at the New Gallery in 1898, the photograph records the painting and frame when it was in the collection of its first owner, the Earl of Wharncliffe. In Walker's photograph, it is evident that the frame was created not merely as an accent but as an integral part of the painting.

It was not unusual for the Pre-Raphaelites and artists of the Aesthetic Movement to design their own purpose-built frames. Given his father's work as a gilder and carver, Burne-Jones was especially familiar with the fabrication of frames, and he frequently incorporated custom designs into his work.[34] The *Briar Rose* series, executed during 1870–90 (fig. 27), serves as one striking example of Burne-Jones's pointed integration of framing to amplify the impact and reception of his paintings. Purchased as a group of four canvases by Alexander Henderson, Lord Faringdon (1850–1934), Burne-Jones designed a frame that knitted the panels together into a continuous frieze across three walls that envelops the viewer.[35] The frame designed by Burne-Jones for *King Cophetua and the Beggar Maid*, however, is particularly notable for the way it extends the architectural elements depicted in the painting, creating an illusion of perspectival recession. The upper and lower corners of the pilasters on either side of the frame intersect with the edges of the painted throne within the picture plane to create a sense of receding space. Amplifying the illusion, the frame, in turn, seemingly extends the interior scene depicted in the painting, allowing it to project forward into the room where the viewer stands. Such an

26 * Emery Walker, *King Cophetua and the Beggar Maid by Edward Burne-Jones*, 1898. Photograph.
National Portrait Gallery, London, NPG CAP00483

27 * Edward Burne-Jones, *The Legend of the Briar Rose*, installed in the saloon at Buscot Park, Oxfordshire, 1870–90. The Faringdon Collection Trust at Buscot Park, Oxfordshire

incorporation of the frame into its surroundings is most commonly found in Renaissance altarpieces, such as Giovanni Bellini's 1488 *Frari Triptych* (fig. 28).[36] In describing the function of the frame in Bellini's work and in the *Frari Triptych* in particular, the art historian Rona Goffen observed,

> *the frame is understood both as the terminus of the fictive architecture and also as the point (or plane) where the two worlds, sacred and mundane, meet and coincide. Thus the holy realm inhabited by the Madonna and saints seems to be accessible from our own, and the place where the one may be entered from the other is the altar.*[37]

In other words, the use of an illusionistic interior and architectural frame in a religious altarpiece allows the painting to facilitate a point of direct contact with the divine.

With *King Cophetua*, Burne-Jones harnessed this quality of the architectural altarpiece frame, transforming his monumental painting into a permeable threshold where the secular and spiritual worlds converge. The strong verticality and vertiginous height of the painting enhance this effect still more, approximating the scale and impact of an altarpiece. By adopting this traditional format Burne-Jones not only imbued the folktale with an aura of spiritual consequence, but also forged a consecrated space that dictated its own terms of engagement.[38] Whether placed on the wall of a gallery or a wealthy home, the painting therefore disrupts the site by creating a gateway that opens onto an immersive utopian vision of the world that might be if art is made free for all. The original structure

28 * Giovanni Bellini, Frari Altarpiece (*Madonna and Child with Saints Nicholas, Peter, Mark, and Benedict*), 1488. Basilica of Sta. Maria Gloriosa dei Frari, Venice

and appearance of the frame is thus vital to the impact of the painting as a complete decorative object, an effect that was obscured throughout most of the twentieth century and has only recently been recovered.

"The goldsmith's art": King Cophetua and the Paradox of Luxury

By choosing to combine two mimetic systems in *King Cophetua*, perspectival recession and haptic facture, Burne-Jones created a palpable tension between surface and depth. This visual conflict amplifies the dynamic tensions central to the theme of the painting, between male and female, rich and poor, strong and vulnerable. The viewer is drawn forward into the seemingly dimensional space through the perspectival recession created by the frame and the lines of the throne. The haptic intensity of the material objects then captivates the eye, which luxuriates over each sensual texture. The more one gazes on this minutely worked surface, the more the image slips away and becomes not a story, but a densely woven pattern of materiality.[39] Presented on an immense scale, this detailed exactness threatens to become phenomenologically overwhelming.

The unique somatic experience of decorative materiality represented a common thread throughout the contemporary reviews and accounts of *King Cophetua and the Beggar Maid*. Repeatedly, viewers emerged with an overpowering sense of tactility and an atmospheric, immersive opulence of color and textures. For example, *The Times*'s reviewer of the Grosvenor Gallery exhibition in 1884 enthused: "Cophetua sits below, glorious and radiant in the colours that king may wear or painter imagine, in steel armour, plate, and chain, with a robe of many tints thrown over him; the crown which he holds is resplendent with jewels, and the brass at his feet and all around him is bright and gleaming."[40] Similarly, *The Spectator*'s reviewer described how "the flashes of colour from gold and steel, from jewelled crown, and scattered flowers, and clinging robe, seem literally to glow and fade almost as a flame pales and glistens in the darkness."[41] Fernand Khnopff also recalled an analogous experience at the Paris Universal Exposition: "[Cophetua] holds on his knees the finely modeled crown of dark metal lighted up with the scarlet rubies and coral, and his face, in clear-cut profile, is raised in silent contemplation. The scene is incredibly sumptuous: costly stuffs glisten and gleam, luxurious pillows of purple brocade shine in front of the chased gold paneling."[42]

Finally, in her overview of Burne-Jones's career published a decade after the debut of *King Cophetua*, Cartwright Ady seems to hit on the essence of this unique quality of the painting: "The most costly marbles and richest draperies, the brightest hues of blue and purple, of rose and violet, adorn the throne where the maid of low degree sits in her plain grey robe; the chased armour of her royal lover and the crown which he bears in his hand are marvels of the goldsmith's art."[43] Moreover, Cartwright Ady's phrase "the goldsmith's art" echoes an especially revealing quotation from Burne-Jones himself on his treatment of surface and painterly technique:

> *I love to treat my pictures . . . as a goldsmith does his jewels. I should like every inch of surface to be so fine that if all were burned or lost, all but a scrap from one of them, the man who found it might say, 'Whatever this may have represented it is a work of art, beautiful in surface and quality and colour.'*[44]

This statement, a rare and therefore significant instance of Burne-Jones offering an insight into his working process, seemingly establishes a binary interpretive element that conforms to Prettejohn's theorization of his paintings as crafted "presences in the world."[45] For Burne-Jones, the import of each painting derived not just from the figurative imagery and the narrative they suggest, but also from the tiniest square of canvas surface and the careful decorative labor to which it attests.

Amid this overabundance of surface detail, the proffered crown held by King Cophetua centers and balances the viewer, synecdochically bearing the narrative, symbolic, and material burden of the painting (fig. 29). Firmly grasping this precious jeweled object, the figure of Cophetua becomes a surrogate for the viewer, a site of somatic connection between flesh and burnished metal. This touch of hands to crown, moreover, reminds the

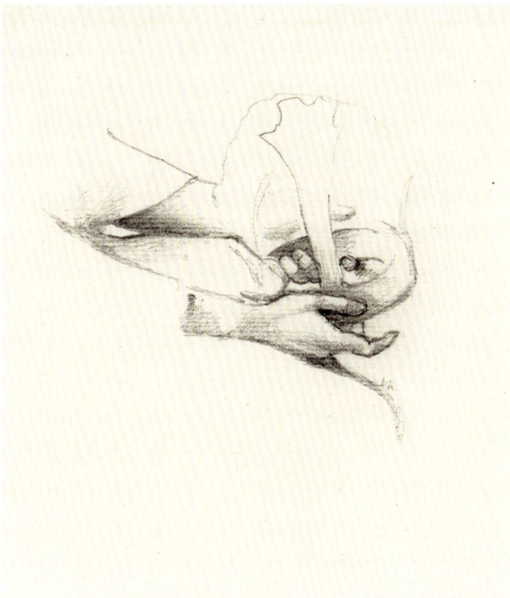

29 * Edward Burne-Jones, *King Cophetua and the Beggar Maid* (detail of fig. 21)

30 * Edward Burne-Jones, *Study of Hands for King Cophetua and the Beggar Maid*, undated. Graphite on paper, 19.4 × 18.1 cm. Tate, London, N05182

31 * Edward Burne-Jones, *King Cophetua and the Beggar Maid – Studies for Cophetua*, 1883–84. Pencil on laid paper, 30.4 × 18.8 cm. Birmingham Museum & Art Gallery, 1972P73

viewer of the material and metaphorical sacrifice Cophetua is about to make, offering his wealth, his kingdom, and his arms in service to the woman seated above him. The golden, bejeweled crown both stands as a potent symbol of wealth and capitalistic acquisition, and appositely represents Burne-Jones's technical aims of attaining the "goldsmith's art."

The careful treatment and subtle development of the crown as a core feature of the composition is evident in two surviving preparatory studies, which reveal the symbolic significance of this object as part of the larger conceit of the painting. Here Burne-Jones elaborated the exact position and shape of the crown, in addition to determining the king's physical relationship with it. The first drawing has been titled *Study of Hands for King Cophetua and the Beggar Maid* and is in the Tate (fig. 30), while the second, *King Cophetua and the Beggar Maid – Studies for Cophetua*, is in the Birmingham Museums & Art Gallery (fig. 31).[46] In the Tate study, Burne-Jones was focused on developing the shape and proportion of the crown in relationship to Cophetua's hands and body. The crown is too small, with only the base clearly drawn and no jeweled details, but the suggestion

32 ∗ Edward Burne-Jones, *The Last Sleep of Arthur in Avalon*, c. 1881–98. Oil on canvas, 279 × 650 cm.
Museo de Arte de Ponce, Puerto Rico, Luis A. Ferré Foundation, Inc., 63.0369

of the curled and twisted metal is present. Similarly, in the Birmingham study, although more of Cophetua's body has been included and there is more assurance to the treatment, overall there is a lack of detail, particularly for the crown. At this stage, it is the contact between hands and crown, the relationship between fingers and metal, that Burne-Jones appears to have been working out over both drawings. The looseness of the grip, with the forefinger of the right hand and the thumb of the left hand (particularly in the Tate study) held away from the crown, denotes a balancing and even a buoyancy to the weighty object. However, this grip also seems to tighten from one study to the next, until in the final painting Cophetua's fingers are drawn firmly around the base of the crown. He is not just holding the golden object, but feeling its presence. The tightened fingers of the left hand in particular suggest the slightest hint of reluctance about offering up this weighty, wealthy object that confers earthly power on the wearer.

As with many of the unique and significant objects found in Burne-Jones's paintings, this crown was based on an actual copper model, from which he made his detailed studies. In an article written several years after Burne-Jones's death, the artist's son Philip recalled his father's practice of working from small models during the preparatory stage of his paintings: "In addition to the great number of careful studies in pencil for heads,

33 * Edward Burne-Jones, *The Last Sleep of Arthur in Avalon* (detail of fig. 32)

34 * Edward Burne-Jones, *Portrait Head of King Cophetua*, c. 1883–84. Oil on canvas, 56 × 42 cm. Private collection

hands, feet, etc., little models in wax or other materials were nearly always prepared, from which further drawings were made, and it was from such small models that he studied the lights and shades on the throne of 'King Cophetua.'"[47] With careful specifications, Burne-Jones commissioned the copper model for Cophetua's crown, along with the shield and armor, from the metalworker, designer, and architect W. A. S. Benson.[48] Aymer Vallance observed in 1900 that the crown "was evidently a favourite of the artist's," appearing in no fewer than three major works in addition to *King Cophetua*, namely *The Last Sleep of Arthur in Avalon* (c. 1881–98; figs. 32 and 33), the second panel of the *Briar Rose* series, *The Council Chamber* (1885–90), and the first panel of the *San Graal* tapestries, *The Summons* (1890–91).[49] This creation of the crown as a physical object beyond the fictive space of the painted canvas presents an interesting study in the significance of mimesis for Burne-Jones. Of the many possibilities suggested by this fascinating act of meta-craft, one compelling explanation may lie with Burne-Jones's fidelity to Ruskin's "truth to nature" dictum.[50] While his images exist outside the quotidian sphere of the modern, each object is nonetheless grounded in reality, recognizable and faithful to the rules of physical existence. By familiarizing himself with the creation and craftsmanship of the crown as an actual object, and the nature of the true "goldsmith's art," Burne-Jones would have been greatly aided in his aim of conferring on each fictive material its own painterly quality.

It is intriguing that Benson not only created a copper version of the crown for the painting, but also served as a model for the figure of Cophetua (fig. 34).[51] A close friend of Burne-Jones and Morris, Benson became a leading figure in the Arts and Crafts Movement. In 1877, Burne-Jones met Benson's sister by chance at a performance by Richard Wagner, and both siblings soon became acquaintances. It is perhaps not surprising that they were attracted to one another, given how closely Benson's biography mirrored that of Morris. Benson was born to privilege, but abandoned a career in law, as well as his Oxford education and his social standing, in order to become a craftsman. In 1880, with the enthusiastic support of Burne-Jones and Morris, he started a metalworking studio, writing to his mother, "I must make something or be miserable."[52] In 1883, the year in which Burne-Jones worked most intensely on *King Cophetua*, Benson was also actively collaborating with Morris on designing a model cottage for artisans at the new Manchester Art Museum in Ancoats. The following year, Benson was instrumental in founding the Art Workers Guild, as well as the Home Arts and Industries Association, "set up to promote craft classes among the poor."[53] Later, Benson helped to lead the Arts and Crafts Exhibition Society and eventually took over Morris & Co. in 1904.

In selecting Benson as a model for Cophetua, Burne-Jones transformed the king into a personification of the artist, who weighs his handicraft between his fingers and contemplates its true import. Just as the king must seemingly reconcile himself to the sacrifice of his crown, so too must the artist reconcile himself to the capitalist art market that makes his craft possible. Cophetua's conundrum plagued Burne-Jones and Morris as they catered to the whims of "the swinish rich."[54] Cophetua as a figure of the artist is just as much a prisoner in the golden cage as the allegorical representation of art embodied by the beggar maid. Artist and art, each is bound by a system that keeps them beholden to the demands of the rich sequestered in their beautifully decorated homes while many are forced to exist in poverty with the cruel ugliness of industry. As Cophetua weighs his choice, it is the beggar maid who directly confronts the privileged classes with her poignant stare at the viewer. She seems to ask, "would you selfishly keep all of this beauty for yourself, locked away, or would you, like Cophetua, offer up your treasures for the sake of love?"[55]

"Fresh strenuous paganism": King Cophetua at the Grosvenor Gallery, London, 1884

Burne-Jones considered the fate of his paintings, whether locked away in the homes of wealthy patrons or offered for sale like common commodities on the walls of London's galleries, to be an unsatisfactory compromise. In a letter written two years after the debut of *King Cophetua* at the Grosvenor Gallery, Burne-Jones openly declared his frustration: "I do from my soul hate all the conditions of modern art – exhibitions, and the money dealings – O heaven, they are vile to contamination and disgrace."[56] Georgiana Burne-Jones later clarified this stance: "He did not, of course, wish his work unseen, but the whole system of exhibitions was distasteful to him, and an easel picture but a makeshift: what he always sought for was to design on a large scale for special places and to paint his pictures *in situ*."[57] On another occasion, Burne-Jones lamented, "I hate hung up pictures & like them to be a part of the wall."[58] Trained outside the academy system, Burne-Jones never felt comfortable with the compromises foisted on him by any of the artistic or exhibiting societies in which he grudgingly participated. He resigned from one institution after another, including the Old Water Colour Society in 1870, the Grosvenor Gallery in 1887, and the Royal Academy in 1893.[59] As he once wrote to George Howard, "It seems I am always resigning something or other, though I should have said I was a peaceable fellow enough."[60] In a more indignant mood, he proclaimed to Rooke, "I'm a born rebel, that's my position and utility in the world. I am not and never was, fitted to belong to any institutions."[61]

The opening of the Grosvenor in 1877 coincided with Burne-Jones's involvement in the E.Q.A. In the aftermath of the failure of the E.Q.A., when Burne-Jones committed himself to the creation and proliferation of his art with renewed efforts, the Grosvenor provided a highly visible venue to exhibit his work to the public. Burne-Jones was hailed as the gallery's leading light as soon as it was launched. In the words of Georgiana Burne-Jones, "From that day he belonged to the world in a sense that he had never done before, for his existence became widely known and his name famous."[62] Over the succeeding years, some hailed Burne-Jones as the preeminent head of a new school of art, the successors to the Pre-Raphaelite Brotherhood, while others derided his work as decadent and suspiciously sensuous. Such qualms arose in large part because of the worshipful and elitist aura of the Grosvenor. According to the art historian Colleen Denney, the Grosvenor Gallery was attended by a rarefied "cult of worshippers," led by the fashionable and aristocratic Sir Coutts and Lady Lindsay, who held up Burne-Jones and his fellow painters as "high priests of a new religion of art."[63] In many ways, this circle of devotees came to overshadow Burne-Jones's art and reputation, heavily informing the reception of his paintings in London.

Although the avant-garde Grosvenor Gallery permitted artists a degree of autonomy not experienced at the Royal Academy, it nonetheless represented a compromise. Ornamented and furnished to resemble a private, aristocratic home, the Grosvenor Gallery exemplified the hoarding of wealth and beauty by the privileged classes against which

Cophetua's sacrifice protests (fig. 35).[64] When *King Cophetua and the Beggar Maid* appeared at the Grosvenor in the summer of 1884, its defiant critique of the institution itself was not acknowledged in the press. Consequently, the reception was not nearly as striking as the one the painting later received in Paris against the backdrop of the Universal Exposition.

Four contemporary reviews of the painting afford the opportunity to assess its reception on its debut in London. These reviews include three anonymous critiques of the exhibition, written for *The Times*, *The Spectator*, and *The Art Journal* respectively, along with Claude Phillips's monographic essay on Burne-Jones in *The Magazine of Art* the following year. Taken together, these critiques provide a comprehensive overview of the initial reaction to the painting in England. Most notable of all is their marked similarity, with each seemingly dwelling on the same set of themes.

35 * "Interior of the Grosvenor Gallery – West Gallery," *Illustrated London News*, May 5, 1877. Wood engraving

The first point on which nearly all the authors could agree was that, among the many works on view that year at the Grosvenor, *King Cophetua* was most worthy of exceedingly high praise. The critic for *The Art Journal* forthrightly declared it to be "the picture of the year."[65] The article in *The Spectator* elaborated that "this is not only the grandest picture [Burne-Jones] has ever painted, but it is the greatest picture which the pre-Raphaelite school has produced, and one of the greatest of modern times." The author continued, "To-day, and while the canvas holds together, this will be a great picture; and the really great pictures of the world are very few and very precious."[66] Finally, *The Times* printed perhaps the highest praise of all, proclaiming *King Cophetua and the Beggar Maid* "not only the finest work that Mr. Burne-Jones has ever painted, but... one of the finest pictures ever painted by an Englishman." According to this critic, the painting dominated the exhibition, much as it would the Universal Exposition five years later in Paris; the "superb picture... far transcends all else in the gallery... and scarcely leaves the visitor any eyes for the rest of the display."[67]

These critics, moreover, each identified the same two aspects of *King Cophetua* that defined it as a successful and eminent work, namely, the display of technical skill and the elevated ideal expressed in the narrative. I have already cited several examples of the almost overwhelming sense of atmospheric sumptuousness and intricately realized materiality, the "goldsmith's art," observed by several viewers. These observations were also paired with more concrete evaluations of Burne-Jones's technical achievement and demonstrable workmanship. The critic for *The Times* wrote, "it is from the technical point of view that the triumph of the painter is most complete." For this author, "this picture is, above all things, a triumph of work. Every inch of it... is finished with the most scrupulous care."[68] The review in *The Spectator* also praised the painting for its "perfect workmanship," remarking on the "combination of great technical excellence of handiwork, with that exquisite sense of beauty."[69] Claude Phillips in *The Magazine of Art* agreed that, particularly in the treatment of the metalwork, "the painter has shown really marvellous technical skill."[70]

As for the conceptual aspects of the painting, the story of the wealthy king sacrificing all for the love of an impoverished woman, the critics for *The Times* and the *Art Journal* found a timeless and poignant appeal in the scene, but refrained from extrapolating the overt critique of wealth disparity implicit within it. The *Art Journal* review stated, "It is the idea, the inspiration of the picture which makes it so fine, and raises it to the level of the great masters of a bye-gone age."[71] That in *The Times* made an even bolder claim for universality: "It is a story which explains itself; and even those who have never heard of King Cophetua will understand that the picture marks a phase of the never-ending history of beauty triumphing over strength, of love breaking down the barriers of caste and social pride.... His story is one that touches all the world; it is of universal interest."[72] In contrast, the critic for *The Spectator* countered these claims of universality by projecting that in future years the painting would stand as a wonder to the world, but would be enigmatic and inscrutable, a mysterious relic much like the ancient Egyptian pyramids were to the people of the nineteenth century.[73]

Underlying these predominantly celebratory evaluations of *King Cophetua and the Beggar Maid*, however, are the echoes of prior charges laid against Burne-Jones. These concerns are particularly apparent in the near-obsessive preoccupation with the manliness and virility of the figure of King Cophetua. Some of these descriptions have been noted in the discussion of Cophetua as a type of Mars. However, the mention of the king's masculinity is so prevalent that there are many more instances to include. For example, the critic for *The Times* described Cophetua as "a hero. Of passion, perhaps, he might have had more, but not of manliness, not of beauty, not of worship."[74] Meanwhile, the author for the *Art Journal* wrote, "We feel the high nature of the man.... he is chivalrous and noble. He is a young and beautiful Don Quixote."[75] Phillips offered perhaps the most revealing discussion of the importance of Cophetua's masculinity by marking this as the greatest achievement of the painting, representing a more significant development in the career of the painter than even the display of technical skill:

> *The noble figure of the king . . . is yet a conception distinctly human and virile, breathing forth a man's passion, chastened and subdued, yet intense and true. This is an advance, or rather a transformation, which, if we could venture to hope that it would be sustained, would justify the highest hopes. What might not Mr. Burne-Jones yet achieve with his brilliant fancy and now complete technical accomplishment, if he should succeed in infusing into his highly-wrought creations and delicately elaborated fancies a more virile force, a higher and closer sympathy with humanity, a more real and profound significance?*[76]

Phillips makes plain that Cophetua's masculinity is seen as a progressive, even evolutionary step, in Burne-Jones's growth as a painter. The celebration of the figure of Cophetua is not meant to be contained within the work itself, but to encourage Burne-Jones to extend this "virile force" into his other conceptions.

In keeping with this critical thread, the beggar maid was also approvingly described as possessing distinctly feminine characteristics. As an apt foil to her companion, she was most often discussed as expressing womanly purity and chastity. For example, the critic for *The Times* referred to "the strength of her maiden purity."[77] Similarly, *The Art Journal* described her "simple beauty and purity."[78] Finally, the critic for *The Spectator*, whose review was the most reserved, did not appear sufficiently convinced of Cophetua's virility or the beggar maid's purity. The author instead found a "strangeness" and "weariness" to the painting in keeping with the artist's frequently noted "peculiar intellectual – perhaps half-spiritual – sensuousness."[79]

These remarks respond to a longstanding indictment against Burne-Jones, a widely held perception of his failure to display appropriate gender traits and an acceptable normative sexuality in his work. An example of this prior strain of criticism can be found in a review of the second Grosvenor Gallery Summer Exhibition, in 1878, for the *Magazine of Art*:

> *As to the value, in a larger sense, of [Burne-Jones's] art . . . we most seriously protest against it (with a reverence for its genius and a tenderness for its beauty) as unmasculine, and – what is worse from a purely artistic standpoint – self-consciously imitative; nay, unintelligently imitative, for this is not classical, this is not medieval, feeling and thought; it is fresh strenuous paganism, emasculated by false modern emotionalism.*[80]

Three years later, Wilfred Meynell raised similar concerns, again in the context of a review of the Grosvenor Gallery in *The Magazine of Art*: "The moral tendency of Mr. Burne-Jones's pictures does not satisfy us. Effeminacy, even when it is associated with some aesthetic sentiment, is not a wholesome moral temper. But it is distinctly unwholesome when it is associated, as in the present instance, with suggestions of a low moral tone and a very apparent pessimism."[81] Part of the success of *King Cophetua and the Beggar Maid* in London was the belief that he had, at last, overcome these faults and was turning toward more suitable displays of morality as would befit one of the leading artists of the nation. In the end, the aura of the Grosvenor Gallery overpowered the critical response to *King Cophetua*, and still, to a certain degree, manages to shroud the painting with lingering suspicions of decadent escapism. Although it was immediately recognized as a momentous and significant painting, it was not until it appeared at the Paris Universal Exposition that the work seemed to find its true voice, becoming provocative and epiphanic.

"The revenge of art on life": King Cophetua at the Universal Exposition, Paris, 1889

Shortly after the 1889 Universal Exposition in Paris, London critic F. G. Stephens remarked on the distinct difference in the reception that *King Cophetua and the Beggar Maid* received in these two cities: "[*King Cophetua*] astonished the French painters and compelled them to regard English art from a – to them – altogether fresh and very unexpected point of view. Deep as was the impression made in London by this picture, on Frenchmen it had a far greater and graver influence."[82] Within the context of the Grosvenor Gallery, *King Cophetua* earned distinguished praise. However, for some who viewed the painting in Paris, the experience of *King Cophetua* was transformative and revelatory. As much as Burne-Jones was venerated with a near religious fervor by some in London, this ardent circle of admirers also curtailed the reception of his work. The ultimate impact of the painting was, in many ways, restricted by the politics of the Aesthetes and their followers. In Paris, freed from many of the preconceptions held by English viewers, and set against the backdrop of an international exhibition of art, industry, and imperialism, *King Cophetua* took on a new life.[83] In contrast to the burlesque of the Universal Exposition, the painting attained an air of immediacy and intensity, particularly in the recollections of Robert de la Sizeranne and Fernand Khnopff.[84] According to Khnopff, "This artist's dream, deliciously bewildering, had become the real; and at this moment it was the elbowing and struggling reality that seemed a dream, or rather a nightmare."[85]

The Universal Exposition commemorated the centennial of the French Revolution and an appropriately grand gateway was commissioned to set this international exhibition apart (fig. 36). The winning design was a 984-foot tower designed by the industrial engineer Gustave Eiffel. Constructed of prefabricated wrought-iron standardized parts, it became the tallest manufactured structure in the world and stood as a self-conscious embodiment of progress and modernity. Perhaps indicative of the overall tenor of the

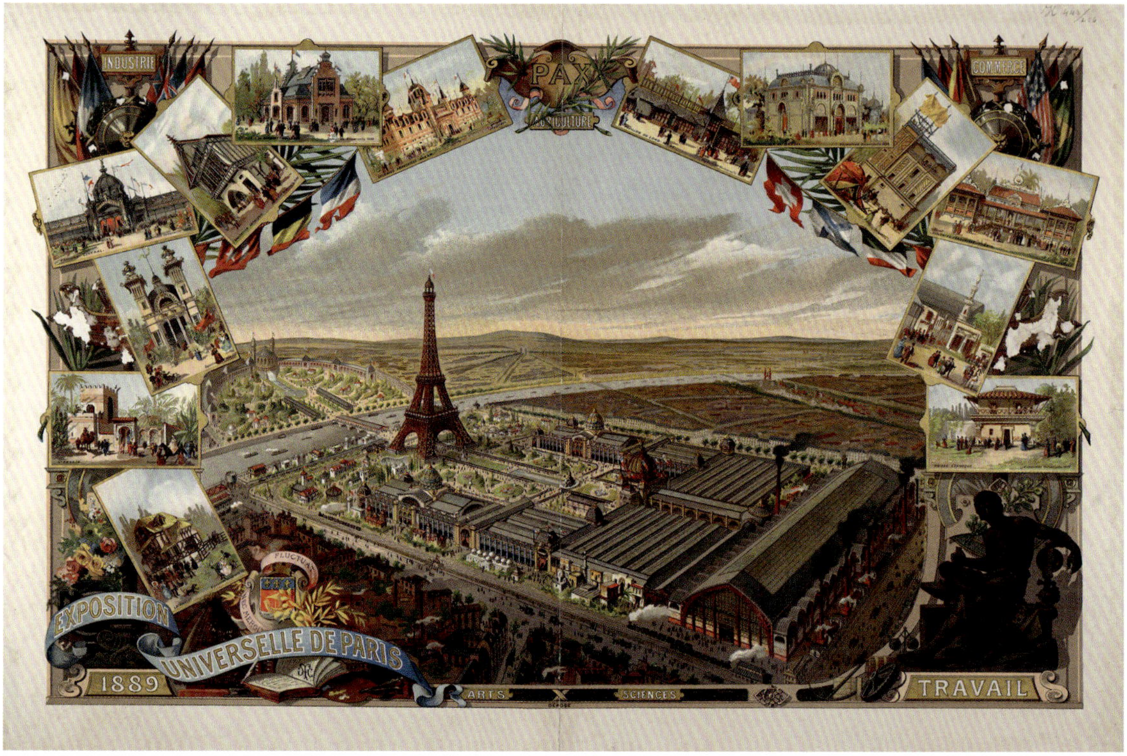

36 * *View of Exposition Universelle de Paris*, 1889. Engraving, 23 × 15.6 cm. Collection of Universitäts und Landesbibliothek Darmstadt

Exposition, the pragmatic Eiffel undertook the project for the potential profits it could bring, and not to enter the annals of architectural history.[86] The Eiffel Tower, dominating the skyline and setting the tone for the Exposition, garnered a mixture of revulsion and adulation. Viewers passed beneath the curving triumphal archways, glittering with a fresh coat of iridescent paint, and entered the main concourse on the Champ de Mars. Here they encountered an array of exhibits, but the most striking structure by far (apart from the Eiffel Tower) was the Galerie des Machines.

While its lofty counterpart went on to become a definitive national landmark, the subsequently demolished Galerie des Machines made an equally impressive impact on the public.[87] The behemoth gallery, the largest enclosed space in the world at the time, was an architectural descendant of Joseph Paxton's Crystal Palace, which housed the Great Exhibition of 1851 in London, and thus provides something of an insight into what Burne-Jones's reaction would have been had he attended the Paris Exposition nearly forty years later. Burne-Jones visited the Crystal Palace in 1854, after its relocation to Sydenham on the outskirts of London. He was not repelled, but he nonetheless foresaw a disheartening future of cold industrial spaces to come:

> *In its gigantic wearisomeness, in its length of cheerless monotony, iron and glass, glass and iron, I grew more and more convinced of the powerlessness of such material to effect an Architecture. Its only claim to our admiration consists in its size, not in those elements in which lies the true principle of appreciation, form and colour: its form is necessarily rigid and mechanical, its colour simple transparency and a painfully dazzling reflection.*[88]

Ruskin, among others, shared Burne-Jones's apathy in the face of an architecture that seemed to represent an erasure of history and memory through the mechanized removal of the trace of a human hand.[89] Some visitors to the Galerie des Machines experienced this same sense of revulsion and dismay, but for the majority the elephantine structure was hailed as evidence of an "innocent modernity, wondrous and magical by implication and uncontaminated by architectural fashions." Upon crossing the threshold of this cathedral of industry, many more marvelous spectacles awaited. Here, viewers could experience such innovations as "the latest bicycles, spectacular displays of electric lighting, demonstrations of Edison's phonograph, telephones," and innumerable other novelties.[90] Moreover, the two-storied hall was so vast that a crane-like "rolling bridge" was especially fabricated for the purpose of transporting visitors across its cavernous expanse.[91] Encased within a cage of iron larger than St. Pancras station in London, the modern industrial world was laid out before the viewer in all its dizzying glory.

One final aspect of the *Weltanschauung* of the Universal Exposition was found on the opposite end of the Champ de Mars from the Galerie des Machines. Beyond the gateway of the Eiffel Tower and bordering the banks of the Seine, symbolically located in a liminal space on the boundaries of the showcase of civilization and modernity, were the colonial exhibits. The organizers were determined to improve on all prior international exhibitions in scope and scale, and these too were expanded to include not just goods and products of imperial territories, but also living representatives of the indigenous populations, put on display in simulacra of their home villages. The Universal Exposition thereby exemplified all that Burne-Jones and Morris inveighed against in the modern era: insatiable capitalist materialism, lifeless industrial architecture, and callous imperialist acquisition.

Having imbibed these myriad diversions, head filled with mesmerizing visions of whirling machines and a lavish treasure trove of material goods, the visitor might happen to wander into the Palais des Beaux Arts. Acclimatized to the hyperactive amusements on view elsewhere, most were drawn to equally easily accessible paintings. In the words of Khnopff, "The public stood... before military or *genre* pictures: it was attracted by the

37 * Jules Breton, *The Shepherd's Star*, 1887. Oil on canvas, 102.8 × 78.7 cm. Toledo Museum of Art (Toledo, Ohio), Gift of Arthur J. Secor, 1922.41

cheap fascinations of an amusing subject or a pretty story; but it was very evidently thinner; the number of chance visitors grew less and less."[92] The majority of works on display, organized by nationality, were of what is generally termed the realist or naturalist school.[93] Many of these paintings depicted a sort of sentimentalized poverty, either through quaint images of the urban poor or pastoral scenes of rural peasantry.[94] Works such as Walter Gay's *Charity* and Jules Breton's *The Shepherd's Star* (fig. 37) softened the image of poverty, aestheticizing the harsh conditions of rural labor, thereby assuaging the guilt of the middle-class viewer, and bolstering the perception that this was the proper place of the poor.[95]

In order to reach the English Art Section, located toward the rear of the ground floor of the Palais des Beaux Arts, a visitor would have enacted a kind of pilgrimage. Persistence would have been rewarded with the growing remoteness of the throng and the hushed calm that pervaded the deep interior of the art exhibit. Upon entering the English Art Section, the viewer would at last have encountered Burne-Jones's *King Cophetua and the Beggar Maid*, flanked by George Frederic Watts's two paintings, *Mammon* (fig. 38) and *Hope* (fig. 39).[96] There can be little doubt that these two works by Watts, a longtime friend and colleague of Burne-Jones, served as powerful complements to *King Cophetua*. Indeed, a little more than a year before the Universal Exposition, Watts himself had expressed a desire to show his work alongside Burne-Jones's, and it is perhaps no coincidence that their paintings were displayed together.[97] However, it was *King Cophetua* alone that left a forceful impression on the visitors to the Universal Exposition. The placement of *Mammon* and *Hope* amplified the central themes of the painting, transforming the monumental secular altarpiece into a triptych. *Mammon*, in particular, drew out the latent theme of capitalist greed as a destructive force in *King Cophetua*. And yet, it was Burne-Jones's painting that lingered in the imagination, that elicited a conversionary response, and earned newfound admiration for the artist from a generation of Continental admirers.

Why did the advantage fall to *King Cophetua*? First, while *Mammon* presents the viewer with a commanding, spiritually iconic condemnation of wealth and avarice, it wallows in the bodily ugliness of greed. This cruel grotesque presented a more severe and forthright reprimand, but a far less palatable one, than *King Cophetua*, which draws the viewer in with an irresistible, somatic experience of beauty. It does not chastise, but rather proposes a challenge to be taken up, a vision of what might be as well as the means to achieve it. Second, and perhaps most striking, was the sharp contrast in the material qualities of the two canvases. The broad, loose brushstrokes and rich, but muted and shadowy tones of *Mammon* would have been thrown into stark relief beside the meticulous treatment, textural depth, and brilliant luminosity of the surface of *King Cophetua*.

Following Burne-Jones's death in 1898, both Sizeranne and Khnopff chose to center their commemorative essays on their still-vivid memories of the contrast between the frenetic atmosphere of the Universal Exposition and the quietly confrontational vision of *King Cophetua and the Beggar Maid*. As an artist, Khnopff highlighted the visceral, emotional, and unexpectedly ennobling experience of encountering "this work of intense beauty." "The spectator was enwrapped by this living atmosphere of dream-love and of spiritualised fire, carried away to a happy intoxication of soul, a dizziness that clutched the spirit and bore it high up, far, far away, too far to be any longer conscious of the brutal presence of the crowd."[98] This passionate response suggests that, for Khnopff, the painting represented a cerebral and spiritually uplifting alternative to the mundane exist-

38 ∗ George Frederic Watts, *Mammon*, 1884–85. Oil on canvas, 183 × 106 cm. Tate, London, N01630

39 ∗ George Frederic Watts, *Hope*, 1886. Oil on canvas, 142.2 × 111.8 cm. Tate, London, N01640

ence touted by the Exposition. The supposed splendors of modern industry were exposed as shallow and ephemeral diversions in contrast to the epiphanic revelation elicited by the contemplation of Burne-Jones's painting. Sizeranne was simultaneously bolder and more concrete in his declaration of the political significance of the painting for any who encountered it, stating simply, "It was a revelation." He elaborated on the acute disparity between the experience of the Exposition and the realm presented to the viewer within Burne-Jones's painting, as well as the implicit condemnation of modernity:

All round this room were others, where emblems and signs of strength and luxury were collected from all the nations of the world – pyramids, silvered or gilt, represented the amount of precious metal dug year by year out of the earth; palaces and booths contained the most sumptuous products of the remotest isles – and here behold a king laying his crown at the feet of a beggar-maid for her beauty's sake![99]

Sizeranne found not only an attack on material greed in *King Cophetua*, but also recognized the critique of imperialism contained within this painting of a chivalric knight setting aside his arms before his beloved. "There might be seen the most highly wrought instruments of war; cannons, models of armour-plated ships, and torpedoes," he commented on most of the exhibition, but "here was a knight duly clad in iron, bowing in his strength before weakness for innocence' sake." Finally, in a declaration that should silence any doubts as to the inherent socialist connotations of this image, Sizeranne concluded that *King Cophetua and the Beggar Maid* depicted "the Apotheosis of Poverty."[100]

When conceiving *King Cophetua and the Beggar Maid*, Burne-Jones was probably not working with the aim of setting his monumental painting against the backdrop of a garish and frenzied international exhibition. And yet, this crucible of the ills and excesses

40 ✷ Joseph Nash, *International Exhibition, Hyde Park, London, 1862, showing Victorian Section with pillar of gold*. Watercolor and pencil, 22.6 × 30.2 cm. State Library of Victoria, Melbourne

41 * Philip Webb and Edward Burne-Jones for Morris, Marshall, Faulkner, & Co., *The Backgammon Players*, 1861. Oil on pine, leather, brass, copper, 185.4 × 114.3 × 53.3 cm. Metropolitan Museum of Art, New York, Rogers Fund, 1926, 26.54

of modernity exponentially heightened viewers' perception of the themes and ideals encompassed in this symbolically rich painting. In 1862, the year in which Burne-Jones abandoned his first attempt to paint the story, he participated in another international exhibition. Held in South Kensington, this exhibition built on the precedent established by the Crystal Palace in 1851. However, in keeping with the trend that continued throughout the century, the exhibition minimized the themes of moral and national improvement, replacing these goals with more overt celebrations of commercialism, materialism, and exotic eclecticism.[101] The cultural values evinced by the 1862 exhibition can perhaps best be exemplified by one of the most popular displays, a large pyramid of gold meant to represent the mining wealth of Australia, itself an imperial possession (fig. 40). An outraged reviewer deemed the entire exhibition to be "an immense shrine set up to the great god, Mammon."[102] Amid this avaricious excess, Burne-Jones offered his own antidote in the form of a carefully hand-crafted cabinet (fig. 41). Designed by Philip Webb and deco-

42 * Edward Burne-Jones, *Love Among the Ruins*, 1894. Oil on canvas, 95.3 × 160 cm. Wightwick Manor, West Midlands, National Trust Collections, NT 1288953

rated with a scene of backgammon players, the cabinet was placed in the Medieval Court along with other examples of the work of the newly founded firm of Morris, Marshall, Faulkner & Co.[103] In its own way, this unassuming cabinet was a small protest against the age, one that foreshadowed the much more strident opposition asserted by the final incarnation of *King Cophetua and the Beggar Maid* in Paris many years later.

The success of *King Cophetua and the Beggar Maid* at the Universal Exposition of 1889 had major repercussions for Burne-Jones's international reputation.[104] Not only did his fame begin to spread across France, Spain, Germany, and Belgium, but Burne-Jones was also established as an artistic revolutionary. He grew in international public estimation to become an artist of significance, a relevant commentator on the modern condition, experiencing something of a liberation and rebirth across Europe. In a separate discussion of the work of Burne-Jones, Sizeranne made this point plain. Describing *Love Among the Ruins* (fig. 42), he directly confronted the "escapist" perception of the artist:

It is perfectly true that he does not paint dresses from Worth, or furniture from the Stores. He should be congratulated thereupon. But it is an immense error, made by realists in search of modern superficiality, to think that his works suggest fewer contemporary pictures, fewer existing interests, because they are farther apart from our daily life than the illustrations of the Graphic, *and the* Illustrated News. *This is proved by the permanent impression they leave on anyone who has seen them. For myself, I never looked at some of his works without a revival of the anxieties and realities of the passing hour.*[105]

For Sizeranne, *Love Among the Ruins* was not just "a vision of ancient days," but "the very figure of humanitarian and social unreason, of the great unreason of the immediate future, on the gloomy horizon of our struggles, our doubts, and our despairs."[106]

Khnopff again echoed Sizeranne's assessment of Burne-Jones as an artist of international social consequence. According to Khnopff, Burne-Jones taught European artists how to "liberate their sensations and ideas from the hampering weight of material hindrances and bonds." Burne-Jones once again became a somewhat reluctant leader, but this time among a burgeoning group of artists that came to be known as the Symbolists: "The name of Burne-Jones became a watchword, a standard hailed with the enthusiasm of younger men in the new effort for idealism, the most vigorous artistic movement of later days."[107] Burne-Jones welcomed this new appreciation, but he also regarded it with trepidation. When he was awarded the Cross of the Légion d'Honneur in 1889 following the exhibition he expressed his gratitude: "I have not for many a day had such comfort and pleasure, in matters that affect my work, as the sympathy that has been shewn to me in France: I cannot tell you how it has cheered me."[108] Nonetheless, the influx of French visitors to his studio over the following years was somewhat bewildering, prompting a sarcastic Morris to liken the new wave of devotees to the French invasion of England at the Battle of Hastings.[109]

In addition to these visits, Burne-Jones began to correspond with a number of European artists, including the French Symbolist painter Pierre Puvis de Chavannes. Over the next decade, Burne-Jones's paintings and drawings were increasingly requested for European exhibitions, while prints and photographs after his work began to circulate widely. In addition to Khnopff, Burne-Jones became a notable influence on such artists as Gustave Moreau, Odilon Redon, Sâr Péladan, Paul Gauguin, and Pablo Picasso, the last of whom expressed an admiration for Burne-Jones's "white skinned maidens."[110] The spread of his international popularity in the years following the 1889 Parisian Universal Exposition attests to Burne-Jones's lasting influence on modern art, secured, in large part, by the potent and enduring radical impact of *King Cophetua and the Beggar Maid*.

Chapter Three

Myth and Mimesis

THE *PERSEUS* SERIES AS MODERN *PARAGONE*

In *The Baleful Head* (1885–87), the concluding canvas of Burne-Jones's unfinished *Perseus* series (1875–98), Perseus and Andromeda meet in a fecund, walled garden beneath the fruited branches of an apple tree (fig. 43). The right hands of the two lovers intertwine as they intimately bow forward over a reflective basin of water, which reveals the severed head of Medusa held aloft between them. Crowned in writhing snakes, the face of the lethal Gorgon is hauntingly serene in death. The mirrored surface of the water safely reflects Medusa's fatal visage back to Perseus and Andromeda, as well as to the viewer. As the culminating scene of Burne-Jones's planned series, *The Baleful Head* does not depict heroic action, but a quiet and introspective denouement after Perseus has slain Medusa and saved Andromeda, who in turn wishes to look on the forbidden head for herself. This final painting in the cycle expresses the allegorical scope of the ancient legend as illuminated and elaborated by Burne-Jones, revealing themes of love and loss, sacrifice and redemption, death and renewal.

The composition of *The Baleful Head* evokes both Classical and medieval precedents, employing iconography from the fall of Adam and Eve, as well as traditional matrimonial hand-clasping ceremonies.[1] By alluding to original sin and redemptive sacrament at once, Burne-Jones created a vision of paradise that is simultaneously lost and regained in a single, poignant gesture, as the hands of Perseus and Andromeda meet over the reflective water. From this moment of physical as well as spiritual union, an invocation of touch at the spatial and thematic center of the work, the eye is drawn toward the play of reflections, the triangulated gazes that revolve around the upraised and sightless head of Medusa. The

43 * Edward Burne-Jones, *The Baleful Head*, 1885–87. Oil on canvas, 150 × 130 cm.
Staatsgalerie, Stuttgart, Inv. 3110

mythological monster is not depicted here as an object of horror, but as one of aesthetic contemplation, her closed eyes suggesting a state of internal meditation. The Gorgoneion is traditionally interpreted as an apotropaic device, while post-Freudian psychoanalytic theory has posited the snake-haired woman as a displacement of male castration fears.[2] Here, however, Burne-Jones harnesses the potential of Medusa, and by extension the Perseus legend as a whole, as an allegory of mimesis.[3] With her unique ability to turn flesh into stone with a glance, Medusa is a corporeal sculptor capable of freezing a body in time. Perseus, in turn, employs his own mode of image-making to overcome his deadly foe by looking on Medusa through the mediating power of reflection. This mitigation is doubly enacted in *The Baleful Head*, for just as Andromeda may safely gaze on Medusa through the mirroring surface of the fountain, so too is the viewer granted the power to see what must otherwise be concealed through the lens of artistic representation. In other words, the reflective pool at the core of the composition synecdochically conjures the canvas itself, calling attention to the unique capacity for painting to convey a revelatory vision.

Commissioned by Arthur Balfour in 1875 for the music room of his London residence at 4 Carlton Gardens, the *Perseus* series was a significant project for Burne-Jones, intended as a holistic and immersive site-specific work. For reasons that remain unclear, he was never able to bring the series to a satisfactory conclusion, leaving four of the eight paintings unfinished at his death in 1898 and the plan for a complete decorative interior in a prominent St. James's property unrealized. Consequently, the series has struggled to take its place as perhaps the defining work of Burne-Jones's career, one that occupied his mind, labor, and studio for well over twenty years. While *King Cophetua and the Beggar Maid* allowed Burne-Jones to explore the disruptive potential of a single monumental canvas, the multiple-panel format of the *Perseus* series enabled him to exceed the individual boundaries of each painting to create an embodied kinesthetic experience. The series was designed to engage not just the eyes, but also the body in motion, as the viewer physically traverses the space from one painting to the next. Elaborating on the latent themes of vision and transformation in the ancient legend of Perseus, Burne-Jones revived the Renaissance tradition of the *paragone*, harnessing the productive tension between sculpture and painting, the haptic and the optic. With the serial canvas format, he aimed to achieve the type of phenomenological aesthetic encounter he sought in large-scale decorative programs, like mosaic, tapestry, and stained glass, while simultaneously facilitating an interrogation of the medium of painting and the limitations of mimesis.[4]

"Many a day shall I have of heartbreak before it is done": The Origins and Development of the *Perseus* Series

Burne-Jones began the *Perseus* series in 1875, but his interest in the myth can be traced back a decade, to William Morris's adaptation of the legend in his poem "The Doom of King Acrisius." Written in 1865 and published as part of the first volume of *The Earthly Paradise* in 1868, "The Doom of King Acrisius" appears as a story for the month of April in the calendar-year conceit of Morris's narrative cycle. Throughout the development of *The Earthly Paradise*, Morris collaborated with Burne-Jones on a scheme to produce a fully illustrated text. In a sketchbook dated to c. 1865–67, Burne-Jones drafted a list of twenty-eight possible subjects from "The Doom" to be translated into woodblock illustrations for the planned edition, which unfortunately never came to fruition.[5] Although Burne-Jones's interpretation of the *Perseus* legend continued to evolve, it is useful to begin with a detailed discussion of Morris's version of the tale before examining the trajectory of the series commission and its subsequent reception.

In the introduction to her edition of *The Earthly Paradise*, Florence Boos argues for the centrality of the narrative poem not only to Morris's literary development, but also to the emergence of his egalitarian views on art and society. Boos describes the overarching themes of *The Earthly Paradise* as "the nature of time, fate, and failed endeavor," declaring, "at its deepest the poem becomes a sustained meditation on the creation of identity through shared grief, memory, and love."[6] Set in the fourteenth century, *The Earthly Paradise* emulates the structure of Chaucer's *Canterbury Tales* and Boccaccio's *Decameron*, with an outer and inner framing narrative and two sets of alternating tales, drawn from Classical and medieval sources and told by the "Elders" and "Wanderers," respectively. The poem cycle is introduced by a narrator who professes to be an "idle singer of an empty day." This narrator laments his feeling of temporal dislocation: "Dreamer of dreams, born out of my due time, / Why should I strive to set the crooked straight?"[7] The inner framing structure proceeds to echo this feeling of historical displacement and visionary reverie with the exhortation:

Forget six counties overhung with smoke,
Forget the snorting steam and piston stroke,
Forget the spreading of the hideous town;
Think rather of the pack-horse on the down,
And dream of London, small and white and clean,
The clear Thames bordered by its gardens green.[8]

Throughout *The Earthly Paradise*, Morris sought to demonstrate the ability of myths and folktales to convey eternal concepts, forging connections between past and present.

According to Boos, "In *The Earthly Paradise*, Morris's near-mystical beliefs in historical empathy become the deep structure of the *singer*'s great endeavor."[9] Much like *A Dream of John Ball*, the narrative poem functioned as an extended exploration of resonant themes culled from the past as a way to shape the future.

In Morris's retelling, "The Doom of King Acrisius" becomes a heroic quest narrative and *bildungsroman*, exploring the rivaling impulses of seduction and love, exile and belonging, prophecy and free will. He adapted his narrative from several Classical sources, notably Ovid's *Metamorphoses* (8 CE), but also infused the myth with medieval and chivalric motifs, drawing aspects from William Caxton's *The Recuyell of the Historyes of Troy* (1464).[10] Unfolding against a perpetual backdrop of stormy seas and rocky coastlines, the tale begins with King Acrisius, who is told that the future son of his daughter Danaë will one day kill him. To prevent this prophecy from being fulfilled, Acrisius builds a tower to imprison Danaë and preserve her chastity. This aspect of the myth echoes the fairytale of the Briar Rose, with a beautiful young maiden sequestered from the world and awaiting her rescue. Locked within her tower, Danaë is visited by Jove (Zeus) in the form of light, which washes over her in waves of "shining gold." Morris imbues this passage with allusions to the Virgin Mary and the Annunciation. Danaë is described as lying "like an ivory image" amid the rays of golden light. When she awakens, Jove takes the form of "a gold-robed man," who tells her to "have no fear of me, / And have no shame," bringing the news that she will bear a son.[11] Upon learning of his grandson's birth, Acrisius casts Danaë and the infant Perseus adrift on the sea in a casket, where they wash ashore on the island of Seriphos and are rescued by a shepherd, Dictys. Many years later, when Perseus is grown, King Polydectes, ruler of Seriphos, desires the still-beautiful Danaë. Polydectes seeks to remove her from the protection of her son by challenging Perseus to kill the monstrous Medusa. Despairing of the impossibility of this task, Perseus is aided by the goddess Pallas (Athena), who presents him with a sword, a polished shield, a cap that renders him invisible, and the winged sandals of Hermes.

Thus armed, Perseus goes to find the Graiae, the three immortal sisters of the Gorgons who were born blind and share one eye between them.[12] With his winged sandals, Perseus flies to a distant, cold, and gray land, where "the leaden tideless sea" surrounds a palace built of a strange metal. Within, he finds the Graiae, described by Morris as dreadful and wrinkled crones clad in white gowns and blue cloaks who crouch on the dais of a marble hall. The narrator relates a chilling scene:

And as they sat they crooned a dreary song,
Complaining that their lives should last so long,
In that sad place that no one came anear,

In that wan place desert of hope and fear;
And singing, still they rocked their bodies bent,
And ever each to each the eye they sent.[13]

Perseus steals their single eye and refuses to return it until the crones tell him how to find Medusa and their other two sisters. The Graiae at last relent, Perseus returns the eye, and he flies back across the sea to continue his quest.

When Perseus arrives in the land of the Gorgons, he encounters not a fiendish beast but a figure of pity. Medusa conforms to the Victorian type of the fallen woman, dressed in a thin red gown with a jeweled belt gifted by her seducer, Neptune.[14] The snakes that encircle her golden tresses and writhe over her body are a constant torment. Moreover, she laments her exile from the beauty of the natural world, declaring: "O was it not enough to take away / The flowery meadows and the light of day? . . . / To take away sweet sounds and melodies, / The song of birds, the rustle of the trees." When Perseus slays Medusa, it is presented as an act of mercy: "she fell upon the ground, / And felt no more of all her bitter pain."[15] Perseus, made invisible by Pallas's cap, flees the enraged Gorgons, tucking Medusa's head safely away in a wallet.[16] Perseus next encounters a king of giants feasting in his palace, a figure who is identified as Atlas in Ovid's account, but whom Morris leaves unnamed.[17] The giant threatens Perseus, who unveils Medusa's head, transforming him and his fellows into stone.

Perseus continues his flight over the sea, until he catches sight of Andromeda, naked and chained to a rock as a sacrificial offering to a monster that has been terrorizing her city. Perseus slays the creature, a "slimy loathsome coil," with Pallas's sword, freeing Andromeda from her fetters. He then relates his tale to the young woman as they perch beside the water after her rescue. Curious to know the truth of his fantastic quest, she begs Perseus to show her the severed head of Medusa reflected up from the smooth surface of a tide pool, asking, "May I not see this marvel of the lands / So mirrored, and yet live?"[18] In the aftermath of Andromeda's dramatic rescue, this passage emphasizes the importance of vision and reflection as a crucial recurrent theme throughout the myth. When viewed directly, the Gorgoneion retains Medusa's deadly power to freeze any who behold it. However, through the mediating surface of a mirroring pool, Andromeda may cast her gaze unharmed.

Upon learning that Andromeda is the daughter of King Cepheus and Queen Cassiope of Joppa, Perseus asks for Andromeda's hand in marriage. At their wedding feast, however, Andromeda's former betrothed, Phineus, attacks with a group of armed soldiers. Perseus once more wields Medusa's head, turning Phineus and his men to stone. Perseus and Andromeda sail back to Seriphos, where he proclaims Dictys king. The story at last concludes with Perseus fulfilling the prophecy of his birth by accidentally killing his grandfather, King Acrisius, in a stone-throwing contest at Thessaly. Back in the narrative schema of *The Earthly Paradise*, Morris follows "The Doom of King Acrisius" with a return to the "Wanderers," who ponder the significance of the story: "So mused the Wanderers, and awhile might deem / That world might not be quite an empty dream, / But dim foreshadowings of what yet might come."[19] This temporal shift, from a mythic past to a prophetic future, signals to the reader that the tale of Perseus and Danaë contains relevant insights for the Victorian age.

By 1865, Morris and Burne-Jones had begun to envision *The Earthly Paradise* as a collaborative project that would bring together word and image to extend the import of the poem cycle. They embarked on a scheme to produce a fully illustrated edition of Morris's text with woodcuts designed by Burne-Jones.[20] May Morris later wrote that Burne-Jones's illustrations were not after-thoughts, but integral to her father's vision for the narrative poem: "Even while he was writing," she recalled, "he saw the episodes as pictures and noted in his margins hints for the wood cuts that Burne-Jones and he were to make for the beautifying of his poems."[21] Between 1865 and 1869, Burne-Jones created numerous designs for several of the tales, including "The Story of Cupid and Psyche," "Pygmalion and the Image," and "The Hill of Venus." He also sketched out the detailed list of planned illustrations for "The Doom of King Acrisius." Despite their shared dedication to the illustrated edition of *The Earthly Paradise*, the scheme proved impracticable given their resources at the time, and they ultimately abandoned the project. Morris was not able to produce the illustrated texts he envisioned until the founding of the Kelmscott Press in 1890.

Although Burne-Jones did not illustrate an edition of Morris's *The Earthly Paradise*, he modified and developed his designs over time, and they became the foundation for several key works. His illustrations for "The Story of Cupid and Psyche" were adapted into individual paintings as well as a cycle for George Howard's dining room at 1 Palace Green, Kensington, which he began in 1872. The paintings were later completed by Walter Crane in 1881. Similarly, the Pygmalion illustrations were condensed into four canvases and executed as both a small set of oils in 1868–69 and later as a larger set in 1875–78 (see figs 90–93).

When Balfour approached Burne-Jones in 1875 about decorating the drawing room of his London home, the artist quickly suggested the Perseus legend as a suitable subject.[22] Balfour's patronage allowed Burne-Jones to return to the unrealized designs for "The Doom of King Acrisius," and thereby draw out his own resonant themes that built on, but also diverged from, Morris's text. Rendered as an unfolding frieze, Burne-Jones's *Perseus* series retained an emphasis on temporality, fate, sacrifice, and love, while delving more deeply into the latent themes of vision, transformation, and mimesis as a way of exploring the capaciousness of the medium of painting itself.

In assessing the appeal of this commission for Burne-Jones, it is worth considering the prominence of Balfour as a patron, as well as the significance of No. 4, Carlton Gardens, a notable St. James's residence.[23] An idealistic and independently wealthy young man of twenty-six, Balfour was at the outset of his career when he met Burne-Jones. Later dubbed "Bloody Balfour" for his suppression of Irish Home Rule, he went on to serve as a staunchly conservative Tory Prime Minister from 1902 to 1905, diverging drastically from Burne-Jones's own radical political views. At the time, however, Balfour was a leading figure in the elite, artistically minded social circle known as "the Souls," whom Burne-Jones described as "very delightful and amiable and so young that it is painful."[24] He was entranced on his introduction to Burne-Jones, writing in his autobiography, "I at once fell a prey both to the man and his art."[25] Balfour proved an amenable and patient patron, granting the artist free rein in selecting not only the subject of the series to adorn his drawing room, but also its scale.[26] The artist quickly expanded the conception of the project from a series of canvases to a holistic and enveloping aesthetic environment of interconnected paintings and decorative reliefs. Although Burne-Jones expressed his displeasure with the "pompous Neo-classicism" of the architecture of Carlton Gardens, he nonetheless embraced the opportunity to, as he stated, "clear a little space as a sort of testimony," by redesigning the drawing room as an expansive decorative cycle.[27]

Located in the heart of London's political district, Carlton Gardens represented a distinguished setting for Burne-Jones's *Perseus* series. Part of a prestigious development initially designed by John Nash, the street is close to the Houses of Parliament, Whitehall, Buckingham Palace, and St. James's Palace. Carlton Gardens and neighboring Carlton House Terrace have been home to leading figures of the British government and aristocracy from the nineteenth century to today.[28] Before Balfour purchased the property, it had been home to the two-term Prime Minister, Henry Palmerston, from 1847 to 1855. Later, George Curzon lodged there in 1898, just before his appointment as Viceroy of India. It was Balfour's primary residence from 1874 to 1929, except for his time at 10 Downing Street from 1898 to 1905. The *Perseus* series was, therefore, designed not only for an influential young patron, but also approximated the kind of site-specific municipal commission that Burne-Jones eagerly sought, despite being sequestered in a private, aristocratic home. Intended as an enveloping artistic vision that entirely altered Balfour's drawing room, the series had the potential to enact Frederic Jameson's definition of a radical utopian space. As Jameson argues in *Archaeologies of the Future* (2005), utopian visions achieve their power in opposition to the everyday, operating as "an imaginary enclave within real social space."[29] Nestled within the residential quarter of London's privileged political class,

44 * "The Dining-Room of Mr. Balfour's Official Residence (No. 10, Downing Street)," *The Sphere* 8, no. 104 (January 18, 1902), p. 74

the *Perseus* series would have served as a moment of disruption, physically and imaginatively transporting the viewer to Burne-Jones's aesthetic realm of myth and mimesis.

Although this vision was never fully realized, it is notable that several panels from the unfinished cycle were ultimately displayed in the dining room of 10 Downing Street, briefly placing Burne-Jones's work at the center of British governance. In 1902, a photograph of the room was published in both *The Sketch* and *The Sphere* (fig. 44).[30] The version of *Perseus and the Graiae* in gilded gesso on wood is hung prominently over the banqueting table, while the oil on canvas version of *Perseus and the Sea Nymphs* appears to the right. Although a posthumous substitute for Burne-Jones's original vision, the series nonetheless hung as a conspicuous backdrop to Balfour's dinners with leading British politicians and international heads of state at the outset of the twentieth century.

In his initial proposal to Balfour, Burne-Jones envisioned the series as a cycle of ten panels forming a continuous frieze that merged seamlessly with the architectural fabric of the drawing room through a gilded plaster border of acanthus leaves, to be contributed by Morris.[31] This first conceptual stage of the project is preserved in a set of cartoons (figs. 45–7) that trace the quest narrative of Perseus: *The Call of Perseus, Perseus and the Graiae, Perseus and the Nereids, The Finding of Medusa, The Death of Medusa (The Birth of Pegasus and*

45 * Edward Burne-Jones, *The Call of Perseus*, *Perseus and the Graiae*, and *Perseus and the Nereids*, 1875–76. Gouache, gold paint, and ink on paper, 36.7 × 102.7 cm. Tate, London, N03456

46 * Edward Burne-Jones, *The Finding of Medusa*, *The Death of Medusa (The Birth of Pegasus and Chrysaor)*, and *Perseus Pursued by the Gorgons*, 1875–76. Gouache, gold paint, and ink on paper, 36.8 × 128.4 cm. Tate, London, N0345-7

47 ∗ Edward Burne-Jones, *Atlas Turned to Stone, The Rock of Doom and the Doom Fulfilled, The Court of Phineas,* and *The Baleful Head*, 1875–76. Gouache, gold paint, and ink on paper, 36.7 × 148.7 cm. Tate, London, N03458

Chrysaor), Perseus Pursued by the Gorgons, Atlas Turned to Stone, The Rock of Doom and the Doom Fulfilled, The Court of Phineas, and *The Baleful Head*. It is evident that Burne-Jones was already shifting away from Morris's "The Doom of King Acrisius" in this early rendering. He included two further episodes from the legend, as well as altering key details. In the first panel, Athena gives Perseus a sword and a mirror, rather than a shield. It is not until the third panel that Perseus is presented with the winged sandals of Hermes, a pouch (or *kibisis*) capable of containing the head of Medusa, and a helmet belonging to Hades that renders the wearer invisible, all given to him by three Nymphs, or Naiads.[32] Burne-Jones also planned to depict the birth of Pegasus and Chrysaor, children of Neptune, who emerge from the body of Medusa at the time of her death.[33] Finally, he replaced Morris's description of the king of the giants feasting in his hall with a depiction of Atlas Telamon holding up the heavens. In this legend, Zeus punishes Atlas for his role in the Titanomachy by forcing him to support the sky.[34]

In his preliminary concept for the series, Burne-Jones confronted the boundaries between decorative art and painting in several key ways. Beyond the ten panels knitted together with the engaged frame of acanthus leaves in gilded gesso, he also recommended

extensive changes to the existing fabric of Balfour's drawing room, including wood paneling and stained-glass windows.[35] He urged Balfour, "The whole room should be in harmony and the whole should look as if nothing was an afterthought but all had naturally grown together."[36] Further blurring the lines between painting, sculpture, and decorative art, Burne-Jones designed four of the ten scenes to be executed not as oils on canvas but as bas-relief panels in gilded gesso on wood. Three of these panels were intended for placement above two doorways and a fireplace, as indicated in the initial cartoon. These relief panels suggest historical precedents familiar to Burne-Jones, alluding in part to the Parthenon sculptures on display at the British Museum, as well as the use of raised elements in Mantegna's *Triumphs of Caesar* (c. 1484–92) at Hampton Court Palace.[37] However, as part of an integrated decorative scheme in the nineteenth century, they were also highly experimental and innovative.

In 1876, *The Academy* published a note on the planned *Perseus* series that highlighted the novelty and importance of the bas-relief gesso panels, as well as the ornamental qualities of the commission overall. The anonymous author of this account described the projected enlivening effect on the viewer of the transition from the decorative border to the bas-relief panels to the paintings, with each medium interacting with and enriching the other:

These panels, besides their service in completing the relation of the legend, have an important function in bringing the larger paintings into harmony with the decorative woodwork that surrounds and frames both panel and picture. For in the treatment of these subordinate subjects the painter has not attempted complete realisation, but has worked out the design, upon the oaken panel for background, with a system of colouring that is partly conventional and determined by the requirements of decorative effect. Thus, without any sense of abrupt transition, the eye passes on from the rich framework of purely ornamental design, executed in the tones of the woodwork, to the series of panels where invention and expression are still under control, and thence to the larger paintings, where the imagination is permitted to be free and the colouring to be strong and vivid.[38]

As I will explore later in this chapter, only *Perseus and the Graiae* was executed in gesso, in 1877 (see fig. 66). However, this one panel conveys an approximate sense of the overall effect as originally conceived. The panel features four figures in raised and gilded gesso silhouetted against a gold-brushed wooden ground. The flickering lights of the fireplace and lamps in Balfour's drawing room would have heightened the animated appearance of these dynamically posed figures. Undulating lines and glittering, sumptuous surface texture would prompt haptic engagement, conjuring the memory of touch as the eye moved from smooth armored plate to interlocking chainmail to striated drapery, all in the guise of a subject exploring the theft of sight.

Such a use of bas relief is in keeping with the Renaissance concept of *rilievo*, or the dynamic effect of light and shadow produced through the interplay of raised surface and flat ground. Walter Pater, in particular, seized on the significance of *rilievo* in his discussion of the Renaissance *paragone* in the work and writings of Leonardo and Michelangelo. For Pater, low relief was capable of overcoming the "special limitation of sculpture," creating an illusion of movement through its mutability and light-catching surface texture, what he termed "those last refinements of shadow."[39] Indicative of his own engagement with *rilievo*, Burne-Jones not only chose to integrate bas relief into his monumental *Perseus* series, but also selected four significant moments of material transformation and haptic knowledge from the legend as the subjects for the gesso panels: Perseus's encounter with the three Graiae; the emergence of Pegasus and Chrysaor from the fallen body of Medusa; the turning of Atlas to stone; and the defeat of Phineus and his men. Together, these four episodes illuminate Burne-Jones's particular interpretation of the Perseus myth, highlighting tactility, mutability, and sensorial allure.

Arrayed across Balfour's drawing room, the series as initially designed would have prompted both a kinesthetic and haptic response from the viewer. As an immersive, site-specific environment, the complete decorative program would have drawn the viewer across the space, guided by the enveloping acanthus border to follow Perseus's quest from one episode to the next in a physical as well as visual progression. Moreover, each of these episodes would have conjured the memory of touch through iconographical invocations of the sculptural integrated with actual passages of raised and gilded gesso surfaces. When Burne-Jones ultimately chose to abandon the wooden panels as well as the gesso border, rendering the entire series as a set of paintings, he nonetheless retained the emphasis on *rilievo*, sculptural form, and haptic engagement suggested by the bas-relief experiments in gesso. Through subject, composition, and brushwork, the *Perseus* series repeatedly evokes the textures of raised stone and chased metal, the shadowed and dimensional rhythms of architectural ornament, and the calligraphic legibility of a monumental sculptural frieze.

The development of Burne-Jones's *Perseus* series over the next two decades was marked by periods of intense work and intermittent pauses. As his studio record reveals, Burne-Jones moved from one Perseus subject to another and back again, sometimes with gaps of several years in between as other projects occupied his time. Returning to the Medusa episodes in 1890 after completing his *Briar Rose* series, he wrote, "And now I am working at Perseus for the patient and kind Arthur Balfour. Medusa is to be very fine and costs me much trouble... many a day shall I have of heartbreak before it is done."[40] The sporadic quality of Burne-Jones's labor on the series, rather than suggesting a trivial status for the works in his larger oeuvre, highlights its role as a constant touchstone in his practice. The series was a magnum opus to which he frequently returned, but which he could never quite resolve. Between 1876 and 1885, he created a complete set of ten large gouache studies, which he displayed in his garden studio until his death (figs. 48–57).[41] In this iteration, he eliminated *The Court of Phineas* and divided the scene of Perseus's discovery of Andromeda and slaying of the monster into two separate panels.[42] He also added a Latin inscription in golden letters against a blue background above the scene of *Perseus and the Graiae*. Written by the scholar Richard Claverhouse Jebb, this text summarizes the key episodes of the legend.[43] The decision to pair this précis of the myth with the Graiae episode, the second panel in the series, suggests its thematic importance to the series overall. This set was subsequently purchased by Alexander Henderson, Lord Faringdon, who also owned Burne-Jones's *Briar Rose* series. Today, the set remains intact and on display in a dedicated space at the Southampton City Art Gallery.

By 1887, Burne-Jones had pared down the series to eight paintings, removing two of the subjects originally designed as gesso panels, *The Birth of Pegasus and Chrysaor* and *Atlas Turned to Stone*, and eliminating the text inscription from *Perseus and the Graiae*. The final incarnation of the series, an amalgamation of finished and unfinished oil paintings and full-scale gouache cartoons, was given to Balfour after Burne-Jones's death in 1898 and is now in the Staatsgalerie, Stuttgart. Thus constituted, the ultimate version of the series

TOP ROW ∗ 48 ∗ Edward Burne-Jones, *The Call of Perseus*, 1876–85. Gouache on paper laid on linen canvas, 152.5 × 127 cm. Southampton City Art Gallery, Inv. No 100

49 ∗ Edward Burne-Jones, *Perseus and the Graiae*, 1876–85. Gouache on paper laid on linen canvas, 152.5 × 170.5 cm. Southampton City Art Gallery, Inv. No. 101

50 ∗ Edward Burne-Jones, *Perseus and the Sea Nymphs*, 1876–85. Gouache on paper laid on linen canvas, 152.8 × 126.4 cm. Southampton City Art Gallery, Inv. No. 102

51 ∗ Edward Burne-Jones, *The Finding of Medusa*, 1876–85. Gouache on paper laid on linen canvas, 152.5 × 137.7 cm. Southampton City Art Gallery, Inv. No. 103

BOTTOM ROW ∗ 52 ∗ Edward Burne-Jones, *The Death of Medusa I*, 1876–85. Gouache on paper laid on linen canvas, 124.5 × 116.9 cm. Southampton City Art Gallery, Inv. No. 109

53 ∗ Edward Burne-Jones, *The Death of Medusa II*, 1876–85. Gouache on paper laid on linen canvas, 152.5 × 136.5 cm. Southampton City Art Gallery, Inv. No. 104

54 ∗ Edward Burne-Jones, *Atlas Turned to Stone*, 1876–85. Gouache on paper laid on linen canvas, 152.5 × 190 cm. Southampton City Art Gallery, Inv. No. 105

55 * Edward Burne-Jones, *The Rock of Doom*, 1876–85. Gouache on paper laid on linen canvas, 154 × 128.6 cm. Southampton City Art Gallery, Inv. No. 107

56 * Edward Burne-Jones, *The Doom Fulfilled*, 1876–85. Gouache on paper laid on linen canvas, 153.8 × 138.4 cm. Southampton City Art Gallery, Inv. No. 106

57 * Edward Burne-Jones, *The Baleful Head*, 1876–85. Gouache on paper laid on linen canvas, 153.7 × 129 cm. Southampton City Art Gallery, Inv. No. 108

58 ∗ Edward Burne-Jones, *The Call of Perseus*, 1877. Oil on canvas, 152.5 × 127 cm.
Staatsgalerie, Stuttgart, Inv. 3103

59 * Edward Burne-Jones, *Perseus and the Graiae*, 1892. Oil on canvas, 153.5 × 170 cm. Staatsgalerie, Stuttgart, Inv. 3105

60 ∗ Edward Burne-Jones, *Perseus and the Sea Nymphs*, 1877. Oil on canvas, 153 × 127 cm.
Staatsgalerie, Stuttgart, Inv. 3104

61 * Edward Burne-Jones, *The Finding of Medusa*, c. 1876–90. Chalk and gouache on paper, 152 × 137 cm. Staatsgalerie, Stuttgart, Inv. 3106

62 * Edward Burne-Jones, *The Death of Medusa*, c. 1876–90. Chalk and gouache on paper, 152 × 137 cm. Staatsgalerie, Stuttgart, Inv. 3107

63 * Edward Burne-Jones, *The Rock of Doom*, 1884–88. Oil on canvas, 155 × 130 cm.
Staatsgalerie, Stuttgart, Inv. 3108

64 ∗ Edward Burne-Jones, *The Doom Fulfilled*, 1888. Oil on canvas, 155 × 140.5 cm.
Staatsgalerie, Stuttgart, Inv. 3109

65 * Edward Burne-Jones, *Perseus and Andromeda*, 1876. Oil on canvas, 152.2 × 229 cm. Art Gallery of South Australia, Adelaide, Elder Bequest Fund 1902, 0.329

includes four finished oil paintings: *Perseus and the Graiae*, 1892 (fig. 59), *The Rock of Doom*, 1884–88 (fig. 63), *The Doom Fulfilled*, 1888 (fig. 64), and *The Baleful Head* (see fig. 43). It also includes two unfinished oil paintings: *The Call of Perseus* (fig. 58) and *Perseus and the Sea Nymphs* (fig. 60), both begun in 1877. The least resolved episodes are the two of Medusa, which are rendered in chalk and gouache on paper: *The Finding of Medusa* (fig. 61) and *The Death of Medusa* (fig. 62), both c. 1876–90.[44] In addition to the two primary "sets" and numerous preparatory studies, there are two alternate oil paintings: a version of *Perseus and Andromeda* created and left unfinished in 1876 (fig. 65), which depicts both episodes occurring synchronously on the same canvas, and a small version of *Perseus and the Graiae*, exhibited at the Grosvenor Gallery in 1882 and now in a private collection. Apart from the main panels of the series, Burne-Jones also created three versions of *Danaë and the Brazen Tower* in 1872 (see fig. 98), 1876, and 1887–88, representing a prelude to Perseus's quest.

Unwieldy, unconventional, and left forever incomplete by the artist's early death at sixty-four, Burne-Jones's *Perseus* series refuses to conform to expectations, or yield a single unitary interpretation. Given the complexities of the series, from its unfinished state to its multipart composition, scholars have often struggled to grapple with the complete cycle as a holistic work.[45] Since the 1980s, the dominant strain of critical inquiry has framed the series as an allegory of masculine sexual frustration and gender anxieties in the Victorian era. The paired canvases depicting the rescue of Andromeda, *The Rock of Doom* and *The Doom Fulfilled*, have received the majority of attention from this perspective, prompting accusations that Burne-Jones was indulging in sadomasochistic fantasies of desire and penetration.[46] The locus of this psychosexual tension is most overtly perceived in the suggestive contrast between Perseus's tightly armored body and Andromeda's dually exposed flesh, her sinuous form revealed from both front and back simultaneously, and further reinforced through the irresistibly phallic implications of the serpentine creature that thrusts its way across the canvas. That monster, moreover, echoes the coiled tangle of snakes that encircle the head of Medusa, whose presence is thereby invoked despite being hidden from view.[47]

This interpretive emphasis on male heteronormative sexual anxieties in the *Perseus* series is heavily indebted to Sigmund Freud's "Medusa's Head" (written 1922, published 1940), which explicates the function of the Medusa myth as an allegorical expression of masculine castration fears:

> *The sight of Medusa's head makes the spectator stiff with terror, turns him to stone. Observe that we have here once again the same origin from the castration complex and the same transformation of affect! For becoming stiff means an erection. Thus in the original situation it offers consolation to the spectator: he is still in possession of a penis, and the stiffening reassures him of the fact.*[48]

Freud's elucidation of the apotropaic power of the Medusa head as conjuring both the fear of castration and its mitigation became so pervasive in the twentieth century that it is now nearly impossible to discuss the Perseus myth and Gorgoneion imagery except via a psychoanalytic lens. While such an approach has significant potential, especially for illuminating the construction of gender roles and the negotiation of sexual desire in the Victorian era, it is also highly reductive and privileges the male, heteronormative gaze. By advancing a single narrative, these arguments ignore the visual and aesthetic specificity of Burne-Jones's *Perseus* series and occlude other equally compelling and insightful lines of inquiry.

More recently, however, Fabian Fröhlich and Caroline Arscott have introduced new approaches to the series while attempting to take the whole scope of the cycle into account. In 2009, Fröhlich contributed a substantial essay on the series to *Edward Burne-Jones: The Earthly Paradise*, the catalogue accompanying the exhibition at the Staatsgalerie, Stuttgart. Although it is not the central focus of his essay, Fröhlich illuminates key moments of aesthetic self-reflexivity throughout his discussion, suggesting the recurrent theme of the process of mimesis within Burne-Jones's series, the tension between sculpture and the corporeal body, and the repeated meditation on painting as an act of representation.[49] Similarly, Arscott adopts a corporeal interpretation of the series that emphasizes "the armoured body" of Perseus as a site for the "interface of flesh and metal." This Perseus is akin to a cyborg, as his amalgamated, fused, and articulated armor renders his figure into a hyper-masculine "machine-body."[50] Arscott also notes the undercurrent of aesthetic self-reflexivity that permeates the cycle as a whole. Much like Fröhlich, she intersperses observations on the role of craft, mimesis, and visuality throughout her analysis.[51] Her corporeal paradigm foregrounds embodied sensation as a central principle driving the series. In dialogue with this work, it is my contention that Burne-Jones not only drew on the well-established trope of Medusa and the Gorgoneion as evocative of visuality and representation in the series, but also seized on the opportunity offered by the tale to engage with questions of aesthetic contemplation, reflectivity, and artistic practice in the age of modernity.

"Ever each to each the eye they sent": Sight, Touch, and the Sculptural Fragment

In 1878, Burne-Jones debuted the boundary-defying bas-relief panel *Perseus and the Graiae* at the second annual exhibition of the Grosvenor Gallery (fig. 66).[52] Although it was to function chronologically and spatially as the second scene in the series, this gilded gesso panel was the first work to be completed and displayed before the public. Measuring a striking 5 × 5½ feet and inscribed with a Latin précis of the legend in raised gold letters, *Perseus and the Graiae* resisted categorization with its unusual blend of word and image, painting and sculpture, the decorative and the monumental. By exhibiting this panel first, and by embedding the text of the legend in summary form over half the pictorial plane, Burne-Jones was asserting the centrality of the lesser-known sisters to his interpretation of the Perseus legend, as well as declaring his experimental approach to the medium. *Perseus and the Graiae* boldly proclaimed that the crux of Burne-Jones's approach to the series resided not in Medusa's deadly gaze but in the Graiae's blindness. The artist thereby, crucially, accentuated that which is heightened by the absence of sight: the sense of touch.[53] Burne-Jones challenges the viewer not simply to look at the scene before them, but also to engage with it as an embodied, corporeal encounter. Accentuating the haptic possibilities of the sculptural, *Perseus and the Graiae* meditates on the tension between visual and tactile knowledge. Just as Perseus steals the eye of the Graiae to discover the knowledge he needs to overcome Medusa, Burne-Jones metaphorically steals the eye of the viewer, embarking on a perceptual journey to train the senses to experience the world anew.

With a rich mixture of textural qualities, from the visible grain of the panel to the metallic brilliance of the raised and gilded gesso, *Perseus and the Graiae* encourages the viewer to luxuriate in visual pleasure, all while depicting the theft of sight. This bas-relief incarnation of the scene is simultaneously a work about the deprivation of the senses and the heightening of embodied material experience. With heads bowed and eyes closed, the three sisters crouch beside each other across the bottom third of the picture plane, perched atop a rocky landscape subtly suggested with spare, charcoal-like brushstrokes. The undulating lines of their draped garments are rendered in a warm rose gold. In contrast to these rippling folds, the hands and heads of the figures are painted in monochromatic tones directly onto the wood, with the exception of the golden streaks that flicker across their wind-blown hair. The grisaille of the hands and faces seems to sink into the background, allowing their glimmering, sculpted bodies to command the viewer's attention. Mere inches apart, the Graiae are suspended in a moment of eternal isolation, their swaying, dance-like motion perpetually frozen. Here, Burne-Jones echoes the description of the sisters in Morris's "The Doom of King Acrisius": "And singing, still they rocked their bodies bent, / And ever each to each the eye they sent."[54] Departing from Morris's text, however, Burne-Jones's sisters are not ghastly crones but graceful maidens with lithe outstretched limbs. The blinded sisters extend their hands, prominently arranged across the panel, in unmistakable gestures of sensorial searching, groping through the darkness for the reassurance of a tactile connection with another body they will seemingly never find.[55]

Perseus arcs balletically above the Graiae, tightly clad in metallic armored plates and intricately realized loops of chainmail executed in a cold, silver tone that contrasts with the roseate robes of the women. Unlike the sightless sisters below him, Perseus's eyes are open and his body bends forward with purpose. Balancing his torqued form with one hand clutching his thigh, he stretches his other hand forward in order to hold out, between forefinger and thumb, a single raised pearl, picked out in yellow gold and surrounded by delicate rays of light (fig. 67). The golden hue of the purloined eye matches the raised letters of the Latin inscription above. Evoking ancient monumental sculptural friezes, *Perseus and the Graiae* dazzles the eye and beckons the hand, encouraging the viewer to interrogate the liminal boundary between the optical effects of two-dimensional painted surface and the haptic quality of three-dimensional bas relief.

It seems that the rebellious Burne-Jones was overtly challenging the liberal policies of the Grosvenor Gallery, which allowed each artist to determine the works they submitted for display. By selecting the experimental and, for some, baffling *Perseus and the Graiae* at what was only the second annual exhibition, Burne-Jones exposed the limits of artistic autonomy by defying the hierarchical divisions between painting, sculpture, and the decorative arts at this avant-garde institution. Despite its location in the marginal space of the

66 * Edward Burne-Jones, *Perseus and the Graiae*, 1877. Silver and gold leaf, gesso and oil on oak, 170.2 × 153.2 cm. Amgueddfa Cymru – National Museum Wales, Cardiff, NMW A 29299

FACING PAGE * 67 * Edward Burne-Jones, *Perseus and the Graiae* (detail of fig. 66)

vestibule, or perhaps because of this, *Perseus and the Graiae* became the sensation of the spring 1878 season. According to one popular journal, the work was a *de rigueur* topic of conversation among the fashionable set: "The neglected Graiae find themselves suddenly famous, and public copies of the meritorious Classical Dictionary of Dr. Smith open nat-

urally at the letter G."[56] Critical response ranged from the laudatory to the derogatory to the merely bemused. A reviewer for *British Architect* praised its "wonderful weird power," while suggesting that Burne-Jones could have furthered the decorative effect by using other precious materials for the heads and hands, such as ivory or mother of pearl.[57] By contrast, a writer for *The Magazine of Art* dismissed *Perseus and the Graiae* as "a barbarism which shocks the eyes."[58] Another reviewer declared the panel an esoteric experiment in a "primitive style" that was quite simply "odder than anything else which [Burne-Jones] has ever done."[59] The critic L. S. Cook was more entranced with the spectacle of the shocked visitors to the Grosvenor as they mused over this uncanny panel: "The astonishment and puzzle of the spectators at this extraordinary work of art of Mr. Burne-Jones's is a sight not to be speedily forgotten."[60] *Perseus and the Graiae* perplexed even William Michael Rossetti, who wrote, "The effect, close to the eye, is cold, shiny, and crinkled: no doubt, however, it is not quite fair or reasonable to estimate the effect until the series shall be placed *in situ* – whatever its destined position may be, for this is not explained in the catalogue."[61]

Rossetti's commentary also suggests that, although Burne-Jones may have been eager to share his new work in progress, *Perseus and the Graiae* suffered when divorced from its function as part of a series in a dedicated space with an enveloping decorative framework.

The recurrent theme across these initial reviews was a shared confusion over the derivation of the unusual mixed-media composition, as well as the exact materials employed. A majority of critics described *Perseus and the Graiae* as a bas relief consisting of plates of chased metal affixed to the wooden support, rather than gilded and painted gesso, fostering the illusion that the panel was a collage-like assemblage.[62] This mistaken identification of the medium further contributed to the conflicting accounts of the possible sources of inspiration for this combination of painting and relief. One reviewer likened *Perseus and the Graiae* to "early Japanese art," while another suggested "a strange Chinese picture... with little conventional figures standing out in relief from the ground," and a third alluded to the use of "real precious stones in the medieval pictures of Madonnas and saints."[63] Indeed, the unsettling impact of *Perseus and the Graiae*'s appearance at the Grosvenor may have been an intrinsic part of the conceptualization of the series, signaling the bold quality of the experimental gesso panel. The range of responses signals not a failure but, rather, the work's radical, subversive quality and Burne-Jones's willingness to confound the expectations of his audience.

As a rarely depicted subject in the visual arts, *Perseus and the Graiae* presented Burne-Jones with an opportunity to declare his unique approach through compositional and iconographic innovation. Unlike the more familiar episodes of the legend, such as the slaying of Medusa or the rescue of Andromeda, Perseus's encounter with the Graiae remains a relatively obscure chapter of the story. As the reviews of the Grosvenor Gallery exhibition attested, visitors were perplexed not just by the medium of the panel, but also by the subject matter. According to Daniel Ogden's survey (2008) of the Perseus myth, descriptions of the Graiae can be found in fifth-century BCE Greek accounts, when the legend "reached its canonical form." In *Prometheus Bound*, attributed to Aeschylus, the Graiae are described as "long-lived girls, three, swan-shaped, with a common eye and a single tooth." The Graiae, like the Gorgons, were daughters of Phorcys and Ceto, and featured as one of several groupings of three women frequently linked to the Perseus legend, including the Nymphs (or Naiads) and the Hesperides. Surviving portrayals from antiquity are scarce; Ogden notes that there are "no more than six, all on vases made between ca. 460 BCE and the Hellenistic period. We find no swans here, just disappointingly ordinary women, their blindness vestigially indicated by closed eyes."[64] Although Burne-Jones sought out ancient pictorial precedents for the *Perseus* series, especially from Greek vase paintings in the British Museum, it is unlikely that he encountered any of these little-known examples.[65]

Absent existing visual models for the three Graiae, Burne-Jones may have drawn on other resonant configurations of three supernatural women for inspiration. As a mythic trope, the Graiae could be likened to the three Fates, or Moirai, as well as the three Norns of Norse tradition, thus broadening the range of possible visual allusions.[66] Exploring Burne-Jones's use of Classical precedents, Fröhlich suggests, "As guardians of ancient wisdom, he sees [the Graiae] as belonging in the same tradition as the Parthenon goddesses in the British Museum."[67] The marble sculptures from the Parthenon were a vital touchstone for Burne-Jones's working practice from the 1860s and throughout his career, as they were for many nineteenth-century British artists.[68] In *Perseus and the Graiae*, Burne-Jones evokes the three female sculptures from the East Pediment of the Parthenon, designated by the British Museum as Figures K, L, and M (fig. 68). Designed by the Greek sculptor Pheidias in the fifth century BCE, these three figures are now often commonly identified as the goddesses Hestia, Dione, and Aphrodite. However, through the early twentieth century, they were commonly referred to as the "Three Fates."[69]

In addition to the typological allusion to the Fates, modeling the Graiae after the Parthenon sculptures would have forged a connection between Burne-Jones's experimental bas relief and the revival of interest in the Pheidian tradition of ancient monumental chryselephantine sculpture. G. F. Watts, in particular, was a vocal advocate for Pheidias as

68 * Pheidias, figures of three goddesses (K, L, and M), from the East Pediment of the Parthenon, 438–32 BCE. Marble, 123 × 233 cm. British Museum, London, 1816,0610.97

an exemplar for the possibilities of modern sculpture. Watts praised the power of ancient sculptural polychromy, with precious materials like gold leaf and ivory in chryselephantine cult statues, to achieve a sense of awe in the viewer.[70] Although Pheidias's monumental *Athena Parthenos* was destroyed, Watts found the rough, striated, and broken drapery of the marble "Three Fates" to be suggestive of the grace, as well as the color, of the lost colossal sculpture: "In the best sculpture," he wrote, "you feel the palpitations of colour, the elements of a picture; you unconsciously see it painted!"[71] In keeping with Watts's conception of the Pheidian ideal, Burne-Jones's experimental engagement with color, texture, and decorative materiality in *Perseus and the Graiae* may also invoke the ancient tradition of chryselephantine sculpture, and sculptural polychromy more broadly, with the capacity to spark wonder and promote affective engagement on the part of the viewer.

Although Burne-Jones ultimately discarded the concept of interspersed decorative panels in the *Perseus* series, completing only *Perseus and the Graiae* in gilded gesso on wood, he experimented further with decorative polychromy and sculptural relief over the next decade. Having once praised tapestry as deliciously "halfway between painting and ornament," the artist seems to have felt similarly about the unique qualities of bas relief in gesso.[72] Indeed, Burne-Jones expressed a particular affinity for the sculptural medium, declaring, "If ever my eyes grow dim . . . I will give up painting and take to sculpture." He went on to stress the durability of sculpture, a belief he also expressed about mosaic, arguing that "It is the fate of all pictures and books to be burnt, it is only a matter of time: but sculpture has a chance of living in some form or other."[73] This emphasis on the resilience of sculpture was consistent with Burne-Jones's desire to create work that would endure through the cyclical rise and fall of civilizations.

In the last year of Burne-Jones's life, Thomas M. Rooke recorded the artist's lament on the reluctance of the public to commission or even appreciate works in the medium, saying, "It's a delightful thing, but people won't come to me for [such work]. They expect painting of me and don't want gesso."[74] Consequently, Burne-Jones's works in gesso were largely created as personal gifts, and often with the assistance of other specialists in the medium, including Kate Faulkner, Matthew Webb, and Osmund Weeks, who may have contributed to the creation of *Perseus and the Graiae*.[75] Notable examples of Burne-Jones's other work in gilded and painted gesso include his memorial tablet for Laura Lyttelton (fig. 69), a cassone featuring *The Garden of the Hesperides* (1888; Birmingham Museums and Art Gallery), and *Cupid's Hunting Fields* (fig. 70), which bears strong compositional similarities to *The Death of Medusa*.[76] Between 1880 and 1886, Burne-Jones also collaborated with the sculptor Edgar Boehm on *The Battle of Flodden Field*, a large-scale panel in painted *gesso duro* created for the library of George Howard's Naworth Castle. These experiments demonstrate Burne-Jones's contributions to the revival of sculptural polychromy and the

69 ∗ Edward Burne-Jones, *A Peacock* (memorial tablet for Laura Lyttelton), 1886. Oil and gilt gesso on wood, 237.5 × 133 × 20 cm. Victoria and Albert Museum, London, P.85-1938

70 ∗ Edward Burne-Jones, *Cupid's Hunting Fields*, 1880. Oil and gold paint on gesso relief on mahogany panel, 99.7 × 76.5 cm. Delaware Art Museum, Wilmington, purchased in memory of Betty Bancroft, 1977-330

emergence of the New Sculpture movement in the later nineteenth century, inspiring the work of artists such as Alfred Gilbert, George Frampton, and Edward Onslow Ford.[77]

When Burne-Jones eventually discarded the plan for interspersed bas-relief panels in the *Perseus* series, he exchanged a literal three-dimensionality of surface for the bolder invocation of haptic sensation through paint alone. In the final oil on canvas version of *Perseus and the Graiae* (see fig. 59), he deepened his exploration of the quality and materials of painting in dialogue with sculpture, in keeping with the Renaissance *paragone*.[78] Set in a bleak and desolate landscape, shrouded with mist and suffused with a stygian darkness, the three Graiae adopt the same crouched poses as in the bas relief.[79] Now, however, they are perched precariously at the edge of a rocky precipice, encircled by a forbidding terrain of barren, windswept mountains that fill the space formerly occupied by the Latin text. Through the vaporous atmosphere, the Graiae stretch out their evocative hands, arrayed across the canvas like musical notes, summoning the desire for a tactile connection. While the raised and gilded gesso of the panel formed a dimensional contrast between the exposed flesh of the figures and their metallic garments, here the same effect is achieved through tonal variation. The warm golden hue of the sisters' skin captures the eye against the receding cool blue of the rocky topography, drapery, and armor. No longer built up in sculptural relief, the painted surface of the canvas itself becomes a study in textural contrasts. Burne-Jones rendered the hazy, mountainous landscape in thinned paintstrokes and subtle, smoky tints that rival Whistler's most ethereal nocturnes.[80] By contrast, the Graiae's drapery is composed of thickly built-up, gestural brushstrokes in chalky lead white against a dark ground that mimic the striated curves of sculpted marble, particularly reminiscent of the broken lines of Pheidias's "Three Fates." Burne-Jones also devoted careful attention to the rendering of sculptural materials throughout the scene: the slick, obdurate opacity of the rock; the cold, smooth burnish of Perseus's metal armor; and even the alabaster luminosity of the flesh of the figures.

In its oil form, Burne-Jones's *Perseus and the Graiae* invokes another key pictorial precedent, Leonardo da Vinci's *The Virgin of the Rocks* (fig. 71).[81] The sense of foggy atmosphere, the rocky enclosed landscape, the cool color palette, and even the figural arrangement all suggest an affinity with Leonardo's oil-on-panel altarpiece. In particular, the play of hand gestures across Burne-Jones's panel resembles the compositional dynamics of Leonardo's painting, guiding the eye from figure to figure, while foregrounding the dialectic between touch and sight. Indeed, a surviving study of hands for the *Perseus and the Graiae* attests to Burne-Jones's attentive treatment of this element of the painting (fig. 72). In the final version, the Graia to the far left of Burne-Jones's painting presents an almost perfect mirror image of Leonardo's Virgin, both with heads tilted down and eyelids lowered, their right and left hands an exact inverse of the other figure. Indeed, Burne-Jones widened the gap between forefinger and thumb for the Graia's left hand in the translation of the composition from bas relief to canvas, not only aligning the pose more closely with that of the Virgin, but also mimicking Perseus's own left hand pressed against his thigh.

If the striated drapery in the painted version of *Perseus and the Graiae* invoked the Parthenon sculptures and Pheidian monumental chryselephantine sculpture, then the prominently arrayed hands offered a similarly forceful invocation of Leonardo and, by association, his theories of the dialogue between painting and sculpture. By overtly alluding to *The Virgin of the Rocks*, Burne-Jones was not merely demonstrating his intimate

71 * Leonardo da Vinci, *The Virgin of the Rocks* (*Madonna of the Rocks*), c. 1483–86. Oil on wood transferred to canvas, 1.9 × 1.2 m. Musée du Louvre, Paris, Inv. 777

72 * Edward Burne-Jones, *Study of the Hands of the Graiae for Perseus and the Graiae, the Perseus Series*, c. 1875–92. Pencil on paper, 27.2 × 17.9 cm. Courtesy of Bonhams

familiarity with a significant Old Master painting. He was signaling his engagement with contemporary art theory surrounding Leonardo, the *paragone*, and the concept of *rilievo*. Lene Østermark-Johansen in 2011 explored the impact of Walter Pater's theorization of the *paragone* as a comparative model of artistic media on his contemporaries, with particular emphasis on Burne-Jones as his "visual counterpart." According to Østermark-Johansen, the concept of *rilievo* was central to Pater's understanding of the *paragone*: "In Renaissance art theory, *rilievo* was frequently employed as a term denoting volume in painting, as a term uniting the art forms of sculpture and painting. As a word full of affective connotations, 'relief,' as an art form, an art theoretical concept, and a stylistic ideal, becomes crucial for Pater's aesthetic theories." The hybrid relationship between flat ground and elevated form found in sculptural relief becomes a potent metaphor in both the plastic and literary arts for the dialectic between light and dark, surface and depth, the spatial and the temporal, the spiritual and the material. Pater thus placed particular emphasis on "relief" and its nuanced associations, stressing the importance of the Parthenon sculptures as the pinnacle of *rilievo*, as well as Leonardo da Vinci's "Treatises on Art."[82]

For Leonardo, *rilievo* was an effect best captured in painting, which appeals to the intellectual sense of sight over the base physical sense of touch. As he wrote, "Painting is a matter of greater mental analysis, of greater skill, and more marvelous than sculpture, since necessity compels the mind of the painter to transform itself into the very mind of nature, to become an interpreter between nature and art."[83] The appraisal of the *paragone* as expressed by Leonardo influenced other nineteenth-century art theorists in addition to Pater, including notably Baudelaire. Reviewing the Salon of 1846, the latter cited the indexical qualities of sculpture as rendering it less intriguing than painting. According to the art historian Alex Potts (in 2000), for Baudelaire, "A sculpture . . . is a palpable thing that even the most untutored can seize upon and marvel at. Painting, by contrast, is possessed of a 'singular mystery that cannot be touched by the fingers.'"[84] The concept of *rilievo* is a means to access the haptic through the optic, to conjure sculpture's sensorial memory of touch through paint alone.[85]

For Pater and his contemporaries, the revival of sculpture in modernity was necessarily predicated on *rilievo* as a tool for the reanimation of what was perceived of as a dead art. *Rilievo*, then, like Pater's concept of *Andersstreben*, was a means to test the boundaries between art forms and access the possibility of hybridity.[86] Østermark-Johansen singles out Burne-Jones in dialogue with Pater, describing the artist's aesthetic as specifically "derived from sculptural relief," as evidenced by his use of "monochromatic colour harmonies, figures caught in a compressed space between a planar surface and a decorative background, the emphasis on surface, texture and repetition."[87] Curiously, Østermark-Johansen comments only briefly on Burne-Jones's gesso-on-panel designs for the *Perseus* series. However, her description of his *Annunciation* (1876; Lady Lever Art Gallery, National Museums Liverpool) as an exploration in paint of "marble and alabaster, architecture, relief and freestanding sculpture" closely aligns with my own interpretation of the oil *Perseus and the Graiae*, and the *Perseus* series overall.[88]

Taking up this thread from Østermark-Johansen, I contend that the *paragone* served as an animating principle for the *Perseus* series, made manifest through repeated allusions to the sculptural fragment. While the concept of *rilievo* is perhaps most overtly expressed in *Perseus in the Graiae*, both in the initial gilded gesso panel and in the translation to oil on canvas, the dialectical tension between sculpture and painting, light and shadow, vision and tactility, materiality and spirituality, infuses the series as a whole. Moreover, Burne-Jones employed the serial format in order to immerse the viewer in this extended meditation on the *paragone*, the effect building from one canvas to the next. Through this enactment of a dialogue between the sculptural and the painted surface, the series functioned as an exploration of what Prettejohn has termed the "shared artistic problem" of Aestheticism. In *Art for Art's Sake* (2007), Prettejohn argues that what unites Aestheticism is the open-ended question of "what art might be, if not for the sake of anything else."[89] Prettejohn posits that this question can only be answered through artistic investigation, rather than theorization. With the *Perseus* series, Burne-Jones attempted to articulate his own response to the debates over the form and function of painting in modernity by reviving the *paragone*.

That sculpture, and particularly the ancient sculptural fragment, functioned as an integral component of the series is evident in the many surviving nude figural studies, the recurrent iconographical quotations of celebrated Classical and Renaissance sculptural forms, and the cool, grisaille color palette that pervades the cycle until the concluding canvas. The following list, by no means exhaustive, indicates the depth of Burne-Jones's sculptural engagement beyond *Perseus and the Graiae*. Beginning with *The Call of Perseus*, the full-length nude body of the male hero as seen in a study from 1877 (fig. 73) emulates elements of the Belvedere Torso from the Vatican (fig. 74), as well as Michelangelo's *Dying Slave* (fig. 75).[90] Early designs for *Perseus and the Sea Nymphs* (figs. 76 and 77) indicate that Burne-Jones shifted his arrangement to echo more overtly the ancient sculptural group of the *Three Graces* (fig. 78).[91] In a nude study for one of the Gorgon sisters in *The Finding of Medusa* (fig. 79), the pose appears modeled after the ancient Roman sculptural type of the *Crouching Venus* (fig. 80). Paul Leprieur likened Burne-Jones's Medusa to the colossal fragment known as the "Medusa Ludovisi," a cast of which was owned by Sidney Colvin and later entered the Fitzwilliam Museum (fig. 81).[92] Pegasus in *The Death of Medusa I* recalls the rearing horses of the Panathenaic procession of the Parthenon frieze (fig. 82). A nude study for the fallen figure of Medusa (fig. 83), with her pale, stone-colored flesh and headless, fragmented form, powerfully evokes both the reclining river-god Ilissos from the West Pediment of the Parthenon, as seen from the back, as well as *The Dying Gaul* (fig. 84).[93] In the last scene of the series, *The Baleful Head*, Burne-Jones not only drew on a Roman sarcophagus fragment for the hand-joining pose of Perseus and Andromeda (fig. 85), but also evoked the *Medusa Rondanini*, a Roman copy after an original sculpture attributed to Pheidias (fig. 86), in the sightless head upraised between them.[94] This near-obsessive

73 * Edward Burne-Jones, *Study for Perseus in The Call of Perseus*, 1877. Pencil on paper, 26.8 × 178 cm. Staatsgalerie, Stuttgart, C 1977/2670

74 * Apollonius, *Belvedere Torso*, 1st century BCE. Marble, h. 159 cm. Pio Clementino Museum, Vatican, Cat. 1192

75 * Michelangelo Buonarroti, *Dying Slave*, 1513–15. Marble, h. 215 cm. Musée du Louvre, Paris, MR 1590

76 * Edward Burne-Jones, *Design for Perseus and the Sea Nymphs*, c. 1875. Pencil on paper, 16.1 × 11.2 cm. Staatsgalerie, Stuttgart, C 1971/2120

77 * Edward Burne-Jones, *Design for Perseus and the Sea Nymphs*, c. 1875. Pencil on paper, 32.1 × 17.7 cm. Staatsgalerie, Stuttgart, C 1971/2121

78 * *The Three Graces*, Roman copy of the 2nd century CE after Hellenistic original. Restored 1609 by Nicolas Cordier. Marble, 119 × 85 cm. Musée du Louvre, Paris, MA 287, MR 211

79 * Edward Burne-Jones, *Study for figure of a Gorgon in the Perseus Series*, 1876. Graphite on paper, 27.1 × 17.8 cm. Fitzwilliam Museum, Cambridge, No. 2020

80 * *Crouching Aphrodite*, Roman copy of 2nd century CE, after Hellenistic original of 3rd century BCE. Marble, 125 × 53 × 65 cm. Royal Collection Trust, RCIN 69746

81 * *Medusa Ludovisi* (or *Sleeping Fury*), 2nd century CE. Marble, h. 46 cm. Palazzo Altemps, Museo Nazionale Romano, INV. 8650

82 * Pheidias, Block XXIV from the North Frieze of the Parthenon: Chariot and Marshal, 438–32 BCE. Marble. British Museum, London, 1816,0610.28

83 ∗ Edward Burne-Jones, *The Death of Medusa (a fragment)*, c. 1876–85. Oil on canvas, 63 × 79 cm. Private collection

84 ∗ *The Dying Gaul* (or *The Dying Galatian* or *The Dying Gladiator*), late 3rd century BCE. Roman copy of Hellenistic sculpture. Marble, h. 93 cm. Capitoline Museum, Rome, MC0747

85 ∗ Roman sarcophagus, c. 160 BCE. Marble, 98.4 × 78 × 11 cm. British Museum, London, 1805,0703.143

86 ∗ *Medusa Rondanini*, Roman copy after Pheidias, *Head of Medusa*, c. 500–430 BCE. Marble, h. 40 cm. Glyptothek, Munich

quotation of sculptural forms far exceeds a mere demonstration of Burne-Jones's mastery of ancient and Renaissance sculptural precedents. Instead, the reiterated allusions foster a sense of continual oscillation between painting and sculpture, vision and tactility, the optic and the haptic, which builds as the viewer progresses from one passage to the next, physically traversing the space along with the mythological hero.

With *Perseus and the Graiae*, Burne-Jones signaled the importance of vision and its inverse, blindness. The tiny pearl pinched between Perseus's thumb and finger represents a world plunged into darkness for the three gray sisters who balance perilously on their stony ledge. Devoid of sight, the figures stretch out their hands, forced to rely solely on touch as they seek their stolen eye. The painting creates a sympathetic reaction for the viewer, evoking potent sensorial memories of the utility of touch in the absence of sight. Rendered in shades of marble, granite, metal, and glass, the sculptural allusions that bind the series together amplify this haptic sensation. The immersive, serial format of the encompassing program creates a cumulative impact, a sense of entrapment in a frozen world of fractured sculptural bodies that builds from one moment to the next. At last, this oppressive sense of stasis is alleviated by an alternative thread that emerges in the latter half of the series with *The Rock of Doom* and *The Doom Fulfilled*. Here, although sculptural form and haptic sensation are still dominant, the fraught encounter of Perseus and Andromeda represents reciprocal vision and the possibility of material transformation as a way to restore to vitality, connection, and true sight.

"The subtle bloom of beauty": Vision, Transformation, and Awakening

If the Graiae are ossified and isolated stone masses crouching alone in a cold and mountainous landscape, then in *The Rock of Doom* and *The Doom Fulfilled* (see figs. 63 and 64) Perseus and Andromeda usher in the awakening of form. Whereas the Graiae blindly reach out in search of a human connection forever beyond their grasp, the young couple exchange reciprocal glances through wide-open eyes that see and acknowledge the other. In the context of the series, Perseus's rescue of Andromeda appears not only as an enactment of the *paragone*, but also as a rejoinder to the tactile deprivation of the Graiae. Andromeda is depicted not as a flesh and blood woman cowering naked in fear but as a stone effigy seemingly coming into being. Placing the myth of Medusa in dialogue with the legend of Pygmalion, these paired canvases that occupy the climax of the painted series allowed Burne-Jones to continue his exploration of the *paragone* in the context of nineteenth-century debates over aesthetic theory. In this passage of the series, he investigates the ability of painting to surpass sculpture through the depiction of physical metamorphosis, of a figure coming to life, and the mutual recognition in a shared gaze.

As elaborated earlier in this chapter, previous scholarship has largely fixated on psychosexual critiques of *The Rock of Doom* and *The Doom Fulfilled* as fantasies of phallic penetration predicated on Victorian male heteronormative desires and frustrations. However, although the viewer's attention may initially be piqued by the charged nature of the encounter of man, woman, and coiled beast, it is the richly realized sculptural texture and calligraphic lines that draw and hold the eye: from the interlocking, incised metallic plates that form a carapace or exoskeleton around Perseus's virile, but vulnerable body; to the ivory polish of Andromeda's glowing skin as she rotates in precisely calibrated counterpoise; to the slick serpent, whose leathery hide is not scaly but burnished to a sheen, possessing the sleek sting of a whiplash.[95] Moreover, the interlaced knot formed by the monster's body undulates rhythmically across the canvas of *The Doom Fulfilled*, guiding the eye along its twists and turns as one might follow a procession across a frieze.[96] If the serpent recalls ebony or bronze, then Andromeda's revolving figure is unmistakably marble, a Praxitelean Aphrodite, seen from the front and the back in sequential rotation, a solid form undergoing metamorphosis into a living body. Burne-Jones no doubt took inspira-

87 * Edward Burne-Jones, *The Rock of Doom* (detail of fig. 63)

tion for this element from Ovid, who recounts how Perseus almost mistook Andromeda for a marble statue, so still and pale was she on the rock as she helplessly awaited her fate.[97] When properly paired, with *The Rock of Doom* on the left and *The Doom Fulfilled* on the right, the two paintings allow Andromeda's figure to be seen "in the round," an enactment yet again of the *paragone*, with one glance at the diptych performing the perambulatory movement of the viewer around a sculpture.[98]

Although Andromeda's nude form is the most overt representation of a body bared before the viewer, Perseus is also portrayed in a moment of unveiling. Burne-Jones depicts him in the act of removing his helmet, revealing his previously hidden figure. Significantly, Andromeda does not avert her gaze in shame when Perseus manifests before her. Her chin is lowered, but her eyes are raised as she looks directly, unabashedly, back at her rescuer (fig. 87). It is an instant of human connection, an exchange of gazes that acknowledges not just the external desire for the body but also recognition of an internal soul. In *The Doom Fulfilled*, Perseus has replaced his helmet, obscuring his body from Andromeda and the monster alike. With Perseus now invisible to her, the unchained Andromeda stares instead into the chilling white eyes of the sea-serpent (fig. 88). She must trust in her rescuer's tangible presence, creating a further commentary on vision, doubt, and faith.

The sculptural quality of the figure of Andromeda, her idealized female form and placid expression in the face of mortal peril, unnerved some contemporary viewers. When the two canvases were first displayed at the New Gallery in 1888, Cosmo Monkhouse praised them as "full of beauty," noting especially their metallic quality: "They are both painted in that scheme of colour which Mr. Burne Jones has chosen more than once for heroic designs . . . a scheme akin to work in various metals, bronze and copper, and

88 * Edward Burne-Jones, *The Doom Fulfilled* (detail of fig. 64)

silver and gold. . . . The pictures are intended to be a power to the soul as well as a pleasure to the eyes."[99] But Monkhouse expressed concern over Andromeda's lack of terror in the face of her impending sacrifice and Perseus's battle with the monster. The critic for *The Times*, meanwhile, described the paintings as depicting "not so much action as the spirit of action."[100] When considered within the *Perseus* series overall, however, these paired canvases represent a moment of transition, where the isolation and deprivation of the previous scenes shift into reunion and revivification. The series turns with Andromeda's revolution in space, her calm mien a signal of a shift in perceptual awareness and cognizance.

With their dominant themes of transformation, mutual recognition, and awakening, *The Rock of Doom* and *The Doom Fulfilled* function as a variant of the legend of Pygmalion and Galatea. The story of Pygmalion was a popular subject in the nineteenth century, in large part because it offered painters the opportunity to meditate on the act of artistic creation itself, as well as revisiting the Renaissance *paragone*. In the tale, a reclusive sculptor falls in love with his own carved figure of a woman, who is then brought to life by Venus. The legend thus explores craft, aesthetic contemplation, and the distinction between lust and love. Morris drafted his own version of the tale, "Pygmalion and the Image," for *The Earthly Paradise*. In her extended exploration of the story of Pygmalion in nineteenth-century literature (2001), Essaka Joshua argues for Morris's poetic interpretation as a meditation on desire. Joshua notes that the youthful protagonist evolves from a lust for the external form of his sculpture to a more mature love of the living woman. "In this case," she comments, "an interest in the purely physical is portrayed as an obsession; an interest in the physical and the spiritual together (i.e. the statue-woman with a soul) is lauded as love."[101] For Morris, Pygmalion's maturation from desire for the external body to acknowledgment of Galatea's soul arises through aesthetic epiphany, reinforcing the importance of the arts for personal and social evolution.

After completing a number of studies for Morris's "Pygmalion and the Image" as part of their scheme to illustrate *The Earthly Paradise*, between 1875 and 1878 Burne-Jones went on to create a four-part oil on canvas series depicting the myth (figs. 90–93). In his own Pygmalion narrative, Burne-Jones suggests not only the revival of beauty and the arts but also the elevation of spiritual devotion over physical desire.[102] Alison Smith in *The Victorian Nude* (1996) noted not only the frequent recurrence of Pygmalion imagery in the nineteenth century but also the particular quality of Burne-Jones's Galatea, in terms that recall Andromeda in *The Rock of Doom* and *The Doom Fulfilled*: "Burne-Jones tempers the overtly erotic overtones of the subject by presenting Galatea in the stages of transition between the world of image-making and life," Smith points out. "White and marmoreal, she is no simulacrum of living flesh."[103] Similarly, Østermark-Johansen explores Burne-Jones's *Pygmalion* series in the context of Pater and the *paragone*, arguing for the emphasis on "the issue of touch and creation" and the dialogue between painting and sculpture: "Burne-Jones demonstrates that he can outdo marble and sculpture in paint. He can render nude figures from the front, the back and the sides, he can render polished marble floors and white lifeless marble, and he can turn marble into flesh."[104] Although Østermark-Johansen does not extend this analysis to the *Perseus* series, I contend that *The Rock of Doom* and *The Doom Fulfilled* perform a similar enactment of the *paragone*. Burne-Jones both displays figures in the round, and demonstrates his ability to depict Andromeda as a sculptural form transforming into a living body.

The potential for the Pygmalion legend to thematize material metamorphosis in the Victorian era is perhaps best exemplified by Watts's 1868 painting *The Wife of Pygmalion: A Translation from the Greek* (fig. 89). Rather than present a single scene or a serial illustration of the legend, Watts condenses the tale down to one charged moment, the instant in which Pygmalion's marble creation changes from cold stone to living flesh, the animated body serving as a metaphor for painterly mimesis. Algernon Swinburne was the first to note the intermedial character of Watts's painting in his review of the Royal Academy Exhibition of 1868, stating that, with this canvas, the artist had proven that "a picture may share the gracious grandeur of a statue, a statue may catch something of the subtle bloom of beauty proper to a picture."[105] Prettejohn has described Watts's *Wife of Pygmalion* as a key work for establishing the core tenets of Aestheticism:

> *The picture makes an exquisitely succinct summary of the set of ideas that had emerged . . . around the phrase "art for art's sake." It is exclusively to do with beauty, not merely*

89 * George Frederic Watts, *The Wife of Pygmalion, A Translation from the Greek*, 1868. Oil on canvas, 66.7 × 53.3 cm. Buscot Park, Oxfordshire

90 ∗ Edward Burne-Jones, *Pygmalion and the Image – The Heart Desires*, 1878. Oil on canvas, 76.3 × 99 cm.
Birmingham Museum & Art Gallery, 1903P23

91 ∗ Edward Burne-Jones, *Pygmalion and the Image – The Hand Refrains*, 1878. Oil on canvas, 76.3 × 99 cm. Birmingham Museum & Art Gallery, 1903P24

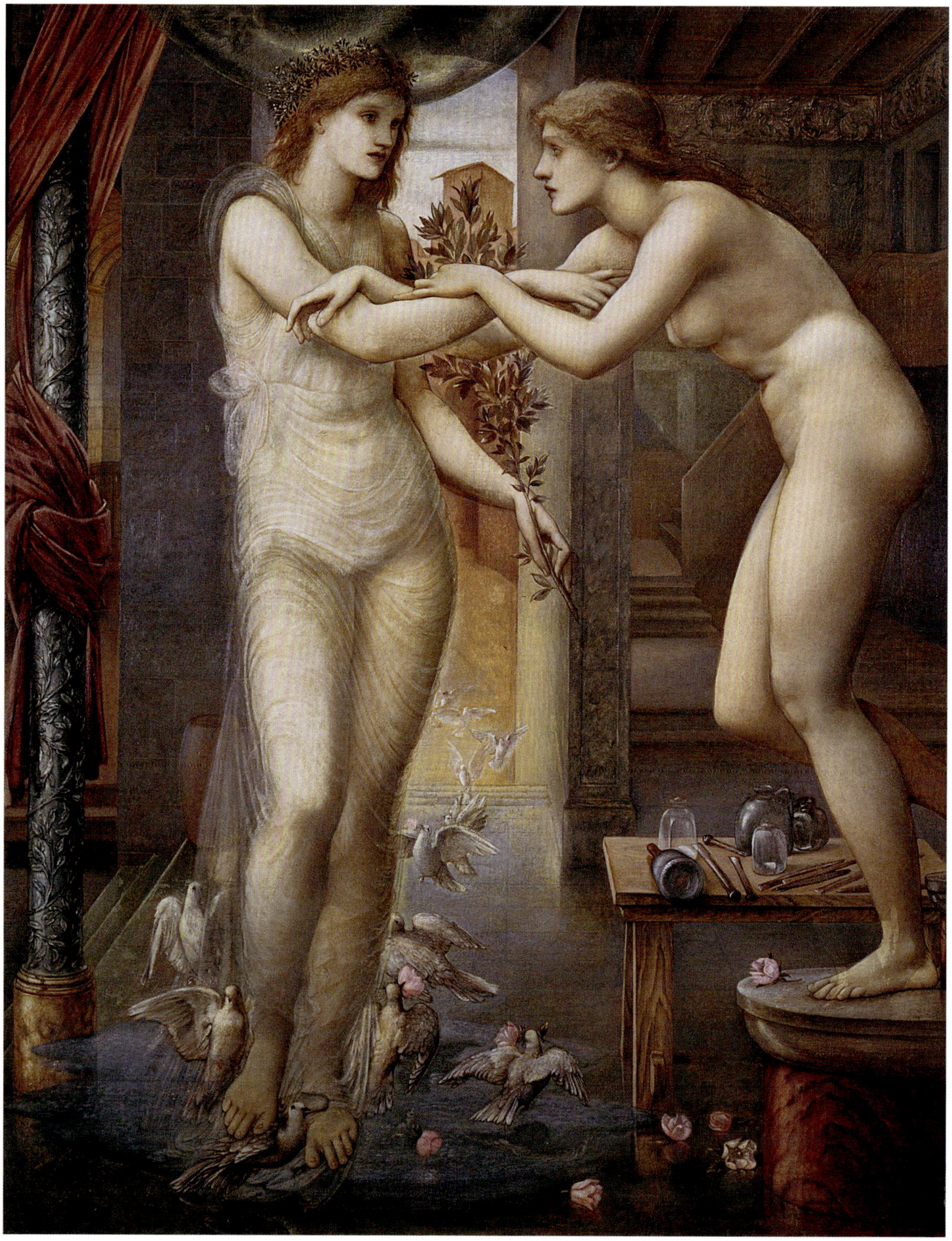

92 ⁎ Edward Burne-Jones, *Pygmalion and the Image – The Godhead Fires*, 1878. Oil on canvas, 76.3 × 99 cm.
Birmingham Museum & Art Gallery, 1903P25

93 ✶ Edward Burne-Jones, *Pygmalion and the Image – The Soul Attains*, 1878. Oil on canvas, 76.3 × 99 cm. Birmingham Museum & Art Gallery, 1903P26

in formal terms, but in its subject-matter.... Moreover the picture does not narrate this story; it enacts it through its own technical processes.[106]

In other words, Watts explores the very act of painting, portraying the instant in which a figure manifests as a presence in the world through the application of colored pigment on canvas.[107] With the enlivening of Andromeda's body, from sculpted form to animate corporeal presence, *The Rock of Doom* and *The Doom Fulfilled* perform an analogous transformative awakening.

The correspondence between the two myths also extends to the figures of Pygmalion and Medusa as foils – the one longing to change stone into flesh, the other petrifying flesh into stone. If the two are mythological counterparts, they represent the difference between death and life, oblivion and sentience, physical isolation and mutual recognition. Commenting on Swinburne's poetry, Østermark-Johansen has explicated the close affinity between the legend of Pygmalion and the myth of Medusa in the context of nineteenth-century Aestheticism.[108] Using as a case study the reception of Michelangelo's sculpture *Night* from the Medici Chapel in Florence (fig. 94), of which Burne-Jones owned a cast, she posits the conceptual link of sculpture, stasis, and revivification. The state of a sculpted figure could be likened either to a metaphorical sleep, "the hybrid state between life and death," a dream from which one could awaken, or to death, with the possibility of resurrection.[109] If a quiescent sculpture suggests aesthetic autonomy and solipsistic pleasure, then by extension a sensate figure, a figure coming into consciousness, signals aesthetic reciprocity, an engagement with the viewer through embodied experience. The enactment of reciprocal vision distinguishes *The Rock of Doom* and *The Doom Fulfilled* from both Watts's *Pygmalion* and Burne-Jones's own *Pygmalion* series. This exchange of gazes between Perseus and Andromeda, the acknowledgment of one soul by another, the act of seeing and being seen, expresses a human connection and a shared awakening within the enclosed spatial reality of the *Perseus* series.

In his original configuration of the series, as well as in the penultimate set of gouache paintings, Burne-Jones incorporated another significant moment of material transformation between the death of Medusa and the rescue of Andromeda through the figure of Atlas Telamon (fig. 95). Burne-Jones chose to represent Atlas not as the king of giants described in Morris's "The Doom of King Acrisius" but as the Titan compelled to hold up the heavens whom Perseus turns to stone by wielding Medusa's head, conflating two mythological variants. Initially intended for a bas-relief panel, the Atlas Telamon turned to stone allowed Burne-Jones to incorporate allusions to the *Farnese Atlas*, a 2nd century BCE Roman copy of a Hellenistic Greek original, which notably features depictions of the constellations derived from the legend of Perseus and Andromeda on the celestial orb (fig.

94 * Michelangelo Buonarroti, *Night* from the tomb of Giuliano, Duke of Nemours, 1519–34. Marble. Medici Chapel, Florence

96). Burne-Jones also modeled the figure after Michelangelo's *Prisoner*, commonly known as *Atlas* (fig. 97). The Atlas episode thus permitted Burne-Jones to incorporate another set of allusions to significant ancient and Renaissance sculptural precedents, as well as providing another chance to depict corporeal metamorphosis. As seen in the gouache cartoon, the heroic, nude body of Atlas is caught in the exact moment of metamorphosis, serving as a visual inverse of Andromeda's awakening to follow. Atlas's petrified flesh is portrayed in a blue-green shade suggestive of stone, or perhaps patinated bronze. The swirling celestial sphere balanced on his shoulders provides another instance of fluid

95 ∗ Edward Burne-Jones, *Atlas Turned to Stone* (detail of fig. 54)

96 ∗ *Farnese Atlas*, 2nd century CE. Roman copy of Hellenistic original. Marble, h. 2.1 m. Museo Archeologico Nazionale, Naples

97 ∗ Michelangelo Buonarroti, *Prisoner* (*Atlas*), 1530–34. Marble, h. 277 cm. Galleria dell'Accademia, Florence

form alchemically frozen in time.[110] Perseus performs an act of mercy, relieving Atlas of his eternal burden, as well as his isolation in a barren landscape devoid of other life. The inclusion of this scene crucially prepares the viewer to encounter Andromeda as a sculptural form, similarly undergoing an evolutionary and alchemical change. This visual dialogue between the figures of Atlas and Andromeda also reiterates the need to consider the *Perseus* series as an unfolding progression, rather than a set of isolated images.

"May I not see this marvel of the lands so mirrored, and yet live?": Mimesis, Reflection, and Vision Restored

With the final panel of the *Perseus* series, *The Baleful Head*, the promise of human connection through the operation of shared vision suggested in *The Rock of Doom* and *The Doom Fulfilled* is realized and extended beyond the hermetic world of the canvas to include the viewer. Perseus's journey has taken us from the bleak, devastated home of the Graiae, where no plant can grow and no human connection seems possible, to a thriving and nourishing environment where two lovers unite beneath a heavily fruited apple tree. In stark contrast to the tactile and emotional deprivation of *Perseus and the Graiae*, *The Baleful Head* (see fig. 43) marks a moment of reassuring physical and spiritual union, as the hands that sought an absent touch meet and tightly grasp at the center of the image.

The trajectory of the series has progressed from barrenness to fecundity, from rocky desolation to fertile rebirth, from isolation to connection. Having immersed the viewer in muted gray-blue tones and unyielding sculptural forms, journeying from the land of the Graiae to the sea-swept shores of Andromeda's rocky prison, Burne-Jones finally transports the viewer to this overwhelmingly lush garden bursting with vibrant color and sumptuous surfaces. He forges an overt typological link between Perseus and Andromeda, who stand with fallen apples strewn about their feet, and Adam and Eve in Paradise, with the snake-haired Medusa occupying the place of the serpent.[111] Moreover, the enclosed garden setting also invokes medieval Marian iconography of the *hortus conclusus*. This allusion to the Virgin is further reinforced by *Danaë Watching the Building of the Brazen Tower* (fig. 98), painted by Burne-Jones in 1872 as a work related to, but distinct from, the *Perseus* series.[112] Just as in Morris's "The Doom of King Acrisius," Danaë is represented as a type of the Virgin Mary, depicted in a walled garden beside a fruited tree and a flowing fountain. This prominently positioned fountain, in turn, echoes the central raised pool in *The Baleful Head*. Attesting to Burne-Jones's capacious symbolic program, the octagonal shape of the fount and the marble patterning additionally recall the Fountain of Life in Jan van Eyck's *Adoration of the Mystic Lamb* (fig. 99).[113] The Fountain of Life is another multivalent symbol that could suggest baptism, the Eucharist, and the heavenly Jerusalem.

98 * Edward Burne-Jones, *Danaë Watching the Building of the Brazen Tower*, 1872. Oil on panel, 17.8 × 26 cm. Harvard Art Museums/ Fogg Museum, Cambridge, Massachusetts, 1943.189, Bequest of Grenville L. Winthrop

99 * Jan van Eyck, *Adoration of the Mystic Lamb* (Ghent Altarpiece, detail), 1432. Oil on panel. St. Bavo Cathedral, Ghent

By layering allusions to the Fall, the Annunciation, and the apocalyptic return to Paradise, *The Baleful Head* may be productively compared to Burne-Jones's illustration *When Adam Delved and Eve Span*, as well as his design for mosaic, *The Tree of Life*. Yet again, Burne-Jones depicts a simultaneous enactment of the Fall and a redemptive return to Paradise through the renewal of nature, the acknowledgment of human fellowship, and the mediating surface of art. Here, however, by also invoking the iconography of marital union, he suggests a further interpretation. In exploring Burne-Jones's engagement with androgyny, Shearer West reflected on the analogous emphasis on love in his work: "in Jewish legend, the original Adam of Genesis was an androgynous being – a combination of heart and soul. The separation of Adam through the creation of Eve resulted in a divisive universe." For Burne-Jones, West argues, love was a means to repair this originary rift of man and woman, heart and soul, "not as merely a sexual but also a spiritual union."[114] Paralleling Pygmalion's maturation from physical desire to spiritual devotion, the symbolic marriage ceremony between Perseus and Andromeda is not merely the promised consummation implied by the libidinal forces of *The Rock of Doom* and *The Doom Fulfilled* but also the recuperative joining together of two souls through love. Medusa, presiding over this matrimonial scene of Perseus and Andromeda, is less the temptress than the Christ-like sacrifice that facilitated their return to prelapsarian harmony.

While the Graiae foreground the sense of sight in tension with the sense of touch, their Gorgon sister Medusa shifts the narrative toward the power of visual representation and artistic creation.[115] In the nineteenth century, Medusa was largely perceived as a figure of mimesis, not as an embodiment of Freudian castration fears. Jean-Pierre Vernant, in his seminal anthropological text on the cultural role of mythology, *Mortals and Immortals* (1991), argued that the fundamental premise of the ancient legend of Perseus is an elucidation of the operation of vision and representation; there is "one theme central to this chain of episodes: the eye, the gaze, the reciprocity of seeing and being seen."[116] Similarly, as Thomas Albrecht asserts regarding Medusa and Victorian aesthetics, "Any painting of Medusa's head... can potentially be interpreted as an allegory about the mitigating power of art."[117] Thus, the reflective surface of the fountain at the core of the composition plays a narrative role, allowing Andromeda to look on Medusa without harm, while simultaneously giving visual form to the metaphorical concept of art as a mirror.[118] The horror and danger of Medusa's head becomes not a threat but an object of beauty and contemplation. In turn, much like Andromeda, the viewer is awakened to the power of art and representation to mirror the world back on itself through a new and revivifying lens.

The development of Burne-Jones's composition for *The Baleful Head* reveals the increasing importance of reflection, as the mirrored head of Medusa moved from the base of the image to its center. His early designs for the image, in 1875, as seen in his initial car-

100 ∗ Edward Burne-Jones, *The Baleful Head* (detail of fig. 47)

101 ∗ Edward Burne-Jones, *Study for The Baleful Head*, 1875. Pencil on paper, 12.6 × 7.9 cm. Staatsgalerie, Stuttgart, Inv. 1971/2119

102 ∗ Dante Gabriel Rossetti, *Perseus and Andromeda* (*Aspecta Medusa*), c. 1865. Pencil on paper, 35.3 × 30.5 cm. Birmingham Museum & Art Gallery, 1904P348

toon for Balfour (fig. 100) and a subsequent pencil study (fig. 101), were markedly different from the final oil on canvas. This first iteration of the image is more closely aligned with the scene in Morris's "Doom of King Acrisius." Here, the two figures perch at the edge of a pool of water, Perseus standing upright, with Medusa's head held above as Andromeda bends forward, clinging to her rescuer's waist. This arrangement was an overt allusion to an unexecuted painting by Dante Gabriel Rossetti, *Aspecta Medusa*, which now exists only as a sketch (fig. 102).[119] Rossetti's figural arrangement, in turn, was derived from a fresco in Pompeii, then recently discovered. In this lesser-known episode of the legend, Perseus appears not as a warrior, but arguably as an artist, formulating a means to portray Medusa's deadly visage safely through replication.[120] Albrecht, describing both Rossetti's and Burne-Jones's works, stresses this moment of mirroring as an allegorical act of mimesis, writing, "The central place the myth gives to the motif of reflection thus underscores the myth's potential relevance to the topic of representation as such."[121] When Burne-Jones altered his composition through a series of sketches in approximately 1876, he began by shifting the scene from a rocky seaside pool to a fountain in an enclosed Edenic garden. He then repositioned the heads of Perseus and Andromeda until they adopted a horizontal relationship, their faces placed across from each other looking down into the basin, with Medusa between them (fig. 103). These new sketches moved reflection, an act of mimesis, a picture within a picture, to the very core of *The Baleful Head*.

This configuration, the sacred joining of hands before a reflective surface, strongly evokes another painting by Jan van Eyck, the 1434 *Arnolfini Portrait* (fig. 104). Acquired by London's National Gallery in 1842, this work depicting a scene of marital union became a touchstone for the Pre-Raphaelites, a persuasive model for early Renaissance absorptive

103 ∗ Edward Burne-Jones, sketchbook with designs for *The Baleful Head*, c. 1876. Pencil on paper. Victoria and Albert Museum, London, E. 9-1955, f. 35

104 ∗ Jan van Eyck, *Double Portrait of a Giovanni Arnolfini and His Wife*, 1434. Oil on wood panel, 83.8 × 57.2 cm. National Gallery, London, NG186

visuality. As Prettejohn has cogently argued, the *Arnolfini Portrait* offered a new paradigm of pictorial logic, a devotional visual mode that immersed the viewer in a world of rich, luminous textures and exacting details, demanding prolonged attention from the viewer, and addressing the very process of artistic creation. According to Prettejohn, the quotation of the mirror in Pre-Raphaelite painting need not be exact, but the allusion was always specific and pointed; for the Pre-Raphaelites, "Mirrors [became] associated with art-making in many different ways. On a basic level the mirror reflection can be a metaphor or analogue for the activity of representational painting: a mirror reflects reality just as a representational painting does."[122] Vernant, indeed, described the emergence of the mirror as an element of the Perseus legend in the context of mimesis:

> *From this perspective, the mimetic activity of artists who fashion images is analogous to other phenomena, which, this time, are not products of a human operation but of a divine art – natural phenomena, for example, like reflections in water, figures in mirrors, shadows, and visions in dreams. . . . The painter's work is thus comparable to that universe of reflections a mirror produces when it is turned from all sides by the hand that wields it.*[123]

The mirror, with its reflective powers, enacts the operation of painting as a mimetic act. By concluding with an image that links the mimetic mythology of Medusa with van Eyck's mirror as an immersive visual tool, Burne-Jones placed the *Perseus* series in dialogue with the larger debates central to nineteenth-century Aestheticism over the efficacy, role, and function of painting.

Mirroring, much like the sculptural, is a recurrent visual motif throughout the *Perseus* series. Beginning with *The Call of Perseus*, Burne-Jones made the significant iconographical choice to depict Athena gifting Perseus with a mirror, rather than the reflective shield suggested in some accounts of the legend. This substitution draws out latent parallels with the allegorical figure of Truth, who is often depicted with a mirror as her attribute. Similarly, in *Perseus and the Sea Nymphs*, the glassy pool of water beneath the feet of the nymphs provides yet another moment of insistent reflectivity, while the doubled body of Andromeda implies the operation of a mirror displaying front and back simultaneously. At the conclusion of the series, the mirrored fount in *The Baleful Head* metaphorically invokes the mimetic process of paint on canvas.

If Medusa is a corporeal sculptor, turning men to stone with a glance, then Perseus is a figure of the painter, allowing Andromeda, and by extension the viewer, to glimpse the forbidden through the mirror of art. The *Perseus* series guides the viewer through an immersive, embodied kinesthetic encounter with the sculptural and with haptic sensation, an aesthetic quest that concludes, at last, with a meditation on art's capacity as a mirror on the world. The series closes by answering Andromeda's request of Perseus in Morris's "The Doom of King Acrisius," "May I not see this marvel of the lands / So mirrored, and yet live?"[124] As the eye is drawn along the exchange of glances, from Perseus to Andromeda, it follows a double mitigation, from the figures represented above to their reflected simulacra in the pool below (fig. 105). Just at the moment when the viewer feels themselves slipping into a *mise en abyme*, the reverie of all-encompassing visual immersion is broken by the interruptive presence of a single leaf floating on the surface. This leaf ruptures the illusion, calling attention to its own mimetic artifice, highlighting the dis-

105 * Edward Burne-Jones, *The Baleful Head* (detail of fig. 43)

tance between nature and its representation, the fictive and the real. As Perseus returned the eye to the Graiae, so too does Burne-Jones return the power of vision to the viewer, who must now turn from the immersive aesthetic experience of this mythic realm to the harsh light of the quotidian world, with senses trained anew.

Burne-Jones dedicated more than twenty years of his career to the *Perseus* commission. And yet, with his death in 1898, the cycle was left unfinished. The exact reason is impossible to determine conclusively. Perhaps Balfour's increasingly conservative political views soured the project for Burne-Jones. Perhaps he simply became distracted with other, more pressing endeavors. Or perhaps he thought he would live another decade to see it through. Whether there was one determining factor, or a convergence of issues, the series will forever remain an incomplete utterance. This unfinished state is particularly problematic given its serial format, which is necessarily dependent on all parts in the sequence to achieve its full impact. At the time of Burne-Jones's death, the central encounter between Perseus and Medusa remained the least resolved episode. Georgiana Burne-Jones recorded that it was "the Medusa part of the legend which attracted him most"; indeed, in 1875 he began work for Balfour by researching depictions of Medusa in the British Museum.[125] This sequence should be the dramatic highlight of Perseus's quest, the achievement of the goal that first sets him on his fated path. And yet, it is also a moment of intense violence, as a man shrouded from view approaches an unsuspecting woman and brutally beheads her before fleeing from the desperate pursuit of her anguished sisters.

The surviving studies and versions of *The Finding* and *The Death of Medusa* are a testament to Burne-Jones's struggles with the composition, as well as his attempts to align them thematically with the rest of the series. From the initial cartoon of 1875 to the gouache set, Burne-Jones made several significant changes. In *The Finding of Medusa*, the setting is changed from a forest, where the Gorgons hide amid bare tree trunks, to a rocky mountainous landscape more akin to that found in *Perseus and the Graiae*. The proposed bas-relief panel of *The Death of Medusa I* (see fig. 52), with its pointed allusions to the Parthenon sculptures, was slightly altered in the depiction of Chrysaor, who becomes a Michelangelesque nude, while Perseus's figure shifts from draped to armored. Finally, *The Death of Medusa II* (see fig. 53) was spatially condensed, shifted from a horizontal to a vertical orientation. This modification heightens the tension of the moment, as the panicked Gorgon sisters crowd into the upper left corner of the composition, creating a claustrophobic sensation while they search in vain for their attacker. Their dual orientations, one forward and the other backward, echo Andromeda's sculptural rotation in *The Rock of Doom* and *The Doom Fulfilled*. Considered as a pair, *The Death of Medusa I* and *II* in the gouache set similarly double the fallen figure of Medusa. Her headless form rotates from a frontal orientation, to a more vulnerable rear-facing posture, her slumping back and bare feet exposed. Both render Medusa's body in chalky white brushstrokes strongly reminiscent of the porous, chipped surface of ancient marble. At the instant of her beheading, Medusa becomes a sculptural fragment, succumbing to the fate of her own victims.

In the final *Perseus* set given to Balfour after Burne-Jones's death, the murderous stroke itself is elided with the removal of the bas relief *Death of Medusa I*. Instead, the viewer is left with only the prelude and the aftermath, while the gruesome act itself

106 * *Demeter of Knidos*, 350–30 BCE. Marble, h. 152 cm. British Museum, London, 1859,1226.26

107 * Edward Burne-Jones, study for *The Finding of Medusa*, 1885. Graphite on paper, 23.4 × 18.1 cm. Fitzwilliam Museum, Cambridge, Inv. No. 2021

resides only in the imagination. Morris's Medusa in "The Doom of King Acrisius" is a piteous figure, a fallen woman cursed for her sexual transgression and calling out for release from her agony, whereas Burne-Jones's Medusa may be tragic, but she is neither monstrous nor pathetic. Her majestic form occupies more than a third of the composition, swathed in rich folds of drapery more akin to the *Demeter of Knidos* (fig. 106) than a seductive Venus.[126] Although Burne-Jones experimented with a mask-like face of horror in an early study (fig. 107), the elegant features of Medusa are more haunting than ghastly. Her windblown locks suggest serpentine forms, but no snakes appear. It is Medusa, not Perseus, who seems heroic, standing to confront her tragic fate. For his part, the invisible Perseus stares into his mirror at the reflection of Medusa, hesitating in a moment of reluctance before fulfilling his duty. In this envisioning, Medusa is not a monster but a doomed prophetess staring out into a vision of the future only she can see. This is the dialectical crux of the series, the death that is necessary for life, the sacrifice that enables redemption. As Burne-Jones himself prophesied for his country and modernity, "someday it will all change violently...but I don't want to see it or foresee it or dwell upon it....I want nothing else, but to paint & paint."[127] This central passage of violent revolutionary upheaval enables love, rebirth, and hope to return to the world, but the price is a painful one to "dwell upon."

Burne-Jones's *Perseus* series was, then, an extended meditation on the *paragone* in response to the open question of painterly mimesis in modernity. With *Perseus and the Graiae*, the artist foregrounded haptic sensation and the sculptural, the painted series recalling the form and qualities of a monumental frieze. With *The Rock of Doom* and *The Doom Fulfilled*, he explored the similarities between the legends of Perseus and Pygmalion as a way to engage with material transformation and reciprocal vision. Finally, with *The Baleful Head*, the series concludes with a meditation on mirroring as a metaphor for the operation of mimesis in paint. Ultimately, the tensions of the series remain unresolved as a holistic work, given its unfinished state and Burne-Jones's unrealized vision of installing the completed paintings as an immersive decorative program at Balfour's residence in Carlton Gardens. The series will remain, as Prettejohn remarks of Aestheticism itself, an "open-ended question," an exploration of the *paragone* in the modern age that strives for an answer, but ceased short of a resolution.[128]

Chapter Four

"Art and the Beauty of the Earth"

BURNE-JONES'S ROMAN MOSAICS

When Burne-Jones reflected back on the works that best fulfilled his aims and ambitions as an artist, he frequently cited his design for the mosaic *The Tree of Life* (fig. 108). The composition formed part of his expansive mosaic cycle for the American Episcopal Church of St. Paul's Within the Walls, Rome, completed between 1881 and 1894 (fig. 109). Created for the second chancel arch, *The Tree of Life* is the visual and conceptual core of the mosaic program. In addition to his typical working drawings, Burne-Jones executed a colossal and highly detailed cartoon in watercolor and gouache, heightened with gold, at one-ninth scale. He exhibited this mammoth study as part of his retrospective at the New Gallery in 1892, and later displayed the watercolor prominently in the hall of his London home, where it remained until his death.[1] Burne-Jones regretted that *The Tree of Life* had not received the same recognition as his oil paintings: "There was that design of the Christ (the man and woman with the fruits of the earth) no one even looked at it when it was shewn in the New Gallery. They only saw that it wasn't oil-painted; and yet it said as much as anything I have ever done."[2] Despite, or perhaps bearing out, this declaration, *The Tree of Life*, along with the Roman mosaic cycle as a whole, remains comparatively overlooked in Burne-Jones's oeuvre.

A cogent and kinetic decorative design, *The Tree of Life* merges the Fall, the Crucifixion, and the apocalyptic return to paradise found in the Book of Revelation, forging an innovative and radical iconography of Christian salvation. Describing his composition to his patron and confidant Frances Horner while it was in progress, Burne-Jones explained the core elements of the arch mosaic:

108 ✱ Edward Burne-Jones, cartoon for *The Tree of Life*, 1888. Watercolor and gouache, 181 × 242 cm. Victoria and Albert Museum, London, 584-1898

I shall make the design I had set my heart on – of a great flowering tree growing all over the space; myriads of leaves to it, every leaf as big as a man's hand, and in the tree a very pale Christ – and on one side of it, Adam – and on the other, Eve, and two toddles, and these shall stand for mankind and Christ shall have outstretched arms on the tree, as if he were on a cross, but there will be no cross. He will be hovering in the tree of life.[3]

109 * Nave interior, 1881–94, St. Paul's Within the Walls, Rome

Christ occupies the center of the design, wearing a crown of thorns and with arms extended in the pose of the cross. However, this Christ is not the Man of Sorrows, nor is he crucified. His body is free from any sign of trauma or suffering, the palms upturned and the head slightly bowed in a gesture of blessing and forgiveness.[4] Christ is flanked not by St. John and Mary but by the figures of Adam and Eve with their infant children Cain and Abel. In the first chapter of this book, I explored how the design for *The Tree of Life* developed concurrently with Burne-Jones's revival of the iconography of the Labors of Adam and Eve. Accordingly, the couple's redemptive toil on the earth remains a potent presence in this composition, signified by the golden ripening corn on the left side of the arch beside Adam. The white flowering lily of the Annunciation appears alongside Eve in the corresponding position on the right, entangled with thorns to suggest the pain of childbirth.

For this new interpretation of traditional Christian iconography, Burne-Jones chose to inscribe a Latin quotation from St. John's Gospel 16:33 at the base of the arch: "IN MUNDO PRESSURAM HABEBITIS SED CONFIDITE EGO VICI MUNDUM" ("In the world ye shall have tribulation: but be of good cheer; I have overcome the world"). This promise of mercy was delivered by Christ to his disciples following the Last Supper on the eve of the Crucifixion. Moreover, the verse follows a passage in which Christ likens himself to a vine, with each of his disciples as branches that will bear fruit (15:5). This carefully selected inscription sends a forthright message of compassion and hope, sustained by the sacred regenerative force of nature. *The Tree of Life* thus reformulates the central tenets of Christian salvation, celebrating not just the redemption of humanity but the concurrent resurgence of all organic life.

Indeed, it is the vibrant, flourishing tree that animates and defines the composition. Rendered in lush shades of emerald and azure, the tree is further enlivened by flowing bands of gold paint that course through the branches and outline every heart-shaped leaf. Serpentine and rhythmically intertwined boughs rise from the base of the design, and explode outwards to fill the sky, while protectively enfolding each of the human figures. The tree possesses an almost corporeal quality, the curving limbs resembling a system of veins or bronchi. Carefully considering the architectural features of the intended space, Burne-Jones designed the mosaic to echo the curves of the trefoil arch in the sweeping lines of the composition, from the grassy slopes of the terrain, to the golden strip of sky, to the spiraling structure of the tree. The terrestrial and celestial realms are bound together through an assertion of the omnipresence of the sacred in all living things. Exemplifying Ruskin's precept for the repair of society, "There is no wealth but life," *The Tree of Life* proposes an ecological model of regeneration and prosperity.[5] Countering the ruinous impact of industrialization on the individual and the environment in the nineteenth century, Burne-Jones's bold vision proposed the ennobled human body in harmony with the revival of a thriving natural world as the key to achieving redemption.[6]

In all, the commission, design, and execution of Burne-Jones's mosaics for St. Paul's Within the Walls spanned well over a decade. However, the timeline is somewhat difficult to decipher, because of both the nature of Burne-Jones's working process and the numerous financial setbacks suffered by the project. It appears that Robert J. Nevin, the rector of the American Episcopalian congregation of St. Paul's, first broached the idea to him in 1881, perhaps suggesting that the project, if successful, would eventually cover multiple surfaces. Burne-Jones began with the apse, making the cartoons between 1881 and 1883. Between 1883 and 1885, he worked with Morris, his studio assistant Thomas M. Rooke, Nevin, and Giovanni Castellani of the Venezia-Murano Company to translate his designs into mosaic. After the unveiling of *Christ Enthroned in the Heavenly Jerusalem* (see fig. 126) on the apsidal semi-dome in 1885, Burne-Jones began a flurry of designs for the remaining surfaces of the church, eventually creating the cartoons for the arches, choir, and entrance wall before 1888. *The Annunciation* and *The Tree of Life* were unveiled together in 1894 on the choir and chancel arches, respectively. The design for the entrance wall, *The Fall of Lucifer*, was never executed in mosaic, but exists as a large-scale watercolor (see fig. 129).[7]

Much like the *Perseus* series, the Roman mosaics allowed Burne-Jones the scope and freedom to create an absorptive, embodied, and transformative aesthetic experience on a monumental scale. However, unlike the commission from Balfour, the Roman mosaics would not be locked away in a wealthy private home. Instead, the expansive decorative project for a dedicated ecclesiastical interior fulfilled his desire to create immersive spaces of contemplation and devotion that were also publicly accessible and liberated from the art market, epitomizing the work that he found to be the most urgent and meaningful. When describing his fraught relationship with exhibitions and the privileged status of the commodified painted canvas, Burne-Jones pointedly selected the mosaics for St. Paul's Within the Walls as exemplifying his ideal mode of artistic practice, stating that he wanted to "fill all the [church] with lasting, unsaleable pictures."[8] Working in the ancient medium of mosaic, he embraced the opportunity to leave an enduring artistic legacy that would exist beyond the grasp of capitalist acquisition. Across the soaring arches and apse of St. Paul's, he unfolded an innovative vision of an ecological apocalypse and redemption. Alongside the pioneering ecocritical philosophy of Ruskin and Morris, the mosaic cycle of St. Paul's Within the Walls becomes Burne-Jones's reciprocal call for environmental regeneration from out of the industrial devastation of the nineteenth century.

110 * Edward Burne-Jones, *The Mill*, 1870–82. Oil on canvas, 91.3 × 198.1 cm.
Victoria and Albert Museum, London CAI.8

"So which shall we have, art or dirt?": Ruskin, Morris, and Ecocriticism

In Burne-Jones's painting *The Mill* (fig. 110), three women dance on the grassy bank of a river, while a laureled figure accompanies their graceful movements on an archaic stringed instrument. An idyllic reverie of sensual pleasure, *The Mill* seemingly epitomizes Pater's principle that "all art constantly aspires towards the condition of music."[9] The painting's title has often been dismissed as a mere pretext for the creation of an evocative mood through lush color and decorative line.[10] However, insistent details throughout the painting suggest that much more is at stake in this vision of harmonic order and tranquility. On the opposite bank, five male figures appear in the middle of undressing to bathe in the crystalline waters. Parallel to their bathing counterparts, on the right side of the composition, two workers carry bags of flour to a waiting boat. These figures reveal that the scene is indeed one of labor and production, depicting a fully functioning mill that blends in with its peaceful surroundings, actively fostering a thriving natural environment. The mill exists, therefore, not as a mere backdrop to the painting, but as a means of asserting that labor and beneficent industry can be compatible with a world of earthly beauty and aesthetic pleasure.

In 1871, shortly after Burne-Jones began painting *The Mill*, Ruskin admonished the working men of England about the dangers of despoiling the land, the air, and most especially the water. In the fifth letter of *Fors Clavigera*, he wrote:

> *[Y]our power over the rain and river-waters of the earth is infinite.... You might have the rivers of England as pure as the crystal of the rock; beautiful in falls, in lakes, in living pools.... Or you may do always as you have done now, turn every river of England into a common sewer, so that you cannot so much as baptize an English baby but with filth, unless you hold its face out in the rain; and even that falls dirty.*[11]

Ruskin perceived industrial pollution as an act of desecration, introducing contaminants that would injure the bodies as well as the souls of succeeding generations. In Burne-Jones's idealized depiction of British manufacturing, the polluted waters have been exchanged for a clean and placid pool where the laboring male body can be refreshed and restored. Indeed, Burne-Jones modeled his scene on one of sacred baptism, incorporating unmistakable allusions to Piero della Francesca's *The Baptism of Christ* (after 1437), acquired by the National Gallery in 1861 (fig. 111). The three dancing women of *The Mill* echo the three angels of *The Baptism of Christ*, while the flight of birds behind them evokes the dove of the Holy Spirit. Moreover, the disrobing figure who stands with his shirt half-lifted from his body, in the background directly below the clasped hands of the dancing women, mirrors a

111 * Piero della Francesca, *The Baptism of Christ*, after 1437.
Egg tempera on poplar, 167 × 116 cm. National Gallery, London, NG665

prominent figure in the altarpiece who is removing his clothing in order to follow Christ in the sacred cleansing ritual. Responding to Ruskin's apocalyptic prediction that all sources of fresh water would be transformed into sewers, Burne-Jones presents the viewer with the sanctification of productive labor, blessed by an uncontaminated, nourishing river.

In 1881, just as Burne-Jones was working on *The Mill* with renewed energy in advance of its debut at the Grosvenor Gallery, Morris delivered his groundbreaking ecosocialist lecture, "Art and the Beauty of the Earth," at Burslem Town Hall.[12] Addressing the artisans and industrialists of this Staffordshire pottery manufacturing center, Morris asserted that the renewal of the arts, essential to the renewal of society, could not be achieved without first healing and preserving natural resources: "Of all the things that is likely to give us back popular art in England, the cleaning of England is the first and the most necessary. Those who are to make beautiful things must live in a beautiful place." The damage inflicted on nature by industry must be undone and replaced with new methods of production that would restore the earth: "If we accept art we must atone for what we have done and pay the cost of it. We must turn this land from the grimy back-yard of a workshop into a garden." His lecture could be summarized with the one potent rhetorical question he posed for his Staffordshire audience, "So which shall we have, art or dirt?"[13]

Burne-Jones, who grew up in "the grimy streets of Birmingham," perceived the systemic impact of environmental waste with the same urgency as Ruskin and Morris.[14] With *The Mill*, he offered his own ecological model of production, immersing the viewer in a world where not only the arts but the earth and ennobled human labor can also aspire to the condition of music. Burne-Jones's restorative mill stands in sharp contrast to the smokestacks, soot, and filth of a typical Victorian industrial works. Here, the utilitarian factory of blackened bricks has been replaced with rhythmically arcing passageways and warm glowing stone. Muddied streets and blighted soil have been transformed into fertile forests and soft grass, where women dance to seraphic music. This interdependence of art, sustaining labor, and a thriving natural environment forms a utopian ideal expressed throughout Burne-Jones's work and practice. The mosaic cycle for St. Paul's in Rome represents this ethos at its fullest expression, as a progressive narrative of ecological destruction and renewal that unfolds down the length of the nave, culminating in the glittering triumph of the *Heavenly Jerusalem* in the apse. Through the direct address of the visual arts, Burne-Jones condemned the destruction of the natural environment and the corresponding implications for human life on the earth in dialogue with the groundbreaking ecocritical philosophy of Ruskin and Morris.

As early as the 1860s, Ruskin argued for a connection between the devaluation of the natural world and the alienating force of a competitive, materialistic economic system. In his essay "Unto this Last" (1860), Ruskin linked the concept of real prosperity not with capital but with the garden. Describing the fulfilling toil offered by the garden, as well as the natural beauty and abundance of the untended landscape, Ruskin wrote:

> *No scene is continually and untiringly loved, but one rich by joyful human labour; smooth in field; fair in garden; full in orchard; trim, sweet, and frequent in homestead. . . . As the art of life is learned, it will be found at last that all lovely things are also necessary; – the wild flower by the wayside, as well as the tended corn.*[15]

Later, in "Traffic" (1864), Ruskin urged readers to atone for the sin of worshiping Mammon by turning to nature in reverence: "I am trying to prove to you the honour of your houses and your hills; not that the Church is not sacred – but that the whole Earth is."[16] In his most overtly ecological text, "The Storm-Cloud of the Nineteenth Century" (1884), Ruskin read the signs of a coming apocalypse in the sky like an Old Testament prophet, discerning a correlation between moral corruption and meteorological disturbance, between the blighted earth and the blighted heart of humanity.[17] Brian J. Day defines Ruskin's stance as a "moral ecology": "The ecological implications of the lecture rest on Ruskin's belief in the interrelatedness of the divine, natural, and human economies, his belief that nature polluted by human economic activities signifies humankind's alienation from both God and nature, and the need for moral reformation."[18] Although expressed in the language and ideology of religious condemnation, Ruskin's writings on environmental pollution and its effect on human quality of life produced significant advances that rivaled developments in Victorian scientific environmental theory.[19]

Morris, furthering the work of his mentor Ruskin, argued even more forcefully for the link between economic conditions, social oppression, and the devastation of the environment.[20] Jonathan Bate proclaimed Morris a father of "the green movement," deeming his contributions to ecosocialism to be more significant than those of Karl Marx.[21] Just as Morris's socialism was rooted in his artistic practice, so too did this aesthetic imperative lead him to acknowledge the need to respect the beauty of the natural environment, thereby broadening the scope of his vision for radical ecological change.[22] The correlation between economic conditions and the destruction of the natural world was a central aspect of Morris's contribution to ecological thought. In other words, if a society is motivated by greed and financial gain alone, then natural resources will be depleted according to profitability rather than the relative health of the environment and the human life within it. Morris thus argued for a holistic and cooperative economic structure which would allow the arts and productive labor to flourish in accord with the environment. Elizabeth C. Miller has demonstrated Morris's prescient attitude toward sustainability in producing volumes for the Kelmscott Press, which although expensive, were designed to minimize waste in production and consumption. The press, for Miller, "articulated a central premise of Morris's socialism. It modeled a form of production grounded in beauty, materials, durability, and good labor practices, even for bookmaking, that most utilitarian of arts."[23] This sustainable approach extended across much of his artistic practice, particularly after the establishment of the Merton Abbey factory works for Morris & Co. in 1881.

Located on the banks of the Wandle River on the site of a former Huguenot silk factory, Merton Abbey was an ideal spot to establish expansive craft workshops in the middle of gardens and greenery (fig. 112), but still within easy reach of London. Production began

112 * Lexden Lewis Pocock, *The Pond at William Morris's Works at Merton*, c. 1880s. Watercolor, 13.97 × 23.18 cm. Victoria and Albert Museum, London, P.34-1924

in 1882, with vats for dying, warehouse space for printing chintzes and producing monumental stained-glass windows, as well as weaving fabric, carpets, and tapestries.[24] Charles Harvey and Jon Press demonstrated that the factory at Merton was not a pure realization of a utopian ideal.[25] However, the works should nonetheless be acknowledged as achieving, to the extent possible at the time, an economically viable approach to sustainable craft production in a harmonious natural setting that benefited both the maker and the user.

In 1886, the American poet Emma Lazarus visited Morris and toured Merton Abbey. Lazarus described the premises as an "un-factory," which seemed actively to nourish the environment as well as the workers:

> *Scrupulous neatness and order reigned everywhere in the establishment; pleasant smells as of dried herbs exhaled from clean vegetable dyes, blent with wholesome odours of grass and flowers and sunny summer warmth that freely circulated through open doors and windows. Nowhere was one conscious of the depressing sense of confinement that usually pervades a factory; there was plenty of air and light.*[26]

She observed a sense of "frank comradeship" among the workers, with the beauty of their work keeping the artisans from feeling like cogs in a machine: "the lovely play of colour and beauty of texture of the fabrics issuing from under their fingers relieved their work of that character of purely mechanical drudgery."[27] H. C. Marillier, who documented the history of the works in 1927, reiterated this description, presenting Merton as an idyllic retreat: "The factory was framed in a lovely setting of meadows and willows.... Through it all ran the pleasant river Wandle, then full of trout, and suitable for dyeing... an oasis of quiet industry."[28] Finally, describing the production of *haute-lisse* tapestries there, A. B. Bence-Jones yet again noted the verdant setting and the general contentment of the artisans:

> *The quietude and peace of the surroundings are very noticeable. There is an absence of noise, for all the work done is hand work and there is nothing in the buildings to suggest the modern factory. The appearance of the workers, nearly all of whom have been trained and taught their business at the Merton Abbey Works, is suggestive of artists rather than operators. The outside surroundings are in keeping – trees, gardens, grass and water.*[29]

With an emphasis on communal practice, sustainability, and a sense of social responsibility, the works at Merton Abbey closely approximated Morris's ideal vision of art, labor, and nature in harmony. A productive factory on the banks of a clean river, surrounded by greenery, it was Burne-Jones's vision of *The Mill* come to life.

Unlike Ruskin and Morris, Burne-Jones did not leave behind his own corresponding verbal treatise on the interconnected principles of pleasurable labor on the land, true social fellowship, the quotidian practice of the arts, and a sympathetic appreciation of nature and the cycles of the earth. Instead, he expressed his ideals through the visual arts, where the health or distress of the natural world echoes the narrative themes of the work, as in the *Perseus* series. Perhaps his most overt expression of his environmental ideals can be found in the mosaic cycle for St. Paul's, Rome. Unfolding across the surfaces of the church in glittering tesserae, Burne-Jones's mosaics present a vision of ecological salvation in the symbolic language of Christian apocalypse and redemption.

"My heart was full of mosaics": Designing for Eternity

Reporting on the progress of Burne-Jones's mosaics in 1890, the art critic and Pre-Raphaelite brother F. G. Stephens emphasized the perceived permanence of the medium. Stephens predicted it would be, of all Burne-Jones's work, the most likely to survive the test of time:

> *Judging the future by the past, it may be sadly as well as safely said that the time will come when, of the works of our living master, those only will remain to describe*

> *which it is my present honourable task. When The Days of Creation have faded from their canvases, and Day and Night, Cophetua, The Silver Stairs [sic], The Four Seasons, The Legend of Perseus, The Legend of the Briar Rose, and all the rest of that galaxy of imagination and treasury of jewellery in lovely colours... have perished... [the mosaics] will endure unchanged until the Protestant church erected in Rome for citizens of the United States of North America shall "Tumble down, and in the dust lie level laid."*[30]

Despite their remote location, far removed from the London art world and fixed in place, the Roman mosaics were repeatedly described as the work by which Burne-Jones would one day be remembered. In 1893, Malcolm Bell reiterated this assessment, describing the mosaic cycle as "[I]n all human probability, the work by this painter which will longest survive the chances and changes of destroying time. Ghirlandajo is reported to have said that he alone designed for eternity, who worked in mosaic, and it is in that enduring and resplendent material that Burne-Jones has written his name for all posterity to read."[31] Although Burne-Jones privately lamented that his mosaic designs would not be understood by his contemporaries, he nonetheless shared the view that the medium promised to persist long into the future – and apart from the marketplace. In another letter to Horner, he wrote, "Its [*sic*] one of those things I do outside painting, far away from it.... I am doing my best but it isn't a picture and few will understand it. It is something between sculpture and architecture... and it can't be sold and will be in Rome and will last for ever. That's why I like doing them."[32] This pervasive association of mosaics with the eternal derived in part from the mosaic revival that had arisen in Victorian Britain around mid-century. Several prominent failures in fresco, most notably the rapid deterioration of those in the House of Lords, coincided with the rise of the Italian glass manufacturer Antonio Salviati and the launch of his commercial mosaic firm, the Compagnia Venezia Murano.[33] In comparison with the often fugitive and fragile fresco medium, perceived as particularly vulnerable to the damp English climate, the ancient art of mosaic was hailed as a durable and expressive alternative.[34] For Burne-Jones, however, his belief in the power and persistence of mosaics also derived from several notable encounters with extant Byzantine examples while traveling in Italy as a young artist.

His passion for the ancient medium can be traced back to his second journey to Italy in the summer of 1862. This trip was arranged and paid for by Ruskin, who served as guide, patron, and father figure. Ushering Burne-Jones through the treasures of Italy, Ruskin directed him to study the works he thought would most benefit the fledgling artist's nascent technical skills and practice. The pair were accompanied by Georgiana, so the tour was also a honeymoon for the couple, lending an air of romance to their memories of this formative experience.[35] The newlyweds briefly parted ways with Ruskin in Milan,

113 * Interior view toward apse, Sta. Maria dell'Assunta, 7th–12th century, Torcello

continuing alone to view Giotto's frescoes in the Scrovegni Chapel in Padua before settling in Venice for three weeks.

There can be little doubt that the opulent mosaics of St. Mark's, dating from the eleventh to the thirteenth centuries, left an indelible impression on Burne-Jones. However, it was the island of Torcello that lingered longest in his imagination. Burne-Jones and Georgiana spent a memorable day touring this ancient town on the Laguna Veneta; he wrote to Ruskin that "[Georgie] and I went early to Torcello and confided much poetic sentiment to each other on the occasion – it was lovely beyond all words."[36] Many years later, Burne-Jones told Mary Gladstone that of the places she must visit in Venice, Torcello came second only to the Piazetta of St. Mark's. He instructed her just as Ruskin had once advised him: "Row out to Torcello, be sure, that's the mother city, and where grass is once was a real city, for centuries too.... There are two places where the history of Venice is most told, and the air is full of it – one is the Piazetta...and the other place is Torcello."[37] Torcello had once surpassed Venice as the most powerful and populous city on the lagoon, but had fallen into decay after the twelfth century. While much of this island's former glory had long since disappeared, the cathedral of Sta. Maria dell'Assunta, with its eleventh- and twelfth-century mosaics (fig. 113), still stood as a poignant reminder of past greatness. Surrounded by ruins and the resurgence of nature, the cathedral at Torcello testified to the unique quality of the mosaic medium to transcend the ebb and flow of time, to endure undimmed and largely intact through the rise and fall of civilizations. Subsequent visits to Rome, in 1871, and especially Ravenna, in 1873, introduced Burne-Jones to a wider sample of mosaics, thereby increasing his understanding of Byzantine iconographic and stylistic conventions.[38] For Burne-Jones, the mosaic medium was not merely durable, but spoke of the cyclical nature of the ages: the inevitability of the death of a society, as well as the possibility of its rebirth.

It was in the middle of the seminal journey to Italy in 1862 that Burne-Jones first felt compelled to execute his own monumental decorative scheme in mosaic. As he shared his passion for the medium with Ruskin, the two began to imagine an entire chapel covered from floor to ceiling in mosaic. Burne-Jones wrote to his benefactor of their grand plans:

> *My heart was full of mosaics!... I want nothing but this chapel.... I wanted above all things a time to talk over this very serious matter – for it is no little thing and we must do something wise – not for fear of the scornful... but because of the glorious company of artists, for which we have put down our names for election. And I wanted to talk for three hours with you, as to whether a divine barn like the Arena Chapel would not be after all better than our many-domed vision – with a barrel roof that should hold our hierarchies and symbols and gods – and clear walls with windows only on one side – a clean space for our histories.... it is my dream.*[39]

While this youthful scheme never came to fruition, Burne-Jones's letter elucidates several key traits that later compelled him to accept the commissions for St. Paul's, Rome.[40] To begin, Burne-Jones acknowledges that the dreamed-of chapel would not be understood or appreciated by their contemporaries, but that he and Ruskin would instead be working for posterity, to add their names to "the glorious company of artists" who had come before and the many generations that would come after. The suggestion of two alternate interiors, a "divine barn like the Arena Chapel" as opposed to a "many-domed vision," probably inspired by St. Mark's, defines Burne-Jones's understanding of the mosaic medium as akin to fresco. Both mosaic and fresco effectively function as two-dimensional public decorative media designed as an integral and permanent part of a building. Finally, his desire for a "clean space" on which to spread "our hierarchies and symbols and gods... our histories" implicitly defines the ideal commission as one for a new, or even purpose-built, architectural space, a personal chapel that could be fashioned after their own beliefs, not those of a patron or a particular religious doctrine.

Two decades later, Morris articulated his own insights into the history and significance of mosaic as a decorative art during the Byzantine era. The emergence of Morris's theories of the Byzantine, and particularly his emphasis on mosaics, coincided with the beginning of Burne-Jones's designs for St. Paul's, suggesting yet again how their respective work continued in active dialogue and intellectual exchange during this time.[41] In his essay "The History of Pattern-Designing" (1882), Morris presents mosaic as the primary decorative vehicle for the rise of a natural, egalitarian, and pleasurable mode of artistic creation:

> *It is perhaps in the noble craft of the mosaic, which is a special craft of the Roman name, that the foreshadowing of the new art is best seen. In the remains of this art you may note the growing formation of more mysterious and more connected, as well as freer and more naturalistic, design. . . . in short, there is a sign in them of the coming wave of that great change which was to turn late Roman art, the last of the old, into Byzantine art, the first of the new.*[42]

Morris argues that it was with the advent of the Byzantine era that art began to free itself from the constraints of tyrannical political rule, the strict bounds of religious doctrine, and even the dictates of race. In Morris's view, Byzantine art, as the herald of the Gothic, planted the seeds of a universal artistic phenomenon that would eventually spread across Europe and Asia, from India to Iceland, Persia to Paris, like a propagating vine.[43] The global flourishing of the arts initiated in the Byzantine era served as a gauge for the correlative rise in the ability of the individual to take pleasure in labor.[44]

This great epoch of artistic creation was predicated not only on the existence of social and economic freedom in a given culture, but also on the extent to which that community coexisted in harmony with nature.[45] Accordingly, Morris pointedly employs organic metaphors to describe this "living" artistic tradition. For example, he likens the development and dissemination of Byzantine and Gothic art over the course of the medieval era to the growth of a great tree: "Its very first roots were spreading when the Roman Empire was tending towards disruption; its last heavily fruited branches were aloft in the air when feudal Europe first felt shaken by the coming storm of revolution in Church and State." Referring to the abundant vegetal scrolls that unite late Roman and early Christian mosaic design, Morris argues that the new style of ornament excelled because of its closer imitation of naturalistic growth. While these scrolls emerged in Roman art, "the real connected pattern where one member grows naturally and necessarily out of another, where the whole thing is alive as a real tree or flower is, all this is an invention of what followed Roman art."[46] Morris does not provide a specific example, but a probable source for this observation may have been the fifth-century apse mosaic in the atrium of S. Giovanni in Fonte, the Lateran Baptistery, Rome (fig. 114). Here, lush vines in green and gold unfurl in spiral patterns across a midnight-blue ground, a celebration of the bounty of nature merged seamlessly with subtle Christian iconography in the form of six jeweled crosses encircling the top of the semi-dome and crowned with a single lamb. Freed from the constraints of Roman classical tyranny and not yet reined in by Christian doctrine, this

114 * Interior atrium, S. Giovanni in Fonte, 5th century. Mosaic. Lateran Baptistery, Rome

vibrant transitional work may have been a crucial touchstone for both Morris and Burne-Jones, illuminating the possibilities of Byzantine art and the mosaic medium.

In seeking to revive not only mosaic but also the centrality of organic ornament indicative of a flourishing natural world, Burne-Jones signaled a hope for a concurrent resurgence of what he and Morris perceived as the cultural and political aspects associated with the era, including human fellowship, rewarding labor, and the thriving of the arts across the globe. To suggest the degree to which these political principles were integral to Burne-Jones's treatment of the mosaic medium and the limits of his willingness to compromise his ideals, it is worth considering a significant project that he rejected. In 1891, Burne-Jones was offered a mosaic commission for four semi-domes in St. Paul's Cathedral, London.[47] To decorate such a renowned building at the very heart of London would have provided the artist with the kind of public platform he prized above all others. Accordingly, he hesitated to decline, writing to the architect George Frederick Bodley in response to his proposal:

> *I know the spaces you mean, and in the abstract am very glad to undertake work which, like this, would be for a public building and upon the larger scale to which I find myself*

> *more and more inclining in design, whilst the fact of its necessary permanence in the place for which it was designed would be additionally attractive to me.*[48]

When he later wrote of refusing to accept the mosaic commission, Burne-Jones suggested that Christopher Wren's Baroque structure was completely at odds not just with his own artistic aims but with the Byzantine stylistic conventions best suited to mosaic work.

However, Burne-Jones's rejection of the commission was motivated by more than his objections to the architectural style. He was repelled by the idea of adorning what he termed the "central edifice of metropolitan devotion." In a sardonic letter to his son Philip, Burne-Jones mocked St. Paul's as a cathedral dedicated to the worship of Mammon:

> *I suppose you know the opening form of prayer used there – "We, members of the stock exchange and of several banking companies (limited) gathered together in this handsome building which the city of London erected at a vast outlay, humbly approach thy throne, O God, beseeching thee to turn thy all-seeing eye upon our present financial difficulties, which threaten to overturn the commercial pre-eminence of our city. It cannot be wholly unknown to thee, O God, that ever since the Argentine bankruptcy our affairs &c.," and so it goes on, rather a long form. Phil, dear, I assure you no other kind of prayer is possible in such a place, and so I was pleased to find that the Book of Common Prayer used there opens with this appeal.*[49]

This private invective is further evidence of his fundamental opposition to capitalist mercantilism, and exposes his view of St. Paul's Cathedral as a bastion of pecuniary greed. It was not fellowship or redemption that united this congregation but competition and profit.

When Burne-Jones accepted the commission to create "unsaleable" mosaics for St. Paul's in Rome, he emphasized their exclusion from the art market, and therefore the impossibility of their becoming transmogrified into capital, as a primary appeal. Although he feared that his mosaic work was ultimately "an unthankful task that no one will ever care for," he persisted in the knowledge that the cycle for this St. Paul's would remain as an integral part of its architectural setting; it could not be sold or hidden away by a wealthy patron.[50] In surveying the nineteenth-century Byzantine revival, J. B. Bullen singles out this quality in Burne-Jones's approach to mosaic: "Unlike [William] Burges, who was fascinated by the purely decorative potential of mosaic, or [William] Butterfield, who was strongly motivated by religious impulses, Burne-Jones saw in this work the possibility of creating democratic art along the lines suggested by William Morris."[51] Mosaics could endure undimmed through the passing centuries, forever appealing to all humanity through what Burne-Jones perceived as the universal legibility, accessibility, and potency of this visual mode. Burne-Jones's choice to structure the decorative scheme as a narrative of ecological apocalypse and redemption aligns with his belief that capitalist acquisitiveness and industrial destruction could only be overcome through a resanctification of the earth. The vision he spread out across the blank surfaces of St. Paul's in Rome was one that rejected the materialism of the age, depicting a munificent Christ offering the viewer salvation as "a gift of the people to the people." His work portrayed the unfettered and unquantifiable bounties of a fertile green earth, reaped not with capital but with pleasurable labor and life-affirming beauty.[52]

An Ecological Apocalypse: The Mosaics

The American Episcopal Church of St. Paul's Within the Walls was intended from its inception as a bold declaration of change and modernity in Rome. Under the direction of Nevin, the construction of St. Paul's was just one component of a widespread urban revival of Rome in the latter part of the nineteenth century that sought to transform the city into a suitable capital for a newly unified Italy. Following the invasion of the city by Italian troops under the command of Victor Emmanuel II in 1870, control of Rome was wrested away from the Pope. Patterning their plans after the prominent example set by Baron Haussmann in Paris, the fledgling Italian government began widening Rome's streets, demolishing its slums, and erecting new state buildings.[53] Along with the restructuring of the physical fabric of Rome, the government also instituted a policy of religious tolerance, thereby allowing Protestant congregations to build houses of worship within the walls of the formerly exclusively Catholic city.[54] Nevin was quick to take advantage of this shift in the political atmosphere, as well as the broader changes in the urban landscape. Rushing to claim the distinction of constructing the first Protestant church within city limits, he arranged for the cornerstone of St. Paul's to be laid alongside the newly forged central axis of modern Rome, the Via Nazionale, on 25 January, 1873.[55] Nevin also promptly secured the services of the English architect George Edmund Street, a popular participant in the Victorian Gothic Revival who was responsible for numerous secular and ecclesiastical building projects and major restorations throughout Britain and Europe. Street's design for St. Paul's was the embodiment of Victorian architectural eclecticism and as a result has been variously described as northern Italian Gothic, neo-Romanesque, and Byzantine in style (fig. 115).[56] Such an anomalous choice of architecture against the backdrop of Rome was no doubt a purposeful statement on the part of Nevin, who desired to render his Protestant independence visually evident, and earn quick recognition for his neophyte church.[57]

Upon the consecration of St. Paul's in 1876, the interior remained largely undecorated due to a lack of funding, although Street's creation of a bare, semi-domed apse clearly suggests that mosaics were part of his initial plan. Four years later, in July 1881, the first mosaic commission was officially offered to Burne-Jones. Georgiana Burne-Jones observed the simultaneous irony and allure of the proposition, writing: "In July I find a letter containing mention of a large scheme of mosaic which occupied Edward for years afterwards. It was for the American Protestant Episcopal Church at Rome – an incongruity not lost upon him – but the architect, Mr. G. E. Street, was a friend, and the chance of working on so large a scale was irresistible."[58] The choice of Burne-Jones may appear somewhat surprising, given not only the large number of American artists then living in Rome, but also his lack of experience working with the medium. Georgiana Burne-Jones perceptively credited his friendship with Street as playing a decisive role in his selection, for the pair had collaborated on a number of ecclesiastical decorative projects.[59] Perhaps even more significantly, not long before the commission was offered, Street and Burne-Jones had campaigned together to stop the planned restoration of St. Mark's, Venice.[60]

115 ✱ G. E. Street, *OS drawing of St Paul American Church, Rome, Italy, No. 12 - Part of West Elevation*, c. 1872–80. Paul Mellon Centre for Studies in British Art, London (Ref: PRJ/4/12/1, Paul Joyce Archive, GB3010)

Speaking out in defense of St. Mark's, renowned for its rich Byzantine mosaics, Burne-Jones is more than likely to have shared his enthusiasm for designing in the medium with Street. In addition to Street's endorsement, however, Nevin would also have been drawn to the further prestige of having an artist of Burne-Jones's stature adorn his fledgling church. By this time, Burne-Jones was not only the leading painter of the Grosvenor Gallery but also an internationally acclaimed ecclesiastical decorative artist renowned for his prolific stained-glass window designs for Morris & Co.

The commission proceeded in two phases, commencing with the design of the apsidal semi-dome, *Christ Enthroned in the Heavenly Jerusalem*, in 1881 (see fig. 126). After the successful installation of this first trial mosaic in 1885, Burne-Jones began designing mosaics that would span the entirety of the church, including the two arches, the choir wall, and the entrance wall. Unfortunately, due in part to delays in securing the funding, only *The Annunciation* and *The Tree of Life* (see figs. 117 and 123) were executed (on the choir and chancel arches, respectively) before Burne-Jones's death in 1898. Several years later, in 1905, the church commissioned Rooke to create *The Earthly Paradise* for the choir, working from a small gouache cartoon and several rough sketches by Burne-Jones. Although Rooke endeavored to remain as faithful as possible to Burne-Jones's original concept, the disparity in the composition, style, color, and production of the choir mosaic renders it distinctly his work rather than that of the late artist.[61] Therefore, in this chapter, I address only the original mosaic cycle as it appeared after the unveiling of the arch mosaics in 1894, with the supplement of any surviving working drawings to suggest how Burne-Jones might have completed the scheme had time and finances allowed.

Creating the first mosaic, *Christ Enthroned*, became a fraught and time-consuming process. Burne-Jones, accustomed to working in partnership with Morris on the execution of his designs in stained glass and, later, tapestry, struggled to achieve his desired effect with the commercial collaborative process of modern mosaic production. When the medium was revived in the nineteenth century, primarily through Salviati's Venezia-Murano Company, a new process of applying the tiles was developed. Under the ancient system, tiles were laid *in situ*, applied directly to the wall surface with plaster, resulting in a marked variability of tile angles and sizes and a shimmering and multifaceted surface. The modern process, by contrast, was made significantly more efficient through the application of tiles to a cartoon in the studio, before shipping the completed sections to the final site to be mounted as one panel. This method lowered costs and greatly sped up the process, but resulted in a more mechanical, or "slick," appearance for the finished mosaic.[62]

Given the shortcomings of this industrialized process, as well as its associations with commercial mass-production, Burne-Jones was reluctant to give over his designs entirely to the Venezia-Murano Company.[63] When he accepted the mosaic commission

116 * Architectural model designed by Edward Burne-Jones for *Christ Enthroned in the Heavenly Jerusalem*, c. 1881–85. Plaster, wood, tempera, and gold, 61 × 100.3 cm. Victoria and Albert Museum, London, 365-1895

for St. Paul's, Burne-Jones therefore sought to temper the effects of this industrial method on the appearance and production of his designs by painstakingly dictating as much of their translation by the workers of Venezia-Murano as possible. As a guide, he painted his design for *Christ Enthroned* onto a wood and plaster scale model of the semi-dome (fig. 116). Then he selected the individual tesserae for every element of the design by hand, with Morris's assistance. He wrote detailed instructions to the overseer of the works in Venice, Giovanni Castellani, on how the colors and form of the mosaic should be executed.[64] In a letter included with the first trial work for the apse mosaic, Burne-Jones explained:

> *I send you also a list of the numbered tesserae – classified for the guidance of the workmen.... I send also a drawing of one of the heads and part of a nimbus and wing, with tesserae arranged in the way I feel the mosaic should be executed – if the workmen had this set up before them I believe it would help them – they would soon fall into the way of designing the flow of the lines, and although at first the work might go slowly,*

& prove... costly I believe you would not regret it. I cannot enough repeat & insist on this point that... all workmanly means [should be] taken to avoid the mechanical look of much modern mosaic.[65]

Even with his carefully articulated directions, or perhaps because of them, the result of this first attempt was disastrous, and the scheme threatened to collapse.

Burne-Jones immediately sent off an impassioned letter to Rooke, who had gone to Venice to intercede. The artist expressed his utter despair over the mosaic sample, fearing that he had baffled the workers:

Have I bewildered them? have I frightened them?... Draw them and colour them a face from the ancient work.... Forget that it is I that am concerned – suppose it is an old cartoon found and that it is desirable to render it, translate it, make it effective – VISIBLE, INTELLIGIBLE at a distance, at a good height... the gradation of colour delicate and soft.... It must be done or I will destroy my cartoons and hand back the money.[66]

The letter attests to Burne-Jones's appreciation of the importance of legibility in public, decorative design, as well as his desire to achieve the effect of ancient mosaic. Castellani replied, in an attempt to reassure the artist and save the project:

It is not the mosaic as we are used to make, or as we understand. We are obliged for doing it to unlearn all that in a very long practice of our art we had apprized.... Your letter therefore did not surprise me; only I regretted not to have been left free to do as we are used to do, and to have been so exposed before you as being totally incapable of performing our duty and doing justice to your beautiful cartoons.[67]

Lacking the means to restore the lost techniques of mosaic work in the manner of the decorative arts objects produced through Morris & Co., such precise instructions were Burne-Jones's only way to encourage the reform of the craft. He may have offended the workers, but the risk was justified in his eyes if it would enable him to avoid "the mechanical look of much modern mosaic." In the end, through the intervention of both Rooke and Nevin, Castellani and his workers came to understand what was expected of them, and the remainder of the mosaics were executed in a manner which satisfied Burne-Jones.[68]

Through this vast decorative program rendered in an adamantine medium, Burne-Jones sought to foster a space for aesthetic as well as spiritual contemplation inside the church of St. Paul's. Harnessing the experiential as well as temporal power of this ancient communal art form, Burne-Jones's mosaics were designed as a holistic, immersive experience for the viewer, with the hope of prompting revelatory awakenings much like his own experience at Beauvais Cathedral (see Chapter One). Throughout the cycle, themes of

117 ∗ Edward Burne-Jones, *The Annunciation*, 1894. Mosaic, St. Paul's Within the Walls, Rome

FOLLOWING PAGES ∗ 118 ∗ Edward Burne-Jones, *The Annunciation* (detail of fig. 117)

natural destruction and rebirth emerge as central to the apocalyptic narrative. Entering off the bustling Via Nazionale, not far from Rome's new central train station, the visitor slowly adjusts to the hushed, cool interior. The glittering gold mosaics of the apse emerge from the darkness, drawing the viewer down the central aisle. The choir arch (fig. 117), which partially obscures the chancel arch and much of the upper portion of the apsidal semi-dome, is the first clearly visible part of the mosaic program as the viewer processes forward.

In this scene of the Annunciation, the essential elements are present, as a humble Mary in white robes bows her haloed head, and clasps her hands in prayer on the miraculous arrival of the angel Gabriel who descends from the heavens before her (fig. 118). However, Burne-Jones chose to unfold this holy scene within a barren desert, rendering

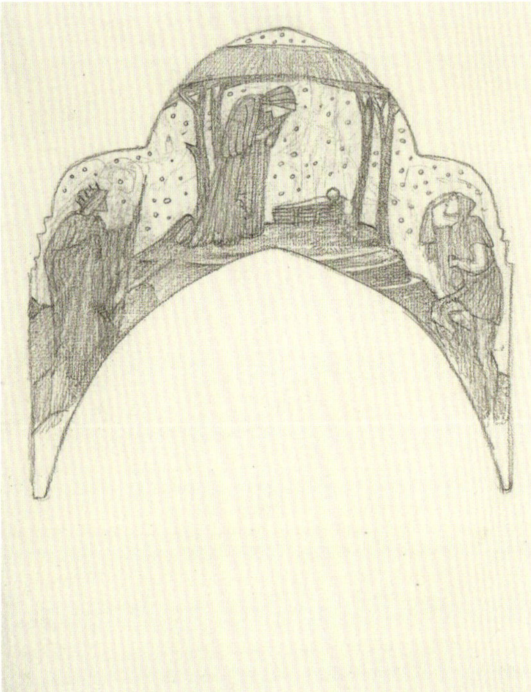

119 ∗ Edward Burne-Jones, "The 'Secret' Book of Designs," 1885–98, no. 417. Album, 37 × 29.4 cm. British Museum, 1899-7-13-417

120 ∗ Edward Burne-Jones, "The 'Secret' Book of Designs," 1885–98, no. 408. Album, 37 × 29.4 cm. British Museum, 1899-7-13-408

it difficult at first to reconcile with existing iconographic traditions. Executed largely in matte or opaque mosaic tiles, the bleak, arid landscape is laid out in pale, somber shades of brown, green, and slate, set against a smoldering crepuscular sky of reds and oranges. Further amplifying the incongruity of the scene, Mary is depicted with the unusual attribute of a water jar.[69] As a symbol of the Incarnation, this empty jar may denote the theological concept of Mary as the sacred human vessel who would receive the word of God made flesh. In addition, Burne-Jones may also have been drawing on an apocryphal legend that told of Mary going forth to fill a water jar beyond the gates of Nazareth.[70] And yet, alone in a rocky terrain with only scattered, shallow pools of water, Mary's task appears futile.

In his preparatory drawings for the mosaics in "The 'Secret' Book of Designs," Burne-Jones experimented with several subjects for the arch mosaics, including the Fall, the Expulsion, and a wintry Nativity scene set on a rocky hilltop (fig. 119). When he settled on the concept of the Annunciation, his first composition depicted the two central fig-

121 ∗ Edward Burne-Jones, "The 'Secret' Book of Designs," 1885–98, no. 411. Album, 37 × 29.4 cm.
British Museum, 1899-7-13-411

ures and the water jar in approximately the same spatial arrangement, but with a clearly delineated river running down from the mountains and encircling the landscape (fig. 120). Rather than bare rock and sand, the landscape is dotted with grass and spring flowers, while several trees appear in the distance, the resurgence of life already in progress. By contrast, his next design was starkly somber in tone, more closely resembling the final mosaic (fig. 121). A small rivulet of water runs down from the mountains, but the ground is completely devoid of life, apart from several blackened tree trunks. Below, a small inset sketch suggests a single lily plant beside an empty door in the lower corner of the arch. In the final arch mosaic, the bleak, scorched wilderness remains, with the thin rivulet of water flowing from the hills on the right accompanied by several desiccated puddles. Notably, in the lower left corner, Burne-Jones replaced the lily with a mother pelican, tearing her breast to sustain her offspring with her own blood.

122 * Edward Burne-Jones, *The Pelican in Her Piety*, 1880–81. East window, St. Martin's Church, Brampton, Cumbria

The pelican was a prevalent medieval Christian symbol evoking Christ's sacrifice. According to Adolphe Napoléon Didron's 1843 *Iconographie chrétienne*, "The pelican, lacerating her breast that her young may be nourished by her blood, is an appropriate figure of Jesus, dying, and shedding his blood for the salvation of mankind."[71] While this notion was biologically inaccurate, the pelican became a potent visual emblem of the Passion and, in particular, the blood that flowed from Christ's side. Burne-Jones featured the pelican and her young in other ecclesiastical designs, including in the central lower light of the east window of St. Martin's Church, Brampton, Cumbria (fig. 122). As a maternal figure of Christ, the pelican aligns mother and child in their nurturing relationship toward humanity, as well as their sacrifice for the sake of redemption.

The presence of the pelican in *The Annunciation* arch mosaic accords with Christian typological symbolism, prefiguring the appearance of Christ himself in the chancel arch, *The Tree of Life*. However, the pelican also suggests that the fauna of the earth decline or flourish with the health of the environment. For Ruskin, along with water and air, the third element necessary for life is earth. Lamenting the effects of industrial exploitation on the land, Ruskin perceived a world turned to toxic dust:

> *Then for the third, Earth – meant to be nourishing for you, and blossoming. You have learned about it, that there is no such thing as a flower; and as far as your scientific*

123 * Edward Burne-Jones, *The Tree of Life*, 1894. Mosaic, St. Paul's Within the Walls, Rome

> *hands and scientific brains, inventive of explosive and deathful, instead of blossoming and life-giving, Dust, can contrive, you have turned the Mother-Earth, Demeter, into the Avenger-Earth, Tisiphone – with the voice of your brother's blood crying out of it, in one wild harmony round all its murderous sphere.*[72]

Standing alongside the self-sacrificing pelican in a scorched desert, Mary and her water jar promise the hope of regeneration for humanity, the earth, and all organic life. Burne-Jones unveils the broadly resonant elements of the Annunciation narrative: themes of both human and environmental rebirth, of the possibility of a wasteland transforming into verdant field and forest, of life flourishing from barrenness, of the nurturing mother and Mother Earth.

This promised resurgence of organic life is brought to vivid fruition as the viewer proceeds further down the pavement of the central aisle, from the stark but expectant scene of *The Annunciation* to the lush triumph of *The Tree of Life* (fig. 123). The space once occupied by Mary on the right of *The Annunciation* is now filled with the figure of Eve and her two children, while the angelic Gabriel floating on the left side of the arch gives way to the earthly body of Adam, his feet firmly planted on a grassy slope. From out of the empty and barren ground that marked the center of *The Annunciation* now sprouts the colossal Tree of Life, from which Christ makes a gesture of blessing and forgiveness. Rather than the suffering and censure of the Crucifixion, the salvation and redemption of humanity is envisioned as the tripartite apotheosis of a flourishing natural world, the human body ennobled through labor, and the harmonic rhythms of decorative art.

Much like his choice to revive the ancient Christian symbol of the mother pelican, Burne-Jones drew on the Byzantine tradition of the Living Cross for his re-envisioning of the Crucifixion. The apocryphal legend of the Living Cross varies across different sources, but the essence of the tale is that Seth, the son of Adam, was sent to paradise by his ailing father to retrieve the healing oils of the Tree of Life. The archangel Michael refused his request, but instead gave Seth a shoot from the tree to plant over his father's grave. The tree that grew from this seedling would eventually be cut down and the cross of the Crucifixion hewn from its branches, thus bestowing the gift of immortality on the human soul through the sacrifice of Christ.[73] In accordance with the popularity of these legends, a corresponding imagery of the Living Cross developed across early and medieval Christian ecclesiastical works. The twelfth-century apse mosaic of S. Clemente in Rome, depicting *Christ and the Cross as Tree of Life* (fig. 124), is one example that Burne-Jones undoubtedly encountered during his time in the city.[74] This effulgent mosaic, with its spiraling, serpentine vines adorned with flowers and exotic birds set against a brilliant gold ground, in turn emulates early Byzantine works such as the apse mosaic in the Lateran Baptistery. At the center of the apse is a deep blue cross bearing an attenuated and crucified Christ surrounded by twelve doves, while to either side appear the figures of Mary and John. This Living Cross is not rendered as a tree, but the proliferating scrolls of plants that dominate the composition emanate from a lush and leafy oasis at its base that recalls the appearance of the Tree of Life set beside the Water of Life in the Book of Revelation.[75] Here, Christ's sacrifice directly facilitates abundant life, and, much like Burne-Jones's *The Tree of Life*, it is this flourishing organic decoration that seems to command devotion.

While he was certainly inspired by the iconography of the Living Cross, Burne-Jones's interpretation deviates radically from these sources. As Alan Crawford observed, "Medieval Christianity had an image of the cross as the tree of life, but Burne-Jones's image is all tree, all life, and no cross."[76] The tree, more so than the human figures, is the beating heart of the composition, the source of life and redemption residing in a revitalized organic world. In *The Magazine of Art* in 1895, an anonymous critic praised the design

124 ∗ *Christ and the Cross as Tree of Life*, c. 1100–28. Apse mosaic, S. Clemente, Rome

as a fundamentally decorative work, which features at its core not a depiction of a tree, but "a perfect symbol of a tree." The writer likened the tree to an anthropomorphic body:

> *The "Tree of Life" . . . is a marvel of learned and elaborate workmanship. . . . in its carrying out it is allowed to become wholly conventional in its balanced pattern of rhythmical and sinuous lines, with its skeleton brought boldly forward and the heart-shaped mass of its fibrous foliage spreading and waving till it entirely fills and is lost behind the topmost cusps and the small arc above them.*[77]

Indeed, during his development of *The Tree of Life* mosaic in "The 'Secret' Book of Designs," Burne-Jones experimented with a design for an arch mosaic where the figural elements are dissolved entirely and replaced with a verdant copse (fig. 125). The intertwined branches and intricately twisting trunks of the trees fill the space from end to end. This Edenic vision simultaneously celebrates the divinity of nature, particularly the universal form of the sacred tree, and the radical potential of the decorative.

Amplifying the capaciousness of the Tree of Life as a symbol for the redemption of humanity and the natural world, Burne-Jones's composition could also hold allusions to

125 * Edward Burne-Jones, "The 'Secret' Book of Designs," 1885–98, no. 405. Album, 37 × 29.4 cm. British Museum, London, 1899-7-13-405

the Norse tradition of Igdrasil. Writing in 1904, Fortunée De Lisle made this connection, describing Burne-Jones's design as merging pagan mythology with ancient Christian iconography: "In the centre rises the Tree of Life – Igdrasil, whose boughs reach into heaven, and whose roots into hell."[78] According to Norse mythology, Igdrasil is a divine organic entity that holds up the heavens, stretches throughout the earth, and houses the three Norns (akin to the Fates) at its roots. The medieval compendium of Norse legends, the *Poetic Edda*, gives a prominent place to Igdrasil in the Norse apocalypse, Ragnarok. The *Poetic Edda* also includes a reference to the legend of Odin, who sacrificed himself on Igdrasil's branches in order to release the knowledge of runes into the world. While not directly tied to Igdrasil, Norse mythology describes the first human couple, Askr and Embla, as each formed by the gods from an ash and an elm tree, respectively. Both Morris and Burne-Jones were deeply conversant with Norse mythology, and the resonances between the design for *The Tree of Life* and the mythology of Igdrasil cannot be coincidental.[79]

Finally, in transforming his Crucifixion into a celebration of the bounty of organic life, Burne-Jones was also harnessing the association of the tree with both the Expulsion from Eden in Genesis 3:22–4 and the Book of Revelation 22:1–3. The Tree of Life figures prominently in the latter's vision of the Heavenly Jerusalem:

> *Then he showed me the river of the water of life, bright as crystal, flowing from the throne of God and of the Lamb through the middle of the street of the city; also, on either side of the river, the tree of life with its twelve kinds of fruit, yielding its fruit each month; and the leaves of the tree were for the healing of the nations. There shall no more be anything accursed, but the throne of God and of the Lamb shall be in it.*[80]

Arrayed across the chancel arch mosaic, *The Tree of Life* serves as a gateway to the shimmering apsidal semi-dome mosaic, *Christ Enthroned in the Heavenly Jerusalem* (fig. 126). Within the spatial configuration of the church, therefore, *The Tree of Life* binds together earth and heaven, transporting the viewer to paradise alongside Adam and Eve.

For his design of *Christ Enthroned*, Burne-Jones remained largely faithful to the Byzantine tradition of placing an enthroned and youthful Christ in Majesty at the heart of the mosaic. He followed such precedents as the sixth-century apse of S. Vitale, Ravenna (fig. 127), and the twelfth-century *Ascension* mosaic in the central dome of St. Mark's, Venice. In Burne-Jones's rendering, Christ is ensconced before the golden walls of the Heavenly Jerusalem, while to either side appear five archangels standing guard at the gates of paradise. This apocalyptic vision was also drawn from the Book of Revelation, in which John is shown the radiant walls of the Heavenly Jerusalem ringed with twelve gates and twelve angels.[81] Choosing to depict one half of a presumably symmetrical configuration, Burne-Jones presented the viewer with six gates; standing before them appear, from left to right, Uriel, guardian of the sun; Michael, the warrior bearing a shield and spear; Gabriel, the angel of the Annunciation holding a white lily; Chemuel, bearing the San Graal; and finally, Zophiel, guardian of the moon.[82] The portal on Christ's right hand remains empty, a gaping void at the very center of the apse. This forbiddingly unguarded gate evokes the legend of Lucifer, the archangel who rebelled against God and was cast down from the heavens.[83]

While it was informed by traditional Byzantine iconography, insistent environmental visual cues pervade Burne-Jones's design for *Christ Enthroned*, suggesting that Burne-Jones shifted his apocalyptic vision to encompass the renewal of nature alongside the salvation of the human soul. Beginning with the enthroned Christ in Majesty, he selected the more obscure attribute of an earthly globe, echoing the apse mosaic of S. Vitale (see image on p. 162). The prominent globe is also strongly reminiscent of those found in his 1872–76 six-panel watercolor *The Days of Creation* (fig. 128). This ecological orb, with its

126 ∗ Edward Burne-Jones, *Christ Enthroned in the Heavenly Jerusalem*, 1885. Mosaic.
St. Paul's Within the Walls, Rome

compressed view of meadows, mountains, and sparkling sky, was frequently noted by commentators as a dominant feature of the mosaic. For example, in 1890, F. G. Stephens called attention to the globe and its detailed landscape: "The great and central figure is that of the Son of God, Who holds on His knee with His left hand the great sphere of crystal in which are mystically reflected the earth, blue sky, and wavy sea full of flecks of light."[84] The terrestrial landscape at the prominent spatial and ideological focal point of the apse

127 * *Christ the Redeemer* (or *Christ between Two Angels, S. Vitalis, and Bishop Ecclesius*), 6th century. Mosaic, S. Vitale, Ravenna

128 * Edward Burne-Jones, *The Days of Creation*, 1870–76, photographed in their original frame (Sotheby's, London, June 13, 1934). Harvard Art Museums/Fogg Museum, Cambridge, Massachusetts, Bequest of Grenville L. Winthrop, 1943.454

is a salient visual cue, alerting the viewer to a prevailing environmental current that runs throughout the cycle as a whole.

At the base of Christ's heavenly throne the four rivers of paradise flow forth to create what one reviewer termed a "circumambient flood" around the base of the semi-dome.[85] Echoing the scene in the orb above, the four streams cascade over a mountainous landscape, dotted by passing clouds and enclosed within the arc of a rainbow, before merging to become one gushing river. The banks of this river are comprised of vividly colored geological patterns that fill the space above the pale blue waves. These interlocking organic shapes, which resemble the striated curves of volcanic geodes or slices of marble, are also suggested by a passage in Revelation where the foundations of heaven are described as "adorned with every jewel."[86] This innovative depiction of a sea of jewels is also a self-referential decorative gesture toward the myriad glass and stone tiles that comprise the geological mosaic medium itself. Lastly, as viewers gaze back up the curve of the apse and around from left to right, they are met on either side with the celestial figures of Uriel and Zophiel, the guardians of the sun and moon, personifications of day and night. The orbiting solar and lunar celestial bodies reinforce the cyclical progression of life on earth, a perpetual rise and fall that promises a new dawn after the dark of night.

Epilogue: The Rebel Artist

With Burne-Jones's death in 1898, his vision for St. Paul's Within the Walls, as with the *Perseus* series, was left unfinished. Although Rooke sought to complete the project with the choir mosaic *The Earthly Paradise*, Burne-Jones's designs for the entrance wall were never implemented. Consequently, as the composition now stands, his decision to conjure the specter of Lucifer with the empty portal beside Christ in the apse appears somewhat inexplicable. In his original concept for the church, Burne-Jones planned to depict Lucifer's expulsion from heaven at the opposite end of the nave. When it became evident that the composition would never be executed in mosaic, he translated the abandoned design into the monumental 1894 watercolor *The Fall of Lucifer* (fig. 129) and exhibited it at the New Gallery in 1895.[87] Suggested by another passage from Revelation, 12:7–10, the composition depicts Satan and his cohort of rebel angels being "thrown down to earth" by the archangel Michael after a heavenly battle.[88] Consistent with the rest of the mosaic cycle, however, the Apocalyptic source facilitates the investigation of a broader theme.

129 ✱ Edward Burne-Jones, *The Fall of Lucifer*, 1894. Gouache and gold paint on paper laid on canvas stretched over board, 245 × 118 cm. Private collection

NECQUE·LOCUS·INVENTUS
EST·EORU·AMPLIUS·IN·COELO
ET·PROIECTUS·EST·DRACO·ILLE·MAGNUS·SERPENS·ANTIQUUS·ET·ANGELI·EIUS·CUM·ILLO·MISSI·SUNT·PROPTEREA·LAETAMINI·COELI·ET·QUI
HABITATIS·IN·EIS·VAE·TERRAE·ET·MARI·QUIA·DESCENDIT·DIABOLUS·AD·VOS·HABENS·IRAM·MAGNAM·SCIENS·QUOD·MODICUM·TEMPUS·HABET·
ET·FACTUM·EST·PROELIUM·MAGNUM·IN·COELO·MICHAEL·ET·ANGELI·EIUS·PROELIA
BANTUR·CUM·DRACONE·ET·DRACO·PUGNABAT·ET·ANGELI·EIUS·ET·NON·VALUERUNT
AUDIVI·VOCEM·MAGNAM·IN·COELO·DICENTEM·NUNC·FACTA·EST·SA
LUS·ET·VIRTUS·ET·REGNUM·DEI·NOSTRI·ET·POTESTAS·CHRISTI·EIUS·

130 ∗ *Genesis* (detail), Lothian Bible, Oxford, England, c. 1220. Vellum, leaf 47.6 × 32 cm.
Morgan Library, New York, MS M.791, fol. 4v. Gift of Philip Hofer, May 1935

Surviving statements suggest that Burne-Jones identified Lucifer as a figure of the artist engaged in a Promethean struggle with the gods to create visions of beauty that exceeded nature, for which he was punished with the curse of eternal darkness.[89] *The Fall of Lucifer*, therefore, functions not only as an Apocalyptic image, but also as an allegory of the perils inherent in the act of artistic creation and rebellion.

Taken together with the empty portal at the core of the apse mosaic, Burne-Jones's choice to call attention to Lucifer's absence may also have invoked the concept of the tenth choir. In describing the depiction of Genesis on the frontispiece of the thirteenth-century Lothian Bible (fig. 130), Jeffrey F. Hamburger has explained the notable absence of angels in one section of the heavenly host to the right of God the Father, Christ, and the dove of the Holy Spirit as a motif derived from the Book of Enoch: "The inchoate band to the left of the Trinity represent[s] the tenth choir once occupied by Lucifer and his cohorts. To this empty space mankind shall be elevated at the end of time, a motif that points to the ultimate reconciliation of God and nature."[90] The vacancy left by the "tenth choir" when God banished Lucifer and his rebel angels from heaven allows room for redeemed humanity to take their place in heaven. The empty portal in the apse mosaic beside Christ, therefore, would have created a perpetual, cyclical rise and fall across the nave of the church. The banishment of Lucifer and his angels on the entrance wall would have ushered the viewer toward the desolation of *The Annunciation*, the verdant rebirth of *The Tree of Life*, and at last to the *Heavenly Jerusalem*, where Christ and humanity are reconciled. Much like the mosaics of Torcello, this vision of an ecological apocalypse could survive long after its sponsoring civilization crumbled around it, transcending temporal limitations to speak across the ages, offering hope for the renewal and redemption of the earth to future generations.

Chapter Five

"Making God manifest"

THE NATIVITY AS EMBODIMENT AND THE ADORATION AS WITNESS

In May 1898, Burne-Jones recorded the very last entry in his working list, a notebook documenting his major projects year by year spanning more than four decades, writing that he "saw the Hawarden window finished this month."[1] The entry refers to *The Nativity*, the west window of St. Deiniol's, the parish church of Hawarden in northern Wales (fig. 131). This stained-glass window was commissioned by Mary Gladstone as a tribute to her parents, Catherine and William Gladstone.[2] Sadly, death haunted the creation of the window from first to last. Mary's initial letters proposing the window arrived in the summer of 1896, coinciding with Morris's illness and then death in October that year. Plunged into mourning for his lost friend and partner, Burne-Jones worked intermittently on the design for the Hawarden window over the next year. In Morris's absence, Burne-Jones was required to execute more aspects of the window than he had with most of his previous stained-glass projects. He not only designed the cartoon, he also traveled to Merton Abbey several times to supervise the translation of the drawing by John Henry Dearle and the artisans of Morris & Co. During this time, William Gladstone's own health began to fail and he died on May 19, 1898, never having seen the completed window. In a letter of June 5, Burne-Jones wrote to Mary Gladstone after the unveiling, "I was really happy making that window.... I felt more content than I usually am with work carried out by other hands. they [*sic*] tried very hard at the works, one & all, to make it good."[3] Less than two weeks later, on June 17, 1898, Burne-Jones himself died from heart failure, leaving behind a studio filled with projects that forever remain unfinished. Although he could not have known that *The Nativity* at Hawarden would be his last completed work, it nonetheless

stands as a poignant memorial to Burne-Jones and his career, offering a divine vision of hope and salvation inseparably fused with loss and mourning.

In the window, Burne-Jones embraced the limitations and demands, as well as the radical possibilities, of the stained-glass medium. Stretching across four lights and the tracery above, the design fosters the illusion that the viewer is a direct witness to the Incarnation, the moment when God became one with mortal flesh. Representing the foundational miracle of Christian belief, the Incarnation has frequently been symbolized as light emerging from darkness.[4] To render the Nativity in stained glass, therefore, symbolically extends the visual metaphor from iconography to medium.[5] Comprised largely of pieces of blue and white glass, punctuated by passages of ruby red, the chromatic shards evoke the colors of the Virgin, as well as the Passion and Christ's future sacrifice. The window does not take a purely "pictorial" approach, disappearing to reveal the scene unfolding in a fictive realm beyond. Instead, the dynamic unification of each integral part constitutes the manifestation of the divine. The translucent colored glass, the continuous compositional field, the network of opaque lead lines, and the intersecting stonework combine to render the Incarnation as the process of the divine coming into being.

Mary and the newborn Christ constitute the theological, visual, and emotional core of the composition. Stretched diagonally across the two central lights, the Virgin cradles her son in her arms as both lie on a bed of straw. With her eyes closed, Mary supports Christ's swaddled body with one hand, while the other gently caresses the back of his head, turned toward her own. Recalling sculptural funerary monuments, their recumbent bodies are shrouded in drapery, which tinges the tender embrace of mother and child with sorrow and foreboding. The surrounding figures serve as empathetic models for the viewer, performing acts of witness and reverence. Five angels kneel at the lower edge of the window, while seven more, standing behind a simple wattle fence, fill the upper portions. Of this latter grouping of angels, three hold musical instruments, two clasp their hands in prayer, and two place their right hands to their cheeks in wonder. In keeping with traditional depictions of the Nativity, Burne-Jones collapses the episode of Christ's birth with the Adoration of the Shepherds, who appear on the right, and the Adoration of the Magi, who appear on the left. A rustic thatched roof surmounts the tableau, sheltering mother and child, while three more angels float in the sky above, drifting diagonally upward across the tracery. In the topmost quatrefoil, the central angel holds aloft a star, a point of celestial light at the apex of the window. In this apocalyptic vision of the Nativity,

131 * Edward Burne-Jones, designer, Morris & Co., *The Nativity*, 1896–98.
Stained glass, St. Deiniol's, Hawarden, Wales

the old heaven and earth are shattered like so many fragments of glass, in order for a new world to emanate from the generative embrace of mother and child, reconstituted as pure color and radiant light.[6]

Exploring the subjects of the Nativity and the Adoration through several key works across Burne-Jones's career and a range of media, this chapter examines his expression of the intertwined concepts of manifestation, embodiment, and witness as analogous to the process of artistic labor, contemplation, and revelatory awakening. Paring down the Adorations and the Nativity to their essence, Burne-Jones created an embodied, empathetic vision with a bold social commentary in interrelated projects executed over nearly four decades and designed largely for ecclesiastical spaces, including altarpieces, tapestry, and stained glass.

"The eternal being born": The Incarnation and the Embodiment of the Divine

While the works considered in this chapter span from Burne-Jones's first major independent painting commission as an emerging artist in 1861 to his last stained-glass window in 1898, there is a notable concentration of Nativities and of Adorations in the years 1887 and 1888. During this time, Burne-Jones began four versions of the subject in as many different media: a *Nativity* stained-glass window for St. Philip's, Birmingham (1887; see fig. 156); *The Adoration of the Magi* tapestry for Exeter College, Oxford (1887–88; see fig. 138); *The Star of Bethlehem*, a watercolor for the new Municipal Museum and Art Gallery, Birmingham (1887–91; see fig. 140); and the pendant paintings *The Nativity* and *The King and the Shepherd* for St. John's, Torquay (1888; see figs. 145 and 146).[7] While Morris was actively engaged in socialist political agitation, Burne-Jones seemingly found an increased urgency in this focal point of Christian mythology. His interpretation of these subjects was profoundly informed by the doctrine of the Incarnation, which in turn became an egalitarian model for aesthetic creation and epiphany.

In 1893, shortly after his retrospective exhibition at the New Gallery, Burne-Jones offered a rare articulation of what Georgiana Burne-Jones termed his "religion of art" during a conversation with the scholar Sebastian Evans. This private dialogue was transcribed at length in the *Memorials*, indicative of Georgiana Burne-Jones's belief in its importance in understanding the core motivations of her husband's artistic practice. One particular passage is worth quoting at length:

> *Day of Judgment? It is a synonym for the present moment – it is eternally going on. It is not so much as a moment – it is just the line that has no breadth between past and*

> *future. There is not – cannot be, if you think it out – any other Day of Judgment. It is not in the 'nature of things.' The Dies irae dies illa is everlastingly dissolving the ages into ashes everywhere. It is Nature herself, natura, not past or future, but the eternal being born, the sum of things as they are.... If we believe that things as they are can be made better than they are, and in that faith set to work to help the betterment to the best of our ability however limited, we are, and cannot help being, children of the Kingdom. If we disbelieve in the possibility of betterment, or don't try to help it forward, we are and cannot help being damned.... Of course you can translate it into any religious language you please; Christian, Buddhist, Mahometan, or what not. 'Have you faith?' I suppose means the same thing. Faith, not amount of achievement – which, at best, must be infinitesimally small – that is the great thing. Have you faith, my dear? Do you ever think of this poor old woman, our Mother, trudging on and on towards nothing and nowhere, and swear by all your gods that she shall yet go gloriously some day, with sunshine and flowers and chanting of her children that love her and she loves? I can never think of collective humanity as brethren and sisters; they seem to me 'Mother' – more nearly Mother than Mother Nature herself. To me, this weary, toiling, groaning world of men and women is none other than Our Lady of the Sorrows. It lies on you and me and all the faithful to make her Our Lady of the Glories. Will she ever be so? Will she? Will she? She shall be, if your toil and mine, and the toil of a thousand ages of them that come after us can make her so!*[8]

This quotation illuminates, in forceful tones, Burne-Jones's dedication to his pursuit of art as a secular ministry. Contrary to his frequent characterization as an escapist who retreated into nostalgic reveries of the past, Burne-Jones here proclaims his embrace of the present moment as the instant of salvation and renewal, the apocalyptic "eternal being born." Moreover, this declaration reinforces the seriousness of purpose with which he approached his artistic labor as a means of enacting change in the world, his "toil" in service of the core belief "that things as they are can be made better."

Burne-Jones also clarifies here that his profound engagement with Christian theology is not a commitment to one religious creed. He espouses faith in nature and collective humanity, conceptualized as not just "Mother" but more particularly under the Virgin Mary's title *Mater Dolorosa*. Burne-Jones's erudite grasp of Christian philosophy, doctrine, and symbolism informed his myriad decorative commissions for ecclesiastical interiors, many in collaboration with Morris, as well as his painting practice. However, when he abandoned his original calling to embrace a life of art, he also turned away from the Church of England, refusing to adhere to Anglican dogma. Instead, Burne-Jones the artist experimented with Christian iconography in order to express what he perceived as universal truths in the hope of transforming "Our Lady of the Sorrows," the suffering of humanity, into "Our Lady of the Glories."[9]

Taking this testimony of his most deeply held beliefs into account, Burne-Jones's depictions of the Virgin Mary, particularly in the context of the Nativity, reveal a new significance. Burne-Jones concluded his discussion with Evans by stating, "That was an awful thought of Ruskin's, that artists paint God for the world.... Think of what it means. It is the power of bringing God into the world – making God manifest. It is giving back her Child that was crucified to Our Lady of the Sorrows."[10] This final statement asserts the importance of the artist in rendering the divine accessible and tangible for the viewer, in "making God manifest." The Incarnation, a core tenet of Christianity, is the theological doctrine that defines this manifestation, the moment at which God takes on mortal form as Christ, whose sacrifice allows for the redemption of humanity. The essence of the Incarnation can be found in its etymology: *incarno*, to make flesh, to bring life into being. The Incarnation was a particular interest of the nineteenth-century Oxford Movement generally, and especially of John Henry Newman and John Keble, both of whom were essential early influences for Burne-Jones.[11] In her examination of the Incarnation in the poetry of Christina Rossetti, the literary scholar Mary Arseneau wrote (in 1993), "The Tractarians saw the incarnation as the vital core of the Church, its sacraments, and God's plan for humanity's redemption." And for many there is, as Arseneau pointed out, a connection between Christ's Incarnation and the manifestation of "earthly beauty": "the incarnation establishes a principle of analogy between the earthly and the divine, making nature the symbol of the divine and forging a link between the spiritual and the physical."[12] The Incarnation thus extends from the single moment of God's embodiment in human form to the manifestation of the divine in nature and collective humanity.

When Rooke directly questioned him on the number of iterations of the Nativity and the Adoration he had completed across a range of media throughout his career, Burne-Jones replied:

> *I love Christmas carol Christianity. I couldn't do without mediaeval Christianity. The central idea of it and all it has gathered to itself made the Europe that I exist in. The enthusiasm and devotion, the learning and the art, the humanity and romance, the self denial and splendid achievement that the human race can never be deprived of, except by cataclysm that would all but destroy man himself – all belong to it.*[13]

The phrase "Christmas carol Christianity" may at first appear trivializing, conjuring frivolous Victorian Yuletide merriment. To the contrary, however, this declaration asserts Burne-Jones's commitment to the underlying tenets of hope, equality, and salvation expressed in the ancient Christian faith and especially the story of the Nativity. For

Burne-Jones, "Christmas carol Christianity" signified an embrace of this parable of the rise of the humble and poor above the wealthy and powerful, a vision of salvation for all humankind and the divine incarnate in nature. Seeking to cull universal truths from the ancient Christian legends, Burne-Jones found the Nativity appropriate for the visual expression of human fellowship and emotional connection, with the procreative bond between mother and child promising redemption and the world remade. The Incarnation and its expression in the Nativity also revealed the power of material and spiritual transformation. As demonstrated by the preceding discussion of the *Perseus* series, investigating the metamorphic possibilities inherent in the process of aesthetic creation was a vital component of Burne-Jones's practice. The Nativity as an iconographic subject thus gave him another opportunity to meditate on the radical possibilities of aesthetic transformation, this time in the visual language of Christian symbolism.

If the Incarnation lies at the heart of the Nativity, then witness and revelation form the essence of the Adoration of the Shepherds and of the Magi. In his study of 1997 of Andrea Mantegna's *The Adoration of the Magi* (c. 1495–1505), the curator Dawson W. Carr described the latter Biblical episode as "one of the earliest revelations of Jesus' identity as the Son of God, and one of the first instances of Christian worship." The two incidents derive from different accounts, with the Adoration of the Shepherds described in Luke 2:8–20 and the Adoration of the Magi in Matthew 2:1–12. However, they are frequently depicted together, along with hosts of heavenly angels, in order to represent the vast scope of Christ's divine revelation. The poor and the wealthy, the young and the old, the celestial and mundane: all equally witness the miracle of the Incarnation and the promise of salvation. Moreover, as Carr argued, in the fifteenth century, the three magi were increasingly represented as continental allegories of Europe, Asia, and Africa, lending the scene a global and imperial significance.[14] The Adoration of the Shepherds and of the Magi allowed Burne-Jones to incorporate representative figures for collective humanity gathered in solidarity as witnesses to the moment of transformation, of the divine incarnate, and salvation.

Embodied witness through active visual observation was also fundamental to early Pre-Raphaelite painting. Indeed, Ruskin's dictum in *Modern Painters* to "Go to nature in all singleness of heart . . . rejecting nothing, selecting nothing and scorning nothing" called artists to witness the divine in nature.[15] If God is made manifest through earthly beauty, truth to nature functions as an act of devotion performed by the artist and conveyed, in turn, to the viewer through exactingly detailed observations. In the third volume of *Modern Painters*, Ruskin went on to proclaim, "the greatest thing a human soul ever does in this world is to see something, and tell what it saw in a plain way. . . . To see clearly is poetry, prophecy, and religion, – all in one."[16] Ruskin compelled his readers to find a clarity of vision, to perceive the divine in the world, as well as the destruction of that divinity in modernity. Following Ruskin's mandate, depictions of the Adoration enabled Burne-Jones to demonstrate the vital importance of the viewer as witness, an active participant in the transformative aesthetic vision, whose role is "to see something, and tell what it saw in a plain way." Shortly after Burne-Jones's death in 1898, the *Quarterly Review* observed this quality as a defining aspect of his legacy, stating that he sought to "make life beautiful... to keep alive the sense of a world that is out of sight, and to show how the troubled waves of human life may dimly reflect the beauty and mystery of God."[17] For Burne-Jones, the artist's role was to make the divine manifest, to create work in the visual arts that would convey salvation. The viewer, in turn, performed an act of witness analogous to the shepherds and magi, with the hopes of achieving a revelatory awakening, a glimpse of the sacred in nature and collective humanity.

"The self-abasement of wealth and power": The Adoration of the Magi

While working on his design for the tapestry *Adoration of the Magi* (designed 1887–88, executed 1888–90; see fig. 138), Burne-Jones wrote to Ruskin about the significance of the call to witness for the shepherds and the kings. "Do you remember ages ago, in Milan it was," Burne-Jones asked, "when in the impudence of youth I said I liked the subject of the Shepherds best, and you straightway blew me up, and said 'No, Ned, they had everything to gain by coming, and it was greater grace in the kings to leave their kingdoms and come.' At which I was abashed and fell to thinking."[18] At the outset of his career in 1861, Burne-Jones executed two versions of an altarpiece featuring the Adoration of the Magi (see figs. 133 and 134). More than a quarter of a century later, in 1887, he again returned to the theme in two prominent works, the tapestry featuring *The Adoration of the Magi* and a watercolor, *The Star of Bethlehem* (1887–91; see fig. 140). Across these three major commissions, the Adoration of the Magi afforded Burne-Jones another opportunity to condemn luxury and materiality, as well as to critique artistic and social hierarchies of the day. Reiterating the central question of *King Cophetua and the Beggar Maid*, Burne-Jones's Adorations confront their viewers with images of the sacrifice of wealth and power for the sake of humility, poverty, and love. Each work asks us to contemplate whether we would have the courage to follow the example of the magi in acknowledging the sacred in all humanity and in the natural world.

In 1860, the Gothic Revival architect George Frederick Bodley commissioned Burne-Jones, then a young and relatively inexperienced artist, to paint an altarpiece for the Church of St. Paul, Brighton.[19] This commission was not only a significant milestone in his burgeoning career, but also presented him with the exceptional opportunity to create

132 * The chancel of St. Paul's, Brighton, with *The Annunciation* and *The Adoration of the Magi*, c. 1870. Albumen print. Regency Society of Brighton and Hove

an altarpiece for a Victorian church.[20] The unusual choice to feature a painted altarpiece in St. Paul's reflects the influence of the Oxford Movement on Bodley as well as the vicar of the church, the Reverend Arthur Wagner.[21] For his first major oil on canvas commission, Burne-Jones created a triptych with the subject of *The Adoration of the Kings and Shepherds* at the center and *The Annunciation* divided across the wings (fig. 133). He completed the altarpiece in early 1861, brought it to St. Paul's, and was immediately dissatisfied with the result. According to Georgiana Burne-Jones, he felt the triptych was "too elaborate to tell its story clearly from a distance."[22] At this early juncture, he came to understand that clarity and legibility were essential for public spaces and ecclesiastical settings. To suit the church better, he proposed creating a second altarpiece, which was finished by the end of the year (figs. 132 and 134).[23] For this second version of the triptych, Burne-Jones

133 ✱ Edward Burne-Jones, *The Annunciation* and *The Adoration of the Magi*, 1861. Oil on canvas, 108.6 × 156.2 cm (center), 108.6 × 73.7 cm (side panels). Tate, London, N04743

simplified the composition to *The Adoration of the Magi*, while the *Annunciation* on the wings remained largely the same, with single kneeling figures of the angel Gabriel on the left and the Madonna on the right.

Both versions of the altarpiece are notable for their unconventional approach to technique and iconography, traits that came to distinguish Burne-Jones's treatment of the subject throughout his career. The first version, *The Annunciation* and *The Adoration of the Kings and Shepherds*, is rendered in sumptuous deep red tones, enriched by a brilliant gilded sky with accents of shimmering gold throughout.[24] Paint is applied with a thick

impasto, visibly raised from the canvas in decorative patterns, most notable in the golden cloth behind Gabriel and the patterned background behind the head of the Virgin. In the second version, *The Annunciation* and *The Adoration of the Magi*, Burne-Jones retained the palette of rich reds, but reduced the gold sky to only a thin strip running along the top of the canvas. The decorative patterning of the fabrics is also simplified, allowing the figures more prominence.

In keeping with his aim of refining and clarifying the composition, Burne-Jones also reduced the number of figures in the central panel from eleven to six. The first version is densely populated, depicting the Holy Family, three magi, two shepherds, and three female attendants. Following the precedent of the Pre-Raphaelite circle, in turn inspired by Renaissance examples, Burne-Jones used his friends as models for several of the fig-

134 * Edward Burne-Jones, *The Annunciation* and *The Adoration of the Magi*, 1861. Oil on canvas, 108 × 156.5 cm (center), 108 × 77.3 cm (side panels). Private collection

ures. Morris inspired the first king, who kneels and proffers his golden crown intertwined with laurel leaves before the Virgin and infant Christ.[25] On the upper right the first shepherd, playing the bagpipes, was modeled after Swinburne, while the other is a self-portrait. An Italian man identified by Georgiana Burne-Jones as Ciamelli, known for his "bush of blue-black hair," modeled for the king in armor.[26] Although there is no record of the model who posed for the African king, his carefully realized features suggest that

they were studied from life. Wearing a distinctive red turban and placed near the center of the canvas, this magus occupies a prominent position in the composition and the symbolic program of the altarpiece.

With the subject shifted in the second version of the triptych to the *Adoration of the Magi* (fig. 134), the role of the black magus becomes even more pronounced. Burne-Jones removed both shepherds along with three attendant female figures, creating a more tightly focused composition. The Virgin and Child are seated on the left, with Mary's feet resting on a pile of straw scattered with red flowers, while Joseph perches protectively behind them. Occupying more than half of the composition, the three magi appear before the Holy Family, standing rather than kneeling. Although the third king, dressed again in armor, has removed his helmet, the first king is only just reaching up to lift his crown as he looks on the infant. The black magus no longer hovers behind his fellow kings, but occupies a more visible space in the front of the picture plane between them.

Burne-Jones's choice to feature an African magus was in keeping with an iconography that had emerged in the visual arts at the dawn of European global expansion in the fifteenth century.[27] Although they are not named in the Bible, the three magi became known as Balthazar, Melchior, and Caspar in later texts.[28] They were also frequently depicted as figures representing youth, maturity, and old age. The first portrayal of one of the magi as a black African king apparently dates to the mid-fourteenth century, and this figure was most often identified as the youngest magus, Balthazar.[29] This visual representation first gained popularity in Northern Europe, especially Germany, and was later adopted in Italy. It imbued the three magi with another layer of allegorical allusion, as the kings came to symbolize Europe, Asia, and Africa, the three known continents.[30] The stately procession of the kings bearing gifts allowed artists to incorporate details of opulence and magnificence into depictions of the Adoration of the Magi. With the magi serving as continental allegories, artists could also devote particular attention to the exotic goods increasingly available through global trade and plunder.[31] Mantegna's *Adoration of the Magi* triptych of c. 1460 (fig. 135) is one of the earliest examples of this model for the three magi in Italy.[32]

Burne-Jones was familiar with Anna Jameson's 1850 *Legends of the Madonna*, another possible source for his interpretation of the Adoration of the Magi. Jameson noted this shift in depictions of the magi to include the black African king:

> *In the legends of the fourteenth century the kings had become distinct personages, under the names of Caspar (or Jasper), Melchior, and Balthasar: the first being always a very aged man with a long white beard; the second a middle-aged man; the third is young, and frequently he is a Moor or negro, to express the king of Ethiopia or Nubia, and also to indicate that when the Gentiles were called to salvation, all the continents and races of the earth, of whatever complexion, were included.*[33]

Jameson's account of the emergence of the youngest magus as the king of Ethiopia or Nubia emphasizes the global scope of the evangelizing mission of the Christian church. Depictions of the black magus, especially in the guise of youth, could be used to justify the forced subjugation and conversion of non-Christians in Africa and around the world. Indeed, it is not coincidental that the black African magus in European art arose concurrently with the enslavement and forced migration of the people of Africa under imperial expansion and colonization. Even after the abolition of slavery in the British Empire,

135 * Andrea Mantegna, *Scenes from the Life of Christ: The Adoration of the Magi* (detail), c. 1460. Tempera on panel, 77 × 72 cm. Gallerie degli Uffizi, Florence

paintings such as Thomas Jones Barker's *The Secret of England's Greatness* of c. 1861–63 (fig. 136) reinforced the importance of Christian evangelizing as validation for the spread of the empire.[34] With an African king kneeling to accept the gift of a Bible from Queen Victoria, dressed in a blue and white gown that unmistakably alludes to the Virgin Mary, Barker's painting echoes imagery of the Adoration of the Magi as part of its pro-imperial rhetoric.

By contrast, Burne-Jones's *Adoration of the Magi*, created around the same time that Barker began his paean to the British Empire under Victoria, openly rebukes such imperial ambition, and declares racial equality before the divine. In the final iteration of his

136 * Thomas Jones Barker, *The Secret of England's Greatness* (*Queen Victoria presenting a Bible in the Audience Chamber at Windsor*), c. 1862–63. Oil on canvas, 167.6 × 213.8 cm. National Portrait Gallery, London, Purchased 1974, NPG 4969

triptych for St. Paul's, Brighton, Burne-Jones chose to depict the three magi as physically joined through clasped hands. The king in armor at the far right grasps the lowered left hand of the African king, whose upraised right hand holds the left hand of the king closest to the Holy Family. This gesture of brotherhood could be interpreted as paternalistic, with the black African magus physically guided towards salvation by his fair-skinned companions. However, the black king is not presented as meek or inferior. With fair-skinned and dark-skinned fingers tenderly intertwined, the gesture of solidarity presented by the three magi evokes a common abolitionist emblem depicting clasped hands. For example, a copper abolitionist token produced in Burne-Jones's native Birmingham around 1796 features two joined hands encircled with the motto "May slavery & oppression cease throughout the world" (figs. 137a and b).[35] Notably, Burne-Jones's creation of this second version in 1861 coincided with the outbreak of the American Civil War.[36] His decision not only to depict a black African magus, but to feature him tightly grasping the hands of a

137 a and b ∗ Roger Dixon, artist; William Lutwyche, manufacturer; Soho Mint, Birmingham, "Am I Not A Man And A Brother" Anti-Slavery Conder Token (recto and verso), c. 1796. Copper, d. 2.8 cm. Yale University Art Gallery, New Haven, Connecticut, 2001.87.3462

fair-skinned king and a fair-skinned knight, appears to be a gesture of protest.[37] The three kings approach the Virgin and Child in fellowship and brotherhood, equally present as witnesses to the manifestation of the divine and the promise of salvation.

More than two decades later, Burne-Jones returned to the theme with two major public commissions, the tapestry (fig. 138) created for Exeter College Chapel, Oxford, and *The Star of Bethlehem* (see fig. 140), a monumental watercolor painted for the recently opened Birmingham Museum and Art Gallery.[38] Intended for two cities that held particular importance during Burne-Jones's formative years, both works confront the inequities of the modern age of luxury that transcend their respective ecclesiastical and secular contexts. Describing *The Star of Bethlehem* in 1893, Malcolm Bell, one of Burne-Jones's early biographers, emphasized the subversive message at its heart, and by extension the story of the Adoration of the Magi: "Individually and collectively, [the Magi] are all exquisite, and the self-abasement of wealth and power before the weak majesty of a homeless mother and her babe has never found a truer or a fairer exposition."[39] Employing two decorative media for two prominent urban settings, Burne-Jones persuasively critiqued contemporary economic injustice in the language of Christian allegory.

In August 1886, John Prideaux Lightfoot, Rector of Exeter College, Oxford, wrote to Morris requesting a tapestry for a dedicated site in the chapel of his alma mater.[40] Both Morris and Burne-Jones were deeply disappointed by their educational experience

FOLLOWING PAGES ∗ 138 ∗ Edward Burne-Jones, designer, for Morris & Co., *The Adoration of the Magi*, 1887–90. Tapestry wool and silk, 264 × 396 cm. Exeter College Chapel, Oxford

IN MEMORIAM

ANTISSIMÆ · JOHANNIS · PRIDEAUX · LIGHTFOOT

at Exeter and they left the college without receiving their degrees. Indeed, Burne-Jones later recalled, "At Exeter they were all pedants, starched and stiff, nothing human about them."[41] However, their relationship with the university improved over the years and both were awarded honorary degrees in 1883. This commission promised a lasting legacy at Oxford that would impart their ideals of art, labor, nature, and human fellowship to future generations of students. Morris immediately replied with enthusiasm:

> *I need hardly say that it would give me such pleasure to do anything for our chapel, and I should be specially pleased to do the piece of tapestry from Burne-Jones designs, as it would make, I feel sure, a very suitable ornament. I do not think you need to go further to look for a subject, since the one you suggest seems a very good one from every point of view, and especially would suit the genius of tapestry completely; I feel sure that Burne-Jones would agree with me in this.*[42]

Within days, Morris traveled to Oxford to view the proposed position of the tapestry on the south side of the chapel choir. Designed by George Gilbert Scott in 1859, the chapel had been executed in a French Gothic Revival style inspired by the Sainte-Chapelle in Paris.[43] Morris wrote again to Lightfoot, on September 7, 1886 that "I have seen the place in our chapel for which tapestry was suggested as a decoration; it seems to me a very suitable place for the kind of work, as we could make the colour both harmonious & powerful, so that it would not be overpowered by the stained glass above it."[44] Although Morris does not specify the proposed subject, Burne-Jones soon began a cartoon of *The Adoration of the Magi*.[45] In 1887, Burne-Jones described the tapestry with marked enthusiasm, writing, "It will be a blaze of colour and look like a carol."[46]

The Adoration of the Magi represented the first significant tapestry commission for the newly established weaving department of Morris & Co. at the Merton Abbey works. Morris revived the traditional *haute-lisse* method of weaving, which required greater skill on the part of the weaver in contrast to mechanized modern tapestry production. He installed three looms in the spacious and bright workshops, first training John Henry Dearle and then a team of young apprentices from working-class neighborhoods of London.[47] Morris praised tapestry as "the noblest of the weaving arts... in which there is nothing mechanical: it may be looked upon as a mosaic of pieces of colour made up of dyed threads, and is capable of producing wall ornament of any degree of elaboration within the proper limits of duly considered decorative work."[48] For Burne-Jones, the tapestry medium represented a crucial opportunity to create legible and accessible decorative designs. He once described it as "halfway between painting and ornament" – in fact, he continued, "I know nothing that's so deliciously half way."[49] Burne-Jones was the primary figural designer for the tapestries produced by Morris & Co., but he also appreciated that the medium was

139 * Edward Burne-Jones, *Adoration of the Magi*, 1888. Cartoon for tapestry, photographic paper heightened with bodycolor and watercolor, 240 × 376 cm. Victoria and Albert Museum, London, E.5012-1919

fundamentally a communal craft, a work of fellowship, requiring multiple designers and weavers to work collaboratively to create the finished object.

Following the established procedure at Morris & Co. for stained glass as well as tapestry cartoons, in 1888 Burne-Jones produced a scale drawing of *The Adoration of the Magi*, which was then photographically enlarged and heightened with gouache (fig. 139). This cartoon is worth considering in detail, as it established the composition for the weavers at Merton Abbey to follow, as well as Burne-Jones's own adaptation of the design for *The Star of Bethlehem*. At the far left, the Holy Family appears amid a rustic woodland setting. The Virgin and Child sit on a pile of straw beneath a humble thatched shelter supported by thin tree trunks and enclosed by a wattle fence. Joseph stands behind them, his heavily robed body slightly bowed in greeting. He holds a bundle of twigs in his arms, while an axe lies at his feet surrounded by several small stumps, suggesting he has crafted the modest sanctuary. At the center of the composition, an angel with long flowing robes hovers just above the ground, with toes not quite touching the grass. A gleaming star, held aloft in the angel's upraised hands, casts a luminous glow on the scene. From the right side of the composition, the three magi approach, echoing Joseph with their heads lowered. Unlike in the Brighton altarpiece, the magi are not holding hands, but instead tightly grasp their gifts for the infant Christ, indicating their worldly power and wealth. Much of the cartoon appears in grisaille, emphasizing the sculptural quality of the figures. However, Burne-Jones carefully elaborated certain passages in color to aid the weavers, including the red briar roses, the jeweled crown resting on the ground before the Virgin, the ornate armor of the knight, and the dark complexion of the African king.[50]

Weaving commenced at Merton Abbey in 1888 and *The Adoration of the Magi* was completed early in 1890. The final tapestry achieves Burne-Jones's vision of brilliant color, dominated by red and gold in the detailed garments of the figures, set against the cool blues and greens of the dark woodland setting, evocative of an English forest. Perhaps the most pronounced change between the cartoon and the finished tapestry is the profusion of flowers that surround the figures. According to A. B. Bence-Jones, who chronicled the creation of the *Holy Grail* tapestry series (1890–94), the apprentice weavers at Morris & Co. were tasked with contributing these flowers, only vaguely indicated in Burne-Jones's cartoon: "the working of [the] flowers and their disposition on the tapestry was left mainly to the workers' discretion. In most cases they had the living flowers before them from which to work; and the success with which they have met, is some measure of the interest they felt in their work."[51] Flowers plucked straight from the Merton Abbey gardens were brought to the weavers to study as they worked and, accordingly, each flower can be identified as a distinct botanical specimen.[52] Not only were the weavers able to adopt a "truth to nature" working practice, they also achieved a degree of agency over their craft. Not merely beholden to Burne-Jones's design, they actively contributed to the finished tapestry.

Following its completion in 1890, *The Adoration of the Magi* was briefly displayed at the Oxford Street showrooms of Morris & Co. in London at Easter. A contemporary reviewer pronounced the tapestry "so perfect, indeed, in every detail, that there is nothing left to desire, and one feels inclined to linger over it until its perfections have been fully grasped."[53] After its debut in London, the tapestry was installed in Exeter College Chapel, set within a purpose-built wooden frame.[54] Subsequently, Morris & Co. received commissions for nine additional weavings of the tapestry over the next seventeen years from a diverse group of patrons, ranging from Eton College to the Manchester Municipal School of Art.[55] A testament to its popularity and appeal, the later weavings of the tapestry were dispersed among public and private collections around the globe, including France, Germany, Australia, and Russia.[56]

In 1887, while he was at work on the design for the tapestry, the Corporation of Birmingham commissioned Burne-Jones to create a painting for their new museum and art gallery. As a lasting legacy for the city of his birth, Burne-Jones adapted his tapestry composition into a monumental watercolor, *The Star of Bethlehem* (fig. 140). As a child raised in industrial Birmingham, Burne-Jones had felt deprived of the art and culture that he craved.[57] In the latter half of the nineteenth century, as the curator Victoria Osborne writes, the people of Birmingham increasingly sought to combat the image of their city as "ugly and philistine – a place both architecturally and culturally barren."[58] A native son at the peak of his artistic career, Burne-Jones was upheld as an example of what Birmingham could achieve. In 1880, he was approached by the mayor, Joseph Chamberlain, to play a public role in the city's renaissance as President of the Royal Birmingham Society of Artists. While Burne-Jones appreciated the gesture, he expressed anxiety over the expectation of a lecture. Writing to Morris, he explained, lamenting, "I have lots to say of course & could say it informally about art & its relation to life... but looking at the people I should like to serve of all others, namely the people I was born amongst, I think I could better serve them by carrying on my accustomed work."[59] Rather than a pompous speech, Burne-Jones believed his paintings and designs for the decorative arts would best communicate his hopes and aims to the people of his hometown.[60]

Instead, Burne-Jones's direct address to the people of Birmingham took the form of *The Star of Bethlehem*, a missive transcribed in pigment on paper to an epicenter of British industrialization. Completed in 1891, *The Star of Bethlehem* was first displayed at the New Gallery in London, where it garnered substantial attention.[61] A reviewer for *The Antiquary* described the watercolor as immersive and meditative, writing, "it is emphatically a picture that grows on the gazer and gradually wins its way."[62] This assessment echoes the description of *The Adoration of the Magi* tapestry, once again emphasizing the need for prolonged engagement and absorptive looking. In the fall of that year, *The Star of Bethlehem* was brought to its permanent home in Birmingham and showcased as part of an exhibition of Pre-Raphaelite art (fig. 141).[63] The monumental watercolor has remained a key fixture of the collection of the museum into the twenty-first century.

FOLLOWING PAGES * 140 * Edward Burne-Jones, *The Star of Bethlehem*, 1887–91. Watercolor and bodycolor with scraping on ten sheets of J. Whatman Turkey Mill Kent paper dated 1882 or 1883, on stretcher, 256 × 386.8 cm. Birmingham Museum & Art Gallery, 1891P75

141 * *The Star of Bethlehem* on display, Birmingham Museum & Art Gallery, 1891. Photograph from glass plate negative

The choice to execute the work as a watercolor is yet another example of Burne-Jones defying the artistic hierarchies of the day by testing the boundaries between painting and the decorative arts.[64] Measuring eight feet high and more than twelve feet long, the watercolor was virtually unprecedented in size, requiring ten sheets of Whatman paper pieced together.[65] With the use of watercolor on paper, Burne-Jones may also have sought to emulate the effect of fresco, reinforcing the status of this monumental painting as akin to a permanent mural for a civic context.[66] In translating the design from tapestry to watercolor, Burne-Jones retained the same rich detail and engaging figural presence of *The Adoration of the Magi* tapestry. However, he adopted a much cooler palette, dominated by blues, purples, and greens, with touches of pink and gold. Notably, he removed the halos from the figures, leaving only a subtle glow around the heads of Mary and Christ. He also devoted particular attention to the costumes of the magi, embellishing their meticulously embroidered robes with significant heraldic details. In a key point of divergence from the tapestry, he incorporated intricate symbols on the robes of the first and third kings. Those of the first and eldest king feature roundels depicting St. George slaying the Dragon along the bottom hem, a traditional emblem of England that came to symbolize the spirit of imperial conquest arrayed in chivalric righteousness. The costume of the Ethiopian king is perhaps the most ornate, featuring a band of dancing angels encircling the lower portion, as well as an elaborately detailed wooden boat with a fruit tree on its sail. Burne-Jones repeated this motif in several sketchbooks, experimenting with different variations of trees either sprouting directly from boats or depicted on sails, signaling its importance. In the context of the Biblical narrative, the emblem could evoke the journey of the magi from across the sea, while also alluding to the Tree of Life and the return to paradise promised by the birth of Christ. However, the visual association between the sailing ship with a fruit tree and the Ethiopian king also conjures allegorical representations of imperial subjects and commodities in the nineteenth century.

With *The Star of Bethlehem*, Burne-Jones presented one of the leading industrial centers of Britain with a salient condemnation of luxury, materiality, and power in "the Century of Commerce."[67] Morris, in his address "The Art of the People" to the Birmingham Society of Arts and School of Design in 1879, denounced consumerism and the privileging of luxury goods as fostering a system of economic enslavement. "Yes," he proclaimed, "luxury cannot exist without slavery of some kind or other, and its abolition will be blessed, like the abolition of other slaveries, by the freeing both of the slaves and of their masters."[68] Employing the traditional associations of the three magi with opulence, exoticism, and global expansion, Burne-Jones recast the legend in *The Star of Bethlehem* as a challenge to what he termed Britain's "material empire."[69] Collectively, the three magi embody British power and imperial ambition, alluding to political governance in the form of the elderly king, martial strength in the figure of the knight, and the imperial subject represented by the African king. Gathered together as witnesses of the divine incarnate, their presence asserts the universal scope of salvation. The three magi remind the viewer that God's redemption included, in Anna Jameson's words, "all the continents and races of the earth, of whatever complexion."[70] However, their presence in an English woodland also functions as a potent rebuke to imperial aggression abroad and the corresponding oppression of poverty and powerlessness within the imperial center. *The Star of Bethlehem* subverts the established social, economic, and artistic hierarchies of modernity in much the same way as Burne-Jones's monumental painting *King Cophetua and the Beggar Maid*. In both works, exquisite objects of luxurious craft and rich materiality are offered up before impoverished humanity and the humble beauty of nature. But *The Star of Bethlehem* enlarges the scope of the central message of *King Cophetua* through the rhetoric of Christian iconography.

One of the most striking features of both *The Adoration of the Magi* tapestry and *The Star of Bethlehem* watercolor is the ornate crown that the first king has removed and placed on the ground. This crown is nearly identical to that worn by the Virgin in Jan van Eyck's

Adoration of the Mystic Lamb (fig. 142). Burne-Jones made a detailed drawing after this crown in a sketchbook dating from around 1859, with careful annotations for each fictive flower (fig. 143). Theologically, the crown laid before Mary signals her future place as Queen of Heaven. However, laid on the grass and surrounded by delicate sprigs of lily of the valley, the sumptuously wrought crown with its ornate floral decoration is brought into direct comparison with the living blooms that surround the Holy Family. Presented as the pinnacle of fine artistic workmanship, the crown proves to be little more than a poor simulacrum of the divine incarnate in nature. Lavishly adorned with costly jewels, this golden crown is an object of pure luxury devoid of functional purpose, other than as a signal of power, prestige, and wealth for the wearer. The material value of this precious ornament, and the coveted supremacy and status that it symbolizes, is eclipsed not only by the abundant flora, but more importantly by a tiny baby, born into poverty. Moreover, the infant on Mary's lap is approximately the same size as the crown at her feet, eliciting a potent visual comparison. The question posed to the viewer by *King Cophetua* is raised once again in *The Star of Bethlehem*: would you sacrifice your worldly goods and privileges for the sake of one impoverished child of God? What is the worth of gold and jewels compared to flesh and blood? With the removal of the halos from the figures in *The Star of Bethlehem*, this challenge is made all the more relevant and immediate, as if the scene could be occurring in present-day Britain and not a remote or mythical Biblical past.

142 * Jan van Eyck, *Adoration of the Mystic Lamb* (detail of Ghent Altarpiece), 1432. Oil on panel. St. Bavo Cathedral, Ghent

The perception of contemporary relevance was reinforced by Burne-Jones's decision to employ a recognizably English woodland setting. When *The Star of Bethlehem* was on view at the New Gallery in 1891, several reviewers commented on the forest backdrop and native flora, describing the scene as unmistakably English. For example, Julia Cartwright noted the "red roses" and "harebells" that "spring up in the green English woodland" around the Virgin and Child. Similarly, the reviewer for *The Antiquary* described Burne-Jones's "daring boldness of artistic license" in depicting "an English orchard background of blossoming boughs" for this "Eastern incident."[71] By setting the Biblical scene in an English landscape, Burner-Jones echoed one of the central messages of Morris's second address to the Birmingham Society of Arts and School of Design in 1880. Morris, asked to speak on art, instead turned his attention to what he deemed a more pressing

143 ∗ Edward Burne-Jones, *Study of crown, after Jan van Eyck*, c. 1859. Pencil and watercolor on paper, 19 × 26.4 cm. Victoria and Albert Museum, London, E.9-1955

issue, the destruction of the landscape in the name of industrial progress, saying, "I must now speak of something else, of possessions which should be common to all of us, of the green grass, and the leaves, and the waters, of the very light and air of heaven, which the Century of Commerce has been too busy to pay any heed to."[72]

Morris reiterated that all those who profess to care about art must also care for the landscape, while praising the importance of simplicity over luxury. He lauded the humble, the useful, and the beautiful over the ornate, costly, and lavish, and explained that the basis for all art resides in the simplest forms of construction:

> *The art of house-building begins it all: if we did not know how to dye or to weave; if we had neither gold, nor silver, nor silk; and no pigments to paint with, but half-a-dozen ochres and umbers, we might yet frame a worthy art that would lead to everything, if we had but timber, stone, and lime, and a few cutting tools to make these common things not only shelter us from wind and weather, but also express the thoughts and aspirations that stir in us.*[73]

This rustic architecture that not only shelters, but also expresses "the thoughts and aspirations that stir in us," is brought to life in the shelter and fence built by Joseph. A carpenter by trade, Joseph does not have gold or jewels to adorn the Virgin and Child. Instead, he has crafted a sanctuary hewn from the simple materials he has gathered in the English forest and the wood he has chopped with his own hands. This vernacular art, the wattle in particular, is a primitive form of weaving, the essential impulse that informed the production of the refined textiles worn by the three magi, and even the medium of tapestry itself.[74] But the simple garments, thatched roof, and trellised briar roses that surround the Holy Family are more precious than the opulent objects brought by the magi. In creation and consumption, these humblest forms of craft, available to all, acknowledge the divine incarnate in nature and ennoble the divine in all humanity.

The most distinctive iconographic innovation of both the watercolor and the tapestry is that of the angel hovering at the center of the composition holding a star. As I have mentioned, the angel garnered significant attention and comment at the New Gallery. Cartwright praised the inventive depiction of the angel and star: "the real originality of the conception lies in the star itself, which is borne aloft by a radiant seraph." M. H. Spielmann expressed mixed feelings about the painting overall, but nonetheless described the angel as a "beautiful, disquieting figure." Claude Phillips, who similarly found fault with the painting's "peculiar vein of mysticism," also reserved particular admiration for the angel, describing it as a "beautiful figure" who appears "holding a globe of fire.... This strange, radiant figure, resembling a statue from Chartres or Rheims, into which the glow of life should have been infused, is the one part of the 'Adoration' which is in truth worthy of Mr. Burne-Jones at his best."[75]

From early compositional sketches, it is evident that Burne-Jones devoted significant attention to the placement of this angel, who first appears in a sketch of c. 1886–87 at the far left behind Mary (fig. 144). Situated at the center, the divine emissary guides the magi to the Holy Family. The angel's strong verticality also creates a bridge between heaven and earth, the celestial and the mundane. Moreover, as the only figure to face fully forward, the angel forges a third link with the viewer, who is thereby incorporated as another witness to the scene. This web of rich and poor, human and divine, witness and manifestation is

144 * Edward Burne-Jones, sketch for *Adoration of the Magi*, c. 1886–87. Pencil and colored crayons on paper, 10.3 × 17.5 cm. Victoria and Albert Museum, London, E.9-1955

held together by the point of light poised on the angel's outstretched fingertips. The "globe of fire" brought from heaven to earth embodies the light of revelation and witness that emerges from out of the darkness with the incarnation of the divine in humanity and the natural world. This star illuminates not the splendors of material luxury and privilege, but the immaterial wonders of human fellowship, natural beauty, and divine love available to all who allow themselves to be guided toward salvation.

"And the Word became flesh": The Nativity, The King and the Shepherd, and Empathetic Connection

In 1888, Burne-Jones created two monumental pendant paintings for the church of St. John the Evangelist, Torquay: *The King and the Shepherd* and *The Nativity* (figs. 145 and 146).[76] Twenty-three years earlier, in 1865, Burne-Jones designed a portrayal of the New Jerusalem for the soaring east window of St. John's (fig. 147). A depiction of the interior

:TRANSEAMUS:USQUE:BETHLEHEM:ET:VIDEAMUS:

145 * Edward Burne-Jones, *The King and the Shepherd*, 1888. Oil on canvas, 206.4 × 316.2 cm. Carnegie Museum of Art, Pittsburgh: Heinz Family Fund, 1997.26.1

:PROPTER:MISERIAM:INOPUM:ET:GEMITUM:PAUPERIS:

146 * Edward Burne-Jones, *The Nativity*, 1888. Oil on canvas, 205.7 × 316.2 cm. Carnegie Museum of Art, Pittsburgh: Heinz Family Fund, 1997.26.2

147 * Edward Burne-Jones, designer, for Morris, Marshall, Faulkner, & Co., *The Church Triumphant in the Heavenly Jerusalem* (*The New Jerusalem*), 1865. Stained glass. St. John the Apostle, Torquay

dated to 1869 (fig. 148) reveals that G. E. Street, the architect of St. John's, included space for two large paintings flanking the altar on the north and south walls of the chancel, in dialogue with Burne-Jones's east window.[77] Torquay, a seaside Devonshire resort, was relatively remote, and the payment for the commission was nominal. However, as Burne-Jones explained to his friend, the bookseller and author Frederick S. Ellis in 1889, the project presented him with the rare opportunity to work *in situ* on a large scale with virtual autonomy of subject and composition, fulfilling his desire for "public work" in "public buildings and in choirs and places where they sing." He admitted, "it is true I can be lured to folly when I am asked to paint for a church."[78]

It is notable that Burne-Jones defines the church as a "public building" and that the paintings constituted, for him, his long-sought goal of "public work."[79] Although Christian churches were ostensibly open to all, individuals might nonetheless have felt deterred

148 ∗ *Chancel of St. John's Church at Torquay 1869*, from Charles L. Eastlake, *A History of the Gothic Revival* (London: Longmans, Green; New York: Scribner, Welford, 1872), facing p. 325

from entering based on their faith, race, ethnicity, or social status, a perception that remains for some today. Despite this potential barrier to entry, ecclesiastical settings could ideally be communal and egalitarian sites where viewers are primed for contemplative and immersive engagement.[80] Ecclesiastical art, therefore, has an ostensibly broader appeal and accessibility for the general public, with clear advantages over paintings and other elite objects of consumption intended for the private homes of the wealthy or for "palaces of art" like the Grosvenor. This was particularly true of stained glass, which was perceived in terms of the tradition of the *Biblia Pauperum*. As an article in *The Review of Reviews* stated shortly after Burne-Jones's death, "The stained glass window of the church, the cathedral, or the college constitute the picture gallery of the multitude. Here Burne-Jones did good work."[81] Indeed, even today, while municipal museums and art galleries often have limited hours, prohibitive entry fees, or are located in major metropolitan centers, stained-glass windows designed by Burne-Jones can be readily accessed by diverse communities in small parish churches across the United Kingdom and around the globe.[82]

The pendant paintings for St. John's, *The Nativity* and *The King and the Shepherd*, are strikingly spare in contrast to Burne-Jones's usual technique for paintings. Rendered in loose, gestural brushstrokes, each canvas measures more than six feet by ten feet and was originally displayed about twelve feet above the pavement of the church.[83] The figures are draped in soft pastel fabrics that stand out against a dark forest background surmounted by a narrow strip of golden sky. After his earlier experience designing the altarpiece for St. Paul's, Brighton, Burne-Jones understood that legibility, clarity, and an innovative iconographic approach were imperative when designing for the large interior of a church with an elaborate decorative program. In his concurrent decorative projects, *The Star of Bethelehem* watercolor and *The Adoration of the Magi* tapestry, Burne-Jones censured luxury and privilege before the wonders of nature and human fellowship. In *The Nativity* and *The King and the Shepherd*, he pared down these core moments of the Christian faith to an even starker form, drawing out a potent message of egalitarianism and empathetic connection rendered as a prophetic vision.

The two scenes represented an opportunity to create another work exploring the Incarnation and the act of witness for an ecclesiastical context, and they allowed Burne-Jones to work in dialogue with his previous stained-glass designs for the east window, "the Church Triumphant in the Heavenly Jerusalem."[84] Bound together through a symbolic program rather than a continuous compositional field, the design is largely comprised of groupings of figures divided into two tiers and arrayed across five lights with a tracery above, including a rose window. As the Reverend Basil Airy, the vicar of the church, explained in *A Brief History of St. John's Torquay* (1902), the overall design of the east window emphasizes the role of angels in guiding all of humanity toward salvation. The outermost lights on each side represented "the twofold aspect of angelic life; in the two upper panels are Angels in the act of adoration; in the two lower are Angels ministering to humanity – the Angel to the right is leading a man, that to the left is leading a woman, into the Golden City." Airy continues, "The other lights contain representative characters of various orders of men and women who will be found in the New Jerusalem."[85] These included a panoply of historical figures, including saints, martyrs, prophets, kings, and bishops. However, the framing figures, the man and woman led by angels, represent ordinary, anonymous individuals, suggesting the egalitarianism of the New Jerusalem. Further emphasizing the broad scope of this community of the blessed, the top tier of the central light depicts a group of women representing "virgins and matrons," joined by a child and a baby. With Christ in Majesty above at the center of the rose window, the isolated figures spread across the individual lights and tiers join in a revelatory vision of communal harmony. The living congregation assembled before the altar and below the window would form a corresponding gathering, indicating that all are welcome and embraced in the new vision of the divine. When Burne-Jones returned many years later to create two paintings to flank this east window and altar, he retained an emphasis on the dual themes of "adoration" and "ministering to humanity," with angels once again serving as guides to salvation for figures both within and beyond the composition.

Although rendered as two canvases, the pendant paintings of *The Nativity* and *The King and the Shepherd* form a continuous whole. Burne-Jones utilized the separation of the paintings across the chancel, as well as the window above the altar, to engage the viewer in an immersive, embodied sensorial experience. Designed for the north wall of the chancel, *The King and the Shepherd* was on the left when facing the altar. Here Burne-Jones collapsed the Adoration of the Shepherds and the Adoration of the Magi, condensing the two traditional groups into one representative figure each. He also elided the temporal distance between them, depicting the two figures approaching the Nativity simultaneously. On the left of the composition, a pale angel grasps the hand of a king, who carries a jeweled casket in his other hand. The king wears an ornate crown and lavish orange robes, bearing some similarity to the first magus in *The Star of Bethlehem*.[86] On the right, a second angel leads a man, who journeys empty-handed and in tattered clothing, across the stark, wooded landscape.

Much like *King Cophetua and the Beggar Maid*, the composition reinforces an inversion of dominant social hierarchies. Above the heads of the four figures and the outlines of the trees, a Latin inscription appears across the sky. This text glosses the scene below and is a devotional cue to the viewer: "Transeamus usque Bethlehem, et videamus verbum quod factum est, quod fecit Dominus" (Luke 2:15). This conventional passage is taken from the Nativity narrative, and translated reads, "Let us go over to Bethlehem and see this thing that has happened which the Lord has made known to us." On its own, this text is perfectly apposite to the subject; however, in the context of the two pendant paintings, it foregrounds sight and bearing witness: *videamus*, "let us go and see."[87] In his own description of these paintings, Burne-Jones declared that *The King and the Shepherd* was an allegory of "the poor and rich man."[88] Notably, he placed the "poor" man, the first to follow the directive to go and see the revelation of the divine in Bethlehem, closer to the altar in St. John's. This emphasized that the humble and impoverished preceded the wealthy and elite in witnessing and acknowledging the embodiment of God on earth.

The directive posed in the inscription, to go and see, to witness the Incarnation, would also compel the viewer in St. John's to turn from *The King and the Shepherd* to the pendant painting on the south wall of the chancel. In this canvas, the composition is once again boldly simplified, reduced to its key elements. The Virgin Mary, draped in white,

149 * Giotto di Bondone, *Nativity* (detail), Scrovegni Chapel, Padua, c. 1305–6. Fresco

150 * Giotto di Bondone, *Lamentation* (detail), Scrovegni Chapel, Padua, c. 1305–6. Fresco

lies on a humble bed of straw and sticks, cradling the infant Christ in her arms. A simple thatched roof on rough-hewn tree trunks shelters their sleeping forms. Joseph sits at Mary's feet, crouched and hooded in a pale orange robe. Turned away from the viewer, he holds an open book. The left side of the composition is occupied by three angels holding implements of the Passion, who solemnly observe the miraculous moment between the new mother and child. Evocative of a pale dusk or dawn, the composition is rendered in subdued shades of peach, pink, and gold. Once again, the landscape background is spare, depicting an expanse of bare earth hemmed in by a thick wall of shadowy trees and deep green foliage.[89]

Across the gilded sky, Burne-Jones inscribed *The Nativity* with another text. Rather than a traditional quotation from Luke or Matthew, he chose instead a passage from the Vulgate: "Propter miseriam inopum et gemitum pauperis nunc exsurgam dicit Dominus" (Psalm 11:6; "By reason of the misery of the needy, and the groans of the poor, now will I arise, saith the Lord").[90] An Old Testament passage with apocalyptic connotations, this choice of quotation was unprecedented, reinforcing the interpretation of the two paintings as a radical assertion of the Christian mandate to redress social inequities. The implications are undeniably political, binding Burne-Jones's depiction of the mystery of the Incarnation to the conditions of Victorian Britain. This call to witness was reinforced through physical immersion in the chancel of St. John's. With Burne-Jones's paintings and stained glass in active dialogue, viewers are poised between the "poor and rich man" on one side, the Nativity on the other, and the vision of all society gathered together in the New Jerusalem in the east window above. Wealth and poverty dissolve as congregants are commanded to truly "go and see" the miracle unfolding before them.

While *The King and the Shepherd* establishes a radical social framework, *The Nativity* focuses the attention on the primary objects of devotion, Mary with the infant Christ. Burne-Jones chose to depict Mary recumbent on a bed of straw and woven branches, rather than kneeling in prayer or enthroned with Christ on her lap. According to both Ruskin and Anna Jameson, this iconography derives from the Byzantine tradition and indicates that Mary is resting in the aftermath of the birth.[91] More than a mere allusion to historical precedents, this allowed Burne-Jones to access the pathos and immediacy of the scene, capturing the raw emotional encounter between an exhausted postpartum mother and her beloved child, face to face at last. For the pose of Mary, Burne-Jones may have been inspired by Giotto's *Nativity* fresco in the Scrovegni Chapel in Padua (c. 1305–6; fig. 149). Beyond compositional similarities, Burne-Jones captures the typological intensity fostered in the thematic program of the chapel, where the embrace of the mother and her dead child in *The Lamentation* (fig. 150) closely and painfully mimics the first tender caress of her newborn in *The Nativity*. In Burne-Jones's painting, the promise of new life and

151 * Edward Burne-Jones and Edgar Boehm, *Memorial for Charles Howard and Mary Parke*, 1879–81. Bronze and Purbeck marble, 97.5 × 142.5 cm. Lanercost Priory, Cumbria

152 * *The Nativity* (detail of fig. 151)

the shadow of death similarly coexist in harrowing proximity, as the angels carrying the implements of the Passion hover beside Mary's bed.

Shrouded in cold, white sculptural drapery, the intertwined bodies of Mary and Christ appear as marble effigies, their sepulchral forms evocative of a bier as much as a bed.[92] Mary's lifeless pallor is only enlivened at the point of bodily contact, skin to skin, with the infant Christ. Like Galatea, she seemingly turns from stone to flesh before the viewer. There are overt parallels to Burne-Jones's investigation of the sculptural in the *Perseus* series (see figs. 43 and 58–64). Once again, here Burne-Jones tests the potentiality of the sculptural expressed though paint, an experiment in embodied haptic vision that challenges viewers not just to look, but to feel the scene before them. Through the generative touch of child to mother, inert matter becomes flesh and the miracle of the Incarnation appears as a reciprocal act. Immersed in this vision, viewers experience the unique capacity of paint to render the liminal state between life and death, and to represent the process of coming into being, of making the divine manifest.

This empathetic mode of vision, which invokes the perilous juxtaposition of birth and death, recalls an earlier depiction of the Nativity by Burne-Jones, in an 1879–81 bronze bas-relief memorial panel (fig. 151) for Lanercost Priory, Cumbria. Commissioned by George Howard in honor of his parents, Charles Howard and Mary Parke, the monument was created in collaboration with the sculptor Edgar Boehm.[93] The plaque features portraits of the Howards with *The Nativity* below Mary and *The Lamentation* below Charles. In the former, the Virgin Mary reclines on a raised bed, her eyelids lowered, while she cradles the tiny infant Christ in her hands (fig. 152). Thick swaths of cloth envelop both mother and child, as if they are still corporeally joined as one, before extending outward in evocative swirls that seem to fill the shallow space of the panel. Joseph huddles at their feet, his head resting heavily in his hand, his eyes closed. He appears to be in a state of mourning or exhaustion, much more than prayer or exaltation. This figure reinforces the disquieting sense that the birthing bed and deathbed are one.

The memorial was commissioned after the death of Charles Howard in 1879, but it also honors Mary Parke, who had died more than three decades earlier in 1843 following complications after the birth of George, their only child. Such tragedies were all too common in the Victorian era, given the high rate of infant and maternal mortality. Burne-Jones's own mother, Elizabeth Coley, died mere days after his birth, having previously lost a daughter, Edward's only sibling, in infancy. Burne-Jones also experienced the harrowing loss of his second son, Christopher, weeks after his premature birth, when Georgiana contracted scarlet fever and nearly died as well. For contemporary viewers, imagery of pregnancy and birth would have triggered anxiety and hope in equal measure, invoking personal memories of loss intermingled with joy. The painful juxtaposition of birth and

153 * Edward Burne-Jones, *Study for the Nativity*, c. 1887. Pencil on paper laid down on board, 40 × 61.9 cm. Sold Sotheby's November 8, 2012, lot 77

death for mother and child in *The Nativity* is reinforced by its pair, *The Lamentation*, which features two female figures cradling the body of Christ beside an open tomb. Rendered in the dynamic tactility and sensorial engagement of sculptural relief, both panels would have elicited a strong empathetic response from nineteenth-century viewers, driven by memory and lived experience as much as theological doctrine. The same poignancy pervades *The Nativity* painting for St. John's, Torquay, where the forms of mother and child are locked in a liminal embrace between sleep and waking, death and life.

Given the intensity of this emotional and memorial appeal, the figure of Joseph seated at Mary's feet performs a crucial intermediary role between the viewer and the postpartum mother and child. Rather than turning in profile toward Mary and the infant Christ as depicted in the Lanercost panel, Joseph crouches with his back to the viewer, holding a book. In a preparatory pencil sketch for *The Nativity* (fig. 153), Burne-Jones initially portrayed Joseph in a pose similar to that in *The Star of Bethlehem*, standing to the side of the manger, with his head and back slightly bowed in reverence. As the composition developed, he drastically altered Joseph's posture and role, shifting him to the foot of the raised bed, and facing him away from the picture plane. Burne-Jones may have once again drawn inspiration from Giotto, merging the seated and sleeping Joseph in *The Nativity* with the cloaked and hooded figure turned away from the viewer on the far left of *The Lamentation*. With his back turned and his head covered, Joseph becomes a surrogate for the viewer as witness, allowing a projection of the self into the unfolding vision of *The Nativity*.

The seated Joseph suggests another crucial referent, Sandro Botticelli's 1500 *Mystic Nativity* (fig. 154). Acquired by the National Gallery in 1878, it was singled out for praise in the nineteenth century as an evocative and innovative depiction of the Incarnation and Adoration of Christ. Notably, Botticelli's painting was also interpreted as an allegory for the turbulent politics of Florence in 1500.[94] According to Jameson, Botticelli treated the Nativity "as a mystery," rather than an event. She asserts that the painting "is indeed a comprehensive poem, a kind of hymn on the Nativity, and might be set to music," and describes the painting as "full of meaning, religious as well as political."[95] Introducing novel iconography and inscribed in Greek with references to the Book of Revelation, Botticelli's painting demonstrated the latent possibilities of the Incarnation and Adoration to convey emotional intensity while also serving as a social commentary. Sidney Colvin observed these qualities of the painting as well: "It is assuredly no fancy to discern, in the assertion of a profound and burning brotherhood between heaven and earth, the key-note of this painting, this lyric of redemption, for such it is."[96]

Burne-Jones did not borrow directly, but instead captured the tone and spirit of Botticelli's *Mystic Nativity* with several pointed allusions. The figure of Joseph is perhaps the most pronounced similarity between the two paintings, with Burne-Jones echoing the crouched posture and reflective attitude of Botticelli's version. Colvin took particular note of this figure in the Botticelli, describing Joseph as "a huddled figure of admirable spirit and expression, and for your connoisseur the great point in the picture – sits away from us, intent and humble."[97] The prominent role of the angels as guides to representative figures of "redeemed humanity" in Botticelli's painting also finds a corresponding treatment in Burne-Jones's *The King and the Shepherd*. In his approach to the subject overall, Burne-Jones emulated the prophetic and apocalyptic qualities of Botticelli's painting, presenting the Nativity as a moment of revolutionary transformation and radical possibility.

To reinforce this visionary quality of *The Nativity* and *The King and the Shepherd*, Burne-Jones also chose to depict Joseph with an open book on his lap (fig. 155).[98] This may have been another allusion to Botticelli's *Mystic Nativity*, where three angels perched on the roof of the shelter above the Holy Family hold an open book. However, he was also invok-

154 ∗ Sandro Botticelli, *Mystic Nativity*, 1500. Oil on canvas, 108.6 × 74.9 cm.
National Gallery, London, NG1034

ing the medieval and Renaissance iconographic tradition of Joseph as a prophetic figure reading from a book.[99] According to Carolyn C. Wilson in her study of 2001, the attribute of a book aligned Joseph with Old Testament prophets, as well as the Apostle Peter. Moreover, with Joseph serving as the first witness to the Incarnation, his possession of an open book asserts the newborn Christ as the Logos, the Word made flesh.[100] Although the text is obscured, suggesting several possible Biblical allusions, the prominence of the volume itself invokes the Gospel of John and the Christian Logos. The relevant passages seem to materialize on the page of Joseph's book: "In the beginning was the Word, and the Word was with God, and the Word was God.... In him was life; and the life was the light of men.... And the Word became flesh and dwelt among us" (John 1:1, 4, 14). Huddled and holding his open book, Joseph is performing an act of witness to the newborn child as a fulfillment of the promise of salvation, the "light of men" who dwells among us.

Depicting Joseph as a reader holds crucial significance for Burne-Jones's two pendant paintings. The portion of the page glimpsed over Joseph's shoulder is covered with lines of text, illegible though clearly visible even from a distance. Its appearance suggests that the book is an illuminated manuscript, although it also resembles an early Renaissance

155 * *The Nativity* (detail of fig. 146)

printed text. With its strong, black lettering and red titling, the book also prefigures the works of the Kelmscott Press, founded three years after the completion of this painting. Just as Mary cradles her child, so too does Joseph caress the book, his fingers interleaved with the pages. Since Joseph is placed near to eye level at the lower edge of the canvas, the viewer is made aware of the tactile pleasures of the act of reading such a book, while the bowed back of Joseph suggests the prolonged engagement that comes with immersion in a text. This figure of Joseph, through his act of reading, models vision as both absorptive and haptic for the viewer. Moreover, with his back turned, Joseph serves as a conduit, a visual site of contact and projection, between the viewer and the painting. Joseph is a visual punctum, both facilitating access to the Word made flesh and breaking the reverie, returning the viewer again to the world, much like a reader who has closed a book and sees the world with newly opened eyes.

"The eternal being born": The Nativity Windows of St. Philip's, Birmingham, and St. Deiniol's, Hawarden

The subject of the Nativity allowed Burne-Jones to depict the manifestation of the divine as embodied in collective humanity and nature. The Adoration, in turn, facilitated an egalitarian examination of the role of the individual as witness to this revelation. His altarpieces for St. Paul's, Brighton, emphasized a radical message of equality before God, while *The Adoration of the Magi* tapestry and *The Star of Bethlehem* watercolor rebuked luxury and power amid cities that privileged both. The pendant paintings of *The Nativity* and *The King and the Shepherd* paired an allegory of the rich and the poor with an empathetic, embodied depiction of birth and death. With the medium of stained glass, particularly in the Nativity windows created for St. Philip's, Birmingham in 1886–88 (fig. 156) and for St. Deiniol's, Hawarden in 1898 (see fig. 131), Burne-Jones was able to seize on yet another aspect of this profound Christian subject. Utilizing the inherent properties of glass, Burne-Jones rendered the Incarnation as a generative moment of light emerging from darkness. Just as sand, ash, and minerals combine at high heat to create glass, a material that exists in a liminal state between solidity and fluidity, so too is the embodiment of the divine at the moment of the Incarnation seemingly constituted in an ephemeral flux of colored light held together in a net of opaque metal bars and framed in stone. The fragmented nature of the medium allowed Burne-Jones to create an apocalyptic vision of the world as simultaneously fractured and remade, with the viewer as not just witness but active participant.

In the aftermath of Morris's death in 1896, Burne-Jones regarded his few remaining window commissions with a sense of finality. As he explained to Rooke, "I'm finishing off all these outstanding [stained glass] cartoons and then think to do no more, I don't see why I should, do you? It's sad to think of anything ever coming to an end, but everything has to finish up someday or other and I don't think any time can be more appropriate than now, do you?"[101] These last windows, including *The Nativity* at Hawarden, were the valediction of his career in stained glass, which had spanned more than four decades and number more than seven hundred cartoons.[102] The vast majority of these designs were created for Morris & Co. Although their working practice was deeply collaborative, it is generally understood that Burne-Jones was responsible for the figures while Morris designed the backgrounds. Morris also supervised the artisans who executed the cartoons in colored glass, and the placement of the metal joins.[103]

In a letter to Mary Gladstone discussing the initial stages of the commission for the west window of St. Deiniol's, Burne-Jones emphasized the qualities he felt were most essential in stained glass. Unlike a painted altarpiece, a stained-glass window is not a picture and "cannot teach anything." Instead, "it is at best a kind of splendid ornament where the colour matters most, & the enclosing lines of lead next." He declares that lead lines should not be perceived as a nuisance, but are rather "part of the beauty of the work and as interesting as the lines of masonry in a wall – & the more of them the merrier – & the deeper the colour looks . . . it is a very limited art and its limitations are its strength, & compel simplicity."[104] On another occasion, he praised the beneficial constraints of designing for an inherently architectural medium: "I love to work in that fettered way, and am better in a prison than the open air always."[105]

Throughout his private correspondence and public treatises on stained glass, Morris reiterated many of Burne-Jones's perceptions of the medium. In 1883, he wrote to Ruskin at Burne-Jones's behest to describe their preference for pot-metals, where the color is intrinsic to the glass and not applied, as well as the minimal use of added shading through silver stain or enamels. After an explanation of the different types of glass available and techniques for achieving the desired colors, Morris wrote,

> *All the glass is very thick . . . in some of the pot-metals, notably the blues the difference between one part of a sheet [and] another is very great. This variety is very useful to*

FOLLOWING PAGES * 156 * Edward Burne-Jones, designer, for Morris & Co., *The Nativity*, 1887–88. Stained glass. St. Philip's Cathedral, Birmingham

157 * Edward Burne-Jones, designer, for Morris & Co., *The Ascension*, 1885. Stained glass. St. Philip's Cathedral, Birmingham

158 * Edward Burne-Jones, designer, for Morris & Co., *The Crucifixion*, 1888. Stained glass. St. Philip's Cathedral, Birmingham

INRI

> *us in getting a jewel-like quality which is the chief charm of painted glass.... You will understand that we rely almost entirely for our colour on the actual colour of the glass; and the more the design will enable us to break up the pieces, and the more mosaic-like it is, the better we like it.*[106]

By prioritizing the "jewel-like quality" of "the actual colour of the glass," Morris sought to maximize transparency and legibility. The shared goal of Burne-Jones and Morris was to achieve a dynamic interplay between pure colored light transmitted through the glass, and pure darkness created by the lead lines and architectural structure of the window.

In 1890, Morris published an entry on "Glass, Painted or Stained" in *Chambers's Encyclopaedia*. Describing the method that he terms "mosaic glass," Morris repeatedly emphasizes the need for clarity: "The qualities needed in the design, therefore, are beauty and character of outline; exquisite, clear, precise drawing of incident, such especially as the folds of drapery. The whole design should be full of clear, crisp, easily-read incident... Whatever key of colour may be chosen, the colour should always be clear, bright, and emphatic." He stresses the need for stained-glass windows to be "pieces of ornamental glazing which... should also tell stories in a simple straightforward manner." However, he also insists that this simplicity does not equate to meaninglessness or triviality. Instead, he asserts that "the expression of thought and emotion" is vital to the success of a stained-glass window.[107] The ideal window conveys meaning through the alignment of subject, decorative rhythm, color, and a visual appeal to the senses and the mind.

Given these criteria, the Nativity is particularly well suited to stained glass, bringing together the medium with the subject in a dynamic way that heightens the impact of both. As the moment when the Incarnation is made manifest, the Nativity has often been understood metaphorically as light emerging from darkness, which is also the central property of stained glass. As Madeline H. Caviness argued (in 1996), in late medieval theological doctrine, light held a symbolic and substantive role in the Incarnation and its realization in the birth of Christ: "the very fact that the physical matter of light could pass through the physical matter of glass, leaving it intact, constituted a miracle comparable to Christ being conceived and born by the Virgin." Caviness also asserted that glass not only held significant theological implications for the Nativity, but also occupied an intercessory role between the earthly realm and the divine; in the medieval era, "both its transparency and its color were held to mediate between the Creator (lux) and the opaque material world."[108] This liminal state of stained glass between the material and the evanescent was also acknowledged and celebrated by Burne-Jones's contemporaries. For example, H. Arthur Kennedy, another stained-glass artist, praised "the representation of visionary subjects" as ideal for stained glass, "with its strength and mystery of colour."[109]

Christopher W. Whall, a leading stained-glass artist of the Arts and Crafts movement, proclaimed that "windows should 'dream,' and should be so treated as to look like what they are, the apertures to admit the light."[110]

In November 1886, at the same time that Morris was finalizing the commission for *The Adoration of the Magi* tapestry at Exeter, he was also exchanging letters with the architect Julius Alfred Chatwin regarding two proposed stained-glass windows for the Church of St. Philip, Birmingham.[111] A fellow Birmingham native, Chatwin was responsible for enlarging the English Baroque church originally designed by Thomas Archer between 1708 and 1725. The previous year, in 1885, Burne-Jones and Morris had worked with Chatwin to create a towering stained-glass window, *The Ascension* (fig. 157), in the new chancel at the east end of the church. In 1886 Chatwin then wrote to Morris on behalf of their patron, Emma Chadwick Villers-Wilkes, to commission two new flanking windows to complete the scheme for the chancel.[112] Morris relayed Burne-Jones's wish to design a "Nativity or visit of the Magi on the north side & the Crucifixion treated as an event (and not mystically)...on the South Side."[113] Evidently having strong opinions on the design of the windows, Villers-Wilkes expressed concern at various points over the "cattle" that might appear in a Nativity or "anything horrifying" depicted in the Crucifixion.[114] Burne-Jones continued to insist on the importance of a Nativity window, countering with the suggestion of a Nativity (minus ox and ass) in one window and the Adoration of the Magi in the other. Eventually, Villers-Wilkes was persuaded, through Chatwin and Morris, to accept the original plan, with reassurances that they would "be perfectly serious and solemn."[115]

In 1888, *The Nativity* and *The Crucifixion* (fig. 158) were unveiled in the chancel at St. Philip's, followed in 1897 by *The Last Judgment* (see fig. 162), an echoing window in the baptistery at the west end of the church that completed the decorative scheme.[116] Given that Burne-Jones was baptized at St. Philip's and his childhood home on Bennett's Hill was a short walk from the church, the commission was no doubt deeply personal.[117] However, the windows were not driven by a nostalgic impulse. Together with *The Star of Bethlehem*, they represented an opportunity to address the city of his birth and the people of Birmingham. In a letter to George Howard, Burne-Jones wrote, "I am doing my best to illuminate contemporary darkness in that dilapidated fortress of Liberalism."[118] Burne-Jones here employed the medium of stained glass not only to engage viewers in an immersive, embodied aesthetic experience, but also to make manifest an alternative vision of the world as a rebuke to the modern industrial city of Birmingham.

The expansive windows of St. Philip's have frequently been singled out for praise as among Burne-Jones's greatest achievements in the decorative arts, and a pinnacle of stained-glass design in the nineteenth century.[119] They are notable, in particular, for their

159 * Interior, St. Philip's Cathedral, Birmingham, designed by Thomas Archer 1708–25, extended by Julius Alfred Chatwin c. 1885–97

divergence from the typical Gothic Revival format of the majority of stained glass produced by Morris & Co. Although the chancel was enlarged by Chatwin, the shape of the soaring arched windows echoes those found in Archer's original Georgian architecture (fig. 159). Without stonework mullions or tracery, the vast and uninterrupted apertures of the chancel allowed Burne-Jones to treat each window as a continuous compositional field. For some critics, this uninterrupted expanse threatened to undermine the medium by transforming a stained-glass window into merely a painting on glass.[120] However, this treatment of stained glass as a single scene that extends across the window was not isolated to St. Philip's. As Martin Harrison has argued, this choice can be traced back to some of Burne-Jones's earliest designs for stained glass.[121] For example, in 1862, Burne-Jones submitted an initial design of "The Court of Heaven" for the east window of St. Michael and All Angels, Lyndhurst, Hampshire, as a single scene of paradise unfolding across seven lights and tracery. Although the final window as executed divided the figures into discrete, banded sections, the preliminary concept suggests that Burne-Jones was already experimenting with this approach to stained glass. In the last decade of his career, he was able to return to this style more frequently, and the windows for St. Philip's and St. Deiniol's demonstrate the advantages of approaching the composition as one extended pictorial plane.

Rendered in vivid ruby reds and deep sapphire blues, and punctuated by dazzling passages of white, *The Nativity* window of St. Philip's, Birmingham, achieves the brilliant jewel-like tones so prized by Burne-Jones and Morris. The dynamic composition unfolds in rippling waves, which extend out and up from the tiny figure of Christ at the bottom of the window. This spiraling quality is enhanced by the outward curve of the glass, following the rounded shape of the chancel and intensifying the perception of simultaneous suspension and movement. Sheltered by an imposing rock outcrop, the infant Christ lies asleep on bare stone. Mary kneels alongside in adoration, while Joseph and three angels bow their heads and clasp their hands in prayer. This traditional depiction of the Nativity in a cave, rather than a barn or manger, served as another symbolic invocation of Christ as the embodiment of light emerging from the darkness.[122] Burne-Jones harnessed this metaphorical association with the cave, creating a passage of dark indigo glass that fills a substantial portion of the lower half of the window, suggesting deep shadows through which light struggles to penetrate.

Another notable feature of Burne-Jones's composition is the shallow riverbed that curves around the stony perch where Christ rests. The stream flows from the bottom left corner of the window to the right before bowing back to disappear into the recesses of the cave. This stream is a pronounced feature of the photographically enlarged and retouched working cartoon (fig. 160), and is also evident in a large watercolor adapted from the window composition and rendered in shades of blue, with highlights of white gouache and gold (fig. 161). It guides the eye into the composition, the first of several spiraling curves that wend their way through the window from bottom to top and back again along its concave structure. The stream fulfills Christian theological symbolism, evocative of the rivers of paradise, as well as the sacrament of baptism and the concept of rebirth through salvation. However, the shallow waterway also asserts the elemental qualities of the scene, and suggests the flow of time on a geological scale. The sedimen-

160 ∗ Edward Burne-Jones, *The Nativity: Design for Stained Glass*, c. 1887–88. Watercolor drawing, photographic enlargement, 571.5 × 236.2 cm. Victoria and Albert Museum, London, E.224-1911

161 ∗ Edward Burne-Jones, *The Nativity*, 1887. Matte opaque paint, with gold paint, on two joined sheets of paper, mounted to cloth, stretched over a strainer, 144.1 × 58.7 cm. Huntington Library, San Marino, California

tary layers exposed in the rock at the base of the window echo the striations of the great arching ledge that forms the roof of the cavern. This suggests the power of even a gentle flow of water to wear away obdurate stone, a force that can begin small and placid, but eventually enact earth-shattering change.

In her compelling examination of *The Nativity* window of St. Philip's, Caroline Arscott has argued not only for Burne-Jones's self-conscious engagement with the stained-glass medium, but also identified the geological and biological forces at work in the composition.[123] She equates the infant Christ to a generative force of replication, aligning the Nativity with organic processes of birth and growth across the natural world:

> *The Christ-child lies at the conceptual centre of the composition, all the bending and extension of forms are organized around this little nub of life, which has already started the miraculous process of subdivision.... There is a fairly straightforward theological implication, that Christ is the source of life, but Burne-Jones's St Philip's windows use the medium of the stained glass to nuance this point in a novel way.*[124]

Arscott likens the fragmented pieces of glass, bound together through rhythmically patterned metallic joins, to the building blocks of all matter. The theological implication of this realization of the process of embodiment is "to find God or spirit in every thing and to conceive of a burgeoning macrocosm where the organic building blocks get divided and reunited in a benign bulking up."[125] She not only embraces Burne-Jones's stained glass as theologically and artistically radical, but also suggests an extreme application of Ruskinian "truth to nature." From the cellular to the cosmic, the microcosm to the macrocosm, Burne-Jones reveals nature to be organized around a central principle of vitality that pulses outward from the womb-like cave, through water and rock, reaching to the heavens. The lead lines are arranged in concentric arcs that ascend upward from Christ through the dark recesses of the grotto and across the ledge that divides the lower and upper portions of the composition. As the composition shifts from the Nativity to the Annunciation to the Shepherds, Burne-Jones extends his radical claim of unity from the natural to the social world.

The subterranean realm of water and rock that dominates the lower half of the window gives way to bare-leafed trees, the setting for the Annunciation to the Shepherds. On the left, a tightly clustered flock of sheep gathers on top of the ledge: a pale cream, they appear as a continuation of the stone, differentiated only by the little heads that peek above the crush of woolly bodies. To the right, the three shepherds echo the arc of the cave, perched behind the ledge, each in monochromatic robes of orange, magenta, and blue. They gaze back toward the left as a phalanx of red-robed and red-winged angels descend from the heavens to fill the arch at the top of the window.

As Burne-Jones once confessed to Ruskin, he preferred the Annunciation to the Shepherds, which fundamentally asserts that the poor and humble were the first to witness and acknowledge the manifestation of the divine.[126] Not only are the social hierarchies once again visually reversed, with the lowly shepherds occupying the heights of the window, but there is also a declaration of fellowship between heaven and earth. Throughout the composition, Burne-Jones once again alludes to Botticelli's *Mystic Nativity*, particularly in Mary's posture, as well as the depiction of the newborn resting on rock in a cave. Burne-Jones also emulated the suggestion of a community forged between angels and humanity as shared witnesses to the revelation of the divine. He thereby harnessed the apocalyptic connotations of the Nativity and suggested a new paradise on earth. As light emerges from darkness, the world is reborn and all life remade in the image of the divine, pulsing through the chain of being, from water to rock to animal to plant to human to angel.

Given this revelatory quality of *The Nativity*, its most fitting counterpart in St. Philip's is *The Last Judgment* window (fig. 162). Located beneath the bell tower in the baptistery at the west end of the church, *The Last Judgment* was created a decade later, in 1897. Much like *The Nativity*, the window is rendered in vibrant jewel tones of red, blue, and white, with a dynamic and rhythmic composition that extends from the figural arrangement to the patterning of the colored glass fragments. At the top of the arched window, Christ sits enthroned, robed in white and crowned with green thorns. Around him, the same red-winged and red-robed angels as in *The Nativity* form a dynamic swirling mass that obscures the sky behind. Beneath this encircling heavenly host, men, women, and children perch tenuously on uneven paving stones, joined in solidarity as they look upward. The skyline behind them is filled with toppling gray towers that are collapsing into oblivion. A crowned figure dressed in red and wearing a white turban stands to the far right, facing away from the viewer. Reminiscent of the oldest king in *The Adoration of the Magi* tapestry (see fig. 138), this figure asserts that rich and poor alike are all subject to the same fate.

Once again aligning the treatment of the medium with the subject, Burne-Jones fostered the illusion that the cataclysmic destruction of the cityscape is not limited to the scene, but extends to the surface of the pictorial plane itself. The very material of the window threatens to fracture and break apart. But just as the viewer perceives this menacing instability, the collapse of physical and fictive space, the patterns of the composition appear to reformulate the very matter of the world. Far from ignoring the English Baroque architecture of St. Philip's, Burne-Jones seized on the contrast between the stark visibility of the echoing windows that line the nave, and the vibrant, dynamic vision of

162 * Edward Burne-Jones, designer, for Morris & Co., *The Last Judgment*, 1897.
Stained glass. West window, St. Philip's Cathedral, Birmingham

the stained-glass windows in the chancel and baptistery. The clear glass panes that flood the rest of the church with unfiltered light also give a view onto the industrial city of Birmingham, which encloses the church on all sides. Looking from the living city beyond the nave to the vision of apocalyptic destruction and renewal, the window fosters the illusion that this fracturing and reformulating of the world extends from the stained glass to the fabric of the modern city. Burne-Jones's apocalyptic vision is thus one of devastating upheaval, but in its wake, there is hope for transformative rebirth. Just as fragmented shards of colored glass may be unified by a dark web of metal joins into a cohesive whole, the window explores, in both form and subject, how rich and poor, heaven and earth, the material and the immaterial, may be united under the light of salvation.

In St. Deiniol's, Hawarden, *The Nativity* window (see fig. 131) is gentler and more somber in tone, but no less innovative in its approach to rendering the Incarnation in stained glass. There is an apocalyptic quality to this rendering of the Nativity, located in the west end of the church. The window functions as a meditation on death as much as birth, serving as a memorial to Gladstone, Morris, and Burne-Jones himself. On a visit to Merton Abbey during the creation of the window, Burne-Jones found the works of Morris & Co. "such a pretty place... but so ghost-ridden to me."[127] Reclining on her bed of straw and cradling the infant in her arms, Mary once again recalls a funerary monument, a reminder of the tenuous line between birth and death. The figures amassed around them, including the magi and the shepherds, invoke an egalitarian message of equality, while also modeling devotional looking, immersive engagement, and epiphanic revelation. Although designed for a Gothic Revival window, divided across four lights and the tracery above, Burne-Jones adopted a continuous-field composition. Acknowledging the architectural structure of the window, from the outer stone framing to the inner lead bars, he bound the narrative scene together by creating a dynamic interplay of light, color, patterning, and subject. This treatment of the stained-glass window forges the illusion that the miraculous vision is alchemically manifesting within the medium itself. As colored light emerges from the darkness, Burne-Jones transforms the viewer into an active witness to the Incarnation of the divine. With his final stained-glass window, he sought to fulfill his aim "of bringing God into the world – making God manifest. It is giving back her Child that was crucified to Our Lady of the Sorrows."[128]

163 * *The Nativity* (detail of fig. 156)

Conclusion

"It was not a fault, it was a force"

THE WHEEL OF FORTUNE

Burne-Jones's painting *The Wheel of Fortune* (1875–83) depicts a poet, a king, and a slave suspended on a mammoth golden wheel (fig. 164). A colossal allegorical figure of Fortune stands beside them, one hand resting against the wheel's inner rim. Rendered in a cool palette of blue, gray, ivory, and gold, *The Wheel of Fortune* derives from a common medieval iconographic tradition signifying the cruelty of fate. Much like the *Perseus* series, Burne-Jones's painting serves as a modern *paragone*, employing the visual language of Classical and Renaissance sculpture. The pale bodies of the three men suggest either marble coming to life, or flesh turning to stone. Similarly, Fortune's gray drapery is thickly striated with white, evocative of an ancient cult statue. The sway of her hip against the hub of the wheel and her contrapposto stance promise movement that is perpetually suspended. Along the lower edges of the painting, broken marble columns and splintered pilasters suggest the remnants of a once great civilization consumed by the ravages of time. Plants have begun to push their way through cracks in the pavement and walls as nature slowly reclaims the ancient urban landscape. There is a subtle but insistent ecological message of environmental renewal in the wake of destruction.

The painting is at once enigmatic and starkly simple, attesting to the inevitable ascendency of the poor and oppressed over the powerful and privileged. The focal point of the canvas features the foot of the slave pressed painfully against the crowned head of the king, who is oblivious to the impending turn of the wheel. As with *King Cophetua and the Beggar Maid*, some contemporaries perceived the radical political critique presented in Burne-Jones's painting, while others refused to acknowledge its revolutionary inversion

of class hierarchies. An anonymous article written in *The Review of Reviews* in 1898 shortly after Burne-Jones's death hints at the failure of his elite patrons to recognize the censure found within his paintings: "'The Wheel of Fortune,' in which the foot of the slave in the ascendant treads upon the crown of the king of yesterday, suggested only the rack and the wheel of torture to many who saw it."[1] But *The Wheel of Fortune* indicates the pervasive egalitarian message embedded in all of Burne-Jones's work – not restricted to his collaborative projects with Morris. The oblivious king is unaware that his reign is ending, his supremacy as fragile as the crystal scepter in his hand or the delicate chains that hold the legs of the slave.

The king, the slave, and Fortune herself all appear with their eyes closed. However, at the very bottom of the canvas, about to be pressed down into the earth by the next rotation of the wheel, the laureled poet looks up, his eyes alert and awake. While the medieval trope of the Wheel of Fortune presented fate as inevitable, the upturned gaze of the artist indicates that perhaps these futures are not yet fixed. In the distance, faint golden rays shine through apertures in the stone, reinforcing the liminality of the painting overall. Poised between dawn and dusk, the fall of the old and the rise of the new, death and life, the poet may yet be able to awaken his fellows to the possibility of breaking the wheel itself.

Following his revelatory encounter with *King Cophetua and the Beggar Maid* at the Paris Universal Exposition of 1889, Robert de la Sizeranne wrote to Burne-Jones to learn more about his work and approach to art. The French critic stressed the contemporary relevance he perceived in Burne-Jones's painting as a protest against the materialism and alienation of modernity. Acknowledging that this aspect of his work was not always understood, Burne-Jones replied, "'It is a matter of just complaint... that I seem to my contemporaries to stand outside of their aspirations and desires so perpetually – seem to more than I really do.... it was not a fault, it was a force."[2] In fact, Burne-Jones remained consistently true to his quest to confront the age through the vital address of the visual arts. Again and again, across a wide range of media, he advocated for the need to awaken from the industrial devastation of the nineteenth century through the revival of artistic handicraft and pleasurable labor, the return to an intimate appreciation of nature, and the realization of social equality through fellowship, each intrinsically bound to the other. He saw around him a world almost impossibly broken, and strove to instill in others the desire to put the fractured pieces back together. Despite this, however, it is undeniable that many of his contemporaries overlooked this radical message, and succeeding genera-

164 * Edward Burne-Jones, *The Wheel of Fortune*, 1875–83. Oil on canvas, 199 × 100 cm. Musée d'Orsay, Paris, R. F. 1980-3

tions of artists, critics, and viewers have disdained his vision as reactionary, escapist, and irrelevant to the teleological progression of modern art.

Although a substantial lineage of artists inspired by Burne-Jones and his work could be traced from the nineteenth century to the present, this kind of influence alone would not have been how the artist measured the success of his career. Like his great friend William Morris, Burne-Jones rejected the ethos of competitive capitalism and the endless chain of winners and losers. Instead, they perceived time moving along the spiral, embracing an ebb and flow, a waxing and waning, spanning centuries. The teenaged rebellion of Burne-Jones and Morris against the flawed and troubled world of their day was inspired by art from the medieval past, and the two culled its lessons for a distant future they wished to bring into being. Morris's personal motto was the Latin phrase *Ars Longa, Vita Brevis*: in other words, life may be short, but art endures.[3] In keeping with Fredric Jameson's theory of utopian disruption forming a "pocket of stasis" from which to reflect back on and critique the world, Burne-Jones left behind a series of aesthetic havens to inspire generations to come.[4] From the intimate encounter with *When Adam Delved and Eve Span* in the tactile pages of Morris's handcrafted volume, to the overwhelming sumptuousness of *King Cophetua and the Beggar Maid* in the galleries of the Tate; from the soaring arches and apse of St. Paul's Within the Walls, Rome, glittering with mosaics, to countless stained-glass windows in small churches scattered around the globe – in all these places, Burne-Jones's legacy persists.

Notes

Introduction

1 John Christian and Penelope Marcus, eds., *Burne-Jones: The Paintings, Graphic, and Decorative Work of Sir Edward Burne-Jones, 1833–98* (London: Arts Council of Great Britain, 1975).

2 John Christian, "Introduction," in ibid., 11.

3 Stephen Wildman and John Christian, eds., *Edward Burne-Jones: Victorian Artist-Dreamer* (New York: Metropolitan Museum of Art, 1998).

4 Ibid., 319–20.

5 See e.g. Roberta Smith, "In Love With the Past and a Vision of Perfect Beauty," *The New York Times*, June 5, 1998.

6 Alison Smith, ed., *Edward Burne-Jones* (London: Tate Enterprises, 2018). For an example of the continued use of the quotation in 2018, see Rowan Pelling, "Why It's Time to Embrace the Mad, Androgynous Art of Burne-Jones," *The Telegraph*, October 6, 2018, https://www.telegraph.co.uk/art/what-to-see/time-embrace-mad-androgynous-art-burne-jones, accessed August 7, 2019.

7 Cosmo Monkhouse, "Introduction," in *Exhibition of Drawings and Studies by Sir Edward Burne-Jones, Bart.* (London: Burlington Fine Arts Club, 1899), vii. The shortened form of the quotation was much more prevalent, beginning with an essay on Burne-Jones's contribution to the decorative arts published as a special issue of *The Art Journal* in 1900: Aymer Vallance, "The Decorative Art of Sir Edward Burne-Jones, Bart.," *The Art Journal* Easter Art Annual (1900): 31. It appears again in this shortened form in Fortunée de Lisle, *Burne-Jones* (New York: Dodge Publishing, 1904), 173.

8 E. Burne-Jones to Helen Mary "May" Gaskell, n.d., British Library, London, Add. 54218, ff. 92–7.

9 Ibid., f. 93.

10 It is also notable that Monkhouse replaced the word "divining" with "divinely" when he published the quotation, removing the connotations of prophecy and visions.

11 *The Collected Works of William Morris*, vol. 12: *The Story of Sigurd the Volsung and the Fall of the Niblungs* (Cambridge: Cambridge University Press, 2012), 124–8.

12 Georgiana Burne-Jones wrote that her husband struggled with some of the more violent passages in the text when Morris asked him to create illustrations for this edition; *Memorials of Edward Burne-Jones*, 2 vols (London: Lund Humphries, 1993), vol. 2, 269–70. However, it is also evident that Burne-Jones was thoroughly versed in the narrative and Morris's interpretation of the story.

13 Florence Boos, "'The Banners of the Spring to Be': The Dialectical Pattern of Morris's Later Poetry," *English Studies: A Journal of English Language and Literature* 81, no. 1 (2000): 23. Boos describes Brynhild's vision as of a "day of better things," written "in language that recalls Christ's view of the kingdoms of the earth" (27).

14 Burne-Jones to Gaskell, Add. 54218, ff. 95–6; Morris, *Story of Sigurd*, 128.

15 Elizabeth Carolyn Miller, *Slow Print: Literary Radicalism and Late Victorian Print Culture* (Stanford, Cal.: Stanford University Press, 2013), 32–81. In her description of Morris's engagement with print culture as "utopian aestheticism," Miller draws on a body of scholarship in English literature that distinguishes between branches of the Aesthetic Movement. For example, Regenia Gagnier, "A Critique of Practical Aesthetics," in *Aesthetics and Ideology*, ed. George Lewis Levine (New Brunswick, N.J.: Rutgers University Press, 2006), 264–82, identifies a divide between decadents, concerned with their own freedom, and "the liberatory aesthetics of the Victorian socialist aesthetes," who wished to enable the freedom of others. Similarly, Ruth Livesey, *Socialism, Sex, and the Culture of Aestheticism in Britain, 1880–1914* (Oxford: Oxford University Press, 2009), 35–6, explores the nuanced differences among Ruskin's, Pater's, and Morris's approaches to aestheticism, arguing that Morris fostered a "somatic aesthetic theory": "For Morris the tradition of the productive hand, rather than the culture of the consuming, tasteful mind was the source of aesthetic transformation: a transformation that could therefore be led by popular revolution and not by doses of culture *de haute en bas*." See also Ch. 1 above.

16 Miller, *Slow Print*, 35, 36–7.

17 Fredric Jameson, *Archaeologies of the Future: The Desire Called Utopia and Other Science Fictions* (London: Verso, 2005), xii; see also xi–xiv, 12–16, 186–7, 231, 279; Jameson capitalizes "Utopia" and "Utopian" throughout.

18 Ibid., 231–2: "It is the very principle of the radical break as such, its possibility, which is reinforced by the Utopian form, which insists that its radical difference is possible and that a break is necessary."

19 Fredric Jameson, *The Cultural Turn: Selected Writings on the Postmodern 1983–1998* (London: Verso, 1998), 134–5.

20 I have chosen to use the term "radical" to describe Burne-Jones's relationship to Victorian society, art, and politics. This choice derives in part from Miller's discussion of the term in *Slow Print*, 8–9. She describes the capaciousness of the term, which can embrace attitudes that do not align specifically with one political party, but nonetheless function as a protest against dominant social and political trends. Burne-Jones's political affiliations at times tended towards Liberalism and at other times towards socialism, and he often expressed views that were even more extreme. The term "radical" thus acknowledges his stance outside normative political boundaries, while not falsely aligning him with any one group. It is also a term that was applied to Burne-Jones and his work by contemporaries; see De Lisle, *Burne-Jones*, 177.

21 Burne-Jones, quoted in G. Burne-Jones, *Memorials*, vol. 1, 84. The quotation is a reference to Alfred Tennyson's *In Memoriam* (1850), where he writes of "the faithless coldness of the times."

22 Elizabeth Prettejohn, *Art for Art's Sake: Aestheticism in Victorian Painting* (London: Paul Mellon Centre for Studies in British Art, 2007), 238.

23 In ibid., the chapter on Burne-Jones (233–53) starts from the same supposition as this book, arguing that the artist-dreamer paradigm is an inherently flawed and largely fictionalized construction. Moreover, Prettejohn reinforces the claim that it was Morris who deserted their shared avant-garde quest to confront the world through art by pursuing the more traditional route of political protest. She writes: "Burne-Jones later described this period as 'the only time when I failed Mr. Morris.' But in a sense it was Morris who had betrayed their shared vision, by abandoning his hopes for art in favour of a more conventional course of political action" (249). Prettejohn also demonstrates how Burne-Jones's paintings operated on the "political principle" of decorative materiality, writing that as his canvases gained increasingly larger proportions they were "no longer easel paintings at all. Now they are unequivocally decorative art: they are presences in the world, elements in an environment that they transform by their being" (238). She further reinforced this approach to Burne-Jones in her "Burne-Jones: Intellectual, Designer, People's Man," in Smith, *Edward Burne-Jones*, 13–21. I will return to Prettejohn's scholarship on Burne-Jones, and nineteenth-century British art more broadly, throughout this book.

24 In her biography of Burne-Jones, *The Last Pre-Raphaelite: Edward Burne-Jones and the Victorian Imagination* (London: Faber and Faber, 2011; Cambridge, Mass.: Harvard University Press, 2012), Fiona MacCarthy perpetuated this perceived division between Morris and

Burne-Jones. Indeed, the book serves as a companion volume of sorts to her biography of Morris, *William Morris: A Life for Our Time* (London: Faber and Faber, 1994), and she repeatedly sets the two apart rather than embracing what they achieved together. In her introduction, MacCarthy states that Burne-Jones "was the greater artist although Morris was unarguably the greater man" (xxii). She dwells much more on Burne-Jones's supposed sexual insecurity than his radical artistic vision. For a more in-depth discussion of MacCarthy's two biographies and her treatment of Burne-Jones's work and politics, see Andrea Wolk Rager, "Review of *The Last Pre-Raphaelite: Edward Burne-Jones and the Victorian Imagination* by Fiona MacCarthy (Harvard UP, 2012)," *Victorian Studies* 56, no. 1 (2013): 113–15.

25 Julia Mary Cartwright Ady, "The Life and Work of Sir Edward Burne-Jones," *The Art Journal* (Christmas 1894): 1. Cartwright Ady and Burne-Jones developed a close friendship following the publication of her art criticism; for more on their relationship and conversations, see her *A Bright Remembrance: The Diaries of Julia Cartwright 1851–1924*, ed. Angela Emanuel (London: Weidenfeld and Nicolson, 1989).

26 Cartwright Ady, "Life and Work," 32.

27 Henry Wilson, "The Work of Sir Edward Burne-Jones: More Especially in Decoration and Design," *The Architectural Review* 1 (May 1897): 277–8.

28 Robert de la Sizeranne, *English Contemporary Art*, ed. H. M. Poynter (London: A. Constable, 1898), 239–40.

29 "Art.III.-1. Sir Edward Burne-Jones," *The Quarterly Review* (October 1898): 359.

30 Ibid.

31 Joseph Jacobs, "Some Recollections of Sir Edward Burne-Jones," *The Nineteenth Century: A Monthly Review* (January 1899): 131.

32 See Thomas M. Rooke, "Memoirs of Thomas Matthews Rooke: typescript: or, Notes of conversations among the Pre-Raphaelite Brotherhood," typescript, National Art Library, Victoria and Albert Museum, London, 86.RR.52.

33 According to Tim Barringer, *Men at Work: Art and Labour in Victorian Britain* (New Haven and London: Yale University Press, 2005), 17, this is analogous to what Ruskin termed "reading." Barringer writes that "the intention is to reject a polarity in which contextual readings and formal analysis are seen as mutually exclusive; to insist, in other words, on the mutual interdependence of the two terms that form the compound – even paradoxical – disciplinary label, 'art history'." Similarly, Prettejohn, *Art for Art's Sake*, 6, writes: "I believe that there is an urgent need, not to supplant the contextual approaches that have been dominant in recent decades, but to create alongside them a new art history that makes works of art its primary concern …"

34 William Morris, *A Dream of John Ball and a King's Lesson* (London: Kelmscott Press, 1892).

35 Robert de la Sizeranne, "In Memoriam: Sir Edward Burne-Jones, Bart., A Tribute from France," *The Magazine of Art* 22 (1898): 513–15.

36 De Lisle, *Burne-Jones*, 2.

37 Ibid., 177.

One ✱ "An ideal of the world"

1 Burne-Jones to May Gaskell, dated in pencil "May–June 1894?" in unknown hand, British Library, London, Add. 54217, vol. 2, ff. 231–5.

2 Burne-Jones, quoted in Georgiana Burne-Jones, *Memorials of Edward Burne-Jones*, 2 vols (London: Lund Humphries, 1993), vol. 1, 114–15.

3 Ibid., 84.

4 Burne-Jones to Gaskell, Add. 54217, ff. 231–5; Burne-Jones states that it was "thirty-seven years" earlier, which would date the letter to 1892.

5 For more on Burne-Jones's designs for Bradfield, see Malcolm Bell, *Sir Edward Burne-Jones: A Record and Review*, 4th edn. (London: George Bell & Sons, 1899), 63–4; Aymer Vallance, "The Decorative Art of Sir Edward Burne-Jones, Bart.," *The Art Journal* Easter Art Annual (1900): 2; A. C. Sewter, *The Stained Glass of William Morris and His Circle*, 2 vols (New Haven, Conn.: Yale University Press, 1974), vol. 2, 1; Alan Crawford, "Burne-Jones as a Decorative Artist," in *Edward Burne-Jones: Victorian Artist-Dreamer*, ed. Stephen Wildman and John Christian (New York: Metropolitan Museum of Art, 1998), 6; Suzanne Fagence Cooper, *Pre-Raphaelite Art in the Victoria and Albert Museum* (London: V&A Publications, 2003), 147.

6 Vallance, "Decorative Art", 2, writes about *Adam and Eve After the Fall*: "When the Rev. J. Keble saw the

window in 1859, two years after it was designed, he was so much impressed that he wrote some verses for it on the text 'In the sweat of thy face shalt thou eat bread' (Gen. iii. 19)."

7 The frontispiece first appeared as an etching in the Reeves & Turner edition of 1888, William Morris, *A dream of John Ball; and, A king's lesson: (reprinted from the "Commonweal")* (London: Reeves & Turner, 1888), then as a woodcut in William Morris, *A Dream of John Ball and a King's Lesson* (London: Kelmscott Press, 1892).

8 See e.g. Stephen F. Eisenman, "Communism in Furs: A Dream of Prehistory in William Morris's *John Ball*," *The Art Bulletin* 87, no. 1 (March 2005): 92–110; see also Elizabeth Carolyn Miller, *Slow Print: Literary Radicalism and Late Victorian Print Culture* (Stanford, Cal.: Stanford University Press, 2013).

9 Elizabeth Prettejohn, *Art for Art's Sake: Aestheticism in Victorian Painting* (London: Paul Mellon Centre for Studies in British Art, 2007), 233–53, esp. 248–9 also argues for this reassessment of Burne-Jones's work, particularly in the light of the divergence with Morris over socialism. For her, Burne-Jones's artistic practice was in itself a "political principle," one that governed his entire career. She argues that it was Morris who adopted the more conservative approach to social reform by turning to political solutions, betraying Burne-Jones at this critical moment.

10 G. Burne-Jones, *Memorials*, vol. 2, 97. The same sentiment was later expressed by F. E. Hansford and G. A. C. Evans, *The Story of the Grange North End Crescent Fulham* (London: Fulham History Society Publications No. 1, 1953), 14, their pamphlet on the history of the Grange, the Burne-Joneses' home in Fulham, southwest London: "It was at this time [c. 1875] that Morris's mind was turning towards active Socialism. Although this never threatened the friendship between Burne-Jones and Morris, it gave the latter less time to spend with his friend. It made them reserved in conversation, which was something hitherto unknown to them, for they had always had complete sympathy with one another. Burne-Jones's disapproval of Morris's interest in active work of this sort was based on his belief that it meant a loss of valuable time that, in his opinion, should have been devoted entirely to Art."

11 Henry George, *Progress and Poverty: An Enquiry into the Cause of Industrial Depressions, and of Increase of Want with Increase of Wealth: The Remedy* (New York: Walter J. Black, 1879).

12 Burne-Jones to Mary Gladstone, November 1883, British Library, Add. 46246, ff. 153–4.

13 For more on Mary Gladstone's political role in her father's administration, see Sheila Gooddie, *Mary Gladstone: A Gentle Rebel* (Chichester: John Wiley & Sons, 2003), 129–46; see also Phyllis Weliver, *Mary Gladstone and the Victorian Salon: Music, Literature, Liberalism* (Cambridge: Cambridge University Press, 2017).

14 See e.g. Burne-Jones's letter to Mary Gladstone about his frustration over the Anglo-Egyptian War, July–September 1882, British Library, Add. 46246, f. 144. See also Thomas M. Rooke, "Memoirs of Thomas Matthews Rooke: typescript: or, Notes of conversations among the Pre-Raphaelite Brotherhood," National Art Library, Victoria and Albert Museum, London, 86.RR.52, 93, 96–7.

15 Burne-Jones sought William Gladstone's approval of a forthcoming publication in protest against the Russian pogroms. He described a number of atrocities and in particular defended the suffering Jewish populations of "poor artisans and industrious people"; E. Burne-Jones to William Gladstone, January 7, 1882, British Library, Add. 44474, ff. 18–20. In a subsequent letter to Mary Gladstone, February 2, 1882, Add. 46246, ff. 129–32, Burne-Jones wrote of attending a meeting on the matter and compared the situation to the earlier Balkan conflict. He stressed that this committee was much less politically motivated, writing "I hope it will spread & spread & become a roar – I went to the meeting yesterday & was glad to find the majority there were Liberals – but indeed all opinions, creeds & races were represented in a way and I hope every city in England will do the same"; see also ff. 127–8.

16 E. Burne-Jones to George Howard, n.d. [1878], Castle Howard Archives, J22/27/86.

17 For a thorough description of the British response to the Balkan crisis of 1875–78, along with a discussion of Morris's involvement, see Arthur Kyle Davis, Jr., "William Morris and the Eastern Question," in *Humanistic Studies in Honor of John Calvin Metcalf*, ed. James Southall Wilson (Charlottesville: University of Virginia Press, 1941), 28–47; see also G. Burne-Jones, *Memorials*, vol. 2, 73–5, 83–4.

18 William Morris, "To the Working-Men of England," May 1877, repr. in E. P. Thompson, *William Morris: Romantic to Revolutionary* (London: Lawrence & Wishart, 1955; New York: Pantheon, 1977), 193.

19 Ruskin replied to Burne-Jones's letter at the start of the conflict on December 8, 1876: "I hope neither Morris nor you will retire wholly again out of such spheres of effort. It seems to me especially a time when the quietest men should be disquieted, and the meekest self-asserting"; quoted in G. Burne-Jones, *Memorials*, vol. 2, 73.

20 Burne-Jones to Norman Grosvenor, Friday 11 or 16 [month unknown] 1876, private collection of Lady Tweedsmuir, repr. in Penelope Fitzgerald, *Edward Burne-Jones: A Biography* (1975; Stroud: Sutton Publishing, 1997), 163–4.

21 For Georgie Burne-Jones's particularly passionate recollection of the demonstration in January 1878, see her *Memorials*, vol. 2, 83–4.

22 Unfortunately, I have been unable to locate any surviving copies of this platform ticket. Aymer Vallance, *The Life and Work of William Morris* (London: Studio Editions, 1986), 222, mentions that at least one example was still in existence in 1897, but it remains untraced.

23 William Morris, February 20, 1878, quoted in J. W. Mackail, *The Life of William Morris*, 2 vols (New York: Dover, 1899), vol. 1, 362.

24 As Prettejohn has observed, *Art for Art's Sake*, 284, Burne-Jones's choice has "been attributed to some sort of conservatism on [his] part," which, moreover, may have led to "the conventional perception that there is something conservative, too, about [his] art."

25 Thompson, *William Morris*.

26 Ibid., 274; Thompson repeats this implicit critique of Burne-Jones as "Sir" later in the text, 627, n. 2.

27 In *The Labour Annual* of 1899, Burne-Jones is included in a list of artists perceived as socialists, and criticized for this stance, alongside Morris, Walter Crane, and G. F. Watts; see Joseph Edwards, ed., *The Labour Annual 1899* (London: Clarion Co., 1899).

28 Prettejohn, *Art for Art's Sake*, 233–53, esp. 248–9 also argues for this reassessment of Burne-Jones's work, particularly given the divergence with Morris over socialism.

29 G. Burne-Jones, *Memorials*, vol. 2, 96–7, my emphasis.

30 J. Bruce Glasier, *William Morris and the Early Days of the Socialist Movement* (London: Longmans, Green, and Co., 1921), 51–2, 113.

31 Morris quoted in ibid., 51–2.

32 Burne-Jones to Ford Madox Brown, September 13, 1885, Huntington Manuscripts, Huntington Library, San Marino, Cal., HM 12213; typescript, Fitzwilliam Museum, Cambridge, Burne-Jones Papers, Box 2, f. 2.

33 Sidney Colvin, *Memories & Notes of Persons & Places 1852–1912*, 2nd edn. (New York: Charles Scribner's Sons, 1922), 59.

34 Rooke, "Memoirs," 481.

35 Julia Mary Cartwright Ady, *A Bright Remembrance: The Diaries of Julia Cartwright 1851–1924*, ed. Angela Emanuel (London: Weidenfeld and Nicolson, 1989), 209, under her entry for Saturday, November 14, 1896.

36 For more on the Labors of Adam and Eve in the medieval era, see Michael Camille, "'When Adam Delved': Laboring on the Land in English Medieval Art," in *Agriculture in the Middle Ages: Technology, Practice, and Representation*, ed. Del Sweeney (Philadelphia: University of Pennsylvania Press, 1995), 259–61.

37 Ibid., 250–58.

38 Ibid., 259–61, noting in general that the image of Eve with spindle and distaff was widely used throughout the medieval era; for the earliest emergence of Eve's apocryphal task of spinning or weaving see Penny Howell Jolly, *Made in God's Image? Eve and Adam in the Genesis Mosaics at San Marco, Venice* (Berkeley: University of California Press, 1997), 114 n. 2.

39 Camille, "When Adam Delved," 261.

40 Ibid., 247–76; for more on the *Adam Delving* window, see Madeline H. Caviness, *The Early Stained Glass of Canterbury Cathedral* (Princeton, N.J.: Princeton University Press, 1977), 26, 52, 104, 113–14, 137.

41 Ruskin described these bas-reliefs as part of his "Mornings in Florence" series; John Ruskin, "Mornings in Florence: Being Simple Studies of Christian Art, For English Travellers," *The Works of John Ruskin*, ed. E. T. Cook and Alexander Wedderburn, 39 vols (London: George Allen, 1906), vol. 23, 281–457.

42 Ruskin, ibid., 417, describes the import of the scene: "The meaning of [this] myth is, as I read it, that men and women must both eat their bread with toil. That the first duty of man is to feed his family, and the

first duty of the woman to clothe it. That the trees of the field are given us for strength and for delight, and that the wild beasts of the field must have their share with us."

43 Morris praised *The Mirror of Salvation*: "some of these cuts are to my mind far away the best woodcuts ever done…at once decorative, and serious with the devotional fervour of the best side of the Middle Ages"; Morris to J. H. Middleton, January 20, 1891, quoted in Mackail, *Life of William Morris*, vol. 2, 254; see also William Morris, "On the Woodcuts of Gothic Books," *Journal of the Society of Arts* 40 (February 1892): 250.

44 Camille, "When Adam Delved," 270.

45 Robin M. Jensen, "The Fall and Rise of Adam and Eve in Early Christian Art and Literature," in *Interpreting Christian Art: Reflections on Christian Art*, ed. Heidi J. Hornik and Mikeal C. Parsons (Macon, Ga: Mercer University Press, 2003), 42–6. For Scriptural citation of this redemptive cycle, see 1 Corinthians 15:22: "For as in Adam all die, so also in Christ shall all be made alive." For a detailed discussion of Burne-Jones's relationship to typological Christian philosophy and the redemption of Eve in Mary, see Kathy M. Bullough, "Serpents, Angels and Virgins: The Virgin Mary as 'Second Eve' in the Art of Edward Burne-Jones," *Religion and the Arts* 4, no. 4 (2000): 463–90.

46 Stephen Prickett, "The Bible in Literature and Art," in *The Cambridge Companion to Biblical Interpretation*, ed. John Barton (Cambridge: Cambridge University Press, 1998), 164. Eisenman, "Communism in Furs," 106, also argues that *A Dream of John Ball* is an example of the Christian typological tradition.

47 Morris, Marshall, Faulkner & Co. did produce a large, multi-figure light for the east window of All Saints, Middleton Cheney, in 1864–65, which included an Adam with spade and an Eve with distaff and spindle, designed by Ford Madox Brown and Morris, respectively; see Sewter, *Stained Glass*, vol. 2, 133, 275.

48 The *Eve Spinning* window at Lamerton was destroyed by fire within months of its completion and the design was never executed again; ibid., vol. 2, 109.

49 For a detailed discussion of Burne-Jones's mosaics for St. Paul's Within the Walls, see Ch. 4 here.

50 "The 'Secret' Book of Designs" sketchbook, British Museum, London, Acc. 1899-7-13-322–544; see also G. Burne-Jones, *Memorials*, vol. 2, 118.

51 Richard Dorment, "Burne-Jones and the Decoration of St. Paul's American Church, Rome" (Ph.D. diss., Columbia University, 1976), 25–50.

52 Morris, *Dream of John Ball*, 227–8.

53 Ibid., 218.

54 Eisenman, "Communism in Furs," 100; Miller, *Slow Print*, 54–64.

55 Michael Holzman, "The Encouragement and Warning of History: William Morris's A Dream of John Ball," in *Socialism and the Literary Artistry of William Morris*, ed. Florence S. Boos and Carole G. Silver (Columbia: University of Missouri Press, 1990), 115 similarly argues for the significance of the act of enframing as indicative of the working relationship between Morris and Burne-Jones: "Morris's characteristic artistic production, in whatever medium, was the border or frame, a boundary between art and life, perhaps a wall to keep the world of industrialism away from the delicate designs of Burne-Jones."

56 Bell, *Burne-Jones*, 64–5, noted that Burne-Jones exhibited his preparatory drawing for the frontispiece at the first exhibition of the New Gallery in the spring of 1888, which further demonstrates his commitment to this image as part of his own oeuvre.

57 There is also an iconographical tradition that depicts Mary spinning in the manner of Eve in the Labors: see Gail McMurray Gibson, "The Thread of Life in the Hand of the Virgin," in *Equally in God's Image: Women in the Middle Ages*, ed. Julia Bolton Holloway, Constance S. Wright, and Joan Bechtold (New York: Peter Lang, 1990), 46–54.

58 Ibid., 49.

59 As will be explored later in this book, Burne-Jones was keenly aware of how paintings could be traded among the wealthy, subsumed into capitalist culture like any other commodity. Indeed, part of the primary appeal of the mosaics for St. Paul's Within the Walls was their necessary exclusion from the economic system. He once wrote, "[the mosaics] can't be sold and will be in Rome and will last for ever. That's why I like doing them"; Burne-Jones to Frances Horner, n.d., Burne-Jones Papers, Fitzwilliam Museum, Box XXVII/8, f. 42.

60 Charles Rowley was an avid promoter of the Arts and Crafts Movement and the Pre-Raphaelite circle. He brought Morris to Manchester to give lectures,

visited Kelmscott, supported the foundation of Manchester City Art Gallery, promoted Ford Madox Brown's murals in Manchester Town Hall, and commissioned a number of designs and crests from Walter Crane for the publications of the Ancoats Brotherhood; Charles Rowley, *Fifty Years of Work Without Wages* (London: Hodder and Stoughton, 1911); see also Eisenman, "Communism in Furs," 104; William Morris, *A Note by William Morris on His Aims in Founding the Kelmscott Press*, ed. William S. Peterson (New York: Grolier Club, 1996), 46.

61 This image of primitive spinning may have held particular significance for the workers of the Ancoats neighborhood of Manchester, which, according to Rowley himself, *Fifty Years*, 137, "was the home of fine spinning"; Rowley also included a reprint of *When Adam Delved and Eve Span* as an illustration (195).

62 When "The 'Secret' Book of Designs" was acquired by the British Museum, W. Roberts, "Our National Museums and Galleries: Recent Acquisitions: The British Museum: The Burne-Jones Drawings," *The Magazine of Art* 24 (1900): 453 particularly noted the sketches of Adam and Eve: "The subject of 'Adam and Eve' is one which Sir Edward Burne-Jones handled with much skill, and of which we have his finished ideas in the Kelmscott Press 'Golden Legend,' and also in the fine cartoon, entitled 'Labour,' which appeared in *The Daily Chronicle*, February 11th, 1895"; see also Bell, *Burne-Jones*, 64–5; Vallance, "Decorative Art," 20. There seems to be some discrepancy as to who was responsible for redrawing and enlarging *When Adam Delved and Eve Span* for *The Daily Chronicle*: Vallance, *Life and Work of William Morris*, 396 states specifically that it was Burne-Jones himself who oversaw the translation. However, according to William S. Peterson, *The Kelmscott Press: A History of William Morris's Typographical Adventure* (Oxford: Clarendon Press, 1991), 149–51 it was in fact Burne-Jones's friend and collaborator Robert Catterson-Smith who "redrew the frontispiece on a larger scale…"

63 Harold J. Laski, "The Social Philosophy of William Morris," *Speeches in Commemoration of William Morris* (Walthamstow: Buck Bros. & Harding, 1934), 21. Laski also noted seeing copies of *Songs for Socialists* and *News from Nowhere*, stating that the revolutionary possibility of Morris's art came from his realization "that once men and women make up their minds to bring beauty into their lives and to pay the price of bringing that beauty, they can change the foundations of their civilisation"; Laski's speech was "delivered at a Town's Meeting held in The Baths Hall, Walthamstow, on Saturday, 24th March, 1934."

64 Several scholars have sought to examine the unique relationship to history and social evolution found in *A Dream of John Ball*, as well as the ways in which the story fulfils the broader goal of educating the working classes; see esp. Holzman, "Encouragement and Warning"; see also Florence Boos, "Alternative Victorian Futures: 'Historicism,' Past and Present and A Dream of John Ball," in *History and Community: Essays in Victorian Medievalism*, ed. Florence S. Boos (New York: Garland, 1992), 3–37. That the medieval dream vision was also commonly employed as an educational tool may have influenced Morris's choice to employ this mode. According to Alice Loftin, "Visions," in *Dictionary of the Middle Ages*, ed. Joseph R. Strayer, vol. 12 (New York: Charles Scribner's, 1989), 476, "A dream vision, linking two or more worlds or levels of reality…records the process of an education – the dreamer's – so that readers or hearers may profit from it"; see also Eisenman, "Communism in Furs," 93–5.

65 Eisenman, "Communism in Furs," 92, also notes the emphasis placed on visual analysis in *A Dream of John Ball*, writing that Morris "provided detailed descriptions of the antique costumes of his protagonists…and of the architecture and decoration of churches, taverns, and houses. Indeed, numerous passages better reveal the eye of the designer than the ear of the novelist."

66 For more on the Peasants' Revolt, see J. A. Raftis, "Social Change Versus Revolution: New Interpretations of the Peasants' Revolt of 1381," in *Social Unrest in the Late Middle Ages*, ed. Francis X. Newman (Binghamton, N.Y.: Medieval & Renaissance Texts & Studies, 1986), 3–22; Mark O'Brien, *When Adam Delved and Eve Span: A History of the Peasants' Revolt of 1381* (Cheltenham: New Clarion Press, 2004).

67 Jean Froissart, *Chronicles of England, France, Spain and the Adjoining Countries, illustrated from the French editions by Thomas Johnes* (London: George Routledge and Sons, 1868), 652–63.

68 Camille, "When Adam Delved," 265, summarizing recent research, states that the couplet is thought

to date back to at least the time of the Adam window of Canterbury Cathedral (c. 1178–80) and is believed "to have been circulating in oral tradition long before the fourteenth century"; see fig. 6 and n. 42 above. However, the phrase might be attributable to Richard Rolle of Hampole (c. 1300–1349), a "hermit and mystical writer" who is credited with writing this poem: "When Adam dalfe and Eue spane/ Go spire if thou may spede [ask if you can],/ Where was than the pride of man,/ That now merres his meed? [spoils his reward]" For this claim see John Ayto, *Brewer's Dictionary of Phrase and Fable*, 17th edn. (New York: Cassell, 2005), 1479.

69 For other interpretations of the causes and development of the Peasants' Revolt, see Holzman, "Encouragement and Warning," 265; Raftis, "Social Change," 17.

70 Froissart, *Chronicles*, vol. 2, 654.

71 In 1889, Burne-Jones lamented having left his copy of Froissart in London when he went to his seaside home in Rottingdean, a casual reference, but one that testifies to the ongoing bond between Burne-Jones and this text, suggesting habitual reading over many years; G. Burne-Jones, *Memorials*, vol. 2, 199; see also Rooke, "Memoirs," 389–90.

72 Eisenman, "Communism in Furs," 92, 97; see also Holzman, "Encouragement and Warning," 100–01.

73 Eisenman, "Communism in Furs," 97–9, argues that the legacy of the Peasants' Revolt persisted among the working classes and political radicals as a "popular ideology of insurrection," fostering "a kind of subterranean cult of John Ball and Wat Tyler." Morris "believ[ed] that he was fanning a revolutionary ember that still glowed in popular consciousness."

74 William Morris, *A Dream of John Ball*, in *The Collected Works of William Morris*, vol. 16 (London: Longmans, Green, and Co., 1912), 215.

75 Ibid., 215.

76 Ibid., 217–18.

77 John Ruskin, *The Stones of Venice* (1853), in *Works*, vol. 10, 180–269.

78 Ibid., 193–4.

79 Ibid., 237.

80 Ibid., 269.

81 William Morris, "The Prospects of Architecture in Civilisation" (1882), in *Collected Works*, vol. 22 (London: Longmans, Green, and Co., 1914), 126.

82 Morris, *Dream of John Ball*, 225.

83 Ibid., 264.

84 Ibid., 287.

85 Ibid: "I got up presently, and going to the window looked out on the winter morning.... On the other side of the water the few willow-trees left us by the Thames Conservancy looked doubtfully alive against the bleak sky and the row of wretched-looking blue-slated houses...and the road in front of the house was sooty and muddy at once, and in the air was that sense of dirty discomfort which one is never quit of in London."

86 Ibid., 288.

87 Cynthia Hahn, "Vision," in *A Companion to Medieval Art: Romanesque and Gothic in Northern Europe*, ed. Conrad Rudolph (London: Wiley-Blackwell, 2006), 46.

88 See Loftin, "Visions," 476 who describes the medieval dream vision as "an ideal and often symbolic landscape in which a dreamer meets an authoritative figure who imparts a religious or secular doctrine."

89 Peter Brown, "On the Borders of the Middle English Dream Visions," in *Reading Dreams: The Interpretation of Dreams from Chaucer to Shakespeare*, ed. Peter Brown (Oxford: Oxford University Press, 1999), 26–7: "Not unusually the [dream vision] setting is a natural one, and the time spring or summer....The landscapes through which they move, and which so beguile them, have a marked tendency to be idealized, to resemble paradise."

90 Thompson, *William Morris*, 674, 675.

91 John Goode, "William Morris and the Dream of Revolution," in *Literature and Politics in the Nineteenth Century*, ed. John Lucas (London: Methuen, 1971), 279, 239, respectively.

92 Thompson, *William Morris*, 694. Holzman, "Encouragement and Warning," 115 also comments on the importance of the dream mode: "This dream form matters. It is in dreams that we refuse those parts of reality that we dislike, constructing, each one of us, a utopia of gratification. The dream is the last defense of the individual against a social world that is threatening, punishing, or merely insufficiently rewarding."

93 Fredric Jameson, *Archaeologies of the Future: The Desire Called Utopia and Other Science Fictions* (London: Verso, 2005), 15; see also Miller, *Slow Print*, 36.

94 Miller, *Slow Print*, 58.

95 Jameson, *Archaeologies of the Future*, 16 described this concept of utopian visions as enacting a world of the future: "The Utopians, however, reflect this still non-revolutionary blindness as to possible modifications in the power system; and this blindness is their strength insofar as it allows their imagination to overleap the moment of revolution itself and posit a radically different 'post-revolutionary' society."

96 This description refers to a copy in the Huntington Library, 108405, originally from the collection of Sanford and Helen Berger.

97 Morris commissioned handmade linen paper from Joseph Batchelor for the press. The paper for this text bears the "Primrose" watermark. See Paul Needham, *William Morris and the Art of the Book* (New York: Pierpont Morgan Library, 1976), 125–6.

98 John Burnett, *A History of the Cost of Living* (1969), 241, quoted in Sylvia Wolf, "'Mrs. Cameron's Photographs, Priced Catalogue': A Note on Her Sales and Process," in *Julia Margaret Cameron's Women*, ed. Sylvia Wolf (New Haven and London: Yale University Press for the Art Institute of Chicago, 1998), 212.

99 William Morris, *News from Nowhere*, in *Collected Works*, vol. 12, 37. For more on the Kelmscott Press, sustainability, and durability, as well as the comparison of a Kelmscott book to the pipe, see Elizabeth C. Miller, "Sustainable Socialism: William Morris on Waste," *The Journal of Modern Craft* 4, no. 1 (2011): 7–25.

100 See Morris's famous dictum to create an "art which is to be made by the people and for the people, as a happiness to the maker and the user," in "The Art of the People" (1879), in *Collected Works*, vol. 22, 47.

101 Cartwright Ady, *Bright Remembrance*, 197.

102 Burne-Jones to Charles Eliot Norton, December 8, 1894, Pierpont Morgan Library, repr. in Needham, *William Morris*, 138–9.

103 Morris, "On the Woodcuts," 248.

104 Morris, *A Note*, 4.

105 William Morris, "The Ideal Book," in *William Morris on Art and Design*, ed. Christine Poulson (Sheffield: Sheffield Academic Press, 1996), 151–2.

106 Morris, "On the Woodcuts," 257.

107 By extension, when Burne-Jones claimed of his book illustrations, "if you drag me out of my encasings it will be like tearing a statue out of its niche & putting it into a museum," he similarly invokes the dynamics of architectural preservation, whereby an architectural fragment or cast might be removed to a space of memorialization, but will effectively have ended its life as a functional structure of living memory. This implies that book illustrations and books themselves are also containers of memory; Burne-Jones to Charles Eliot Norton, December 8, 1894, Morgan Library, New York, repr. in Needham, *William Morris*, 138–9.

108 William Morris, "The Manifesto of the Socialist League" (1885), repr. in Thompson, *William Morris*, 739. Eisenman, "Communism in Furs," 107 also stresses the importance of this concept to interpreting the socialist message of *A Dream of John Ball*. This vision of history progressing on a spiral represented a radical challenge to the dominant "Whig" accounts of British history, such as those of Thomas B. Macaulay, Sir John Seeley, and James A. Froude, which emphasized a gradual progression toward the triumph of the middle class and the development of constitutional liberties as a process excluding the peasantry and working classes; see Herbert Butterfield, *The Whig Interpretation of History* (London: G. Bell and Sons, 1959); John W. Burrow, *A Liberal Descent: Victorian Historians and the English Past* (Cambridge: Cambridge University Press, 1981).

Two * "The Apotheosis of Poverty"

1 For more on the Paris Universal Exposition, see Elizabeth Gilmore Holt, *The Expanding World of Art, 1874–1902*, vol. 1 (New Haven and London: Yale University Press, 1988); Tim Benton, "Exhibiting Modernity: The 1889 Universal Exhibition and the Eiffel Tower," in *The Challenge of the Avant-Garde*, ed. Paul Wood (New Haven and London: Yale University Press, 1999), 156–63. Portions of this chapter were previously published in Andrea Wolk Rager, "'The Revenge of Art on Life': Beauty, Modernity, and Edward Burne-Jones's *King Cophetua and the Beggar Maid*," in *A Companion to Nineteenth-Century Art*, ed. Michelle Facos (Hoboken, N.J.: Wiley-Blackwell, 2019), 51–68.

2 The two primary first-hand accounts of encountering *King Cophetua* at the Exposition are found in Robert de la Sizeranne, "In Memoriam: Sir Edward Burne-Jones, Bart., A Tribute from France," *The Magazine of Art* 22 (1898): 513–20; Fernand Khnopff, "In Memoriam: Sir Edward Burne-Jones, Bart.: A Tribute

from Belgium," ibid., 520–26; see also F. G. Stephens, "Mr. E. Burne-Jones, A.R.A., as a Decorative Artist," *Portfolio* 20 (1889): 214; Julia Mary Cartwright Ady, "The Life and Work of Sir Edward Burne-Jones," *The Art Journal* (Christmas 1894): 23; Georgiana Burne-Jones, *Memorials of Edward Burne-Jones* (1904), 2 vols (London: Lund Humphries, 1993), vol. 2, 139, 201.

3 Sizeranne, "In Memoriam," 513, 515.

4 G. Burne-Jones, *Memorials*, vol. 2, 139; see also Martin Harrison and Bill Waters, *Burne-Jones*, 2nd edn. (London: Barrie & Jenkins, 1990), 144–5.

5 Sizeranne, "In Memoriam," 519.

6 Alfred Tennyson, "The Beggar Maid," in *The Works of Alfred Lord Tennyson* (Ware, Herts: Wordsworth Editions, 1998), 211.

7 Thomas Percy, *Reliques of Ancient English Poetry* (1765; New York: Thomas Y. Crowell & Co., 1876), 80–82; see also W. S. Taylor, "King Cophetua and the Beggar Maid," *Apollo* 97 (1973): 148–50; Stephen Wildman and John Christian, eds., *Edward Burne-Jones: Victorian Artist-Dreamer* (New York: Metropolitan Museum of Art, 1998), 252–3.

8 It is unclear why Burne-Jones chose to discard the work in 1862, but Georgiana reported, *Memorials*, vol. 1, 253 that he suffered from recurring depression while struggling over this first version: "I work daily at Cophetua and his Maid. I torment myself every day – I never learn a bit how to paint. No former work ever helps me – every new picture is a new puzzle and I lose myself and am bewildered – and it's all as it was at the beginning years ago. But I will kill myself or else Cophetua shall look like a King and the beggar like a Queen, such as Kings and Queens ought to be."

9 Duncan Robinson, "Letter to the Editor: Burne-Jones's King Cophetua and the Beggar Maid," *Apollo* 97 (1973): 626; the studies are part of a sketchbook now in the Fitzwilliam Museum, Cambridge. Robinson states that the dating is difficult to pinpoint, but from the surrounding studies it can be fairly conclusively tied to c. 1875.

10 Robinson, ibid., notes the similarities to Burne-Jones's *Annunciation*, painted around the same time, 1876–79.

11 See e.g. Harrison and Waters, *Burne-Jones*, 141–4; Taylor, "King Cophetua"; Wildman and Christian, *Edward Burne-Jones*, 253.

12 M. H. Spielmann, "In Memoriam, III: Sir Edward Burne-Jones, Bart.," *The Magazine of Art* 21 (1898): 528.

13 In *Men at Work: Art and Labour in Victorian Britain* (New Haven and London: Yale University Press, 2005), 21–81, Tim Barringer employs the designation of "secular altarpiece" to describe Ford Madox Brown's monumental achievement of artistic labor, *Work* (1852–65). Indeed, *King Cophetua and the Beggar Maid* shares much with *Work*, particularly the challenge each posed to contemporary social, economic, and artistic hierarchies. I am deeply indebted to Barringer's discussion of Brown's *Work*, particularly as a secular altarpiece.

14 Claude Phillips, "Edward Burne-Jones," *The Magazine of Art* 8 (1885): 292; see also G. Burne-Jones, *Memorials*, vol. 2, 26, 227.

15 Harrison and Waters, *Burne-Jones*, 141–4; Taylor, "King Cophetua," 151–2.

16 While Burne-Jones never records having seen the painting, it is likely that he saw it during one of his three separate journeys to Paris, in 1855, 1862, and 1878; see G. Burne-Jones, *Memorials*, vol. 1, 114, 241, vol. 2, 82. Additionally, a popular engraving after the painting by Francesco Novelli in 1804 was widely circulated throughout the nineteenth century; see Michael Bryan, *Dictionary of Painters and Engravers* (London: George Bell and Sons, 1889), 217; Rodolfo Signorini, "The Creation of Adam: A Detail in Mantegna's Madonna Della Vittoria," *Journal of the Warburg and Courtauld Institutes* 59 (1996): 303 n. 1.

17 Taylor, "King Cophetua," 151.

18 A contemporary critic observed the sacred air of the painting, implicitly likening the beggar maid to the Virgin Mary, writing that she faces her destiny "as some saint might face the Beatific Vision, in the strength of her maiden purity"; "The Grosvenor Gallery: First Notice," *The Times*, May 1, 1884.

19 See e.g. Wildman and Christian, *Edward Burne-Jones*, 141. For a thorough discussion of the popularization of Botticelli, see Michael Levey, "Botticelli and Nineteenth-Century England," *Journal of the Warburg and Courtauld Institutes* 23, no. 3–4 (1960): 291–306; see also Mark Evans and Stefan Weppelmann, *Botticelli Reimagined* (London: V&A Publications, 2016).

20 Elizabeth Prettejohn, *Modern Painters, Old Masters: The Art of Imitation from the Pre-Raphaelites to the*

First World War (New Haven and London: Paul Mellon Centre for Studies in British Art, 2017), 162–3.

21 Levey, "Botticelli," 300; Penelope Fitzgerald, *Edward Burne-Jones: A Biography* (1975; Stroud: Sutton Publishing, 1997), 155.

22 See Ronald Lightbown, *Sandro Botticelli*, 2 vols (Berkeley: University of California Press, 1978), vol. 2, 55.

23 Fitzgerald, *Edward Burne-Jones*, 155. At the time of the Barker auction in 1874, the National Gallery already possessed six paintings by Botticelli and his followers, all acquired after 1855. Two more were purchased in 1878, bringing its holdings to ten paintings by the close of the century.

24 Patricia Rubin, "The Seduction of Antiquity," in *Manifestations of Venus: Art and Sexuality*, ed. Caroline Arscott and Katie Scott (Manchester: Manchester University Press, 2003), 33.

25 "Grosvenor Gallery," *The Times*.

26 "London Spring Exhibitions: The Grosvenor and the Water-Colour Societies," *The Art Journal* (1884): 21.

27 Burne-Jones to Mary Gladstone, July–September 1882, British Library, Add. 46246, f. 144.

28 Burne-Jones quoted in Thomas M. Rooke, "Memoirs of Thomas Matthews Rooke: typescript: or, Notes of conversations among the Pre-Raphaelite Brotherhood," typescript, National Art Library, Victoria and Albert Museum, London, 86.RR.52, 93.

29 Ibid., 96–7.

30 Caroline Arscott and Katie Scott, "Introducing Venus," in *Manifestations of Venus*, 5, 7.

31 Burne-Jones in Rooke, "Memoirs," 458.

32 Fitzgerald, *Edward Burne-Jones*, 199 states that Burne-Jones drew "his brush-handle round [the head of the beggar maid] to mark the paint," further highlighting and separating the figure from the treatment of her surroundings.

33 Alastair Johnson, "Re-Altering the Glazing Alterations of a Burne-Jones Frame," in *Conserving Context: Relating Object Treatment to Collections and Settings*, ed. Gerry Alabone (London: Archetype, 2014), 72.

34 See Paul Mitchell and Lynn Roberts, "Burne-Jones's Picture Frames," *The Burlington Magazine* 142, no. 1167 (2000): 362–70.

35 For more on the *Briar Rose* series and Burne-Jones's use of framing, see Andrea Wolk Rager, "'Smite this Sleeping World Awake': Edward Burne-Jones and *The Legend of the Briar Rose*," *Victorian Studies* 51, no. 3 (2009): 438–50.

36 Although he does not identify Bellini in particular, Johnson, "Re-Altering the Glazing Alterations," 76 suggests this connection: "Burne-Jones deliberately chose the design of a Renaissance altarpiece frame to perform a traditional role, similar to that in a church: as a continuation in relief of the architectural setting contained within the painting…" Burne-Jones, an admirer of Bellini's work, would undoubtedly have encountered this painting and several similar examples during his two visits to Venice. In 1898, he wrote to a friend visiting Venice, "whenever you see Bellini give him my adoration, for none is like him – John, that is, for his brother I only respect"; G. Burne-Jones, *Memorials*, vol. 2, 335. Mitchell and Roberts, "Burne-Jones's Picture Frames," 368 also suggest Carlo Crivelli's *Madonna della Rondine* from the National Gallery, London, as another possible source for the design.

37 Rona Goffen, *Piety and Patronage in Renaissance Venice: Bellini, Titian, and the Franciscans* (New Haven and London: Yale University Press, 1986), 40. Similarly, Goffen in "Bellini, S. Giobbe and Altar Egos," *Artibus et Historiae* 7, no. 14 (1986): 60 wrote: "The fictive architecture of the pictures is completed by the actual architecture of the frame.… Thus the sacred realm of the holy beings is extended into our own world, and the place where the one may be approached from the other is, literally and metaphorically, the altar."

38 Prettejohn, *Modern Painters*, 135–8 describes the paintings of Rossetti and Burne-Jones as "altarpieces for an age of doubt." But "they do not simply take up the traditional form of the altarpiece and empty out its religious content.… By imitating some of the features of the old religious paintings, the Victorian artists are exploring what it was that made them powerful; at the same time, they are inventing those sources of artistic power afresh."

39 Elizabeth Prettejohn, *Art for Art's Sake: Aestheticism in Victorian Painting* (New Haven and London: Paul Mellon Centre for Studies in British Art, 2007), 251.

40 "Grosvenor Gallery," *The Times*.

41 "Grosvenor Gallery: First Notice," *The Spectator*, May 10, 1884, 614.

42 Khnopff, "In Memoriam," 522.

43 Cartwright Ady, "Life and Work," 23. In likening Burne-Jones's art to that of a goldsmith, Cartwright Ady was perhaps drawing another implicit connection between the Victorian artist and Botticelli. Ruskin, in particular, emphasized that Botticelli was trained as a goldsmith before he became a painter. According to Ruskin, "Ariadne Florentina: Six Lectures on Wood and Metal Engraving" (1876), in *The Works of John Ruskin*, ed. E. T. Cook and Alexander Wedderburn, 39 vols (London: George Allen, 1906), vol. 22, 427–8 Botticelli retained the exacting sense of detail, line, and color he learned while practicing this early artisanal trade, skills which enhanced his painting: "I have before pointed out to you the importance of training by the goldsmith. Sandro got more good of it, however, than any of the other painters so educated, – being enabled by it to use gold for light to colour, in a glowing harmony never reached with equal perfection, and rarely attempted in the later schools. To the last, his paintings are partly treated as work in niello; and he names himself, in perpetual gratitude, from this first artisan master"; see also John Ruskin, "The Schools of Art in Florence," in *Works*, vol. 23, 265–6.

44 Burne-Jones quoted in Spielmann, "In Memoriam," 528.

45 Prettejohn, *Art for Art's Sake*, 238, 243, 249, 251. For more on the potential for Pre-Raphaelite painting to function in a radical, decorative mode, as both objects and political assertions, see Morna O'Neill, "Arts and Crafts Painting: The Political Agency of Things," *British Art Studies*, Issue 1, https://dx.doi.org/10.17658/issn.2058-5462/issue-01/moneill.

46 Another preparatory study of Cophetua's crown and hands, similar to that in the Tate, is *Study of a Hand Carrying a Crown*, 1883, pencil with terracotta wash on paper, 29 × 22.5 cm, Wightwick Manor, West Midlands, National Trust Collections (NT 1288074).

47 Philip Burne-Jones, "Notes on Some Unfinished Works of Sir Edward Burne-Jones, Bt.," *The Magazine of Art* 24 (1901): 161–2. In addition to including a photograph of the model for Cophetua's copper crown, this article also illustrates several similar working models, including a helmet and sword for the *Perseus* series, several musical instruments for *The Sleep of Arthur in Avalon*, the wooden chariot for *The Passing of Venus*, and a ship with three sails for *The Sirens*.

48 Aymer Vallance, "The Decorative Art of Sir Edward Burne-Jones, Bart.," *The Art Journal* Easter Art Annual (1900): 28.

49 Ibid.

50 John Ruskin, "Modern Painters II" (1846), in *Works*, vol. 3, 624.

51 W. A. S. Benson, *Drawing, Its Histories and Uses* (Oxford: Oxford University Press, 1925), 21. Georgiana Burne-Jones, *Memorials*, vol. 2, 81, 112 wrote that Benson's sister was a model for the "Perseus pictures" and that Benson also sat for the figure of Pygmalion. Benson was an architect as well as a designer and metalworker, and helped with the remodeling of the "little house at Rottingdean," including designing the furniture.

52 Avril Denton, "W. A. S. Benson: A Biography," in *W. A. S. Benson: Arts and Crafts Luminary and Pioneer of Modern Design*, ed. Ian Hamerton (Woodbridge: Antique Collectors' Club, 2005), 51.

53 Alan Crawford, "W. A. S. Benson, Machinery, and the Arts and Crafts Movement in Britain," *The Journal of Decorative and Propaganda Arts* 24 (2002): 99.

54 Attributed to William Morris by W. R. Lethaby, *Philip Webb and His Work* (Oxford: Oxford University Press, 1935), 94.

55 As Prettejohn, *Art for Art's Sake*, 253 eloquently states, the viewer is given the choice between "a world of Wealth without Beauty" and "a world of Beauty without Wealth."

56 Burne-Jones to Francis Horner, June 1886, Fitzwilliam Museum, Cambridge, Burne-Jones Papers, Box XXVII, f. 5. Fittingly, he juxtaposed this comment with a discussion of his mosaics in Rome, works which, as will be explained in Ch. 4 here, transcended the restrictive parameters of his painting practice.

57 G. Burne-Jones, *Memorials*, vol. 2, 13.

58 Burne-Jones to Helen Mary Gaskell, n.d., British Library, Add. 54218, f. 285.

59 For more on Burne-Jones's role in the very public break-up of the Grosvenor Gallery, see "Correspondence with Sir Coutts Lindsay, 1887, concerning Grosvenor Gallery," National Arts Library, Victoria and Albert Museum, London, 40.G, Box I.

60 Burne-Jones to George Howard, November 1887, Castle Howard Archives, J22/27/369.

61 Burne-Jones, quoted in Rooke, "Memoirs," 137.

62 G. Burne-Jones, *Memorials*, vol. 2, 75.

63 Colleen Denney, *At the Temple of Art: The Grosvenor Gallery, 1877–1890* (London: Associated University Presses, 2000), 67.

64 Ibid., 59: "In essence... Lindsay duplicated at his gallery some of the most private and comfortable features of the private temple of the English country house, because he sought to convey the ideas of his gallery as a temple of domestic virtue, a private sanctuary, or safe haven, conducive to private contemplation and worship of art." Burne-Jones, along with Ruskin, strongly objected to the décor of the Grosvenor from the beginning. One of the novel radical changes to exhibition display introduced by the Grosvenor was to hang each artist's work together as a group and to give ample wall space to view and contemplate each painting, rather than the floor-to-ceiling hang of the Royal Academy. However, Burne-Jones felt that this intention was undermined by the initial gaudy red damask wall hangings, which detracted from the color of the paintings. His disapproval indicates his awareness that the gallery was meant to resemble a wealthy home: "I know in private houses that one's work is always destroyed by carpets and hangings, but in this Gallery, for a little, one's colour ought to rest and tell as one meant it to"; quoted in G. Burne-Jones, *Memorials*, vol. 2, 78. For more on the decoration of the Grosvenor and Burne-Jones's reaction, see ibid., 69–70, 77–9; Denney, *At the Temple*, 48–59; Christopher S. Newall, *The Grosvenor Gallery Exhibitions: Change and Continuity in the Victorian Art World* (Cambridge: Cambridge University Press, 1995), 10–15.

65 "London Spring Exhibitions," *The Art Journal*, 221.

66 "Grosvenor Gallery," *The Spectator*, 614, 615.

67 "Grosvenor Gallery," *The Times*.

68 Ibid.

69 "Grosvenor Gallery," *The Spectator*, 614–15.

70 Phillips, "Burne-Jones." The critic for *The Art Journal* also admired "the fine drawing"; "London Spring Exhibitions," 221.

71 "London Spring Exhibitions," *The Art Journal*, 221.

72 "Grosvenor Gallery," *The Times*.

73 "Grosvenor Gallery," *The Spectator*, 614.

74 "Grosvenor Gallery," *The Times*.

75 "London Spring Exhibitions," *The Art Journal*, 221.

76 Phillips, "Burne-Jones," 292–4.

77 "Grosvenor Gallery," *The Times*.

78 "London Spring Exhibitions," *The Art Journal*, 221.

79 "Grosvenor Gallery," *The Spectator*, 614–15.

80 "The Grosvenor Gallery: Second Notice," *The Magazine of Art* (1878): 81, my emphasis.

81 Wilfred Meynell, "The Winter Exhibition at the Grosvenor Gallery," *The Magazine of Art* 4 (1881): 180.

82 Stephens, "Mr. E. Burne-Jones," 214.

83 Fitzgerald, *Edward Burne-Jones*, 220–21 writes: "it so happened that the *Cophetua* made the best possible contrast to the glittering Paris of the Expo, which the Tour Eiffel, although not quite ready in time, epitomised."

84 Sizeranne, "In Memoriam," 513–20; Khnopff, "In Memoriam," 520–26. These two articles are the most thorough in delineating the experience of viewing the painting at the Universal Exposition. However, it is evident from other contemporary accounts that Burne-Jones's exhibit in 1889 left a lasting impression in Paris. For example, for his retrospective at the New Gallery in 1893, the French art critic Baronne Madeleine Deslandes (1866–1929) contributed an extensive article, "Edward Burne-Jones," *Le Figaro*, May 7, 1893, which begins by recalling his paintings at the Salon du Champ de Mars four years previously, "l'exposition des oeuvres du grand peintre de l'Angleterre, Edward Burne-Jones," then proceeds to devote a substantial portion to *King Cophetua*.

85 Khnopff, "In Memoriam," 522.

86 Benton, "Exhibiting Modernity," 158: "Eiffel had coolly assessed the project as a money-winning venture..."

87 Holt, *Expanding World of Art*, vol. 1, 70; see also Petra ten-Doesschate Chu, *Nineteenth-Century European Art* (New York: Harry N. Abrams, 2003), 430–31.

88 Burne-Jones quoted in G. Burne-Jones, *Memorials*, vol. 1, 101.

89 John Ruskin, "The Opening of the Crystal Palace: Considered in Some of Its Relations to the Prospects of Art," in *Works*, vol. 12, 417–32. Ruskin uses his discussion as an opportunity to expose the crimes of architectural neglect and, perhaps worse in his opin-

ion, campaigns of architectural restoration then occurring across Europe: "We shall wander through our palaces of crystal, gazing sadly on copies of pictures torn by cannon-shot, and on casts of sculpture dashed to pieces long ago. We shall gradually learn to distinguish originality and sincerity from the decrepitudes of imitation and palsies of repetition; but it will be only in hopelessness to recognize the truth, that architecture and painting can be 'restored' when the dead can be raised, – and not till then" (429).

90 Benton, "Exhibiting Modernity," 156, 158.

91 Chu, *Nineteenth-Century European Art*, 431.

92 Khnopff, "In Memoriam," 520–22.

93 Benton, "Exhibiting Modernity," 158.

94 For an overview of the works displayed, see Chu, *Nineteenth-Century European Art*, 435–49. The Impressionists and Post-Impressionists were excluded from the official art exhibits; however, smaller shows of their work could be found beyond the official grounds of the Exposition.

95 For more on Gay's *Charity* at the Universal Exposition of 1889, see Annette Blaugrund, *Paris 1889: American Artists at the Universal Exposition* (New York: Harry N. Abrams, 1989), 153–4; for Breton's *The Shepherd's Star*, see Annette Bourrut Lacouture, *Jules Breton, Painter of Peasant Life* (New Haven and London: Yale University Press, 2002), 253.

96 Khnopff, "In Memoriam," 520–22 also described the English Art Section: "As you went on from room to room a reverent hush was felt till at last, in the central hall of the English section – which contained, among other works, those of Lord Leighton, of Millais, of Alma-Tadema, and Orchardson, and on one side the strong crimsons of Watts's 'Mammon,' and the cruelly far-away blue of his 'Hope' – there appeared, like a queen, supreme and glorious, the lovely picture by Burne-Jones, 'King Cophetua and the Beggar-Maid,' in the place of honour, the centre of a panel, with its beautiful frame of pale gold pilasters ornamented with scrolls…"

97 Burne-Jones wrote to Watts, February 1888, Burne-Jones Papers, Fitzwilliam Museum, Box XXVI, f. 99, "I keep remembering your words that you wanted to shew your pictures side by side with mine and nothing that ever was said to me will be more remembered than these, and still I hope you will, though I dread to say a word to influence you"; and previously, July 5, 1885, ibid., f. 97 Burne-Jones referred to himself as Watts's "godchild…"

98 Khnopff, "In Memoriam," 522.

99 Sizeranne, "In Memoriam," 513, 515.

100 Ibid., 515.

101 Paul Greenhalgh, "The Art and Industry of Mammon: International Exhibitions, 1851–1901," in *The Victorian Vision: Inventing New Britain*, ed. John M. MacKenzie (London: V&A Publications, 2001), 265–79.

102 *Dublin University Magazine*, 1862, 132, quoted in ibid., 272.

103 Wildman and Christian, *Burne-Jones*, 75.

104 This was not the first time that Burne-Jones's work had been seen in Paris. His painting *Merlin and Vivien* (also known as *The Beguiling of Merlin*, 1873–74) had appeared in the 1878 Universal Exposition, but it was not until 1889 that he truly came into the public eye in Europe.

105 Robert de la Sizeranne, *English Contemporary Art*, ed. H. M. Poynter (London: A. Constable, 1898), 239–40.

106 Ibid., 243–4.

107 Khnopff, "In Memoriam," 526.

108 Burne-Jones quoted in G. Burne-Jones, *Memorials*, vol. 2, 202.

109 William Morris to Helen Mary Gaskell, 1893, British Library, Add. 54217, vol. 1, ff. 164–6. De la Sizeranne, "In Memoriam," 515 also wrote of this French invasion: "The upshot of these reflections was that a great many young Frenchmen determined on an extraordinary, and to us somewhat alarming step: on crossing the Channel – and lo! they discovered England!"

110 Pablo Picasso quoted in Roland Penrose, *Picasso: His Life and Work*, 3rd edn. (Berkeley: University of California Press, 1981), 37, quoted in Andrew Wilton and Robert Upstone, eds., *The Age of Rossetti, Burne-Jones, & Watts: Symbolism in Britain, 1860–1910* (London: Tate Gallery, 1997), 33; see also Laurence des Cars, "Edward Burne-Jones and France," in Wildman and Christian, *Burne-Jones*, 25–40.

Three * Myth and Mimesis

1 Suggesting an Edenic setting, *The Baleful Head* sees a man, woman, and serpentine monster meet

among the laden limbs of an apple tree. The painting is closely related to Burne-Jones's design for a stained-glass window, *The Fall of Man* (1873–74), where the devil has the body of a snake with a female head and torso. For more on the typological connection of Perseus and Andromeda with Adam and Eve, see Adrienne Auslander Munich, *Andromeda's Chains: Gender and Interpretation in Victorian Literature and Art* (New York: Columbia University Press, 1989), 125. The joined hands evoke the traditional iconography of the *dextrarum iunctio*; Burne-Jones may have modeled the scene after a Roman sarcophagus fragment in the British Museum (c. 160 BCE); see Fabian Fröhlich, "The Perseus Series," in *Edward Burne-Jones: The Earthly Paradise*, ed. Christofer Conrad and Annabel Zettel (Ostfildern: Hatje Cantz, 2009), 131. Similarly, *The Baleful Head* echoes the depiction of the marriage of Louis of Anjou in Jean Froissart's *Chronicles* in the British Library (c. 1470–72); Martin Harrison and Bill Waters, *Burne-Jones*, 2nd edn. (London: Barrie & Jenkins, 1990), 64 point out the similarities between this illumination from the "Harley Froissart" and Burne-Jones's design for a stained-glass window, *The Marriage of Sir Tristram* (1862). An early sixteenth-century Netherlandish tapestry depicting the wedding of Perseus and Andromeda portrays the couple with hands joined in a similar fashion to *The Baleful Head*. Now in the Cleveland Museum of Art (1927.487), the tapestry formerly belonged to Sir Edgar Speyer (1862–1932), a founding patron of the Whitechapel Art Gallery. Burne-Jones may have encountered the tapestry in London before it entered Speyer's collection, although no records exist to support the connection apart from the striking visual similarities.

2 The term "Gorgoneion" is used of a representation of the Gorgon's head. For an overview of theoretical approaches to Medusa as a mythological figure, see Marjorie Garber and Nancy J. Vickers, eds., *The Medusa Reader* (New York: Routledge, 2003), 1–7. For a recent survey of Medusa imagery in art, see Kyriaki Karoglou, "Dangerous Beauty: Medusa in Classical Art," *Metropolitan Museum of Art Bulletin* 75, no. 3 (2018).

3 For a discussion of Medusa as an allegory of mimesis, see Jean-Pierre Vernant, *Mortals and Immortals: Collected Essays*, ed. Froma I. Zeitlin (Princeton, N.J.: Princeton University Press, 1991), 135–8, 164–84; see also Rainer Mack, "Facing Down Medusa (An Aetiology of the Gaze)," *Art History* 25, no. 5 (November 2002): 571–604. For a discussion of Medusa and mimesis in the Victorian era, see Thomas Albrecht, *The Medusa Effect: Representation and Epistemology in Victorian Aesthetics* (Albany: State University of New York Press, 2009), 1–21.

4 For more on Burne-Jones's approach to painting in series, particularly a comparison between the *Perseus* and *Briar Rose* series, see Elizabeth Prettejohn, "The Series Paintings," in *Edward Burne-Jones*, ed. Alison Smith (London: Tate Enterprises, 2018), 169–94.

5 Sketchbook, Fitzwilliam Museum, Cambridge, 1070(2). Many thanks to Rebecca Virlag and Nicholas Robinson for their assistance in securely dating this sketchbook. For more on the planned collaboration between Morris and Burne-Jones on an illustrated version of *The Earthly Paradise*, see Joseph R. Dunlap, *The Book That Never Was* (New York: Oriole Editions, 1971).

6 Florence Boos, "Volume One: Introduction," in William Morris, *The Earthly Paradise*, ed. Florence Boos (New York: Routledge, 2002), 6; her introduction is a comprehensive overview of the themes and reception.

7 Morris, *Earthly Paradise*, vol. 1, 52.

8 Ibid., 69.

9 Boos, "Volume One," 23.

10 Florence Boos, "Notes: The Doom of King Acrisius: The Classical Tale for April," in Morris, *Earthly Paradise*, vol. 1, 265.

11 Morris, *Earthly Paradise*, vol. 1, 278.

12 There are several common spellings of "Graiae," including "Graiai" and "Graeae." Throughout, I will use the spelling adopted by Morris and Burne-Jones, "Graiae," singular "Graia," except where quoting authors who employed one of the other spellings.

13 Morris, *Earthly Paradise*, vol. 1, 297.

14 See also Fröhlich, "Perseus Series," 117.

15 Morris, *Earthly Paradise*, vol. 1, 303, 304.

16 The word "wallet" is used by Morris, ibid., 305 n. 69 in place of the term "kibisis," the bag or sack that could safely contain Medusa's head. According to Boos, this bag derives from Apollodorus, whereas in Ovid, Perseus does not cover the head as he flies and the drops of blood become snakes as they fall to the ground.

17 Ibid., 306 nn. 73, 75. The mythological Atlas was a Titan; however, in Ovid's version of the legend,

he appears as a giant. Morris describes the figure as a giant but does not explicitly use the name "Atlas."

18 Ibid., 316, 317.

19 Ibid., 342.

20 Initially, there were plans for Morris and Burne-Jones, along with Jane Morris and Georgiana Burne-Jones, to carve the woodblocks for the illustrations themselves.

21 May Morris, *William Morris: Artist, Writer, Socialist* (Oxford: Blackwell, 1936), vol. 1, 402, quoted in Dunlap, *Book That Never Was*, 10.

22 For more on Balfour and the commission, see Arthur James, First Earl of Balfour, *Chapters of Autobiography*, ed. Mrs. Edgar Dugdale (London: Cassell, 1930), 233–4; see also Jane Abdy and Charlotte Gere, *The Souls* (London: Sidgwick & Jackson, 1984), 30–39.

23 For more on Burne-Jones's relationship to Balfour as a patron and the circumstances of the *Perseus* commission, see Melody Barnett Deusner, *Aesthetic Painting in Britain and America: Collectors, Art Worlds, Networks* (New Haven and London: Paul Mellon Centre for Studies in British Art with Yale University Press, 2020), 33–69.

24 Burne-Jones to George Howard, [1875], Castle Howard Archives, J22/27/47.

25 Balfour, *Chapters of Autobiography*, 233.

26 In ibid., 233–4 Balfour writes, "I had bought Number 4 Carlton Gardens in the year 1871, and the house remained in my possession during the rest of my active life. It so happens that the principal drawing-room was, as London drawing-rooms go, long and well lit, and the happy thought occurred to me to ask my new friend to design for it a series of pictures characteristic of his art. This must have been in the early 'seventies, but alas! his death in 1898 separated us before his designs in every case were quite finished. The subject I left entirely to him. The choice of the Perseus Legend was therefore not mine, but I have never regretted it."

27 Burne-Jones to Balfour, May 27, 1875, in Balfour Papers, 1872–September 1886, British Library, Add. 49838, cited in Fröhlich, "Perseus Series," 108.

28 For a description of the history of Carlton Gardens and Carlton House Terrace, see G. H. Gater and F. R. Hiorns, eds., *St. Martin-in-the-Fields, Part 3: Trafalgar Square & Neighbourhood*, vol. 20 in *Survey of London* (London: Country Life for London County Council, 1940), 77–87.

29 Fredric Jameson, *Archaeologies of the Future: The Desire Called Utopia and Other Science Fictions* (London: Verso, 2005), 15–16, 231; see also Elizabeth Carolyn Miller, *Slow Print: Literary Radicalism and Late Victorian Print Culture* (Stanford, Cal.: Stanford University Press, 2013), 35–7.

30 "The Opening of Parliament by King Edward VII: Scenes in the Governmental City of Westminster," *The Sphere* 8, no. 104 (January 18, 1902): 74; "Small Talk of the Week: The Premier's London Home," *The Sketch*, December 10, 1902; see also George A. Wade, "10, Downing Street," *The Pall Mall Magazine*, February 1901.

31 Kurt Löcher, *Der Perseus-Zyklus von Edward Burne-Jones* (Stuttgart: Staatsgalerie Stuttgart, 1973), 38 argued that there is a direct comparison to Morris's *Acanthus* wallpaper of the same year.

32 Daniel Ogden, *Perseus* (London and New York: Routledge, 2008), 40–41 suggests that the water nymphs first appear in the Perseus legend at the end of the sixth century BCE, depicted on a set of vases.

33 This portion of the legend derives from Hesiod's *Theogony* (c. 700–650 BCE); ibid., 35.

34 This iteration of Atlas was not traditionally linked with Perseus, but Hesiod and Ovid link Atlas to the Gorgons; see Fröhlich, "Perseus Series," 125.

35 For more on the decoration of 4 Carlton Gardens and the planned integration of the *Perseus* paintings into the interior design, see Deusner, *Aesthetic Painting*, esp. 36–47; see also Fröhlich, "Perseus Series," 103–4.

36 Burne-Jones to Balfour, May 27, 1875, Balfour Papers 1872–September 1886.

37 Burne-Jones suggested Mantegna's *Triumphs of Caesar* as a model for the *Perseus* series in an early letter to Balfour for the commission (ibid.); see also Fröhlich, "Perseus Series," 104.

38 "Notes and News," *The Academy*, March 11, 1876, 249.

39 Walter Pater, *The Renaissance: Studies in Art and Poetry* (1893), ed. Donald L. Hill (Berkeley: University of California Press, 1980), 50; see Alex Potts, *The Sculptural Imagination: Figurative, Modernist, Minimalist* (New Haven and London: Yale University Press, 2000), 68–9;

for a discussion of Pater and *rilievo*, see Lene Østermark-Johansen, *Walter Pater and the Language of Sculpture* (Farnham: Ashgate, 2011), esp. 16–25.

40 Burne-Jones quoted in Georgiana Burne-Jones, *Memorials of Edward Burne-Jones* (1904; London: Lund Humphries, 1993), vol. 2, 208.

41 For a discussion of the *Perseus* gouache series in Burne-Jones's studio, see e.g. Fernand Khnopff, "In Memoriam: Sir Edward Burne-Jones, Bart.: A Tribute from Belgium," *The Magazine of Art* 21 (1898): 525.

42 According to Burne-Jones's working list, he painted a large-scale combined canvas depicting both moments of the rescue of Andromeda occurring simultaneously, as indicated in the initial cartoon (unfinished, Art Gallery of South Australia, Adelaide, 0.329). It seems that he then set aside the Andromeda episode for a time. By 1884–85, he had settled on dividing the episode into two canvases. The completed oils were exhibited together in 1888 at the New Gallery; see Burne-Jones, "List of my designs," 23, 35, Fitzwilliam Museum, Cambridge.

43 The passage translates as: "Pallas Athene with her urging spurred Perseus to action and equipped him with arms. The blind sisters of the Gorgons revealed to him the remote home of the nymphs. From there he went with wings on his feet and with his head shrouded in darkness, and with his sword he struck the one Gorgon who was subject to death – the others were immortal. Her two sisters arose and pursued him. Next he turned Atlas to stone, the sea-serpent was slain and Andromeda rescued and the comrades of Phineus became lumps of rock. Then Andromeda looked with wonder in a mirror at the dreadful Medusa"; Stephen Snoddy and Esta Jones, eds., *The Perseus Series: Sir Edward Coley Burne-Jones* (Southampton: Southampton City Art Gallery, 1998), 22. For the attribution to Jebb, see "The Grosvenor Gallery," *British Architect*, May 24, 1878, 239; see also Stephen Wildman and John Christian, eds., *Edward Burne-Jones: Victorian Artist-Dreamer* (New York: Metropolitan Museum of Art, 1998), 223.

44 Burne-Jones exhibited the four finished canvases during his lifetime: *The Baleful Head* at the Grosvenor Gallery in 1887; *The Rock of Doom* and *The Doom Fulfilled* at the New Gallery in 1888; and *Perseus and the Graiae* at the Paris Salon in 1893; Christian and Marcus, *Burne-Jones*, 59–62.

45 The most comprehensive studies of the series as a whole have emerged from the Staatsgalerie, which acquired Balfour's set in 1971. Shortly after, Kurt Löcher published a concise, meticulously researched overview of the series, *Der Perseus-Zyklus*, gathering together many of the surviving studies and working drawings. Löcher suggested numerous visual sources for Burne-Jones's iconography, spanning ancient and Renaissance prototypes, from examples of ancient Greek vase painting in the British Museum to Michelangelo's *ignudi* from the Sistine ceiling. Drawing on the precedent of Morris's "The Doom of King Acrisius," Löcher also stressed the myth as a chivalric quest for salvation. In 2002, Fabian Fröhlich devoted his doctoral dissertation to the series: "Frauen Im Spiegel. Der Perseus-Zyklus von Edward Burne-Jones" (University of Kassel, 2002). In 2009, he adapted it into his "Perseus Series" for the catalogue *Edward Burne-Jones: The Earthly Paradise*. Other notable accounts of the series can be found in Wildman and Christian, *Edward Burne-Jones*, 221–33; Snoddy and Jones, *Perseus Series*; Ogden, *Perseus*, 138–43.

46 See e.g. Joseph Kestner, "Edward Burne-Jones and the Nineteenth-Century Fear of Women," *Biography* 7, no. 2 (Spring 1985): 95–122; Munich, *Andromeda's Chains*, 117–31; Liana de Giroliani Cheney, "Edward Burne-Jones's 'Andromeda': Transformation of Historical and Mythological Sources," *Artibus et Historiae* 25, no. 49 (2004): 197–227; Alicia Craig Faxon, "The Pre-Raphaelites and the Mythic Image: Iconographies of Women," *Visual Resources* 27, no. 1 (March 2011): 77–89.

47 Munich, *Andromeda's Chains*, 117 discusses Burne-Jones's series as a typological exploration of the "dangers of both male and female sexuality"; frequently, Burne-Jones's brief affair with the artist Maria Zambaco is used to support claims of his alleged fear of women and female sexuality as supposedly expressed in the *Perseus* series, e.g. by Kestner, "Burne-Jones," 112–15; Cheney, "Burne-Jones's 'Andromeda,'" 217; Craig Faxon, "Pre-Raphaelites and the Mythic Image," 288.

48 Sigmund Freud, "Medusa's Head" (1922, pub. 1940), repr. in Garber and Vickers, *Medusa Reader*, 85.

49 Fröhlich, "Perseus Series," 127, 134.

50 Caroline Arscott, *William Morris and Edward Burne-Jones: Interlacings* (New Haven and London: Paul

Mellon Centre for Studies in British Art, 2008), 53; full discussion of the series, 53–86. Arscott generates a new approach by placing the series in the context of the modern, mechanized military industrial complex that arose in the nineteenth century; while demonstrating the extent to which Burne-Jones's armored Perseus functions as "a certain kind of militaristic fantasy" (82), Arscott also allows for a degree of resistance and ambivalence that prevents the series from being usurped by Balfour's Tory hawkishness.

51 E.g., ibid., 67 Arscott relates the apotropaic function of the Gorgoneion frequently found on depictions of Athena's shield as analogous to the operation of art in ancient Greek society: "The function of the shield is that of art, where art is redemptive; it is akin to the Apollonian recuperation of Dionysian force"; moreover, when discussing the shift from gesso on wood to oil on canvas for *Perseus and the Graiae*, Arscott observes the association between reflective metal and the operation of vision: "The metallic sheen, the 'grey and steely' tones of the picture are less stunning... than the gold and silver of the gesso reliefs, but the sheen nevertheless functions analogously to the reflectivity of the reliefs as a form of heightened visual experience at the moment of the failure of sight" (83).

52 For a discussion of this 1878 version of *Perseus and the Graiae*, see Claire Jones, "Perseus and the Graiae," in *Sculpture Victorious: Art in an Age of Inventions, 1837–1901*, ed. Martina Droth, Jason Edwards, and Michael Hatt (New Haven and London: Yale Center for British Art in association with Yale University Press, 2014), 390–93.

53 As Arscott, *Morris and Burne-Jones*, 63 argues, "This gesso work realizes the groping panic of the three crouching sisters, deprived by Perseus of their single eye, by evoking the uncertain mapping of topography solely through the sense of touch by means of the ridges and hollows of the swirling bas-relief design." Fröhlich, "Perseus Series," 115 also notes the emphasis on sight and blindness in his discussion.

54 Morris, *Earthly Paradise*, vol. 1, 297.

55 In his initial listing of designs for "The Doom of King Acrisius," Sketchbook 1070(s), f. 77, repr. in Löcher, *Perseus-Zyklus*, 48, Burne-Jones seems to confuse the Graiae's blindness with Perseus's invisibility when he reaches the Gorgons: for the 11th illustration, he writes, "Lands at Graiae – snatching eye Graiae not looking at him because he's invisible – make them looking different ways?"

56 "Uses of Modern Art," *Saturday Review*, May 25, 1878, 651.

57 "Grosvenor Gallery," *British Architect*, 239.

58 "The Grosvenor Gallery (Concluding Notice)," *The Magazine of Art* 1 (January 1878): 111.

59 "The Picture Galleries," *Saturday Review*, June 1, 1878, 692.

60 L. S. Cook, "Among the Pictures," *University Magazine*, June 1878, 739.

61 W. M. Rossetti, "The Grosvenor Gallery (First Notice)," *The Academy*, May 18, 1878, 447.

62 This confusion over media seems to have largely arisen from Henry Blackburn, ed., *Grosvenor Notes* (London: Chatto and Windus, 1878), 48, which included this erroneous description: "The first of a series of designs (in yellow and white metal fastened on wood) to illustrate the tale of Perseus: the inscription (by Professor Jebb) sets forth the subject of the whole series..." For repeated descriptions of this inaccurate identification of the medium, see "Grosvenor Gallery," *British Architect*, 239; Rossetti, "Grosvenor Gallery," 447; Cook, "Among the Pictures," 739. This confusion over whether Burne-Jones had experimented with metal plates on wood or canvas, rather than gesso, has persisted, and may be due in part to the fact that the gesso version remained in the Balfour family until 2008, when it was donated to the National Museum Wales. As noted above, there is also one small canvas of *Perseus and the Graiae* completed in 1882, and now in a private collection, which could possibly have been adorned with metal plates, although this seems unlikely; for a small image of this version, see Löcher, *Perseus-Zyklus*, 99. For the persistence of the metal plate description, see e.g. Harrison and Waters, *Burne-Jones*, 120; Wildman and Christian, *Burne-Jones*, 224; Arscott, *Morris and Burne-Jones*, 81.

63 "Grosvenor Gallery," *Magazine of Art*, 111; Cook, "Among the Pictures," 739; "Picture Galleries," *Saturday Review*, respectively.

64 Ogden, *Perseus*, 56.

65 Indeed, some of the now known depictions had either not yet been excavated or their subject matter identified at the time. It is possible that Burne-Jones

was familiar with a more recent iteration, Henry Fuseli's *Perseus Returning the Eye to the Graiai* (1790–1800; Birmingham Museums and Art Gallery), although the composition of this pen and ink drawing does not bear any resemblance to Burne-Jones's version. Writing in 1893, after the exhibition of the later oil on canvas *Perseus and the Graiae* at the Paris Salon, Paul Leprieur, "La Légende de Persée, par M. Burne-Jones," *Gazette des Beaux-Arts* 10, no. 6 (December 1, 1893): 471 declared the composition to be unique: "C'est un des motifs de la légende qui semble avoir exercé, d'ailleurs, sur l'imagination de M. Burne-Jones la plus grande séduction, celui pour lequel il a visiblement de secrètes préférences, sans doute parce qu'il y a mis le plus de lui-même, et que, n'en ayant trouvé nulle part, que je sache, le prototype figuré, il en peut être dit proprement l'inventeur."

66 Richard Jenkyns, *Dignity and Decadence: Victorian Art and the Classical Inheritance* (London: HarperCollins; Cambridge, Mass.: Harvard University Press, 1992), 267 likens what he describes as "the three weird sisters" of *Perseus and the Graiae* to the Norns, noting that they evoke Wagner's *Götterdämmerung*.

67 Fröhlich, "Perseus Series," 113–15; Löcher, *Perseus-Zyklus*, 13.

68 See John Christian, "Burne-Jones and Sculpture," in *Pre-Raphaelite Sculpture: Nature and Imagination in British Sculpture, 1848–1914*, ed. Benedict Read and Joanna Barnes (London: Henry Moore Foundation with Lund Humphries, 1991), 77–91. In 1875, at the outset of the *Perseus* commission, Georgiana Burne-Jones, *Memorials*, vol. 2, 59 described her husband visiting the British Museum in order to study "all the most ancient ways of pourtraying [*sic*] Medusa"; Burne-Jones also owned casts of the figures of Theseus and Ilissus and displayed them in his drawing-room; Christian, "Burne-Jones and Sculpture," 81. For detailed discussion of the reception of these sculptures and their impact on the understanding of Greek sculpture in the nineteenth century, see Elizabeth Prettejohn, *The Modernity of Ancient Sculpture: Greek Sculpture and Modern Art from Winckelmann to Picasso* (London: I.B. Tauris, 2012), 38–103, esp. 68–72.

69 E.g. Cecil Smith, "The Central Groups of the Parthenon Pediments," *The Journal of Hellenic Studies* 27 (1907): 248.

70 See Stephanie Brown, "Indefinite Expansion: Watts and the Physicality of Sculpture," in *Representations of G. F. Watts: Art Making in Victorian Culture*, ed. Colin Trodd and Stephanie Brown (Aldershot: Ashgate, 2004), 90–91; see also M. S. Watts, *George Frederic Watts*, 3 vols (London: Macmillan, 1912), vol. 3, 23.

71 Watts, *Watts*, vol. 1, 141, quoted in Prettejohn, *Modernity of Ancient Sculpture*, 68.

72 Burne-Jones quoted in Thomas M. Rooke, "Memoirs of Thomas Matthews Rooke: typescript: or, Notes of conversations among the Pre-Raphaelite Brotherhood," National Art Library, Victoria and Albert Museum, London, 86.RR.52, 232. Walter Crane, "Notes on Gesso Work," *The Decorator and Furnisher* 24, no. 1 (April 1894): 21 expressed the same assessment: "Decorative design in gesso stands, it may be said, midway between painting and sculpture, partaking in its variations of the characters of each in turn – the younger sister of both, holding, as it were, the hands of each; playful, light-hearted, familiar, associated in turn with all kinds of domestic furniture and adornment."

73 Notes by Lady Lewis (private collection), cited in Christian, "Burne-Jones and Sculpture," 77, 90 n. 3. Although they do not survive, sculptural models were also an integral aspect of Burne-Jones's working practice. Working collaboratively with Georgiana, he produced models out of common materials such as tin or deal for the armor, crowns, swords, and other fantastical accessories that appear in his paintings. Particular effort was made to create models for the *Perseus* series; G. Burne-Jones, *Memorials*, vol. 2, 61. Burne-Jones may also have become closely acquainted with sculptural technique and practice through his relationship with Zambaco, an accomplished sculptor who later worked in the studio of Auguste Rodin. Zambaco's artistic exchange with Burne-Jones has not received sufficient scholarly attention.

74 Rooke, "Memoirs," 483.

75 Matthew Webb, "On Gesso, with Some Designs for Finger-Plates," *The Decorator and Furnisher* 26, no. 2 (May 1895): 61 noted the particular appeal of gesso as a sculptural medium for painters, explaining that "much of its manipulation is practically that of painting it on with the brush," while also describing the brilliant effects that could be achieved by combining gilding with oil paints. Burne-Jones sometimes spells Osmund

Weeks's name as "Weekes," leading to some confusion; e.g. Burne-Jones to George Howard, n.d., Castle Howard Archives, J22/27/355.

76 Burne-Jones created two versions of the monumental memorial tablet for Laura Lyttelton (née Tennant), who died aged twenty-four after the birth of her first child and within one year of her marriage. One tablet, rendered in stark white plaster, was placed in the church of St. Andrew's, Mells, Somerset. Burne-Jones kept the second version, which he painted and gilded, and displayed at his London home. Further attesting to his belief in the resilience of gesso, he described the memorial tablet as "durable as granite and enduring till the Judgment Day"; G. Burne-Jones, *Memorials*, vol. 2, 166.

77 For discussions of Burne-Jones's influence on New Sculpture and polychromy, see e.g. Christian, "Burne-Jones and Sculpture," 86–90; Jason Edwards, *Alfred Gilbert's Aestheticism: Gilbert Amongst Whistler, Wilde, Leighton, Pater and Burne-Jones* (London: Routledge, 2006).

78 Burne-Jones chose to exhibit this final version of *Perseus and the Graiae* at the Paris Salon of 1893 where, according to Claude Phillips, "The Salons II," *The Magazine of Art* (January 1893): 388 the painting proved "a piquant novelty to the Parisians, hungering just now … for some form of modern, semi-decorative mysticism …" Attesting to the public fascination with *Perseus and the Graiae*, Leprieur, "Légende de Persée," examined the series as a whole, illustrating an etching after the painting by Félix-Stanislas Jasinski; *Perseus and the Graiae* thus circulated widely as a print in France.

79 Of the oil version of *Perseus and the Graiae*, Fröhlich, "Perseus Series," 115 writes, "Perseus's calling appears to have taken him into a supernatural twilight realm. The mist-swathed gloom of the place reflects the hero's own dread and he acts as if he, too, had been deprived of the sense of sight, groping blindly until his fingers close around the barely visible, bead-sized object of his desire – the eye of the Graiae."

80 Østermark-Johansen, *Walter Pater*, 203 similarly likens Burne-Jones's treatment of surface in the *Briar Rose* series to Whistler's nocturnes.

81 I have chosen to illustrate Leonardo's first version, from the Louvre, which Burne-Jones may have seen during his travels to Paris. The second version (c. 1491/2–99 and 1506–8), was acquired by the National Gallery, London in 1880. The link to the Louvre version is much more compelling, given the greater emphasis on the gestural arrangement of the hands. Fröhlich, "Perseus Series," 115 also notes the "clear parallels" between *The Virgin of the Rocks* and *Perseus and the Graiae*, especially the female figure at left.

82 Østermark-Johansen, *Walter Pater*, 164, 16, 18, 16, respectively.

83 Leonardo, "Treatise on Painting," trans. A. Philip McMahon (1956), repr. in Robert Klein and Henri Zerner, eds., *Italian Art 1500–1600: Sources and Documents* (Evanston, Ill.: Northwestern University Press, 1966), 7.

84 Baudelaire, *Oeuvres complètes* (1961), 943, quoted in Potts, *Sculptural Imagination*, 62.

85 In addition to Pater and Baudelaire, other art theorists including A. F. Rio, Ruskin, and Swinburne stressed the importance of *rilievo* as a central concept in the *paragone*; Østermark-Johansen, *Walter Pater*, 27.

86 Ibid., 116. The term *Andersstreben*, loosely translated as "other-striving," is unique to Pater and scholars have struggled to trace the exact origin; Østermark-Johansen (148) argues that it probably derives from Pater's reading of Baudelaire, not an original German source.

87 Ibid., 164; 164–203 elaborate Burne-Jones's deeply considered visual enactment of modern theories of the *paragone* in works as diverse as *The Golden Stairs* (1876–80), the *Pygmalion* series (1875–78), and *The Days of Creation* (1870–76), drawing not only on Leonardo, but also Michelangelo and Botticelli, as well as Pater, Swinburne, and Baudelaire.

88 Ibid., 198, 192.

89 Elizabeth Prettejohn, *Art for Art's Sake: Aestheticism in Victorian Painting* (New Haven and London: Paul Mellon Centre for Studies in British Art, 2007), 2.

90 The nude figure of Perseus seen at left appears similar to an *ignudo* from Michelangelo's Sistine Chapel ceiling in the initial cartoon for Balfour. However, Burne-Jones altered the pose in later versions. By the final canvas, the figure resembles Hippolyte Flandrin's painting, *Study (Young Male Nude Seated beside the Sea)* (1836; Musée du Louvre, Paris). This painting is, in itself, a study of the male nude form in dialogue with sculptural precedents.

91 Burne-Jones made a separate study after a *Three Graces* sculptural group, as seen in his sketchbook, Victoria and Albert Museum, London, 91.D.40. The pose of Perseus in this scene could also echo another *ignudo* from the Sistine ceiling.

92 Leprieur, "Légende de Persée," 473.

93 In addition to a cast of *Ilissos*, Burne-Jones also owned replicas of *Dionysus* from the Parthenon, and Michelangelo's *Night* and *Day* from the Medici Chapel in Florence; Christian, "Burne-Jones and Sculpture," 81; John Christian and Penelope Marcus, *Burne-Jones: The Paintings, Graphic and Decorative Work of Sir Edward Burne-Jones, 1833–98* (London: Arts Council of Great Britain, 1975), 98.

94 Fröhlich, "Perseus Series," 117.

95 For more on this particular quality of Perseus's armor, see Arscott, *Morris and Burne-Jones*, 66. Fröhlich, "Perseus Series," 127 observes the sculptural quality of Andromeda, stating that she "is depicted standing on her plinth like a classical Venus, as pale as marble and in perfect contrapposto."

96 Burne-Jones's engagement with the sculptural went even further here, as he created clay models as visual aids. In an undated latter to George Howard, Castle Howard Archives, J22/27/41, he wrote, "I have all this week wasted my time making a clay image of Perseus and all next week will be wasted making a snake round it. But, I know no other way of getting what I want, and my arm so aches with using wet clay that I can hardly frame the letters to make this intelligible."

97 Ovid, "The Story of Perseus," *Metamorphosis*, trans. Rolfe Humphries, repr. in Garber and Vickers, *Medusa Reader*, 32. Several scholars have noted this particular allusion to Ovid, e.g. Ogden, *Perseus*, 141; Fröhlich, "Perseus Series," 127.

98 In the initial 1875 cartoon and in an early oil on canvas version (Art Gallery of South Australia, Adelaide, 0.329), the two episodes in the rescue of Andromeda were shown as one image.

99 Cosmo Monkhouse, "The New Gallery," *The Academy*, June 2, 1888, 383.

100 *The Times*, May 9, 1888, cited in Wildman and Christian, *Burne-Jones*, 222.

101 Essaka Joshua, *Pygmalion and Galatea: The History of a Narrative in English Literature* (Aldershot and Burlington, Vt: Ashgate, 2001), 87–8. For more on Morris's "Pygmalion and the Image," see Jane Thomas, "Morris and the Muse: Gender and Aestheticism in William Morris's 'Pygmalion and the Image,'" in *Writing on the Image: Reading William Morris*, ed. David Latham (Toronto: University of Toronto Press, 2007), 61–72.

102 Burne-Jones created two versions of the Pygmalion series. The first in 1868–69 was commissioned by Euphrosyne Cassavetti, Zambaco's mother. Given Zambaco's work as a sculptor, this series could be further evidence of a collaborative exchange between the two artists in testing the boundaries of sculptural and painted media; see Wildman and Christian, *Burne-Jones*, 215–21; Simon Oberholzer, "Edward Burne-Jones's Pygmalion," in *Edward Burne-Jones: The Earthly Paradise*, ed. Christopher Conrad and Annabel Zettel (Ostfildern: Hatje Cantz Verlag, 2009).

103 Alison Smith, *The Victorian Nude: Sexuality, Morality, and Art* (Manchester: Manchester University Press, 1996), 200.

104 Østermark-Johansen, *Walter Pater*, 196, 198. For more on Burne-Jones's *Pygmalion* series as an exploration of intertextuality and metamorphosis, rather than psychosexual obsession, see Amelia Yeates, "Poetic Narrative in William Morris's and Edward Burne-Jones's Pygmalion Project," in *Poetry in Pre-Raphaelite Paintings: Transcending Boundaries*, ed. Sophie Andres and Brian Donnelly (New York: Peter Lang, 2018), 107–20.

105 Algernon Swinburne, "Notes on Some Pictures of 1868," cited in Joshua, *Pygmalion and Galatea*, 88.

106 Elizabeth Prettejohn, *Beauty and Art 1750–2000* (Oxford: Oxford University Press, 2005), 140; see also Prettejohn's discussion of Watts's painting in *Art for Art's Sake*, 55–8; see also Prettejohn, "Between Homer and Ovid: Metamorphosis of the 'grand style,'" in *Representations of G. F. Watts: Art Making in Victorian Culture*, ed. Colin Trodd and Stephanie Brown (Aldershot and Burlington, Vt: Ashgate 2004), 49–64.

107 Joshua, *Pygmalion and Galatea*, 91 also observes this transformative quality of Watts's painting.

108 Lene Østermark-Johansen, "Between the Medusan and the Pygmalian: Swinburne and Sculpture," *Victorian Literature and Culture* 38 (2010): 21–37.

109 Østermark-Johansen, "Between the Medusan," 32.

110 The figures glimpsed in Atlas's starry orb derive from the zodiac constellations, suggesting a further element of the Perseus myth that appealed to Burne-Jones. According to the folklorist Joseph Jacobs, writing shortly after the artist's death, "Some Recollections of Sir Edward Burne-Jones," *The Nineteenth Century: A Monthly Review*, January 1899, 127, Burne-Jones was particularly interested in the prominence of the Perseus legend in the constellations, indicative, perhaps, of the primal elements of the myth: "He had also a scholar's sense of the suitable problem to be investigated. Thus he pointed out the large predominance of the Perseus myth in Greek astronomy. Cassiopeia, Cepheus, Perseus, Andromeda fill up a much larger portion of the heavens than could be accounted for by their prominence in Greek myth"; see also Cheney, "Burne-Jones's 'Andromeda,'" 206. Cheney notes Burne-Jones's astrological interest in the Perseus legend, suggesting that Burne-Jones was also referencing an Iranian celestial globe made by Muhammad ibn Hilal al-Munajjim al Mawsili in 1275–76, known as the "Malcolm celestial globe" after Major-General Sir John Malcolm, who gave it to the British Museum from 1871. I have not found evidence to support this suggestion, but it is an interesting one.

111 Other scholars have noted the typological allusion to Adam, Eve, and the serpent in the Garden of Eden, as well as the Virgin of the Annunciation, e.g. Fröhlich, "Perseus Series," 134–5; Munich, *Andromeda's Chains*, 117, 121–3.

112 There is some dispute on the dating of this painting between the Ashmolean and the Fogg. Burne-Jones created two versions, one in 1872 and the other in 1876, both given to William Graham. The orientation of the Fogg painting is horizontal, as opposed to the vertical format of the Ashmolean version, which more closely aligns to the Glasgow *Tower of Brass* (1888). Therefore, I date this Fogg version to 1872 and the pencil study to c. 1872.

113 Burne-Jones made careful studies from color reproductions after Van Eyck's *Adoration of the Mystic Lamb* early in his career, and allusions to the painting can be found throughout his work; e.g. a sketchbook dated to c. 1859 includes careful studies from the crown of the enthroned Virgin (see fig. 143). For more on Burne-Jones's copies after the *Adoration*, see Alison Smith, *Reflections: Van Eyck and the Pre-Raphaelites* (London: National Gallery Company, 2017), 20–22, 80. The similarities between the two fountains is even more pronounced in a preparatory drawing for *Danaë and the Brazen Tower* (1869–70, sold Bonhams Auctioneers UK, 2011). For more on Burne-Jones's admiration for Van Eyck, particularly *The Arnolfini Portrait* (1434; National Gallery), see G. Burne-Jones, *Memorials*, vol. 2, 189, 306; see also Elizabeth Prettejohn, *Modern Painters, Old Masters: The Art of Imitation from the Pre-Raphaelites to the First World War* (New Haven and London: Paul Mellon Centre for Studies in British Art, 2017), 58, 60–63.

114 Shearer West, *Fin De Siècle: Art and Society in an Age of Uncertainty* (Woodstock, N.Y.: Overlook Press, 1994), 81.

115 In his chapter addressing the importance of materiality, the painted surface, and mediation in the work of Burne-Jones, David Peters Corbett, *The World in Paint: Modern Art and Visuality in England, 1848–1914* (University Park: Pennsylvania State University Press, 2004), 71 briefly asserts that the *Perseus* series, particularly *The Baleful Head*, expresses a "central interest in the thematics of sight."

116 Vernant, *Mortals and Immortals*, 135; perhaps not coincidentally, the cover shows a detail of *The Baleful Head*.

117 Albrecht, *Medusa Effect*, 5.

118 Fröhlich, "Perseus Series," 134 notes the self-referential "picture-in-a-picture" of this central mirroring element in *The Baleful Head*, although he argues for this device as a mitigation of the sexual threat represented by Medusa.

119 There is also a chalk study for the head of Andromeda, 1867 (sold at Christie's, London, December 18, 1984). Rossetti began the painting as a commission for C. P. Matthews and wrote an accompanying poem of the same title. His work on *Aspecta Medusa* in 1865–67 coincided with Morris's writing of *The Earthly Paradise* and Burne-Jones's planned illustrations. In a letter dated to 1867, Burne-Jones wrote to George Howard, Castle Howard Archives, J22/27/423, about the painting: "Rossetti is beginning a large picture of Perseus showing the Gorgon's head to Andromeda, in the pool – a glorious composition, in his grand manner: and a great thing for us to look forward to…"

120 See Laurence Roussillon, "Aspecta Medusa: The Many Faces of Medusa in the Painting and Poetry of Dante Rossetti," *The Journal of Pre-Raphaelite Studies* 11 (2002): 5–18, interpreting this moment as an enactment of gender roles: "the warning not to look at Medusa but at her reflection in the water expresses the idea that one should not try to depict reality as it is, but to transform it through 'fundamental brainwork.' In that sense the role of the artist is akin to that of Perseus. Like him he has to use cunning devices to avoid confronting the gaze of his model, and use her seductive power to enchant the viewer and turn her into a work of art. In this process the canvas is the 'wave' of the water, the purifying and idealizing medium of art" (13).

121 Albrecht, *Medusa Effect*, 20.

122 Prettejohn, *Modern Painters*, 81.

123 Vernant, *Mortals and Immortals*, 166. Mack, "Facing Down Medusa," 593–4 echoes this claim.

124 Morris, *Earthly Paradise*, vol. 1, 317.

125 G. Burne-Jones, *Memorials*, vol. 2, 60.

126 Burne-Jones owned a cast of the head of this *Demeter*; Christian, "Burne-Jones and Sculpture," 81; Christian and Marcus, *Burne-Jones*, 94.

127 Burne-Jones to Mary Gladstone, 1883, British Library, Add. 46246, f. 154.

128 Prettejohn, *Art for Art's Sake*, 2.

Four * "Art and the Beauty of the Earth"

1 See Georgiana Burne-Jones, *Memorials of Edward Burne-Jones*, 2 vols (1904; London: Lund Humphries, 1993), vol. 2, 238–49; Robert de la Sizeranne, "In Memoriam: Sir Edward Burne-Jones, Bart., A Tribute from France," *The Magazine of Art* 22 (1898): 520.

2 Burne-Jones quoted in Thomas M. Rooke, "Memoirs of Thomas Matthews Rooke: typescript: or, Notes of conversations among the Pre-Raphaelite Brotherhood," National Art Library, Victoria and Albert Museum, London, 86.RR.52, 22.

3 Burne-Jones to Frances Horner, [c. 1891], Burne-Jones Papers, Fitzwilliam Museum, Cambridge, Box XXVII/8, f. 37.

4 Indeed, Burne-Jones also referred to the design as *The Tree of Forgiveness*; G. Burne-Jones, *Memorials*, vol. 2, 349. Alan Crawford, "Burne-Jones as a Decorative Artist," in *Edward Burne-Jones: Victorian Artist-Dreamer*, ed. Stephen Wildman and John Christian (New York: Metropolitan Museum of Art, 1998), 16 also noted these unique qualities of the mosaic: "The arms of Christ in front of the tree are spread out, as in Byzantine images where Christ does not hang in suffering but triumphs over death. Only here the arms are spread more in blessing than in triumph. The tree flourishes.... To either side, where we would normally see the Virgin Mary and Saint John, are Adam and Eve and their children, an arrangement that moves the focus of the scene from the event itself to the significance of the event. This is a most benign redemption, an image about growth and the possibility of blessing in life."

5 John Ruskin, "Unto This Last" (1860, 1862), in *The Works of John Ruskin*, ed. E. T. Cook and Alexander Wedderburn, 39 vols (London: George Allen, 1906), vol. 17, 105.

6 As Crawford, "Burne-Jones as a Decorative Artist," 16 wrote, "The Tree of Life is an instance where Burne-Jones actually developed Christian imagery..."

7 The majority of the preparatory designs for these mosaics can be found in "The 'Secret' Book of Designs," British Museum, London, 1899-7-13-322–544. However, lacking funding, Nevin seems not to have been able officially to commission the first arch mosaic, the *Annunciation*, until 1890. This was completed in 1892, but not unveiled until 1894. *The Tree of Life* was commissioned in 1891, with final designs completed in 1892; it was begun in mosaic in 1893, and unveiled in 1894.

8 Burne-Jones to Horner, June 1886, Burne-Jones Papers, Box XXVII/8, f. 5.

9 Walter Pater, *The Renaissance: Studies in Art and Poetry*, ed. Donald L. Hill (1893; Berkeley: University of California Press, 1980), 105.

10 E.g. Wildman and Christian, *Burne-Jones*, 250–52.

11 John Ruskin, "*Fors Clavigera*: Letter 5: The White-Thorn Blossom" (1871), in *Works*, vol. 27, 92.

12 According to Burne-Jones, "List of my designs," Fitzwilliam Museum, Cambridge, 27–9 he began painting *The Mill* in 1870, but returned to it in 1881, with two entries documenting work for that year, before completing it in 1882.

13 William Morris, "Art and the Beauty of the Earth" (1881), in *The Collected Works of William Morris*,

34 vols (London: Longmans, Green, and Co., 1914), vol. 22, 169–70, 173, 172, respectively.

14 Burne-Jones to Horner, n.d., Burne-Jones Papers, Box XXVII/8, f. 23.

15 Ruskin, "Unto this Last," 111.

16 John Ruskin, "Traffic" (1864), in *Crown of Wild Olive*, 11th edn. (Orpington: George Allen, 1898), 87.8

17 John Ruskin, "The Storm-Cloud of the Nineteenth Century" (1884), in *Works*, vol. 34, 1–80.

18 Brian J. Day, "The Moral Intuition of Ruskin's 'Storm-Cloud,'" *Studies in English Literature* 45, no. 4 (Autumn 2005): 918.

19 As Jonathan Bate noted in his pioneering ecocritical text on Romanticism and the environment, *Romantic Ecology: Wordsworth and the Environmental Tradition* (London: Routledge, 1991), 59, Ruskin argued for the essential role of trees to the cleansing of the air, the healthy circulation of water, and the prevention of drought; see also Ruskin, "*Fors Clavigera*," 91–2.

20 For studies on Morris's contribution to ecological thought, see Raymond Williams, "Socialism and Ecology," in *Resources of Hope*, ed. Robin Gable (London: Verso, 1989), 210–26; Paddy O'Sullivan, "The Struggle for the Vision Fair: Morris and Ecology," *The Journal of the William Morris Society* 8, no. 4 (Spring 1990): 5–9; Florence S. Boos, "An Aesthetic Ecocommunist: Morris the Red and Morris the Green," in *William Morris: Centenary Essays*, ed. Peter Faulkner and Peter Preston (Exeter: University of Exeter Press, 1999), 21–46; Stephen F. Eisenman, "Class Consciousness in the Design of William Morris," *Journal of the William Morris Society* 15, no. 1 (Winter 2002): 17–37; Nicholas Frankel, "The Ecology of Decoration: Design and Environment in the Writings of William Morris," *The Journal of Pre-Raphaelite Studies* 12 (Fall 2003): 58–85; Bradley J. Macdonald, "William Morris and the Vision of Ecosocialism," *Contemporary Justice Review* 7, no. 3 (2004): 287–304; Elizabeth C. Miller, "Sustainable Socialism: William Morris on Waste," *The Journal of Modern Craft* 4, no. 1 (2011): 7–25; Elizabeth C. Miller, "William Morris, Extraction Capitalism, and the Aesthetics of Surface," *Victorian Studies* 57, no. 3 (Spring 2015): 395–404.

21 Bate, *Romantic Ecology*, 55. For an in-depth comparison of Morris and Marx on ecology, see Macdonald, "William Morris," 288–93.

22 As Macdonald argues, "William Morris," 296, "What we then see is that Morris's socialism was a logical outgrowth of his thinking on the arts. And, importantly, it is the commitment to beauty and naturalist forms that always moved his vision of socialism in an ecological direction"; see also Frankel, "Ecology of Decoration," 70–74.

23 Miller, "Sustainable Socialism," 23.

24 H. C. Marillier, *History of the Merton Abbey Tapestry Works* (London: Constable and Co., 1927), 15.

25 Charles Harvey and Jon Press, *William Morris: Design and Enterprise in Victorian Britain* (Manchester: Manchester University Press, 1991), 131–56.

26 Emma Lazarus, "A Day in Surrey with William Morris," *Century Illustrated Magazine* 32, no. 3 (July 1886): 390–91.

27 Ibid., 391; she continued, 392: "That the workman shall take pleasure in his work, that decent conditions of light and breathing-space and cleanliness shall surround him, that he shall be made to feel himself not the brainless 'hand,' but the intelligent co-operator, the *friend* of the man who directs his labor, that his honest toil shall inevitably win fair and comfortable wages, whatever be the low-water record of the market-price of men, that illness or trouble befalling him during the term of his employment shall not mean dismissal and starvation – these are some of the problems of which Mr. Morris's factory is a noble and successful solution."

28 Marillier, *History*, 13.

29 A. B. Bence-Jones, "The Stanmore Tapestry: Some notes on the Sanc Graal Arras, worked by William Morris, J. H. Dearle and others, for Stanmore Hall," typescript (1893–95), National Art Library, Victoria and Albert Museum, London, 86.W.4, p. 89.

30 F. G. Stephens, "Mr. E. Burne-Jones's Mosaics at Rome," *The Portfolio* 21 (January 1890): 102. Stephens appears to be paraphrasing James Shirley's poem, "Death the Leveller" (1659), "The glories of our blood and state / Are shadows, not substantial things; / There is no armour against Fate; / Death lays his icy hand on kings: / Sceptre and Crown / Must tumble down, / And in the dust be equal made / With the poor crooked scythe and spade"; *The Book of Elizabethan Verse*, ed. William Stanley Braithwaite (London: Chatto & Windus, 1908) 643.

31 Malcolm Bell, *Sir Edward Burne-Jones: A Record and Review*, 4th edn. (London: George Bell & Sons, 1899), 70. For more references to the durability of mosaics, and predictions that Burne-Jones's would outlast all his other works, see "Mosaics by Sir Edward Burne-Jones at Rome," *The Magazine of Art* (January 1895): 256; Aymer Vallance, "The Decorative Art of Sir Edward Burne-Jones, Bart.," *The Art Journal* Easter Art Annual (1900): 14.

32 Burne-Jones to Horner, [1892], Burne-Jones Papers, Box XXVII/8, ff. 41–2.

33 For a summary of the widespread frustration with fresco and the perception of fragility and risk associated with the medium in nineteenth-century Britain, see Clare A. P. Willsdon, *Mural Painting in Britain, 1840–1940: Image and Meaning* (Oxford: Oxford University Press, 2000), 24–5.

34 E.g. in 1862, Matthew Digby Wyatt, "On Pictorial Mosaic as an Architectural Embellishment," *The Builder*, March 22, 1862, 199, wrote, "Mural painting must in our climate ever have to contend with elements, certain to shorten its ephemeral beauty. If attempted in real fresco, damp, fog, and frost speedily fasten upon its very vitals, tending to set the lime against the oxides and other pigments, which in time are eaten away, as even in Italy we frequently see them, into nothingness. Fresco secco is still less permanent. Tempera, or distemper, I need not waste a word upon. Oil or encaustic painting involves the use of vehicles darkening, turning yellow, shrinking irregularly, and ultimately often detaching themselves from the ground to which they are applied. What, then, is left to us, if we would have our decorations live after we have ceased to live?" The answer was the "nearly imperishable" medium of mosaic. For a similar discussion of the risks of fresco in an English climate, as opposed to the durability of mosaic, see A. H. Layard, "Mosaic Decoration," *The Builder*, December 5, 1868, 887–8. For more on Salviati and his contribution to the revival of mosaic in the nineteenth century, see J. B. Bullen, *Byzantium Rediscovered* (London: Phaidon, 2003), 142–5.

35 G. Burne-Jones, *Memorials*, vol. 2, 241–9.

36 Burne-Jones to John Ruskin, June 1862, Burne-Jones Papers, Box IV/2,, f. 3.

37 Burne-Jones to Mary Gladstone, October 1879, British Library, London, Add. 46246, ff. 25–6.

38 Bell, *Burne-Jones*, 83–4 argued that Ravenna, much like Torcello, would have demonstrated to Burne-Jones the ability of the mosaic medium to resist the destructive forces of time: "when, in 1882, the chance came to him to decorate in the same fashion the American Protestant Church which had been built by Mr. Street the English architect in the Via Nazionale at Rome, he recollected and profited well by the lessons he then learned."

39 Burne-Jones to Ruskin, n.d. [c. 1862], formerly collection of Kenneth A. Lohf, New York, bequeathed to the Morgan Library, New York, MA5160, quoted in Richard Dorment, "Burne-Jones and the Decoration of St. Paul's American Church, Rome" (Ph.D. diss., Columbia University, 1976), 100.

40 The idea of this abandoned chapel, the "divine barn" inspired by Giotto's Scrovegni Chapel, lingered in Burne-Jones's mind, even after he began the first mosaic design for St. Paul's in Rome: on 15 March 1883, Burne-Jones Papers, Box XXV/7, f. 24, he wrote to Ruskin, "You and I will yet build us a bower and have our mosaics which none of them shall ever see."

41 It can hardly be a coincidence that Morris's earnest study and theorization of the Byzantine era as the pivotal precursor to the Gothic, in his estimation the only era in which art truly flourished, dates to the formative stages of his friend's mosaic commission. Bullen, *Byzantium Rediscovered*, 165 concurs that Burne-Jones's work probably informed Morris's words on mosaics and the Byzantine era.

42 William Morris, "The History of Pattern-Designing" (1882), in *Collected Works*, vol. 22, 222.

43 In another lecture, "Art and the Beauty of the Earth," 158–9 Morris described this spread of artistic freedom around the world through the Byzantine, and later Gothic: "All people east of the Atlantic felt this art; from Bokhara to Galway, from Iceland to Madras, all the world glittered with its brightness and quivered with its vigour. It cast down the partitions of race and religion also. Christian and Mussulman were made joyful by it; Kelt, Teuton, and Latin raised it up together; Persian, Tartar, and Arab gave and took its gifts from one another."

44 Morris, ibid., 158 also emphasized the liberty of art during the Byzantine era, declaring, "art was free. Whatever a man thought of, that he might bring

to light by the labour of his hands, to be praised and wondered at by his fellows..."

45 Addressing the early growth of the Gothic in Britain, Morris, "History of Pattern-Designing," 230 describes the humble artistic achievements of his cultural ancestors: "they built their homes and temples ...if not so majestically as many peoples have done, yet in such sweet accord with the familiar nature amidst which they dwelt"; for more evidence of the development of Morris's theorization of the Byzantine in tandem with his ecological philosophy, see Morris, "Art and the Beauty of the Earth," 155–74, esp. 157–9.

46 Morris, "History of Pattern-Designing," 207, 222.

47 For more on Burne-Jones's rejection of the mosaics for St. Paul's, London, see G. Burne-Jones, *Memorials*, vol. 2, 217. His name was circulated in association with these long-planned mosaics from as early as 1884, when an anonymous author, "Fine-Art Gossip," *Athenaeum*, July 1884, 89 favourably reviewed his first work for St. Paul's, Rome: "Mr. E. Burne-Jones has nearly completed a number of cartoons of gigantic figures in colour for the mosaic decorations of the dome of the American Protestant Church in the Via Nazionale, Rome. The artist has adapted the style of the quasi-Byzantine mosaics at Ravenna to the architecture of Street's great work, and in delineating a Majesty...has illustrated a grand conception of the subject. Its simplicity will recommend it to those who have undertaken to direct the decoration of the dome of St. Paul's." The mosaic commission was eventually given instead to William Blake Richmond, whose mosaics would spread throughout much of the church, far exceeding the original semi-domes offered to Burne-Jones; for discussion of these, see Bullen, *Byzantium Rediscovered*, 146–51; for examination of the earlier, failed campaigns to execute mosaics there, see also Alison Inglis, "A Victorian High Renaissance Scheme for the Dome of St Paul's Cathedral, London," *Fabrications* 10 (1999): 79–99.

48 Burne-Jones to George Frederick Bodley, 1891, quoted in G. Burne-Jones, *Memorials*, vol. 2, 218.

49 Burne-Jones to Philip Burne-Jones, [after 1891], in ibid., 219–20.

50 Burne-Jones, probably to Horner, n.d., quoted in ibid., 134: "but for the sake of many ancient loves I am doing it; for love of Venice and Ravenna and the seven impenetrable centuries between them, and for love of many old studies and odds and ends of things I like – Talmud and Aquinas, and I don't know what."

51 Bullen, *Byzantium Rediscovered*, 153.

52 Morris, "The Prospects of Architecture in Civilisation," in *Collected Works*, vol. 22, 134 wrote that art should be "a gift of the people to the people, a thing which everybody can understand, and everyone surround with love, it will be a part of every life, and a hindrance to none."

53 For summaries of the transformation of Rome in the late nineteenth century, see Judith Rice Millon, *St. Paul's Within the Walls Rome: A Building History and Guide, 1870–1980* (Dublin, N.H.: William L. Bauhan, 1982), 19–24; Elizabeth Gilmore Holt, *The Expanding World of Art, 1874–1902*, vol. 1 (New Haven and London: Yale University Press, 1988), 269; see also "Modern Work in Rome," *The Builder* 11, no. 1991 (April 2, 1881): 393–4.

54 The Pope had tolerated Protestant services in Rome only inside foreign embassies. The American and British Protestant congregations, comprised largely of tourists and artists visiting the city, were forced to hold joint services in a converted granary just beyond the Porta del Popolo. The site was far from ideal and all but unbearable in the summer heat; see Millon, *St. Paul's*, 20–21.

55 Holt, *Expanding World of Art*, 269 wrote that the Via Nazionale was constructed so as to "cut through the city to connect the railway station and the Baths of Diocletian to the Piazza Venezia, the Via Vittorio Emmanuele, and the Corso"; Millon, *St. Paul's*, 24 termed the Via Nazionale "the first new street of modern Rome."

56 According to several sources, Street's direct inspiration was the twelfth-century Basilica di S. Zeno in Verona; Dorment, "Burne-Jones," 5; Millon, *St. Paul's*, 27.

57 Nevin's efforts to achieve distinction were noted by an anonymous critic for *The Builder*, "Modern Work in Rome," 393 who wrote in 1881: "It is not often that a new church in a prominent position becomes an adornment in a city famous for its architectural beauty, but certainly the eminent English architect who has so skilfully designed the Church of St. Paul in the magnificent new Via Nazionale has sought successfully inspiration for, and most happily availed himself of, the peculiar features of the little Gothic work that is

to be found in the Eternal City"; See also Dorment, "Burne-Jones," 5–8.

58 G. Burne-Jones, *Memorials*, vol. 2, 114.

59 Burne-Jones's relationship with Street dated back to 1855, when Morris became an apprentice in the architect's firm. When Morris later chose to become a designer and decorative artist instead of an architect, he and Burne-Jones carried out a number of ecclesiastical commissions in cooperation with Street. However, this working relationship had also been repeatedly strained over disagreements about the issue of architectural restoration since the founding of the Society for the Protection of Ancient Buildings (SPAB) by Morris in 1877. In brief, Morris refused from that point onward to carry out new decorative commissions for older buildings whose restorations he felt were injurious. Street, however, largely continued with the practice. Burne-Jones also notably designed a stained-glass window and two pendant paintings for Street's church of St. John the Evangelist, Torquay, discussed in Ch. 5 here. For more on the selection of Burne-Jones for the mosaics and his relationship with Street, see Dorment, "Burne-Jones," 13–15.

60 W. A. S. Benson, quoted in W. N. Bruce, "Memoir: Introduction," in W. A. S. Benson, *Drawing, Its Histories and Uses* (London: Oxford University Press, 1925), xxii, vividly recalled meeting Burne-Jones, Morris, and Street on the platform of Paddington Station in 1880 (though Benson may have been mistaken on the year, as Burne-Jones's letters suggest the meeting may have been in November 1879). All three were heading off to Oxford to give speeches against the St. Mark's restorations. Benson noted in particular that Street was carrying "specimens of mosaics" to demonstrate the kinds of work that would be done to St. Mark's. Georgiana Burne-Jones, *Memorials*, vol. 2, 95–6 noted that the preservation of St. Mark's was so important to her husband that he broke his vow not to give public addresses in order to protest against the planned restorations at this meeting. For evidence of Burne-Jones's protests against the restoration of St. Mark's, see his letters to Mary Gladstone, British Library, Add. 46246, ff. 30–36, and to William Gladstone, Add. 44508, ff. 125–8.

61 For full discussion of Rooke's creation of the choir mosaic, see Dorment, "Burne-Jones," 51–6.

62 See W.H.R., "Architectural Mosaic III: Mediaeval Mosaic," *The Building News*, April 4, 1879, 348: "In the old work there is an endless sparkle and diversity of tint, which frequently contrast painfully with modern restorations in the old buildings. The modern artist has aimed at a fineness, smoothness, and regularity which the old workmen seemed not to care for; and with the result that while the modern work glistens painfully like a single sheet of burnished metal, which some have compared to a 'copper cauldron' effect – the old work, having been fixed by the method described, it was impossible to bring each separate piece of glass into an absolutely true place, and consequently they are all seen at thousands of angles, differing some widely and some microscopically, but all reflecting light at different degrees. This it was, combined with a judicious coarseness of execution in work placed at a distance from the eye, which happily gave to the old mosaics that glorious brilliancy and variety which they retain to the present day, and which the modern mosaicist would do well to emulate."

63 The artist had at first hoped that Street could act as a mediator in this process and, accordingly, the two had begun working closely on the preliminary designs for the apse. Unfortunately, Street died unexpectedly in December 1881, and Burne-Jones nearly abandoned the project at this early stage; Burne-Jones to George Howard, February 1882, Castle Howard Archives, quoted in Dorment, "Burne-Jones," 74: "the Roman Church I shall give up – Street is dead who could have stood between me + the cloth + could have helped me also with the workmen – but I cannot + will not be hurried about work – + I shall write this week + throw up the affair – having already wasted many a precious hour upon it – but I see it would be a life of torment + I am not fit for it…"

64 G. Burne-Jones, *Memorials*, vol. 2, 114, 141.

65 Burne-Jones to G. Castellani, c. 1884, Dept. of Paintings, Drawings and Prints, Fitzwilliam Museum, Cambridge. Acc. 1085A, ff. 1–2.

66 Burne-Jones to Rooke, 1884, quoted in G. Burne-Jones, *Memorials*, vol. 2, 142–3.

67 Castellani to E. Burne-Jones, 1884, quoted in ibid., 143–4; Georgiana notes that she preserved the "Italian idiom" of the original letter.

68 Rather than risk the confusion that resulted

from Burne-Jones's first method of translating the design into tesserae (listing each by number according to the portion of the composition), the artist developed a slightly different system for the arch mosaics. According to Dorment, "Burne-Jones," 81, Burne-Jones instead sent "packets of tesserae appropriately labeled with the part of the composition for which they were to be used. On the other hand, with the cartoons the artist sent a compositional study marked with the old numbering system."

69 Burne-Jones had first introduced the water jar as a Marian attribute in an earlier oil version of *The Annunciation* (1876–79; Lady Lever Art Gallery, National Museums Liverpool). However, the two compositions drastically diverge over the locations in which Mary attempts to fulfill her task. The painting depicts her standing beside a well set on the outskirts of a city, while the mosaic shifts to the much harsher setting of the desert.

70 Walter Lowrie, *Fifty Years of S. Paul's American Church, Rome* (Rome: The Rector, 1926), 77 stated that, rather than portraying Mary engaged in a domestic chore, such as sewing or reading, "Burne-Jones preferred an early and more poetical legend, according to which Mary had gone without the gate of the town to draw water from the fountain when she heard the voice of an angel." Dorment, "Burne-Jones," 76 writes that Mary's water pitcher can be traced to "the apocryphal Book of James or Protoevangelism (XI:1): 'And she took the pitcher and went forth to fill it with water, and lo a voice saying: Hail, thou art highly favoured; the Lord is with thee, blessed art thou among women.'"

71 Adolphe Napoléon Didron, *Christian Iconography; or, The History of Christian Art in the Middle Ages*, ed. Margaret Stokes, trans. E. J. Millington, 2 vols. (1843; repr. London: George Bell and Sons, 1886), vol. 1, 343. For Burne-Jones's appreciation of Didron, see Rooke, *Memoirs*, 12. For more on the pelican as an emblem of Christ, see H. J. Smith, *Illustrated Symbols and Emblems of the Jewish, Early Christian, Greek, Latin, and Modern Churches* (Philadelphia: T. S. Leach & Co., 1900), 67.

72 Ruskin, "*Fors Clavigera*: Letter 5," 92–3.

73 Didron, *Christian Iconography*, 367–9. For one of the significant medieval sources of the legend, see Jacobus de Voragine, *The Golden Legend: Readings on the Saints*, trans. William Granger Ryan, 2 vols. (Princeton, N.J: Princeton University Press, 1993), vol. 1, 277–80.

74 Dorment, "Burne-Jones," 118–19 also identifies the apse mosaic of S. Clemente as a possible inspiration for *The Tree of Life*. For more on the iconography of this mosaic in comparison to other medieval representations of the Tree of Life, see Rab Hatfield, "The Tree of Life and the Holy Cross: Franciscan Spirituality in the Trecento and the Quattrocento," in *Christianity and the Renaissance: Image and Religious Imagination in the Quattrocento*, ed. Timothy Verdon and John Henderson (Syracuse, N.Y.: Syracuse University Press, 1990), 136–7.

75 Hatfield, "Tree of Life," 136–7.

76 Crawford, "Burne-Jones as a Decorative Artist," 16.

77 "Mosaics by Sir Edward Burne-Jones," 260, 259, respectively.

78 De Lisle, *Burne-Jones* (New York: Dodge Publishing, 1904), 147.

79 The philosopher Thomas Carlyle, whom Burne-Jones admired, elucidated the possible symbolic resonances between Odin and Christ, as well as Igdrasil and the Tree of Life, in his 1841 text *On Heroes, Hero-Worship and the Heroic in History* (London: Oxford University Press, 1974).

80 Dorment, "Burne-Jones," 86 also notes the significance of this passage to elucidating the connection between *The Tree of Life* and *Christ Enthroned*.

81 Revelation 21:10–12: "[the angel] carried me away to a great, high mountain, and showed me the holy city Jerusalem coming down out of heaven from God, having the glory of God, its radiance like a most rare jewel, like a jasper, clear as crystal. It had a great, high wall, with twelve gates, and at the gates twelve angels..."

82 Lowrie, *Fifty Years*, 88; Angela Thirkell, *Three Houses* (London: Oxford University Press, 1931; Wakefield, R.I.: Moyer Bell, 1998), 117; see also G. Burne-Jones, *Memorials*, vol. 2, 114. The scale model of the apse, made by Burne-Jones after measurements provided by Street, reveals that the artist initially included Raphael instead of Uriel, and also had the angels appear in a different order (from left to right, Chemuel, Gabriel, Michael, Raphael, and Zophiel). He also labeled each angel in gold and included the name "Azael," suggest-

ing he may have considered Azrael, the angel of death, rather than Lucifer, for the empty portal.

83 According to Angela Thirkell, *Three Houses*, 117 the original cartoon for Lucifer's empty gate contained "flickering flames," in order to signal his descent into hell. However, for unknown reasons, the flames were excluded from the final composition; see G. Burne-Jones, *Memorials*, vol. 2, 114.

84 Stephens, "Mr. E. Burne-Jones's Mosaics," 107. Previously, in 1884, an anonymous author for *The Athenaeum*, "Fine-Art Gossip," 89 similarly wrote: "In the centre of one side of the cupola Christ appears in majesty, holding on His knee that Crystal Sphere 'which is an image of the mighty world' to be"; again, a writer for *The Times*, "A Mosaic by Mr. Burne-Jones," April 14, 1886 observed, "The Lord is represented in the freshness and eternal youth of the glorified body...and in the hollow of his left he bears the world, a wonderful ball like those in the famous picture of 'The Days of Creation.'...His feet rest on a rainbow, and below from the foundation of the throne there flow the four rivers of the Gospel, which spread abroad and cover all the world"; see also "Mosaics by Sir Edward Burne-Jones," 257. In a more recent description of this orb, Bullen, *Byzantium Rediscovered*, 154 wrote, "[Christ's] orb has become a crystal ball in which we can see the earth, the water and the sky entwined together."

85 "Fine-Art Gossip," 89.

86 Revelation 21:18–20: "The wall was built of jasper, while the city was pure gold, clear as glass. The foundations of the wall of the city were adorned with every jewel; the first was jasper, the second sapphire, the third agate, the fourth emerald, the fifth onyx, the sixth carnelian, the seventh chrysolite, the eighth beryl, the ninth topaz, the tenth chrysoprase, the eleventh jacinth, the twelfth amethyst"; such jewel imagery recurs frequently in Revelation, and this sea of precious stones in Burne-Jones's mosaic could refer to multiple descriptions of the Heavenly Jerusalem, as in Revelation 4:1–6: "lo, a throne stood in heaven, with one seated on the throne! And he who sat there appeared like jasper and carnelian, and round the throne was a rainbow that looked like an emerald...and before the throne there is as it were a sea of glass, like crystal..." Dorment, "Burne-Jones," 74 also cites this passage as a general referent for *Christ Enthroned*. Finally, in the working letter to Castellani, c. 1884, Acc. 1085A, f. 11, Burne-Jones describes this passage as "foundations of jewelled work..."

87 See G. Burne-Jones, *Memorials*, vol. 2, 257; Rooke, "Memoirs," 65.

88 "Now war arose in heaven, Michael and his angels fighting against the dragon; and the dragon and his angels fought, but they were defeated and there was no longer any place for them in heaven. And the great dragon was thrown down, that ancient serpent, who is called the Devil and Satan, the deceiver of the whole world – he was thrown down to earth, and his angels were thrown down with him. And I heard a loud voice in heaven, saying, 'Now the salvation and the power and the kingdom of our God and the authority of his Christ have come'"; this passage was inscribed in Latin on the frame of *The Fall of Lucifer*, though, as Dorment notes, "Burne-Jones," 44–6 Burne-Jones inverts the passage: in this new configuration, the declaration from heaven that the Salvation of Christ has come precedes the battle.

89 In an undated letter to Frances Horner, Burne-Jones Papers, Box XXVII/8, ff. 43–4, Burne-Jones wrote: "The gods are jealous and they hate artists especially who mimic their work and better it. All that is an old story and I could tell you a thousand things about it. That's why they hated Prometheus, and killed Icharus, and ham-strung Volund – nay isn't there a remote wild tale about the cause of the fray in Heaven, and why Lucifer fell who was a mighty artist. Did you know that the blackness of night is made by his hosts still falling? Poor artists, say I." Similarly, Georgiana Burne-Jones, *Memorials*, vol. 2, 348 recorded her husband as stating, "I feel very sorry for the devil; that is why I painted him beautiful, as a fallen angel. He tried to make himself equal with God, and so he fell. I would not have him pushed out of Paradise. No, he found heaven was gone, and there was only blackness"; she also noted that Burne-Jones intended the title of *The Fall of Lucifer* to be changed to *Paradise Lost*. This would represent the third title that was attached to this composition, for Burne-Jones also called it in its earlier state *The Fall of the Rebel Angels*.

90 Jeffrey F. Hamburger, "Speculations on Speculation: Vision and Perception in the Theory and Practice of Mystical Devotion," in *Deutsche Mystik im*

Abendländischen Zusammenhang: Neu Erschlossene Texte, Neue Methodische Ansätze, Neue Theoretische Konzepte, ed. Walter Haug and Wolfram Schneider-Lastin (Tübingen: Max Niemeyer Verlag, 2000), 374.

Five ∗ "Making God manifest"

1 Burne-Jones, "List of my designs," Fitzwilliam Museum, Cambridge, 43.

2 Catherine Glynne and William Gladstone were married in St. Deiniol's in 1839 and resided in nearby Hawarden Castle. Mary Gladstone married the Reverend Harry Drew, the curate of St. Deiniol's, in 1886, and was subsequently known by her married name, Mary Gladstone Drew; however, for the sake of clarity, I refer to her as Mary Gladstone.

3 Burne-Jones to Mary Gladstone, June 5, 1898, Gladstone Papers, British Library, London, Add. 46246, ff. 240–41.

4 In his examination of Mantegna's depictions of the Adoration of the Magi, Dawson W. Carr, *Andrea Mantegna: The Adoration of the Magi* (Los Angeles: Getty Museum Studies on Art, 1997), 64–5, described light penetrating darkness as a key visual, as well as theological, metaphor for the Incarnation. In early Renaissance depictions of the Annunciation and the Nativity, the Incarnation was often symbolized by the depiction of light passing through glass that remains intact. Mary was likened to a pure glass vessel, her virginity remaining intact in much the way that light is able to pass through glass; see Shirley Neilsen Blum, "Hans Memling's 'Annunciation' with Angelic Attendants," *Metropolitan Museum Journal* 27 (1992): 46.

5 For more on the perception of stained glass as a metaphor for the Incarnation in the medieval era, see Madeline H. Caviness, *Stained Glass Windows* (Turnhout: Brepols, 1996), 58.

6 Throughout this chapter, I will be using "apocalyptic" as it was widely understood in the nineteenth century, suggesting revelation and prophecy, more so than destruction.

7 During this time, Burne-Jones also created an unexecuted design of the Nativity as an arch mosaic for St. Paul's Within the Walls, Rome (c. 1885–88; see Ch. 4 above). If this design is included, the total is five major projects in five different media.

8 Georgiana Burne-Jones, *Memorials of Edward Burne-Jones* (London: Lund Humphries, 1993), vol. 2, 256–7.

9 Similarly, Fiona MacCarthy, "'As Good Work as I Do': Burne-Jones and Stained Glass," *The Journal of Stained Glass* 35 (2011): 11 observes, "Burne-Jones may ... have lost his religious faith in formal terms but he had retained his deep emotional attachment to what he called 'Christmas Carol Christianity,' the power of the ancient Christian imagery, the mysteries inherent to those well-known Christian narratives. In a sense the loss of faith had freed him to interpret the old stories from the Bible in new ways."

10 Burne-Jones quoted in G. Burne-Jones, *Memorials*, vol. 2, 257. He made a similar statement to Rooke: "The Christian idea of a God who wanted to see what it was like to be one of the men he had made is about the biggest notion mankind ever got hold of"; Thomas M. Rooke, "Memoirs of Thomas Matthews Rooke: typescript: or, Notes of conversations among the Pre-Raphaelite Brotherhood," National Art Library, Victoria and Albert Museum, London, 86.RR.52, 201.

11 Reflecting back on his early influences, Burne-Jones wrote to Frances Horner, n.d., Burne-Jones Papers, Fitzwilliam Museum, Cambridge, Box XXVII/8, f. 23 that in his formative years, Newman "taught me so much I do mind – things that will never be out of me.... in an age of materialism, he taught me to venture all on the unseen."

12 Mary Arseneau, "Incarnation and Interpretation: Christina Rossetti, the Oxford Movement, and 'Goblin Market,'" *Victorian Poetry* 31, no. 1 (Spring 1993): 80, 81.

13 Rooke, "Memoirs," 61.

14 Carr, *Mantegna*, 84, 55–7, 63–4, 77–81, respectively; see also Paul H. D. Kaplan, *The Rise of the Black Magus in Western Art* (Ann Arbor, Mich.: UMI Research Press, 1985).

15 John Ruskin, "Modern Painters II" (1846), in *The Works of John Ruskin*, ed. E. T. Cook and Alexander Wedderburn, 39 vols (London: George Allen, 1906), vol. 3, 624.

16 John Ruskin, "Modern Painters III" (1856), in ibid., vol. 5, 333.

17 "Art.III.-1. Sir Edward Burne-Jones," *The Quarterly Review* (October 1898): 359.

18 Burne-Jones quoted in G. Burne-Jones, *Memorials*, vol. 2, 176–7.

19 Bodley had originally been asked to create a reredos for the church. As Georgiana Burne-Jones recalled, ibid., vol. 1, 224, "The commission came through our friend Mr. G. F. Bodley, who unselfishly suggested that the church should have a painted altarpiece instead of a reredos, which he himself had been asked to design, and that Edward should be the artist employed." For an overview of the commission, see Ronald Parkinson, "Two Early Altar-Pieces by Burne-Jones," *Apollo* 102, no. 165 (November 1, 1975): 320–23; for discussions of the commission and altarpiece, see also Allen Staley, *The New Painting of the 1860s: Between the Pre-Raphaelites and the Aesthetic Movement* (New Haven and London: Paul Mellon Centre for Studies in British Art and Yale University Press, 2011), 348–51; Michael Hall, *George Frederick Bodley and the Later Gothic Revival in Britain and America* (New Haven and London: Paul Mellon Centre for Studies in British Art and Yale University Press, 2014), 48–9.

20 Alison Smith, "Apprentice to Master: 1856–70," in *Edward Burne-Jones*, ed. Alison Smith (London: Tate Enterprises, 2018), 55 explains that "painted altarpieces were rare in the Church of England, due to a long-standing emphasis on the word above material culture and altarpieces in particular being associated with Roman Catholic idolatry." Elizabeth Prettejohn, *Modern Painters, Old Masters: The Art of Imitation from the Pre-Raphaelites to the First World War* (New Haven and London: Paul Mellon Centre for Studies in British Art, 2017), 127 also notes that Burne-Jones took the opportunity to experiment with how an altarpiece might function in modernity, writing of the Brighton triptychs, "Far from being 'establishment' projects, these are experimental works by artists who are seeing what a modern altarpiece – should there be such a thing – might look like."

21 Bodley was not the architect of the church, but an active parishioner and an early supporter of Burne-Jones's career; see Hall, *Bodley*, 48–9.

22 G. Burne-Jones, *Memorials*, vol. 1, 224.

23 The first altarpiece was given to the estate of Pre-Raphaelite collector Thomas Plint. Later, in 1867, Bodley found the altarpiece for sale as "an old Italian picture," and purchased it for himself; ibid. The two altarpieces were shown together at the Arts Council exhibition in 1975; John Christian and Penelope Marcus, eds., *Burne-Jones: The Paintings, Graphic and Decorative Work of Sir Edward Burne-Jones, 1833–98* (London: Arts Council of Great Britain, 1975), 36–7. The second altarpiece was sold by St. John's Church in 1975 and is now in the collection of Baron Lloyd-Webber.

24 Georgiana Burne-Jones, *Memorials*, vol. 1, 224 suggests that the second version of the triptych is executed on a gold ground, but does not clarify if this was true for the first version.

25 The choice to depict Morris as the first king kneeling before the infant Christ was perhaps in homage to the recent birth of Morris's first child, Jane (later known as Jenny), in January of that year. Differing accounts suggest that both Jane Morris and Georgiana Burne-Jones modeled for the Virgin, although the figure does not clearly resemble either woman; see e.g. Linda Parry, ed., *William Morris* (London: Philip Wilson Publishers with the Victoria and Albert Museum, 1996), 118–19.

26 G. Burne-Jones, *Memorials*, vol. 1, 262 describes Ciamelli as a frequent model for her husband: "He ground an organ on the streets and sang to it very finely out of his southern heart when he was not sitting, and sometimes brought it with him when he came to sit."

27 For the seminal text on this subject, see Kaplan, *Rise of the Black Magus*; for another helpful overview of the black African magus, see Carr, *Mantegna*, 51–81.

28 Kaplan, *Rise of the Black Magus*, 21. Kaplan argues that there is textual evidence dating to the early medieval period that the magi were also interpreted as symbolic of the Gentiles of the world, lending validity to global Christian missionary crusades. Moreover, one of the magi became linked to Ethiopia as early as the sixth century.

29 Ibid., 85–6. Kaplan notes that although the names were well established by the twelfth century, they were not always consistent in their relative ages. There are several variant spellings of Balthazar, including Balthasar and Balthassar, as well as for Caspar, including Jasper and Gaspar. Burne-Jones does not assign names to his magi in any surviving texts or sketches of which I am aware. Given the confusion and discrepancies, I have chosen not to use these names unless directly quoting sources that do so.

30 Carr, *Mantegna*, 63.

31 Ibid., 57–8.

32 Ibid., 77. Burne-Jones particularly noted this painting in the Uffizi during his third visit to Italy in 1873, making a detailed study of the standing Virgin and Child in the right-hand panel; Sketchbook 1070 (5), f. 4, Fitzwilliam Museum, Cambridge. It is likely that he also encountered Albrecht Dürer's *Adoration of the Magi* (1504), which depicts the black African magus, while in the Uffizi. As Prettejohn, *Modern Painters*, 125–7 argues, Burne-Jones also appears to be referencing paintings by Giotto, Carpaccio, and Giorgione; she writes of the altarpieces that "specific points of reference have scarcely been interrogated, still less the intricate and ingenious ways in which they are combined."

33 Anna Jameson, *Legends of the Madonna*, ed. Estelle M. Hurll (1850; Boston: Houghton, Mifflin and Company, 1900), 254.

34 For more on Barker's painting, see Jan Marsh, "Icon of the Age: 'Africa,' Victoria and The Secret of England's Greatness," in *Black Victorians: Black People in British Art, 1800–1900*, ed. Jan Marsh (Aldershot: Manchester Art Gallery and Birmingham Museums and Art Gallery with Lund Humphries, 2005), 57–67.

35 The other side of the token features the widely circulated image of a kneeling figure in chains, encircled by the words "Am I Not a Man and a Brother?" This imagery was produced as a medallion by Thomas Wedgwood, although without the clasped hands on the reverse. For more on this token, see Timothy Barringer, Gillian Forrester, and Barbaro Martinez-Ruiz, *Art and Emancipation in Jamaica: Isaac Mendes Belisario and His Worlds* (New Haven, Conn.: Yale Center for British Art, 2007), 296–7; on the Wedgwood medallion and other abolitionist emblems, see Marcus Wood and James Raven, "'The Abolition Blunderbuss': Free Publishing and British Abolition Propaganda, 1780–1838," in *Free Print and Non-Commercial Publishing Since 1700*, ed. James Raven (London: Routledge, 2000), 67–92.

36 According to Burne-Jones's working list, he began the first version of the altarpiece in 1860, finished it in 1861, and then created the second version in that year. The American Civil War officially began in April 1861, but southern states had already started seceding from the union by January; see "List of my designs," 4–5.

37 Unfortunately, while there are numerous contemporary reviews that mention the black African magus in Burne-Jones's later *Adoration of the Magi* tapestry and *The Star of Bethlehem* watercolor, I have not been able to find more than passing reference to these two early altarpieces in nineteenth-century texts. Given that the first version was sold to Bodley just a few years later as "an Italian picture," they do not seem to have been widely known as part of Burne-Jones's oeuvre.

38 During the intervening years, Burne-Jones created several designs of the Adoration of the Magi for stained glass. They were mostly small scenes intended for predella windows below single figures, and adapted iconography that is more fully elaborated in his larger works discussed in this chapter. However, the figure of the black African magus continued in these designs. According to A. C. Sewter, *The Stained Glass of William Morris and His Circle*, 2 vols (New Haven, Conn.: Yale University Press, 1974), vol. 2, 302–3, between 1864 and 1885 Burne-Jones created five designs for stained glass depicting the *Adoration of the Magi* and a sixth titled *Magi Led by Angel with Star*. Three of these feature a black African magus, including those for Castle Howard and Jesus College, Cambridge, and three do not. However, the three that do were reused for other Morris & Co. windows a total of eighteen times during Burne-Jones's lifetime, while the windows that do not were only reused four times (not including posthumous reuse by Morris & Co). In other words, Burne-Jones's stained-glass windows featuring a black African magus were more than four times as prevalent during his lifetime. This statistic does not include the Hawarden Nativity window, which also features a black African magus. It is safe to assume that the patrons commissioning the windows may have determined some of the figures. When designing in other media, including painting and tapestry, Burne-Jones always included the black magus.

39 Malcolm Bell, *Sir Edward Burne-Jones: A Record and Review*, 4th edn. (London: George Bell & Sons, 1899), 94.

40 William Morris, *The Collected Letters of William Morris*, ed. Norman Kelvin (Princeton, N.J.: Princeton University Press, 1984), 2b:572.

41 Burne-Jones quoted in Julia Mary Cartwright Ady, *A Bright Remembrance: The Diaries of Julia Cartwright*

1851–1924, ed. Angela Emanuel (London: Weidenfeld and Nicolson, 1989), 165.

42 Morris, *Collected Letters*, 2b:572.

43 See Geoffrey Tyack, "Gilbert Scott and the Chapel of Exeter College, Oxford," *Architectural History* 50 (2007): 125–48.

44 Morris, *Collected Letters*, 2b:574.

45 Stephen Wildman and John Christian, eds., *Edward Burne-Jones: Victorian Artist-Dreamer* (New York: Metropolitan Museum of Art, 1998), 293 suggest that Burne-Jones may already have begun designing the subject based on a sketch in sketchbook E.9-1955, Victoria and Albert Museum, London, but it also includes designs for the stained-glass windows at St Philip's, Birmingham, which date to 1887.

46 Burne-Jones quoted in G. Burne-Jones, *Memorials*, vol. 2, 176.

47 Linda Parry, *William Morris Textiles* (London: V&A Publications, 2013), 124–63.

48 William Morris, "Textiles," in *Arts and Crafts Essays by Members of the Arts and Crafts Exhibition Society* (London: Longmans, Green, and Co., 1899), 23.

49 Burne-Jones quoted in Rooke, "Memoirs," 232.

50 In 1906–7, Walter Taylor, a weaver for Morris & Co., produced a careful study of the African king's head by tracing Burne-Jones's cartoon; see Marsh, *Black Victorians*, cat. 95, p. 174.

51 A. B. Bence-Jones, "The Stanmore Tapestry: Some notes on the Sanc Graal Arras, worked by William Morris, J. H. Dearle and others, for Stanmore Hall," typescript, National Art Library, Victoria and Albert Museum, London, 1893–95 (86.W.4), 79.

52 Linda Parry, "The Tapestries of Edward Burne-Jones," *Apollo* 165 (November 1975): 326.

53 Review in *The Queen*, April 26, 1890, quoted in Parry, *William Morris Textiles*, 145. The language is strikingly similar to that used to describe the *Briar Rose* series, which was on view concurrently [in April 1890] at Toynbee Hall.

54 The tapestry remains *in situ* in Exeter College Chapel. In 2018, it received conservation treatment and a new glazing that has helped to restore its original appearance.

55 The commission by the Manchester School of Art for their new museum in 1894 is perhaps one of the most interesting and significant of the later weavings of *The Adoration of the Magi*. As Imogen Hart, *Arts and Crafts Objects* (Manchester: Manchester University Press, 2010), 193 explains, the tapestry formed the central focus in the Textile Court, the first room encountered when entering the museum. There the ecclesiastical and aesthetic aspects of the tapestry were intertwined: "Looking at the plan of the Textile Court, we can see that the tapestry took the position of an altarpiece within a space strikingly suggestive of a nave and transept. The display format thus appears to present the tapestry for contemplation as the epitome of design achievement."

56 According to Parry, *William Morris Textiles*, 145, "Ten versions of this tapestry were made between 1890 and 1907. As well as that for Exeter College, others were made for: Wilfred Scawen Blunt for Newbuildings Place, Shipley, West Sussex (woven 1890–94); Manchester Corporation (1894); Eton College (1895); the Museum für Kunst und Gewerbe, Hamburg (1900); Sir George Brookman (1901), now in the Art Gallery of South Australia, Adelaide; S. I. Shchukin (1902), now in the Hermitage Museum, St. Petersburg; Guillaume Mallet for his Edwin Lutyens-designed home Le Bois des Moutiers, near Dieppe, France (woven in 1904), later sold to Yves St Laurent, the fashion designer, and now in the Musée d'Orsay, Paris; the Colman family (1906), now in Norwich Castle Museum and Art Gallery; and finally, in 1907, for St Andrew's Church, Roker, near Newcastle."

57 Burne-Jones later recalled, "So all alone I was in my mind, and untaught away there in Birmingham, with nothing for it to fasten on but details of the dowdiest existence"; Rooke, "Memoirs," 468–9.

58 Victoria Osborne, "'A New Order of Things': The Pre-Raphaelite Legacy and Art in Birmingham," in *Victorian Radicals: From the Pre-Raphaelites to the Arts & Crafts Movement*, ed. Martin Ellis, Victoria Osborne, and Tim Barringer (New York: American Federation of Arts, 2018), 73.

59 Here is the passage in full: "The difficulty would be the lecture; a thing as you know so utterly out of my way, which I could not possibly make light of, & should have for many reasons to prepare with utmost carefulness. What have I to say that Ruskin & you have not said already? And although you might answer justly that constant reiterations of even a few truths is a nec-

essary & helpful part of our work, still it would take me much time to put anything that occurred to me in a new form, & all my habits of labour for many years now have been carrying me further & further from the possibility of easily expressing myself in words. I have lots to say of course & could say it informally about art & its relation to life, but I do really think that the labour of shaping it into a presentable form would be out of all proportion to usefulness, & that many an hour would be better spent over my ordinary work, – I don't mean to say to my own advantage but looking at the people I should like to serve of all others, namely the people I was born amongst, I think I could better serve them by carrying on my accustomed work. If such an offer came from any other town I should not hesitate a moment to think it over, but in this case I have thought about it & what I could say, & how like an impertinent sermon a great deal of what might have to be said would be – the first time I appeared among them too – & I believe not said well enough to give me the right to say it, & if you could make this a little clear to them I should be very glad, & if you could say too that I am not unmindful of their claims upon me & am grateful for their interest in me, – please make this clear"; E. Burne-Jones to Morris, February 1880, Burne-Jones Papers, Box XXV/7, f. 1.

60 In a subsequent letter to Chamberlain declining the request, Burne-Jones asserted his support, agreeing to lend works to an exhibition and to make suggestions on the new art gallery in an exchange of letters or discussion in person: "I would sooner exhibit at Birmingham than anywhere & with all my heart I am hoping that one day I may be of more practical use to my native place than I have been"; Burne-Jones to J. H. Chamberlain, March 14, 1881, ibid., f. 5. In 1885, in honor of the opening of the Birmingham Museum & Art Gallery, Burne-Jones was asked again to serve as president and finally acquiesced, on condition of not giving a public lecture. Instead, he devoted his time to visiting the students of the School of Art, who showed him their work. Burne-Jones was invigorated by the visit and given new hope for Birmingham: "Something in my time with you in Birmingham has set fresh hope in my heart.... The visit made me younger and is like a fresh impulse to me.... And Birmingham shall be a famous City, of white stone, full of brave architecture, carved and painted"; quoted in G. Burne-Jones, *Memorials*, vol. 2, 156. For more on Burne-Jones and the Birmingham Museum & Art Gallery, see Osborne, "New Order," 80–81; see also Amy Woodson-Boulton, *Transformative Beauty: Art Museums in Industrial Britain* (Stanford, Cal.: Stanford University Press, 2012), 21–32, 121–6.

61 Recalling the display of *The Star of Bethlehem* at the New Gallery, Bell, *Burne-Jones*, 13–14 wrote, "All Londoners who then, for a brief period, saw with admiration the breadth and certainty of treatment in a material so difficult on so large a scale, the rich and varied glow of colour, the beauty of the design, and the delicacy of the feeling, may be pardoned for envying their Midland brethren the enduring companionship of such a treasure, which should prove a constant stimulus to students born in happier times, since, apart from the technical lessons to be gained from it, there may be seen how little unfavourable surroundings at the beginning have prevailed against the innate faculties tardily developed, but matured by invincible determination and patience." The reviews of the New Gallery exhibition overwhelmingly described the work as one of the most notable paintings on view that year. There was a mixed response, but many, both favorable and unfavorable, focused on the cool color palette and unusual iconography. Nearly every reviewer, even those who criticized the watercolor, commented on the angel with the star as an innovative and notable aspect of the composition; see M. H. Spielmann, "Current Art," *The Magazine of Art* (January 1891): 253–63; "The Picture Galleries," *The Saturday Review*, May 2, 1891, 532–3; "The New Gallery," *The Graphic*, May 9, 1891, 528; "The Antiquary Among the Pictures," *The Antiquary* 23 (June 1891): 241–7; Julia Cartwright, "The Pictures of the Year," *The National Review* 17, no. 100 (June 1891): 466–76; Claude Phillips, "The Summer Exhibitions at Home and Abroad," *Art Journal* (June 1891): 183–90.

62 "The Antiquary Among the Pictures," 245.

63 Burne-Jones did not attend the opening, but Morris delivered the opening address. See Osborne, "A New Order of Things," 78–80.

64 Similarly, see Woodson-Boulton, *Transformative Beauty*, 125, "On its own terms, however, the painting challenges the boundaries between painting and weaving, artist and artisan, and beauty and truth."

65 Osborne, "New Order," 78.

66 Phillips, "Summer Exhibitions," 184 made this comparison to fresco, although he did not find the attempt quite successful, writing that the picture was "on a vaster scale than anything the master has yet attempted, and painted in a curious water-colour, or rather body-colour medium, which aims at reproducing the fresh bright tints, though it cannot give the swiftness and decision of true fresco." Executing the painting required Burne-Jones to use a portable staircase, which was featured in a widely circulated photograph of *The Star of Bethlehem* in progress in 1890. He likened the physically demanding process to the voyage of the magi: "I have journeyed as many miles already as ever the kings travelled"; quoted in G. Burne-Jones, *Memorials*, vol. 2, 209.

67 William Morris, "The Beauty of Life, Delivered before the Birmingham Society of Arts and School of Design, February 19, 1880," in *The Collected Works of William Morris*, 34 vols (London: Longmans, Green, and Co., 1912–14), vol. 22, 61, 73.

68 William Morris, "The Art of the People" (1879), in ibid., 48.

69 Burne-Jones quoted in Rooke, "Memoirs," 93, 96.

70 Jameson, *Legends of the Madonna*, 254.

71 Cartwright, "Pictures of the Year," 471; "The Antiquary Among the Pictures," 245.

72 Morris, "Beauty of Life," 70; it is in this lecture that Morris uttered his now famous dictum, "Have nothing in your houses that you do not know to be useful, or believe to be beautiful" (76).

73 Ibid., 70, 73–4.

74 The wattle entwined with roses is a self-referential quotation of the *Trellis* wallpaper pattern, c. 1862–64, one of the earliest designs for wallpaper created by Morris shortly after moving into Red House. This wallpaper even includes several songbirds, much like the birds in the lower left of both *The Adoration of the Magi* and *The Star of Bethlehem*.

75 Cartwright, "Pictures of the Year," 471; Spielmann, "Current Art," 259; Phillips, "Summer Exhibitions," 185. "The Antiquary Among the Pictures," 245, also took particular notice of the angel: "The poetry of this remarkable composition comes out strongest in the angel. Modelled after the Byzantine style, this angel in conventional attitude is just alighting with sandalled feet, and holds between upraised palms the tenderly glowing and devoutly-sheltered star that had led the Magi from their distant Eastern home."

76 The church is now St. John the Apostle. The two paintings were sold by the church in 1989 to help pay for repairs. After entering the collection of Baron Lloyd-Webber, they were acquired by the Carnegie Museum, Pittsburgh in 1996. The church later acquired two high-quality replicas, so parishioners and visitors experience an approximation of the original impact.

77 The church was completed by G. E. Street's son, Arthur Edmund Street. It is unclear if G. E. or Arthur suggested Burne-Jones for the commission. According to Charles Eastlake, *A History of the Gothic Revival* (London: Longmans, Green; New York: Scribner, Welford, 1872), 325, it was common practice for G. E. Street to design churches to be completed as money became available, allowing for a more ambitious scheme to be built over time. This was the case for St. John's, Torquay, which was completed in stages, beginning with the chancel in 1864. The rest of the church followed in 1871, and the tower was completed in 1885. The decorative scheme also seems to have developed as funds were available. The drawing in ibid., facing 325 shows a rectangular space flanking the altar which appears to suggest paintings. However, given that mosaic was used in other parts of the church, it is possible these spaces could have been for large mosaic panels. See Basil Reginald Airy, *A Brief History of St. John's Torquay* (Torquay: Andrew Iredale, 1902).

78 E. Burne-Jones to F. S. Ellis, January 16, 1889, Burne-Jones Papers, Box XXVI/7, f. 125.

79 Georgiana Burne-Jones excerpted this statement for the first chapter of the second volume of *Memorials* (13), supporting her discussion of his rejection of exhibitions and the "easel picture."

80 Caroline Arscott, *William Morris and Edward Burne-Jones: Interlacings* (New Haven and London: Paul Mellon Centre for Studies in British Art, 2008), 207 also establishes this desire for public work and immersive spaces to Burne-Jones's stained glass, as well as his mosaics: "the advantage of placing his work in a church was that a church potentially offered a public space incorporating beauty of form, sweet sounds, a sense of spirituality and the opportunity for contemplation."

81 "Character Sketch," *The Review of Reviews* 18 (December 1898): 25.

82 Sewter's two-volume catalogue, *Stained Glass of William Morris and His Circle*, remains the most comprehensive overview of the large number and diverse locations of the windows designed by Burne-Jones and his fellow artists at Morris & Co. However, this may not be exhaustive and the project of tracing and documenting all of the firm's windows would be worth revisiting. For more on Burne-Jones's particular contribution to stained glass, see "Burne-Jones," ed. Sandra Coley, special issue, *The Journal of Stained Glass* 35 (2011).

83 The display height of 12 ft off the ground is described in Airy, *Brief History*, 13.

84 Ibid., 11; see also Sewter, *Stained Glass*, vol. 2, 188.

85 Airy, *Brief History*, 11.

86 Bell, *Burne-Jones*, 74 notes this similarity: "the Magus on the left with his jeweled robes and golden casket bears a striking resemblance to the venerable figure in the great Birmingham water-colour."

87 Ruskin emphasized this translation of Luke 2:15 in "Fors Clavigera: Letter 12: The Prince's Lesson" (1871), in *Works*, vol. 28, 209, as "Let us go and see," as part of his Christmas letter that focuses on the Nativity.

88 Burne-Jones to Ellis, January 16, 1889, Burne-Jones Papers, Box XXVI/7, f. 125. In addition, Burne-Jones also twice described the paintings in his working list for the year 1888, "List of my designs," 35–6: firstly, "I designed and began two pictures for a church of a King & a shepherd led by an angel in one picture – and the Nativity in the other"; secondly, he describes them as "pictures of The Nativity & the angels with the rich & poor men for a church at Torquay, and they were sent there in the middle of December."

89 Despite the schematic quality of this forest backdrop, Cartwright once again identified it as a recognizably "English woodland," setting the Nativity on familiar soil; Julia Mary Cartwright Ady, "The Life and Work of Sir Edward Burne-Jones," *The Art Journal* (Christmas 1894): 25–6.

90 This is the translation in the King James Bible, where it is Psalm 12:5. See also Airy, *Brief History*, 16; Louise Lippincott, "Victorian Masterworks Come to Pittsburgh from Andrew Lloyd Webber," *Carnegie Magazine*, October 1997, https://carnegiemuseums.org/magazine-archive/1997/sepoct/feat1.html, accessed July 7, 2015.

91 E.g. John Ruskin, *Giotto and his Works in Padua* (1853), in *Works*, vol. 24, 74; Jameson, *Legends of the Madonna*, 244.

92 Lippincott, "Victorian Masterworks," also observes the funereal qualities of *The Nativity* and the likely connection to Giotto's Scrovegni Chapel.

93 For an overview of this Howard commission, as well as Burne-Jones's other major sculptural collaborations with Boehm, see Mark Stocker, "Edward Burne-Jones, Edgar Boehm, and The Battle of Flodden Field," *Apollo* 158, no. 498 (August 2003): 10–11.

94 Botticelli's *Mystic Nativity* was acquired by W. Fuller Maitland in 1837 and exhibited on several occasions in Britain, including the Manchester Art Treasures exhibition of 1857 and the Royal Academy in 1871. It was thus widely known even before it entered the National Gallery in 1878; see John Pope-Hennessy, *Botticelli: The Nativity* (London: Percy Lund Humphries, 1946). Prettejohn, *Modern Painters*, 130 notes the particular importance of this painting for Dante Gabriel Rossetti and explores the connection to *The Blessed Damozel* (1875–78).

95 Jameson, *Legends of the Madonna*, 243.

96 Sidney Colvin, "A 'Nativity,' by Sandro Botticelli," *The Portfolio* (January 1871): 27.

97 Ibid.

98 Burne-Jones had previously depicted Joseph with an open book in his *Nativity* stained-glass window of 1873–74 for Jesus College Chapel, Cambridge. This small scene was included as a predella below a large figure of St. Matthew, also holding an open book. Two figures flanking Matthew are the Persian Sibyl, also with an open book, and the Cumaean Sibyl.

99 One notable example of Joseph reading a book is Andrea del Sarto's *Holy Family* lunette fresco in the cloister of SS. Annunziata in Florence, often called *The Madonna del Sacco* (1525). This fresco was reproduced in a chromolithograph by the Arundel Society in 1862, and it is likely that Burne-Jones either saw the original during his visits to Italy, or was familiar with the print. For more examples of Joseph depicted with a book, see Carolyn C. Wilson, *St. Joseph in Italian Renaissance Soci-*

ety and Art: New Directions and Interpretations (Philadelphia: Saint Joseph's University Press, 2001), 44, 212 n. 109.

100 Ibid., 44, 78.

101 Burne-Jones, [c. October 10, 1896], quoted in Rooke, "Memoirs," 279.

102 This number derives from Douglas Schoenherr's meticulous "Edward Burne-Jones's Account Books with Morris & Company (1861–1900): An Annotated Edition," in "Burne-Jones," special issue, *The Journal of Stained Glass* 35 (2011): 115: he estimates that Burne-Jones created "786 drawings, which include 719 cartoons, counting each light as one cartoon, thirty-one cases of touching up cartoons, twenty-one preparatory designs, and fifteen scale drawings." Offering another estimate, Sewter, *Stained Glass*, vol. 1, 46 calculated that at his peak in the 1870s, Burne-Jones produced a cartoon on average "every eight and a half days." For general discussions of the stained glass of Morris & Co., as well as Burne-Jones's role as a designer, see Sewter, *Stained Glass*; Martin Harrison, *Victorian Stained Glass* (London: Barrie & Jenkins, 1980); Martin Harrison, "Church Decoration and Stained Glass," in Parry, *William Morris*, 106–15, cat. nos. 116–35; Arscott, *Morris and Burne-Jones*, 39–62; *Journal of Stained Glass* 35 (2011); Peter Cormack, *Arts & Crafts Stained Glass* (New Haven and London: Paul Mellon Centre for Studies in British Art, 2015), 19–25; see also Morris & Co. Ltd., *A Note on the Morris Stained Glass Work* (London: Morris & Company, Ltd., n.d. [after 1919]).

103 For Burne-Jones's division of labor with Morris when creating stained glass, see Schoenherr, "Burne-Jones's Account Books," 78–119; his article contains a detailed exploration of these account books, now in the Fitzwilliam Museum, Cambridge. Schoenherr argues, and I fully concur, that Burne-Jones's humorous tone throughout these was not only a long-running joke between two friends, but also suggested the absurdity that he found in treating Morris like a capitalist businessman. For another discussion of their shared working practice in stained glass, see Cormack, *Arts & Crafts Stained Glass*, 19–25. From the founding of Morris, Marshall, Faulkner, & Co. in 1861, Burne-Jones was one of several designers in stained glass, but when the firm became Morris & Co. in 1875, he became the primary designer for stained glass.

104 Burne-Jones to Mary Gladstone Drew, 1896, British Library, Add. 46246, f. 216.

105 Burne-Jones quoted in G. Burne-Jones, *Memorials*, vol. 2, 159.

106 Morris to Ruskin, April 15, 1883, *Collected Letters*, 2a:184; original emphasis. Burne-Jones had also written to Ruskin two months earlier, February 14, 1883, Burne-Jones Papers, Box XXV/7, ff. 21–2, describing what he understood of Morris's attempts to get the most brightly colored glass. He describes urging Morris to make his own glass, rather than purchase from other firms. It seems there was some hope that this could be done at Merton Abbey, but there were limitations on the lease that prevented them from installing the necessary kilns. Burne-Jones admits to not fully understanding the desired qualities in the glass, especially the thickness or thinness of the sheet. However, he does express familiarity with some of the chemistry, including needing to add copper to create ruby glass: "I have urged him when he wants a deep ruby to steal his wife's gold ornaments and boil them up and make a red for himself." See also Cormack, *Arts & Crafts Stained Glass*, 24–5.

107 William Morris, "Glass, Painted or Stained (1890)," in *William Morris on Art and Design*, ed. Christine Poulson (Sheffield: Sheffield Academic Press, 1996), 44, 48, 49; he also stressed that shading should be minimal: "the object of the methods of shading is to keep the shadows as clear, and to dull the glass as little as the explanation or expression of the subject will admit of" (43).

108 Caviness, *Stained Glass Windows*, 58.

109 H. Arthur Kennedy, "An Art Not Generally Understood," *The Contemporary Review* 55 (1889): 440; he specifically praises depictions of "the prophets and the Apocalypse" as well suited to stained glass.

110 C. W. Whall, *Stained Glass Work: A Text-Book for Students and Workers in Glass* (repr. London: Sir Isaac Pitman & Sons, 1920), 94.

111 St. Philip's became the cathedral for the diocese of Birmingham in 1905. Given that this postdates Burne-Jones's death, I will refer to it as a church rather than a cathedral when discussing the creation of the stained glass, unless quoting other authors.

112 Emma Villers-Wilkes was the sole inheritor of a substantial fortune from her family's metalworking

firm, which specialized in copper and brass kitchen and catering equipment; it eventually became Lee and Wilkes Ltd and remained in operation through the late twentieth century. Villers-Wilkes was unmarried and a devout Anglican. See Joe Hunt, "Miss Wilkes's Windows," in *Edward Burne-Jones: 1833–1898: A Commemorative Centenary Issue of The Review of the Pre-Raphaelite Society* (Birmingham: Pre-Raphaelite Society, 1998), 26–38.

113 Morris to Julius Alfred Chatwin, November 1, 1886, *Collected Letters*, 2b:587.

114 For the sequence of letters between Morris and Chatwin, see ibid., 2b:587, 2b:591, 2b:592, 2b:594, 2b:595, 2b:596; see also Hunt, "Miss Wilkes's Windows," 26–38.

115 Morris to J. A. Chatwin, November 30, 1886, *Collected Letters*, 2b:596.

116 *The Last Judgment*, from a separate commission to the chancel windows, was dedicated to H. B. Bowlby, the Rector of St. Philip's and Bishop of Coventry.

117 In his account book for Morris & Co., Burne-Jones wrote in his entry for *The Nativity* and *The Crucifixion* windows in St. Philip's in 1887: "I mention parenthetically that in that very church at the tender age of a few weeks I was enlisted amongst the rank and file of the church militant"; Burne-Jones Papers, Account Book, vol. 2, 1883–97, 26.

118 E. Burne-Jones to George Howard, September 3, 1887, Castle Howard Archives, J22/27/367. Howard himself had only recently served as a Liberal MP (for East Cumberland, 1879–80, 1881–85).

119 E.g., in his obituary for Burne-Jones, Ford Madox Hueffer, "Sir Edward Burne-Jones," *The Contemporary Review* 186 (August 1898): 186, stated, "One is almost tempted to declare them the highest attainment of the artist, almost of the century." Cormack, *Arts & Crafts Stained Glass*, 23 writes, "Many would regard these as the supreme nineteenth-century achievement in the art."

120 Aymer Vallance, "The Decorative Art of Sir Edward Burne-Jones, Bart.," *The Art Journal* Easter Art Annual (1900): 10 adopted this line of criticism, describing *The Last Judgment* as "rather a deep-toned picture than, strictly regarded, a painted-glass window."

121 Martin Harrison, "'Pure Gold, Clear as Glass': Burne-Jones in Transition and the Lyndhurst New Jerusalem," *The Journal of Stained Glass* 35 (2011): 67–77.

122 See e.g. Carr, *Mantegna*, 64–5; Jameson, *Legends of the Madonna*, 244.

123 For Arscott's full discussion of Burne-Jones, stained glass, and the windows of St. Philip's, see *Morris and Burne-Jones*, 203–23.

124 Ibid., 216.

125 Ibid., 217.

126 Burne-Jones, [July 21, 1889?], quoted in G. Burne-Jones, *Memorials*, vol. 2, 176–7.

127 Burne-Jones quoted in ibid., 339.

128 Ibid., 257.

Conclusion

1 "Character Sketch," *The Review of Reviews* 18 (December 1898): 25.

2 Robert de la Sizeranne, "In Memoriam: Sir Edward Burne-Jones, Bart., A Tribute from France," *Magazine of Art* 22 (1898): 519.

3 This Latin aphorism has two predominant, interrelated interpretations. One widely understood meaning is that craft or skill takes long to master, but life is short. I have chosen to adopt the alternate interpretative possibility here: life is short, but art endures. I believe Morris and Burne-Jones would have understood and appreciated the dual significance of the phrase.

4 Fredric Jameson, *Archaeologies of the Future: The Desire Called Utopia and Other Science Fictions* (London: Verso, 2005), xii.

Bibliography

Archives

British Library, London
- Balfour Papers
- Burne-Jones Letters
- Cockerell Papers
- Ashley Manuscripts
- Gladstone Papers

British Museum, London
- Edward Burne-Jones, "The 'Secret' Book of Designs," 1899-7-13-322–544

Castle Howard Archives
- Letters from Edward Burne-Jones to George Howard, J22/27

Fitzwilliam Museum, Cambridge
- Burne-Jones Papers, including account books with Morris & Co. (1861–97) and "List of my designs" (1862–98; working list of paintings)
- Acc. 1085A, Burne-Jones correspondence with Antonio Salviati

Huntington Library, Art Collections, and Botanical Gardens, San Marino, California
- William Morris Papers
- Autograph Letters and Drawings by Sir Edward Burne-Jones
- Burne-Jones Collection
- William Morris Collection
- William Morris Papers
- Kelmscott Press Books

National Art Library, Victoria and Albert Museum, London
- Bence-Jones, A. B., "The Stanmore Tapestry: Some notes on the Sanc Graal Arras, worked by William Morris, J. H. Dearle and others, for Stanmore Hall" (1893–95), 86.W.4
- "Correspondence with Sir Coutts Lindsay, 1887, concerning Grosvenor Gallery," 40.G, Box I
- Rooke, Thomas M., "Memoirs of Thomas Matthews Rooke: typescript: or, Notes of conversations among the Pre-Raphaelite Brotherhood," 86.RR.52

Yale Center for British Art, New Haven, Connecticut
- Edward Coley Burne-Jones Letters to Cornell Price (MSS 45)
- Edward Burne-Jones Letters to John Ruskin (MSS 56)

Published Sources

Journals
- *The Academy*
- *The Antiquary*
- *The Art Journal*
- *The Athenaeum*

British Architect
The Builder
The Building News
The Graphic
The Magazine of Art
The Quarterly Review
The Review of Reviews
The Saturday Review
The Sketch
The Spectator
The Sphere
The Times

Abdy, Jane, and Charlotte Gere. *The Souls*. London: Sidgwick & Jackson, 1984

Airy, Basil Reginald. *A Brief History of St. John's Torquay*. Torquay: Andrew Iredale, 1902

Albrecht, Thomas. *The Medusa Effect: Representation and Epistemology in Victorian Aesthetics*. Albany: State University of New York Press, 2009

Arscott, Caroline. *William Morris and Edward Burne-Jones: Interlacings*. New Haven and London: Paul Mellon Centre for Studies in British Art, 2008

——, and Katie Scott, eds. *Manifestations of Venus: Art and Sexuality*. Manchester: Manchester University Press, 2003

Arseneau, Mary. "Incarnation and Interpretation: Christina Rossetti, the Oxford Movement, and 'Goblin Market.'" *Victorian Poetry* 31, no. 1 (Spring 1993): 79–93

Ayto, John, ed. *Brewer's Dictionary of Phrase and Fable*. 17th edn. New York: Cassell, 2005

Barringer, Tim. *Men at Work: Art and Labour in Victorian Britain*. New Haven and London: Yale University Press, 2005

——, Gillian Forrester, and Barbaro Martinez-Ruiz. *Art and Emancipation in Jamaica: Isaac Mendes Belisario and His Worlds*. New Haven, Conn.: Yale Center for British Art, 2007

Bate, Jonathan. *Romantic Ecology: Wordsworth and the Environmental Tradition*. London: Routledge, 1991

Bell, Malcolm. *Sir Edward Burne-Jones: A Record and Review*. 4th edn. London: George Bell & Sons, 1899

Benson, W. A. S. *Drawing, Its Histories and Uses*. London: Oxford University Press, 1925

Benton, Tim. "Exhibiting Modernity: The 1889 Universal Exhibition and the Eiffel Tower." In *The Challenge of the Avant-Garde*, ed. Paul Wood. New Haven and London: Yale University Press, 1999, 156–63

Blackburn, Henry, ed. *Grosvenor Notes*. London: Chatto and Windus, 1878

Blaugrund, Annette. *Paris 1889: American Artists at the Universal Exposition*. New York: Harry N. Abrams, 1989

Blum, Shirley Neilsen. "Hans Memling's 'Annunciation' with Angelic Attendants." *Metropolitan Museum Journal* 27 (1992): 43–58

Boos, Florence S. "An Aesthetic Ecocommunist: Morris the Red and Morris the Green." In *William Morris: Centenary Essays*, ed. Peter Faulkner and Peter Preston. Exeter: University of Exeter Press, 1999, 21–46

——. "Alternative Victorian Futures: 'Historicism,' Past and Present and A Dream of John Ball." In *History and Community: Essays in Victorian Medievalism*, ed. Florence S. Boos. New York: Garland, 1992, 3–37

——. "'The Banners of the Spring to Be': The Dialectical Pattern of Morris's Later Poetry." *English Studies: A Journal of English Language and Literature* 81, no. 1 (2000): 14–40

Braithwaite, William Stanley, ed. *The Book of Elizabethan Verse*. London: Chatto & Windus, 1908

Brown, Peter. "On the Borders of the Middle English Dream Visions." In *Reading Dreams: The Interpretation of Dreams from Chaucer to Shakespeare*, ed. Peter Brown. Oxford: Oxford University Press, 1999, 22–50

Brown, Stephanie. "Indefinite Expansion: Watts and the Physicality of Sculpture." In *Representations of G. F. Watts: Art Making in Victorian Culture*, ed. Colin Trodd and Stephanie Brown. Aldershot: Ashgate, 2004, 83–108

Bruce, W. N. "Memoir: Introduction." In W. A. S. Benson, *Drawing, Its Histories and Uses*. London: Oxford University Press, 1925, vii–xxxiii

Bryan, Michael. *Dictionary of Painters and Engravers*. London: George Bell and Sons, 1889

Bullen, J. B. *Byzantium Rediscovered*. London: Phaidon, 2003

Bullough, Kathy M. "Serpents, Angels and Virgins: The Virgin Mary as 'Second Eve' in the Art of Edward Burne-Jones." *Religion and the Arts* 4, no. 4 (2000): 463–90

Burne-Jones, Georgiana. *Memorials of Edward Burne-Jones* (1904). 2 vols. London: Lund Humphries, 1993

Burne-Jones, Philip. "Notes on Some Unfinished Works of Sir Edward Burne-Jones, Bt." *The Magazine of Art* 24 (1901): 159–67

Burrow, John W. *A Liberal Descent: Victorian Historians and the English Past*. Cambridge: Cambridge University Press, 1981

Butterfield, Herbert. *The Whig Interpretation of History*. London: G. Bell and Sons, 1959

Camille, Michael. "'When Adam Delved': Laboring on the Land in English Medieval Art." In *Agriculture in the Middle Ages: Technology, Practice, and Representation*, ed. Del Sweeney. Philadelphia: University of Pennsylvania Press, 1995, 247–76

Carlyle, Thomas. *On Heroes, Hero-Worship and the Heroic in History* (1841). London: Oxford University Press, 1974

Carr, Dawson W. *Andrea Mantegna: The Adoration of the Magi*. Los Angeles: Getty Museum Studies on Art, 1997

Cars, Laurence des. "Edward Burne-Jones and France." In *Edward Burne-Jones: Victorian Artist-Dreamer*, ed. Stephen Wildman and John Christian. New York: Metropolitan Museum of Art, 1998, 25–40

Cartwright Ady, Julia Mary. *A Bright Remembrance: The Diaries of Julia Cartwright 1851–1924*. Ed. Angela Emanuel. London: Weidenfeld and Nicolson, 1989

——. "The Life and Work of Sir Edward Burne-Jones." *The Art Journal* (Christmas 1894): 1–34

——. "The Pictures of the Year." *The National Review* (June 1891): 466–76

Caviness, Madeline H. *The Early Stained Glass of Canterbury Cathedral*. Princeton, N.J.: Princeton University Press, 1977

——. *Stained Glass Windows*. Turnhout: Brepols, 1996

Cheney, Liana de Giroliani. "Edward Burne-Jones's 'Andromeda': Transformation of Historical and Mythological Sources." *Artibus et Historiae* 25, no. 49 (2004): 197–227

Christian, John. "Burne-Jones and Sculpture." In *Pre-Raphaelite Sculpture: Nature and Imagination in British Sculpture, 1848–1914*, ed. Benedict Read and Joanna Barnes. London: Henry Moore Foundation with Lund Humphries, 1991, 77–91

——, and Penelope Marcus, eds. *Burne-Jones: The Paintings, Graphic and Decorative Work of Sir Edward Burne-Jones, 1833–98*. London: Arts Council of Great Britain, 1975

Chu, Petra ten-Doesschate. *Nineteenth-Century European Art*. New York: Harry N. Abrams, 2003

Coley, Sandra, ed. "Burne-Jones." Special issue, *The Journal of Stained Glass* 35 (2011)

Colvin, Sidney. *Memories & Notes of Persons & Places 1852–1912*. 2nd edn. New York: Charles Scribner's Sons, 1922

——. "A 'Nativity,' by Sandro Botticelli." *The Portfolio* (January 1871): 25–8

Cook, L. S. "Among the Pictures." *University Magazine* (June 1878): 732–41

Corbett, David Peters. *The World in Paint: Modern Art and Visuality in England, 1848–1914*. University Park: Pennsylvania State University Press, 2004

Cormack, Peter. *Arts & Crafts Stained Glass*. New Haven and London: Paul Mellon Centre for Studies in British Art, 2015

Craig Faxon, Alicia. "The Pre-Raphaelites and the Mythic Image: Iconographies of Women." *Visual Resources* 27, no. 1 (March 2011): 77–89

Crane, Walter. "Notes on Gesso Work." *The Decorator and Furnisher* 24, no. 1 (April 1894): 21

Crawford, Alan. "W. A. S. Benson, Machinery, and the Arts and Crafts Movement in Britain." *The Journal of Decorative and Propaganda Arts* 24 (2002): 94–117

——. "Burne-Jones as a Decorative Artist." In *Edward Burne-Jones: Victorian Artist-Dreamer*, ed. Stephen Wildman and John Christian. New York: Metropolitan Museum of Art, 1998, 5–24

Dakers, Caroline. *The Holland Park Circle: Artists and Victorian Society*. New Haven and London: Yale University Press, 1999

Davis, Jr., Arthur Kyle. "William Morris and the Eastern Question." In *Humanistic Studies in Honor of John Calvin Metcalf*, ed. James Southall Wilson. Charlottesville: University of Virginia Press, 1941, 28–47

Day, Brian J. "The Moral Intuition of Ruskin's 'Storm-Cloud.'" *Studies in English Literature* 45, no. 4 (Autumn 2005): 917–33

Denney, Colleen. *At the Temple of Art: The Grosvenor Gallery, 1877–1890*. London: Associated University Presses, 2000

Denton, Avril. "W. A. S. Benson: A Biography." In *W. A. S. Benson: Arts and Crafts Luminary and Pioneer of Modern Design*, ed. Ian Hamerton. Woodbridge: Antique Collectors' Club, 2005, 40–67

Deslandes, Madeleine. "Edward Burne-Jones," *Le Figaro*, May 7, 1893

Deusner, Melody Barnett. *Aesthetic Painting in Britain and America: Collectors, Art Worlds, Networks*. New Haven and London: Paul Mellon Centre for Studies in British Art with Yale University Press, 2020

Didron, Adolphe Napoléon. *Christian Iconography; or, The History of Christian Art in the Middle Ages* (1843). Ed. Margaret Stokes, trans. E. J. Millington. 2 vols. London: George Bell and Sons, 1886

Dorment, Richard. "Burne-Jones and the Decoration of St. Paul's American Church, Rome." Ph.D. diss., Columbia University, 1976

Dunlap, Joseph R. *The Book That Never Was*. New York: Oriole Editions, 1971

Eastlake, Charles L. *A History of the Gothic Revival*. London: Longmans, Green; New York: Scribner, Welford, 1872

Edwards, Jason. *Alfred Gilbert's Aestheticism: Gilbert Amongst Whistler, Wilde, Leighton, Pater and Burne-Jones*. London: Routledge, 2006

Edwards, Joseph, ed. *The Labour Annual 1899*. London: Clarion Co., 1899

Eisenman, Stephen F. "Class Consciousness in the Design of William Morris." *Journal of the William Morris Society* 15, no. 1 (Winter 2002): 17–37

——. "Communism in Furs: A Dream of Prehistory in William Morris's *John Ball*." *The Art Bulletin* 87, no. 1 (March 2005): 92–110

Evans, Mark, and Stefan Weppelmann. *Botticelli Reimagined*. London: V&A Publications, 2016

Fagence Cooper, Suzanne. *Pre-Raphaelite Art in the Victoria and Albert Museum*. London: V&A Publications, 2003

Fitzgerald, Penelope. *Edward Burne-Jones: A Biography*. 1975. Stroud: Sutton Publishing, 1997

Frankel, Nicholas. "The Ecology of Decoration: Design and Environment in the Writings of William Morris." *The Journal of Pre-Raphaelite Studies* 12 (Fall 2003): 58–85

Fröhlich, Fabian. "Frauen Im Spiegel. Der Perseus-Zyklus von Edward Burne-Jones." Ph.D. diss., University of Kassel, 2002

——. "The Perseus Series." In *Edward Burne-Jones: The Earthly Paradise*, ed. Christofer Conrad and Annabel Zettel. Ostfildern: Hatje Cantz, 2009, 103–35

Froissart, Jean. *Chronicles of England, France, Spain and the Adjoining Countries, illustrated from the French editions by Thomas Johnes*. London: George Routledge and Sons, 1868

Gagnier, Regenia. "A Critique of Practical Aesthetics." In *Aesthetics and Ideology*, ed. George Lewis Levine. New Brunswick, N.J.: Rutgers University Press, 2006, 264–82

Garber, Marjorie, and Nancy J. Vickers, eds. *The Medusa Reader*. London and New York: Routledge, 2003

Gater, G. H., and F. R. Hiorns, eds. *St. Martin-in-the-Fields, Part 3: Trafalgar Square & Neighbourhood*. In *Survey of London*. Vol. 20. London: Country Life for London County Council, 1940

George, Henry. *Progress and Poverty: An Enquiry into the Cause of Industrial Depressions, and of Increase of Want with Increase of Wealth: The Remedy*. New York: Walter J. Black, 1879

Gibson, Gail McMurray. "The Thread of Life in the Hand of the Virgin." In *Equally in God's Image: Women in the Middle Ages*, ed. Julia Bolton Holloway, Constance S. Wright, and Joan Bechtold. New York: Peter Lang, 1990, 46–54

Glasier, J. Bruce. *William Morris and the Early Days of the Socialist Movement*. London: Longmans, Green, and Co., 1921

Goffen, Rona. *Piety and Patronage in Renaissance Venice: Bellini, Titian, and the Franciscans*. New Haven and London: Yale University Press, 1986

——. "Bellini, S. Giobbe and Altar Egos." *Artibus et Historiae* 7, no. 14 (1986): 57–70

Gooddie, Sheila. *Mary Gladstone: A Gentle Rebel*. Chichester: John Wiley & Sons, 2003

Goode, John. "William Morris and the Dream of Revolution." In *Literature and Politics in the Nineteenth Century*, ed. John Lucas. London: Methuen, 1971, 221–80

Greenhalgh, Paul. "The Art and Industry of Mammon: International Exhibitions, 1851–1901." In *The Victorian Vision: Inventing New Britain*, ed. John M. MacKenzie. London: V&A Publications, 2001, 265–79

Hahn, Cynthia. "Vision." In *A Companion to Medieval Art: Romanesque and Gothic in Northern Europe*, ed. Conrad Rudolph. London: Wiley-Blackwell, 2006, 44–64

Hall, Michael. *George Frederick Bodley and the Later Gothic Revival in Britain and America*. New Haven and London: Paul Mellon Centre for Studies in British Art and Yale University Press, 2014

Hamburger, Jeffrey F. "Speculations on Speculation: Vision and Perception in the Theory and Practice of Mystical Devotion." In *Deutsche Mystik im Abendländischen Zusammenhang: Neu Erschlossene Texte, Neue Methodische Ansätze, Neue Theoretische Konzepte*, ed. Walter Haug and Wolfram Schneider-Lastin. Tübingen: Max Niemeyer Verlag, 2000, 353–408

Hansford, F. A., and G. A. C. Evans. *The Story of the Grange North End Crescent Fulham*. London: Fulham History Society Publications No. 1, 1953

Harrison, Martin. *Victorian Stained Glass*. London: Barrie & Jenkins, 1980

——. "Church Decoration and Stained Glass." In *William Morris*, ed. Linda Parry. London: Philip Wilson Publishers with the Victoria and Albert Museum, 1996, 106–15

——. "'Pure Gold, Clear as Glass': Burne-Jones in Transition and the Lyndhurst New Jerusalem." *The Journal of Stained Glass* 35 (2011): 67–77

——, and Bill Waters. *Burne-Jones*. 2nd edn. London: Barrie & Jenkins, 1990

Hart, Imogen. *Arts and Crafts Objects*. Manchester: Manchester University Press, 2010

Harvey, Charles, and Jon Press. *William Morris: Design and Enterprise in Victorian Britain*. Manchester: Manchester University Press, 1991

Hatfield, Rab. "The Tree of Life and the Holy Cross: Franciscan Spirituality in the Trecento and the Quattrocento." In *Christianity and the Renaissance: Image and Religious Imagination in the Quattrocento*, ed. Timothy Verdon and John Henderson. Syracuse, N.Y.: Syracuse University Press, 1990, 132–60

Holmes, Emily A. *Flesh Made Word: Medieval Women Mystics, Writing, and the Incarnation*. Waco, Tex.: Baylor University Press, 2013

Holt, Elizabeth Gilmore. *The Expanding World of Art, 1874–1902*. Vol. 1. New Haven and London: Yale University Press, 1988

Holzman, Michael. "The Encouragement and Warning of History: William Morris's A Dream of John Ball." In *Socialism and the Literary Artistry of William Morris*, ed. Florence S. Boos and Carole G. Silver. Columbia: University of Missouri Press, 1990, 98–116

Howell Jolly, Penny. *Made in God's Image? Eve and Adam in the Genesis Mosaics at San Marco, Venice*. Berkeley: University of California Press, 1997

Hueffer, Ford Madox. "Sir Edward Burne-Jones." *The Contemporary Review* 186 (August 1898): 181–95

Hunt, Joe. "Miss Wilkes's Windows." In *Edward Burne-Jones: 1833–1898: A Commemorative Centenary Issue of The Review of the Pre-Raphaelite Society*. Birmingham: Pre-Raphaelite Society, 1998, 26–38

Inglis, Alison. "A Victorian High Renaissance Scheme for the Dome of St Paul's Cathedral, London." *Fabrications* 10 (1999): 79–99

Jacobs, Joseph. "Some Recollections of Sir Edward Burne-Jones." *The Nineteenth Century: A Monthly Review* (January 1899): 126–31

James, Arthur, First Earl of Balfour. *Chapters of Autobiography*. Ed. Mrs. Edgar Dugdale. London: Cassell, 1930

Jameson, Anna. *Legends of the Madonna* (1850). Ed. Estelle M. Hurll. Boston: Houghton, Mifflin and Company, 1900

Jameson, Fredric. *Archaeologies of the Future: The Desire Called Utopia and Other Science Fictions*. London: Verso, 2005

——. *The Cultural Turn: Selected Writings on the Postmodern 1983–1998*. London: Verso, 1998

Jenkyns, Richard. *Dignity and Decadence: Victorian Art and the Classical Inheritance*. London: HarperCollins; Cambridge, Mass.: Harvard University Press, 1992

Jensen, Robin M. "The Fall and Rise of Adam and Eve in Early Christian Art and Literature." In *Interpreting Christian Art: Reflections on Christian Art*, ed. Heidi J. Hornik and Mikeal C. Parsons. Macon, Ga: Mercer University Press, 2003, 25–52

Johnson, Alastair. "Re-Altering the Glazing Alterations of a Burne-Jones Frame." In *Conserving Context: Relating Object Treatment to Collections and Settings*, ed. Gerry Alabone. London: Archetype, 2014, 69–81

Jones, Claire. "Perseus and the Graiae." In *Sculpture Victorious: Art in an Age of Inventions, 1837–1901*, ed. Martina Droth, Jason Edwards, and Michael Hatt. New Haven and London: Yale University Press with the Yale Center for British Art, 2014, 390–93

Joshua, Essaka. *Pygmalion and Galatea: The History of a Narrative in English Literature*. Aldershot and Burlington, Vt: Ashgate, 2001

Kaplan, Paul H. D. *The Rise of the Black Magus in Western Art*. Ann Arbor, Mich.: UMI Research Press, 1985

Karoglou, Kyriaki. "Dangerous Beauty: Medusa in Classical Art." *Metropolitan Museum of Art Bulletin* 75, no. 3 (2018)

Kennedy, H. Arthur. "An Art Not Generally Understood." *The Contemporary Review* 55 (1889): 427–42

Kestner, Joseph. "Edward Burne-Jones and the Nineteenth-Century Fear of Women." *Biography* 7, no. 2 (Spring 1985): 95–122

Khnopff, Fernand. "In Memoriam: Sir Edward Burne-Jones, Bart.: A Tribute from Belgium." *The Magazine of Art* 21 (1898): 520–26

Klein, Robert, and Henri Zerner, eds. *Italian Art 1500–1600: Sources and Documents*. Evanston, Ill.: Northwestern University Press, 1966

Lacouture, Annette Bourrut. *Jules Breton, Painter of Peasant Life*. New Haven and London: Yale University Press, 2002

Laski, Harold J. "The Social Philosophy of William Morris." In *Speeches in Commemoration of William Morris*, ed. John Drinkwater, Holbrook Jackson, and Harold J. Laski. Walthamstow: Buck Bros. & Harding, 1934, 17–21

Layard, A. H. "Mosaic Decoration." *The Builder*, December 5, 1868, 887–8

Lazarus, Emma. "A Day in Surrey with William Morris." *Century Illustrated Magazine* 32, no. 3 (July 1886): 388–97

Leprieur, Paul. "La Légende de Persée, par M. Burne-Jones." *Gazette des Beaux-Arts* 10, no. 6 (December 1, 1893): 462–77

Lethaby, W. R. *Philip Webb and His Work*. Oxford: Oxford University Press, 1935

Levey, Michael. "Botticelli and Nineteenth-Century England." *Journal of the Warburg and Courtauld Institutes* 23, no. 3–4 (1960): 291–306

Lightbown, Ronald. *Sandro Botticelli*. 2 vols. Berkeley: University of California Press, 1978

Lippincott, Louise. "Victorian Masterworks Come to Pittsburgh from Andrew Lloyd Webber." *Carnegie Magazine* (October 1997), https://carnegiemuseums.org/magazine-archive/1997/sepoct/feat1.html

Lisle, Fortunée de. *Burne-Jones*. New York: Dodge Publishing, 1904

Livesey, Ruth. *Socialism, Sex, and the Culture of Aestheticism in Britain, 1880–1914*. Oxford: Oxford University Press, 2009

Löcher, Kurt. *Der Perseus-Zyklus von Edward Burne-Jones*. Stuttgart: Staatsgalerie Stuttgart, 1973

Loftin, Alice Cornelia. "Visions." In *Dictionary of the Middle Ages*, ed. Joseph R. Strayer. New York: Charles Scribner's, 1989, vol. 12, 475–8

Lowrie, Walter. *Fifty Years of S. Paul's American Church, Rome*. Rome: The Rector, 1926

MacCarthy, Fiona. *The Last Pre-Raphaelite: Edward Burne-Jones and the Victorian Imagination*. London: Faber and Faber, 2011; Cambridge, Mass.: Harvard University Press, 2012

——. *William Morris: A Life for our Time*. London: Faber and Faber, 1994

——. "'As Good Work as I Do': Burne-Jones and Stained Glass." *The Journal of Stained Glass* 35 (2011): 8–16

Macdonald, Bradley J. "William Morris and the Vision of Ecosocialism." *Contemporary Justice Review* 7, no. 3 (2004): 287–304

Mack, Rainer. "Facing Down Medusa (An Aetiology of the Gaze)." *Art History* 25, no. 5 (November 2002): 571–604

Mackail, J. W. *The Life of William Morris*. 2 vols. New York: Dover, 1899

Marillier, H. C. *History of the Merton Abbey Tapestry Works*. London: Constable and Co., 1927

Marsh, Jan. "Icon of the Age: 'Africa,' Victoria and The Secret of England's Greatness." In *Black Victorians: Black People in British Art, 1800–1900*, ed. Jan Marsh. Aldershot: Manchester Art Gallery and Birmingham Museums and Art Gallery with Lund Humphries, 2005, 57–67

Meynell, Wilfred. "The Winter Exhibition at the Grosvenor Gallery." *The Magazine of Art* 4 (1881): 180

Miller, Elizabeth Carolyn. *Slow Print: Literary Radicalism and Late Victorian Print Culture*. Stanford, Cal.: Stanford University Press, 2013

——. "William Morris, Extraction Capitalism, and the Aesthetics of Surface." *Victorian Studies* 57, no. 3 (Spring 2015): 395–404

——. "Sustainable Socialism: William Morris on Waste." *The Journal of Modern Craft* 4, no. 1 (2011): 7–25

Millon, Judith Rice. *St. Paul's Within the Walls Rome: A Building History and Guide, 1870–1980*. Dublin, N.H.: William L. Bauhan, 1982

Mitchell, Paul, and Lynn Roberts. "Burne-Jones's Picture Frames." *The Burlington Magazine* 142, no. 1167 (2000): 362–70

"Modern Work in Rome." *The Builder*, 11, no. 1991 (April 2, 1881)

Monkhouse, Cosmo. "Introduction." In *Exhibition of Drawings and Studies by Sir Edward Burne-Jones, Bart*. London: Burlington Fine Arts Club, 1899, vii–xx

——. "The New Gallery." *The Academy*, June 2, 1888, 383–4

Morris, William. *The Collected Letters of William Morris*. Ed. Norman Kelvin. 4 vols. Princeton, N.J: Princeton University Press, 1984

——. *The Collected Works of William Morris, with Introductions by His Daughter May Morris*. 24 vols. London: Longmans, Green, and Co., 1910–15

——. *A Dream of John Ball* (1886–87). In *Collected Works*, vol. 16, 213–88

——. *A Dream of John Ball; and, A king's lesson: (reprinted from the "Commonweal")*. London: Reeves & Turner, 1888

——. *A Dream of John Ball and a King's Lesson*. London: Kelmscott Press, 1892

——. *The Earthly Paradise*. Ed. Florence Boos. 2 vols. New York: Routledge, 2002

——. *News From Nowhere* (1890). In *Collected Works*, vol. 16, 1–211

——. *A Note by William Morris on His Aims in Founding the Kelmscott Press*. Ed. William S. Peterson. New York: Grolier Club, 1996

——. *The Story of Sigurd the Volsung and the Fall of the Niblungs* (1876). In *Collected Works*, vol. 12

——. "Art and the Beauty of the Earth" (1881). In *Collected Works*, vol. 22, 155–74

——. "The Art of the People" (1879). In *Collected Works*, vol. 22, 28–50

——. "The Beauty of Life, Delivered before the Birmingham Society of Arts and School of Design, February 19, 1880." In *Collected Works*, vol. 22, 51–80

——. "Glass, Painted or Stained" (1890). In *William Morris on Art and Design*, ed. Christine Poulson. Sheffield: Sheffield Academic Press, 1996, 42–50

——. "The History of Pattern-Designing" (1882). In *Collected Works*, vol. 22, 206–34

——. "The Ideal Book" (1893). In *William Morris on Art and Design*, ed. Christine Poulson. Sheffield: Sheffield Academic Press, 1996, 144–52

——. "On the Woodcuts of Gothic Books." *Journal of the Society of Arts* 40 (February 1892): 247–60

——. "The Prospects of Architecture in Civilisation" (1881). In *Collected Works*, vol. 22, 119–52

——. "Textiles." In *Arts and Crafts Essays by Members of the Arts and Crafts Exhibition Society*. London: Longmans, Green, and Co., 1899, 22–38

Morris & Co. Ltd. *A Note on the Morris Stained Glass Work*. London: Morris & Company, Ltd., n.d. [after 1919]

"A Mosaic by Mr. Burne-Jones." *The Times*, April 14, 1886

Munich, Adrienne Auslander. *Andromeda's Chains: Gender and Interpretation in Victorian Literature and Art*. New York: Columbia University Press, 1989

Needham, Paul. *William Morris and the Art of the Book*. New York: Pierpont Morgan Library, 1976

Newall, Christopher S. *The Grosvenor Gallery Exhibitions: Change and Continuity in the Victorian Art World*. Cambridge: Cambridge University Press, 1995

O'Brien, Mark. *When Adam Delved and Eve Span: A History of the Peasants' Revolt of 1381*. Cheltenham: New Clarion Press, 2004

O'Neill, Morna. "Arts and Crafts Painting: The Political Agency of Things," *British Art Studies*, Issue 1, https://dx.doi.org/10.17658/issn.2058-5462/issue-01/moneill

O'Sullivan, Paddy. "The Struggle for the Vision Fair: Morris and Ecology." *The Journal of the William Morris Society* 8, no. 4 (Spring 1990): 5–9

Oberholzer, Simon. "Edward Burne-Jones's Pygmalion." In *Edward Burne-Jones: The Earthly Paradise*, ed. Christopher Conrad and Annabel Zettel. Ostfildern: Hatje Cantz Verlag, 2009, 67–77

Ogden, Daniel. *Perseus*. London and New York: Routledge, 2008

Osborne, Victoria. "'A New Order of Things': The Pre-Raphaelite Legacy and Art in Birmingham." In *Victorian Radicals: From the Pre-Raphaelites to the Arts & Crafts Movement*, ed. Martin Ellis, Victoria Osborne, and Tim Barringer. New York: American Federation of Arts, 2018, 71–87

Østermark-Johansen, Lene. *Walter Pater and the Language of Sculpture*. Farnham: Ashgate, 2011

——. "Between the Medusan and the Pygmalian: Swinburne and Sculpture." *Victorian Literature and Culture* 38 (2010): 21–37

Parkinson, Ronald. "Two Early Altar-Pieces by Burne-Jones." *Apollo* 102, no. 165 (November 1, 1975): 320–23

Parry, Linda. *William Morris Textiles*. London: V&A Publications, 2013

——. "The Tapestries of Edward Burne-Jones." *Apollo* 165 (November 1975): 324–8

——, ed. *William Morris*. London: Philip Wilson Publishers with the Victorian and Albert Museum, 1996

Pater, Walter. *The Renaissance: Studies in Art and Poetry* (1893). Ed. Donald L. Hill. Berkeley: University of California Press, 1980

Pelling, Rowan. "Why It's Time to Embrace the Mad, Androgynous Art of Burne-Jones." *The Telegraph*. October 6, 2018, https://www.

telegraph.co.uk/art/what-to-see/time-embrace-mad-androgynous-art-burne-jones
Percy, Thomas. *Reliques of Ancient English Poetry* (1765). New York: Thomas Y. Crowell & Co., 1876
Peterson, William S. *The Kelmscott Press: A History of William Morris's Typographical Adventure*. Oxford: Clarendon Press, 1991
Phillips, Claude. "Edward Burne-Jones." *The Magazine of Art* 8 (1885): 286–94
——. "The Salons II." *The Magazine of Art* 16 (1893): 386–93
——. "The Summer Exhibitions at Home and Abroad." *The Art Journal* (June 1891): 183–90
Pope-Hennessy, John. *Botticelli: The Nativity*. London: Percy Lund Humphries, 1946
Potts, Alex. *The Sculptural Imagination: Figurative, Modernist, Minimalist*. New Haven and London: Yale University Press, 2000
Prettejohn, Elizabeth. *Art for Art's Sake: Aestheticism in Victorian Painting*. New Haven and London: Paul Mellon Centre for Studies in British Art, 2007
——. *Beauty and Art 1750–2000*. Oxford: Oxford University Press, 2005
——. *Modern Painters, Old Masters: The Art of Imitation from the Pre-Raphaelites to the First World War*. New Haven and London: Paul Mellon Centre for Studies in British Art, 2017
——. *The Modernity of Ancient Sculpture: Greek Sculpture and Modern Art from Winckelmann to Picasso*. London: I.B. Tauris, 2012
——. "Between Homer and Ovid: Metamorphosis of the 'grand style.'" In *Representations of G. F. Watts: Art Making in Victorian Culture*, ed. Colin Trodd and Stephanie Brown. Aldershot and Burlington, Vt: Ashgate, 2004, 49–64
——. "Burne-Jones: Intellectual, Designer, People's Man." In *Edward Burne-Jones*, ed. Alison Smith. London: Tate Enterprises, 2018, 13–21
——. "The Series Paintings." In *Edward Burne-Jones*, ed. Alison Smith. London: Tate Enterprises, 2018, 169–94
Prickett, Stephen. "The Bible in Literature and Art." In *The Cambridge Companion to Biblical Interpretation*, ed. John Barton. Cambridge: Cambridge University Press, 1998, 160–80
Raftis, J. A. "Social Change Versus Revolution: New Interpretations of the Peasants' Revolt of 1381." In *Social Unrest in the Late Middle Ages*, ed. Francis X. Newman. Binghamton, N.Y.: Medieval & Renaissance Texts & Studies, 1986, 3–22
Rager, Andrea Wolk. "'The Revenge of Art on Life': Beauty, Modernity, and Edward Burne-Jones's *King Cophetua and the Beggar Maid*." In *A Companion to Nineteenth-Century Art*, ed. Michelle Facos. Hoboken, N.J.: Wiley-Blackwell, 2019, 51–68
——. "Review of *The Last Pre-Raphaelite: Edward Burne-Jones and the Victorian Imagination* by Fiona MacCarthy (Harvard UP, 2012)," *Victorian Studies* 56, no. 1 (2013): 113–15
——. "'Smite this Sleeping World Awake': Edward Burne-Jones and *The Legend of the Briar Rose*." *Victorian Studies* 51, no. 3 (2009): 438–50
Roberts, W. "Our National Museums and Galleries: Recent Acquisitions: The British Museum: The Burne-Jones Drawings." *The Magazine of Art* 24 (1900): 453
Robinson, Duncan. "Letter to the Editor: Burne-Jones's King Cophetua and the Beggar Maid." *Apollo* 97 (1973): 626
Rossetti, W. M. "The Grosvenor Gallery (First Notice)." *The Academy*, May 18, 1878, 446–7
Roussillon, Laurence. "Aspecta Medusa: The Many Faces of Medusa in the Painting and Poetry of Dante Rossetti." *The Journal of Pre-Raphaelite Studies* 11 (2002): 5–18
Rowley, Charles. *Fifty Years of Work Without Wages*. London: Hodder and Stoughton, 1911
Rubin, Patricia. "The Seduction of Antiquity." In *Manifestations of Venus: Art and Sexuality*, ed. Caroline Arscott and Katie Scott. Manchester: Manchester University Press, 2003, 24–38
Ruskin, John. *Giotto and his Works in Padua* (1853). In *Works of John Ruskin*, vol. 24, 1–123
——. *Modern Painters* II (1846). In *Works of John Ruskin*, vol. 3

——. *Modern Painters* III (1856). In *Works of John Ruskin*, vol. 5
——. *The Stones of Venice* (1851–53). In *Works of John Ruskin*, vol. 10, 180–269
——. *The Works of John Ruskin*, ed. E. T. Cook and Alexander Wedderburn. 39 vols. London: George Allen, 1906
——. "Ariadne Florentina: Six Lectures on Wood and Metal Engraving" (1876). In *Works of John Ruskin*, vol. 22, 289–490
——. "*Fors Clavigera*: Letter 5: The White-Thorn Blossom" (1871). In *Works of John Ruskin*, vol. 27, 79–97
——. "Mornings in Florence: Being Simple Studies of Christian Art, For English Travellers" (1875). In *Works of John Ruskin*, vol. 23, 281–457
——. "On the Woodcuts of Gothic Books." *Journal of the Society of Arts* 40 (February 1892): 250
——. "The Opening of the Crystal Palace: Considered in Some of Its Relations to the Prospects of Art" (1854). In *Works of John Ruskin*, vol. 12, 417–32
——. "The Schools of Florence" (1894). In *Works of John Ruskin*, vol. 23, 188–307
——. "The Storm-Cloud of the Nineteenth Century" (1884). In *Works of John Ruskin*, vol. 34, 1–80
——. "Traffic" (1864). In *Crown of Wild Olive*. 11th edn. Orpington: George Allen, 1898, 72–114
——. "Unto This Last" (1860, 1862). In *Works of John Ruskin*, vol. 17, 25–114
Schoenherr, Douglas E. "Edward Burne-Jones's Account Books with Morris & Company (1861–1900): An Annotated Edition." "Burne-Jones," special issue. *The Journal of Stained Glass* 35 (2011): 78–119
Sewter, A. C. *The Stained Glass of William Morris and His Circle*. 2 vols. New Haven, Conn.: Yale University Press, 1974
Signorini, Rodolfo. "The Creation of Adam: A Detail in Mantegna's Madonna Della Vittoria." *Journal of the Warburg and Courtauld Institutes* 59 (1996): 303–4
Sizeranne, Robert de la. *English Contemporary Art*. Ed. H. M. Poynter. London: A. Constable, 1898
—— "In Memoriam: Sir Edward Burne-Jones, Bart., A Tribute from France." *The Magazine of Art* 22 (1898): 513–20
Smith, Alison. *Reflections: Jan van Eyck and the Pre-Raphaelites*. London: National Gallery Company, 2017
——. *The Victorian Nude: Sexuality, Morality, and Art*. Manchester: Manchester University Press, 1996
——. "Apprentice to Master: 1856–70." In Smith, *Edward Burne-Jones*, 45–73
——, ed. *Edward Burne-Jones*. London: Tate Enterprises, 2018
Smith, Cecil. "The Central Groups of the Parthenon Pediments." *The Journal of Hellenic Studies* 27 (1907): 242–8
Smith, H. J. *Illustrated Symbols and Emblems of the Jewish, Early Christian, Greek, Latin, and Modern Churches*. Philadelphia: T. S. Leach & Co., 1900
Smith, Roberta. "In Love With the Past and a Vision of Perfect Beauty." *The New York Times*, June 5, 1998
Snoddy, Stephen, and Esta Jones, eds. *The Perseus Series: Sir Edward Coley Burne-Jones*. Southampton: Southampton City Art Gallery, 1998
Spielmann, M. H. "Current Art." *The Magazine of Art* 14 (January 1891): 253–63
——. "In Memoriam, III: Sir Edward Burne-Jones, Bart." *The Magazine of Art* 21 (1898): 528
Staley, Allen. *The New Painting of the 1860s: Between the Pre-Raphaelites and the Aesthetic Movement*. New Haven and London: Paul Mellon Centre for Studies in British Art and Yale University Press, 2011
Stephens, F. G. "Mr. E. Burne-Jones, A.R.A., as a Decorative Artist." *Portfolio* 20 (November 1889): 214–19
——. "Mr. E. Burne-Jones's Mosaics at Rome." *Portfolio* 21 (January 1890): 101–8
Stocker, Mark. "Edward Burne-Jones, Edgar Boehm, and The Battle of Flodden Field." *Apollo* 158, no. 498 (August 2003): 10–14
Taylor, W. S. "King Cophetua and the Beggar Maid." *Apollo* 97 (1973): 148–50

Tennyson, Alfred. "The Beggar Maid" (1842). In *The Works of Alfred Lord Tennyson*. Ware, Herts: Wordsworth Editions, 1998

Thirkell, Angela. *Three Houses*. London: Oxford University Press, 1931; Wakefield, R.I.: Moyer Bell, 1998

Thomas, Jane. "Morris and the Muse: Gender and Aestheticism in William Morris's 'Pygmalion and the Image.'" In *Writing on the Image: Reading William Morris*, ed. David Latham. Toronto: University of Toronto Press, 2007, 61–72

Thompson, E. P. *William Morris: Romantic to Revolutionary*. London: Lawrence & Wishart, 1955; New York: Pantheon, 1977

Tyack, Geoffrey. "Gilbert Scott and the Chapel of Exeter College, Oxford." *Architectural History* 50 (2007): 125–48

Vallance, Aymer. *The Life and Work of William Morris*. London: Studio Editions, 1986

——. "The Decorative Art of Sir Edward Burne-Jones, Bart." *The Art Journal* Easter Art Annual (1900): 1–32

Vernant, Jean-Pierre. *Mortals and Immortals: Collected Essays*. Ed. Froma I. Zeitlin. Princeton, N.J.: Princeton University Press, 1991

Voragine, Jacobus de. *The Golden Legend: Readings on the Saints*. Trans. William Granger Ryan. 2 vols. Princeton, N.J.: Princeton University Press, 1993

Wade, George A. "10, Downing Street." *The Pall Mall Magazine*, February 1901

Watts, M. S. *George Frederic Watts*. 3 vols. London: Macmillan, 1912

Webb, Matthew. "On Gesso, with Some Designs for Finger-Plates." *The Decorator and Furnisher* 26, no. 2 (May 1895): 61–4

Weliver, Phyllis. *Mary Gladstone and the Victorian Salon: Music, Literature, Liberalism*. Cambridge: Cambridge University Press, 2017

West, Shearer. *Fin De Siècle: Art and Society in an Age of Uncertainty*. Woodstock, N.Y.: Overlook Press, 1994

Whall, C. W. *Stained Glass Work: A Text-Book for Students and Workers in Glass*. Repr. London: Sir Isaac Pitman & Sons, 1920

Wildman, Stephen, and John Christian, eds. *Edward Burne-Jones: Victorian Artist-Dreamer*. New York: Metropolitan Museum of Art, 1998

Williams, Raymond. "Socialism and Ecology." In *Resources of Hope*, ed. Robin Gable. London: Verso, 1989, 210–26

Willsdon, Clare A. P. *Mural Painting in Britain, 1840–1940: Image and Meaning*. Oxford: Oxford University Press, 2000

Wilson, Carolyn C. *St. Joseph in Italian Renaissance Society and Art: New Directions and Interpretations*. Philadelphia: Saint Joseph's University Press, 2001

Wilson, Henry. "The Work of Sir Edward Burne-Jones: More Especially in Decoration and Design." *The Architectural Review* (March 1897): 171–81; (April 1897): 225–34; (May 1897): 273–81

Wilton, Andrew, and Robert Upstone, eds. *The Age of Rossetti, Burne-Jones, & Watts: Symbolism in Britain, 1860–1910*. London: Tate Gallery, 1997

Wolf, Sylvia. "'Mrs. Cameron's Photographs, Priced Catalogue': A Note on Her Sales and Process." In *Julia Margaret Cameron's Women*, ed. Sylvia Wolf. New Haven and London: Yale University Press for the Art Institute of Chicago, 1998, 208–18

Wood, Marcus, and James Raven. "'The Abolition Blunderbuss': Free Publishing and British Abolition Propaganda, 1780–1838." In *Free Print and Non-Commercial Publishing Since 1700*, ed. James Raven. London: Routledge, 2000, 67–92

Woodson-Boulton, Amy. *Transformative Beauty: Art Museums in Industrial Britain*. Stanford, Cal.: Stanford University Press, 2012

Wyatt, Matthew Digby. "On Pictorial Mosaic as an Architectural Embellishment." *The Builder*, March 22, 1862

Yeates, Amelia. "Poetic Narrative in William Morris's and Edward Burne-Jones's Pygmalion Project." In *Poetry in Pre-Raphaelite Paintings: Transcending Boundaries*, ed. Sophie Andres and Brian Donnelly. New York: Peter Lang, 2018, 107–20

Photograph Credits

Images have been provided by and are reproduced courtesy of the owners or custodians of the works of art. Images for which additional photographic credit is due are listed below.

The Cleveland Museum of Art, licensed under CC0: 1; © Victoria and Albert Museum, London: 2, 69, 103, 108, 112, 116, 139, 143, 144, 160; © Andrew Taylor: 3; © William Morris Gallery, London Borough of Waltham Forest: 4, 18, 20; © The British Library Board: 5; © Angelo Hornak/Alamy Stock Photo: 6; © Scala/Art Resource, NY: 7, 74, 94, 97, 99, 113, 127, 142; © Bodleian Libraries, University of Oxford: 8; Courtesy of the Huntington Art Museum, San Marino, California: 9, 10, 19, 161 (Purchased with funds from an anonymous donor and gift of Dr. Charles H. Strub and Mrs. John Wilson, by exchange, 2017.20); © Peter Hildebrand: 11, 147; © The Trustees of the British Museum: 12, 13, 14, 15, 68, 82, 85, 106, 119, 120, 121, 125; © Andrea Rager: 16, 148, 151; © Ashmolean Museum, University of Oxford: 17; Photo: Tate: 21, 22, 29, 30, 38, 39, 45, 46, 47, 133; © The Fitzwilliam Museum, Cambridge: 23, 79, 107; © RMN-Grand Palais/Art Resource, NY: 24, 71, 78; © The National Gallery, London: 25; © National Portrait Gallery, London: 26, 136; © The Faringdon Collection Trust at Buscot Park: 27, 89; © Cameraphoto Arte, Venice/Art Resource, NY: 28; Birmingham Museums Trust, licensed under CC0: 31, 90, 91, 92, 93, 102, 140, 141; Courtesy of Peter Nahum, Renate Nahum, Agency: 34; © Illustrated London News Ltd/Mary Evans: 35, 44; © National Trust Photographic Library/Derrick E. Witty/Bridgeman Images: 42; © bpk Bildagentur/Staatsgalerie Stuttgart/Art Resource, NY: 43, 58, 59, 60, 61, 62, 63, 64; © Southampton City Art Gallery/Paul Carter/Bridgeman Images: 48, 49, 50, 51, 52, 53, 54, 55, 56, 57; © Amgueddfa Cymru – National Museum Wales: 66; Photo: © Delaware Art Museum: 70; © Staatsgalerie, Stuttgart: 73, 76, 77, 101; © Erich Lessing/Art Resource, NY: 75; Royal Collection Trust/© Her Majesty Queen Elizabeth II 2021: 80; © Scala/Ministero per i Beni e le Attività culturali/Art Resource, NY: 81; © Christie's Images/Bridgeman Images: 83; © Steven Zucker: 84; © Staatliche Antikensammlung und Glyptothek, Munich, Germany/Bridgeman Images: 86; © Museo Archeologico Nazionale, Naples, Campania, Italy/Luisa Ricciarini/Bridgeman Images: 96; © President and Fellows of Harvard College: 98, 128; © Giorgio Morara/Alamy Stock Photo: 104; © Andrea Manchée/St. Paul's Within the Walls: 109; © Victoria and Albert Museum, London/Bridgeman Images: 110; © National Gallery, London/Bridgeman Images: 111, 154; © Ivan Vdovin/Alamy Stock Photo: 114; © Maurizio Badolato: 117, 118, 123, 126; © Alastair Carew-Cox/Bridgeman Images: 122, 131, 156, 157, 158, 159, 162; © Vito Arcomano/Alamy Stock Photo: 124; © Morgan Library & Museum, New York: 130; © Peter Barritt/Alamy Stock Photo: 135; Published with permission of the Rector and Scholars of Exeter College, Oxford and Studio8 photography: 138; © Carnegie Museum of Art, public domain: 145, 146; © Alfredo Dagli Orti/Art Resource, NY: 149, 150; Courtesy of Sotheby's: 153; © RMN-Grand Palais/Gérard Blot/Art Resource, NY: 164; © Paolo Romiti/Alamy Stock Photo: detail on p. 162

Index

NOTE: Page numbers in italics refer to illustrations. Page numbers followed by *n.* and a number refer to information in a note. Works and discussion of works by Burne-Jones and Morris appear at the end of their index entries. B-J = Edward Burne-Jones.